DATE DUE

FEB 0 8 2012	
OCT 0 6 2016	
DEC 1 5 2016	

BRODART, CO.   Cat. No. 23-221

IN DEFENSE OF LOST CAUSES

IN DEFENSE OF LOST CAUSES

SLAVOJ ŽIŽEK

VERSO

London • New York

First published by Verso 2008
Copyright © Slavoj Žižek 2008
All rights reserved

The moral right of the author has been asserted

3 5 7 9 10 8 6 4

Verso
UK: 6 Meard Street, London W1F 0EG
USA: 180 Varick Street, New York, NY 10014-4606
www.versobooks.com

Verso is the imprint of New Left Books

ISBN-13: 978-1-84467-108-3

British Library Cataloguing in Publication Data
A catalogue record for this book is available from the British Library

Library of Congress Cataloging-in-Publication Data
A catalog record for this book is available from the Library of Congress

Typeset in Cochin by Hewer Text UK Ltd, Edinburgh
Printed in the USA by Maple Vail

Alain Badiou was once seated amongst the public in a room where I was delivering a talk, when his cellphone (which, to add insult to injury, was mine — I had lent it to him) all of a sudden started to ring. Instead of turning it off, he gently interrupted me and asked me if I could talk more softly, so that he could hear his interlocutor more clearly . . . If this was not an act of true friendship, I do not know what friendship is. So, this book is dedicated to Alain Badiou.

Contents

Introduction: Causa Locuta, Roma Finita

Roma locuta, causa finita — the decisive words of authority that should end a dispute, in all its versions, from "the Church synod has decided" to "the Central Committee has passed a resolution" and, why not, "the people has made clear its choice at the ballot box" . . . However, is not the wager of psychoanalysis the opposite one: let the Cause itself speak (or, as Lacan put it, "I, the truth, speak"), and the Empire (of Rome, that is, contemporary global capitalism) will fall apart? *Ablata causa tolluntur effectus*: when the cause is absent, the effects thrive (*Les effets ne se portent bien qu'en absence de la cause*). What about turning this proverb around? When the cause intervenes, the effects are dispelled . . .[1]

However, *which* Cause should speak? Things look bad for great Causes today, in a "postmodern" era when, although the ideological scene is fragmented into a panoply of positions which struggle for hegemony, there is an underlying consensus: the era of big explanations is over, we need "weak thought," opposed to all foundationalism, a thought attentive to the rhizomatic texture of reality; in politics too, we should no longer aim at all-explaining systems and global emancipatory projects; the violent imposition of grand solutions should leave room for forms of specific resistance and intervention . . . If the reader feels a minimum of sympathy with these lines, she should stop reading and cast aside this volume.

Even those who otherwise tend to dismiss "French" postmodern theory with its "jargon" as an exemplary case of "bullshit" tend to share its aversion towards "strong thought" and its large-scale explanations. There is indeed a lot of bullshitting going on these days. Unsurprisingly, even those who popularized the notion of "bullshit," such as Harry Frankfurt, are not free from it. In the endless complexity of the contemporary world, where things, more often than not, appear as their opposites — intolerance as tolerance, religion as rational common sense, and so on and so forth — the temptation is great to cut it short with a violent gesture of "No bullshit!" — a gesture which seldom amounts to more than an impotent *passage à l'acte*. Such a desire to draw a clear line of demarcation between sane truthful talk and "bullshit" cannot but reproduce as truthful talk the predominant ideology itself. No wonder that, for Frankfurt himself, examples of "no bullshit" politicians are Harry Truman, Dwight Eisenhower, and, today, John McCain[2]—as if the pose of outspoken personal sincerity is a guarantee of truthfulness.

The common sense of our era tells us that, with regard to the old distinction between *doxa* (accidental/empirical opinion, Wisdom) and Truth, or, even more radically, empirical positive knowledge and absolute Faith, one should draw a line between what one can think and do today. At the level of common sense, the furthest one can go is enlightened conservative liberalism: obviously, there are no viable alternatives to capitalism; at the same time, left to itself, the capitalist dynamic threatens to undermine its own foundations. This concerns not only the economic dynamic (the need for a strong state apparatus to maintain the market competition itself, and so on), but, even more, the ideologico-political dynamics. Intelligent conservative democrats, from Daniel Bell to Francis Fukuyama, are aware that contemporary global capitalism tends to undermine its own ideological conditions (what, long ago, Bell called the "cultural contradictions of capitalism"): capitalism can only thrive in the conditions of basic social stability, of intact symbolic trust, of individuals not only accepting their own responsibility for their fate, but also relying on the basic "fairness" of the system—this ideological background has to be sustained through a strong educational, cultural apparatus. Within this horizon, the answer is thus neither radical liberalism *à la* Hayek, nor crude conservatism, still less clinging to old welfare-state ideals, but a blend of economic liberalism with a minimally "authoritarian" spirit of community (the emphasis on social stability, "values," and so forth) that counteracts the system's excesses—in other words what Third Way social-democrats such as Blair have been developing.

This, then, is the limit of common sense. What lies beyond involves a Leap of Faith, faith in lost Causes, Causes that, from within the space of skeptical wisdom, cannot but appear as crazy. And the present book speaks from within this Leap of Faith—but why? The problem, of course, is that, in a time of crisis and ruptures, skeptical empirical wisdom itself, constrained to the horizon of the dominant form of common sense, cannot provide the answers, so one *must* risk a Leap of Faith.

This shift is the shift from "I speak the truth" to "the truth itself speaks (in/through me)" (as in Lacan's "matheme" of the analyst's discourse, where the agent speaks from the position of truth), to the point at which I can say, like Meister Eckhart, "it is true, and the truth says it itself."[3] At the level of positive knowledge, it is, of course, never possible to (be sure that we have) attain(ed) the truth—one can only endlessly approach it, because language is ultimately always self-referential, there is no way to draw a definitive line of separation between sophism, sophistic exercises, and Truth itself (this is Plato's problem). Lacan's wager is here the Pascalean one: the wager of Truth. But how? Not by running after "objective" truth, but by holding onto the truth about the position from which one speaks.[4]

There are still only two theories which imply and practice such an engaged notion of truth: Marxism and psychoanalysis. They are both struggling theories, not only theories about struggle, but theories which are themselves engaged in a struggle: their histories do not consist in an accumulation of neutral knowledge, for they are marked by schisms, heresies, expulsions. This is why, in both of them, the relationship between theory and practice is properly dialectical, in other words, that of an irreducible tension: theory is not just the conceptual grounding of practice, it simultaneously accounts for why practice is ultimately doomed to failure—or, as Freud put it concisely, psychoanalysis would only be fully possible in a society that would no longer need it. At its most radical, theory is the theory of a failed practice: "This is why things went wrong . . ." One usually forgets that Freud's five great clinical reports are basically reports on a partial success and ultimate failure; in the same way, the greatest Marxist historical accounts of revolutionary events are the accounts of great failures (of the German Peasants' War, of the Jacobins in the French Revolution, of the Paris Commune, of the October Revolution, of the Chinese Cultural Revolution . . .). Such an examination of failures confronts us with the problem of fidelity: how to redeem the emancipatory potential of these failures through avoiding the twin trap of nostalgic attachment to the past and of all-too-slick accommodation to "new circumstances."

The time of these two theories seems over. As Todd Dufresne recently put it, no figure in the history of human thought was more wrong about all the fundamentals of his theory than Freud[5]—with the exception of Marx, some would add. And, indeed, in liberal consciousness, the two now emerge as the main "partners in crime" of the twentieth century: predictably, in 2005, the infamous *The Black Book of Communism*, listing all the Communist crimes,[6] was followed by *The Black Book of Psychoanalysis*, listing all the theoretical mistakes and clinical frauds of psychoanalysis.[7] In this negative way, at least, the profound solidarity of Marxism and psychoanalysis is now displayed for all to see.

There are nonetheless signs which disturb this postmodern complacency. Commenting on the growing resonance of Alain Badiou's thought, Alain Finkelkraut recently characterized it as "the most violent philosophy, symptomatic of the return of radicality and of the collapse of anti-totalitarianism"[8]—an honest and surprised admission of the failure of the long and arduous work of all kinds of "anti-totalitarians," defenders of human rights, combatants against "old leftist paradigms," from the French *nouveaux philosophes* to the advocates of a "second modernity." What should have been dead, disposed of, thoroughly discredited, is returning with a vengeance. One can understand their despair: how can it be that, after having explained for decades not only in scholarly treatises, but also in the mass media, to anyone who wanted to listen (and to many who did not) the dangers of totalitarian "Master-Thinkers," this kind of philosophy is returning in its most violent form? Have people not caught on that the time of such dangerous utopias is over? Or are we dealing with some strange ineradicable blindness, or an innate anthropological constant, a tendency to succumb to totalitarian temptation? Our proposal is to turn the perspective around: as Badiou himself might put it in his unique Platonic way, true ideas are eternal, they are indestructible, they always return every time they are proclaimed dead. It is enough for Badiou to *state* these ideas again clearly, and anti-totalitarian thought appears in all its misery as what it really is, a worthless sophistic exercise, a pseudo-theorization of the lowest opportunist survivalist fears and instincts, a way of thinking which is not only reactionary but also profoundly *reactive* in Nietzsche's sense of the term.

Linked to this is an interesting struggle which has been going on recently (not only) among Lacanians (not only) in France. This struggle concerns the status of the "One" as the name of a political subjectivity, a struggle which has led to many broken personal friendships (say, between Badiou and Jean-Claude Milner). The irony is that this struggle is taking place among ex-Maoists (Badiou, Milner, Lévy, Miller, Regnault, Finkelkraut), and between "Jewish" and "non-Jewish" intellectuals. The question is: is the name of the One the result of a contingent political struggle, or is it somehow rooted in a more substantial particular identity? The position of "Jewish Maoists" is that "Jews" is such a name which stands for that which resists today's global trend to overcome all limitations, inclusive of the very finitude of the human condition, in radical capitalist "deterritorialization" and "fluidification" (the trend which reaches its apotheosis in the gnostic-digital dream of transforming humans themselves into virtual software that can reload itself from one hardware to another). The name "Jews" thus stands for the most basic *fidelity* to what one is. Along these lines, François Regnault claims that the contemporary Left demands of Jews (much more than of other ethnic groups) that they "yield with regard to their name"[9]—a reference to Lacan's ethical maxim "do not yield with regard to your desire" . . . One should remember here that the same shift from radical emancipatory politics to the fidelity to the Jewish name is already discernible in the fate of the Frankfurt School, especially in Horkheimer's later texts. Jews here are the exception: in the liberal multiculturalist perspective, all groups can assert their identity—except Jews, whose very self-assertion equals Zionist racism . . . In contrast to this approach, Badiou and others insist on the fidelity to the One which emerges and is constituted through the very political struggle of/for naming and, as such, cannot be grounded in any particular determinate content (such as ethnic or religious roots). From this point of view, fidelity to the name "Jews" is the obverse (the silent recognition) of the defeat of authentic emancipatory struggles. No wonder that those who demand fidelity to the name "Jews" are also those who warn us against the "totalitarian" dangers of any radical emancipatory movement. Their politics consists in accepting the fundamental finitude and limitation of our situation, and the Jewish Law is the ultimate mark of this finitude, which is why, for them, all attempts to overcome Law and tend towards all-embracing Love (from Christianity through the French Jacobins to Stalinism) must end up in totalitarian terror. To put it succinctly, the only true solution to the "Jewish question" is the "final solution" (their annihilation), because Jews *qua objet a* are the ultimate obstacle to the "final solution" of History itself, to the overcoming of divisions in all-encompassing unity and flexibility.

But is it not rather the case that, in the history of modern Europe, those who stood for the striving for universality were precisely atheist Jews from Spinoza to Marx and Freud? The irony is that in the history of anti-Semitism Jews stand for both of these poles: sometimes they stand for the stubborn attachment to their particular life-form which prevents them from becoming full citizens of the state they live in, sometimes they stand for a "homeless" and rootless universal cosmopolitanism indifferent to all particular ethnic forms. The first thing to recall is thus that this struggle is (also) *inherent* to Jewish identity. And, perhaps, this Jewish struggle is our central struggle today: the struggle between fidelity to the Messianic impulse and the *reactive* (in the precise Nietzschean sense) "politics of fear" which focuses on preserving one's particular identity.

The privileged role of Jews in the establishment of the sphere of the "public use of reason" hinges on their subtraction from every state power—this position of the "part of no-part" of every organic nation-state community, not the abstract-universal nature of their monotheism, makes them the immediate embodiment of universality. No wonder, then, that, with the establishment of the Jewish nation-state, a new figure of the Jew emerged: a Jew resisting identification with the State of Israel, refusing to accept the State of Israel as his true home, a Jew who "subtracts" himself from this state, and who includes the State of Israel among the states towards which he insists on maintaining a distance, living in their interstices—and it is *this* uncanny Jew who is the object of what one cannot but designate as "Zionist anti-Semitism," a foreign excess disturbing the nation-state community. These Jews, the "Jews of the Jews themselves," worthy successors of Spinoza, are today the only Jews who continue to insist on the "public use of reason," refusing to submit their reasoning to the "private" domain of the nation-state.

This book is unashamedly committed to the "Messianic" standpoint of the struggle for universal emancipation. No wonder, then, that to the partisans of the "postmodern" *doxa* the list of lost Causes defended here must appear as a horror show of their worst nightmares embodied, a depository of the ghosts of the past they put all their energies into exorcizing: Heidegger's politics as the extreme case of a philosopher seduced by totalitarian politics; revolutionary terror from Robespierre to Mao; Stalinism; the dictatorship of the proletariat . . . In each case, the predominant ideology not only dismisses the cause, but offers a replacement, a "softer" version of it: not totalitarian intellectual engagement, but intellectuals who investigate the problems of globalization and fight in the public sphere for human rights and tolerance, against racism and sexism; not revolutionary state terror, but the self-organized decentralized multitude; not the dictatorship of the proletariat, but the collaboration among multiple agents (civil-society initiatives, private money, state regulation . . .). The true aim of the "defense of lost causes" is not to defend Stalinist terror, and so on, as such, but to render problematic the all-too-easy liberal-democratic alternative. Foucault's and, especially, Heidegger's political commitments, while acceptable in their basic motivation, were clearly "right steps in the wrong direction"; the misfortunes of the fate of revolutionary terror confront us with the need—not to reject terror *in toto*, but—to reinvent it; the forthcoming ecological crisis seems to offer a unique chance of *accepting* a reinvented version of the dictatorship of the proletariat. The argument is thus that, while these phenomena were, each in its own way, a historical failure and monstrosity (Stalinism was a nightmare which caused perhaps even more human suffering than fascism; the attempts to enforce the "dictatorship of the proletariat" produced a ridiculous travesty of a regime in which precisely the proletariat was reduced to silence, and so on), *this is not the whole truth*: there was in each of them a redemptive moment which gets lost in the liberal-democratic rejection—and it is crucial to isolate this moment. One should be careful not to throw out the baby with the dirty water— although one is tempted to turn this metaphor around, and claim that it is the liberal-democratic critique which wants to do this (say, throwing out the dirty water of terror, while retaining the pure baby of authentic socialist democracy), forgetting thereby that the water was originally pure, that all the dirt in it comes from the baby. What one should do, rather, is to throw out the baby before it spoils the crystalline water with its excretions, so that, to paraphrase Mallarmé, *rien que l'eau n'aura eu lieu dans le bain de l'histoire*.

Our defense of lost Causes is thus not engaged in any kind of deconstructive game in the style of "every Cause first has to be lost in order to exert its efficiency as a Cause." On the contrary, the goal is to leave behind, with all the violence necessary, what Lacan mockingly referred to as the "narcissism of the lost Cause," and to courageously accept the full actualization of a Cause, including the inevitable risk of a catastrophic disaster. Badiou was right when, apropos the disintegration of the Communist regimes, he proposed the maxim: *mieux vaut un désastre qu'un désêtre*. Better a disaster of fidelity to the Event than a non-being of indifference towards the Event. To paraphrase Beckett's memorable phrase, to which I shall return many times later, after one fails, one can go on and fail better, while indifference drowns us deeper and deeper in the morass of imbecilic Being.

A couple of years ago, *Premiere* magazine reported on an ingenious inquiry into how the most famous endings of Hollywood films were translated into some of the major non-English languages. In Japan, Clark

Gable's "Frankly, my dear, I don't give a damn!" to Vivien Leigh from *Gone With the Wind* was rendered as: "I fear, my darling, that there is a slight misunderstanding between the two of us"—a bow to proverbial Japanese courtesy and etiquette. In contrast, the Chinese (in the People's Republic of China) rendered the "This is the beginning of a beautiful friendship!" from *Casablanca* as "The two of us will now constitute a new cell of anti-fascist struggle!"—struggle against the enemy being the top priority, far above personal relations.

Although the present volume may often appear to indulge in excessively confrontational and "provocative" statements (what today can be more "provocative" than displaying even a minimal sympathy for or understanding of revolutionary terror?), it rather practices a displacement along the lines of the examples quoted in *Premiere*: where the truth is that I don't give a damn about my opponent, I say that there is a slight misunderstanding; where what is at stake is a new theoretico-political shared field of struggle, it may appear that I am talking about academic friendships and alliances . . . In such cases, it is up to the reader to unravel the clues which lie before her.

I

THE STATE OF THINGS

1 Happiness and Torture in the Atonal World

Human, all too human

In contrast to the simplistic opposition of good guys and bad guys, spy thrillers with artistic pretensions display all the "realistic psychological complexity" of the characters from "our" side. Far from signaling a balanced view, however, this "honest" acknowledgment of our own "dark side" stands for its very opposite, for the hidden assertion of our supremacy: we are "psychologically complex," full of doubts, while the opponents are one-dimensional fanatical killing machines. Therein resides the lie of Spielberg's *Munich*: it wants to be "objective," presenting moral complexity and ambiguity, psychological doubts, the problematic nature of revenge, of the Israeli perspective, but, what its "realism" does is redeem the Mossad agents still further: "look, they are not just cold killers, but human beings with their doubts—*they* have doubts, whereas the Palestinian terrorists . . ." One cannot but sympathize with the hostility with which the surviving Mossad agents who really carried out the revenge killings reacted to the film ("there were no psychological doubts, we just did what we had to do") for there is much more honesty in their stance.[1]

The first lesson thus seems to be that the proper way to fight the demonization of the Other is to subjectivize her, to listen to her story, to understand how she perceives the situation—or, as a partisan of the Middle East dialogue put it: "An enemy is someone whose story you have not heard."[2] Practicing this noble motto of multicultural tolerance, Iceland's authorities recently imposed a unique form of enacting this subjectivization of the Other. In order to fight growing xenophobia (the result of increasing numbers of immigrant workers), as well as sexual intolerance, they organized what they called "living libraries": members of ethnic and sexual minorities (gays, immigrant East Europeans or blacks) are paid to visit an Icelandic family and just talk to them, acquainting them with their way of life, their everyday practices, their dreams, and so on — in this way, the exotic stranger who is perceived as a threat to our way of life appears as somebody we can empathize with, with a complex world of her own . . .

There is, however, a clear limit to this procedure. Can we imagine inviting a Nazi thug to tell us his story? Are we ready to affirm that Hitler was an enemy because his story hadn't been heard? A Serb journalist recently reported a strange piece of news from the politician who, after long painful talks, convinced Slobodan Milošević in his villa to surrender to the police and let himself be arrested. Milošević said yes and then asked to be allowed to go to the first floor of the villa to attend to some business. The negotiator, afraid that Milošević was going to commit suicide, expressed his doubts, but Milošević calmed him down, saying that he had given his word to his wife, Mira Markovic, that he would wash his hair before leaving. Does this personal-life detail "redeem" the horrors that resulted from Milošević's reign, does it make him "more human"? One can well imagine Hitler washing Eva Braun's hair — and one does not have to imagine, since we already know that Heydrich, the architect of the Holocaust, liked to play Beethoven's late string quartets with friends in the evenings. Recall the couple of "personal" lines that usually conclude the presentation of a writer on the back cover of a book: "In his free time, X likes to play with his cat and grow tulips . . ." — such a supplement which "humanizes" the author is ideology at its purest, the sign that he is "also human like us." (I was tempted to suggest for the cover of one my books: "In his free time, Žižek likes to surf the internet for child pornography and to teach his small son how to pull the legs off spiders . . .")

Our most elementary experience of subjectivity is that of the "richness of my inner life": this is what I "really am," in contrast to the symbolic determinations and mandates I assume in public life (father, professor, philosopher). The first lesson of psychoanalysis here is that this "richness of our inner life" is fundamentally a fake: a screen, a false distance, whose function is, as it were, to save my appearance, to render palpable (accessible to my imaginary narcissism) my true social-symbolic identity. One of the ways to practice the critique of ideology is therefore to invent strategies to unmask this hypocrisy of "inner life" and its "sincere" emotions, in the manner systematically enacted by Lars von Trier in his films:

My very first film, *The Orchid Gardener*, opened with a caption stating that the film was dedicated to a girl who had died of leukaemia, giving the dates of her birth and death. That was entirely fabricated! And manipulative and cynical, because I realized that if you started a film like that, then the audience would take it a lot more seriously.[3]

There is much more than manipulation at work here: in his feminine trilogy (*Breaking the Waves, Dancer in the Dark, Dogville*), von Trier provokes us in our innermost being, stirring up automatic sympathy with the ultimate archetypal image of the victimized woman who, with her heart of gold, suffers pain. Through his "manipulation," he displays the lie of this sympathy, the obscene pleasure we gain from seeing the victim suffer, and thereby disturbs our self-satisfaction. Does this mean, however, that my "truth" is simply in my symbolic identity obfuscated by my imaginary "inner life" (as a simplistic reading of Lacan seems to indicate, opposing the subject of the signifier to the imaginary ego)?

Let us take a man who, deep down, cultivates sadistic fantasies while in public life he is polite, follows rules, and so forth; when he goes online to express those fantasies in a chat room, say, he is showing his truth in the guise of a fiction. But is it not the case, on the contrary, that the polite persona is the truth here and the sadistic fantasies serve as a kind of defense? As in a new version of the old Jewish joke: "You are polite, so why do you act as if you were polite?" Is not, then, the internet, where we supposedly express on screen our deepest truths, really a site for the playing out of defensive fantasies that protect us from the banal normality that is our truth?[4]

Two cases are to be distinguished here. When I am a brutal executive who, deep within myself, feel that this is just a public mask and that my true Self discloses itself in my spiritual meditations (and imagine my friends telling people: "His brutal business efficiency shouldn't deceive you — he is really a very refined and gentle person . . ."), this is not the same as when I am, in real interactions with others, a polite person who, on the internet, gives way to violent fantasies. The site of subjective identification shifts: in the internet case, I think that I really am a polite person, and that I am just playing with violent fantasies, while, as a New Age businessman, I think that I am just playing a public role in my business dealings, while my true identity is my inner Self enlightened through meditation. In other words: in both cases, truth is a fiction, but this fiction is differently located. In the internet case, it is imaginable that, at some point, I will "take off the mask" and explode, that is, carry out my violent fantasies in real life — this explosion will effectively enact "the truth of my Self." In the case of the New Age businessman, my truth is my public persona, and, here, "taking off the mask," enacting my New Age self in reality, namely, *really* abandoning my businessman traits, would involve a real shift in my subjective position. In the two cases, "taking off the mask" thus works differently. In the internet case, this gesture is what Hitler did with actual anti-Semitic measures (realizing anti-Semitic fantasies), a false act, while in the New Age businessman case, would be a true act.

In order to resolve the apparent contradiction, one should reformulate the two cases in the terms of Lacan's triad Imaginary–Symbolic–Real: we are not dealing with two, but with three elements. The dirty fantasies I am playing with on the net do not have the same status as my "true Self" disclosed in my meditations: the first belong to the Real, the second to the Imaginary. The triad is then I–S–R. Or, more precisely, in the internet case, my polite public persona is Imaginary–Symbolic versus the Real of my fantasies, while, in the New Age executive case, my public persona is Symbolic–Real versus my Imaginary "true Self."[5] (And, to take a crucial further theoretical step, in order for this triad to function, one has to add a fourth term, none other than the empty core of subjectivity: the Lacanian "barred subject" ($) is neither my Symbolic identity, nor my Imaginary "true Self," nor the obscene Real core of my fantasies, but the empty container which, like a knot, ties the three dimensions together.)

It is this complex "knot" that accounts for a well-known tragic figure from the Cold War era: those Western leftists who heroically defied anti-Communist hysteria in their own countries with utmost sincerity. They were ready even to go to prison for their Communist convictions and their defense of the Soviet Union. Is it not the very illusory nature of their belief that makes their subjective stance so tragically sublime? The miserable reality of the Stalinist Soviet Union renders the fragile beauty of their inner conviction all the more majestic. This leads us to a radical and unexpected conclusion: it is not enough to say that we are dealing here with a tragically misplaced ethical conviction, with a blind trust that avoids confronting the miserable, terrifying reality of its ethical point of reference. What if, on the contrary, such a blindness, such a violent gesture of refusing-to-see, such a disavowal-of-reality, such a fetishistic attitude of "I know very well that things are horrible in the Soviet Union, but I nonetheless believe in Soviet socialism," is the innermost constituent part of *every* ethical stance? Kant was already well aware of this paradox when he deployed his notion of enthusiasm for the French Revolution in his *Conflict of Faculties* (1795). The Revolution's true significance did not reside in what actually went on in Paris—much of which was terrifying and included outbursts of murderous passion— but in the enthusiastic response that the events in Paris generated in the eyes of sympathetic observers all around Europe:

> The recent Revolution of a people which is rich in spirit, may well either fail or succeed, accumulate misery and atrocity, it nevertheless arouses in the heart of all spectators (who are not themselves caught up in it) a taking of sides according to desires [*eine Teilnehmung dem Wunsche nach*] which borders on enthusiasm and which, since its very expression was not without danger, can only have been caused by a moral disposition within the human race.[6]

The real Event, the dimension of the Real, was not in the immediate reality of the violent events in Paris, but in how this reality appeared to observers and in the hopes thus awakened in them. The reality of what went on in Paris belongs to the temporal dimension of empirical history; the sublime image that generated enthusiasm belongs to Eternity . . . And, *mutatis mutandis*, the same applies for the Western admirers of the Soviet Union. The Soviet experience of "building socialism in one country" certainly did "accumulate misery and atrocity," but it nevertheless aroused enthusiasm in the heart of the spectators (who were not themselves caught up in it).

The question here is: does *every* ethics have to rely on such a gesture of fetishistic disavowal? Is even the most universal ethics not obliged to draw a line and ignore some sort of suffering? What about animals slaughtered for our consumption? Who would be able to continue eating pork chops after visiting an industrial farm in which pigs are half blind and cannot even properly walk, but are just fattened to be killed? And what about, say, the torture and suffering of millions about which we know but choose to ignore? Imagine the effect on one of us if we were forced to watch one single snuff movie of what goes on thousands of times a day around the earth—brutal torture (plucking out of eyes, crushing of testicles, for example)? Would we continue to go on living as usual? Yes—if we were able to somehow forget (suspend the symbolic efficiency) of what we had witnessed.

So, again, does not *every* ethics have to rely on such a gesture of fetishistic disavowal?[7] Yes, every ethics — *with the exception of the ethics of psychoanalysis* which is a kind of anti-ethics: it focuses precisely on what the standard ethical enthusiasm excludes, on the traumatic Thing that our Judeo-Christian tradition calls the "Neighbor." Freud had good reasons for his reluctance to endorse the injunction "Love thy neighbor!"—the temptation to be resisted here is the ethical domestication of the Neighbor. This is what Emmanuel Levinas did with his notion of the Neighbor as the abyssal point from which the call of ethical responsibility emanates: he thereby obfuscated the monstrosity of the Neighbor, the monstrosity on account of which Lacan applied to the neighbor the term Thing (*das Ding*), used by Freud to designate the ultimate object of our desires in its unbearable intensity and impenetrability. One should hear in this term all the connotations of horror fiction: the Neighbor is the (Evil) Thing which potentially lurks beneath every homely human face, like the hero of Stephen King's *The Shining*, a gentle failed writer, who gradually turns into a killing beast and, with an evil grin, goes on to slaughter his entire family.

When Freud and Lacan insist on the problematic nature of the basic Judeo-Christian injunction to "love thy neighbor," they are thus not just making the standard critico-ideological point about how every notion of universality is colored by our particular values and thus implies secret exclusions. They are making a much stronger point about the incompatibility of the Neighbor with the very dimension of universality. What resists universality is the properly *inhuman* dimension of the Neighbor. This brings us back to the key question: does *every* universalist ethics have to rely on such a gesture of fetishistic disavowal? The answer is: every ethics that remains "humanist" (in the sense of avoiding the inhuman core of being-human), that disavows the abyssal dimension of the Neighbor. "Man," "human person," is a mask that conceals the pure subjectivity of the Neighbor.

Consequently, when one asserts the Neighbor as the impenetrable "Thing" that eludes any attempt at gentrification, at its transformation into a cozy fellow man, this does not mean that the ultimate horizon of ethics is deference towards this unfathomable Otherness that subverts any encompassing universality. Following Alain Badiou, one should assert that, on the contrary, *only* an "inhuman" ethics, an ethics addressing an inhuman subject, not a fellow person, can sustain true universality. The most difficult thing for common understanding is to grasp this speculative-dialectical reversal of the singularity of the subject *qua* Neighbor-Thing into universality, not standard "general" universality, but universal singularity, the universality grounded in the subjective singularity extracted from all particular properties, a kind of direct short circuit between the singular and the universal, bypassing the particular.

We should celebrate the genius of Walter Benjamin which shines through in the very title of his early work: *On Language in General and Human Language in Particular*. The point here is not that human language is a species of some universal language "as such" which comprises also other species (the language of gods and angels? Animal language? The language of some other intelligent beings out there in space? Computer language? The language of DNA?): there is no actually-existing language other than human language—but, in order to comprehend this "particular" language, one *has* to introduce a minimal difference, conceiving it with regard to the gap which separates it from language "as such" (the pure structure of language deprived of the insignia of the human finitude, of erotic passions and mortality, of the struggles for domination and the obscenity of power).[8] This minimal difference between inhuman language and human language is clearly a Platonic one. What if, then, we have to turn the standard relationship around: the obverse of the fact that, in Christ, God is fully human, is that *we, humans, are not*. G.K. Chesterton began *The Napoleon of Nothing Hill* with: "The human race, to which so many of my readers belong . . ."—which, of course, does not mean that some of us are not human, but that there is an inhuman core in all of us, or, that we are "not-all human."

The screen of civility

The predominant way of maintaining a distance towards the "inhuman" Neighbor's intrusive proximity is politeness—but what is politeness? There is a gentle vulgar story that plays on the innuendos of seduction: A boy and a girl are saying goodbye late in the evening, in front of her house; hesitantly, he says: "Would you mind if I come in with you for a coffee?", to which she replies: "Sorry, not tonight, I have my period . . ." A polite version would be the one in which the girl says: "Good news, my period is over—come up to my place!", to which the boy replies: "Sorry, I am not in a mood for a cup of coffee right now . . ." This, however, immediately confronts us with the ambiguity of politeness: there is an unmistakable dimension of humiliating brutality in the boy's polite answer—as John Lennon put it in his "Working Class Hero": "you must learn how to smile as you kill."

The ambiguity of politeness is best rendered in Henry James's masterpieces: in this universe where *tact* reigns supreme, where the open explosion of one's emotions is considered as the utmost vulgarity, everything is said, the most painful decisions are made, the most delicate messages are passed over—however, it all takes place in the guise of a formal conversation. Even when I blackmail my partner, I do it with a polite smile, offering her tea and cakes . . . Is it, then, that, while the brutal direct approach misses the Other's kernel, a tactful dance can reach it? In his *Minima Moralia*, Adorno pointed out the utter ambiguity of tact clearly discernible already in Henry James: the respectful consideration for the other's sensitivity, the concern not to violate her intimacy, can easily pass over into the brutal insensitivity for the other's pain.[9] The same spirit, elevated to the level of absurdity, was displayed by Field Marshall von Kluge, the commander of the Army Group Centre on the Russian front. In January 1943, a group of German officers in Smolensk, where the headquarters of the army group was based, was planning to kill Hitler during the latter's visit; the idea was that, during a meal in the mess, some two dozen officers would simultaneously draw their pistols and shoot him, thus rendering the responsibility collective, and also making sure that Hitler's bodyguards would not be able to prevent at least some of the bullets hitting their target. Unfortunately, von Kluge vetoed the plan, although he was anti-Nazi and wanted Hitler dead. His argument was that, by the tenets of the German Officer Corps, "it is not seemly to shoot a man at lunch."[10]

As such, politeness comes close to civility. In a scene from *Break Up*, the nervous Vince Vaughn angrily reproaches Jennifer Anniston: "You wanted me to wash the dishes, and I'll wash the dishes—what's the problem?" She replies: "I don't want you to wash the dishes—I want you to *want* to wash the dishes!" This is the minimal reflexivity of desire, its "terrorist" demand: I want you not only to do what I want, but to do it as if you really want to do it—I want to regulate not only what you do, but also your desires. The worst thing you can do, even worse than not doing what I want you to do, is to do what I want you to do without wanting to do it . . . And this brings us to civility: an act of civility is precisely to feign that I want to do what the other asks me to do, so that my compliance with the other's wish does not exert pressure on her. The movie *Borat* is at its most subversive not when the hero is simply rude and offensive (for our Western eyes and ears, at least), but, on the contrary, when he desperately tries to be polite. During a dinner party in an upper-class house, he asks where the toilet is, whence he then returns with his excrement carefully wrapped in a plastic bag, and asks his hostess in a hushed voice where he should put it. This is a model metaphor of a truly subversive political gesture: bringing those in power a bag of excrement and politely asking them how to get rid of it.

In a perspicuous short essay on civility, Robert Pippin elaborates the enigmatic in-between status of this notion which designates all the acts that display the basic subjective attitude of respect for others as free and autonomous agents, equal to us, the benevolent attitude of transcending the strict utilitarian or "rational" calculation of costs and benefits in relations with others and engaging in trusting them, trying not to humiliate them, and so forth.[11] Although, measured by the degree of its obligatory character, it is more than kindness or generosity (one cannot oblige people to be generous), but distinctly less than a moral or legal obligation. This is what is wrong in politically correct attempts to moralize or even directly penalize modes of behavior which basically pertain to civility (like hurting others with vulgar obscenities of speech, and so on): they potentially undermine the precious "middle ground" of civility, mediating between uncontrolled private fantasies and the strictly regulated forms of intersubjective behavior. In more Hegelian terms, what gets lost in the penalization of un-civility is "ethical substance" as such: in contrast to laws and explicit normative regulations, civility is, by definition, "substantial," something experienced as always-already given, never imposed/instituted as such.[12] Which is why civility participates in all the paradoxes of the "states-that-are-essentially-by-products": it cannot be purposefully enacted — if it is, we have the full right to say that it is fake civility, not a true form. Pippin is right to link the crucial role of civility in modern societies to the rise of the autonomous free individual — not only in the sense that civility is a practice of treating others as equal, free, and autonomous subjects, but in a much more refined way: the fragile web of civility is the "social substance" of free independent individuals, it is their very mode of (inter)dependence. If this substance disintegrates, the very social space of individual freedom is foreclosed.

The properly Marxist notion of the "base" (in contrast with the "superstructure") should not be understood as a foundation which determines and thus constrains the scope of our freedom ("we think we are free, but we are really determined by the base"); one should rather conceive it as the very base (frame, terrain, space) *of* and *for* our freedom. The "base" is a social substance which sustains our freedom — in this sense, the rules of civility do not constrain our freedom, but provide the only space within which our freedom can thrive; the legal order enforced by state apparatuses is the base for our free-market exchanges; the grammatical rules are the indispensable base for our free thought (in order to "think freely," we have to practice these rules blindly); habit as our "second nature" is the base for culture; the collective of believers is the base, the only terrain, within which a Christian subject can be free, and so on. This is also how one should understand the infamous Marxist plea for "concrete, real freedom" as opposed to the bourgeois "abstract, merely formal freedom": this "concrete freedom" does not constrain the possible content ("you can only be truly free if you support our, Communist, side"); the question is, rather, what "base" should be secured for freedom. For example, although workers in capitalism are formally free, there is no "base" that would allow them to actualize their freedom as producers; although there is "formal" freedom of speech, organization, and so forth, the base of this freedom is constrained.

The theoretical point of civility is thus that free subjectivity has to be sustained by feigning. Contrary to what we might expect, however, this is not feigning to perform a free act when one is simply doing what one is under pressure or obliged to do (the most elementary form of it is, of course, the ritual of "potlatch," exchange of gifts, in "primitive" societies). How, then, does civility relate to the set of unwritten rules which *de facto* constrain my freedom while sustaining its appearance? Let us imagine a scene in which, to be polite and not to humiliate the other, I formulate my order to him (since I am in the position of authority towards him, so that he has to obey my orders) as a kind request: "Could you perhaps be so kind as to . . ." (Along the same lines, when powerful or famous people receive an unknown individual, one of the polite forms is to pretend that it is the unknown individual who is doing them a favor by visiting them — "Thank you for being so kind as to pay me a visit . . .") This, however, is not true civility: civility is not simply obligation-feigned-as-free-act; it is rather its exact opposite: *a free act feigned as an obligation.* Back to our example: the true act of civility from someone in power would be for him to feign that he is simply doing something he has to do when, in reality, it is an act of generosity on his part. Freedom is thus sustained by a paradox that turns around the Spinozan definition of freedom as conceived necessity: it is freedom which is feigned necessity.

To put it in Hegelian terms, freedom is sustained by the ethical substance of our being. In a given society, certain features, attitudes, and norms of life are no longer perceived as ideologically marked, they appear as "neutral," as the non-ideological common-sense form of life; ideology is the explicitly posited ("marked" in the semiotic sense) position which stands out from/against this background (like extreme religious zeal, dedication to some political orientation, etc.). The Hegelian point here would have been that it is precisely this neutralization of some features into the spontaneously accepted background which is ideology *par excellence* (and at its most effective) — this is the dialectical "coincidence of the opposites": the actualization of a notion (ideology, in this case) at its coincides with (or, more precisely, appears as) its opposite (as non-ideology). And, *mutatis mutandis*, the same goes for violence: social-symbolic violence unadulterated appears as its opposite, as the spontaneity of the milieu in which we dwell, of the air that we breathe.

This notion of civility is at the very heart of the impasses of multiculturalism. A couple of years ago, there was a debate in Germany about *Leitkultur* (the dominant culture): against abstract multiculturalism, conservatives insisted that every state is based on a predominant cultural space which the members of other cultures who live in the same space should respect. Although liberal leftists attacked this notion as covert racism, one should admit that, if nothing else, it offers an adequate description of the facts. Respect of individual freedoms and rights, even if at the expense of group rights, full emancipation of women, freedom of religion (and of atheism) and sexual orientation, freedom to publicly attack anyone and anything, are central constituent elements of Western liberal *Leitkultur*, and this can be used to respond to those Muslim theologians in Western countries who protest against their treatment, while accepting it as normal that in, say, Saudi Arabia, it is prohibited to practice publicly religions other than Islam. They should accept that the same *Leitkultur* which allows their religious freedom in the West, demands of them a respect for all other freedoms. To put it succinctly: freedom for Muslims is part and parcel of the freedom for Salman Rushdie to write what he wants — you cannot choose the part of Western freedom which suits you. The answer to the standard critical argument that Western multiculturalism is not truly neutral, that it privileges specific values, is that one should shamelessly accept this paradox: universal openness itself is rooted in Western modernity.

And, to avoid any misunderstanding, the same applies to Christianity itself. On May 2, 2007, *L'Osservatore Romano*, the Vatican's official newspaper, accused Andrea Rivera, an Italian comedian, of "terrorism" for criticizing the pope. As a presenter of a televised May Day rock concert, Rivera attacked the pope's position on evolution ("The pope says he doesn't believe in evolution. I agree, in fact the Church has never evolved.") He also criticized the Church for refusing to give a Catholic funeral to Piergiorgio Welby, a victim of muscular dystrophy who campaigned for euthanasia and died in December 2006 after a doctor agreed to unplug his respirator ("I can't stand the fact that the Vatican refused a funeral for Welby but that wasn't the case for Pinochet or Franco"). Here is the Vatican's reaction: "This, too, is terrorism. It's terrorism to launch attacks on the Church. It's terrorism to stoke blind and irrational rage against someone who always speaks in the name of love, love for life and love for man." It is the underlying equation of intellectual critique with physical terrorist attacks which brutally violates the West European *Leitkultur*, which insists on the universal sphere of the "public use of reason," where one can criticize and problematize every-thing—in the eyes of our shared *Leitkultur*, Rivera's statements are totally acceptable.

Civility is crucial here: multicultural freedom also functions only when it is sustained by the rules of civility, which are never abstract, but always embedded within a *Leitkultur*. Within our *Leitkultur*, it is not Rivera but *L'Osservatore Romano* which is "terroristic" with its dismissal of Rivera's simple and reasonable objections as expressions of "blind and irrational rage." Freedom of speech functions when all parties follow the same unwritten rules of civility telling us what kind of attacks are improper, although they are not legally prohibited; civility tells us which features of a specific ethnic or religious "way of life" are acceptable and which are not acceptable. If all sides do not share or respect the same civility, then multiculturalism turns into legally regulated mutual ignorance or hatred.

One of the Lacanian names for this civility is the "Master-Signifier," the set of rules grounded only in themselves ("it is so because it is so, because it is our custom")—and it is this dimension of the Master-Signifier which is more and more threatened in our societies.

Gift and exchange

So what is a Master-Signifier? Apropos school exams, Lacan pointed out a strange fact: there must be a minimal gap, delay, between the procedure of measuring my qualifications and the act of announcing the result (grades). In other words, even if I know that I provided perfect answers to the exam questions, there remains a minimum element of insecurity, of chance, till the results are announced—this gap is the gap between the constative and the performative, between *measuring* the results and *taking note* of them (registering them) in the full sense of the symbolic act. The whole mystique of bureaucracy at its most sublime hinges on this gap: you know the facts, but you can never be quite sure of how these facts will be registered by bureaucracy. The same holds for elections: in the electoral process the moment of contingency, of hazard, of a "lottery," is crucial. Fully "rational" elections would not be elections at all, but a transparent objectivized process.

Traditional (pre-modern) societies resolved this problem by invoking a transcendental source which "verified" the result, conferring authority on it (God, King . . .). Therein resides the problem of modernity: modern societies perceive themselves as autonomous, self-regulated; that is, they can no longer rely on an external (transcendental) source of authority. But, nonetheless, the moment of hazard has to remain operative in the electoral process, which is why commentators like to dwell on the "irrationality" of votes (one never knows which way votes will swing in the last days before elections . . .). In other words, democracy would not work if it were reduced to permanent opinion-polling—fully mechanized and quantified, deprived of its "performative" character. As Claude Lefort pointed out, voting has to remain a (sacrificial) ritual, a ritualistic self-destruction and rebirth of society.[13] The reason is that this hazard itself should not be transparent, it should be minimally externalized/reified: the "people's will" is our equivalent of what the Ancients perceived as the imponderable will of God or the hands of Fate. What people cannot accept as their direct arbitrary choice, the result of a pure contingency, they can do if this hazard is referred to a minimum of the "real"—Hegel knew this long ago, this is the entire point of his defense of monarchy. And, last but not least, the same goes for love: there should be an element of the "answer of the Real" in it ("we were forever meant for each other"), I cannot really accept that my falling in love hinges on a purely aleatory process.[14]

It is only against this background that one can properly locate the function of the Master. The Master is the one who receives gifts in such a way that his acceptance of a gift is perceived by the subject who provided the gift as its own reward. As such, the Master is thus correlative to the subject caught in the double movement of what Freud called *Versagung* (renunciation): the gesture by means of which the subject gives what is most precious to him and, in exchange, is himself turned into an object of exchange, is correlative to the gesture of giving in the very act of receiving. The Master's refusal of exchange is correlative to the re-doubled, self-reflected, exchange on the side of the subject who ex-changes (gives what is most precious to him) and is exchanged.

The trick of capitalism, of course, is that this asymmetry is concealed in the ideological appearance of equivalent exchange: the double non-exchange is masked as free exchange. This is why, as was clear to Lacan, psychoanalysis—not only as a theory, but above all as a specific intersubjective practice, as a unique form of social link—could have emerged only within capitalist society where intersubjective relations are mediated by money. Money—paying the analyst—is necessary in order to keep him out of circulation, to avoid getting him involved in the imbroglio of passions which generated the patient's pathology. This is why a psychoanalyst is not a Master-figure, but, rather, a kind of "prostitute of the mind," having recourse to money for the same reason some prostitutes like to be paid so that they can have sex without personal involvement, maintaining their distance—here, we encounter the func-tion of money at its purest.

There are similarities between analytic treatment and the ritual of potlatch. Marcel Mauss, in his "Essai sur le don,"[15] first described the paradoxical logic of potlatch, of the reciprocal exchange of gifts. Gift and exchange are, of course, opposed in their immanent logic: a true gift is by definition an act of generosity, given without expecting something in return, while exchange is necessarily reciprocal—I give something, expecting something else in exchange. Potlatch is a short-circuit (inter-section) of the two sets: an exchange in the form of its opposite, of two acts of voluntary gift-giving (and the point is, of course, that such acts are not secondary with regard to exchange, but precede and ground it). The same holds for psychoanalytic treatment, in which the analyst is not paid for the work he does in a set of equivalent exchanges (so much for an interpretation of a dream, so much for the dissolution of a symptom, etc., with the ironic prospect of offering a special discount: "buy three dream interpretations and get one for free . . .")—the moment the relationship starts to function like this, we are no longer in the analyst's discourse (social link). But neither is the analyst restoring the patient's mental health out of the goodness of his heart, for free: the analyst's acts have nothing to do with goodness, with helping a neighbor—again, the moment the patient perceives the analyst as acting out of goodness, this can lead even to a psychotic crisis, and trigger a paranoid outburst. So, as in potlach, the exchange between the analyst and the analysand is between two incommensurable excesses: the analyst is paid for nothing, as a gift, his price is always exorbitant (typically, the patients oscillate between complaining that the price is too high and bouts of excessive gratitude—"how can I ever repay you for what you did . . ."), *and* the patient gets some help, an improvement in his condition, as an unintended by-product. As Lacan makes clear, the underlying problem here is how to determine the price of that which has no price.

How, then, are we to resolve the enigma of potlatch? Mauss's solution is a mystical X which circulates in exchange. Claude Lévi-Strauss reduced the mystique to its "rational core": reciprocity, exchange as such—the meaning of reciprocal exchange of gifts is *exchange itself* as the enactment of social link.[16] There is, however, something missing in this Lévi-Straussian solution;[17] it was Pierre Bourdieu[18] who asked here the crucial "Marxist" question as to why (in Marx's words) "Political Economy has indeed analyzed, however incompletely, value and its magnitude, and has discovered what lies beneath these forms. But it has never once asked the question why labor is represented by the value of its product and labor-time by the magnitude of that value."[19] If the secret core of potlatch is the reciprocity of exchange, why is this reciprocity not asserted directly, why does it assume the "mystified" form of two consecutive acts each of which is staged as a free voluntary display of generosity? Here we encounter the paradoxes of forced choice, of freedom to do what is necessary, at its most elementary: I have to do freely what I am expected to do. (If, upon receiving a gift, I immediately return it to the giver, this direct circulation would amount to an extremely aggressive gesture of humiliation, it would signal that I *refused* the other's gift—recall those embarrassing moments when elderly people forget and give us last year's present once again . . .) However, Bourdieu's solution remains all too vulgar Marxist: he evokes hidden economic "interests." It was Marshall Sahlins who proposed a different, more pertinent, solution: the reciprocity of exchange is in itself thoroughly ambiguous; at its most fundamental, it is *destructive* of the social bond, it is the logic of revenge, tit for tat.[20] To cover this aspect of exchange, to make it benevolent and pacific, one has to *pretend* that each person's gift is free and stands on its own. This brings us to potlatch as the "pre-economy of the economy," its zero-level, that is, exchange as the reciprocal relation of two non-productive expenditures. If the gift belongs to Master and exchange to the Servant, potlatch is the paradoxical exchange between Masters. Potlatch is thus simultaneously the zero-level of civility, the paradoxical point at which restrained civility and obscene consumption overlap, the point at which it is polite to behave impolitely.

Ulysses' realpolitik

The obscene underside that haunts the dignity of the Master-Signifier from its very inception, or the secret alliance between the dignity of the Law and its obscene transgression, was first clearly outlined by Shakespeare in *Troilus and Cressida*, his most uncanny play, effectively a postmodern work *avant la lettre*. In his influential *Shakespearean Tragedy*, which set the coordinates of the traditional academic reading of Shakespeare, A.C. Bradley, the great English Hegelian, speaks of

> a certain limitation, a partial suppression of that element in Shakespeare's mind which unites him with the mystical poets and with the great musicians and philosophers. In one or two of his plays, notably in *Troilus and Cressida*, we are almost painfully conscious of this suppression; we feel an intense intellectual activity, but at the same time a certain coldness and hardness, as though some power in his soul, at once the highest and the sweetest, were for a time in abeyance. In other plays, notably in *The Tempest*, we are constantly aware of the presence of this power.[21]

There is truth in this perception: it is as if, in *Troilus*, there is no place for the redemptive quality of metaphysical pathos and bliss which somehow cancels the horrible and ridiculous events that took place. The first difficulty is how to categorize *Troilus*: although arguably the bleakest of Shakespeare's plays, it is often listed as a comedy—correctly, since it lacks dignified tragic pathos.[22] In other words, if *Troilus* is a comedy, then it is for the same reason that all good films about the Holocaust also are comedies: it is a blasphemy to claim that the predicament of prisoners in a concentration camp was tragic—their predicament was so terrifying that they were deprived of the very possibility of displaying tragic grandeur. *Troilus* plays the same structural role in Shakespeare's opus as *Così fan tutte* among Mozart's operas: its despair is so thoroughgoing that the only way to overcome it is through the retreat into fairy-tale magic (*The Tempest* and other late Shakespeare plays; Mozart's *Magic Flute*).

Many of Shakespeare's plays retell an already well-known great story (of Julius Caesar, of English kings); what makes *Troilus* the exception is that, in retelling the well-known story, it shifts the accent to what were in the original minor and marginal characters: *Troilus* is not primarily about Achilles and Hector, Priam and Agamemnon; its love couple is not Helen and Priam, but Cressida and Troilus. In this sense, *Troilus* can be said to prefigure one of the paradigmatic postmodern procedures, that of re-telling a well-known classical story from the standpoint of a marginal character. Tom Stoppard's *Rosencranz and Gildenstern Are Dead* does it with *Hamlet*, while here, Shakespeare himself carries out the move. This displacement also undermines Shakespeare's standard procedure, from his royal chronicles, of supplementing the "big" royal scenes staged in a dignified way with scenes figuring common people who introduce a comic common-sense perspective. In the royal chronicles, these comic interludes strengthen the noble scenes through their contrast to them; in *Troilus*, everybody, even the noblest of warriors, is "contaminated" by the ridiculing perspective which makes us see them either as blind and stupidly pathetic or as involved in ruthless intrigues. The "operator" of this undoing of the tragic dimension, the single agent whose interventions systematically undermine tragic pathos, is Ulysses—this may sound surprising in view of Ulysses' first intervention, at the Greek war council in Act I where the Greek (or "Grecian," as Shakespeare put it, in what now may be called "Bush mode") generals try to account for their failure to occupy and destroy Troy after eight years of fighting. Ulysses inter-venes from a traditional "old values" position, locating the true cause of the Greeks' failure in their neglect of the centralized hierarchical order where every individual is in his proper place:

The specialty of rule hath been neglected.
And look how many Grecian tents do stand
Hollow upon this plain: so many hollow factions.
    [. . .] O when degree is shaked,
Which is the ladder to all high designs,
Then enterprise is sick. How could communities,
Degrees in schools and brotherhoods in cities,
Peaceful commerce from dividable shores,
The primogenity and due of birth,
Prerogative of age, crowns, sceptres, laurels,
But by degree stand in authentic place?

Take but degree away, untune that string,
And, hark, what discord follows. Each thing meets
In mere oppugnancy. The bounded waters
Should lift their bosoms higher than the shores
And make a sop of all this solid globe;
Strength should be lord of imbecility,
And the rude son should strike his father dead.
Force should be right—or rather, right and wrong,
Between whose endless jar justice resides,
Should lose their names, and so should justice too.
Then every thing includes itself in power [. . .]

(I, 3)

What, then, causes this disintegration which ends up in the democratic horror of everyone participating in power? Later in the play, when Ulysses wants to convince Achilles to rejoin the battle, he mobilizes the metaphor of time as the destructive force that gradually undermines the natural hierarchical order: in the course of time, your old heroic deeds will soon be forgotten, your glory will be eclipsed by the new heroes—so if you want to continue shining in your warrior glory, rejoin the battle:

Time hath, my lord,
A wallet at his back,
wherein he puts
Alms for oblivion,
a great-sized monster
Of ingratitudes.
Those scraps are good deeds past,
Which are devoured
as fast as they are made,
Forgot as soon
As done. Perseverance, dear my lord,
Keeps honour bright. To have done is to hang
Quite out of fashion, like a rusty mail
In monumental mock'ry. [. . .]
O, let not virtue seek
Remuneration for the thing it was;
For beauty, wit,
High birth, vigour of bone, desert in service,

Love, friendship, charity, are subjects all
To envious and calumniating time.

(III, 3)

Ulysses' strategy here is profoundly ambiguous. In a first approach, he merely restates his argumentation about the necessity of "degrees" (ordered social hierarchy), and portrays time as the corrosive force which undermines old true values—an arch-conservative motif. However, on a closer reading, it becomes clear that Ulysses gives to his argumentation a singular cynical twist: how are we to fight against time, to keep old values alive? Not by directly sticking to them, but by supplementing them with the obscene realpolitik of cruel manipulation, of cheating, of playing one hero against the other. It is only this dirty underside, this hidden disharmony, that can sustain harmony (Ulysses plays with Achilles' envy, he refers to emulation—the very attitudes that work to destabilize the hierarchical order, since they signal that one is not satisfied by one's subordinate place within the social body). Secret manipulation of envy—that is, the violation of the very rules and values Ulysses celebrates in his first speech—is needed to counteract the effects of time and sustain the hierarchical order of "degrees." This would be Ulysses' version of Hamlet's famous "The time is out of joint; O cursed spite, / That ever I was born to set it right!"—the only way to "set it right" is to counteract the transgression of Old Order with its *inherent transgression*, with crime secretly committed to serve the Order. The price we pay for this is that the Order which thus survives is a mockery of itself, a blasphemous imitation of Order.

This is why ideology is not simply an operation of closure, drawing the line between what is included and what is excluded/prohibited, but the ongoing regulation of non-closure. In the case of marriage, ideology not only prohibits extramarital affairs; its crucial operation is to regulate such inevitable transgressions (say, the proverbial Catholic priest's advice to a promiscuous husband: if you really have needs that your wife cannot satisfy, visit a prostitute discreetly, fornicate and then repent, as long as you do not divorce). In this way, an ideology always admits the failure of closure, and then goes on to regulate the permeability of the exchange with its outside.

Today, however, in our "postmodern" world, this dialectic of the Law and its inherent transgression is given an additional twist: transgression is more and more directly enjoined by the Law itself.

The atonal world

Why does potlatch appear so mysterious or meaningless to us? The basic feature of our "postmodern" world is that it tries to dispense with the agency of the Master-Signifier: the "complexity" of the world should be asserted unconditionally, every Master-Signifier meant to impose some order on it should be "deconstructed," dispersed, "disseminated": "The modern apology for the 'complexity' of the world [. . .] is really nothing but a generalized desire for atonality."[23] Badiou's perspicuous example of such an "atonal" world is the politically correct vision of sexuality, as promoted by gender studies, with its obsessive rejection of "binary logic": this world is a nuanced, ramified world of multiple sexual practices which tolerates no decision, no instance of the Two, no evaluation (in the strong Nietzschean sense). This suspension of the Master-Signifier leaves as the only agency of ideological interpellation the "unnameable" abyss of *jouissance*: the ultimate injunction that regulates our lives in "postmodernity" is "Enjoy!"—realize your potential, enjoy in all manner of ways, from intense sexual pleasures through social success to spiritual self-fulfilment.

However, far from liberating us from the pressure of guilt, such dispensing with the Master-Signifier comes at a price, the price signaled by Lacan's qualification of the superego command: "Nothing forces anyone to enjoy except the superego. The superego is the imperative of *jouissance*—Enjoy!"[24] In short, the decline of the Master-Signifier exposes the subject to all the traps and double-talk of the superego: the very injunction to enjoy, in other words, the (often imperceptible) shift from the permission to enjoy to the injunction (obligation) to enjoy sabotages enjoyment, so that, paradoxically, the more one obeys the superego command, the more one feels guilty. This same ambiguity affects the very basis of a "permissive" and "tolerant" society: "we see from day to day how this tolerance is nothing else than a fanaticism, since it tolerates only its own vacuity."[25] And, effectively, every decision, every determinate engagement, is potentially "intolerant" towards all others.

In his *Logiques des mondes*, Badiou develops the notion of "atonal" worlds (*monde atone*),[26] worlds lacking a "point," in Lacanese: the "quilting point" (*point de capiton*), the intervention of a Master-Signifier that imposes a principle of "ordering" into the world, the point of a simple decision ("yes or no") in which the confused multiplicity is violently reduced to a "minimal difference." None other than John F. Kennedy provided a concise description of this point: "The essence of ultimate decision remains impenetrable to the observer—often, indeed, to the decider himself." This gesture which can never be fully grounded in reasons, is that of a Master—or, as G.K. Chesterton put it in his inimitable manner: "The purpose of an open mind, like having an open mouth, is to close it upon something solid."

If the fight against a world proceeds by way of undermining its "point," the feature that sutures it into a stable totality, how are we to proceed when (as is the case today) we dwell in an atonal world, a world of multiplicities lacking a determinate tonality? The answer is: one has to oppose it in such a way that one compels it to "tonalize" itself, to openly admit the secret tone that sustains its atonality. For example, when one confronts a world which presents itself as tolerant and pluralist, disseminated, with no center, one has to attack the underlying structuring principle which sustains this atonality—say, the secret qualifications of "tolerance" which excludes as "intolerant" certain critical questions, or the secret qualifications which exclude as a "threat to freedom" questions about the limits of the existing freedoms.

The paradox, the sign of hidden complicity between today's religious fundamentalisms and the "postmodern" universe they reject so ferociously, is that fundamentalism also belongs to the "atonal world"—which is why a fundamentalist does not *believe*, he *knows* directly. To put it in another way, both liberal-skeptical cynicism and fundamentalism thus share a basic underlying feature: the loss of the ability to believe in the proper sense of the term. For both of them, religious statements are quasi-empirical statements of direct knowledge: fundamentalists accept them as such, while skeptical cynics mock them. What is unthinkable for them is the "absurd" act of a decision which establishes every authentic belief, a decision which cannot be grounded in the chain of "reasons," in positive knowledge: the "sincere hypocrisy" of somebody like Anne Frank who, in the face of the terrifying depravity of the Nazis, in a true act of *credo qua absurdum* asserted her belief in the fundamental goodness of all humans. No wonder then that religious fundamentalists are among the most passionate digital hackers, and always prone to combine their religion with the latest findings of science: for them, religious statements and scientific statements belong to the same modality of positive knowledge. (In this sense, the status of "universal human rights" is also that of a pure belief: they cannot be grounded in our knowledge of human nature, they are an axiom posited by our decision.) The occurrence of the term "science" in the very name of some of the fundamentalist sects (Christian Science, Scientology) is not just an obscene joke, but signals this reduction of belief to positive knowledge. The case of the Turin shroud is here symptomal: its authenticity would be awful for every true believer (the first thing to do then would be to analyze the DNA of the blood stains and thus solve empirically the question of who Jesus' father was . . .), while a true fundamentalist would rejoice in this opportunity.

We find the same phenomenon in some forms of contemporary Islam: hundreds of books by scientists "demonstrate" how the latest scientific advances confirm the insights and injunctions of the Koran—the divine prohibition of incest is confirmed by recent genetic knowledge about the defective children born of incestuous copulation, and so on and so forth. (Some even go so far as to claim that what the Koran offers as an article of faith to be accepted because of its divine origin is not finally demonstrated as scientific truth, thereby reducing the Koran itself to an inferior mythic version of what has acquired its appropriate formulation in contemporary science.)[27] The same goes also for Buddhism, where many scientists vary the motif of the "Tao of modern physics," that is, of how the contemporary scientific vision of reality as a desubstantialized flux of oscillating events finally confirmed the old Buddhist ontology . . .[28] One is thus compelled to draw the paradoxical conclusion: in the opposition between traditional secular humanists and religious fundamentalists, it is the humanists who stand for belief, while fundamentalists stand for knowledge—in short, the true danger of fundamentalism does not reside in the fact that it poses a threat to secular scientific knowledge, but in the fact that it poses a threat to authentic belief itself.

What we should bear in mind here is how the opposition of knowledge and faith echoes the one between the constative and the performative: faith (or, rather, trust) is the basic ingredient of speech as the medium of social bond, of the subject's engaged participation in this bond, while science—exemplarily in its formalization—reduces language to neutral registration. Let us not forget that science has, for Lacan, the status of the "knowledge in the real": the language of science is not the language of subjective engagement, but the language deprived of its performative dimension, desubjectivized language. The predominance of scientific discourse thus entails the retreat, the potential suspension, of the very symbolic function as the metaphor constitutive of human subjectivity. Paternal authority is irreducibly based on faith, on trust as to the identity of the father: we have fathers (as symbolic functions, as the Name-of-the-

Father, the paternal metaphor), because we do not directly *know* who our father is, we have to take him *at his word* and *trust* him. To put it pointedly, the moment I know with scientific certainty who my father is, fatherhood ceases to be the function which grounds social-symbolic Trust. In the scientific universe, there is no need for such faith, truth can be established through DNA analysis . . . The hegemony of the scientific discourse thus potentially suspends the entire network of symbolic tradition that sustains the subject's identifications. Politically, the shift is from Power grounded in the traditional symbolic authority to biopolitics.

The "worldless" character of capitalism is linked to this hegemonic role of scientific discourse in modernity, a feature clearly identified already by Hegel who wrote that, for us moderns, art and religion no longer obey absolute respect: we can admire them, but we no longer kneel down in front of them, our heart is not really with them — today, only science (conceptual knowledge) deserves this respect. "Postmodernity" as the "end of grand narratives" is one of the names for this predicament in which the multitude of local fictions thrives against the background of scientific discourse as the only remaining universality deprived of sense. Which is why the politics advocated by many a leftist today, that of countering the devastating world-dissolving effect of capitalist modernization by inventing new fictions, imagining "new worlds" (like the Porto Alegre slogan "Another world is possible!"), is inadequate or, at least, profoundly ambiguous: it all depends on how these fictions relate to the underlying Real of capitalism — do they just *supplement* it with the imaginary multitude, as the postmodern "local narratives" do, or do they *disturb* its functioning? In other words, the task is to produce *a symbolic fiction (a truth) that intervenes into the Real*, that causes a change within it.[29]

It is only psychoanalysis that can disclose the full contours of the shattering impact of modernity (in its two aspects: the hegemony of scientific discourse and capitalism) on the way our identity is performatively grounded in symbolic identifications, on the manner in which the symbolic order is counted on to provide the horizon that allows us to locate every experience in a meaningful totality. The necessary obverse of modernity is the "crisis of meaning," the disintegration of the link — identity even — between Truth and Meaning. Since, in Europe, modernization was spread over centuries, we had the time to accommodate to this break, to soften its shattering impact, through *Kulturarbeit*, through the formation of new social narratives and myths, while some other societies — exemplarily the Muslim ones — were exposed to this impact directly, without a protective screen or temporal delay, so their symbolic universe was perturbed much more brutally, they lost their (symbolic) ground with no time left to establish a new (symbolic) balance. No wonder, then, that the only way for some of these societies to avoid total breakdown was to erect in panic the shield of "fundamentalism," the psychotic-delirious-incestuous reassertion of religion as direct insight into the divine Real, with all the terrifying consequences that such a reassertion entails, up to the return with a vengeance of the obscene superego divinity demanding sacrifices. The rise of the superego is another feature that postmodern permissiveness and the new fundamentalism share; what distinguishes them is the site of the enjoyment demanded: our own in permissiveness, God's own in fundamentalism.

From all sides, Right and Left, complaints abound today about how, in our postmodern societies composed of hedonistic solipsists, social bonds are progressively disintegrating: we are increasingly reduced to social atoms, as exemplified by the lone individual hooked on the computer screen, preferring virtual exchanges to contacts with other flesh-and-blood persons, preferring cyber sex to bodily contact, and so forth. However, this very example renders visible what is wrong with the diagnosis on suspended social ties: in order for an individual to immerse herself in the virtual space, the big Other has to be there, more powerful than ever in the guise of cyberspace itself, this directly universalized form of sociality which enables us to be connected with the entire world while sitting alone in front of a screen.

It may seem that Lacan's *doxa* "there is no big Other" has today lost its subversive edge and turned into a globally acknowledged commonplace—everybody seems to know that there is no "big Other" in the sense of a substantial shared set of customs and values, that what Hegel called "objective Spirit" (the social substance of mores) is disintegrating into particular "worlds" (or life styles) whose coordination is regulated by purely formal rules. This is why not only communitarians but even liberal leftists advocate the need to establish new ties of solidarity and other shared values. However, the example of cyberspace clearly demonstrates how the big Other is present more than ever: social atomism can only function when it is regulated by some (apparently) neutral mechanism — digital solipsists need a very complex global machinery to be able to persevere in their splendid isolation.

Was not Richard Rorty the paradigmatic philosopher of such an Other without a privileged link to others? His big Other is the set of neutral public rules which enable each of the individuals to "tell her own story" of dreams and suffering. These rules guarantee that the "private" space of personal idiosyncrasies, imperfections, violent fantasies, and so on, will not spill over into a direct domination of others. Recall one of the latest upshots of sexual liberation: the "masturbate-a-thon," a collective event in which hundreds of men and women pleasure themselves for charity, raising money for sexual- and reproductive-health agencies, and—as the organizers put it—raising awareness and dispelling the shame and taboos that persist around this most commonplace, natural, and safe form of sexual activity. The ideological stance underlying the notion of the masturbathon is marked by a conflict between its form and content: it builds a collective out of individuals who are ready to *share* with others the solipsistic egotism of their stupid pleasure. This contradiction, however, is more apparent than real. Freud already knew about the connection between narcissism and immersion in a crowd, best rendered precisely by the Californian phrase "sharing an experience." And what is crucial is the underlying symbolic pact which enables the assembled masturbators to "share a space" without intruding on each other's space. The more one wants to be an atomist, the more some figure of the big Other is needed to regulate one's distance from others. Perhaps this accounts for the strange, but adequate, impression it is difficult to avoid when one encounters a true hedonist solipsist: in spite of her unconstrained indulgence in personal idiosyncrasies, she strikes us as weirdly impersonal—what she lacks is the very sense of the "depth" of a person.

What, then, is missing in today's social bond, if it is not the big Other?[30] The answer is clear: a small other which would embody, stand in for, the big Other—a person who is not simply "like the others," but who directly embodies authority. In our postmodern universe, every small other is "finitized" (perceived as fallible, imperfect, "merely human," ridiculous), inadequate to give body to a big Other—and, in this way, preserves the purity of the big Other unblemished by its failings. When, in a decade or so, money will finally become a purely virtual point of reference, no longer materialized in a particular object, this dematerialization will render its fetishistic power absolute: its very invisibility will render it all-powerful and omnipresent. The task of radical politics is therefore not to denounce the inadequacy of every small other to stand in for the big Other (such a "critique" only reinforces the big Other's hold over us), but to undermine the very big Other and, in this way, to untie the social bond the big Other sustains. Today, when everyone complains about dissolving social ties (and thereby obfuscating their hold over us, which is stronger than ever), the true job of untying them is still ahead of us, more urgent than ever.

Lacan's standard notion of anxiety is that, as the only affect that does not lie, it bears witness to the proximity of the Real, to the inexistence of the big Other; such anxiety has to be confronted by courage, it should lead to an act proper which, as it were, cuts into the real of a situation. There is, however, another mode of anxiety which predominates today: the anxiety caused by the claustrophobia of the atonal world which lacks any structuring "point," the anxiety of the "pathological Narcissus" frustrated by the fact that he is caught in the endless competitive mirroring of his fellow men (a-a'-a''-a''' . . .), of the series of "small others" none of which functions as the stand-in for the "big Other."[31] The root of this claustrophobia is that the lack of embodied stand-ins for the big Other, instead of opening up the social space, depriving it of any Master-figures, renders the invisible "big Other," the mechanism that regulates the interaction of "small others," all the more all-pervasive.

Serbsky Institute, Malibu

With this shift towards the "atonal world," the obscene solidarity between the Law and its superego underside is supplanted by the hidden solidarity between tolerant permissiveness and religious fundamentalism. A recent scandal in Malibu not only displayed the obscene pact between the biopolitical "therapeutic" approach and the fundamentalist reaction to it, but also the catastrophic ethical price we have to pay for this pact.

In good old Soviet times, the Serbsky Institute in Moscow was the psychiatric flagship for punitive political control; its psychiatrists developed painful drug methods to make detainees talk and extract testimony for use in national security investigations. Underpinning the ability of psychiatrists to incarcerate people was an invented political mental disorder known as ("sluggish *vilotekushchaia* schizophrenia"). Psychiatrists described symptoms thus: a person might appear quite normal most of the time but would break out with a severe case of "inflexibility of convictions," or "nervous exhaustion brought on by his or her search for justice," or "a tendency to litigation" or "reformist delusions." The treatment involved intravenous injections of psychotropic drugs that were so painfully administered that patients became unconscious. The overriding belief was that a person had to be *insane* to be opposed to

Communism. Is this psychiatric approach to politically problematic positions a thing of the past? Unfortunately, no: not only is the Serbsky Institute today happily thriving in Putin's Russia, but, as a recent incident with Mel Gibson indicates, it will soon open a branch in Malibu! Here is Gibson's own description of what happened to him on Friday, July 28, 2006:

> I drove a car when I should not have, and was stopped by the LA County Sheriffs. The arresting officer was just doing his job and I feel fortunate that I was apprehended before I caused injury to any other person. I acted like a person completely out of control when I was arrested, and said things that I do not believe to be true and which are despicable.

It is reported that Gibson said, "F------ Jews . . . The Jews are responsible for all the wars in the world," and asked a deputy, "Are you a Jew?" Gibson apologized, but his apology was rejected by the Anti-Defamation League. Here is what Abraham Foxman, director of the League, wrote:

> Mel Gibson's apology is unremorseful and insufficient. It's not a proper apology because it does not go to the essence of his bigotry and his anti-Semitism. His tirade finally reveals his true self and shows that his protestations during the debate over his film *The Passion of the Christ*, that he is such a tolerant, loving person, were a sham.

Later, Gibson offered a more substantial apology, announcing through a spokesman that he would undergo rehabilitation for alcohol abuse. He added: "Hatred of any kind goes against my faith. I'm not just asking for forgiveness. I would like to take it one step further, and meet with leaders in the Jewish community, with whom I can have a one-on-one discussion to discern the appropriate path for healing." Gibson said he is "in the process of understanding where those vicious words came from during that drunken display." This time, Foxman accepted his apology as sincere:

> Two years ago, I was told by his publicist that he wants to meet with me and have an understanding. I'm still waiting. There is no course, there is no curriculum. We need in-depth conversation. It's therapy—

and the most important step in any therapy is to admit that you have a problem, which is a step he's already taken.

Why waste precious time on such a vulgar incident? For an observer of the ideological trends in the US, these events display a nightmarish dimension: the mutually reinforcing hypocrisy of the two sides, the anti-Semitic Christian fundamentalists and the Zionists, is breathtaking. Politically, the reconciliation between Gibson and Foxman signals an obscene pact between anti-Semitic Christian fundamentalists and aggressive Zionists, whose expression is the growing support of the fundamentalists for the State of Israel (recall Pat Robertson's claim that Sharon's heart attack was divine retribution for the evacuation of Gaza). The Jewish people will pay dearly for such pacts with the devil—can one imagine what a boost anti-Semitism will receive from Foxman's offer? "So if I now say something critical about Jews, I will be forced to submit to psychiatric therapy . . ."

What underlies the final reconciliation is, obviously, an obscene quid pro quo. Foxman's reaction to Gibson's outburst was not excessively severe and demanding; on the contrary, it let Gibson all too easily off the hook. It accepted Gibson's refusal to take full personal responsibility for his words (his anti-Semitic remarks): they were not really his own, it was pathology, some unknown force that took over under the influence of alcohol. However, the answer to Gibson's question "Where did those vicious words come from?" is ridiculously simple: they are part and parcel of his ideological identity, formed (as far as one can tell) to a large extent by his father. What sustained Gibson's remarks was not madness, but a well-known ideology (anti-Semitism).

In our daily life, racism works as a spontaneous disposition lurking beneath the surface and waiting for a "remainder of the day" to which it can attach itself and color it in its own way. I recently read *Man Is Wolf to Man*, Janusz Bardach's (a Polish Jew) memoirs of his miraculous survival in Kolyma, the worst Stalinist camp, in the worst of times when conditions were especially desperate (during World War II).[32] In early 1945, as the result of an amnesty to celebrate the victory over Germany, he was freed but not yet able to leave the region. So, in order to pass the time and earn some money, he accepted a post in a hospital. There, on the advice of a colleague, a doctor, he organized a desperate method of providing the sick and starving prisoners with some vitamins and nutritious foodstuffs. The camp hospital had too large a stock of human blood for transfusions which it was planning to discard; Bardach re-processed it, enriched it with vitamins from local herbs, and sold it back to the hospital. When the higher authorities learned about this, he was almost rearrested: they banned him from practicing what they designated as "organized cannibalism." But he found a way out, replacing human blood with the blood of the deer killed by the Inuit living nearby, and soon developed a successful business . . . My immediate racist association was, of course: "Typical Jews! Even in the worst gulag, the moment they are given a minimum of freedom and space for maneuver, they start trading—in human blood!"

The stakes are much higher when this obscene underside is institutionalized, as in the case of the Catholic priests' pedophilia, a phenomenon that is inscribed into the very functioning of the Church as a socio-symbolic institution. It is therefore not a matter of the "private" unconscious of individuals, but rather of the "unconscious" of the institution itself; not something that happens because the Church has to accommodate itself to the pathological realities of libidinal life in order to survive, but rather an inherent part of the way the institution reproduces itself.[33] This institutional unconscious has nothing to do with any kind of Jungian "collective unconscious," a spiritual substance that encompasses individuals; its status is thoroughly non-psychological, strictly discursive, correlative to the "big Other" as the "reified" system of symbolic coordinates. It is the set of presuppositions and exclusions implied by the public discourse. Consequently, the response to the Church's reluctance to acknowledge its crimes should be that these are indeed crimes and that, if it does not fully participate in their investigation, the Church is an accomplice after the fact; moreover, the Church *as such*, as an institution, must be made to recognize the ways it systematically creates the conditions for such crimes to take place. No wonder that, in contemporary Ireland, when small children have to go out alone, it is becoming standard for their mothers to supplement the traditional warning "Don't talk to strangers!" with a new and more specific one, ". . . and don't talk to priests!"

Consequently, what Gibson needs is not therapy; it is not enough for him to simply admit that "he has a problem" so long as he fails to accept responsibility for his remarks, asking himself in what way his outburst is linked to his Catholicism and functions as its obscene underside. When Foxman offered to treat Gibson's outburst as a case of individual pathology which needs a therapeutic approach, he not only committed the same error as those who want to reduce cases of pedophilia to individual pathologies; much worse, he contributed to the revival of the Serbsky Institute's manner of dealing with problematic political and ideological attitudes as phenomena that call for psychiatric intervention. In the same way that the overriding belief underlying the Serbsky Institute's measures was that a person had to be *insane* to be against Communism, so Foxman's offer implies that a person has to be insane to be anti-Semitic. This easy way out enables us to avoid the key issue: that, precisely, anti-Semitism in our Western societies was—and is—not an ideology displayed by the deranged, but an ingredient of spontaneous ideological attitudes of perfectly *sane* people, of our ideological *sanity* itself. This, then, is where we stand today: a sad choice between Gibson and Foxman, between the obscene bigotry of fundamentalist beliefs and the no less obscene disqualification of problematic beliefs as cases of mental illness that require therapy.

Poland as a symptom

This hidden complicity between the postmodern "atonal world" and the fundamentalist reaction to it explodes when a society enters a crisis of its symbolic identity. A scandal ripped Poland apart in March 2007, the so-called "Oleksy-gate," when a tape of a private conversation was made public. Josef Oleksy, the former Prime Minister and one of the Democratic Left Alliance's (SLD, ex-Communists) leading figures, was revealed to have made disparaging remarks about the SLD politicians, calling them "a bunch of losers and swindlers," cynically boasting that the SLD had really introduced capitalism into Poland, and claiming that the SLD leaders cared nothing about Poland, but just about their own survival and wealth. The truly shocking feature of these tapes is a certain coincidence: Oleksy used exactly the same words as the rightist anti-Communist opponents of the SLD who refused to admit its legitimacy, claiming that it was a party without a proper program, just a network of ex-*nomenklatura* swindlers looking after their own business interests— this harsh external characterization was now confirmed as the inner cynical self-designation of the SLD itself . . . a sure sign that the first task of the new Left in post-Communist states is to reject all links with the ex-Communist "left" parties which, as a rule, are the parties of big capital.

The counterpart to this scandal is the fact that Poland has the distinction of being the first Western country in which the anti-modernist backlash has won, effectively emerging as a hegemonic force: calls for the total ban on abortion, anti-Communist "lustration," the exclusion of Darwinism from primary and secondary education, up to the bizarre idea of abolishing the post of the President of the Republic and proclaiming Jesus Christ the Eternal King of Poland, and so forth, are coming together into an all-encompassing proposal to enact a clear break and constitute a new Polish republic unambiguously based on anti-modernist Christian values. Is, however, this backlash really so dangerous that the Left should accept the liberal blackmail: "the time has come for all of us to unite forces, thwart this threat and reassert liberal-secular modernization"? (Something, incidentally, which cannot but recall the memory of Social-Democratic evolutionists who claimed that, in not yet fully developed countries, the Left should first support the bourgeois project of the modern democratic state, and only in the "second phase" should it move on to radical politics proper, to the overcoming of capitalism and bourgeois democracy . . . It is good to remember that Lenin was thoroughly opposed to this "stageist" approach, reinstituted in later Stalinism with its scholastic distinction between the "lower" and the "higher" stages of Communism.)

The task of the Left is, on the contrary, more than ever to "subtract" itself from the entire field of the opposition between liberal modernization and the anti-modernist backlash.[34] In spite of their zealous pursuit of a positive project of installing stable Christian values into social life, one should never forget that the anti-modernist fundamentalist backlash is a profoundly *reactive* phenomenon (in the Nietzschean sense): at its core, there is not a positive politics, actively pursuing a new social project, but a politics of fear whose motivating force is defense against a perceived threat. Here, reduced to its most elementary contours, is the conservative view of our predicament, whose central feature is that "secular-progressive culture has swept away traditional beliefs":

To replace this loss of spirituality, millions of Europeans have embraced the secular concept of "relativism." According to this way of thinking, there is no absolute truth, no certain right and wrong. Everything is "relative." What is wrong in my eyes might not be wrong in your eyes. By this logic, even heinous acts can be explained, so they should not—in fact, they cannot—be condemned. In other words, no definite judgments about behavior should be made because there are always extenuating circumstances to justify not taking a stand.

The wide acceptance of relativism has rendered Europe weak, confused, and chaotic. Socialist or quasi-socialist governments now provide the necessities of life to their citizens, allowing many Europeans to live entirely within themselves. When that happens to a person, it is hard to rally him or her to a greater cause. Thus, nothing is worth fighting for outside of one's immediate well-being. The only creed is a belief in personal gratification.[35]

How are we to unite this opposition (of traditionalism versus secular relativism) with the other great ideological opposition on which the entire legitimacy of the West and its "War on Terror" relies: the opposition between liberal-democratic individual rights and religious fundamentalism embodied primarily in "Islamo-fascism"? Therein resides the symptomatic inconsistency of the US neoconservatives: while, in domestic politics, they privilege the fight against liberal secularism (abortion, gay marriages, and so on), that is, their struggle is the so-called "culture of life" against the "culture of death," in foreign affairs, they privilege the very opposite values of the liberal "culture of death." One way to resolve this dilemma is the hardline Christian fundamentalist solution, articulated in the works of Tim LaHaye *et consortes*: to unambiguously subordinate the second opposition to the first one. The title of one of LaHaye's latest novels points in this direction: *The Europa Conspiracy*. In this account, the true enemy of the US is not Muslim terrorism, the latter is merely a puppet secretly manipulated by European secularists, who are the true forces of the Antichrist intent on weakening the US and establishing the New World Order under the domination of the United Nations. Opposed to this minority view is the predominant liberal-democratic view which sees the principal enemy in all kinds of fundamentalisms, and perceives US Christian fundamentalism as a deplorable homegrown version of "Islamo-fascism."

The reactive nature of religious fundamentalism is discernible in its hidden reflexive position. Let us take a look at this reflexivity at its (artistic) highest, in the work of Andrei Tarkovsky. Tarkovsky himself, and not only the heroes of his (late) films, stands for the regained immediacy of authentic belief, as opposed to the Western intellectual's doubt and self-destructive distance. But what if the constellation is more complex? The ultimate figure of this direct belief is Stalker—to quote Tarkovsky himself:

I am often asked what this Zone stands for. There is only one possible answer: the Zone doesn't exist. Stalker himself invented his Zone. He created it, so that he was able to bring there some very unhappy persons and impose on them the idea of hope. The room of desires is equally Stalker's creation, yet another provocation in the face of the material world. This provocation, formed in Stalker's mind, corresponds to an act of faith.[36]

What, however, if we take the claim that Stalker invented the Zone literally? What if Stalker, far from directly believing, manipulates, feigns belief, in order to fascinate the intellectuals he brings to the Zone, arousing in them the prospect of belief? What if, far from being a direct believer, he assumes the role of a subject supposed to believe for the eyes of the decadent intellectual observers? What if the truly naive position is that of the intellectual spectator, of his fascination with Stalker's naive belief? And what if the same goes for Tarkovsky himself, who—far from being the authentic Orthodox believer in contrast to Western skepticism—acts out this role in order to fascinate the Western intellectual public?[37] John Gray is therefore right to say that "Religious fundamentalists see themselves as having remedies for the maladies of the modern world. In reality they are symptoms of the disease they pretend to cure."[38]

To put it in Nietzsche's terms: they are the ultimate nihilists, since the very form of their activity (spectacular mediatic mobilization, and so forth) undermines their message. One of the first exponents of early literary modernism, Lautréamont (Isidore Ducasse), followed his provocative *Chants of Maldoror* with *Poésies*, a weird reassertion of traditional morality. At the very beginning of artistic modernity, he thus stages its final paradoxical reversal: when all sources of transgression are exhausted, the only way to break out of the suffocating weariness of the Last Men is to propose traditional attitudes themselves as the ultimate transgression. And the same goes for our popular culture:

What will happen when we run out of new vices? How will satiety and idleness be staved off when designer sex, drugs and violence no longer sell? At that point, we may be sure, morality will come back into fashion. We may not be far from a time when "morality" is marketed as a new brand of transgression.[39]

One should be very precise here: this reversal is not the same as the one, described by Chesterton, in which morality itself appears as the greatest transgression, or law-and-order as the greatest (universalized) crime. Here, in contrast to Chesterton's model, the encompassing unity is not that of crime, but that of the law: it is not morality which is the greatest transgression, it is transgression which is the fundamental "moral" injunction of contemporary society. The true reversal should thus occur *within* this speculative identity of opposites, of morality and its transgression: all one has to do is to shift the encompassing unity of these two terms from morality to transgression. And, since this encompassing unity has to appear as its opposite, we thus have to accomplish a shift from a society in which the Law rules—in the guise of a permanent transgression—to a society in which transgression rules—in the guise of a new Law.[40]

Happy to torture?

This elevation of transgression itself into a moral injunction has a precise name: *happiness as the supreme duty*. No wonder that, over the last decade, the study of happiness emerged as a scientific discipline of its own: there are now "professors of happiness" at universities, "quality of life" institutes attached to them, and numerous research papers; there is even the *Journal of Happiness Studies*. Ruut Veenhoven, its editor-in-chief, wrote:

> We can now show which behaviors are risky as far as happiness goes, in the same way medical research has shown us what is bad for our health. We should eventually be able to show what kind of lifestyle suits what kind of person.[41]

This new discipline has two branches. On the one hand, there is a more sociological approach, based on data gathered from hundreds of surveys measuring happiness across different cultures, professions, religions, social and economic groups. One cannot reproach these researches for cultural bias: they are well aware of how the notion of what constitutes happiness depends on the cultural context (it is only in individualistic Western countries that happiness is seen as a reflection of personal achievement). One also cannot deny that the data collected are often interesting: happiness is not the same thing as satisfaction with one's life (several nations that report low or average life satisfaction at the same time report high percentages of very happy people); the happiest nations—mostly Western and individualistic ones—tend to have the highest levels of suicide; and, of course, the key role of envy—what counts is not what you have so much as what others have (the middle classes are far less satisfied than the poor, for they take as their reference point the very wealthy, whose income and status they will be hard-pushed to match; the poor, meanwhile, take as their reference point the middle earners, who are more within their reach).

On the other hand, there is a more psychological (or, rather, brain-sciences) approach, combining cognitivist scientific research with occasional incursions into New Age meditation wisdom: the exact measuring of brain processes that accompany feelings of happiness and satisfaction, etc. The combination of cognitive science and Buddhism (which is not new—its last great proponent was Francisco Varela) is here given an ethical twist: what is offered in the guise of scientific research is a new morality that one is tempted to call *biomorality*—the true counterpart to today's biopolitics. And indeed, was it not the Dalai Lama himself who wrote: "The purpose of life is to be happy"[42]—*this is not true for psychoanalysis*, one should add. In Kant's description, ethical duty functions like a foreign traumatic intruder that from the outside disturbs the subject's homeostatic balance, its unbearable pressure forcing the subject to act "beyond the pleasure principle," ignoring the pursuit of pleasures. For Lacan, exactly the same description holds for desire, which is why enjoyment is not something that comes naturally to the subject, as a realization of her inner potential, but is the content of a traumatic superego injunction.[43]

Consequently, if one sticks to the end to the "pleasure principle," it is difficult to abandon a radical conclusion. The artificial-intelligence philosopher Thomas Metzinger considers artificial subjectivity possible, especially in the direction of hybrid biorobotics, and, consequently, an "empirical, not philosophical" issue.[44] He emphasizes its ethically problematic character: "it is not at all clear if the biological form of consciousness, as so far brought about by evolution on our planet, is a *desirable* form of experience, an actual *good in itself*."[45] This problematic feature concerns conscious pain and suffering: evolution

> has created an expanding ocean of suffering and confusion where there previously was none. As not only the simple number of individual conscious subjects but also the dimensionality of their phenom-

enal state spaces is continuously increasing, this ocean is also deepening.[46]

And it is reasonable to expect that new artificially generated forms of awareness will create new "deeper" forms of suffering . . . One should be careful to note how this ethical thesis is not an idiosyncrasy of Metzinger as a private person, but is a consistent implication of his theoretical framework: the moment one endorses the full naturalization of human subjectivity, the avoidance of pain and suffering cannot but appear as the ultimate ethical point of reference. The only thing one should add to this is that, if one follows this line of reasoning to the end, drawing all the consequences from the fact that evolution "has created an expanding ocean of suffering and confusion where there previously was none," then one should also renounce human subjectivity itself: we would have had much less suffering if we had remained animals . . . and, to push it yet further, if animals had remained plants, if plants had remained single cells, if cells had remained minerals.

One of the great ironies of our predicament is that this same biomorality, focused on happiness and on preventing suffering, is today invoked as the underlying principle for the justification of torture: we should torture—impose pain and suffering—in order to prevent more suffering. One is truly tempted to paraphrase De Quincey yet again: "How many people began with committing a little act of torture, and ended up embracing as their cause the fight against pain and suffering!" This definitely holds for Sam Harris whose defense of torture in *The End of Faith* is based on the distinction between our immediate state of being impressed by the suffering of others and our abstract notion of others' suffering: it is much more difficult for us to torture a single person than to drop a bomb from a great distance which would cause the more painful death of thousands. We are thus all caught in a kind of ethical illusion, parallel to perceptual illusions. The ultimate cause of these illusions is that, although our power of abstract reasoning has developed immensely, our emotional-ethical responses remain conditioned by millennia-old instinctual reactions of sympathy to suffering and pain that is directly witnessed. This is why shooting someone point-blank is, for most of us, much more repulsive than pressing a button that will kill a thousand absent persons:

Given what many of us believe about the exigencies of our war on terrorism, the practice of torture, in certain circumstances, would seem to be not only permissible but necessary. Still, it does not seem any more acceptable, in ethical terms, than it did before. The reasons for this are, I trust, every bit as neurological as those that give rise to the moon illusion. . . . It may be time to take out our rulers and hold them up to the sky.[47]

No wonder that Harris refers to Alan Derschowitz and his legitimization of torture.[48] In order to suspend this evolutionary conditioned vulnerability to the physical display of others' suffering, Harris imagines an ideal "truth pill," an effective torture equivalent to decaffeinated coffee or diet coke:

> a drug that would deliver both the instruments of torture and the instrument of their utter concealment. The action of the pill would be to produce transitory paralysis and transitory misery of a kind that no human being would willingly submit to a second time. Imagine how we torturers would feel if, after giving this pill to captive terrorists, each lay down for what appeared to be an hour's nap only to arise and immediately confess everything he knows about the workings of his organization. Might we not be tempted to call it a "truth pill" in the end?[49]

The very first lines—"a drug that would deliver both the instruments of torture and the instrument of their utter concealment"—introduces the typically postmodern logic of the chocolate laxative: the torture imagined here is like decaf coffee—we get the result without having to suffer unpleasant side effects. At the Serbsky Institute in Moscow, the already-mentioned psychiatric outlet of the KGB, they did invent just such a drug with which to torture dissidents: an injection into the prisoner's heart zone which slowed down his heart beat and caused terrifying anxiety. Viewed from the outside, the prisoner seemed just to be dozing, while in fact he was living a nightmare.

There is, however, a much more disquieting prospect at work here: the proximity (of the tortured subject) which causes sympathy and makes torture unacceptable is not his mere physical proximity, but, at its most fundamental, the proximity of the Neighbor, with all the Judeo-Christian-Freudian weight of this term, the proximity of the Thing which, no matter how far away it is physically, is always by definition "too close."

What Harris is aiming at with his imagined "truth pill" is nothing less than *the abolition of the dimension of the Neighbor*. The tortured subject is no longer a Neighbor, but an object whose pain is neutralized, reduced to a property that has to be dealt with in a rational utilitarian calculus (so much pain is tolerable if it prevents a much greater amount of pain). What disappears here is the abyss of the infinity that pertains to a subject. It is thus significant that the book which argues for torture is also a book entitled *The End of Faith*—not in the obvious sense of "You see, it is only our belief in God, the divine injunction to love your neighbor, that ultimately prevents us from torturing people!" but in a much more radical sense. Another subject (and, ultimately, the subject as such) is for Lacan not something directly given, but a "presupposition," *something presumed, an object of belief*—how can I ever be sure that what I see in front of me is another subject, not a biological machine lacking any depth?

There is, however, a popular and seemingly convincing reply to those who worry about the recent US practice of torturing suspected terrorist prisoners. It is: "What's all the fuss about? The US are now only (half) openly admitting what not only they were doing all the time, but what all other states are and were doing all the time—if anything, we have less hypocrisy now . . ." To this, one should retort with a simple counter-question: "If the senior representatives of the US mean only this, *why, then, are they telling us this?* Why don't they just silently go on doing it, as they did up until now?" That is to say, what is proper to human speech is the irreducible gap between the enunciated content and its act of enunciation: "You say this, but why are you telling me it openly now?" Let us imagine a wife and husband who coexist with a tacit agreement that they can lead discreet extra-marital affairs; if, all of a sudden, the husband openly tells his wife about an ongoing affair, she will have good reason to be in panic: "If it is just an affair, why are you telling me this? It must be something more!"[50] The act of publicly reporting on something is never neutral, it affects the reported content itself.

And the same goes for the recent open admission of torture: in November 2005, Vice-President Dick Cheney said that defeating terrorists meant that "we also have to work . . . sort of the dark side . . . A lot of what needs to be done here will have to be done quietly, without any discussion"—was he not talking like a reborn Kurtz? So when we hear people like Dick Cheney making their obscene statements about the necessity of torture, we should ask them: "If you just want to torture secretly some suspected terrorists, then why are you saying it publicly?"

That is to say, the question to be raised is: what more is there hiding in this statement that made the speaker enunciate it?

We could note (more than) a hint of what there is when, in the middle of March 2007, Khalid Sheikh Mohammed's confession dominated the headlines of our media. Moral outrage at the extent of his crimes was mixed with doubts. Can his confession be trusted? What if he confessed even more than he did, either because of a vain desire to be remembered as the big terrorist Mastermind, or because he was ready to confess anything in order to stop being subjected to water-boarding and other "enhanced interrogation techniques"? What attracted much less attention was the simple fact that, for the first time, torture was *normalized*, presented as something acceptable. The ethical and legal consequences of it are something to think about.

With all the outcry about the horror of Mohammed's crimes, very little was heard about the fate our societies reserve for the hardest criminals — to be judged and severely punished. It is as if, by the nature of his acts (*and* by the nature of the treatment to which he was submitted by the US authorities), Mohammed is not entitled to the same treatment as even the most depraved murderer of children, namely to be tried and punished accordingly. It is as if *not only the terrorists themselves, but also fight against them has to proceed in a grey zone of legality, using illegal means*. We thus *de facto* have "legal" and "illegal" criminals: those who are to be treated with legal procedures (using lawyers etc.), and those who are outside legality. Mohammed's legal trial and punishment are now rendered meaningless — no court which operates within the frames of our legal system can deal with illegal detentions, confessions obtained by torture, and so on.

This fact says more than it intends. It puts Mohammed almost literally into the position of the living dead, occupying the place of what the Italian political philosopher Giorgio Agamben calls *homo sacer*: legally dead (deprived of a determinate legal status) while biologically still alive — and the US authorities which treat them in this way are also of an in-between status which forms the counterpart to *homo sacer*: acting as a legal power, their acts are no longer covered and constrained by the law — they operate in an empty space that is sustained by the law, and yet not regulated by the rule of law.

So, back to the "realistic" counter-argument: the "War on Terror" *is* dirty, one is put in situations where the lives of thousands depend on information we can get from our prisoners. (Incidentally, the torturing of Mohammed was *not* a case of the "ticking-clock" situation evoked by the advocates of torture as the reason for its legitimization: Mohammed's confession saved no lives.) Against this kind of "honesty," one should stick to the apparent hypocrisy. I can well imagine that, in a very specific situation, I would resort to torture—however, in such a case, it is crucial that I do *not* elevate this desperate choice into a universal principle. Following the unavoidable brutal urgency of the moment, I should simply *do it*. Only in this way, in the very impossibility of elevating what I had to do into a universal principle, do I retain the proper sense of the horror of what I did.

In a way, those who, without outrightly advocating torture, accept it as a legitimate topic of debate, are in a way more dangerous than those who explicitly endorse it. Morality is never just a matter of individual conscience. It only thrives if it is sustained by what Hegel called "objective spirit," the set of unwritten rules which form the background of every individual's activity, telling us what is acceptable and what is unacceptable. For example, the sign of progress in our societies is that one does not need to argue against rape: it is "dogmatically" clear to everyone that rape is wrong, and we all feel that even arguing against it is too much. If someone were to advocate the legitimacy of rape, it would be a sad sign if one had to argue against him—he should simply appear ridiculous. And the same should hold for torture.

This is why the greatest victims of publicly admitted torture are all of us, the public that is informed about it. We should all be aware that some precious part of our collective identity has been irretrievably lost. We are in the middle of a process of moral corruption: those in power are literally trying to break a part of our ethical backbone, to dampen and undo what is arguably civilization's greatest achievement, the growth of our spontaneous moral sensitivity.

Nowhere is this clearer than in a significant detail of Mohammed's confession. It was reported that the agents torturing him submitted themselves to water-boarding and were able to endure it for only ten to fifteen seconds before being ready to confess anything and everything, while Mohammed gained their grudging admiration by enduring it for two and a half minutes, the longest time anyone could remember someone resisting. Are we aware that the last time such statements were part of public discourse was way back in the late Middle Ages when torture was still a public spectacle, an honorable way to test a captured worthy enemy who gained the admiration of the crowd if he bore the pain with dignity? Do we really need this kind of primitive warrior ethics?

Are we, then, aware of what is at the end of this road? When, in the fifth season of *24*, it became clear that the mastermind behind the terrorist plot was none other than the President of the US himself, many of us were eagerly waiting to see if Jack Bauer would also apply to the President—"the most powerful man on earth", "the leader of the free world" (and other Kim-Yong-Il-esque titles that he possesses)—his standard procedure for dealing with terrorists who do not want to divulge a secret that may save thousands of lives. Will he *torture* the President?

Unfortunately, the authors did not risk this redeeming step. But our imagination can go even further, making a modest proposal in Jonathan Swift style: what if part of the procedure to test the candidates for the US presidency were also the public torture of the candidate? Say, a waterboarding of the candidates on the White House lawn, transmitted live to millions? Those qualified for the post of the leader of the free world would be those who could last longer than Mohammed's two and a half minutes.

2 The Family Myth of Ideology

Numerous treatises have been written about the perception of a historical Real in the terms of a family narrative as a fundamental ideological operation: a story about the conflict of larger social forces (classes and so forth) is framed into the coordinates of a family drama. This ideology, of course, finds its clearest expression in Hollywood as the ultimate ideological machine: in a typical Hollywood product, everything, from the fate of the knights of the Round Table through the October Revolution up to asteroids hitting the Earth, is transposed into an Oedipal narrative. (A Deleuzian cannot resist the temptation of pointing out how the main theoretical justification of such familialization is psychoanalysis, which makes it the key ideological machine.)

"Capitalist realism"

Our first step should be to analyze this family narrative at its most elementary, kitsch, level. Exemplary here is Michael Crichton, today's successor of Arthur Hailey, the first great author of "capitalist realism" (whose bestsellers, back in the 1960s—*Hotel, Airport, Cars* . . .—always focused on a particular site of production or complex organization, mixing a melodramatic plot with lengthy descriptions of the site's functions, in an unexpected echo of the Stalinist classics of the late 1920s and 1930s such as Gladkov's *Cement*).[1] Crichton added to the genre a postmodern techno-thriller twist, in accordance with today's predominant politics of fear: he is the ultimate novelist of fear—fear of the past (*Jurassic Park, Eaters of the Dead*), of the nanotechnological future (*Prey*), of Japan's economic strength (*The Rising Sun*), of sexual harassment (*Disclosure*), of robotic technology (*Westworld*), of the medical industry (*Coma*), of alien intrusions (*Andromeda Strain*), of ecological catastrophes (*State of Fear*). *State of Fear*, his most recent book, brings an unexpected final addition to this series of shadowy forces which lurk among us, poised to wreak havoc: America's fiercest enemies are none other than the environmentalists themselves.[2]

As many a critic has noted, Crichton's books are not really novels, they are more like unfinished drafts, prospectuses for screenplays; however, it is this very feature which makes his work interesting for an analysis of contemporary ideology: the very lack of stylistic qualities, the totally "transparent" mode of writing, allows the underlying ideological fantasies to be staged at their embarrassingly desublimated purest, in naked form, as it were. Exemplary here is *Prey*,[3] in which a nanotechnological experiment in a laboratory in the Nevada desert goes horribly wrong; a cloud of nanoparticles—millions of microrobots—escapes. The cloud—visible to observers as a black swarm—is self-sustaining, self-reproducing, intelligent, and it learns from experience, evolving hour by hour. Every effort to destroy it fails.[4] It has been programmed to become a predator; humans are its prey. Only a handful of scientists trapped in the laboratory can halt the release of this mechanical plague on a defenseless world . . . As is always the case in such stories, this "big plot" (the catastrophe that threatens to ruin humanity itself) is combined with the "secondary plot," a set of relations and tensions amongst the group of scientists, with the troubled role-reversal married couple at its center. Jack, the novel's narrator, was the manager of a cutting-edge computer-program division in a media-technology company before he was made a scapegoat for someone else's corruption and fired; now he is a house-husband while his wife, Julia, is the workaholic vice-president of Xymos, the nanotechnology company which owns the Nevada desert laboratory where the catastrophe occurs—erotic, manipulative, and cold, she is a new version of the corporate vixen from *Disclosure*. At the novel's start, Jack has to cope with their three children, discusses Pampers versus Huggies with another father in the supermarket, and tries to control his suspicions that his wife is having an affair.

Far from providing a mere human-interest subplot, this family plot is what the novel really turns on: the cloud of nanoparticles should be conceived of as a materialization of the family's tensions. The first thing that cannot but strike the eye of anyone who knows Lacan is how this swarm resembles what Lacan, in his *Seminar XI*, called "lamella": it appears indestructible, in its infinite plasticity; it always reassembles itself, able to morph into a multitude of shapes; in it, pure evil animality overlaps with machine-like blind insistence. The lamella is an entity consisting of pure surface, without the density of a substance, an infinitely plastic object capable not just of incessantly changing its form, but even of transposing itself from one to another medium: imagine "something" that is first heard as a shrill sound, and then pops up as a monstrously distorted body. A lamella is indivisible, indestructible, and immortal—more precisely, undead in the sense this term has in horror fiction: not sublime spiritual immortality, but the obscene immortality of the "living dead" which, after every annihilation, recompose themselves and clumsily carry on their activities. As Lacan puts it, the lamella does not exist, it insists: it is unreal, an entity of pure semblance, a multiplicity of appearances which seem to envelop a central void—its status is purely fantasmatic. This blind indestructible insistence of the libido is what Freud called the "death drive," and one should bear in mind that the "death drive" is, paradoxically, the Freudian name for its very opposite, for the way immortality appears within psychoanalysis: for an uncanny excess of life, for an "undead" urge which persists beyond the (biological) cycle of life and death, of generation and corruption. Freud equates the death drive with the so-called "compulsion-to-repeat," an uncanny urge to repeat painful past experiences which seems to outgrow the natural limitations of the organism affected by it and to insist even beyond the organism's death. As such, the lamella is "what is subtracted from the living being by virtue of the fact that it is subject to the cycle of sexed reproduction":[5] it precedes sexual difference, it multiplies and reproduces itself by means of asexual self-division.[6] In the novel's climactic scene, Jack holds Julia in his arms while she, unbeknowst to him, is already infected by the swarm and lives in symbiosis with the nanoparticles, receiving from them a superhuman life-power.

> I held her hard. The skin of her face began to shiver, vibrating rapidly. And then her features seemed to grow, to swell as she screamed. I thought her eyes looked frightened. The swelling continued, and began to break up into rivulets, and streams.
>
> And then in a sudden rush Julia literally disintegrated before my eyes. The skin of her swollen face and body blew away from her in streams of particles, like sand blown off a sand dune. The particles curved away in the arc of the magnetic field toward the sides of the room.
>
> I felt her body growing lighter and lighter in my arms. Still the particles continued to flow away, with a kind of whooshing sound, to all corners of the room. And when it was finished, what was left

behind—what I still held in my arms—was a pale and cadaverous
form. Julia's eyes were sunk deep in her cheeks. Her mouth was thin
and cracked, her skin translucent. Her hair was colorless, brittle. Her
collarbones protruded from her bony neck. She looked like she was
dying of cancer. Her mouth worked. I heard faint words, hardly more
than breathing. I leaned in, turned my ear to her mouth to hear.

"Jack," she whispered, "It's eating me." (468–9)

This separation is then undone, the particles return to Julia and revitalize
her:

The particles on the walls were drifting free once more. Now they
seemed to telescope back, returning to her face and body. . ./ And
suddenly, in a *whoosh*, all the particles returned, and Julia was full and
beautiful and strong as before, and she pushed me away from her with
a contemptuous look . . . (471)

In the final confrontation, we then get both Julias side by side, the
glimmering Julia composed of the swarm and the exhausted real Julia:

Julia came swirling up through the air toward me, spiralling like a
corkscrew—and grabbed the ladder alongside me. Except she wasn't
Julia, she was the swarm, and for a moment the swarm was disorganized enough that I could see right through her in places; I could
see the swirling particles that composed her. I looked down and saw
the real Julia, deathly pale, standing and looking up at me, her face a
skull. By now the swarm alongside me become solid-appearing, as I
had seen it become solid before. It looked like Julia. (476)

Here, we are not talking about science, not even problematic science, but
one of the fundamental fantasy scenarii, or, more precisely, the scenario
of the very disintegration of the link between fantasy and reality, so that
we get the two of them, fantasy and reality, the Julia-swarm and the
"real" Julia, side by side, as in the wonderful scene from the beginning of
Terry Gilliam's *Brazil*, where food is served in an expensive restaurant in
such a way that we get on a plate itself a small patty-like cake which looks
(and probably tastes) like excrement, while above the plate, hangs a color
photo which shows us what we are "really eating," namely a nicely
cooked juicy steak . . .

This, then, is how one should read *Prey*: all the (pseudo-)scientific speculations about nanotechnology are here a pretext to tell the story of a husband reduced to a domestic role, frustrated by his ambitious corporate vixen of a wife. No wonder that, at the novel's end, a "normal" couple is recreated: at Jack's side is Mae, the passive but understanding Chinese colleague scientist, silent and faithful, lacking Julia's aggressiveness and ambition.

The production of the couple in Hollywood . . .

A variant of the same motif, the impasse of paternal authority and its restoration, secretly runs through all key Steven Spielberg films—*ET*, *Empire of the Sun*, *Jurassic Park*, *Schindler's List* . . . One should remember that the small boy to whom ET appears was abandoned by his father (as we learn in the very beginning), so that ET is ultimately a kind of "vanishing mediator" who provides a new father (the good scientist who, in the film's last shot, is already seen embracing the mother)—when the new father arrives, ET can leave and "go home." *Empire of the Sun* focuses on a boy deserted by his family in war-torn China and surviving through the help of an ersatz father (played by John Malkovich). In the very first scene of *Jurassic Park*, we see the paternal figure (played by Sam Neill) jokingly threatening the two kids with a dinosaur bone—this bone is clearly the tiny object-stain which, later, explodes into gigantic dinosaurs, so that one can risk the hypothesis that, within the film's fantasmatic universe, the dinosaurs' destructive fury merely materializes the rage of the paternal superego. A barely perceptible detail that occurs later, in the middle of the film, confirms this reading. Neill and the two children, pursued by the monsters, take refuge from the murderous carnivorous dinosaurs in a gigantic tree, where, dead tired, they fall asleep; on the tree, Neill loses the dinosaur bone that was stuck in his belt, and it is as if this accidental loss has a magical effect—before they fall asleep, Neill is reconciled with the children, displaying warm affection and tenderness towards them. Significantly, the dinosaurs which approach the tree the next morning and awaken the sleeping party, turn out to be of the benevolent herbivorous kind . . . *Schindler's List* is, at the most basic level, a remake of *Jurassic Park* (and, if anything, worse than the original), with the Nazis as the dinosaur monsters, Schindler as (at the film's beginning) the cynical, profiteering, and opportunistic parental figure, and the ghetto Jews as threatened children (their infantilization in the film is striking). The story the film tells is about Schindler's gradual rediscovery of his paternal duty towards the Jews, and his transformation into a caring and responsible father. And is *The War of the Worlds* not the latest installment of this saga? Tom Cruise plays a divorced working-class father who neglects his two children; the invasion of the aliens reawakens in him the proper paternal instincts, and he rediscovers himself as a caring father—no wonder that, in last scene, he finally gets the recognition from his son who, throughout the film, despised him. In the mode of eighteenth-century stories, the film could thus also have been subtitled "A story of how a working father is finally reconciled with his son." . . . One can easily imagine the film *without* the bloodthirsty aliens so that what remains is in a way "what it is really about," the story of a divorced working-class father who strives to regain the respect of his two children. Therein resides the film's ideology: with regard to the two levels of the story (the Oedipal level of lost and regained paternal authority; the spectacular level of the conflict with the invading aliens), there is a clear dissymmetry, since the Oedipal level is what the story is "really about," while the external spectacular is merely its metaphoric extension. There is a nice detail in the film's soundtrack which makes clear the predominance of this Oedipal dimension: the aliens' attacks are accompanied by a terrifying one-note low-trombone sound weirdly resembling the low bass and trumpet sound of the Tibetan Buddhist chant, the voice of the suffering, dying evil father (in clear contrast to the "beautiful" five-tones melodic fragment that identifies the "good" aliens in Spielberg's *Encounters of the Third Kind*).

No wonder, then, that the same key discloses the underlying motif of the greatest cinema hit of all times, James Cameron's *Titanic*. Is *Titanic* really a film about the catastrophe of a ship hitting an iceberg? One should be attentive to the precise moment of the disaster: it takes place when the two young lovers (Leonardo Di Caprio and Kate Winslet), immediately after consummating their amorous encounter in the sexual act, return to the ship's deck. This, however, is not all: if this were all, then the catastrophe would have been simply the punishment of Fate for the double transgression (illegitimate sexual act; transgression of the class divisions). What is more crucial is that, on the deck, Kate passionately tells her lover that, when the ship reaches New York the next morning, she will leave with him, preferring a life of poverty with her true love to a false and corrupted existence among the rich; at *this* moment the ship hits the iceberg, in order to *prevent* what would undoubtedly have been the *true* disaster, namely the couple's life in New York. One can safely guess that the misery of everyday life would soon have destroyed their love. The accident thus occurs in order to save their love, in order to sustain the illusion that, had it not happened, they would have lived "happily ever after" . . .

But this is not all. A further clue is provided by the final moments of Di Caprio. He is freezing to death in the cold water, while Winslet is safely floating on a large piece of wood; aware that she is losing him, she cries: "I'll never let you go!", all the while pushing him away with her hands — why? Because he has served his purpose. For, beneath the love story, *Titanic* tells another tale, that of a spoiled high-society girl in an identity crisis: she is confused, does not know what to do with herself, and, much more than her lover, Di Caprio is a kind of "vanishing mediator" whose function is to restore her sense of identity and purpose in life, her self-image (quite literally, also: he sketches her image); once his job is done, he can disappear. This is why his last words, before he disappears into the freezing North Atlantic, are not the words of a departing lover, but, rather, the last message of a preacher, telling her how to lead her life, to be honest and faithful to herself, and so on and so forth. What this means is that Cameron's superficial Hollywood Marxism (his all too obvious privileging of the lower classes and caricatural depiction of the cruel egotism and opportunism of the rich) should not deceive us: beneath this sympathy for the poor, there is another narrative, the profoundly reactionary myth, first fully deployed by Kipling's *Captains Courageous*, of a young rich kid in crisis whose vitality is restored by a brief intimate contact with the full-blooded life of the poor. What lurks behind the compassion for the poor is their vampiric exploitation.

The ridiculous climax of this Hollywood procedure of staging great historical events as the backdrop to the formation of a couple is Warren Beatty's *Reds*, in which Hollywood found a way to rehabilitate the October Revolution itself, arguably the most traumatic historical event of the twentieth century. How, exactly, is the October Revolution depicted in the film? The couple of John Reed and Louise Bryant are in a deep emotional crisis; their love is reignited when Louise watches John on a platform delivering an impassioned revolutionary speech. What then follows is their love-making, intersected with archetypal scenes from the revolution, some of which reverberate in an all too patent manner with the love-making; say, when John penetrates Louise, there is a cut to a street where a dark crowd of demonstrating people envelops and stops a penetrating "phallic" tramway . . . all this against the background of the singing of "The Internationale." When, at the orgasmic climax, Lenin himself appears, addressing a packed hall of delegates, he is more a wise teacher overseeing the couple's love initiation than a cold revolutionary leader. Even the October Revolution is acceptable, if it serves the reconstitution of a couple . . .

To what extent, one might ask, is this Hollywood formula of the creation of the couple as the foreground of a great historical epic present also in other cultures? Let us take a look at the successors of the October Revolution itself—there are surprises awaiting us here.[7]

Take Chiaureli's infamous *The Fall of Berlin* (1948), the supreme case of the Stalinist war epic, the story of the Soviet victory over Hitler's Germany. The film begins in 1941, just prior to the German assault on the USSR; the hero, a Stakhanovite steelworker in love with a local teacher, but too shy to directly approach her, is awarded the Stalin Prize and received by Stalin in his dacha. In a scene which was cut after 1953 and then lost, after the official congratulations, Stalin notices a nervous uneasiness in the hero and asks him what is wrong. The hero tells Stalin about his love problems, and Stalin gives him advice: recite poetry to her, that's the way to win a girl's heart, and so on. Back home, the hero succeeds in seducing the girl, but at the very moment when he is carrying her in his arms into the grass (to make love, in all probability), the bombs from German planes start to fall—this is June 22, 1941. In the ensuing confusion, the girl is taken prisoner by the Germans and taken to a work camp near Berlin, while the hero joins the Red Army, fighting on the front lines to get his love back. At the film's end, when the jubilant crowd of camp prisoners liberated by the Red Army mingles with the Russian soldiers, a plane lands on a field nearby; Stalin himself steps out and walks towards the crowd which greets him joyfully. At that very point, as if again mediated by Stalin's help, the couple are reunited: the girl notes the hero in the crowd; before embracing him, she approaches Stalin and asks him if she can give him a kiss . . . Truly, they don't make them like that any more! *The Fall of Berlin* is effectively the story of a couple reunited: World War II serves as the obstacle to be overcome so that the hero can reach his beloved, like the dragon the knight has to kill to win the princess imprisoned in the castle. The role of Stalin is that of a magician and matchmaker who wisely leads the couple to its reunion . . .

The same interpretive key fits science-fiction catastrophe films. In a recent example of the series of cosmic catastrophe films, Mimi Leder's

Deep Impact (1998), a gigantic comet threatens to hit the Earth and to extinguish all life for millennia; at the end of the film, the Earth is saved due to the heroic and suicidal action of a group of astronauts with atomic weapons; only a small fragment of the comet falls into the ocean east of New York and causes a colossal wave, hundreds of yards high, that flushes the entire northeast coast of the USA, including New York and Washington. This comet-Thing also creates a couple, but an unexpected one: the incestuous couple of the young, obviously neurotic, sexually inactive TV reporter (Tea Leoni) and her promiscuous father (Maximilian Schell), who has divorced her mother and just married a young woman of the same age as his daughter. It is clear that the film is effectively a drama about this unresolved proto-incestuous father–daughter relationship: the threatening comet obviously gives body to the self-destructive rage of the heroine, who is single, and has an obvious traumatic fixation on her father. Flabbergasted by her father's remarriage, she is unable to come to terms with the fact that he has abandoned her for her peer. The President (played by Morgan Freeman, in a politically correct vein) who, in a broadcast to the nation, announces the looming catastrophe, acts as the ideal counterpoint to the obscene real father, as a caring paternal figure (without a noticeable wife!) who, significantly, gives her a privileged role at the press conference, allowing her to ask the first questions. The link of the comet with the dark, obscene underside of paternal authority is made clear through the way the heroine gets in touch with the President: in her investigation, she discovers an impending financial scandal (large illegal government spending) connected with "Elle"—her first idea, of course, is that the President himself is involved in a sex scandal, that "Elle" refers to his mistress; she then discovers the truth: "E.L.E" is a codename for the emergency measures to be taken when an accident that could lead to total extinction of life threatens the Earth, and the government was secretly spending funds building a gigantic underground shelter in which a million Americans would be able to survive the catastrophe.

The approaching comet is thus clearly a metaphoric substitute for paternal infidelity, for the libidinal catastrophe of a daughter facing the fact that her obscene father has chosen another young woman over her. The entire machinery of the global disaster is thus set in motion so that the father's young wife will abandon him, and the father will return (not to his wife, the heroine's mother, but . . .) to his daughter: the culmination of the film is the scene in which the heroine rejoins her father who, alone in his luxurious seaside house, awaits the impending wave. She finds him walking along the shoreline; they make peace with each other and embrace, silently awaiting the wave; when the wave approaches and is already casting its large shadow over them, she draws herself closer to her father, gently crying "Daddy!", as if to search for protection in him, reconstituting the childhood scene of a small girl sheltered by the father's loving embrace, and a second later they are both swept away by the gigantic wave. The heroine's helplessness and vulnerability in this scene should not deceive us: she is the evil spirit who, in the underlying libidinal machinery of the film's narrative, pulls the strings, and this scene of finding death in the protective father's embrace is the realization of her ultimate wish . . . Here we are at the opposite extreme to *The Forbidden Planet*: in both cases we are dealing with the incestuous relationship between father and daughter, yet while in *Forbidden Planet* the destructive monster materializes the *father's* incestuous death wish, in *Deep Impact* it materializes the *daughter's* incestuous death wish. The scene on the waterfront with the gigantic wave sweeping away the embraced daughter and father is to be read against the background of the standard Hollywood motif (rendered famous in Fred Zinneman's *From Here to Eternity*) of the couple making love on the beach, caressed by waves (Burt Lancaster and Deborah Kerr): here, the couple is truly an incestuous one, so the wave is enormous and destructive, not the sootheing ebb and flow of small beach wavelets.

Interestingly enough, the other big 1998 blockbuster variation on the theme of a gigantic comet threatening Earth, *Armageddon*, also focuses on the incestuous father–daughter relationship. Here, however, it is the father (Bruce Willis) who is excessively attached to his daughter: the comet's destructive force gives body to *his* fury at her love affairs with other men of her own age. Significantly, the denouement is also more "positive," not self-destructive: the father sacrifices himself in order to save Earth, that is, effectively—at the level of the underlying libidinal economy—erasing himself in order to bless the marriage of his daughter to her young lover.

. . . and out

Rather surprisingly, one often finds a version of the same family myth underlying even the off-Hollywood art films. Let us begin with Florian Henckel von Donnersmarck's *Das Leben der Anderen* (*The Lives of Others*,

2006), often favorably compared with Ulrich Becker's *Goodbye Lenin*—the claim is that it provides the necessary corrective to *Goodbye Lenin* with its sentimental *Ostalgie*, by providing an insight into the manner in which Stasi terror penetrated every pore of private lives. Is, however, this really the case?

Upon a closer look, an almost inverted image appears: as is the case with many depictions of the harshness of the Communist regimes, *The Lives of Others* misses the true horror of the situation in its very attempt to portray it—how? First, the trigger for the events in the film is the corrupted minister of culture who wants to get rid of the top GDR playwright Georg Dreyman, so that he will be able to pursue unimpeded his affair with Dreyman's partner, the actress Christa-Maria. In this way, the horror inscribed into the very formal structure of the system is relegated to an effect of a personal whim—the point lost is that, even without the minister's personal corruption, with only dedicated and devoted bureaucrats, the system would be no less terrifying.

The writer from whom the minister wants to take the woman is idealized in the opposite manner: if he is such a good writer, both honest and sincerely dedicated to the Communist system, personally close to the top regime figures (we learn that Margot Honecker, the party leader's wife, gave him a book by Solzhenitsyn which is strictly prohibited for ordinary people), how is it that he did not come into conflict with the regime much earlier? How is it that he was not considered at least a little bit problematic by the regime, with his excesses nonetheless tolerated because of his international fame, as was the case with all famous GDR authors from Bertolt Brecht to Heiner Müller and Christa Wolf? One cannot but recall here a witty formula regarding life under a harsh Communist regime: of three features—personal honesty, sincere support for the regime, intelligence—it was possible to combine only two, never all three. If one was honest and supportive, one was not very bright; if one was bright and supportive, one was not honest; if one was honest and bright, one was not supportive. The problem with Dreyman is that he does actually combine all three features.

Second, during a reception at the start of the film, a dissident directly and aggressively confronts the minister, without consequences—if such a thing was possible, was the regime really so terrible? Last, it is Christa-Maria who breaks down and betrays the husband, which later leads to her suicidal flight from the apartment, crushed under the wheels of a truck, whereas in the overwhelming majority of real cases of married couples when a spouse betrayed his partner and spied on her, it was the men who became "IM," "*informelle Mitarbeiter* (informal collaborators)" of the Stasi.[8]

The most extraordinary Cold War love story was the one between Vera Lengsfeld and Knud Wollenberger who, in the now defunct German Democratic Republic, got married and had two children together. After the fall of the Wall, when Vera, a GDR dissident, gained access to her Stasi file, she learned that Knud, a Stasi informer codenamed Donald, had married and lived with her on the orders of his masters, so that he was able to report on her activities; upon learning this, she immediately divorced him and they have not spoken since. Afterwards, Knud sent her a letter explaining that he wanted to shield her and that his betrayal was, in fact, an act of love. Now that he is dying of a galloping form of Parkinson's, Vera has announced that she has forgiven him . . . No wonder Hollywood is considering making a film with Meryl Streep as Vera.[9] Betrayal as an act of love — the formula had already been proposed by John Le Carré in his masterpiece, *A Perfect Spy*.

The only way to account for the shift in *The Lives of Others* is to evoke a weird undercurrent of the story: in a blatant contradiction to the known facts, is the reason for this odd distortion of reality not the secret homosexual undercurrent in the film? It is clear that, in the course of his spying on the couple, Gerd Wiesler becomes libidinally attracted to Dreyman, effectively obsessed by him — it is this affection that gradually pushes him to help Dreyman. After *die Wende*, Dreyman discovers what had gone on by gaining access to his files; following which he reciprocates in amorous terms, including tailing Wiesler who now works as a postman. The situation is thus effectively reversed: the observed victim is now the observer. In the film's last scene, Wiesler goes to a bookstore (the legendary *Karl-Marx-Buchhandlung* on the Stalin Allee, of course), buys the writer's new novel, *Sonata for an Honest Man*, and discovers that it is dedicated to him (designated by his Stasi codename). Thus, to indulge in a somewhat cruel irony, the finale of *The Lives of Others* recalls the famous ending of *Casablanca*: the proverbial "beginning of a beautiful friendship" between Dreyman and Wiesler, with the intrusive female obstacle conveniently disposed of — a true Christological gesture of sacrifice (no wonder her name is Christa-Maria!).

In contrast to this idyll, the very appearance of light-hearted nostalgic comedy in *Goodbye Lenin* is a façade which covers a much harsher underlying reality (signalled at the very beginning by the brutal intrusion of the Stasi into the family home after the husband escapes to the West). The lesson is thus much more desperate than that of *The Lives of Others*: no heroic resistance to the GDR regime was ultimately sustainable, the only way to survive was to escape into madness, to disconnect from reality.

This, of course, in no way implies that *Goodbye Lenin* is without faults of its own. A comparison with another recent political thriller can be of some help here: John Malkovich's *Dancer Upstairs*. In both films, violence is framed by love: the love of a son for his mother (*Goodbye Lenin*), the love of a man for a woman (*Dancer*). In both cases, the function of love is *stricto sensu* ideological: it mystifies and thereby domesticates, renders tolerable, the confrontation with the Real of brutal, traumatic violence—the violence of the GDR regime, as well as of its collapse and the Western takeover; the violence of Sendero Luminoso's ruthless revolutionary terror. While both *Lenin* and *Dancer* confront a recent "radical" political past, significantly, one was a big hit and the other a box-office failure.

Goodbye Lenin tells the story of a son whose mother, an honest GDR believer, has a heart attack on the confused night of the demonstrations which accompanied the forty-year anniversary celebrations in 1991; she survives, but the doctor warns the son that any traumatic experience could cause the mother's death. With the help of a friend, the son thus stages for the mother, who is restricted to her apartment, the smooth continuation of the GDR: every evening, they play on the TV video-recorded fake GDR news, and so on. Towards the film's end, the hero says that the game has gone too far—the fiction staged for the dying mother has become an alternative GDR, reinvented as it should have been . . . Therein resides the key political question, beyond the rather boring topic of *Ostalgie* (which is not a real longing for the GDR, but the enactment of a real parting from it, the acquiring of a distance, detraumatization): was this dream of an "alternative GDR" inherent in the GDR itself? When, in the final fictional TV report, the new GDR leader (the first GDR astronaut) decides to open the borders, allowing the West German citizens to escape consumer terrorism, racism, and the hopeless struggle to survive, it is clear that the need for *such* a utopian escape is real. To put it quite brutally, while *Ostalgie* is widely practiced in today's Germany without causing ethical problems, one (for the time being, at least) cannot imagine publicly practicing a Nazi-nostalgia—"Goodbye Hitler" instead of "Goodbye Lenin." Does this not bear witness to the fact that we are still aware of the emancipatory potential, distorted and thwarted as it was, in Communism but which was completely missing in fascism? The quasi-metaphysical epiphany towards the film's end (when the mother, on her first walk outside the apartment, finds herself face-to-face with a statue of Lenin being transported by helicopter, whose outstretched hand seems to address/interpellate her directly) is thus to be taken more seriously than it may first appear.

The weak point of the film is that (like Roberto Benigni's *Life Is Beautiful*) it sustains an ethics of protecting one's illusions: it manipulates the threat of a second heart attack as the means to blackmail us into accepting the need to protect one's fantasy as the highest ethical duty. Does the film here not endorse unexpectedly Leo Strauss's thesis on the need for a "noble lie"? But is it really that the emancipatory potential of Communism is only a "noble lie" to be staged and sustained for naive believers, a lie which actually only masks the ruthless violence of Communist rule? The mother is the "subject supposed to believe" here: through her, *others* sustain their belief. (The irony is that it is usually the mother who is supposed to be the care-giver, protecting her children from cruel reality.) Is the mother in *Goodbye Lenin* not the one who makes the law on behalf of the (absent) father here? So—since, for Lacan, therein resides the genesis of male homosexuality—the true question is: why is the hero not gay, as he should have been?

In contrast to *Goodbye Lenin*, *Dancer Upstairs* sees no redemptive potential in the figure of Evil with which it is strangely fascinated; it should rather be read as yet another version of Conrad's voyage into the "heart of darkness," epitomized here by the excessive cruelty and ruthlessness of the Sendero Luminoso movement which, so we are told, showed no interest in conquering public opinion with ideological programs, but simply waged its murderous campaign. Rejas, the "honest liberal" police investigator and the film's hero, is split between the corruption of those in power and the absolute Evil of the Revolution. This split is the one between form and content: Rejas supports the *form* of the existing democratic order. Although critical of its present content (the corrupt rapist president, and so on), he rejects the revolutionary "transgression" of the form, the "leap of faith" into the inhuman dimension.

However, the enigma that the film addresses is double: it is not primarily the enigma of the "radical Evil" of Sendero Luminoso terror, but the enigma of Rejas's love-object: how is it possible for a cultivated and beautiful middle-class ballet dancer to be a "fanatical" member of Sendero Luminoso? Why does Yolanda totally reject Rejas at the end?

How to account for the gap that separates this sensitive and beautiful woman from the fanatical and merciless revolutionary that explodes at the end? Therein resides what one is tempted to call the constitutive stupidity of the film (and of the novel on which it is based): publicized as an attempt to "understand" the Sendero Luminoso phenomenon, it is precisely a defense against such an understanding, an attempt to perpetuate the "enigma" it confronts. No wonder that, ultimately, *Dancer Upstairs*—which prides itself on being anti-Hollywood—relies on the basic Hollywood formula of the "production of the couple."

The real Hollywood Left

If even the marginal non-Hollywood productions remain determined by the family motif, where, then, are we to find true exceptions to its rule?

In March 2005, the Vatican itself made a highly publicized statement, condemning in the strongest terms Dan Brown's *The Da Vinci Code* as a book based on lies and which spread false teachings (for example, that Jesus had married Mary Magdalene and that they had descendants—the true identity of the Grail is Mary Magdalene's vagina!), especially regretting the book's popularity among the younger generation searching for spiritual guidance. The absurdity of this Vatican intervention, sustained by a barely concealed longing for the good old days when the infamous Index of prohibited books was still operative, should not blind us to the fact that, while the form is wrong (one almost suspects a conspiracy between the Vatican and the publisher to give a new boost to the sales of the book), the content is basically right: *The Da Vinci Code* does in fact propose a New Age reinterpretation of Christianity in terms of the balance of the masculine and feminine principles, that is, the basic idea of the novel is the reinscription of Christianity into a pagan sexualized ontology: the feminine principle is sacred, perfection resides in the harmonious coupling of the male and female principles . . . The paradox to be accepted here is that, in this case, every feminist should support the Church: it is *only* through the "monotheistic" suspension of the feminine signifier, of the polarity of the masculine and feminine opposites, that the space emerges for what we broadly refer to as "feminism" proper, for the rise of feminine subjectivity. The femininity asserted in the affirmation of the cosmic "feminine principle" is, on the contrary, always a subordinated (passive, receptive) pole, opposed to the active "masculine principle."

This is why thrillers like *The Da Vinci Code* are one of the key indicators of contemporary ideological shifts: the hero is in search of an old manuscript which will reveal some shattering secret which threatens to undermine the very foundations of (institutionalized) Christianity; the "criminal" edge is provided by the desperate and ruthless attempts of the Church (or some hardline faction within it) to suppress this document. This secret focuses on the "repressed" feminine dimension of the divine: Christ was married to Mary Magdalene, the Grail is actually the female body . . . is this revelation really such a surprise? Is the idea that Jesus had sex with Mary Magdalene not rather a kind of obscene open secret of Christianity, a Christian *secret de polichinelle*? The true surprise would have been to go a step further and claim that Mary had really been a transvestite, so that Jesus' lover had been a beautiful ephebe!

The interest of the novel (and, against the suspiciously hasty dismissal of the film, one should say that this holds even more for the film) resides in a feature which, surprisingly, echoes *The X-Files* where the fact that so many things happen "out there" where the truth is supposed to dwell (aliens invading Earth and so on) fills in the void, that is, the much closer truth that nothing (no sexual relation) is going on between the two agents, Mulder and Scully. In *The Da Vinci Code*, the sexual life of Christ and Mary Magdalene is the excess which inverts (covers up) the fact that the sexual life of Sophie, the heroine, Christ's last descendant, is non-existent: *she* is like a contemporary Mary, virginal, pure, asexual; there is no hint of sex between her and Robert Langdom.

Her trauma is that she witnessed the primordial fantasmatic scene of parental copulation, this excess of *jouissance* which totally "neutralized" her sexually: it is as if, in a kind of temporal loop, she was present at the act of her own conception, so that, for her, *all* sex is incestuous and thus prohibited. Here enters Robert who, far from being her lover, acts as her "wild analyst" whose task is to construct a narrative frame, a myth, which will enable her to break out of this fantasmatic captivity, *not* by way of regaining "normal" heterosexuality, but by way of accepting her asexuality and "normalizing" it as part of the new mythic narrative. In this sense, *The Da Vinci Code* belongs in the series we are analyzing: it is not really a film about religion, about the "repressed" secret of Christianity, but a film about a frigid and traumatized young woman who is redeemed, freed from her trauma, provided with a mythical framework that enables her to fully accept her asexuality.

The mythical character of this solution emerges clearly if we contrast

Robert as its proponent to Sir Leigh, the counterpoint to Opus Dei in the film (and novel): he wants to disclose the secret of Mary and thus save humanity from the oppression of official Christianity. The film rejects this radical move and opts for a fictional compromise solution: what is important are not facts (the DNA that would prove the genealogical link between her and Mary and Christ), but what she (Sophie) believes — the movie opts for symbolic fiction against genealogical facts. The myth of being Christ's descendant creates for Sophie a new symbolic identity: at the end, she emerges as the leader of a community. It is at this level of what goes on in terrestrial life that *The Da Vinci Code* remains Christian: in the person of Sophie, it enacts the passage from sexual love to desexualized *agape* as political love, love that serves as the bond of a collective. There is nothing "pre-Freudian" in this solution — it can only appear pre-Freudian if one accepts the crude normative heterosexual version of psychoanalysis according to which, for a woman, everything but "normal" heterosexual desire is pathological. For a true Freudian, on the contrary, "there is no sexual relationship," no standard of normality, but only an inevitable deadlock, and the asexual position of withdrawing from the commerce between the sexes is as good a *sinthom* (a symptomal "knot" which holds a subject together) to deal with this deadlock as any other position.[10]

In spite of this interesting displacement of the standard Hollywood formula, it would be, of course, ridiculous to claim that *The Da Vinci Code* belongs to the Hollywood Left. One has to look for the real Hollywood Left elsewhere — but where? Zack Snyder's *300*, the saga of the three hundred Spartan soldiers who sacrificed themselves at Thermopylae to halt the invasion of Xerxes' Persian army, was attacked as the worst kind of patriotic militarism with clear allusions to the recent tensions with Iran and events in Iraq — are, however, things really so clear? The film should, rather, be thoroughly defended against these accusations.

There are two points to be made. The first concerns the story itself — it is the story of a small and poor country (Greece) invaded by the army of a much larger state (Persia), at that point much more developed, and with advanced military technology — are the Persian elephants, giants and large fire arrows not the ancient version of high-tech weaponry? When the last surviving group of Spartans and their king, Leonidas, are killed by the thousands of arrows, are they not in a way bombed to death by techno-soldiers operating sophisticated weapons from a safe distance, like today's US soldiers who at the push of a button launch rockets from the warships miles away in the Persian Gulf? Furthermore, Xerxes' words when he attempts to convince Leonidas to accept Persian domination, definitely do not sound like those of a fanatical Muslim fundamentalist: he tries to seduce Leonidas into subjection by promising him peace and sensual pleasures if he rejoins the Persian global empire. All he asks from him is the formal gesture of kneeling in acknowledgment of Persian supremacy—if the Spartans do this, they will be given supreme authority over all Greece. Is this not similar to what President Reagan demanded from the Nicaraguan Sandinista government? All they had to do was say "Hey uncle!" to the US . . . And is Xerxes' court not depicted as a kind of multiculturalist different-lifestyles paradise? Everyone participates in orgies there, different races, lesbians and gays, the handicapped, and so forth? Are, then, the Spartans, with their discipline and spirit of sacrifice, not much closer to something like the Taliban defending Afghanistan against the US occupation (or, an elite unit of the Iranian Revolutionary Guard ready to sacrifice itself in the case of an American invasion)? Perspicuous historians have already noted this parallel—this is from the blurb of Tom Holland's *Persian Fire*:

> In the fifth century BC, a global superpower was determined to bring truth and order to what it regarded as two terrorist states. The superpower was Persia, incomparably rich in ambition, gold and men. The terrorist states were Athens and Sparta, eccentric cities in a poor and mountainous backwater: Greece.[11]

Western racist investment in the battle of Thermopylae is evident: it was widely read as the first and decisive victory of the free West against the despotic East—no wonder Hitler and Goering compared the German defeat at Stalingrad in 1943 to Leonidas's heroic death at Thermopylae. However, it is for this very reason that one should invert the perspective. Western cultural racists like to claim that, had the Persians succeeded in subduing Greece, there would today be minarets all over Europe. This stupid claim is doubly wrong: not only would there be no Islam in the case of the defeat of the Greeks (since there would have been no ancient Greek thought and no Christianity, two historical presuppositions of Islam); even more important is the fact that there *are* minarets in many European cities today, and the kind of multicultural tolerance which made this possible was precisely the result of the Greek victory over the Persians.

The main Greek arm against Xerxes' overwhelming military supremacy was discipline and the spirit of sacrifice—and, to quote Alain Badiou:

We need a popular discipline. I would even say . . . that "those who have nothing have only their discipline." The poor, those with no financial or military means, those with no power—all they have is their discipline, their capacity to act together. This discipline is already a form of organization.[12]

In today's era of hedonist permissivity which serves as the dominant ideology, the time has come for the Left to (re)appropriate discipline and the spirit of sacrifice: there is nothing inherently "fascist" about these values.

But even this fundamentalist identity of the Spartans is more ambiguous. A programmatic statement towards the end of the film defines the Greeks' agenda as "against the reign of mystique and tyranny, towards the bright future," further specified as the rule of freedom and reason—which sounds like an elementary Enlightenment program, with even a communist twist! Recall also that, at the film's beginning, Leonidas outrightly rejects the message of the corrupt "oracles" according to whom the gods forbid the military expedition to stop the Persians—as we learn later, the "oracles" who were allegedly receiving the divine message in an ecstatic trance had in fact been paid by the Persians, like the Tibetan "oracle" who, in 1959, delivered the message to the Dalai Lama to leave Tibet and who was—as we now know—on the payroll of the CIA!

But what about the apparent absurdity of the idea of dignity, freedom, and reason, sustained by extreme military discipline, including of the practice of discarding weak children? This "absurdity" is simply the price of freedom—freedom is not free, as they put it in the film. Freedom is not something given, it is regained through a hard struggle in which one should be ready to risk everything. Spartan ruthless military discipline is not simply the external opposite of Athenian "liberal democracy," it is its inherent condition, it lays the foundation for it: the free subject of Reason can only emerge through ruthless self-discipline. True freedom is not a freedom of choice made from a safe distance, like choosing between a strawberry cake and a chocolate cake; true freedom overlaps with necessity, one makes a truly free choice when one's choice puts at stake one's very existence—one does it because one simply "cannot do otherwise." When one's country is under foreign occupation and one is called by a resistance leader to join the fight against the occupiers, the reason given is not "you are free to choose," but: "Can't you see that this is the only thing you can do if you want to retain your dignity?" No wonder that all the eighteenth-century egalitarian radicals, from Rousseau to the Jacobins, imagined republican France as the new Sparta: there is an emancipatory core in the Spartan spirit of military discipline which survives even when we subtract all the historical paraphernalia of Spartan class rule, ruthless exploitation of and terror over their slaves, and so forth—no wonder too that Trotsky himself called the Soviet Union in the difficult years of "war communism" a "proletarian Sparta."

Even more important is, perhaps, the film's formal aspect: the entire film was shot in a warehouse in Montreal, with the entire background and many of the people and objects digitally constructed. The artificial character of the background seems to infect the "real" actors themselves, who often appear like characters from comics brought to life (the film is based on Frank Miller's graphic novel *300*). Furthermore, the artificial (digital) nature of the background creates a claustrophobic atmosphere, as if the story is not taking place in "real" reality with its endless open horizons, but in a "closed world," a kind of relief-world of closed space. Aesthetically, we are here steps ahead of the *Star Wars* and *Lord of the Rings* series: although, in these series also, many background objects and persons are digitally created, the impression is nonetheless one of (real and) *digital actors and objects* (elephants, Yoda, Urkhs, palaces, etc.) *placed in a "real" open world*; in *300*, on the contrary, all the main characters are *"real" actors placed against an artifical background*, a combination which produces a much more uncanny "closed" world of a "cyborg" mixture of real people integrated into an artificial world. It is only with *300* that the combination of "real" actors and objects with a digital environment has come close to creating a truly new autonomous aesthetic space.

The practice of mixing different arts, of including in one artistic form the reference to another, has a long tradition, especially with regard to cinema; many of Hopper's portraits of a woman at an open window, looking out, are clearly mediated by the experience of cinema (they offer a shot without its counter-shot). What makes *300* notable is that in it (not for the first time, of course, but in a way which is artistically much more interesting than, say, Warren Beatty's *Dick Tracy*) a technically more developed art form (digitalized cinema) refers to a less developed form (comics). The effect produced is that of "true reality" losing its innocence, appearing as part of a closed artificial universe, which is a perfect figuration of our socio-ideological predicament.

Those critics who claimed that the "synthesis" of the two art forms in *300* is a failure are thus wrong because they are right: of course the "synthesis" fails, of course the universe we see on the screen is traversed by a profound antagonism and inconsistency, but it is this very antagonism which is an indication of truth.

History and family in Frankenstein

There is, however, a more fundamental question to be raised apropos the family myth as interpretive tool. It seems obvious that the first task of the critique of ideology is, of course, to treat the family narrative as an ideological myth which should be handled like a dream's explicit text, which should be deciphered back into the true struggle obfuscated by the family narrative. What if, however, one follows here the homology with the Freudian logic of dreams to the end, bearing in mind that the true focus of a dream, its "unconscious desire," is not the dream-thought, but something that, paradoxically, inscribes itself into a dream-text through the very mechanisms of the transposition of the dream-thought into the dream-text? In other words, the unconscious desire in a dream is not simply its core which never appears directly, which is distorted by the translation into the manifest dream-text, but the very principle of this distortion—here is Freud's unsurpassed formulation of this paradox:

> The latent dream-thoughts are the material which the dream-work transforms into the manifest dream. [. . .] The only essential thing about dreams is the dream-work that has influenced the thought-material. We have no right to ignore it in our theory, even though we may disregard it in certain practical situations. Analytic observation shows further that the dream-work never restricts itself to translating these thoughts into the archaic or regressive mode of expression that is familiar to you. In addition, it regularly takes possession of something else, which is not part of the latent thoughts of the previous day, but which is the true motif force for the construction of the dream. This indispensable addition [*unentbehrliche Zutat*] is the equally unconscious wish for the fulfillment of which the content of the dream is given its new form. A dream may thus be any sort of thing in so far as you are

only taking into account the thoughts it represents—a warning, an intention, a preparation, and so on; but it is always also the fulfillment of an unconscious wish and, if you are considering it as a product of the dream-work, it is only that. A dream is therefore never simply an intention, or a warning, but always an intention etc., translated into the archaic mode of thought by the help of an unconscious wish and transformed to fulfill that wish. The one characteristic, the wish-fulfillment, is the invariable one; the other may vary. It may for its part once more be a wish, in which case the dream will, with the help of an unconscious wish, represent as fulfilled a latent wish of the previous day.[13]

Every detail is worth analyzing in this marvelous passage, from its implicit opening motto "what is good enough for practice—namely the search for the meaning of dreams—is not good enough for theory," to its concluding redoubling of the wish. Its key insight is, of course, the "triangulation" of latent dream-thoughts, manifest dream-content, and the unconscious wish, which limits the scope of—or, rather, directly undermines—the hermeneutic model of the interpretation of dreams (the path from the manifest dream-content to its hidden meaning, the latent dream-thought), which runs backwards the path of the formation of a dream (the transposition of the latent dream-thought into the manifest dream-content by dream-work). The paradox is that this dream-work is not merely a process of masking the dream's "true message": the dream's true core, its unconscious wish, inscribes itself only through and in this very process of masking, so that the moment we retranslate the dream-content back into the dream-thought expressed in it, we lose the "true motif force" of the dream—in short, it is the process of masking itself which inscribes into the dream its true secret. One should therefore turn around the standard notion of the ever deeper penetration to the core of the dream: it is not that we first penetrate from the manifest dream-content to the first-level secret, the latent dream-thought, and then, in a step further, even deeper, to the dream's unconscious core, the unconscious wish. The "deeper" wish is located in the very gap between the latent dream-thought and manifest dream-content.[14]

A perfect example of this logic in literature is Mary Shelley's *Franken-stein*. A standard Marxist critical point about the novel is that it is focused on the dense family-and-sexuality network in order to obliterate (or, rather, repress) its true historical reference: history is eternalized as a family drama, larger socio-historical trends (from the "monstrosity" of revolutionary terror to the impact of scientific and technological revolutions) are reflected/staged in a distorted manner as Victor Frankenstein's troubles with his father, fiancée, and monstrous progeny . . . While all this is true, a simple mental experiment demonstrates the limitations of this approach: imagine the same story (of Dr Frankenstein and his monster) told as a story of the scientist and his experiment, without the accompanying family melodrama (the monster as the ambiguous obstacle to the sexual consummation of marriage: "I'll be there on your wedding night," and so on)—what we would end up with is an impoverished story, deprived of the dimension which accounts for its extraordinary libidinal impact. So, to put it in Freudian terms: it is true that the explicit narrative is like a dream-text which refers in an encoded way to its true referent, its "dream-thought" (the larger socio-historical dimension), reflecting it in a distorted way; however, it is through this very distortion and displacement that the text's "unconscious wish" (the sexualized fantasy) inscribes itself.

The Romantic notion of monstrosity is to be understood against the background of the distinction, elaborated by Samuel Taylor Coleridge, between Imagination and Fancy: Imagination is a creative power which generates organic and harmonious bodies, while Fancy stands for a mechanical assemblage of parts which do not fit each other, so that the product is a monstrous combination lacking any harmonious unity. In *Frankenstein*, the story of a monster, this topic of monstrosity is not limited to the narrative content; it somehow spills over and pervades other levels. There are three levels of monstrosity/fancy.

1. First, most obviously, the monster reanimated by Victor is mechanically composed of parts, not a harmonious organism.
2. Then, as the novel's social background, social unrest and revolution as a monstrous decomposition of society: with the advent of modernity, traditional harmonious society is replaced by an industrialized society in which people interact mechanically as individuals, following their egotistic interests, no longer feeling that they belong to a wider Whole, and occasionally exploding in violent rebellions. Modern societies oscillate between oppression and anarchy: the only unity that can take place in them is the artificial unity imposed by brutal power.

3. Finally, there is the novel itself, a monstrous, clumsy, inconsistent composite of different parts, narrative modes, and genres.

To these three, one should add a fourth level of monstrosity, that of the interpretations provoked by the novel: what does the monster mean, what does it stand for? It can mean the monstrosity of social revolution, of sons rebelling against fathers, of modern industrial production, of asexual reproduction, of scientific knowledge. We thus get a multitude of meanings which do not form a harmonious whole, but just coexist side by side. The interpretation of monstrosity thus ends up in monstrosity (fancy) of interpretations.

How are to find our way in *this* monstrosity? It is easy to show that the true focus of Mary Shelley's *Frankenstein* is the "monstrosity" of the French Revolution, its degeneration into terror and dictatorship. Mary and Percy Shelley were ardent students of the literature and polemics regarding the French Revolution. Victor creates his monster in the same city, Ingolstadt, that a conservative historian of the Revolution, Barruel—Mary read his book repeatedly—cites as the source of the French Revolution (it was in Ingolstadt that the secret society of Illuminati planned the Revolution). The monstrosity of the French Revolution was described by Edmund Burke precisely in the terms of a state killed and revived as a monster:

> out of the tomb of the murdered monarchy in France has arisen a vast, tremendous, unformed spectre, in a far more terrific guise than any which ever yet have overpowered the imagination, and subdued the fortitude of man. Going straight forward to its end, unappalled by peril, unchecked by remorse, despising all common maxims and all common means, that hideous phantom overpowered those who could not believe it was possible she could at all exist.[15]

Furthermore, *Frankenstein* is dedicated to Mary's father, William Godwin, known for his utopian ideas about the regeneration of the human race. Godwin entertained millennial expectations in *An Enquiry Concerning the Principles of Political Justice* (1793), where he exulted in nothing less than the coming of a new human race. This race, to emerge once over-population had been scientifically brought under control, was to be produced by social engineering, not sexual intercourse. In the novel, Victor says:

A new species would bless me as its creator and source; many happy and excellent natures would owe their being to me. No father could claim the gratitude of his child so completely as I should deserve theirs.

The symbolic association between Godwin and monsters was forged in 1796–1802, when the conservative reaction against him reached its peak. During those years, demons and the grotesque were frequently used to deflate Godwin's theories about the utopian regeneration of humanity. Conservatives depicted Godwin and his writings as a nascent monster that had to be stamped out, lest England were to go the way of revolutionary France. Horace Walpole called Godwin "one of the greatest monsters exhibited by history." In 1800, The *AntiJacobin Review*, which championed the attack upon William Godwin and Mary Wollstonecraft, denounced the couple's disciples as "the spawn of the monster."

Frankenstein does not directly approach its true focus; instead, it tells the story as a depoliticized family drama or a family myth. The characters of the novel re-enact earlier political polemics on the level of personal psychology. In the 1790s, writers such as Edmund Burke had warned of a collective, parricidal monster — the revolutionary regime in France; in the aftermath of the revolution, Mary Shelley scales this symbolism down to domestic size. Her novel re-enacts the monster trope, but it does so from the perspective of isolated and subjective narrators who are locked in parricidal struggles of their own. In this way, the novel can maintain its true topic at a distance, invisible. As we have noted, this is also the standard Marxist critical point about *Frankenstein*: it is focused on the dense family-and-sexuality network in order to obliterate (or, rather, repress) its true historical reference.

But why must *Frankenstein* obfuscate its true historical referent? Because its relationship to this true focus/topic (the French Revolution) is deeply ambiguous and contradictory, and the form of the family myth makes it possible to neutralize this contradiction, to evoke all these incompatible attitudes as parts of the same story. Not only is *Frankenstein* a myth in Lévi-Strauss's sense, an imaginary resolution of real contradictions. One should also follow Lévi-Strauss when he claims that Freud's analysis of the Oedipus myth is another version of the Oedipus myth, to be treated in the same way as the original myth: further variations of a myth try to displace and resolve in another way the contradiction which the original myth tried to resolve. In the case of *Frankenstein*, one should therefore treat as part of the same myth, as its further variation, the cinematic versions (of which there are more than fifty), and the manner they transform the original story. Here are the main moments:

1. *Frankenstein* (the best-known, James Whale's classic from 1931, with Boris Karloff as the monster): its main feature is that it leaves out the subjectivization of the monster (the monster is never allowed to tell the story in the first person, it remains a monstrous Other).
2. In *Frankenstein: The True Story* (1973), Frankenstein creates a handsome young man whom he educates for society, but the creature's body begins to degenerate, turning him against his maker.
3. In *The Bride* (1985), after Frankenstein abandons his original creature as a failure, he creates a beautiful female and educates her to be his perfect mate; but she also escapes his control.
4. In Kenneth Branagh's *Mary Shelley's Frankenstein*, after the monster kills Victor's bride, Victor in a desperate move reassembles and reanimates *her* (the scene culminates in Victor dancing with his reanimated wife).
5. Finally, although it does not directly refer to *Frankenstein*, in Ridley Scott's *Blade Runner* (1982), Police Lt. Deckard is assigned to hunt down and eliminate a group of "replicants," super-human creatures genetically engineered for slave labor, who have rebelled against their creators and are hiding in Los Angeles. The showdown between Deckard and "Batty," the replicant leader, obviously refers to the conflict between Frankenstein and the monster—here, Batty, in the final act of reconciliation, saves Deckard from certain death.

What all these films have in common is that they all reproduce the basic prohibition of the original novel: none of them directly approaches the political topic (the "monstrosity" of social rebellion); they all tell the story through the frame of family/love relations. So in what does the novel's contradictory attitude to its central topic consist?

The motif of the monstrosity of the revolution is a conservative element, and the novel's form (a confession of the principal character at the point of death) is clearly related to a conservative genre popular in Shelley's time, in which, after they are forced to confront the catastrophic results of their dreams about universal freedom and brotherhood, re-pentant ex-radicals renounce their reforming ways. However, Shelley does here something that a conservative would never have done: in the central part of the book, she moves a step further and directly gives a voice to the monster himself who is allowed to tell the story from his own perspective. This step expresses the liberal attitude of freedom of speech at its most radical: everyone's point of view should be heard. In *Frankenstein*, the monster is not a Thing, a horrible object no one dares to confront; he is fully *subjectivized*. Mary Shelley moves inside the mind of the monster and asks what it is like to be labeled, defined, oppressed, excommunicated, even physically distorted by society. The ultimate criminal is thus allowed to present himself as the ultimate victim. The monstrous murderer reveals himself to be a deeply hurt and desperate individual, yearning for company and love.

So it is crucial to see in *what* consists the monster's own story. The monster tells us that his identity as a rebel and murderer was learned, not innate. In direct contradiction to the Burkean tradition of the monster as evil incarnate, the creature tells Frankenstein: "I was benevolent and good; misery made me a fiend." Surprisingly, the monster proves to be a very philosophical rebel: he explains his actions in traditional republican terms. He claims to have been driven to rebellion by the failings of the ruling order. His superiors and protectors have shirked their responsi-bilities towards him, impelling him to insurrection. Monsters rebel not because they are infected by the evils of the godless radical philosophy, but because they have been oppressed and misused by the regnant order. Mary Shelley's source was here her own mother's study, *An Historical and Moral View of the Origin and Progress of the French Revolution* (1794), in which Mary Wollstonecraft, after agreeing with the Burkean conservatives that rebels are monsters, resolutely insists that these monsters are social products. They are not the living dead, nor are they specters arisen from the tomb of the murdered monarchy. Rather, they are the products of oppression, misrule, and despotism under the *ancien régime*. The lower orders are driven to rebellion, they turn against their oppressors in parricidal fashion. It is here that the novel comes closest to politics: the monster develops a radical critique of oppression and inequality: "I heard of the division of property, of immense wealth and squalid poverty; of rank, descent, and noble blood." He speaks in the manner of revolu-tionary-era radicals:

I learned that the possessions most esteemed by your fellow-creatures were, high and unsullied descent united with riches. A man might be respected with only one of these acquisitions, but without either he was considered, except in very rare occasions, as a vagabond and a slave, doomed to waste his powers for the profit of the chosen few.

Here Mary Shelley effectively develops the "dialectic of Enlightenment" 150 years before Adorno and Horkheimer. She goes much further than the usual conservative warnings about how scientific and political progress turns into nightmare, chaos, and violence, how man should retain proper humility in the face of the mystery of creation and not try to become a master of life, which should remain a divine prerogative.

The monster is a pure subject of the Enlightenment: after his reanimation, he is a "natural man," his mind a *tabula rasa*. Left alone, abandoned by his creator, he has to re-enact the Enlightenment theory of development: he has to learn everything from zero-level by reading and by experience. His first months are effectively the realization of a kind of philosophical experiment. The fact that he morally fails, that he turns into a murderous vengeful monster, is not a condemnation of him but of the society which he approaches with the best intentions and a need to love and be loved. His sad fate illustrates perfectly Rousseau's thesis that man is by nature good, and that it is society that corrupts him.

The very fear of progress is not necessarily a conservative motif. Recall that, in Mary Shelley's England, "Luddites," gangs of desperate workers, were destroying industrial machines in protest against the loss of jobs and the greater exploitation that machines meant for them. Furthermore, feminists read *Frankenstein* not as a conservative warning about the dangers of progress, but as a proto-feminist critique of the dangers of masculine knowledge and technology which aim to dominate the world and gain control over human life itself. This fear is still with us today: the fear that scientists will create a new form of life or artificial intelligence which will run out of our control and turn against us.

There is, finally, a fundamental ambiguity that pertains to the very motif of the son's rebellion as a monstrosity—whose rebellion is this in the novel? Rebellion is redoubled: the first rebel against paternal order is Victor himself, and the monster rebels against the rebellious son. Victor rebels against the proper paternal order: his creation of the monster is asexual reproduction, not the normal succession of generations in a family.

This brings us to the Freudian notion of the *Unheimliche* (the uncanny). What is the most *unheimlich* thing, that closest to us and at the same time the object of horror and disgust? *Incest*: the incestuous subject literally stays at home, he does not need to look for his sexual partner outside, *and* he engages in a secret activity which inspires fear and shame in all of us. No wonder, then, that hints of incest occur twice in *Frankenstein*: Walton writes his letters (and, at the novel's end, decides to return) not to his wife, but to his sister; in the first edition of the novel, Victor's bride is his half-sister. (So when the monster is really "there at [the] wedding night" and kills the bride, he prevents at the last moment the consummation of an incestuous union.)

Walton's and Victor's urge to leave home and engage in a risky transgressive act is thus more ambiguous than it may seem: they both do it not out of some pathological blasphemous ambition, but in order to escape the incestuous stuffiness of their home. There must be something wrong at home. Mary's husband, Percy, described what was wrong in his famous sonnet "England in 1819":

An old, mad, blind, despised, and dying king,
Princes, the dregs of their dull race, who flow
Through public scorn—mud from a muddy spring,
Rulers who neither see, nor feel, nor know,
But leech-like to their fainting country cling,
Till they drop, blind in blood, without a blow,
A people starved and stabbed in the untilled field,
An army, which liberticide and prey
Makes as a two-edged sword to all who wield,
Golden and sanguine laws which tempt and slay,
Religion Christless, Godless—a book seal'd,
A Senate—Time's worst statute unrepealed,
Are graves, from which a glorious Phantom may
Burst, to illumine our tempestuous day.

A conservative would reply, of course, that this phantom which may burst from a grave "to illumine our tempestuous day", may turn out not to be so glorious at all, but rather a phantom of murderous revenge like Frankenstein's monster. This brings us to Mary Shelley's contradiction: the contradiction between "oppression and anarchy", between the stifling and oppressive home and the murderous consequences of our attempts to break out of it. Unable to resolve this contradiction, and not willing to confront it directly, she could only tell it as a family myth.

The lesson of all these impasses is not that one should bypass the family myth and turn directly to social reality; what one should do is something much more difficult: to undermine the family myth *from within*. The key testimony of a struggle to achieve this goal is Kafka's letter to his father.

A letter which did arrive at its destination

The 2001 Darwin Award for the most stupid act was posthumously conferred on an unfortunate woman from rural Romania who woke up during her funeral procession. Crawling out of her coffin and realizing what was going on, she ran away in blind terror, only to be hit by a truck on a busy road and instantly killed. So she was put back into the coffin and the funeral procession carried on . . . Is this not the ultimate example of what we call fate—of a letter arriving at its destination?

A letter can also reach its destination precisely insofar as its addressee refuses to receive it—as is the case towards the end of *Troilus and Cressida*, Shakespeare's aforementioned neglected masterpiece, when the deceived lover Troilus rips up and throws away the letter from his Cressida in which she tries to explain her flirtation with Diomedes. We never learn what was in the letter, although the scene cannot but arouse our melodramatic expectations: will Cressida redeem herself, "explain it all"? The force of this expectation accounts for the fact that, throughout the eighteenth century, the version of the play usually performed was Dryden's revision from 1679, in which Cressida is fully redeemed: we learn that she has plotted with her father an escape back to Troy and to Troilus, and that her seeming surrender to Diomedes was merely a ploy to enable that. So, what if Shakespeare wanted to make a point—and not just keep our curiosity in suspension—when he refuses to divulge its content? What if the letter was *meant* to be rejected? The scene to which this letter refers occurred earlier, when, after Cressida and Troilus spend their first (and only) night together, she was delivered by her own father to the Greeks, as part of a cold bargain, in exchange for a Trojan warrior captured by the Greeks. In the Greek camp, she was given as a booty to Diomedes; in his tent, she flirts with him, shamelessly offering herself under the gaze of Troilus, who has been brought to the tent by Ulysses. After Diomedes leaves the tent, she reflects aloud:

> Troilus, farewell! One eye yet looks on thee,
> But with my heart the other eye doth see.
> Ah, poor our sex! This fault in us I find:
> The error of our eye directs our mind.
> What error leads must err. O then conclude:
> Minds swayed by eyes are full of turpitude.
>
> (V, 2)

The key question to be raised here is: what if Cressida had been all the time aware of being observed by Troilus, and just pretended to be thinking aloud alone? What if the entire seduction scene, her shameless attempt to arouse Diomedes' desire, was *staged for Troilus's gaze*? Let us not forget that Cressida announces her split nature already at the lovers' first anxious meeting, when she ominously warns Troilus of how

> I have a kind of self [that] resides with you—
> But an unkind self, that itself will leave
> To be another's fool.
>
> (III, 2)

thereby foreshadowing his bitter statement, after witnessing her flirting with Diomedes, that, in her, there is no "rule in unity itself." This strange internal dislocation of hers is more complex than it may appear: part of her loves him, but this part is "unkind," and, with the same necessity that it linked her to Troilus, will soon push her towards another man. The general lesson of this is that, in order to interpret a scene or an utterance, sometimes, the key thing to do is to *locate its true addressee*. In one of the best Perry Mason novels, the lawyer witnesses a police interrogation of a couple in the course of which the husband tells the policeman in unexpectedly great detail what happened, what he saw, and what he thinks happened—why this excess of information? The solution: this couple committed the murder, and since the husband knew that he and his wife would soon be arrested on suspicion of the murder and kept separated, he used this opportunity to tell his wife the (false) story they should both cling to—the true addressee of his endless talk was thus not the policeman, but his wife.[16]

And thus we come to Franz Kafka's letter to his father, in which he articulated the crisis of paternal authority in all its ambiguity—no wonder that the first impression one gets in reading Kafka's letter is that there is something missing in it, the final twist along the lines of the parable on the Door of the Law ("This door was here only for you . . ."): the father's display of terror and rage is here only for you, you have invested in it, you are sustaining it . . . One can well imagine the real Hermann Kafka as a benevolent and nice gentleman, genuinely surprised at the role he played in his son's imagination.[17]

To put it in Californian style, Kafka had a serious attitude problem with regard to his father. When Kafka identified himself as "Lowy," assuming his mother's name, he located himself in a series which comprises Adorno (who also shifted from father's name, Wiesengrund, to his mother's family name), not to mention Hitler (from Schickelgruber)—all uneasy with assuming the role of the bearer of the paternal name. This is why one of the points in the letter to his father is Kafka's claim that it would have been possible for him to accept (the person of) his father, to establish a non-traumatic relationship with him, if he were his friend, brother, boss, even father-in-law, just not his father . . .

What bothers Kafka is the excessive presence of his father: he is too much alive, too obscenely intrusive. However, this father's excessive presence is not a direct fact: it appears as such only against the background of the suspension of the father's symbolic function. This father's "too-muchness" (as Eric Santner would call it) is ultimately the too-muchness of life itself, the humiliating quality of the father's excess of vitality which undermines his authority—let us note how Kafka's notices his father's

> taste for indecent expressions, which you would produce in the loudest possible voice, laughing about them as though you had said something particularly good, while in point of fact it was only a banal little obscenity (at the same time this again was for me a humiliating manifestation of your vitality).

Again, one should bear in mind the proper order of causality: it is not that his father's excessive vitality undermines his symbolic authority; it is, rather, the other way round, namely, the very fact that Kafka is bothered by his father's excessive vitality already presupposes the failure of symbolic authority.

What is the true function of the Name-of-the-Father? It is, precisely, to allow the subject to "symbolically kill" the father, to be able to *abandon* his father (and the closed family circle) and freely set out on his own path in the world. No wonder, then, that Kafka's reluctance to assume the Name-of-the-Father is the very indication of his failure to break away from his father: what the letter to Kafka's father bears witness to is a subject who was doomed to remain forever in the paternal shadow, caught up with him in a libidinal deadlock. Far from enabling him to elude his father's grasp, Kafka's refusal to accept the father's name is the surest sign of this imprisonment.

Not in any sense a passive victim of his father's terror, Kafka was directing the game (recall from the long debate between the man from the countryside and the Priest, which follows the parable about the Door of the Law in Kafka's *The Trial*, the Priest's claim that the man from the countryside was in the superior position and that the guardian of the door was really subordinated to him). The proof? If there ever was a screen memory, it is the accident from when he was two months old that Kafka claims as the only thing from his childhood of which he has a "direct memory" (and appeals to his father that he should also remember it). It was (re)constructed afterwards, probably from what the parents told Franz about it—but covering what, we may ask? Like the primal scene of the Wolfman, it is a retroactive fantasy:

> There is only one episode in the early years of which I have a direct memory. You may remember it, too. One night I kept on whimpering for water, not, I am certain, because I was thirsty, but probably partly to be annoying, partly to amuse myself. After several vigorous threats had failed to have any effect, you took me out of bed, carried me out onto the *pavlatche* [the Czech word for the long balcony in the inner courtyard of old houses in Prague], and left me there alone for a while in my nightshirt, outside the shut door. I am not going to say that this was wrong—perhaps there was really no other way of getting peace and quiet that night—but I mention it as typical of your methods of bringing up a child and their effect on me. I dare say I was quite obedient afterward at that period, but it did me inner harm. What was for me a matter of course, that senseless asking for water, and then the extraordinary terror of being carried outside were two things that I, my nature being what it was, could never properly connect with each other. Even years afterward I suffered from the tormenting fancy that the huge man, my father, the ultimate authority, would come almost for no reason at all and take me out of bed in the night and carry me out

onto the *pavlatche*, and that consequently I meant absolutely nothing as far as he was concerned.

The gurgling signifying chain of the child intended to provoke the father is like the obscene soft sounds on the phone line from the Castle, or the US marines' marching chants . . . There is thus a hidden link between the "subversive" pre-symbolic babble of the child and the inaccessible Power that terrorizes the Kafkean hero, between superego and id.

The true underlying reproach to the father is not his power and arrogant display of authority, but, on the contrary, his *impotence*, his *lack* of symbolic authority. Are the father's terrifying outbursts of rage (*Wuten*) not so many signs of his basic impotence, signals that his cold and efficient authority has failed? The father himself accounted for his "imperious temperament" as "due to [his] nervous heart condition"—not exactly a sign of power, but, as is clear to Kafka himself, a method of cheap manipulation worthy of a weakling: "the nervous heart condition is a means by which you exert your domination more strongly, since the thought of it necessarily chokes off the least opposition from others." Here is another of the father's ritualistic displays of power: "It was also terrible when you ran around the table, shouting, grabbing at one, obviously not really trying to grab, yet pretending to . . ."—a ridiculous, self-undermining, display of power. Furthermore, what kind of a father feels so threatened by his two-month-old son that he has to undertake the absurdly excessive measure of taking him out of the apartment? A truly authoritative figure would deal with the problem with a cold stare . . . (And, incidentally, in the standard patriarchal family which the Kafka family certainly was, is the first sign of the lack of authority not already the fact that it was the father, not the mother, who came to respond to the child?) It is no less clear that the description of the father's "intellectual domination" is sustained by a barely concealed fear that this obvious fraud, this semblance of authority, will burst like a balloon, laying bare father's stupidity . . .

From your armchair you ruled the world. Your opinion was correct, every other was mad, wild, *meshugge*, not normal. Your self-confidence indeed was so great that you had no need to be consistent at all and yet never ceased to be in the right. It did sometimes happen that you had no opinions whatsoever about a matter and as a result every conceivable opinion with respect to the matter was necessarily wrong, without exception. You were capable, for instance, of running down the Czechs, and then the Germans, and then the Jews, and what is more, not only selectively but in every respect, and finally nobody was left except yourself. For me you took on the enigmatic quality that all tyrants have whose rights are based on their person and not on reason.

No wonder Kafka's "exclusive sense of guilt" has been replaced by "insight into our helplessness, yours and mine."

We have thus to be very precise when we are dealing with the topic of paternal authority: authority is not to be confused with an overbearing, violently intrusive presence. That is to say, one way to read Kafka's bewilderment with regard to his father is to decipher it as the experience of the gap, the contrast, between the ridiculous, pretentious, and impotent figure that is the reality of his father and the immense power he nonetheless exerts: "How can such a pathetic figure nonetheless exert such power?" The answer would then be the socio-symbolic network that invests an empirical person with power, and the gap would be that of symbolic castration. From the traditional rituals of investiture, we know the objects which not only "symbolize" power, but put the subject who acquires them into the position of effectively *exercising* power — if a king holds in his hands the scepter and wears the crown, his words will be taken as the words of a king. Such insignia are external, not part of my nature: I don them; I wear them in order to exert power. As such, they "castrate" me: they introduce a gap between what I immediately am and the function that I exercise (that is, I am never fully at the level of my function). This, however, is *not* the way Kafka experiences his father; the problem for Kafka is rather that his father's bodily presence disturbs the efficacy of the paternal symbolic function. In other words, his father's excessive, almost spectral, towering presence whose impact exceeds the immediate reality of his person is not the excess of the symbolic authority over immediate reality; it is the excess of the fantasmatic obscenity of the Real. In Freudian terms, the problem with Kafka's father is that, in Franz's eyes, he has "regressed" from the agency of symbolic Law to the "primordial father [*Ur-Vater*]."

There are two modes of the Master, the public symbolic Master and the secret Evil Magician who effectively pulls the strings and does his work during the night. When the subject is endowed with symbolic authority, he acts as an appendix to his symbolic title, that is, it is the big Other, the symbolic institution, which acts through him: suffice it to recall a judge, who may be a miserable and corrupted person, but the moment he puts on his robe and other insignia, his words are the words of the Law itself. On the other hand, the "invisible" Master (whose exemplary case is the anti-Semitic figure of the "Jew" who, invisible to the public eye, pulls the strings of social life) is a kind of uncanny double of public authority: he has to act in the shadows, irradiating a phantom-like, spectral omnipotence. The disintegration of the patriarchal symbolic authority, of the Name-of-the-Father, gives rise to a new figure of the Master who is simultaneously our common peer, our "neighbor," our imaginary double, and for this very reason fantasmatically endowed with another dimension of the Evil Genius. In Lacanian terms: the suspension of the ego ideal, of the feature of symbolic identification, that is, the reduction of the Master to an imaginary ideal, necessarily gives rise to its monstrous obverse, to the superego figure of the omnipotent Evil Genius who controls our lives. In this figure, the Imaginary (semblance) and the Real (of paranoia) overlap, due to the suspension of proper symbolic efficiency.

The Kafkean Law is not prohibitive, not even intrusive or imposing: its repeated message to the subject is "You are free to do whatever you want! Don't ask me for orders!"—which, of course, is the perfect superego formula. No wonder that the message of Kafka's father to his son was: "Do whatever you like. So far as I'm concerned you have a free hand. You're of age, I've no advice to give you . . ." The series of the father's "rhetorical methods" as enumerated by Kafka—"abuse, threats, irony, spiteful laughter, and—oddly enough—self-pity"—are the most concise rendering of the superego's ambiguity. Kafka's father was definitely a *luðer*, if ever there was one, a figure out of which an "orgy of malice and spiteful delight" emanated. (The link here is between Kafka and David Lynch: namely, the excessive clownish figures of terrorist authority in *Blue Velvet*, *Wild at Heart*, *Dune*, *Lost Highway* . . .)

The superego's basic trick consists in reproaching the subject for not living up to its high expectations, while simultaneously sabotaging the subject's efforts (or mockingly expressing disbelief in the subject's capacities, and then laughing at the subject's failure). Kafka clearly noticed this paradox apropos of his father's demands that he should become an autonomous person who succeeds on his own:

> But that wasn't what you wanted at all; the situation had, after all, become quite different as a result of all your efforts, and there was no

opportunity to distinguish oneself as you had done. Such an opportunity would first of all have had to be created by violence and revolutions, it would have meant breaking away from home (assuming one had had the resolution and strength to do so and that Mother wouldn't have worked against it, for her part, with other means). But that was not what you wanted at all, that you termed ingratitude, extravagance, disobedience, treachery, madness. And so, while on the one hand you tempted me to it by means of example, story, and humiliation, on the other hand you forbade it with the utmost severity.

This is the obscene superego in its contrast to the Name-of-the-Father: the very injunction "be autonomous," in its mode of operation, sabotages its goal; the very injunction "Be free!" ties the subject up forever in the vicious circle of dependence.

One can retell in these superego terms even the remark allegedly made by Brecht apropos the accused at the Moscow show trials in the 1930s: "If they are innocent, they deserve all the more to be shot." This statement is thoroughly ambiguous—it can be read as the standard assertion of radical Stalinism (your very insistence on your individual innocence, your refusal to sacrifice yourself for the Cause, bears witness to your guilt which resides in privileging your individuality over the larger interests of the party), or it can be read as its opposite, in a radically anti-Stalinist way: if they were in a position to plot and execute the execution of Stalin and his entourage, and were "innocent" (that is, they did not grasp the opportunity), they effectively deserved to die for failing to rid us of Stalin. The true guilt of the accused is thus that, instead of rejecting the very ideological framework of Stalinism and ruthlessly acting against Stalin, they narcissistically fell in love with their victimization and either protested their innocence or became fascinated by the ultimate sacrifice they were making to the party by confessing their nonexistent crimes. So the properly dialectical way of grasping the imbrication of these two meanings would have been to start with the first reading, followed by the common-sense moralistic reaction to Brecht: "But how can you claim something so ruthless? Can such a logic which demands blind self-sacrifice for the accusatory whims of the Leader not function only within a terrifying criminal totalitarian universe? Far from accepting these rules, it is the duty of every ethical subject to fight such a universe with all means possible, including the physical removal (killing) of the totalitarian leadership?" "So you see how, if the accused are innocent, they deserve all the more to be shot—they effectively *were* in a position to organize a plot to rid us of Stalin and his henchmen, and missed this unique opportunity to spare humanity from terrible crimes!" This, again, is the twisted superego logic at its purest: the more you are innocent, the more you are guilty, because your innocence itself (innocence in the eyes of whom? With regard to what? With regard to the obscene criminal power) is the proof of your guilt (of your complicity with this power) . . .

Although Freud uses three distinct terms for the agency that pushes the subject to act ethically—he speaks of the ideal ego (*Idealich*), ego ideal (*Ich-Ideal*), and superego [*Überich*]—as a rule he conflated the three (he often uses the expression *Ichideal oder Idealich* (ego ideal or ideal ego), and the title of chapter III of *The Ego and the Id*) is "The Ego and Superego (Ego Ideal)." Lacan, however, introduces a precise distinction between these three terms: the "ideal ego" stands for the idealized self-image of the subject (the way I would like to be, I would like others to see me); the ego ideal is the agency whose gaze I try to impress with my ego image, the big Other who watches over me and pushes me to give my best, the ideal I try to follow and actualize; and the superego is this same agency in its vengeful, sadistic, punishing aspect. The underlying structuring principle of these tree terms is clearly Lacan's triad Imaginary–Symbolic–Real: the ideal ego is imaginary, what Lacan calls the "small other," the idealized double image of my ego; the ego ideal is symbolic, the point of my symbolic identification, the point in the big Other from which I observe (and judge) myself; the superego is real, the cruel and insatiable agency which bombards me with impossible demands and which mocks my failed attempts to meet them, the agency in the eyes of which I am all the more guilty, the more I try to suppress my "sinful" strivings and live up to its exigencies.

What follows from these precise distinctions is that, for Lacan, the superego "has nothing to do with moral conscience as far as its most obligatory demands are concerned."[18] The superego is, on the contrary, the anti-ethical agency, the stigmatization of our ethical betrayal. So which one of the other two *is* the proper ethical agency? Should we—as some American psychoanalysts propose—set up the "good" (rational-moderate, caring) ego ideal against the "bad" (irrational-excessive, cruel, anxiety-provoking) superego, trying to lead the patient to get rid of the "bad" superego and follow the "good" ego ideal? Lacan opposes this easy way out—for him, the only proper agency is the fourth one, missing from Freud's tripartite list, the one sometimes referred to by Lacan as "the law of desire," the agency which tells you to act in conformity with your desire. The gap between this "law of desire" and the ego ideal (the network of social-symbolic norms and ideals that the subject internalizes in the course of her education) is crucial here. For Lacan, the ego ideal, this seemingly benevolent agency which leads us to moral growth and maturity, forces us to betray the "law of desire" by adopting the "reasonable" demands of the existing socio-symbolic order. The superego, with its excessive feeling of guilt, is merely the necessary obverse of the ego ideal: it exerts its unbearable pressure upon us on behalf of our betrayal of the "law of desire." In short, for Lacan, the guilt we experience under the superego's pressure is not illusory but actual—"the only thing of which one can be guilty is of having given ground relative to one's desire," and the superego's pressure demonstrates that we effectively *are* guilty of betraying our desire.

Back to Kafka: he formulates this same insight apropos the father's reactions to his attempts to get married:

> The fundamental thought behind both attempts at marriage was quite sound: to set up house, to become independent. An idea that does appeal to you, only in reality it always turns out like the children's game in which one holds and even grips the other's hand, calling out: "Oh, go away, go away, why don't you go away?"

What the father was thus preventing is Kafka's marriage: in his case, the father did not act as the guarantor of marriage, as the agent of symbolic authority (see Lacan's thesis that a harmonious sexual relationship can only take place under the cover of the Name-of-the-Father), but as its superego obstacle, as what Freud, in his analysis of E.T.A. Hoffmann's *Sandman*, calls *Liebesstörer*, the obstacle which disturbs/prevents the love relationship. We encounter here the superego paradox at its purest: the father who prevents the love relationship is precisely the obscene father who enjoins us to "do it," to engage in sexual promiscuity without constraints; and, inversely, the father who opens up the space for a love relationship is the father who is the agency of prohibition, of the symbolic Law. That is to say, Kafka's desire for a proper father is not a masochistic desire for subordination to an authority; it is, on the contrary, a desire for freedom and autonomy. The paradox is thus that *freedom from* his father means *assuming his father's name*, which puts them on the same level: "Marriage certainly is the pledge of the most acute form of self-liberation and independence. I would have a family, in my opinion the highest one can achieve, and so too the highest you have achieved." The choice Kafka confronted was between the two ways of escaping from his father, two modes of independence: marriage or writing, *le père ou pire*, his father or the "almost nothing" of writing:

> in my writing, and in everything connected with it, I have made some attempts at independence, attempts at escape, with the very smallest of success; they will scarcely lead any farther; much confirms this for me. Nevertheless it is my duty or, rather, the essence of my life, to watch over them, to let no danger that I can avert, indeed no possibility of such a danger, approach them. Marriage bears the possibility of such a danger.

And he continues,

> the final outcome is certain: I must renounce. The simile of the bird in the hand and the two in the bush has only a fiery remote application here. In my hand I have nothing, in the bush is everything, and yet—so it is decided by the conditions of battle and the exigency of life—I must choose the nothing.[19]

Kafka's self-humiliation, which includes excremental identification ("And so if the world consisted only of me and you, a notion I was much inclined to have, then this purity of the world came to an end with you and, by virtue of your advice, the filth began with me"), is thus profoundly deceptive: it is easy to discern in Kafka's claim that he is "the result of your upbringing and of my obedience" the stratagem of denying one's own libidinal involvement in one's sad fate. The strategy is clear here: *I willingly assume my filth in order for my father to remain pure.* This becomes especially clear when one bears in mind when, precisely, this self-identification with "filth" occurs: at the exact (and most traumatic) point of the letter, when Kafka reports on the (rare) moments when his father offered him "realistic"/obscene advice on how to deal with sex (do it discreetly, have your fun, do not take things too seriously, do not fall for the first girl who offers herself to you, remember they are all the same whores, just use them and move on . . .). For example, Kafka recalls a "brief discussion" that followed the announcement of my latest marriage plans. You said to me something like this: "She probably put on a fancy blouse, something these Prague Jewesses are good at, and right away, of course, you decided to marry her. And that as fast as possible, in a week, tomorrow, today. I can't understand you: after all, you're a grown man, you live in the city, and you don't know what to do but marry the first girl who comes along. Isn't there anything else you can do? If you're frightened, I'll go with you." You put it in more detail and more plainly, but I can no longer recall the details, perhaps too things became a little vague before my eyes, I paid almost more attention to Mother who, though in complete agreement with you, took something from the table and left the room with it. You have hardly ever humiliated me more deeply with words and shown me your contempt more clearly.

The "real meaning" of this advice was clear to Kafka: "what you advised me to do was in your opinion and even more in my opinion at that time, the filthiest thing possible." For Kafka, this displacement of "filth" onto the son was part of the father's strategy to keep himself pure—and it is at this point that Kafka's own identification with "filth" occurs:

> Thus you became still purer, rose still higher. The thought that you might have given yourself similar advice before your marriage was to me utterly unthinkable. So there was hardly any smudge of earthly filth on you at all. And it was you who pushed me down into this filth— just as though I were predestined to it with a few frank words. And so, if the world consisted only of me and you (a notion I was much inclined to have), then this purity of the world came to an end with you and, by virtue of your advice, the filth began with me.

Again, it is here that Kafka cheats: it is not his father's, but *his own*, desperate striving to keep the father pure—it is for Kafka himself that any notion of his father following similar advice (and, consequently, dwelling in "filth") is "utterly unthinkable," which means: totally catastrophic, foreclosed from his universe.

There follows a weird but crucial conclusion: the father's prosopopoeia. In his father's reply as imagined by Kafka, the father imputes to Kafka that whatever he would have done (namely to support or oppose Kafka's marriage plans), it would have backfired and have been twisted by Kafka into an obstacle. The father evokes here the standard logic of (paternal) prohibition and its transgression:

> My aversion to your marriage would not have prevented it; on the contrary, it would have been an added incentive for you to marry the girl, for it would have made the "attempt at escape," as you put it, complete.

One has to be very precise here and avoid confusing this entanglement of the law and its transgression (the law sustained by a hidden call for its own transgression) with the superego proper as its (almost) symmetrically opposite. On the one hand, it is the hidden (non-articulated) injunction "Enjoy! Violate the law!" that reverberates in the explicit prohibition; on the other (much more interesting and uneasy) hand, it is the hidden (non-articulated) injunction to fail that reverberates in the explicit permissive call "Be free! Enjoy!"

The last paragraph does break the vicious cycle of mutual accusations and is thus hesitantly "optimistic," opening up a minimal space of truce and a symbolic pact.

> My answer to this is that, after all, this whole rejoinder—which can partly also be turned against you—does not come from you, but from me. Not even your mistrust of others is as great as my self-mistrust, which you have bred in me. I do not deny a certain justification for this rejoinder, which in itself contributes new material to the characterization of our relationship. Naturally things cannot in reality fit together the way the evidence does in my letter; life is more than a Chinese puzzle. But with the correction made by this rejoinder—a correction I neither can nor will elaborate in detail—in my opinion something has been achieved which so closely approximates the truth that it might reassure us both a little and make our living and our dying easier.

What we have here is effectively a kind of (self-)analysis punctuated by the father's (analyst's) imagined intervention which brings about the conclusion: it is as if Kafka's long, rambling flow finally provokes the analyst's intervention, as a reaction to which Kafka (the analysand) finally enacts the shift in his subjective position, signaled by the obvious but no less odd claim that "this whole rejoinder—which can partly also be turned against you—does not come from you, but from me." The parallel is clear with the conclusion of the parable on the Door of the Law, when the man from the country is told that "this door was here only for you": here too, Kafka learns that all the spectacle of father's outbursts and so forth "was here only for him." Thus the letter to father *did indeed* arrive at its destination—because the true addressee was the writer himself . . .

In this way, Kafka's subjective identification shifts—minimally, but in a way which changes everything—from the "almost nothing" of being (father's) filth to "nothing at all": if all of it "comes from me," my nullity can no longer be (the other's) filth. The move that concludes the letter is thus the one from death to sublimation: Kafka's choice of nothing as one's place, the reduction of his existence to the minimum where "nothing but the place takes place," to paraphrase Mallarmé, creates the space for creative sublimation (literature). To paraphrase yet again Brecht's motto from *The Threepenny Opera*, what is the filth of engaging in small sexual transgressions compared to the filthy purity of writing, of literature as "litturaterre" (Lacan's pun), as the litter defiling the surface of earth?

3   Radical Intellectuals
Or, Why Heidegger Took the Right Step
(Albeit in the Wrong Direction) in 1933

Hiding the tree in a forest

When, in G.K. Chesterton's "The Sign of the Broken Sword" (a story from *The Innocence of Father Brown*),[1] Father Brown explains the mystery to his companion Flambeau, he begins with "what everyone knows":

> Arthur St. Clare was a great and successful English general. [Every-one] knows that after splendid yet careful campaigns both in India and Africa he was in command against Brazil when the great Brazilian patriot Olivier issued his ultimatum. [Everyone] knows that on that occasion St. Clare with a very small force attacked Olivier with a very large one, and was captured after heroic resistance. And [everyone] knows that after his capture, and to the abhorrence of the civilised world, St. Clare was hanged on the nearest tree. He was found swinging there after the Brazilians had retired, with his broken sword hung round his neck.

However, Father Brown notices that something does not fit in this story that everybody knows: St. Clare, who was always a prudent commander, characterized more by a sense of duty than by dashing, made a foolish attack which ended in disaster; Olivier, who was magnanimous to the point of knight errantry and always set free prisoners, cruelly killed St. Clare. To account for this mystery, Father Brown evokes a metaphor:

> "Where does a wise man hide a leaf? In the forest. But what does he do if there is no forest? He grows a forest to hide it in," said the priest in an obscure voice. "A fearful sin. [. . .] And if a man had to hide a dead body, he would make a field of dead bodies to hide it in."

The denouement relies on the hypothesis of the dark corrupted side of the English hero: Sir Arthur St. Clare

> was a man who read his Bible. That was what was the matter with him. When will people understand that it is useless for a man to read his Bible unless he also reads everybody else's Bible? A printer reads a Bible for misprints. A Mormon reads his Bible, and finds polygamy; a Christian Scientist reads his, and finds we have no arms and legs. St. Clare was an old Anglo-Indian Protestant soldier. [. . .] Of course, he found in the Old Testament anything that he wanted—lust, tyranny, treason. Oh, I dare say he was honest, as you call it. But what is the good of a man being honest in his worship of dishonesty?

In the Brazilian jungle, just before the fatal battle, the general encountered an unexpected problem: his accompanying younger officer, Major Murray, had somehow guessed the hideous truth; and as they walked slowly through the jungle, he killed Murray with his sabre. But what could he do now with this body he would have to account for? "He could make the corpse less unaccountable. He could create a hill of corpses to cover this one. In twenty minutes eight hundred English soldiers were marching down to their death." Here, however, things went wrong for the general: the surviving English soldiers somehow guessed what he had done—it was they who killed the general, not Olivier. Olivier (to whom the survivors surrendered) generously set them free and withdrew his troops; the surviving soldiers then tried St. Clare and hanged him, and then, in order to save the glory of the English army, covered up their act by the story that Olivier had had him killed.

The story ends in the spirit of John Ford's westerns which prefer heroic legend to truth (recall John Wayne's final speech to the journalists about the ruthless general played by Henry Fonda, from *Fort Apache*): "Millions who never knew him shall love him like a father—this man whom the last few that knew him dealt with like dung. He shall be a saint; and the truth shall never be told of him, because I have made up my mind at last."

What, then, is the Hegelian lesson of this story? Is it that the simple cynical-denunciatory reading should be rejected? Is it that the gaze which reduces the general's corruption to the truth of his personality is itself mean and base? Hegel described long ago this trap as that of the

Beautiful Soul whose gaze reduces all great heroic deeds to the private base motives of their perpetrators:

> No hero is a hero to his valet, not, however, because the hero is not a hero, but because the valet is — the valet, with whom the hero has to do, not as a hero, but as a man who eats, drinks, and dresses, who, in short, appears as a private individual with certain personal wants and ideas of his own. In the same way, there is no act in which that process of judgment cannot oppose the personal aspect of the individuality to the universal aspect of the act, and play the part of the "moral" valet towards the agent.[2]

Is, then, Father Brown, if not this kind of "moral valet" to the general, then, at least, a cynic who knows that the unpleasant truth has to be covered up for the sake of the public good? Chesterton's theological finesse is discernible in the way he allocates the responsibility for the general's gradual downfall: it is not the general's betrayal of the Christian faith through his moral corruption due to the predominance of base materialist motives. Chesterton is wise enough to depict the cause of the general's moral downfall as inherent to Christianity: the general "was a man who read his Bible. That was what was the matter with him." It was the particular — in this case, Protestant — reading that is held responsible. And can one not say the same about Heidegger's attempt (and also that of Adorno and Horkheimer, and even of Agamben) to lay the blame for the ethico-political catastrophes of the twentieth century on the shoulders of the entire tradition of "Western metaphysics" with its instrumental Reason, and so on and so forth, leading in linear fashion "from Plato to Nato" (or, rather, the gulag)? Sloterdijk has written the following about the leftist global problematization of "Western civilization":

> Through the boundless forms of cultural criticism — say, the reduction of Auschwitz back to Luther and Plato, or the criminalization of Western civilization in its entirety — one tries to blur the traces which betray how close to a class-genocidical system we ourselves were standing.[3]

The only thing one should add here is that the same applies to Heidegger and other former fascists: they too hid their Nazi corpse in the mountain of corpses called Western metaphysics . . . And should one not reject in the same way, as an over-hasty generalization, the liberal popular wisdom according to which philosophers who meddle in politics will always lead to disaster? According to this view, starting with Plato, they either miserably fail or succeed . . . in supporting tyrants. The reason, so the story goes on, is that philosophers try to impose their Notions on reality, violating it—no wonder that, from Plato to Heidegger, they are resolutely anti-democratic (with the exception of a few empiricists and pragmatists), dismissing the "people" as the victim of sophists, at the mercy of a contingent plurality . . . So when those who hold to this commonsensical wisdom hear of Marxists who defend Marx, claiming that his ideas were not faithfully realized by Stalinism, they reply: "Thank God! It would have been even worse had they been fully realized!" Heidegger at least was willing to draw the consequences of his catastrophic experience and concede that those who think ontologically have to err ontically, that the gap is irreducible, that there is no "philosophical politics" proper. It thus seems that G.K. Chesterton was fully justified in his ironic proposal to install a "special corps of policemen, policemen who are also philosophers":

It is their business to watch the beginnings of this conspiracy, not merely in a criminal but in a controversial sense. [. . .] The work of the philosophical policeman [. . .] is at once bolder and more subtle than that of the ordinary detective. The ordinary detective goes to pothouses to arrest thieves; we go to artistic tea-parties to detect pessimists. The ordinary detective discovers from a ledger or a diary that a crime has been committed. We discover from a book of sonnets that a crime will be committed. We have to trace the origin of those dreadful thoughts that drive men on at last to intellectual fanaticism and intellectual crime.[4]

Would not thinkers as different as Popper, Adorno, and Levinas also subscribe to a slightly amended version of this idea, where the political crime is called "totalitarianism" and the philosophical crime is condensed in the notion of "totality"? A straight road leads from the philosophical notion of totality to political totalitarianism, and the task of the "philosophical police" is to detect in a book of Plato's dialogues or a treatise on the social contract by Rousseau that a political crime will be committed. The ordinary political policeman goes to secret organizations to arrest revolutionaries; the philosophical policeman goes to philosophical sym-

posia to detect proponents of totality. The ordinary anti-terrorist policeman tries to detect those preparing to blow up buildings and bridges; the
philosophical policeman tries to arrest those about to deconstruct the
religious and moral foundations of our societies . . .[5]

This position is that of "wisdom": a wise man knows that one should
not "enforce" reality, that a little bit of corruption is the best defense
against great corruption. Christianity is in this sense a form of anti-
wisdom *par excellence*: a crazy wager on Truth, in contrast to paganism
which, ultimately, counts on wisdom ("everything returns to dust, the
Wheel of Life goes on forever . . ."). The fateful limitation of this stance
of wisdom resides in the formalism that pertains to the notion of balance,
of avoiding the extremes. When one hears formulae such as "we need
neither total state control nor totally non-regulated liberalism/individu-
alism, but the right measure between these two extremes," the problem
that immediately pops up is *the measurement of this measure*—the point of
balance is always silently presupposed. Suppose someone were to say:
"We need neither too much respect for Jews, nor the Nazi Holocaust, but
the right measure in between, some quotas for universities and prohibition of public office for the Jews to prevent their excessive influence,"
one cannot really answer at a purely formal level. Here we have the
formalism of wisdom: the true task is to transform the measure itself, not
only to oscillate between the extremes of the measure.

In his otherwise admirable *Holy Terror*, Terry Eagleton seems to fall
into the same trap when he deploys the *pharmakos* dialectic of the excess
of the Sacred, of the Holy Terror as the excess of the Real which should
be respected, satisfied, but kept at a distance. The Real is simultaneously
generative and destructive: destructive if given free rein, but also
destructive if denied, since its very denial unleashes a fury which imitates
it—again a case of the coincidence of opposites. Eagleton here perceives
freedom as such as a *pharmakos*, which becomes destructive when
unhindered. Is, however, this not all too close to a conservative form
of wisdom? Is it not a supreme irony here that Eagleton, arguably the
sharpest and most perspicuous critic of postmodernism, displays here his
own secret postmodern bias, endorsing one of the great postmodern
motifs, that of the Real Thing towards which one should maintain a
proper distance? No wonder that Eagleton professes his sympathy for
conservatives such as Burke and his critique of French Revolution: not
that it was unjust, and so on, but that it exposed the founding excessive
violence of the legal order, bringing to light and re-enacting what should

be at all costs concealed—this is the function of traditional myths. Rejection of these myths, reliance on pure Reason critical of tradition, thereby necessarily ends up in the madness and destructive orgy of Unreason.[6]

Where does Lacan stand with regard to this complex topic referred to by the tiresome and stupid designation "the social role of intellectuals"? Lacan's theory, of course, can be used to throw new light on numerous politico-ideological phenomena, bringing to the fore the hidden libidinal economy that sustains them; but we are asking here a more basic and naive question: does Lacan's theory imply a precise political stance? Some Lacanians (and not only Lacanians), such as Yannis Stavrakakis, endeavor to demonstrate that Lacanian theory directly grounds democratic politics. The terms are well known: "there is no big Other" means that the socio-symbolic order is inconsistent, no ultimate guarantee, and democracy is the way to integrate into the edifice of power this lack of ultimate foundation. Insofar as all organic visions of a harmonious Whole of society rely on a fantasy, democracy thus appears to offer a political stance which "traverses the fantasy," that is, which renounces the impossible ideal of a non-antagonistic society.

The political theorist who serves as a key reference here is Claude Lefort, who was himself influenced by Lacan and uses Lacanian terms in his definition of democracy: democracy accepts the gap between the symbolic (the empty place of power) and the real (the agent who occupies this place), postulating that no empirical agent "naturally" fits the empty place of power. Other systems are incomplete, they have to engage in compromises, in occasional shake-ups, to function; democracy elevates incompleteness into a principle, it institutionalizes the regular shake-up in the guise of elections. In short, S(barred A) is the signifier of democracy. Democracy here goes further than the "realistic" nostrum according to which, in order to actualize a certain political vision, one should allow for concrete unpredictable circumstances and be ready to make compromises, to leave the space open for people's vices and imperfections—democracy turns imperfection itself into a notion. However, one should bear in mind that the democratic subject, which emerges through a violent abstraction from all its particular roots and determinations, is the Lacanian barred subject, $, which is as such foreign to, incompatible with, enjoyment:

Democracy as empty place means for us: the subject of democracy is a barred subject. Our small algebra enables us to grasp immediately that this leaves out the small (a). That is to say: all that hinges on the particularity of enjoyments. The empty barred subject of democracy finds it difficult to link itself to all that goes on, forms itself, trembles, in all that we designate with this comfortable small letter, the small (a). We are told: once there is the empty place, everybody, if he respects the laws, can bring in his traditions and his values. [. . .] However, what we know is that, effectively, the more democracy is empty, the more it is a desert of enjoyment, and, correlatively, the more enjoyment condenses itself in certain elements. [. . .] the more the signifier is "disaffected," as others put it, the more the signifier is purified, the more it imposes itself in the pure form of law, of egalitarian democracy, of the globalization of the market, [. . .] the more passion augments itself, the more hatred intensifies, fundamentalisms multiply, destruction extends itself, massacres without precedent are accomplished, and unheard-of catastrophes occur.[7]

What this means is that the democratic empty place and the discourse of totalitarian fullness are strictly correlative, two sides of the same coin: it is meaningless to play one against the other and advocate a "radical" democracy which would avoid this unpleasant supplement. So, when leftists deplore the fact that today only the Right has passion, is able to propose a new mobilizing imaginary, and that the Left only engages in administration, what they do not see is the structural necessity of what they perceive as a mere tactical weakness of the Left. No wonder that the European project which is widely debated today fails to enflame the passions: it is ultimately a project of administration, not of ideological commitment. The only passion is that of the rightist reaction against Europe — all the leftist attempts to infuse the notion of a united Europe with political passion (such the Habermas–Derrida initiative in the summer of 2003) fail to gain momentum. The reason for this failure is that the "fundamentalist" attachment to *jouissance* is *the obverse, the fantasmatic supplement, of democracy itself.*

What to do, then, once one draws the consequences of this *Unbehagen* in democracy? Some Lacanians (and not exclusively Lacanians) endeavor to attribute to Lacan the position of an internal critic of democracy, a provocateur who raises unpleasant questions without proposing his own positive political project. Politics as such is here devalued as a domain of imaginary and symbolic identifications, as the self, by definition, involves a misrecognition, a form of self-blinding. Lacan is thus a provocateur, in the tradition extending from Socrates to Kierkegaard, and he discerns democracy's illusions and hidden metaphysical presuppositions. The outstanding advocate of this second position is Wendy Brown who, although not a Lacanian, deploys an extremely important and perspicuous Nietzschean critique of the politically correct politics of victimization, of basing one's identity on injury.

A domestication of Nietzsche

Brown reads the postmodern politics of identity based on the wrongs committed to specific groups (the sex–gender–race trinity) as an expression of the ambiguous relationship with the liberal-democratic egalitarian framework of human rights: one feels betrayed by it (with regard to women, blacks, gays . . . the universalist liberal rhetoric did not deliver, it masks continuous exclusion and exploitation), while nonetheless remaining deeply attached to these very ideals. In a refined analysis, Brown demonstrates how the sense of moral outrage emerges in order to find a precarious compromise between a host of inconsistent and opposed attitudes (sadism and masochism, attachment and rejection, blaming the other and feeling one's own guilt). She reads moralizing politics "not only as a sign of stubborn clinging to a certain equation of truth with powerlessness, or as the acting out of an injured will, but as a symptom of a broken historical narrative to which we have not yet forged alternatives."[8] "It is when the telos of the good vanishes but the yearning for it remains that morality appears to devolve into moralism in politics."[9] After the disintegration of the grand, all-encompassing, leftist narratives of progress, when political activity dissolved into a multitude of identity issues, the excess over these particular struggles can only find an outlet in impotent moralistic outrage.

However, Brown takes here a crucial step further and pushes all the paradoxes of democracy to the end, more radically than Chantal Mouffe did with her "democratic paradox." Already with Spinoza and Tocqueville, it became clear that democracy is in itself inchoate — empty, lacking a firm principle — it needs anti-democratic content to fill in its form; as such, it really is constitutively "formal." This anti-democratic content is provided by philosophy, ideology, theory — no wonder that most of the great philosophers, from Plato to Heidegger, were mistrustful of democracy, if not directly anti-democratic:

What if democratic politics, the most untheoretical of all political forms, paradoxically requires theory, requires an antithesis to itself in both the form and substance of theory, if it is to satisfy its ambition to produce a free and egalitarian order?[10]

Brown deploys all the paradoxes from this fact that "democracy requires for its health a nondemocratic element": a democracy needs a permanent influx of anti-democratic self-questioning *in order to remain a living democracy*—the cure for democracy's ills is homoeopathic in form:

> If, as the musings of Spinoza and Tocqueville suggest, democracies tend towards cathexis onto principles antithetical to democracy, then critical scrutiny of these principles and of the political formations animated by them is crucial to the project of refounding or recovering democracy.[11]

Brown defines the tension between politics and theory as the tension between the political necessity to fix meaning, to "suture" textual drift in a formal principle which can only guide us in action, and theory's permanent "deconstruction" which cannot ever be recuperated in a new positive program:

> Among human practices, politics is peculiarly untheoretical because the bids for power that constitute it are necessarily at odds with the theoretical project of opening up meaning, of "making meaning slide," in Stuart Hall's words. Discursive power functions by concealing the terms of its fabrication and hence its malleability and contingency; discourse fixes meaning by naturalizing it, or else ceases to have sway in a discourse. This fixing or naturalizing of meanings is the necessary idiom in which politics takes place. Even the politics of deconstructive displacement implicates such normativity, at least provisionally.[12]

Theoretical analyses which unearth the contingent and inconsistent nature and lack of ultimate foundation of all normative constructs and political projects, "are anti-political endeavors insofar as each destabilizes meaning without proposing alternative codes or institutions. Yet each may also be essential in sustaining an existing democratic regime by rejuvenating it."[13] It is thus as if Brown is proposing a kind of Kantian "critique of deconstructive (anti-democratic) reason," distinguishing between its legitimate and illegitimate use: it is legitimate to use it as a negatively regulative corrective, a provocation, and so on, but it is illegitimate to use it as a constitutive principle to be directly applied to reality as a political program or project. Brown discerns the same ambiguous link in the relationship between state and people: in the same way that democracy needs anti-democracy to rejuvenate itself, the state needs the people's resistance to rejuvenate itself:

> Only through the state are the people constituted as a people; only in resistance to the state do the people remain a people. Thus, just as democracy requires antidemocratic critique in order to remain democratic, so too the democratic state may require democratic resistance rather than fealty if it is not to become the death of democracy. Similarly, democracy may require theory's provision of unliveable critiques and unreachable ideals.[14]

Here, however, in this parallel between the two couples of democracy/anti-democracy and state/people, Brown's argumentation becomes caught up in a strange symptomal dynamic of reversals: while democracy needs anti-democratic critique to remain alive, to shake its false certainties, the democratic state needs the democratic resistance of the people, *not* anti-democratic resistance. Does Brown not confound here two (or, rather, a whole series of) resistances to the democratic state: the anti-democratic "elitist" theoreticians' resistance (Plato–Nietzsche–Heidegger), and popular-democratic resistance against the insufficiently democratic character of the state? Furthermore, is not each of these two kinds of resistance accompanied by its dark shadowy double: brutal cynical elitism that justifies those in power; the violent outbursts of the rabble? And what if the two join hands, what if we have *anti-democratic resistance of the people themselves* ("authoritarian populism")?

Furthermore, does Brown not dismiss all too lightly anti-democratic theorists such as Nietzsche as proposing "unliveable" critiques of democracy? How do we respond to the coming-about of a regime that endeavors to "live" them, such as Nazism? Is it not too simple to relieve Nietzsche of responsibility by claiming that the Nazis distorted his thought? Of course they did, but so did Stalinism distort Marx, for every theory changes (is "betrayed") in its practico-political application, and the Hegelian point to be made here is that, in such cases, the "truth" is not simply on the side of theory—what if the attempt to actualize a theory renders visible the objective content of this theory, concealed from the gaze of the theorist itself?

The weakness of Brown's description is perhaps that she locates the undemocratic ingredient that keeps democracy alive only in the "crazy" theoreticians questioning its foundations from "unliveable" premises — but what about the very *real* undemocratic elements that sustain democracy? Does therein not reside the major premise of Foucault's (Brown's major reference) analyses of modern power: democratic power has to be sustained by a complex network of controlling and regulating mechanisms? In his *Notes Towards a Definition of Culture*, T.S. Eliot, that archetypal "noble conservative," convincingly argued that a strong aristocratic class is a necessary ingredient of a feasible democracy: the highest cultural values can only thrive if they are transmitted through a complex and continuous familial and group background. So when Brown claims that "democracy requires antidemocratic critique in order to remain democratic," a liberal conservative would deeply agree in their warnings against "deMOREcracy": there should be a tension in the opposition between the state and democracy, a state should not simply be dissolved in democracy, it should retain the excess of unconditional power *over* the people, the firm rule of law, to prevent its own dissolution. If the state, democratic though it may be, is not sustained by this specter of the unconditional exercise of power, it does not have the authority to function: power is, by definition, in excess, or else it is not power.

The question here is: who is supplementing whom? Is democracy a supplement to fundamentally non-democratic state power, or is undemocratic theory a supplement to democracy? At what point is the predicate inverted with the subject? Furthermore, apropos "stopping the sliding of meaning," does non-democratic theory as a rule not articulate its horror at democracy precisely because it perceives it as too "sophistic" (for Plato . . .), too involved in the sliding of meaning, so that theory, far from reproaching democracy for the fixity of meaning, desperately wants to impose a stable order on social life? And, furthermore, is this "incessant sliding of meaning" not something that is already a feature of the capitalist economy itself which, in its contemporary dynamic, raises to new heights Marx's old description of its dissolvent power on all fixed identities?

The "homoeopathic" logic evoked by Brown is thus ambiguous. On the one hand, the remedy against an ossified democracy is theoretical anti-democratic critique which shatters its certainties and rejuvenates it.

But, at the same time, there is the opposite homoeopathy: as the saying goes, the only true remedy against the obvious democratic ills is more democracy. This defense of democracy is a variation of Churchill's famous quip that it is the worst of all systems, the only qualification being that there is none better: the democratic project is inconsistent, in its very notion an "unfinished project," but its very "paradox" is its strength, a guarantee against totalitarian temptation. Democracy includes its imperfection in its very notion, which is why the only cure against democratic deficiencies is more democracy.

Thus all the dangers that lurk in democracy can be understood as grounded in these constitutive inconsistencies of the democratic project, as ways of dealing with these inconsistencies, but with the price that, in trying to get rid of the imperfections of democracy, of its non-democratic ingredients, we inadvertently lose democracy itself—recall simply how the populist appeal to a direct expression of the people's General Will, bypassing all particular interests and petty conflicts, ends up stifling democratic life itself. In a Hegelian mode, one is thus tempted to classify Brown's version as the extreme aggravation of the "democratic paradox" to the point of direct self-inconsistency. What, then, would be the (re)solution of this opposition between "thesis" (Lacan as a theorist of democracy) and "antithesis" (Lacan as its internal critic)? We suggest that it is the risky but necessary gesture of rendering problematic the very notion of "democracy," of moving elsewhere—of having the courage to elaborate a positive *liveable* project "beyond democracy."

Is Brown not all too un-Nietzschean in her reduction of "Nietzsche" to a provocative correction of democracy which, through his exaggeration, renders visible the inconsistencies and weaknesses of the democratic project? When she proclaims Nietzsche's implicit (and also explicit) anti-democratic project "unliveable," does she not thereby all too glibly pass over the fact that there were very real political projects which directly referred to Nietzsche, up to and including Nazism, and that Nietzsche himself constantly referred to actual political events around him—say, the "slave rebellion" of the Paris Commune that he found so shattering?[15] Brown thus accomplishes a *domestication* of Nietzsche, the transformation of his theory into an exercise in "inherent transgression": provocations which are not really "meant seriously," but aim, through their "provocative" character, to awaken us from our democratic-dogmatic slumber and thus contribute to the revitalization of democracy itself . . . This is how the establishment likes its "subversive" theorists: harmless gadflies who sting us and thus awaken us to the inconsistencies and imperfection of our democratic enterprise—God forbid that they might take the project seriously and try to *live* it . . .

Michel Foucault and the Iranian event

One of the main anti-totalitarian clichés is that of "intellectuals" (in the infamous Paul Johnson sense of the term) seduced by the "authentic" touch of violent spectacles and outbursts, in love with the ruthless exercise of power which supplements their limp-wristed existence— the long line from Plato and Rousseau to Heidegger, not to mention the standard list of the dupes of Stalinism (Brecht, Sartre . . .). The facile Lacanian defense against this charge would be to point out that the least one can say about Lacanian psychoanalysis is that it renders us immune to such "totalitarian temptations": no Lacanian has ever committed a similar political blunder of being seduced by a mirage of a totalitarian revolution . . .

However, instead of such an easy way out, one should rather heroically accept this "white intellectual's burden." Let us approach it at its most problematic. The contours of the debate about the status of Heidegger's Nazi engagement (was it just a passing mistake of no theoretical significance or was it grounded in his thought itself? Did it contribute to the turn Heidegger's thought took afterwards?) are strangely reminiscent of Michel Foucault's brief engagement on behalf of the Iranian revolution.[16] How could the following lines not evoke a striking parallel with Heidegger?

> Many scholars of Foucault view these writings [on Iran] as aberrant or the product of a political mistake. We suggest that Foucault's writings on Iran were in fact closely related to his general theoretical writings on the discourse of power and the hazards of modernity. We also argue that Foucault's experience in Iran left a lasting impact on his subsequent oeuvre and that one cannot understand the sudden turn in Foucault's writings in the 1980s without recognizing the significance of the Iranian episode and his more general preoccupation with the Orient.[17]

In both cases, one should invert the standard narrative according to which the erroneous engagement awakened the thinker to the limitations of his previous theoretical position and compelled him to radicalize his thought, to enact a "turn" that would prevent such mistakes from occurring again (Heidegger's shift to *Gelassenheit*, Foucault's to the aesthetic of the self): Foucault's Iranian engagement, like Heidegger's Nazi engagement, was in itself (in its form) an appropriate gesture, the best thing he ever did, the only problem being that it was (as to its content) a commitment in the wrong direction.

Rather than reproach Foucault for his "blunder," one should read his turn to Kant a couple of years later as his response to this failed engagement. Foucault is interested in the notion of enthusiasm as Kant deploys it apropos the French Revolution (in his *Conflict of Faculties*, which we already quoted in Chapter 1): as we have already noted, for Kant, its true significance does not reside in what actually went on in Paris—many things there were terrifying, outbursts of murderous passions—but in the enthusiastic response that the events in Paris generated in the eyes of the sympathetic observers all around Europe . . . Did Foucault thereby not propose a kind of meta-theory of his own enthusiasm about the Iranian revolution of 1978–79? What matters is not the miserable reality that followed the upheavals, the bloody confrontations, the new oppressive measures, and so on, but the enthusiasm that the events in Iran stimulated in the external (Western) observer, confirming his hopes in the possibility of a new form of spiritualized political collective.

Was Iran, then, for Foucault the object of "interpassive authenticity," the mythical Other Place where the authentic happens—Cuba, Nicaragua, Bolivia today . . .—and for which Western intellectuals have an inexhaustible need? And, incidentally, one could redeem in the same way not only the enthusiasm evoked by Stalinist Russia in many Western intellectuals and artists in the 1930s and 1940s, but even the enthusiasm stoked in those who were otherwise bitter critics of Stalinism by the Maoist Cultural Revolution: what matters was not the brutal violence and terror in China, but the enthusiasm fired up by this spectacle amongst the Western observers . . . (And—why not?—one could claim the same for the fascination of Nazi Germany for some Western observers in the first four years of Hitler's rule when unemployment fell rapidly, and so on!)

However, the problem with this reading is that, in his interpretation of the Iranian events, Foucault turns this perspective around and opposes the enthusiasm of those engaged in the event to the cold view of the external observer who discerns the larger causal context, the interplay of classes and their interests, and so on and so forth. This shift of the enthusiasm aroused in an external observer to the enthusiasm of those caught in the events is crucial—how are we to *think* the link of these two locations of enthusiasm, the enthusiasm of direct participants and that of external and disengaged (disinterested) observers? The only solution is to "deconstruct" the very immediacy of the lived experience of the direct participants: what if this immediacy is already staged for an observer, for an imagined Other's gaze? What if, in their innermost lived experience, they already imagine themselves being observed? Along these lines, in his last text on Iran ("Is it Useless to Revolt?", from May 1979), Foucault opposes the historical reality of a complex process of social, cultural, economic, political, and so on, transformations to the magical event of the revolt which somehow suspends the network of historical causality—to which it is irreducible:

> The man in revolt is ultimately inexplicable. There must be an uprooting that interrupts the unfolding of history, and its long series of reasons why, for a man "really" to prefer the risk of death over the certainty of having to obey.[18]

One should be aware of the Kantian connotation of these propositions: revolt is an act of freedom which momentarily suspends the nexus of historical causality, that is, in revolt, the noumenal dimension transpires. The paradox, of course, is that this noumenal dimension coincides with its opposite, with the pure surface of a phenomenon: the noumenon not only appears, the noumenal is what is, in a phenomenon, irreducible to the causal network of reality that generated this phenomenon—in short, the *noumenon is phenomenon qua phenomenon.* There is a clear link between this irreducible character of the phenomenon and Deleuze's notion of event as the flux of becoming, as a surface emergence that cannot be reduced to its "bodily" causes. His reply to the conservative critics who denounce the miserable and even terrifying actual results of a revolutionary upheaval is that they remain blind to the dimension of becoming:

> It is fashionable these days to condemn the horrors of revolution. It's nothing new; English Romanticism is permeated by reflections on Cromwell very similar to present-day reflections on Stalin. They say revolutions turn out badly. But they're constantly confusing two different things, the way revolutions turn out historically and people's

revolutionary becoming. These relate to two different sets of people. Men's only hope lies in a revolutionary becoming: the only way of casting off their shame or responding to what is intolerable.[19]

Deleuze refers here to revolutionary explosions in a way which is strictly parallel to Foucault's:

The Iranian movement did not experience the "law" of revolutions that would, some say, make the tyranny that already secretly inhabited them reappear underneath the blind enthusiasm of the masses. What constituted the most internal and the most intensely lived part of the uprising touched, in an unmediated fashion, on an already over-crowded political chessboard, but such contact is not identity. The spirituality of those who were going to their deaths has no similarity whatsoever with the bloody government of a fundamentalist clergy. The Iranian clerics want to authenticate their regime through the significations that the uprising had. It is no different to discredit the fact of the uprising on the grounds that there is today a government of mullahs. In both cases, there is "fear," fear of what just happened last fall in Iran, something of which the world had not seen an example for a long time.[20]

Foucault is here effectively Deleuzian: what interests him are not the Iranian events at the level of actual social reality and its causal interactions, but the evental surface, the pure virtuality of the "spark of life" which only accounts for the uniqueness of the Event. What took place in Iran in the interstice of two epochs of social reality was not the explosion of the People as a substantial entity with a set of properties, but the event of a becoming-people. The point is thus not the shift in relations of power and domination between actual socio-political agents, the redistribution of social control, and so on, but the very fact of transcending—or, rather, momentarily canceling—this very domain, the emergence of a totally different domain of "collective will" as a pure sense-event in which all differences are obliterated, rendered irrelevant. Such an event is not only new with regard to what happened before, it is new "in itself" and thus forever remains new.[21]

However, here, at their most sublime, things start to get complicated. Foucault has to concede that this division was internal to the engaged individuals themselves:

Let's take the activist in some political group. When he was taking part in one of those demonstrations, he was double: he had his political calculation, which was this or that, and at the same time he was an individual caught up in that revolutionary movement, or rather that Iranian who had risen up against the king. And the two things did not come into contact, he did not rise up against the king because his party had made this or that calculation.[22]

And the same division cuts across the entire social body: at the level of reality, there were, of course, multiple agents, complex interactions of classes, the overdetermination of incompatible struggles; however, at the level of the revolutionary event proper, all this was "sublated" into "an absolutely collective will" that united the entire social body against the Shah and his clique. There was no division within the social body, no "class struggle," all—from poor farmers to students, from clergy to disappointed capitalists—wanted the same:

The collective will is a political myth with which jurists and philosophers try to analyze or to justify institutions, etc. It's a theoretical tool: nobody has ever seen the "collective will" and, personally, I thought that the collective will was like God, like the soul, something one would never encounter. I don't know whether you agree with me, but we met, in Tehran and throughout Iran, the collective will of a people.[23]

Foucault opposes here revolt and revolution: "revolution" (in the modern European sense) designates the reinscription of a revolt into the process of strategic-political calculation: revolution is a process by means of which the revolt is "colonized by realpolitik":

"Revolution" gave these uprisings a legitimacy, sorted out their good and bad forms, and defined their laws of development. [. . .] Even the profession of revolutionary was defined. By thus repatriating revolt into the discourse of revolution, it was said, the uprising would appear in all its truth and continue to its true conclusion.[24]

No wonder Foucault compares the appearing of a collective will with two of Kant's noumenal things (God, soul). When the noumenal appears, it is in the guise of ultimate horror—as Foucault is aware:

At this stage, the most important and the most atrocious mingle—the extraordinary hope of remaking Islam into a great living civilization and various forms of virulent xenophobia, as well as the global stakes and the regional rivalries. And the problem of imperialisms. And the subjugation of women, and so on.[25]

What has given the Iranian movement its intensity has been a double register. On the one hand, a collective will that has been very strongly expressed politically and, on the other hand, the desire for a radical change in ordinary life. But this double affirmation can only be based on traditions, institutions that carry a charge of chauvinism, nationalism, exclusiveness, which have a very powerful attraction for individuals. To confront so fearsome an armed power, one mustn't feel alone, nor begin with nothing.[26]

The picture thus becomes blurred. First, Foucault withdraws from overall support for the Iranian revolt (sustained by a hope that an entirely different society will emerge out of it, breaking out of the space of European modernity and its deadlocks) to valorizing only the enthusiastic moment of revolt itself: the European liberals who want to discredit the Iranian events because they ended up in an oppressive theocracy move at the same level as the clergy itself which is reclaiming the revolt in order to justify its rule—they both attempt to reduce the Event to a factor in a political struggle of strategic interests. Then, in a more subtle and surprising move, Foucault discerns *another* ambiguity which cannot be reduced to the difference between the level of pure revolt and the level of multiple sociopolitical interplay: "chauvinism," "virulent xenophobia," the "subjugation of women," and so on, are not signs of the contamination of the Event by sociopolitical reality, they are inherent forces of the Event itself, that is, their mobilization gave the Event the strength to oppose itself to the oppressive political regime and to avoid getting caught in the game of political calculations. It is this very reliance on the "vilest" racist, anti-feminist, etc., motifs that gave the Iranian revolution the power to move beyond a mere pragmatic power struggle. To put it in Badiouian terms, the authentic Event thus becomes indistinguishable from a pseudo-Event.

Are we not dealing here with a kind of Hegelian triad in which the external opposition is gradually internalized, reflected into itself? First, the external opposition of the Iranian revolution in itself (a unique event) and the way it appears to Europeans is internalized into the two aspects of the events themselves: their pragmatic struggle-for-power side, and the side of a unique politico-spiritual Event. Finally, these two aspects are identified as the form and content of the same event: the oppressive misogynist ideology, anti-Semitism, and so forth, are the only ideological materials at the disposal of the Iranians that can sustain the properly metaphysical elevation of the Event—the Event turns into a purely formal feature, indifferent towards its specific historical content. In other words, Foucault ends up at a point at which one should effectively raise the question usually addressed to Badiou: why, then, is Hitler's Nazi "revolution" not also an Event? Does it not share the very features attributed by Foucault to the Iranian revolution? Did we not have there also the spiritual unity of people, undivided into particular subgroups separated by interests, a unity for which individuals were ready to sacrifice themselves? And, as in the case of Iran, was this spirit of unity not sustained by the "vilest" elements of tradition (racism and so on)?

At this point, the only move that remains is to drop this form itself—no wonder, then, that, after his Iranian experience, Foucault withdrew to the topic of the care of the self, of the aesthetics of existence (and, politically, to supporting different human-rights initiatives, which makes him in France a darling of the neoliberal-humanitarian "new philosophers"). Here, one can only venture the hypothesis that the conceptual root of this Foucauldian deadlock is his key notion of the *dispositif*. At first sight, it may appear that Lacan's big Other is the poor cousin of Foucault's notion of the *dispositif*, which is much more productive for social analysis. However, there is the deadlock of the *dispositif* with regard to the status of the subject: first (in his history of madness), Foucault tended to exclude from it the resisting core of subjectivity; then, he shifted his position to its opposite, to the radical inclusion of resistant subjectivity into the *dispositif* (power itself generates resistance, and so on—the themes of his *Discipline and Punish*); finally, he tried to outline the space of the "care of the self" that allows the subject to articulate through self-relating his own "mode of life" within a *dispositif*, and thus to regain a minimum of distance from it. The subject is here always a curve, a disturbance, of the *dispositif*, the proverbial grain of sand that disrupts its smooth running. With Lacan's "big Other," the perspective is completely the opposite: the very "positing" of the big Other is a subjective gesture, that is, the "big Other" is a virtual entity that exists only through the subject's presupposition (this moment is missing in Althusser's notion of the "Ideological State Apparatuses," with its emphasis on the "materiality" of the big Other, its material existence in ideological institutions and ritualized practices—Lacan's big Other is, on the contrary, ultimately virtual and as such, in its most basic dimension, "immaterial").

But let us return to Iran. Foucault's blunder in no way implies that the Iranian revolution was a pseudo-Event (in a Badiouian sense) comparable to the Nazi "revolution": it was an authentic Event, a momentary *opening* that unleashed unprecedented forces of social transformation, a moment in which "everything seemed possible." To detect this dimension, it is enough to follow closely the shifts and reversals of the Iranian events, the gradual closing of the multiple modes of self-organization of the protesting crowds through the takeover of political power by the new Islamic clergy. There was nothing comparable to the effervescent first months after the shah's fall—the constant frantic activity, debates, utopian plans, etc.—in Germany after the Nazi takeover (although there *was* something comparable going on in the first years after the October Revolution). One should not take this qualitative difference as something that concerns only the formal level of events (or, even worse, the group-psychological level, as if the Iranian explosion was more "sincere" than the Nazi one)—its crucial dimension was that of socio-political content: what makes the Iranian explosion an Event was the momentary emergence of something new that pertained to the struggle to formulate an alternative beyond the existing options of Western liberal democracy or a return to pre-modern tradition. The Nazi "revolution" was *never* "open" in this authentic sense.

Foucault was also fully justified in emphasizing Shia Islam's potential for serving as the ideological vehicle for a democratic-egalitarian movement: the opposition Sunni versus Shia is, in political terms, one of hierarchical state organization versus the egalitarian opening of the event. In contrast to both Judaism and Christianity, the two other religions of the book, Islam excludes God from the domain of paternal logic: Allah is not a father, not even a symbolic one—God as One is neither born nor does He give birth to creatures: *there is no place for a Holy Family in Islam.* This is why Islam emphasizes so much the fact that Muhammad himself was an orphan; this is why, in Islam, God intervenes precisely at the moments of the suspension, withdrawal, failure, "blackout," of the paternal function (when the mother or the child are abandoned or ignored by the biological father). What this means is that God remains thoroughly in the domain of the impossible-Real: He is the impossible-

Real beyond the father, so that there is a "genealogical desert between man and God."[27] (This was the problem with Islam for Freud, since his entire theory of religion is based on the parallel of God with the father.) More importantly still, this inscribes politics into the very heart of Islam, since the "genealogical desert" renders impossible a grounding of the community in the structures of parenthood or other bonds based on blood: "the desert between God and Father is the place where the political institutes itself."[28] With Islam, it is no longer possible to ground a community in the mode of *Totem and Taboo*, through the murder of the father, the ensuing guilt bringing brothers together—thence Islam's unexpected actuality. This problem is at the very heart of the (in)famous *umma*, the Muslim "community of believers"; it accounts for the over-lapping of the religious and the political (the community should be grounded directly on God's word), as well as for the fact that Islam is "at its best" when it grounds the formation of a community "out of nowhere," in the genealogical desert, as the egalitarian revolutionary fraternity—no wonder Islam succeeds when young men find themselves deprived of a traditional familial safety network.

This, too, compels us to qualify and limit the homology between Foucault's Iranian engagement and Heidegger's Nazi commitments: Foucault was *right* in engaging himself, he *correctly* detected the emancipatory potential in the events; all insinuations of liberal critics that this was yet another chapter in the sad saga of Western radical intellectuals projecting their fantasies onto an exotic foreign zone of turbulence, which allows them to satisfy *simultaneously* their emancipatory desires *and* their secret "masochistic" longing for harsh discipline and oppression, totally miss the point. So where was his mistake? One can claim that he did the right thing for the wrong reason: the manner in which he theorized and justified his engagement is misleading. The framework within which Foucault operates in his analysis of the Iranian situation is the opposition between the revolutionary Event, the sublime enthusiasm of the united people where all internal differences are momentarily suspended, and the pragmatic domain of the politics of interests, strategic power calculations, and so forth—the opposition which, as we have already seen, directly evokes Kant's distinction between the noumenal (or, more precisely, the sublime which evokes the noumenal dimension) and the phenomenal. Our thesis is here a very precise one: this general frame is too "abstract" to account for different modalities of collective enthusiasm—to distinguish between, say, the Nazi enthusiasm of the people united in its rejection of the Jews (whose effects were undoubtedly real), the enthusiasm of the people united against the stagnating Communist regime, or a properly revolutionary enthusiasm. The difference is simply that the first two are not Events, merely pseudo-Events, because they lacked the moment of a truly utopian opening. This difference is strictly immanent to enthusiastic unity: only in the last case, the common denominator of this unity was the "part of no-part," the "downtrodden," those included in society with no proper place within it and, as such, functioning as the "universal singularity," directly embodying the universal dimension.

This is also why the opposition between noumenal enthusiasm and particular strategic interests does not cover the entire field—if it were so, then we would remain stuck forever in the opposition between emancipatory outbursts and the sobering "day after" when life returns to its pragmatic normal run. From this constrained perspective, every attempt to avoid and/or postpone this sobering return to the normal run of things amounts to terror, to the reversal of enthusiasm into monstrosity. What if, however, *this* is what is truly at stake in a true emancipatory process: in Jacques Rancière's terms, how to unite the political and the police, how to transpose the political emancipatory outburst into the concrete regulation of policing? What can be more sublime than the creation of a new "liberated territory," of a positive order of being which escapes the grasp of the existing order?

This is why Badiou is right to deny the status of an Event to the enthusiasm that followed the collapse of the Communist regimes. When, in the last months of 2001, the Milošević regime in Serbia was finally toppled, many Marxists in the West raised the question: "What about the coal miners whose strike led to the disruption of the electricity supply and thus effectively brought Milošević down? Was that not a genuine workers' movement, which was then manipulated by the politicians, who were nationalists or corrupted by the CIA?" The same symptomatic point emerges apropos of every new social upheaval: in each of these cases, such people identify some working-class movement which allegedly displayed a true revolutionary or, at least, socialist potential, but was first exploited and then betrayed by the pro-capitalist and/or nationalist forces. This way, one can continue to dream that the Revolution is round the corner: all we need is an authentic leadership which would be able to organize the workers' revolutionary potential. If one is to believe them, Solidarność was originally a workers' democratic-socialist movement, later "betrayed" by its leadership which was corrupted by the Church and the

CIA . . . There is, of course, a grain of truth in this approach: the ultimate irony of the disintegration of Communism was that the great revolts (the GDR in 1953, Hungary in 1956, Solidarity in Poland) were originally *workers'* uprisings which only later paved the way for the standard "anti-Communist" movements — before succumbing to the "external" enemy, the regime got a message about its falsity from those whom these "workers' and peasants' states" evoked as their own social base. However, this very fact also demonstrates how the workers' revolt lacked any substantial socialist commitment: in all cases, once the movement exploded, it was smoothly hegemonized by standard "bourgeois" ideology (political freedom, private property, national sovereignty, and so forth).

The trouble with Heidegger

How, then, do things stand with Heidegger's engagement? Was it, in contrast to Foucault's, not just a mistake, but a mistake grounded in his philosophy? There is something profoundly symptomatic in the compulsion of many liberal-democratic critics of Heidegger to demonstrate that Heidegger's Nazi affiliation was not a mere temporary blunder, but in consonance with the very fundamentals of his thought: it is as if this consonance allows us to dismiss Heidegger as theoretically irrelevant and thus to avoid the effort to *think* with and through Heidegger, to confront the uneasy questions he raised against such basic tenets of modernity as "humanism," "democracy," "progress," etc. Once Heidegger disappears from the picture, we can safely carry on with our common concerns about the ethical problems opened up by biogenetics, about how to accommodate capitalist globalization within a meaningful communal life — in short, we can safely avoid confronting what is really new in globalization and biogenetic discoveries, and continue to measure these phenomena with old standards, in the wild hope of a synthesis that will allow us to keep the best of both worlds.

But this, of course, in no way means that we should rehabilitate the standard defense of Heidegger's Nazi episode, which, unsurprisingly, follows yet again the borrowed-kettle formula: (1) Heidegger was never really a Nazi, he just made some superficial compromises in order to save whatever could have been saved for the autonomy of the university; when he realized that this tactic would not work, he consequently stepped down and withdrew from public life. (2) Heidegger was, for a limited period, a sincerely committed Nazi; however, not only did he withdraw once he become aware of his blunder, but the acquaintance with Nazi power precisely enabled him to gain an insight into the nihilism of modern technology as the deployment of the unconditional will-to-power. (3) Heidegger was a Nazi, and there is nothing to reproach him with for this choice: in the early 1930s, it was a perfectly legitimate and understandable choice. This final position is Ernst Nolte's, and it is worth recalling here his book on Heidegger, which brought fresh wind to the sails of the endless debate on "Heidegger and politics"—far from excusing Heidegger's infamous political choice in 1933, it justifies it, or, at least, de-demonizes it, rendering it a viable and meaningful choice. Against the standard defenders of Heidegger whose mantra is that Heidegger's Nazi engagement was a personal mistake of no fundamental consequence for his thought, Nolte accepts the basic claim of Heidegger's critics that his Nazi choice is inscribed into his thought—but with a twist: instead of problematizing his thought, Nolte justifies his political choice as a justifiable option in the late 1920s and early 1930s, given the economic chaos and the threat of Communism:

> Insofar as Heidegger resisted the attempt at the [Communist] solution, he, like countless others, was historically right . . . In committing himself to the [National Socialist] solution perhaps he became a "fascist." But in no way did that make him historically wrong from the outset.[29]

And here is Mark Wrathall's model formulation of the second position:

> Heidegger's work after the war did go some way towards overcoming the political naivete that led to his disastrous involvement with National Socialism. He did this by, first, getting much clearer than he had been about the dangers of the modern world—the dangers which led him to think we need a new world disclosure. Once he was able to articulate the danger of modernity in terms of technology, it became clear that National Socialism was just another modern technological movement (even if it employed technology for reactionary goals).[30]

This passage tells much more than may appear at first glance—the key words in it are the innocuous "just another": is the underlying premise not "even the best of political projects, the most radical attempt to oppose nihilism, remained just another nihilistic movement caught in technology"? There is no horror of Nazism here, Nazism is "just another" in the series, the difference is ontologically insignificant (which is why, for Heidegger, the Allied victory in World War II really decided nothing). Here Heidegger's reference to Hölderlin's famous lines enters: "where the danger is rising, that which can save us—*das Rettende*—also grows . . ."—in order to overcome the danger, one has to push it to the extreme—in short, in order to arrive at the ontological truth, Heidegger had to err ontically. So when Wrathall writes apropos Heidegger's Nazi engagement: "It is disconcerting, to say the least, that Heidegger, who purported to have a unique insight into the movement of world history, proved to be so terribly blind to the significance of the events that played out before his eyes"[31]—a Heideggerian could easily turn this argument around: the "ontic" blindness to the truth of the Nazi regime was a positive condition of his "ontological" insight. However, when defenders of Heidegger claim that his acquaintance with the Nazi exercise of power precisely enabled him to gain an insight into the nihilism of modern technology as the deployment of the unconditional will-to-power, does this line of defense not sound a little bit like the attitude of the proverbial prostitute-turned-preacher who, after her conversion, ferociously attacks carnal sins, claiming that she knows from her own experience how destructive they are? Steve Fuller writes:

> Ironically, Heidegger's intellectual stature may even have been *helped* by the time-honored practice of "learning from the opponent" in which victors indulge after a war. In this respect, Heidegger's political "genius" may lie in having stuck with the Nazis long enough for the Americans to discover him during de-Nazification without ending up being judged an untouchable war criminal whose works had to be banned. As committed anti-Nazis ensconced in Allied countries, Heidegger's existentialist rivals never underwent such intense scrutiny nor subsequently acquired such a mystique for depth and danger.[32]

There is truth in these lines, but it is more complex than Heidegger's mere luck in striking the right balance in the depth of his Nazi engagement: the difficult truth to admit is that Heidegger is "great" *not in spite of, but because of* his Nazi engagement, that this commitment is a key constituent of his "greatness." Imagine a Heidegger without this passage, or a Heidegger who, after World War II, had done what many colleagues expected of him: namely, publicly renounce his Nazi engagement and apologize for it—would this not somehow have occluded the radicality of his insight? Would it not have constrained him to humanitarian political concerns which he so bitterly despised? Miguel de Beistegui makes a perspicuous observation on the fundamental ambiguity of Heidegger's disillusionment with Nazism: it was his "resignation and his disillusionment with what, until the end of his life, and with a touch of regret at not having seen it develop its potential, he referred to as 'the movement'."[33] Is, however, this not the reason why Heidegger's later withdrawal from political commitment also cannot be conceived only in the terms of his insight into the nihilism of contemporary politics? De Beistegui concludes his book with the statement that Heidegger

> will not be caught out in [a belief in the redemptive power of political engagement] twice: having burned his fingers in politics, and lost his illusions in the failure of Nazism to carry out a project of onto-destinal significance, his hopes will turn to the hidden resources of thought, art and poetry, all deemed to carry a historical and destinal power far greater than that of politics.[34]

But is Heidegger's refusal to be caught twice in the act of political engagement and thus burning his fingers again not a negative mode of his continuing melancholic attachment to the Nazi "movement"? (His refusal to engage again in politics was thus similar to a disappointed lover who, after the failure of his relationship, rejects love as such and avoids all further relationships, thereby confirming in a negative way his lasting attachment to the failed relationship.) Is the premise of this refusal not that, to the end of his life, Nazism remained for Heidegger the only political commitment which at least tried to address the right problem, so that the failure of Nazism is the failure of the political as such? It never entered Heidegger's mind to propose—say, in a liberal mode—that the failure of the Nazi movement was merely the failure of a certain kind of engagement which conferred on the political the task of carrying out "a project of onto-destinal significance," so that the lesson to draw was simply a more *modest* political engagement. In other words, what if one concludes from the failure of Heidegger's political experience that what one should renounce is the expectation that a political engagement will have destinal ontological consequences and that one should participate in "merely ontic" politics which, far from obfuscating the need for a deeper ontological reflection, precisely open up a space for it? What if even the very last Heidegger, when he expressed his doubts as to whether democracy was the political order which best fitted the essence of modern technology, had still not learnt the ultimate lesson of his Nazi period, since he continued to cling to the hope of finding an (ontic) political engagement which would fit (be at the level of) the ontological project of modern technology? (Our premise, of course, is that the liberal engagement is not the only alternative: Heidegger was right in his doubt about liberal democracy; what he refused to consider was a radical leftist engagement.)

Therein resides the importance of the link between Heidegger and Hannah Arendt: what is at stake in the difficult relationship between Heidegger and Arendt is Heidegger's much-decried aversion to liberalism and (liberal) democracy, which he continuously, to his death, rejected as "inauthentic," not the idiosyncrasies of their personal liaisons. Arendt was not only opposed to Heidegger along the double axis of woman versus man and a "worldly" Jew versus a "provincial" German, she was (which is much more important) *the first liberal Heideggerian*, the first to try to reunite Heidegger's insights with the liberal-democratic universe. In a closer reading, of course, it is easy to discern what enabled Arendt to support liberalism while maintaining her basic fidelity to Heidegger's insights: her anti-bourgeois stance, her critical dismissal of politics as "interest-group" politics, as the expression of the competitive and acquisitive society of the bourgeoisie. She shared the great conservatives' dissatisfaction with the lack of heroism and the pragmatic-utilitarian orientation of bourgeois society:

> Simply to brand as outbursts of nihilism this violent dissatisfaction with the prewar age and subsequent attempts at restoring it (from Nietzsche to Sorel to Pareto, from Rimbaud and T.E. Lawrence to Juenger, Brecht and Malraux, from Bakunin and Nechayev to Aleksander Blok) is to overlook how justified disgust can be in a society wholly permeated with the ideological outlook and moral standards of the bourgeoisie.[35]

The opposition Arendt mobilizes here is the one between *citoyen* and *bourgeois*: the first lives in the political sphere of public engagement for the common good, of the participation in public affairs, while the second is the egotistic utilitarian fully immersed in the process of production and who reduces all other dimensions of life to their role in enabling the smooth running of this process. In Aristotelian terms, this opposition is that between *praxis* and *poiesis*, between the "high" exercise of virtues in public life, and the "low" instrumentality of labor—the opposition whose echoes reverberate not only in Habermas's distinction between communicative action and instrumental activity, but even in Badiou's notion of the Event (and in his concomitant denial that an Event can take place in the domain of production). Recall how Arendt describes, in Badiouian terms, the suspension of temporality as the defining ontological characteristic of ontic political action: acting, as man's capacity to begin something new, "out of nothing," not reducible to a calculated strategic reaction to a given situation, takes place in the non-temporal *gap* between past and future, in the hiatus between the end of the old order and the beginning of the new which in history is precisely the moment of revolution.[36] Such an opposition, of course, raises a fundamental question formulated by Robert Pippin:

> how can Arendt separate out what she admires in bourgeois culture—
> its constitutionalism, its assertion of fundamental human rights, its
> equality before the law, its insistence on a private zone in human life,
> exempt from the political, its religious tolerance—and condemn what
> she disagrees with—its secularism, its cynical assumption of the
> pervasiveness of self-interest, the perverting influence of money on
> human values, its depoliticizing tendencies, and the menace it poses for
> tradition and a sense of place?[37]

In other words, are these not two sides of the same phenomenon? No wonder then, that, when Arendt is pressed to provide the outline of the authentic "care of the world" as a political practice that would not be contaminated by utilitarian pragmatic calculation of interests, all she can evoke are forms of self-organization in revolutionary situations, from the early American tradition of town-hall meetings of all citizens to revolutionary councils in the German revolution. Not that she is not politically justified in evoking these examples—the problem is that they are "utopian," that they cannot be reconciled with the liberal-democratic political order to which she remains faithful. In other words, is Arendt with regard to liberal democracy not the victim of the same illusion as the democratic Communists who, within the "really-existing socialism," were fighting for its truly democratic instantiation? Arendt is also right when (implicitly against Heidegger) she points out that fascism, although a reaction to bourgeois banality, remains its inherent negation, that is, remains within the horizon of bourgeois society: the true problem of Nazism is not that it "went too far" in its subjectivist-nihilist hubris of exerting total power, but that it *did not go far enough*, namely, that its violence was an impotent acting-out which, ultimately, remained in the service of the very order it despised. (However, Heidegger would also have been right in rejecting Arendt's Aristotelian politics as not radical enough to break out of the nihilist space of European modernity.)

Arendt would thus have been justified in countering Pippin's all-too-easy version of a contemporary political Hegelianism; his basic claim is that while, of course, from today's perspective, Hegel's notion of a rational state no longer works, its limitations are evident, and these very limitations should be addressed in a Hegelian way:

> In some fairly obvious sense and in the historical terms he would have to accept as relevant to his own philosophy, he was wrong. None of these institutional realizations now looks as stable, as rational, or even as responsive to the claims of free subjects as Hegel has claimed, even though such criticisms are often themselves made in the name of such freedom. But the nature of that wrong is, I am arguing, also Hegelian, a matter of being incomplete, not wholly wrong-headed.[38]

In short, it is a matter of an *Aufhebung*, of the immanent self-critique and self-overcoming, of these solutions, not of their outright rejection . . . However, what cannot but strike the eye is the "formalist" character of Pippin's formula: he does not provide any concrete examples that would render it operative. The question is, of course, how far do we have to go in this *Aufhebung* if we are to bring Hegel's project of a rational state of freedom up to today's conditions—how "deeply" is irrationality inscribed into today's bourgeois society so that its critique can still be formulated as a defense of bourgeois society? Do we have to stay within capitalism or risk a move beyond it? These, however, are not Heidegger's concerns: his fundamental move apropos our critical historical moment is to emphasize the underlying sameness of the (ideological, political, economic . . .) choices we confront:

> from the point of view of their onto-historical origin, there is no *real* or *fundamental* difference between the Christian doctrine and Bolshevism, between the biologism and imperialism of Nazism and the forces of

capital (which, today, have permeated all spheres of life), and between vitalism and spiritualism. This, I believe, is at once the strength, and the extraordinary weakness and limitation of Heidegger's position. For on the one hand it allows us to establish continuities and complicities where we thought there were incompatibilities, and to shift the weight of difference to a different terrain (that of the "meaning" or the "truth" of being). On the other hand, though, by revealing such differences as pseudo-differences, he also neutralizes the decisions and choices they often call for, thereby erasing the traditional space of politics and ethics.[39]

Unfortunately, de Beistegui's solution to this deadlock remains all too commonsensical—a balanced approach which takes into account the legitimate demands of both levels:

> whatever our commitments to the deconstruction of metaphysics, and to the struggle for new possibilities of thought and action beyond it, or perhaps on its margins, we continue to live within the metaphysical, technical framework, and so must remain committed to taking seriously, and discriminating between, the many differences, choices and situations we are faced with at the historical, political, religious and artistic level. [. . .] The free relation to technology Heidegger advocates may, after all, also involve an active participation in intra-metaphysical processes, and not just a meditation of its essence. For within technology, there are differences that matter, and to which we cannot—and must not—remain blind. With one critical eye, and the other deconstructive, we may be better equipped to navigate the often treacherous waters of our time.[40]

But what if there is a fundamental discordance between the ontological and the ontic, so that, as Heidegger put it, those who reach ontological truth have to err in the ontic? What if, if we are to see with the ontological eye, our ontic eye has to be blinded?

Ontological difference

When Heidegger speaks of the untruth-concealedness-withdrawal as inherent to the truth-event itself, he has in mind two different levels:

1. On the one hand, the way a man, when engaged in inner-worldly affairs, forgets the horizon of meaning within which he dwells, and even forgets this forgetting itself (exemplary is here the "regression" of Greek thought that occurs with the rise of Sophists: what was the confrontation with the very foundation of our Being turns into a trifling play with different lines of argumentation with no inherent relation to Truth).

2. On the other hand, the way this horizon of meaning itself, insofar as it is an epochal Event, arises against the background of—and thereby conceals—the imponderable Mystery of its emergence, in the same way a clearing in the midst of a forest is surrounded by the dark thickness of the woods.

The same ambiguity repeats itself with regard to the earth as that which resists, remains forever obscure and unfathomable: "There always is something resisting and supporting our practices, and that something is very real."[41] So, on the one hand, the earth designates what resists the meaningful totality of a historical world:

> As a world strives to grow back into the earth, it encounters resistance. In the process, the earth appears in a determinate way in terms of the resistance that the world encounters. In building the cathedral, we discover particular ways in which our practices are limited and constrained. [. . .] Our worlds, and consequently our meaningful relations to things, are always based in something that can't be explained in terms of the prevailing intelligible structure of the world.[42]

On the other hand, however, what is most impenetrable is *the basic structure of the world itself*. For example, when we argue that the modernization of Japan was desirable because it brought about a higher gross domestic product and per capita income, one should raise the more fundamental question:

> But why one should have just those preferences is precisely what is at issue—if one would prefer the pace and style of premodern Japanese life to an increase of per capita income, then the argument that Japan should modernize in order to increase average income will not be persuasive. [. . .] So it seems that the strength of the drive to establish

a new world and destroy the old depends on something withdrawing from view — that is becoming so self-evident that it is no longer open to question: namely, the desirability of the new world itself. This desirability is an earthly thing: it withdraws and shelters the world it supports. [. . .] Our world is supported by our most basic preferences — a taste for efficiency and flexibility — having largely withdrawn from view.[43]

The earth is thus either the impenetrable abyss of the ontic which withdraws from ontological disclosure, or the horizon of this disclosure itself, invisible on account of its excessive self-evidence — we do not see it as such because it is the very medium through which we see everything. One should make the properly Hegelian move of identifying the two levels: the Beyond and the obstacle-screen that distorts our access to Beyond. So this is not simply Heidegger's mistake or confusion (to be resolved or corrected by introducing a further notional distinction: one term for the earth as the darkness of what resists disclosure, another for the invisibility of the very horizon of disclosure). The oscillation between the two levels is what defines the earth.

What this also means is that ontological difference is not "maximal," between all beings, the highest genus, and something else/more/beyond, but, rather, "minimal," the bare minimum of a difference not between beings but between the minimum of an entity and the void, nothing. Insofar as it is grounded in the finitude of humans, ontological difference is that which makes a totalization of "All beings" impossible — ontological difference means that the field of reality is finite. Ontological difference is, in this precise sense, "real/impossible": to cite Ernesto Laclau's determination of antagonism, in it, *external difference overlaps with internal difference*. The difference between beings and their Being is simultaneously a difference within beings themselves; that is to say, the difference between beings/entities and their Opening, their horizon of meaning, always also cuts into the field of beings themselves, rendering it incomplete/finite. Therein resides the paradox: *the difference between beings in their totality and their Being precisely "misses the difference" and reduces Being to another "higher" entity.* The parallel between Kant's antinomies and Heidegger's ontological difference resides in the fact that, in both cases, the gap (phenomenal/noumenal; ontic/ontological) is to be referred to the non-All of the phenomenal–ontic domain itself. However, the limitation of Kant was that he was not able to fully assume this paradox of finitude as constitutive of the ontological horizon: ultimately, he reduced trans-cendental horizon to a way reality appears to a finite being (man), with all of it located into a wider encompassing realm of noumenal reality.

Here there is a clear link with the Lacanian Real which, at its most radical level, is the disavowed X on account of which our vision of reality is anamorphically distorted: it is simultaneously the Thing to which direct access is not possible *and* the obstacle which prevents this direct access, the Thing which eludes our grasp *and* the distorting screen which makes us miss the Thing. More precisely, the Real is ultimately the very shift of perspective from the first to the second standpoint. Recall the well-known Adornian analysis of the antagonistic character of the notion of society: in a first approach, the split between the two notions of society (the Anglo-Saxon individualistic-nominalistic version and the Durkhei-mian organicist notion of society as a totality which preexists individuals) seems irreducible; we seem to be dealing with a true Kantian antinomy which cannot be resolved via a higher "dialectical synthesis," and which elevates society into an inaccessible Thing-in-itself. However, in a second approach, one should merely take note of how this radical antinomy which seems to preclude our access to the Thing *already is the thing itself* — the fundamental feature of today's society *is* the irreconcilable antagon-ism between Totality and the individual. What this means is that, ultimately, the status of the Real is purely parallactic and, as such, non-substantial: it has no substantial density in itself, it is just a gap between two points of perspective, perceptible only in the shift from the one to the other. The parallax Real is thus opposed to the standard (Lacanian) notion of the Real as that which "always returns to its place," namely, as that which remains the same in all possible (symbolic) universes: the parallax Real is rather that which accounts for the very *multiplicity* of appearances of the same underlying Real — it is not the hard core which persists as the Same, but the hard bone of contention which pulverizes the sameness into the multitude of appearances. In a first move, the Real is the impossible hard core which we cannot confront directly, but only through the lenses of a multitude of symbolic fictions, virtual formations. In a second move, this very hard core is purely virtual, actually non-existing, an X which can be reconstructed only retroac-tively, from the multitude of symbolic formations which are "all that there actually is."

It seems that Heidegger was not ready to draw all the consequences from this necessary double meaning of "unconcealedness," which, to put

it bluntly, would have compelled him to accept that "ontological difference" is ultimately nothing but a rift in the ontic order (incidentally, in the
exact parallel to Badiou's key admission that the Event is ultimately
nothing but a torsion in the order of Being). This limitation of Heidegger's thought has a series of philosophical and ethico-political consequences. Philosophically, it leads to Heidegger's notion of historical
destiny which delivers different horizons of the disclosure of Being,
destiny which cannot and should not be in any way influenced by or
dependent on ontic occurrences. Ethico-politically, it accounts for Heidegger's (not simply ethical, but properly ontological) indifference towards the Holocaust, its leveling to just another case of the technological
disposal of life (in the infamous passage from the conference on tech-
nique): to acknowledge the Holocaust's extraordinary/exceptional status
would equal recognizing in it a trauma that shatters the very ontological
coordinates of Being. Does this indifference make him a Nazi?

Heidegger's smoking gun?

There are two of Heidegger's seminars which clearly disturb the official
picture of a Heidegger who only externally accommodated himself to the
Nazi regime in order to save whatever could be saved of the university's
autonomy: *Über Wesen und Begriff von Natur, Geschichte und Staat* (*On the
Essence and Notion of Nature, History, and State*, Winter 1933–34, protocol
conserved in the Deutsches Literaturarchiv, Marbach am Neckar); *Hegel,
über den Staat* (*Hegel, on the State*, Winter 1934–35, protocol also conserved
in the DLA). Significantly, the first of the two is *not* included in the
official *Gesamtausgabe* by Klostermann Verlag—a fact that renders problematic its designation as a "complete edition." These two seminars are
the closest one can get to the proverbial smoking gun, since they enact
precisely what, according to the official Heideggerian *doxa*, did not, could
not, and should not have taken place: full-bodied support for Nazism
formulated and grounded in Heidegger's innermost philosophical project. (It is nonetheless wrong for a philosopher to invest too much into
finding smoking guns: they only confirm what is already there in the
formal structure of a thought.) However, one should not lose one's nerve
too fast here and let oneself fall into the standard liberal condemnation:
Heidegger's failure is not as easy to locate as it may appear. The
atmosphere of Heidegger's political references in his texts and courses
from the 1930s (the examples he uses, etc.) is, as expected, ominous —

suffice it to recall the beginning of the paragraph which questions the being of a state: "A state — it *is*. In what consists its being? In that the state police arrests a suspect [. . .]?"[44] The very example he uses to illustrate what Hegel means by his claim about the speculative identity of the rational and the actual is, again, ominous: "The treaty of Versailles is actual, but not rational."[45]

Heidegger's starting point is a defense of Hegel against the famous proclamation by Carl Schmitt that Hegel died in 1933, when Hitler took over: "It was said that Hegel died in 1933; quite the contrary: it was only then that he first began to live."[46] Why? Heidegger endorses Hegel's thesis on the state as the highest form of social existence: "The highest actualization of human being occurs in the state."[47] He even directly "ontologizes" the state, defining the relationship between the people and the state in terms of ontological difference: "The people, the existing, has a fully determined relationship towards its being, towards the state."[48]

However, in what follows, it soon becomes clear that Heidegger only needs Hegel in order to assert the emerging Nazi "total state" against the liberal notion of the state as a means to regulate the interaction of civil society; he approvingly refers to Hegel's deployment of the limitation of the "external" state, the "state of necessity," the "state of Understanding," the system of civil society:[49] "[. . .] we cannot grasp what Hegel understands as freedom, if we take it as an essential determination of a singular I. [. . .] Freedom is only actual where there is a community of 'I's, of subjects."[50] But Hegel understands by "freedom" *also* this: he insists on the "modern" principle of the individual's "infinite right." For Hegel, civil society is *the* great modern achievement, the condition of actual freedom, the "material basis" of mutual recognition, and his problem is precisely how to *unite* the unity of the state and the dynamic mediation of civil society without curtailing the rights of civil society. The young Hegel, especially in his *System der Sittlichkeit*, was still fascinated by the Greek *polis* as the organic unity of individual and society: here, social substance does not yet stand opposed to individuals as a cold, abstract, objective legality imposed from outside, but as the living unity of "customs," of a collective ethical life in which individuals are "at home," recognizing it as their own substance. From this perspective, cold universal legality is a regression from the organic unity of customs — the regression from Greece to the Roman Empire. Although Hegel soon accepted that the subjective freedom of modernity has to be accepted, that the organic unity of *polis* is forever lost, he nonetheless insisted on a need for some kind of return to renewed organic unity, to a new *polis* that would offer as a counterpart to individuals a deeper sense of social solidarity and organic unity over and above the "mechanistic" interaction and individualist competition of civil society.

Hegel's crucial step towards maturity occurs when he really "abandons the paradigm of the *polis*"[51] by way of reconceptualizing the role of civil society. First, civil society is for Hegel the "state of Understanding," the state reduced to the police apparatus regulating the chaotic interaction of individuals each of whom pursues his egotistic interests—such an individualistic-atomistic notion of freedom and the notion of legal order as imposed on individuals as the external limitation of their freedom are strictly correlative. The need thus arises to pass from this "state of Understanding" to the true "state of Reason," in which the individuals' subjective dispositions are harmonized with the social Whole, in which individuals recognize the social substance as their own. The crucial step occurs when Hegel fully develops the mediating role of civil society: the "system of multilateral dependence" whose ultimate modern form is the market economy, the system in which particular and universal are separated and opposed, in which every individual pursues only his private goals, in which organic social unity decomposes into external mechanic interaction, which is in itself already the reconciliation of the particular and the universal in the guise of the famous "invisible hand" of the market, on account of which, by pursuing private interests at the expense of others, every individual contributes to the welfare of all. It is thus not simply that one has to "overcome" the mechanical/external interaction of civil society in a higher organic unity: civil society and its disintegration play a crucial mediating role, so that the true reconciliation (which does not abolish modern subjective freedom) should recognize how this disintegration is in itself already its opposite, a force of integration. Reconciliation is thus radically *immanent*: it implies a shift of perspective as to what first appears as disintegration. In other words, insofar as civil society is the sphere of alienation, of the separation between subjectivity persisting in its abstract individuality and the objective social order opposing it as an external necessity that curtails its freedom, the resources of reconciliation should be found *in this very sphere (in what, in this sphere, appears "at first sight, as the least spiritual, as the most alienating: the system of needs*"[52]), not in the passage to another "higher" sphere. The structure of this reconciliation in the mature Hegel is, again, that of the Rabinovich joke: "There are two reasons modern society is reconciled with itself. The first is the interaction within civil society . . ." "But that interaction is constant strife, the very mechanism of disintegration, of ruthless competition!" "Well, this is the second reason, since this very strife and competition makes individuals thoroughly interdependent and thus generates the ultimate social bond . . ."

The whole perspective thus changes: it is no longer that the organic *Sittlichkeit* of the *polis* disintegrates under the corrosive influence of modern abstract individuality in its multiple modes (the market economy, Protestantism, and so on), and that this unity should somehow be restored at a higher level: the point of Hegel's analyses of Antiquity, best exemplified by his repeated readings of *Antigone*, is that the Greek *polis* itself was already marked, cut through, by fatal immanent antagonisms (public–private, masculine–feminine, human–divine, free–slaves, etc.) which belie its organic unity. Abstract universal individualism (Christianity), far from causing the disintegration of Greek organic unity, was, on the contrary, the necessary first step towards true reconciliation. With regard to the market, far from being simply a corrosive force, it is market interaction which provides the mediating process which forms the basis of true reconciliation between the universal and the particular: market competition brings people really together, while organic order divides them.

The best indication of this shift in the mature Hegel concerns the opposition of customs and law: for the early Hegel, the transformation of customs into institutionalized law is a regressive move from organic unity to alienation (the norm is no longer experienced as part of my substantial ethical nature, but as an external force that constrains my freedom), while for the mature Hegel this transformation is a crucial step forward, opening up and sustaining the space of modern subjective freedom.[53] It is in total opposition to these Hegelian insights that Heidegger deploys his notion of a "total state":

> We are talking about a *total* state. This state is not a particular domain (among others), it is not an apparatus which is here to protect society (from the state itself), a domain with which only some people have to deal.[54]

> [. . .] the people thus wills and loves the state as its own way and manner to be as a people. The people is dominated by the striving, by *eros*, for the state.[55]

This Eros, of course, implies personification: love is always love for the One, the Leader:

> The Führer-State—the one we have—means the accomplishment of the historical development: the actualization of the people in the Führer.[56]

> It is only the leader's will which makes others into his followers, and community arises out of this relationship of following. The followers' sacrifice and service originate in this living connection, not in their obedience to the constraint of institutions.[57]

> The leader has something to do with the people's will; this will is not the sum of singular wills, but a Whole of a primordial authenticity. The question of the consciousness-of-the-will of a community is a problem in all democracies, which can only be resolved in a fruitful way when one recognizes the leader's will and the people's will in their essentiality. Our task today is to arrange the founding relationship of our communal being in the direction of this actuality of people and leader, where, as its actuality, the two cannot be separated. Only when this basic scheme is asserted in its essential aspect through its application, is true leadership possible.[58]

This, of course, is again totally opposed to Hegel, for whom the head of a rational state should not be a leader, but a king. Why? Let us take a look at Hegel's (in)famous deduction of the rational necessity of hereditary monarchy: the bureaucratic chain of knowledge has to be supplemented by the king's decision as the "completely concrete objectivity of the will" which "reabsorbs all particularity into its single self, cuts short the weighing of pros and cons between which it lets itself oscillate perpetually now this way and now that, and by saying 'I will' makes its decision and so inaugurates all activity and actuality."[59] This is why "the conception of the monarch" is "of all conceptions the hardest for ratiocination, i.e. for the method of reflection employed by the Understanding."[60] In the next paragraph, Hegel further elaborates this speculative necessity of the monarch:

> This ultimate self in which the will of the state is concentrated is, when thus taken in abstraction, a single self and therefore is immediate individuality. Hence its "natural" character is implied in its very

conception. The monarch, therefore, is essentially characterized as this individual, in abstraction from all his other characteristics, and this individual is raised to the dignity of monarchy in an immediate, natural, fashion, i.e. through his birth in the course of nature.[61]

The speculative moment that Understanding cannot grasp is "the transition of the concept of pure self-determination into the immediacy of Being and so into the realm of nature."[62] In other words, while Understanding can well grasp the universal mediation of a living totality, what it cannot grasp is that *this totality, in order to actualize itself, has to acquire actual existence in the guise of an immediate "natural" singularity*.[63] The term "natural" should be given its full weight here: in the same way that, at the end of the *Logic*, the Idea's completed self-mediation releases itself from Nature, collapses into the external immediacy of Nature, the State's rational self-mediation has to acquire actual existence in a will which is determined as directly natural, unmediated, *stricto sensu* "irrational."

While observing Napoleon on a horse in the streets of Jena after the battle of 1807, Hegel remarked that it was as if he had seen the World Spirit riding a horse. The Christological implications of this remark are obvious: what happened in the case of Christ is that God himself, the creator of our entire universe, was walking around as a common individual. This mystery of incarnation is discernible at different levels, up to the parent's speculative judgment apropos a child "Out there our love is walking!", which stands for the Hegelian reversal of determinate reflexion into reflexive determination—the same as with a king, when his subject sees him walking around: "Out there our state is walking." Marx's evocation of reflexive determination (in his famous footnote in chapter 1 of *Capital*) also falls short here: individuals think that they treat a person as a king because he is a king in himself, while, in fact, he is a king only because they treat him as one. However, the crucial point is that this "reification" of a social relation in a person cannot be dismissed as a simple "fetishistic misperception"; what such a dismissal itself misses is something that, perhaps, could be designated as the "Hegelian performative": of course a king is "in himself" a miserable individual, of course he is a king only insofar as his subjects treat him as one; however, the point is that the "fetishistic illusion" which sustains our veneration of a king has in itself a performative dimension—*the very unity of our state, that which the king "embodies," actualizes itself only in the person of a king*. Which is why it is not enough to insist on the need to avoid the "fetishistic trap" and to distinguish between the contingent person of a king and what he stands for: what the king stands for only comes to be in his person, the same as with a couple's love which (at least within a certain traditional perspective) only becomes actual in their offspring.

So far, Hegel seems to say the same thing as Heidegger; there is, however, a key difference, made clear in the Addition to paragraph 280:

> *Addition*: It is often alleged against monarchy that it makes the welfare of the state dependent on chance, for, it is urged, the monarch may be ill-educated, he may perhaps be unworthy of the highest position in the state, and it is senseless that such a state of affairs should exist because it is supposed to be rational. But all this rests on a presupposition which is nugatory, namely that everything depends on the monarch's particular character. In a completely organized state, it is only a question of the culminating point of formal decision (and a natural bulwark against passion. It is wrong therefore to demand objective qualities in a monarch); he has only to say "yes" and dot the "i", because the throne should be such that the significant thing in its holder is not his particular make-up. [. . .] In a well-organized monarchy, the objective aspect belongs to law alone, and the monarch's part is merely to set to the law the subjective "I will".[64]

What is missing in Heidegger is this reduction of the function of the Monarch to the purely formal function of dotting the "i"s, that is, the separation between what, today, we would call the "constative" and the "performative" aspects (or, in Lacan's terms, the chain of knowledge and the Master-Signifier): the "objective aspect" of governing a state, the content of laws and measures (which is the business of the expert bureaucracy), and its transformation into a "subjective" decision of the state that is to be enacted. Heidegger's concept of the Leader confounds precisely the two dimensions Hegel strives to keep apart. The further paradox of Hegel's notion of monarchy is that the king is the constitutive exception which, as such, guarantees the universal legal equality of all other subjects; no wonder that, in contrast to Hegel, Heidegger explicitly rejects equality in favor of a "hierarchy of grades" enforced by the Leader:

> To domination belongs power, which creates a hierarchy of grades through the imposition of the will of the one who rules, insofar as he is actually powerful, i.e., insofar as he disposes those under his rule.[65]

Heidegger—*pace* those who accuse him of leaving out of consideration the "cruel" aspects of ancient Greek life (slavery and so on)—openly draws attention to how "rank and dominance" are directly grounded in a disclosure of being, thereby providing a direct ontological grounding for the social relations of domination:

> If people today from time to time are going to busy themselves rather too eagerly with the *polis* of the Greeks, they should not suppress this side of it; otherwise the concept of the *polis* easily becomes innocuous and sentimental. What is higher in rank is what is stronger. Thus Being, logos, as the gathered harmony, is not easily available for every man at the same price, but is concealed, as opposed to that harmony which is always mere equalizing, the elimination of tension, leveling.[66]

Who, then, is the enemy of such a hierarchical order? The Janus head of non-hierarchical egalitarianism with its two faces, bourgeois-liberal individualism and communist egalitarianism, grounded in "Judeo-Christian" spirituality, which is thus the common source and foundation of both opposed strands of modern politics:

> In accordance to its mode, *Jewish-Christian* domination plays a double game, taking simultaneously the side of the "dictatorship of the proletariat" and the side of the liberal-democratic cultural striving; for some time, this double game will continue to conceal our already-present loss of roots and inability to take essential decisions.[67]

And Heidegger goes even a step further here against the liberal-democratic *doxa*: in the alternative between Communism and liberalism, "English" democratic liberalism is the more dangerous: "The bourgeois-Christian form of English 'Bolshevism' is the most dangerous. Without its annihilation, the modern era will continue to be maintained."[68]

Distrust of democracy is a constant feature of Heidegger's thought, even after the *Kehre*; we find it in his Nietzsche lectures from 1936–37 (where he wrote that "Europe always wants to cling to 'democracy' and does not want to see that this would be a fateful death for it"[69]), as well as in his posthumously published *Spiegel* interview where he expressed his doubt that democracy was the political form that best fits modern technology.

Repetition and the New

So we are back to Chesterton's notion of concealing a body in a pile of corpses: when one condemns Heidegger's entire philosophical edifice as "fascist," one masks one's inability to identify *a* (*one*) corpse—the singular ideological feature which gave a fascist touch to all others—by constructing a *pile* of corpses called "Heidegger's fascist thought." In this way, one concedes too much to the enemy: there is nothing "inherently fascist" in the notions of decision, repetition, assuming one's destiny, and so forth (or, closer to "ordinary" politics, in the notions of mass discipline, sacrifice of the individual for the collective, and so forth). In short, one should not allow the enemy to define the terrain of the battle and its stakes, so that we end up abstractly opposing him, supporting a negative copy of what he wants. To be clear and brutal to the end, there is a lesson to be learned from Hermann Goering's reply, in the early 1940s, to a fanatical Nazi who asked him why he protected a well-known Jew from deportation: "In this city, I decide who is a Jew!" (an answer, incidentally, attributed already to many other German figures who protected their privileged Jews, from Bismarck to Karl Lüger). In this city, it is we who decide what is left, so we should simply ignore liberal accusations of "inconsistency." For example, in his review of the Guevara film *The Motorcycle Diaries*, Paul Berman critically claimed that

> the entire movie, in its concept and tone, exudes a Christological cult of martyrdom, a cult of adoration for the spiritually superior person who is veering toward death—precisely the kind of adoration that Latin America's Catholic Church promoted for several centuries, with miserable consequences. The rebellion against reactionary Catholicism in this movie is itself an expression of reactionary Catholicism. The traditional churches of Latin America are full of statues of gruesome bleeding saints. And the masochistic allure of those statues is precisely what you see in the movie's many depictions of young Che coughing out his lungs from asthma and testing himself by swimming in cold water.[70]

To this, one should simply answer: true, but—so what? Why should revolutionary politics not take over the Catholic cult of martyrdom? And one should not be afraid to go to (what for many liberals would be) the end and to say the same about Leni Riefenstahl. Her work seems to lend itself to a teleological reading, progressing towards its dark conclusion. It began with *Bergfilme* which celebrated heroism and bodily effort in the extreme conditions of mountain-climbing; it went on to her two Nazi documentaries, celebrating the political and sport forms of bodily discipline, concentration, and strength of the will; then, after World War II, in her photo albums, she rediscovered her ideal of bodily beauty and graceful self-mastery in the Nubi African tribe; finally, in the last decades, she learned the difficult art of deep-sea diving and started shooting documentaries about the strange life in the dark depths of the sea.

We thus seem to obtain a clear trajectory from the top to the bottom: we begin with the individuals struggling at the mountain tops and gradually descend, till we reach the amorphous thriving of life itself at the bottom of the sea—is not what she encountered down there her ultimate object, obscene and irresistible eternal life itself, what she was searching for all along? And does this not apply also to her personality? In fact, it seemed that the fear of those who were fascinated by Leni was no longer "When will she die?", but "Will she *ever* die?"—although we rationally knew she would soon die, we somehow did not really believe it, secretly convinced that she would go on forever, so her death was a genuine surprise.

This continuity is usually given a "proto-fascist" twist, as in the exemplary case of Susan Sontag's famous essay on Riefenstahl, "Fascinating Fascism." The idea here is that even her pre- and post-Nazi films articulate a vision of life which is "proto-fascist": Riefenstahl's fascism is deeper than her direct celebration of Nazi politics, it resides already in her pre-political aesthetics of life, in her fascination with beautiful bodies displaying their disciplined movements . . . Perhaps it is time to problematize this topos. Let us take *Das blaue Licht*: is it not possible to read the film also in exactly the opposite way? Is Junta, the lonely and wild mountain girl, not an outcast who almost becomes the victim of a pogrom by the villagers in a manner which cannot but remind us of anti-Semitic massacres? Perhaps it is not an accident that Béla Balázs, Riefenstahl's lover at that time who co-wrote the scenario with her, was a Marxist . . .

The problem is here much more general, it goes far beyond Riefenstahl. Let us take the very opposite of Riefenstahl, Arnold Schoenberg: in the second part of *Harmonienlehre*, his major theoretical manifesto from 1911, he develops his opposition to tonal music in terms which, superficially, almost recall later Nazi anti-Semitic tracts: tonal music has become a "diseased," "degenerate" world in need of a cleansing solution; the tonal system has given in to "inbreeding and incest"; romantic chords such as the diminished seventh are "hermaphroditic," "vagrant," and "cosmopolitan" . . . nothing easier than to claim that such a messianic-apocalyptic attitude is part of the same "spiritual situation" which gave birth to the Nazi "final solution." This, however, is precisely the conclusion one should *avoid*: what makes Nazism repulsive is not the rhetoric of final solution *as such*, but the concrete twist it gives to it.

Another popular topic of this kind of analysis, closer to Riefenstahl, is the allegedly "proto-fascist" character of the mass choreography displaying disciplined movements of thousands of bodies (parades, mass performances in the stadia, and so on); if one finds the same phenomenon also in socialism, one immediately draws the conclusion about a "deeper solidarity" between the two "totalitarianisms." Such a procedure, the very prototype of ideological liberalism, misses the point: not only are such mass performances not inherently fascist; they are not even "neutral," waiting to be appropriated by Left or Right—it was Nazism that stole them and appropriated them from the workers' movement, their original creator. None of the "proto-fascist" elements is *per se* fascist, what makes them "fascist" is only their specific articulation—or, to put it in Stephen Jay Gould's terms, all these elements are "ex-apted" by fascism. In other words, there is no "fascism *avant la lettre*," because *it is the letter itself (the nomination) which makes out of the bundle of elements fascism proper.*

Along the same lines, one should radically reject the notion that discipline (from self-control to body training) is a "proto-fascist" feature—the very predicate "proto-fascist" should be abandoned: it is the exemplary case of a pseudo-concept whose function is to block conceptual analysis. When we say that the organized spectacle of thousands of bodies (or, say, the admiration of sports which demand intense efforts and self-control such as mountain-climbing) is "proto-fascist," we say strictly nothing, we just express a vague association which masks our ignorance. So when, three decades ago, Kung Fu films were popular (Bruce Lee and so forth), was it not obvious that we were dealing with a genuine working-class ideology of youngsters whose only means of success was the disciplined training of their only possession, their bodies? Spontaneity and the "let it all hang out" attitude of indulging in excessive freedoms belong to those who can afford it—those who have nothing have only their discipline. The "bad" form of corporeal discipline, if there is one, is not collective training, but, rather, jogging and body-building as part of the New Age myth of the realization of the self's inner potential — no wonder that the obsession with one's body is an almost obligatory part of the passage of ex-leftist radicals into the "maturity" of pragmatic politics: from Jane Fonda to Joschka Fischer, the "period of latency" between the two phases was marked by the focus on one's own body.

So, back to Riefenstahl, what this means is not that one should dismiss her Nazi engagement as a limited and unfortunate episode. The true problem is to sustain the tension which cuts through her work: the tension between the artistic perfection of her procedures and the ideological project which "co-opted" them. Why should her case be different from that of Ezra Pound, W.B. Yeats, and other modernists with fascist tendencies who long ago became part of our artistic canon? Perhaps, the search for the "true ideological identity" of Riefenstahl is misleading: there is no such identity, she was genuinely inconsistent, blown this way and that as she was caught up in a conflictual forcefield.

To return to Heidegger, in his Nazi engagement, he was not "totally wrong" — the tragedy is that he was *almost right*, deploying the structure of a revolutionary act and then distorting it by giving it a fascist twist. Heidegger was closest to truth precisely where he erred most, in his writings from the late 1920s to the mid-1930s. Our task thus is to *repeat* Heidegger and retrieve this lost dimension/potential of his thought. In 1937–38, Heidegger wrote:

What is conservative remains bogged down in the historiographical; only what is revolutionary attains the depth of history. Revolution does not mean here mere subversion and destruction but an upheaval and recreating of the customary so that the beginning might be restructured. And because the original belongs to the beginning, the restructuring of the beginning is never the poor imitation of what was earlier; it is entirely other and nevertheless the same.[71]

In itself, is this not a wholly pertinent description of the revolution along Benjaminian lines? Recall the example provided by Walter Benjamin: the October Revolution repeated the French Revolution, redeeming its failure, unearthing and repeating the same impulse. Already for Kierkegaard, repetition is "inverted memory," a movement forward, the production of the New, and not the reproduction of the Old. "There is nothing new under the sun" is the strongest contrast to the movement of repetition. So, it is not only that repetition is (one of the modes of) the emergence of the New—*the New can only emerge through repetition*. The key to this paradox is, of course, what Deleuze designates as the difference between the virtual and the actual (and which—why not?—one can also determine as the difference between the Spirit and the Letter). Let us take a great philosopher such as Kant—there are two modes of repeating him: either one sticks to the letter and further elaborates or changes his system, in the spirit of the neo-Kantians (up to and including Habermas and Luc Ferry); or, one tries to regain the creative impulse that Kant himself betrayed in the actualization of his system (that is, to connect to what was already "in Kant more than Kant himself," more than his explicit system, its excessive core). There are, accordingly, two modes of betraying the past. The true betrayal is an ethico-theoretical act of the highest fidelity: one has to betray the letter of Kant in order to remain faithful to (and repeat) the "spirit" of his thought. It is precisely when one remains faithful to the letter of Kant that one really betrays the core of his thought, the creative impulse underlying it. One should bring this paradox to its conclusion: it is not only that one can remain really faithful to an author by way of betraying him (the actual letter of his thought); at a more radical level, the inverse statement holds even more—one can only truly betray an author by way of repeating him, by remaining faithful to the core of his thought. If one does not repeat an author (in the authentic Kierkegaardian sense of the term), but merely "criticizes" him, moves elsewhere, turns him around, and so forth, this effectively means that one unknowingly remains within his horizon, his conceptual field.[72] When G.K. Chesterton describes his conversion to Christianity, he claims that he "tried to be some ten minutes in advance of the truth. And I found that I was eighteen years behind it."[73] Does the same not hold even more for those who, today, desperately try to catch up with the New by way of following the latest "post-" fashion, and are thus condemned to remain forever eighteen years behind the truly New?

In his ironic comments on the French Revolution, Marx opposes the revolutionary enthusiasm to the sobering effect of the "morning after": the actual result of the sublime revolutionary explosion, of the Event of freedom, equality, and brotherhood, is the miserable utilitarian/egotistic universe of market calculation. (And, incidentally, is not this gap even wider in the case of the October Revolution?) However, one should not simplify Marx: his point is not the rather commonsensical insight into how the vulgar reality of commerce is the "truth" of the theater of revolutionary enthusiasm. In the revolutionary explosion as an Event, another utopian dimension shines through, the dimension of universal emancipation which, precisely, is the excess betrayed by the market reality which takes over "the day after"—as such, this excess is not simply abolished, dismissed as irrelevant, but, as it were, *transposed into the virtual state*, continuing to haunt the emancipatory imaginary as a dream waiting to be realized. The excess of revolutionary enthusiasm over its own "actual social base" or substance is thus literally that of an attribute-effect over its own substantial cause, a spectral Event waiting for its proper embodiment.

Only repetition brings out pure difference. When, in his famous analysis in *Being and Time*, Heidegger describes the ex-static structure of *Dasein*'s temporality as the circular movement which goes from future through the past to the present, it is not enough to understand this as a movement in which I, starting from the future (the possibilities opened to me, my projects, and so on), go back to the past (analyze the texture of the historical situation into which I was "thrown," in which I find myself), and, from there, engage in my present in order to realize my projects. When Heidegger characterizes future itself as "having-been" (*gesewene*) or, more precisely, something that "is as having-been" (*gewe-sende*), he locates the future itself into the past—not, of course, in the sense that we live in a closed universe in which every future possibility is already contained in the past, so that we can only repeat, realize, what already is present in the inherited texture, but in the much more radical sense of the "openness" of the past itself: the past itself is not simply "what there was," it contains hidden, non-realized potentials, and the authentic future is the repetition/retrieval of *this* past, not of the past as it was, but of those elements in the past which the past itself, in its reality, betrayed, stifled, failed to realize. It is in this sense that one should today "repeat Lenin": choosing Lenin as one's hero (to paraphrase Heidegger) not in order to follow him and do the same today, but to repeat/retrieve him in the precise sense of bringing out the non-realized potentials of Leninism.

And one should not be afraid to conceive in these terms the very sensitive topic of Heidegger's relation to Nazism. Although it is true that, in contrast to "really-existing socialism," one does not talk about "really-existing fascism" (since we did not experience "actual" fascism as the betrayal of its inherent emancipatory potential), there is nonetheless a philosopher who precisely *did* engage in a kind of critique of "really-existing Nazism" on behalf of its true potential (its "inner greatness") betrayed by its racist-technological nihilistic reality—none other than Heidegger himself, of course. After his much-debated disappointment with the reality of the Nazi regime in 1934, Heidegger's effort throughout the 1930s was effectively to salvage this betrayed "inner greatness," the world-historic potential, of the Nazi movement—therein resides the ultimate political wager of Heidegger's endless variations on the topic of Hölderlin and the fate of Germany.[74]

According to the memoirs of a leading member of the German student movement in the late 1960s,[75] a delegation of student protesters visited Heidegger in 1968, and he professed his full sympathy and support for the students, claiming that they were doing then what he had tried to do in 1933 as rector in Freiburg, although from a different political position. One should not dismiss this claim as Heidegger's hypocritical illusion. What Heidegger was looking for in Nazism (to avoid a misunderstanding: not only due to an accidental error in his personal judgment, but due to the flaws of his theoretical edifice itself) was a revolutionary Event, so that even some measures he imposed on the Freiburg university during his brief tenure as its rector bear witness to his intention to enact there a kind of "cultural revolution" (bringing students together with workers and soldiers—which, in itself, is not a fascist measure, but something Maoists tried to do in the Cultural Revolution). One is thus tempted to apply to Heidegger André Gide's sarcastic comment as regards Théophile Gautier: in 1933, he played a crucial role in German academic politics, it is just that he was not worthy of the role.

From Heidegger to the drive

Although Heidegger's almost phobic oversensitivity to morality can be easily accounted for as an implicit admission of his own ethically repulsive behavior and lack of elementary ethical attitudes, his opponents' insistence on these same features of Heidegger as a person is also false—as if, by demonstrating Heidegger's personal lack of ethics, one can avoid the hard task of confronting the issues posed by Heidegger's thought. There is nonetheless something disturbing in Heidegger's proverbial allergy against any mention of moral considerations; in his reading of Plato in the 1931–32 seminar, he even tries to purify the Platonic *to agathon* from all links with moral goodness through a skillful reference to one of the everyday uses of the exclamation "Good!": "'good!' means: It will be done! It is decided! It has nothing to do with the meaning of *moral* goodness; ethics has ruined the grounding meaning of this word." One can thus easily imagine, at the conclusion of the Wahnsee conference, Heydrich exclaiming: "Good!", using the term in the "authentic" Platonic sense ("It will be done! It is decided!") . . . The fact that there is a real philosophical problem here can be demonstrated by a close reading of Heidegger's seminar on Schelling's "Philosophical Enquiries into the Nature of Human Freedom," in which Heidegger has to admit a dimension of radical Evil which cannot be historicized, that is, reduced to the nihilism of modern technology. It is the merit of Bret Davis to have analyzed in detail this deadlock of Heidegger's thought.

In his close reading of Heidegger, Derrida tried to demonstrate how "Spirit" (*Geist*) is the undeconstructed symptomal point in Heidegger's philosophical edifice;[76] Bret Davis has done the same thing for the notion of the Will.[77] A consensus is gradually emerging in Heidegger studies that there are not two, but, rather, three distinct phases of his thought: the early phase of the analytic of *Dasein* (*Sein und Zeit*); the middle phase of the assertion of heroic historicity (from the conference "What Is Metaphysics?" to the manuscript *Vom Ereignis*—the key text published in *Introduction to Metaphysics*); and the last phase of the withdrawal from technological nihilism into poetry and thought, under the sign of *Gelassenheit*. In his first phase, Heidegger ignores the phenomenon of the Will; in the second phase, it is forcefully asserted, and well beyond Heidegger's Nazi engagement (in the *Vom Ereignis* manuscript, which is usually read as the beginning of late Heidegger, he still speaks of the "will to *Ereignis*"); in the last phase, as the result of Heidegger's confrontation with Nietzsche, the will is, on the contrary, posited as the very core of modern subjectivity, and thus as that which has to be overcome if mankind is to leave behind the nihilism that threatens its very essence. Through a detailed and perceptive analysis, Davis shows how this tripartite division is not self-evident: although not explicitly thematized, the will is not only lurking in the background already in the first phase; much more crucially, it persists to the end, mysteriously popping up in unexpected ways.

Where I disagree with Davis is in how to interpret this strange persistence of the Will, which continues to haunt Heidegger even when its overcoming becomes the very focus of his thought. Under the clear influence of his in-depth knowledge of Japanese Zen Buddhism, Davis reads this persistence as a sign of "*Gelassenheit* as an unfinished project": it basically indicates that Heidegger did not succeed in thoroughly "deconstructing" the will, so that it is up to us, who continue in his path, to finish the job and draw all the consequences from *Gelassenheit*. Our wager is, however, that the persistence of the Will even in the later Heidegger, so brilliantly discerned by Davis, rather demonstrates the insufficiency of Heidegger's critical analysis of modern subjectivity—not in the sense that "Heidegger didn't go far enough, and thus remained himself marked by subjectivity," but in the sense that he overlooked a non-metaphysical core of modern subjectivity itself: the most fundamental dimension of the abyss of subjectivity cannot be grasped through the lens of the notion of subjectivity as the attitude of technological domination.[78] In other words, it is the *symptom* of *Gelassenheit*, an indication of the limitation of this notion itself, not only of our failure to fully develop its potential.[79]

Davis proposes the distinction

> between (1) what Heidegger calls "the will" of subjectivity, a funda-mental (dis)attunement that has risen up and prevailed in a particular epochal history of metaphysics, and (2) what we have (interpretively supplementing Heidegger) called "ur-willing," a non-historical dis-sonant excess which haunts the proper essence of non-willing.[80]

Heidegger directly approaches this point in his reading of a fragment of Anaximander on order and disorder, where he considers the possibility that an entity

> may insist [*bestehen*] upon its while solely to remain more present, in the sense of perduring [*Beständigen*]. That which lingers persists [*beharrt*] in its presencing. In this way it extricates itself from its transitory while. It strikes the wilful pose of persistence, no longer concerning itself with whatever else is present. It stiffens—as if this were the only way to linger—and aims solely for continuance and subsistence.[81]

Davis's thesis is that this "rebellious whiling" refers to a non-historical ur-willing, a willing which is not limited to the epoch of modern subjectivity and its will to power, but belongs to the core of Being itself. This is also why Davis is right in dismissing Hannah Arendt's reading of this "craving to persist" which reduces it to the traditional theological notion of a "wilful rebellion against the 'order' of Creation as such"[82]: this ur-willing is not the egotistic withdrawal-into-itself of a particular creature from the global Order, it is a "perversion" inscribed into this Order itself:

Is there not a problem of "willing" that is an ineradicable aspect of man's ineradicable finitude? Would not a problem of "willing"—even if not that of its specific historical determinations/exacerbations in the epochs of metaphysics—remain even in the other beginning?[83]

What Heidegger clearly saw is what the great Rheinland mystics (Eckhart, Böhme) also saw: the formula of evil as the distance or Fall from divine goodness is not enough; the question to be asked is, how can this distance occur? The only consistent answer is: there has to be an "inversion" in God himself, a struggle, dissonance, already in the very heart of the divine Origin. In the same way, Heidegger grounds the excess of subjectivity, its nihilistic forgetfulness of Being, in a strife/discord in the very heart of Being. Davis draws the same conclusion from Heidegger's oscillations in his reading of Schelling's *Treatise on Freedom*: radical Evil is most brutally exposed

> not in the *faceless defacing* technology of the extermination camps, but rather in the fact that it is possible [. . .] for a person to look another person in the face and, clearly sensing the withdrawal of interiority, wilfully pull the trigger, or point a finger in the direction of the gas chambers. The wickedness of this *face-to-face defacement*—this wicked will to power that wills the murder of the Other as *Other*, in other words, that wills to maintain a recognition of the Other precisely in order to take diabolical pleasure in annihilating his or her otherness—radically exceeds the evil of the calculating machinations of technology.
>
> [. . .] The thoughtless reduction of the Other to a cog in the wheel of technological machination is not yet the wicked will to power that maintains a recognition of the alterity of the Other precisely in order to take diabolical pleasure in conquering her resistance and witnessing her pain. This terrible fact of evil cannot be explained technologically.
>
> Heidegger's history of metaphysics, which proceeds to culminate in the technological will to will [. . .] passes by the abyss of this wicked will to power. After Heidegger therefore, we must step back to think the originary dissonant excess of ur-willing as the root potential, not just of the faceless defacing technological will to will, but also of this wicked face-to-face defacing will to power. Moreover, insofar as human freedom could not be detached from a responsibility with regard to this non-technological evil will to power, a limit in Heidegger's thinking of evil would also mark a limit in his thinking of human freedom.[84]

This, then, is where Heidegger was wrong in his infamous insertion of the Holocaust in the same series as the agricultural exploitation of nature:

> What is "scandalously inadequate" here is that Heidegger's thought appears unable to mark an essential difference between the reduction of vegetables to standing-reserve for the production and consumption of foodstuffs and the lining up of persons to be systematically murdered.[85]

So, what about the counter-argument in Heidegger's defense according to which it is not Heidegger but modern technology itself which reduces vegetables and humans to the same level of available/disposable objects? The answer is clear: Heidegger is simply (and crucially) *wrong* in reducing the Holocaust to a technological production of corpses; there is, in events like the Holocaust, a crucial element of the will to humiliate and hurt the other. The victim is treated as an object in a reflexive way, in order to humiliate him further, in clear contrast to the industrially produced vegetable, where this intention to hurt is absent—in industrialized agriculture, a vegetable simply *is* reduced to an object of technological manipulation.

This is also why the notion of trauma has no place in his universe: does, in Heideggerian terms, the concept of trauma, of a traumatic encounter, not designate precisely the unthinkable point at which an ontic intrusion gets so excessively powerful that it shatters the very ontological horizon which provides the coordinates within which reality is disclosed to us? This is why a traumatic encounter entails a "loss of reality" which has to be understood in the strong philosophical sense of the loss of ontological horizon—in trauma, we are momentarily exposed to the "raw" ontic thing not yet covered/screened by the ontological horizon. This, of course, is what happens when we witness something like the Holocaust: the eclipse of the World itself. One has to take this statement at its most literal: an act of thorough Evil threatens the very World-disclosure.

Davis's solution—to "clearly distinguish [. . .] between the ontological necessity of errancy and the inordinate excess of 'letting oneself be led astray'"[86]—comes dangerously close to the all-too-simple distinction between the ontologically necessary "normal" level of Evil and the ontic "excess" over this "normal" level (something akin to old Herbert Marcuse's distinction between "necessary" libidinal repression and the unnecessary excessive repression). The problem with this solution is that it doubly misses the point. First, it obviously misses Heidegger's point, which is, to the contrary, that the true excess is the ontological "evil" of technological nihilism—compared with it, "ontic" excesses are a minor mishap, so that one might even risk a tasteless Heideggerian paraphrase of Brecht: "What is the slaughter of thousands of enemies compared to the technological reduction of man himself to an object of technological manipulation?" Second, it misses a dimension isolated already by the German mystics from Eckhart onwards: the very non-historical "excessive" basic human evil (the intention to hurt and humiliate the other) is not a simple falling-off from man's ontological essence, but has to be grounded in this ontological essence.

Two further (interconnected) questions are to be raised here. The first one, naive but necessary: does this not ultimately absolve man from responsibility for concrete Evil, when Evil is grounded in the convolutions of Being itself? In other words, the question is "whether Heidegger, in ascribing the origin of evil to a negativity in being itself, implicitly justifies evil as an ontologiocally necessitated errancy."[87] The second, more fundamental-ontological: is this strife in the heart of Being part of its Harmony itself, in the sense that being is the very hidden concord of the struggling poles, or is it a more radical discord, something which derails the very Harmony of Being? Or, as Davis puts it: "Is being a fugue into which all dissonance is in the end necessarily harmonized? Or does evil haunt the gift of being as its non-sublatable dissonant excess?"[88] However, against Davis's claim that the first option "pulls Heidegger's thought back towards the systematicity of idealism,"[89] one should insist that it is, on the contrary, pre-modern (pre-idealist) "paganism" whose ultimate horizon is the higher Harmony of the struggling forces, and that "subjectivity," at its most fundamental, designates precisely a "dissonant excess" which cannot be co-opted into a higher Harmony of the substantial order of Being.

To answer these questions, it is not enough to think "with Heidegger against Heidegger," that is, to push the "unfinished Heidegger project" to its end. In other words, immanent critique is not enough here; one has to abandon Heidegger's basic premise of a diabolical inversion of the "fugue of being". Let us go back to Heidegger's reading of Anaximander. For anyone minimally versed in Freud and Lacan, Heidegger's reading of Anaximander's "disorder" cannot but evoke the Freudian *drive*: his formulation renders perfectly the "stuckness," the fixation, of the drive on a certain impossible point around which it circulates, obeying a "compulsion to repeat." At its most elementary, the drive is a "rebellious whiling" which derails the "natural" flow. So, what if there is *stricto sensu* no world, no disclosure of being, prior to this "stuckness"? What if there is no *Gelassenheit* which is disturbed by the excess of willing, what if it is this very excess-stuckness which opens up the space for *Gelassenheit*? What if it is only against the background of this stuckness that a human being can experience him- or herself as finite/mortal, in contrast to an animal which simply is mortal?

The primordial fact is thus not the fugue of being (or the inner peace of *Gelassenheit*), which can then be disturbed/perverted by the rise of ur-willing; the primordial fact is this ur-willing itself, its disturbance of the "natural" fugue. To put it in yet another way: in order for a human being to be able to withdraw from immersion in the everyday world to the inner peace of *Gelassenheit*, this immersion has first to be broken by the excessive "stuckness" of the drive.

Two further consequences should be drawn from this. First, that human finitude strictly equals infinity: the obscene "immortality"/infinity of the drive which insists "beyond life and death." Second: the name of this diabolical excess of willing which "perverts" the order of being is the subject. The subject thus cannot be reduced to an epoch of Being, to modern subjectivity bent on technological domination—there is, under-lying it, a "non-historical" subject.

Heidegger's "divine violence"

If there is a proposition against which our entire reading is aimed, it is the notion that "Heidegger abandoned his romantic infatuation with strug-gle, and mythical political deeds and sacrifices in favor of a more gentle and receptive form of openness to the earth and sky, mortals and divinities."[90] A subtitle to the present chapter could well have been: "Beware of Gentle Openness!"

What this means with regard to the three phases of Heidegger's thought is that there is a potential breakthrough towards another dimension in phase 2, which gets lost in phase 3: where Heidegger erred most (his Nazi engagement), he came closest to truth. Far from resolving the inconsistencies of phase 2, phase 3 proposes a new paradigm which renders them invisible. In contrast to this assertion of the late, green-*Gelassenheit* Heidegger, one should therefore explore for new openings the very Heidegger of violence, political deeds, and sacrifices. At the level of textual analysis, Gregory Fried[91] has already done a lot of spadework in his deep and pertinent reading of Heidegger's entire opus through the interpretive lens of his reference to Heraclitus's *polemos* (struggle—in German, *Krieg, Kampf*, or, predominantly in Heidegger, *Auseinandersetzung*) from the latter's famous Fragment 53: "War is both father of all and king of all: it reveals the gods on the one hand and humans on the other, makes slaves on the one hand, the free on the other."[92]

As every interpreter of Heraclitus knows, this fragment is to be read as the inversion of the religious vision of the universe as generated and ruled by a divine potency: for someone like Hesiod, God (Zeus) "the father and king of all is"! If we replace Zeus with struggle (war), we get a totally different overall map of the universe: not a hierarchical whole whose local tensions and struggles are controlled by the paternal force of the over- whelming divine One, but the ongoing process of struggle itself as the ultimate reality, as the process out of which all entities as well as their (temporary) order emerge. It is not only that each stable identity of each entity is only temporary, that they all sooner or later disappear, disin- tegrate, return to the primordial chaos; their (temporary) identity itself emerges through struggle, that is, stable identity is something one should gain through the ordeal of struggle, one asserts in confrontation with the other(s) . . . Perhaps this sounds familiar? One can insist that it does— when Heidegger, in his reading of the fragment, insists on how the "struggle meant here is originary struggle, for it allows those who struggle to originate as such in the first place,"[93] do we not have here not so much the usual *Heidegger avec Hitler*, but, rather, the unexpected *Heidegger avec Staline*? For Stalin also, nature and history are a great ongoing process of eternal "struggle between the opposites":

> Contrary to metaphysics, dialectics holds that internal contradictions are inherent in all things and phenomena of nature, for they all have their negative and positive sides, a past and a future, something dying away and something developing; and that the struggle between these opposites, the struggle between the old and the new, between that which is dying away and that which is being born, between that which is disappearing and that which is developing, constitutes the internal content of the process of development, the internal content of the transformation of quantitative changes into qualitative changes.
>
> The dialectical method therefore holds that the process of devel- opment from the lower to the higher takes place not as a harmonious

unfolding of phenomena, but as a disclosure of the contradictions inherent in things and phenomena, as a "struggle" of opposite tendencies which operate on the basis of these contradictions.[94]

Even the "class struggle" is already there in Heraclitus, in the guise of the struggle which "makes slaves on the one hand, the free on the other" . . . According to some sources, one of Heidegger's visitors in the last years of World War II was surprised to see on desk some books on Marxist philosophy; he replied that, since the Soviet Union was going to win the war, he was getting ready to play his role in a new society . . . Apocryphal or not, we can see the inner logic of this anecdote, which resides in the unexpected reverberation between the highest and the lowest, the terse poetic beauty and precision of Heraclitus's ancient wisdom, and the simple brutality of Stalin's dialectical-materialist "world-view."

The other key Greek passage on violence to which Heidegger repeatedly returns is the famous Chorus from *Antigone* on the "uncanny/demonic" character of man. In his reading of this chorus in the *Introduction to Metaphysics*, Heidegger deploys the notion of "ontological" violence that pertains to every founding gesture of the new communal World of a people, accomplished by poets, thinkers, and statesmen:

> Violence is usually seen in terms of the domain in which concurring compromise and mutual assistance set the standard for Dasein, and accordingly all violence is necessarily deemed only a disturbance and an offense. [. . .] The violent one, the creative one who sets forth into the unsaid, who breaks into the unthought, who compels what has never happened and makes appear what is unseen—this violent one stands at all times in daring. [. . .] Therefore the violence-doer knows no kindness and conciliation (in the ordinary sense), no appeasement and mollification by success or prestige and by their confirmation. [. . .] For such a one, disaster is the deepest and broadest Yes to the Overwhelming. [. . .] Essential de-cision, when it is carried out and when it resists the constantly pressing ensnarement in the everyday and the customary, has to use violence. This act of violence, this de-cided setting out upon the way to the Being of beings, moves humanity out of the hominess of what is most directly nearby and what is usual.[95]

As such, the Creator is *"hupsipolis apolis"* (*Antigone*, line 370): he stands outside and above *polis* and its *ethos*, he is unbound by any rules of "morality" (which are only a degenerative form of *ethos*); only as such can he ground a new form of *ethos*, of communal Being in a *polis* . . . —of course, what reverberates here is the topic of an "illegal" violence that founds the rule of the law itself, deployed at the same time in different forms by Walter Benjamin and Carl Schmitt.[96] What accounts for the chilling character of these passages is that, here, Heidegger does not merely provide a new variation on his standard rhetorical figure of inversion ("The essence of violence has nothing to do with ontic violence, suffering, war, destruction, etc.; the essence of violence resides in the violent character of the very imposition/founding of the new mode of the Essence—disclosure of communal Being—itself"); here, Heidegger (implicitly, but clearly) reads this essential violence as something that grounds—or, at least, opens up the space for—the explosions of ontic violence themselves . . . Liberal critics of Heidegger like to dwell on these lines, emphasizing how, in suspending even minimal moral criteria, Heidegger legitimizes the most brutal "ontic" violence of the statesman-creator, and thus paves the way for his own Nazi engagement and support for Hitler as such a statesman-creator who, standing outside and above the communal space of the moribund Weimar Republic, fearlessly shattered its coordinates and thus violently grounded a new communal Being, that of the Germany reawakened in the National Socialist revolution . . .

However, what one is tempted to add here is that, in the case of Nazism (and fascism in general), the constellation of violence is rather the opposite: crazy, tasteless even, as it may sound, the problem with Hitler was that *he was not violent enough*, that his violence was not "essential" enough. Nazism was not radical enough, it did not dare to disturb the basic structure of the modern capitalist social space (which is why it had to focus on destroying an invented external enemy, Jews).

This is why one should oppose the fascination with Hitler which claims that, of course, he was an evil man, responsible for the death of millions— but that he definitely had courage, that he pursued what he wanted with an iron will . . . The point is that this is not only ethically repulsive, but simply *wrong*: no, Hitler did *not* "have the courage" to really change things; he did *not* really act, all his actions were fundamentally *reactions*, that is, he acted so that nothing would really change, he staged a great spectacle of Revolution so that the capitalist order could survive. If one really wants to come up with an act which was truly daring, for which one truly had to "have the courage" to try the impossible, but which was simultaneously a horrific act, an act which caused suffering beyond comprehension, one could nominate Stalin's forced collectivization at the end of 1920s in the Soviet Union — but even here, the same reproach holds: the paradox of the 1928 "Stalinist revolution" was rather that, in all its brutal radicality, *it was not radical enough* in effectively transforming the social substance. Its brutal destructiveness has to be read as an impotent *passage à l'acte*. Far from simply standing for a total forcing of the unnamable Real on behalf of the Truth, Stalinist "totalitarianism" rather designates the attitude of absolutely ruthless "pragmatism," of manipulating and sacrificing all "principles" on behalf of maintaining power.

From this perspective, the irony of Hitler was that his grand gestures of despising bourgeois self-complacency and so on were ultimately in the service of enabling this complacency to continue: far from effectively disturbing the much disparaged "decadent" bourgeois order, far from awakening the Germans from immersion in its degeneracy, Nazism was a dream which enabled them to continue wallowing in it and to postpone an awakening — Germany really awakened only in the defeat of 1945. The worry that Badiou's notion of "courage" (which one needs in order to practice the fidelity to the Event) raises in liberal minds is: but how are we to distinguish "good" (properly evental) courage from "bad" courage — say, were the Nazis who defended Berlin in the winter of 1944–45 or the Muslim terrorists who blow themselves up when they perform suicidal attacks also not truly courageous? One should nonetheless insist that there is no "bad courage": bad courage is always a form of cowardice. The "courage" of the Nazis was sustained by their cowardice concerning attacking the key feature of their society, the capitalist relations of production; the "courage" of the terrorists relies on the "big Other" whose instruments they perceive themselves to be. The true courage of an act is always the courage to accept the inexistence of the big Other, that is, to attack the existing order at the point of its symptomal knot.

Back once more to Heidegger: what this means is that Hitler's violence, even at its most terrifying (the murder of millions of Jews), was all too "ontic," that is, it too was an impotent *passage à l'acte* that revealed the inability of the Nazi movement to be really "*apolis*," to question–confront–shatter the basic coordinates of bourgeois communal being. And what if Heidegger's own Nazi engagement is also to be read as a *passage à l'acte*: a violent outburst that bears witness to Heidegger's inability to resolve the theoretical deadlock he found himself in? The question of how

Heidegger's Nazi commitment relates to his philosophy should thus be recast: it is no longer a question of *adequatio* (correspondence) between Heidegger's thought and his political acts, but of an inherent theoretical deadlock (which, in itself, has nothing to do with Nazism), and the violent *passage* as the only way of escaping it.

This is how one should also reframe the old dilemma, Which was in the beginning the Word or the Act? Logically, it all began with the Word; the Act that followed was a flailing outburst that bore witness to the deadlock of the Word. And the same goes for the Act *par excellence*, the divine act of Creation: it also signals the impasse of God's ratiocinations. In short, here too, the negative aspect of ontological proof holds: the fact that God created the world does not display His omnipotence and excess of goodness, but rather His debilitating limitations.

II

LESSONS FROM THE PAST

4 Revolutionary Terror from Robespierre to Mao

"What do you want?"

In his *Logiques des mondes*, Alain Badiou[1] elaborates the eternal Idea of the politics of revolutionary justice at work from the ancient Chinese "legists" through the Jacobins to Lenin and Mao. It consists of four moments: *voluntarism* (the belief that one can "move mountains," ignoring "objective" laws and obstacles); *terror* (a ruthless will to crush the enemy of the people); *egalitarian justice* (its immediate brutal imposition, with no understanding for the "complex circumstances" which allegedly compel us to proceed gradually); and, last but not least, *trust in the people* — suffice it to recall two examples here, Robespierre himself, his "a great truth" ("the characteristic of popular government is to be trustful towards the people and severe towards itself"), and Mao's critique of Stalin's *Economic Problems of Socialism in the USSR*, where he qualifies Stalin's point of view as "almost altogether wrong. The basic error is mistrust of the peasants".[2]

In modern European history, the first to fully enact the politics of revolutionary justice were the Jacobins in the course of the French Revolution.[3] When, in 1953, Zhou Enlai, the Chinese Prime Minister, was in Geneva for the peace negotiations to end the Korean war, a French journalist asked him what he thought about the French Revolution; Zhou replied: "It is still too early to tell." In a way, he was right: with the disintegration of the "people's democracies" in the late 1990s, the struggle for the historical significance of the French Revolution flared up again. The liberal revisionists tried to impose the notion that the demise of Communism in 1989 occurred at exactly the right moment: it marked the end of the era which began in 1789, the final failure of the statist-revolutionary model which first entered the scene with the Jacobins.

Nowhere is the dictum "every history is a history of the present" more true than in the case of the French Revolution: its historiographical reception has always closely mirrored the twists and turns of political struggles. The identifying mark of all kinds of conservatives is its flat rejection: the French Revolution was a catastrophe from the very beginning, the product of the godless modern mind, it is to be interpreted as God's punishment for humanity's wicked ways, so its traces should be effaced as thoroughly as possible. The typical liberal attitude is a differentiated one: its formula is "1789 without 1793." In short, what the sensitive liberals want is a decaffeinated revolution, or a revolution which does not smell of a revolution. François Furet and others thus try to deprive the French Revolution of its status as the founding event of modern democracy, relegating it to a historical anomaly: there was a historical necessity to assert the modern principles of personal freedom and so forth, but, as the English example demonstrates, the same could have been much more efficiently achieved in a more peaceful way . . . Radicals are, on the contrary, possessed by what Alain Badiou calls the "passion of the Real": if you say A—equality, human rights, and freedom—you should not shirk from its consequences and gather the courage to say B—the terror needed to really defend and assert the A.[4]

And the same goes for the memory of May 1968. Days before the second round of the presidential elections in May 2007, Nicolas Sarkozy formulated the exorcism of the ghost of May 68 as the true choice facing the electorate: "In this election, we should learn whether the inheritance of May 68 is to be perpetuated, or whether it should be liquidated once and for all. I want to turn the page of May 68." While one should defend the memory of 68, one should also bear in mind that the content of this memory is the stake of an ideological struggle—as Daniel Bensaïd and Alain Krivine pointed out recently: "There is their May and ours."[5] The predominant liberal discourse appropriated the May 68 events as the beginning of the end of the traditional Left, as the explosion of youthful energy and creativity, as France's "belated entrance into hedonist modernity." For the Left, on the contrary, May 68 was the unique moment of a general strike which paralyzed France and evoked the specter of the disintegration of state power, the moment of unification of the students' contestation with the workers' protests, part of the larger movement which encompassed student movements in the US, Germany, and Italy.

However, it is all too easy to say that today's Left should simply continue along this path. Something, some kind of historical rupture, effectively took place in 1990: everyone, the contemporary "radical Left" included, is somehow ashamed of the Jacobin legacy of revolutionary terror with its state-centralized character, so that the current *doxa* is that the Left, if it is to regain political efficacy, should thoroughly reinvent itself, finally abandoning the so-called "Jacobin paradigm." In our postmodern era of "emergent properties," chaotic interaction of multiple subjectivities, of free interaction instead of centralized hierarchy, of a multitude of opinions instead of one Truth, the Jacobin dictatorship is fundamentally "not to our taste" (the term "taste" should be given all its historical weight, as a word capturing a basic ideological disposition). Can one imagine anything more foreign to our universe of the freedom of opinions, of market competition, of nomadic pluralist interaction, and so on and so forth, than Robespierre's politics of Truth (with a capital T, of course), whose proclaimed goal is "to return the destiny of liberty into the hands of the truth"? Such a Truth can only be enforced in a terrorist manner:

> If the mainspring of popular government in peacetime is virtue, amid revolution it is at the same time virtue and terror: virtue, without which terror is fatal; terror, without which virtue is impotent. Terror is nothing but prompt, severe, inflexible justice; it is therefore an emanation of virtue. It is less a special principle than a consequence of the general principle of democracy applied to our country's most pressing needs.[6]

This line of argumentation reaches its climax in the paradoxical identification of the opposites: revolutionary terror "sublates" the opposition between punishment and clemency—just and severe punishment of the enemies *is* the highest form of clemency, so that rigor and charity coincide in terror:

> To punish the oppressors of humanity is clemency; to pardon them is barbarity. The rigor of tyrants has only rigor for a principle; the rigor of the republican government comes from charity.[7]

Do we still have ears for such a revolutionary "coincidence of the opposites"—of punishment and charity, of terror and freedom? The popular image of Robespierre is that of a kind of inverted Elephant Man: while the latter had a terribly deformed body hiding a gentle and intelligent soul, Robespierre was a kind and polite person hiding ice-cold cruel determination as signaled by his green eyes. As such, Robespierre serves perfectly today's anti-totalitarian liberals who no longer need to portray him as a cruel monster with a sneering evil smile, as was the case for nineteenth-century reactionaries: everyone is ready to recognize his moral integrity and full devotion to the revolutionary cause, since his very purity is the problem, the source of all trouble, as is indicated by the title of the latest biography of Robespierre, Ruth Scurr's *Fatal Purity*.[8] And, so that no one misses the point, Antonia Fraser, in her review, draws "a chilling lesson for us today": Robespierre was personally honest and sincere, but "[t]he bloodlettings brought about by this 'sincere' man surely warn us that belief in your own righteousness to the exclusion of all else can be as dangerous as the more cynical motivation of a deliberate tyrant."[9] Happy are we who live under cynical public-opinion manipulators, not under the sincere Muslim fundamentalists ready to fully engage themselves in their projects . . . what better proof of the ethico-political misery of our epoch whose ultimate mobilizing motif is the mistrust of virtue!

What, then, should those who remain faithful to the legacy of the radical Left do with all this? Two things, at the very least. First, the terrorist past has to be accepted as *ours*, even — or precisely because — it is critically rejected. The only alternative to the half-hearted defensive position of feeling guilty faced with our liberal or rightist critics is: we have to do the critical job better than our opponents. This, however, is not the entire story: one should also not allow our opponents to determine the terms and topic of the struggle. What this means is that ruthless self-criticism should go hand in hand with a fearless admission of what, to paraphrase Marx's judgment on Hegel's dialectics, one is tempted to call the "rational kernel" of the Jacobin Terror:

> Materialist dialectics assumes, without particular joy, that, till now, no political subject was able to arrive at the eternity of the truth it was deploying without moments of terror. For, as Saint-Just asked: "What do those who want neither Virtue nor Terror want?" His answer is well known: they want corruption — another name for the subject's defeat.[10]

Or, as Saint-Just put it succinctly elsewhere: "That which produces the general good is always terrible."[11] These words should not be interpreted as a warning against the temptation to violently impose the general good on a society, but, on the contrary, as a bitter truth to be fully endorsed.

The further crucial point to bear in mind is that, for Robespierre, revolutionary terror is the very opposite of war: Robespierre was a pacifist, not out of hypocrisy or humanitarian sensitivity, but because he was well aware that war *between* nations as a rule serves as the means to obfuscate revolutionary struggle *within* each nation. Robespierre's speech "On War" is of special importance today: it shows him as a true peace-lover who ruthlessly denounces the patriotic call to war, even if the war is formulated as the defense of the revolution, for it is the attempt of those who want "revolution without revolution" to divert the radicalization of the revolutionary process. His stance is thus the exact opposite of those who need war to militarize social life and take dictatorial control over it.[12] Which is why Robespierre also denounced the temptation to export revolution to other countries, forcefully "liberating" them:

> The French are not afflicted with a mania for rendering any nation happy and free against its will. All the kings could have vegetated or died unpunished on their blood-spattered thrones, if they had been able to respect the French people's independence.[13]

Jacobin revolutionary terror is sometimes (half) justified as the "founding crime" of the bourgeois universe of law and order, in which citizens are allowed to pursue their interests in peace, but one should reject this claim on two accounts. Not only is it factually wrong (many conservatives were quite right to point out that one can achieve bourgeois law and order without terrorist excesses, as was the case in Great Britain — although there is Cromwell to remember . . .); much more important, the revolutionary Terror of 1792–94 was not a case of what Walter Benjamin and others call state-founding violence, but a case of "divine violence."[14] Interpreters of Benjamin wonder what "divine violence" could effectively mean — is it yet another leftist dream of a "pure" event which never really takes place? One should recall here Friedrich Engels's reference to the Paris Commune as an example of the dictatorship of the proletariat:

> Of late, the Social-Democratic philistine has once more been filled with wholesome terror at the words: Dictatorship of the Proletariat. Well and good, gentlemen, do you want to know what this dictatorship looks like? Look at the Paris Commune. That was the Dictatorship of the Proletariat.[15]

One should repeat this, *mutatis mutandis*, apropos divine violence: "Well and good, gentlemen critical theorists, do you want to know what this divine violence looks like? Look at the revolutionary Terror of 1792–94. That was Divine Violence." (And the series can continue: the Red Terror of 1919 . . .) That is to say, one should fearlessly identify divine violence with positively existing historical phenomena, thus avoiding all obscurantist mystification. When those outside the structured social field strike "blindly," demanding *and* enacting immediate justice/vengeance, this is "divine violence"—recall, a decade or so ago, the panic in Rio de Janeiro when crowds descended from the favelas into the wealthy part of the city and started looting and burning supermarkets—*this* was "divine violence" . . . Like biblical locusts, divine punishment for men's sinful ways, it strikes from out of nowhere, a means without an end—or, as Robespierre put it in his speech in which he demanded the execution of Louis XVI:

> Peoples do not judge in the same way as courts of law; they do not hand down sentences, they throw thunderbolts; they do not condemn kings, they drop them back into the void; and this justice is worth just as much as that of the courts.[16]

The "dictatorship of the proletariat" is thus another name for Benjaminian "divine violence" which is outside the law, a violence exerted as brutal revenge/justice—but why "divine"? "Divine" points towards the dimension of the "inhuman"; one should thus posit a double equation: divine violence = inhuman terror = dictatorship of the proletariat. Benjaminian "divine violence" should be conceived as divine in the precise sense of the old Latin motto *vox populi, vox dei*: not in the perverse sense of "we are doing it as mere instruments of the People's Will," but as the heroic assumption of the solitude of a sovereign decision. It is a decision (to kill, to risk or lose one's own life) made in absolute solitude, with no cover from the big Other. If it is extra-moral, it is not "immoral," it does not give the agent the license just to kill with some kind of angelic innocence. The motto of divine violence is *fiat iustitia, pereat mundus*: it is through *justice*, the point of non-distinction between justice and vengeance, that the "people" (the anonymous part of no-part) imposes its terror and makes other parts pay the price—Judgment Day for the long history of oppression, exploitation, suffering—or, as Robespierre himself put it in a poignant manner:

What do you want, you who would like truth to be powerless on the lips of representatives of the French people? Truth undoubtedly has its power, it has its anger, its own despotism; it has touching accents and terrible ones, that resound with force in pure hearts as in guilty consciences, and that untruth can no more imitate than Salome can imitate the thunderbolts of heaven; but accuse nature of it, accuse the people, which wants it and loves it.[17]

And this is what Robespierre is targeting in his famous accusation to the moderates that what they really want is a "revolution without a revolution": they want a revolution deprived of the excess in which democracy and terror coincide, a revolution respecting social rules, subordinated to preexisting norms, a revolution in which violence is deprived of the "divine" dimension and thus reduced to a strategic intervention serving precise and limited goals:

Citizens, did you want a revolution without a revolution? What is this spirit of persecution that has come to revise, so to speak, the one that broke our chains? But what sure judgement can one make of the effects that can follow these great commotions? Who can mark, after the event, the exact point at which the waves of popular insurrection should break? At that price, what people could ever have shaken off the yoke of despotism? For while it is true that a great nation cannot rise in a simultaneous movement, and that tyranny can only be hit by the portion of citizens that is closest to it, how would these ever dare to attack it if, after the victory, delegates from remote parts could hold them responsible for the duration or violence of the political torment that had saved the homeland? They ought to be regarded as justified by tacit proxy for the whole of society. The French, friends of liberty, meeting in Paris last August, acted in that role, in the name of all the departments. They should either be approved or repudiated entirely. To make them criminally responsible for a few apparent or real disorders, inseparable from so great a shock, would be to punish them for their devotion.[18]

This authentic revolutionary logic can be discerned already at the level of rhetorical figures, where Robespierre likes to turn around the standard procedure of first evoking an apparently "realistic" position and then displaying its illusory nature: he often starts with presenting a position or description of a situation as an absurd exaggeration, a fiction, and then goes on to remind us that what, in a first approach, cannot but appear as a fiction, is actually truth itself: "But what am I saying? What I have just presented as an absurd hypothesis is actually a very certain reality." It is this radical revolutionary stance which also enables Robespierre to denounce the "humanitarian" concern with victims of revolutionary "divine violence": "A sensibility that wails almost exclusively over the enemies of liberty seems suspect to me. Stop shaking the tyrant's bloody robe in my face, or I will believe that you wish to put Rome in chains."[19]

Asserting the inhuman

Critical analysis and the acceptance of the historical legacy of the Jacobins overlap in the real question to be raised: does the (often deplorable) actuality of revolutionary terror compel us to reject the very idea of Terror, or is there a way to *repeat* it in today's different historical constellation, to redeem its virtual content from its actualization? We claim here that it *can* and *should* be done, and the most concise formula of repeating the event designated by the name "Robespierre" is to pass from (Robespierre's) humanist terror to anti-humanist (or, rather, inhuman) terror.

In his *Le Siècle*, Alain Badiou detects a sign of the political regression that occurred towards the end of the twentieth century in the shift from "humanism *and* terror" to "humanism *or* terror."[20] In 1946, Maurice Merleau-Ponty wrote *Humanism and Terror*, his defense of Soviet Communism as involving a kind of Pascalean wager that announces the trope which Bernard Williams later called "moral luck": the present terror will be retroactively justified if the society that emerges from it is truly human; today, such a conjunction of terror and humanism is properly unthinkable, the predominant liberal view replaces "and" with "or": either humanism or terror . . . More precisely, there are four variations on this motif: humanism *and* terror, humanism *or* terror, each either in a "positive" or in a "negative" sense. "Humanism and terror" in a positive sense is what Merleau-Ponty elaborated: it sustains Stalinism (the forceful — "terrorist" — engendering of the New Man), and is already clearly discernible in the French Revolution, in the guise of Robespierre's conjunction of virtue and terror. This conjunction can be negated in two ways. It can involve the choice "humanism *or* terror," that is, the liberal-humanist project in all its versions, from dissident anti-Stalinist humanism up to and including today's neo-Habermasians (such as Luc Ferry and Alain Renaut in France) and other defenders of human rights *against* (totalitarian, fundamentalist) terror. Or it can retain the conjunction "humanism *and* terror," but in a negative mode: all those philosophical and ideological orientations, from Heidegger and conservative Christians to partisans of Oriental spirituality and deep ecology, who perceive terror as the truth — the ultimate consequence — of the humanist project itself, of its hubris.

There is, however, a fourth variation, usually left aside: the choice "humanism *or* terror," but with *terror*, not humanism, as a positive term. This is a radical position which is difficult to sustain, but, perhaps, our only hope: it does not amount to the obscene madness of openly pursuing a "terrorist and inhuman politics," but something much more difficult to think through. In contemporary "post-deconstructionist" thought (if one risks this ridiculous designation which cannot but sound like its own parody), the term "inhuman" has gained new weight, especially through the work of Agamben and Badiou. The best way to approach it is via Freud's reluctance to endorse the injunction "Love thy neighbor!" — the temptation to be resisted here is the ethical prettification of the neighbor that we have already noted in the work of Emmanuel Levinas. In a properly dialectical paradox, what Levinas, with all his celebration of Otherness, fails to take into account is not some underlying Sameness of all humans but radically "inhuman" Otherness itself: the Otherness of a human being reduced to inhumanity, the Otherness exemplified by the terrifying figure of the *Muselmann*, the "living dead" in the concentration camps. At a different level, the same goes for Stalinist Communism. In the standard Stalinist narrative, even the concentration camps were a locus of the fight against fascism where imprisoned Communists were organizing networks of heroic resistance — in such a universe, of course, there is no place for the limit-experience of the *Muselmann*, of the living dead deprived of the capacity for human engagement — no wonder that Stalinist Communists were so eager to "normalize" the camps into just another site of the anti-fascist struggle, dismissing the *Muselmänner* as simply those who were too weak to endure the struggle.

It is against this background that one can understand why Lacan speaks of the *inhuman* core of the neighbor. Back in the 1960s, the era of structuralism, Louis Althusser launched the notorious formula of "theoretical anti-humanism," allowing, demanding even, that it be supplemented by *practical humanism*. In our practice, we should act as humanists, respecting the others, treating them as free persons with full dignity, creators of their world. However, in theory, we should equally always bear in mind that humanism is an ideology, the way we spontaneously experience our predicament, and that true knowledge of humans and their history should treat individuals not as autonomous subjects, but as elements in a structure which follows its own laws. In contrast to Althusser, Lacan accomplishes the passage from theoretical to *practical anti-humanism*, that is, to an ethics that goes beyond the dimension of what Nietzsche called the "human, all too human," and confronts the inhuman core of humanity. This does not only mean an ethics which no longer denies, but fearlessly takes into account the latent monstrosity of being-human, the diabolical dimension which exploded in phenomena usually covered by the concept–name "Auschwitz"—an ethics that would be still possible after Auschwitz, to paraphrase Adorno. This inhuman dimension is for Lacan, at the same time, the ultimate bedrock of ethics.

In philosophical terms, this "inhuman" dimension can be defined as that of a subject subtracted from all forms of human "individuality" or "personality" (which is why, in contemporary popular culture, one of the exemplary figures of the pure subject is a non-human—alien, cyborg—who displays more fidelity to the task, more dignity and freedom than its human counterparts, from the Rutger-Hauer android in *Blade Runner* to the Schwarzenegger-figure in *Terminator*). It is against the background of this topic of the sovereign acceptance of death that one should reread the rhetorical turn often referred to as the proof of Robespierre's "totalitarian" manipulation of his audience.[21] This turn took place in the midst of Robespierre's speech in the National Assembly on 11 Germinal Year II (March 31, 1794); the previous night, Danton, Camille Desmoulins, and some others had been arrested, so many members of the Assembly were understandably afraid that their turn would also come. Robespierre directly addresses the moment as pivotal: "Citizens, the moment has come to speak the truth." He then goes on to evoke the fear floating in the room:

> One wants [*on veut*] to make you fear abuses of power, of the national power you have exercised [. . .] One wants to make us fear that the people will fall victim to the Committees [. . .] One fears that the prisoners are being oppressed [. . .].[22]

The opposition is here between the impersonal "one" (the instigators of fear are not personified) and the collective thus put under pressure, which almost imperceptibly shifts from the plural second-person "you" (*vous*) to the first-person "us" (Robespierre gallantly includes himself into the collective). However, the final formulation introduces an ominous twist: it is no longer that "one wants to make you/us fear," but that "one fears," which means that the enemy stirring up fear is no longer outside "you/us," members of the Assembly, it is here, amongst us, amongst the "you" addressed by Robespierre, corroding our unity from within. At this precise moment, Robespierre, in a true master stroke, assumes full subjectivization—waiting a little bit for the ominous effect of his words to be felt, he then continued in the first person *singular*:

> I say that anyone who trembles at this moment is guilty; for innocence never fears public scrutiny.[23]

What can be more "totalitarian" than this closed loop of "your very fear of being guilty makes you guilty"—a weird superego-twisted version of the well-known motto "the only thing to fear is fear itself"? One should nonetheless move beyond the facile dismissal of Robespierre's rhetorical strategy as the strategy of "terrorist culpabilization" and discern its moment of truth: there are no innocent bystanders in the crucial moments of revolutionary decision, because, in such moments, innocence itself—exempting oneself from the decision, going on as if the struggle I am witnessing does not really concern me—*is* the highest treason. That is to say, the fear of being accused of treason *is* my treason, because, even if I "did not do anything against the revolution," this fear itself, the fact that it emerged in me, demonstrates that my subjective position is external to the revolution, that I experience the "revolution" as an external force threatening me.

But what happens subsequently in this unique speech is even more revealing: Robespierre directly addresses the touchy question that has to arise in the mind of his public—how can he himself be sure that he will not be the next in line to be accused? He is not the master exempted from the collective, the "I" outside "we"—after all, he was once very close to Danton, a powerful figure now under arrest, so what if, tomorrow, his proximity to Danton will be used against him? In short, how can Robespierre be sure that the process he unleashed will not swallow him? It is here that his position achieves sublime greatness—he fully accepts that the danger that now threatens Danton will tomorrow threaten him. The reason that he is so serene, that he is not afraid of this fate, is not that Danton was a traitor, while he, Robespierre, is pure, a direct embodiment of the people's Will; it is that he, Robespierre, *is not afraid to die* —his eventual death will be a mere accident which counts for nothing:

> What does danger matter to me? My life belongs to the Fatherland; my heart is free from fear; and if I were to die, I would do so without reproach and without ignominy.[24]

Consequently, insofar as the shift from "we" to "I" can effectively be determined as the moment when the democratic mask falls off and when Robespierre openly asserts himself as a Master (up to this point, we follow Lefort's analysis), the very term "Master" has to be given here its full Hegelian weight: the Master is the figure of sovereignty, the one who is not afraid to die, who is ready to risk everything. In other words, the ultimate meaning of Robespierre's first-person singular ("I") is: I am not afraid to die. What authorizes him is simply this, not any kind of direct access to the big Other, that is, he does not claim that he has direct access to the people's Will which speaks through him. It is against this background that one should recall Mao Zedong's message to the hundreds of millions of downtrodden, a simple and touching message of courage—do not be afraid of the Big Powers: "Bigness is nothing to be afraid of. The big will be overthrown by the small. The small will become big." The same message of courage sustains also Mao's (in)famous stance towards the prospect of a new atomic world war:

> We stand firmly for peace and against war. But if the imperialists insist on unleashing another war, we should not be afraid of it. Our attitude on this question is the same as our attitude towards any disturbance: first, we are against it; second, we are not afraid of it. The First World War was followed by the birth of the Soviet Union with a population of 200 million. The Second World War was followed by the emergence of the socialist camp with a combined population of 900 million. If the imperialists insist on launching a third world war, it is certain that several hundred million more will turn to socialism, and then there will not be much room left on earth for the imperialists [. . .][25]

It is all too easy to dismiss these lines as the empty posturing of a leader ready to sacrifice millions for his political goals (the extension *ad absurdum* of Mao's ruthless decision to starve tens of millions to death in the late 1950s) — the flipside of this dismissive attitude is the basic message: "we should not be afraid." Is this not the *only* correct attitude apropos war: "first, we are against it; second, we are not afraid of it"? (The logic of Mao's argument is very precise here: his "although we are against war, we are not afraid of it" inverts the "imperialists'" true attitude, which is "although we are for war, we are afraid of it"—imperialists are Nietzschean slaves, they need wars, but are afraid to lose their possessions to which they are attached, while the proletarians are the true aristocratic Masters who do not want war (they do not need it), but are not afraid of it, because they have nothing to lose . . .) Mao's argument goes on to its terrifying conclusion:

> The United States cannot annihilate the Chinese nation with its small stack of atom bombs. Even if the US atom bombs were so powerful that, when dropped on China, they would make a hole right through the earth, or even blow it up, that would hardly mean anything to the universe as a whole, though it might be a major event for the solar system.[26]

There is obviously an "inhuman madness" in this argument: is the fact that the destruction of planet Earth "would hardly mean anything to the universe as a whole" not rather poor solace for the extinction of humanity? The argument only works if, in a Kantian way, one presupposes a pure transcendental subject unaffected by this catastrophe—a subject which, although non-existent in reality, *is* operative as a virtual point of reference. Recall Husserl's dark dream, from his *Cartesian Meditations*, of how the transcendental *cogito* would remain unaffected by a plague that would annihilate all humanity: it is easy, apropos this example, to score cheap points about the self-destructive background of transcendental subjectivity, and about how Husserl misses the paradox of what Foucault, in his *Les Mots et les choses*, called the "transcendental-empirical doublet," of the link that forever attaches the transcendental ego to the empirical ego, so that the annihilation of the latter by definition leads to the disappearance of the first. However, what if, fully recognizing this dependence as a fact (and nothing more than this—a bald fact of being), one nonetheless insists on the truth of its negation, the truth of the assertion of the independence of the subject with regard to the empirical individuals *qua* living beings? Che Guevara approached the same line of thought when, in the midst of the unbearable tension of the Cuban missile crisis, he advocated a fearless approach of risking the new world war which would involve (at the very least) the total annihilation of the Cuban people — he praised the heroic readiness of the Cuban people to risk its own disappearance.

Again, there is definitely something terrifying about this attitude — however, this terror is nothing less than the condition of freedom. This is how Yamamoto Jocho, a Zen priest, described the proper attitude of a warrior: "every day without fail he should consider himself as dead. There is a saying of the elders that goes, 'Step from under the eaves and you're a dead man. Leave the gate and the enemy is waiting.' This is not a matter of being careful. It is to consider oneself as dead beforehand."[27] This is why, according to Hillis Lory, many Japanese soldiers in World War II performed their own funerals before leaving for the battlefield:

> Many of the soldiers in the present war are so determined to die on the battlefield that they conduct their own public funerals before leaving for the front. This holds no element of the ridiculous to the Japanese. Rather, it is admired as the spirit of the true samurai who enters the battle with no thought of return.[28]

This preemptive self-exclusion from the domain of the living, of course, turns the soldier into a properly sublime figure. Instead of dismissing this feature as part of fascistic militarism, one should assert it as also constitutive of a radical revolutionary position, which, as Seneca put it long ago in his *Oedipus*, demands of the subject to "search for a way to wander without mixing with the dead, and yet removed from the living."[29]

When, in the flashback scene from Bryan Singer's *The Usual Suspects*, the mysterious Keyser Soeze returns home and finds his wife and small daughter held at gunpoint by the members of a rival mob, he shoots his wife and daughter dead, and then declares that he will pursue the members of the rival gang mercilessly, tracking down their parents, families, and friends, in order to kill them all . . . In a situation of a forced choice, the Soeze-subject makes the crazy, impossible choice of, in a way, striking at himself, at what is most precious to him, and this act, far from amounting to a case of impotent aggression turned towards oneself, rather changes the coordinates of the situation in which the subject found himself: by way of cutting himself loose from the precious object through whose possession the enemy kept him in check, the subject gains the space for a free act. The price of this freedom is, of course, terrible: the only way for the subject to neutralize the guilt of sacrificing his most precious object(s) is to turn himself into a king of the "living dead," to renounce all personal idiosyncrasies and pleasures and to dedicate his entire life to destroying all those who forced him to perform the sacrificial act. Such an "inhuman" position of absolute freedom (in my loneliness, I am free to do whatever I want, nobody has any hold over me) coinciding with absolute subjection to a Task (the only purpose of my life is to enact vengeance) is what, perhaps, characterizes the revolutionary subject at its innermost.

Another "inhuman" dimension of the couple Virtue–Terror promoted by Robespierre is the rejection of habit (in the sense of the agency of realistic compromises). Every legal order (or every order of explicit normativity) has to rely on a complex "reflexive" network of informal rules which tells us how we are to relate to the explicit norms, how we are to apply them: to what extent we are to take them literally, how and when are we allowed, solicited even, to disregard them, and so on—and this is the domain of habit. To know the habits of a society is *to know the meta-rules of how to apply its explicit norms*: when to use them or not use them; when to violate them; when not to choose what is offered; when we are effectively obliged to do something, but have to pretend that we are doing it as a free choice (as in the case of potlatch). Let us refer to the polite offer-meant-to-be-refused: it is a "habit" to refuse such an offer, and anyone who accepts such an offer commits a vulgar blunder. The same goes for many political situations in which a choice is given *on condition that we make the right choice*: we are solemnly reminded that we can say no—but we are expected to reject this offer and enthusiastically say yes. With many sexual prohibitions, the situation is the opposite: the explicit "no" effectively functions as the implicit injunction "do it, but in a discreet way!". Measured against this background, revolutionary-egalitarian figures from Robespierre to John Brown are (potentially, at least) *figures without habits*: they refuse to take into account the habits that qualify the functioning of a universal rule.

Such is the natural dominion of habit that we regard the most arbitrary conventions, sometimes indeed the most defective institutions, as absolute measures of truth or falsehood, justice or injustice. It does not even occur to us that most are inevitably still connected with the prejudices on which despotism fed us. We have been so long stooped under its yoke that we have some difficulty in raising ourselves to the eternal principles of reason; anything that refers to the sacred source of all law seems to us to take on an illegal character, and the very order of nature seems to us a disorder. The majestic movements of a great people, the sublime fervours of virtue often appear to our timid eyes as something like an erupting volcano or the overthrow of political society; and it is certainly not the least of the troubles bothering us, this contradiction between the weakness of our morals, the depravity of our minds, and the purity of principle and energy of character demanded by the free government to which we have dared aspire.[30]

To break the yoke of habit means: if all men are equal, than all men are to be effectively treated as equal; if blacks are also human, they should be immediately treated as such. Let us recall the early stages of the struggle against slavery in the US, which, even prior to the Civil War, culminated in the armed conflict between the gradualism of compassionate liberals and the unique figure of John Brown:

> African Americans were caricatures of people, they were characterized as buffoons and minstrels, they were the butt-end of jokes in American society. And even the abolitionists, as antislavery as they were, the majority of them did not see African Americans as equals. The majority of them, and this was something that African Americans complained about all the time, were willing to work for the end of slavery in the South but they were not willing to work to end discrimination in the North. [. . .] John Brown wasn't like that. For him, practicing egalitarianism was a first step toward ending slavery. And African Americans who came in contact with him knew this immediately. He made it very clear that he saw no difference, and he didn't make this clear by saying it, he made it clear by what he did.[31]

For this reason, John Brown is a key political figure in the history of the US: in his fervently Christian "radical abolitionism," he came closest to introducing the Jacobin logic into the American political landscape:

> John Brown considered himself a complete egalitarian. And it was very important for him to practice egalitarianism on every level. [. . .]

He made it very clear that he saw no difference, and he didn't make this clear by saying it, he made it clear by what he did.[32]

Even today, long after slavery has been abolished, Brown is the polarizing figure in American collective memory; those whites who support Brown are all the more precious—among them, surprisingly, Henry David Thoreau, the great opponent of violence: against the standard dismissal of Brown as bloodthirsty, foolish, and insane, Thoreau painted a portrait of a peerless man whose embracement of a cause was unparalleled; he even goes as far as to liken Brown's execution (he states that he regards Brown as dead before his actual death) to Christ.[33] Thoreau vents his rage at the scores of those who voiced their scorn for John Brown: they could not understand Brown due to their concrete stances and "dead" existences; they are not truly alive, only a handful of men can be said to have lived.

It is, however, this very consistent egalitarianism which also constitutes the limitation of Jacobin politics. Recall Marx's fundamental insight about the "bourgeois" limitation of the logic of equality: capitalist inequalities ("exploitation") are not the "unprincipled violations of the principle of equality," but are absolutely inherent to the logic of equality, they are the paradoxical result of its consistent realization. What we have in mind here is not only the wearisome old motif of how market exchange presupposes formally/legally equal subjects who meet and interact in the market; the crucial moment of Marx's critique of "bourgeois" socialists is that capitalist exploitation does not involve any kind of "unequal" exchange between the worker and the capitalist—this exchange is fully equal and "just," ideally (in principle), the worker gets paid the full value of the commodity he is selling (his labor-power). Of course, radical bourgeois revolutionaries are aware of this limitation; however, the way they try to counteract it is through a direct "terroristic" imposition of more and more *de facto* equality (equal salaries, equal access to health services . . .), which can only be imposed through new forms of formal inequality (different sorts of preferential treatments for the underprivileged). In short, the axiom of "equality" means either not enough (it remains the abstract form of actual inequality) or too much (enforce "terroristic" equality)—it is a formalistic notion in a strict dialectical sense, that is, its limitation is precisely that its form is not concrete enough, but a mere neutral container of some content that eludes this form.

The problem here is not terror as such—our task today is precisely to reinvent emancipatory terror. The problem lies elsewhere: egalitarian political "extremism" or "excessive radicalism" should always be read as a phenomenon of ideologico-political *displacement*: as an index of its opposite, of a limitation, of a refusal effectively to "go to the end." What was the Jacobins' recourse to radical "terror" if not a kind of hysterical acting-out bearing witness to their inability to disturb the very fundamentals of economic order (private property, etc.)? And does the same not go even for the so-called "excesses" of political correctness? Do they also not display the retreat from disturbing the effective (economic and other) causes of racism and sexism? Perhaps, then, the time has come to render problematic the standard topos, shared by practically all "postmodern" leftists, according to which political "totalitarianism" somehow results from the predominance of material production and technology over intersubjective communication and/or symbolic practice, as if the root of political terror resides in the fact that the "principle" of instrumental reason, of the technological exploitation of nature, is extended also to society, so that people are treated as raw stuff to be transformed into New Men. What if it is the exact *opposite* which holds? What if political "terror" signals precisely that the sphere of (material) production is *denied* its autonomy and *subordinated* to political logic? Is it not that all political "terror," from the Jacobins to the Maoist Cultural Revolution, presupposes the foreclosure of production proper, its reduction to the terrain of the political struggle? In other words, what such a postmodern perspective effectively amounts to is nothing less than the abandonment of Marx's key insight into how the political struggle is a spectacle which, in order to be deciphered, has to be referred to the sphere of the economy ("if Marxism had any analytical value for *political* theory, was it not in the insistence that the problem of freedom was contained in the social relations implicitly declared 'unpolitical'—that is, naturalized—in liberal discourse?")[34]

It is at this level that one should search for the decisive moment of a revolutionary process: say, in the case of the October Revolution, not the explosion of 1917–18, not even the civil war that followed, but the intense experimentation of the early 1920s, the (desperate, often ridiculous) attempts to invent new rituals of daily life: how to replace the prerevolutionary marriage and funeral rituals? How to organize the most commonplace interaction in a factory, in an apartment block? It is at this level of what, as opposed to the "abstract terror" of the "great" political revolution, one is tempted to call the "concrete terror" of imposing a new order on quotidian reality, that the Jacobins and both the Soviet and the Chinese revolutions ultimately failed—not for lack of attempts in this direction, for sure. The Jacobins were at their best not in the theatrics of Terror, but in the utopian explosions of political imagination apropos the reorganization of the everyday: everything was there, proposed in the course of the frantic activity condensed into a couple of years, from the self-organization of women to communal homes in which the old were to be able to spend their last years in peace and dignity.[35] The harsh consequence to be accepted here is that this excess of egalitarian democracy over and above the democratic procedure can only "institutionalize" itself in the guise of its opposite, as revolutionary-democratic *terror*.

Transubstantiations of Marxism

In modern history, the politics of revolutionary terror casts its shadow over the epoch which spans from Robespierre to Mao, or, more generally, the disintegration of the Communist bloc in 1990—its last installment was the Maoist Cultural Revolution.

Obviously, the socio-historical context had changed radically between the French Revolution and the Cultural Revolution—to put it in Platonist terms, what unites the two is precisely and only the same "eternal" Idea of revolutionary Justice. In the case of Mao, the question is even whether one can legitimately count him as a Marxist, since the social base of the Maoist revolution was not the working class.

One of the most devious traps which lurk for Marxist theorists is the search for the moment of the Fall, when things took the wrong turning in the history of Marxism: was it already the late Engels with his more positivist-evolutionary understanding of historical materialism? Was it the revisionism and the orthodoxy of the Second International? Was it Lenin?[36] Or was it Marx himself in his late work, after he had abandoned his youthful humanism (as some "humanist Marxists" claimed decades ago)? This entire trope has to be rejected: there is no opposition here, the Fall is to be inscribed in the very origins. (To put it even more pointedly, such a search for the intruder who infected the original model and set in motion its degeneration cannot but reproduce the logic of anti-Semitism.) What this means is that, even if—or, rather, especially if—one submits the Marxist past to ruthless critique, one has first to acknowledge it as "one's own," taking full responsibility for it, not to comfortably reject the "bad" side of things by attributing it to a foreign element (the "bad" Engels who was too stupid to understand Marx's dialectics, the "bad" Lenin who did not grasp the core of Marx's theory, the "bad" Stalin who spoilt the noble plans of the "good" Lenin, and so on).

The first thing we must do is to fully endorse the displacement in the history of Marxism concentrated in two great passages (or, rather, violent cuts): the passage from Marx to Lenin, as well as the passage from Lenin to Mao. In each case, there is a displacement of the original constellation: from the most advanced country (as Marx expected) to a relatively backward country—the revolution "took place in the wrong country"; from workers to (poor) peasants as the main revolutionary agent. In the same way as Christ needed Paul's "betrayal" in order for Christianity to emerge as a universal Church (recall that, amongst the twelve apostles, Paul occupies the place of Judas the traitor, replacing him!), Marx needed Lenin's "betrayal" in order to enact the first Marxist revolution: it is an inner necessity of the "original" teaching to submit to and survive this "betrayal"; to survive this violent act of being torn out of one's original context and thrown into a foreign landscape where it has to reinvent itself—*only in this way is universality born.*

So, apropos the second violent transposition, that of Mao, it is too easy either to condemn his reinvention of Marxism as theoretically "inadequate," as a regression with regard to Marx's standards (it is easy to show that peasants lack substanceless proletarian subjectivity), but it is equally too facile to blur the violence of the cut and to accept Mao's reformulation as a logical continuation or "application" of Marxism (relying, as is usually the case, on the simple metaphoric expansion of class struggle: "today's predominant class struggle is no longer between capitalists and proletariat in each country, it has shifted to the Third versus the First World, bourgeois versus proletarian nations"). The achievement of Mao is here tremendous: his name stands for the political mobilization of the hundreds of millions of anonymous Third World layers whose labor provides the invisible "substance," the background, of historical development—the mobilization of all those whom even such a poet of "otherness" as Levinas dismissed as the "yellow peril", as we see in what is arguably his weirdest text, "The Russo-Chinese Debate and the Dialectic" (1960), a comment on the Soviet–Chinese conflict:

The yellow peril! It is not racial, it is spiritual. It does not involve inferior values; it involves a radical strangeness, a stranger to the weight of its past, from where there does not filter any familiar voice or inflection, a lunar or Martian past.[37]

Does this not recall Heidegger's insistence, throughout the 1930s, that the main task of Western thought today was to defend the Greek breakthrough, the founding gesture of the "West," the overcoming of the pre-philosophical, mythical, "Asiatic" universe, to struggle against the renewed "Asiatic" threat—the greatest adversary of the West was "the mythical in general and the Asiatic in particular"?[38] It is *this* Asiatic "radical strangeness" which is mobilized, politicized, by Mao Zedong's Communist movement. In his *Phenomenology of Spirit*, Hegel introduces his notorious notion of womankind as "the everlasting irony of the community": womankind "changes by intrigue the universal end of the government into a private end, transforms its universal activity into a work of some particular individual, and perverts the universal property of the state into a possession and ornament for the family."[39] In contrast to male ambition, a woman wants power in order to promote her own narrow family interests or, even worse, her personal caprice, incapable as she is of perceiving the universal dimension of state politics. How are we not to recall F.W.J. Schelling's claim that "the same principle carries and holds us in its ineffectiveness which would consume and destroy us in its effectiveness"?[40] A power which, when it is kept in its proper place, can be benign and pacifying, turns into its radical opposite, into the most destructive fury, the moment it intervenes at a higher level, the level which is not its own: *the same* femininity which, within the closed circle of family life, is the power of protective love, turns into obscene frenzy when displayed at the level of public and state affairs . . . In short, it is acceptable for a woman to protest against public state power on behalf of the rights of the family and kinship; but woe to a society in which women endeavor directly to influence decisions concerning the affairs of state, manipulating their weak male partners, effectively emasculating them . . . Is there not something similar in the terror aroused by the prospect of the awakening of the anonymous Asian masses? They are fine if they protest at their fate and allow us to help them (through large-scale humanitarian activity), but not when they "empower" themselves, to the horror of sympathetic liberals, always ready to support the revolt of the poor and dispossessed, so long as it is done with good manners . . .

Georgi M. Derluguian's *Bourðieu's Secret Aðmirer in the Caucasus* tells the extraordinary story of Musa Shanib from Abkhazia, the leading intellectual of this turbulent region whose incredible career passed from Soviet dissident intellectual through democratic political reformer and Muslim fundamentalist war leader up to respected professor of philosophy, his entire career marked by a strange admiration for Pierre Bourdieu's thought.[41] There are two ways to approach such a figure. The first reaction is to dismiss it as a local eccentricity, to treat it with benevolent irony—"what a strange choice, Bourdieu—who knows what this folkloric guy sees in Bourdieu . . .?" The second reaction is to directly assert the universal scope of theory—"see how universal theory is: every intellectual from Paris to Chechnya and Abkhazia can debate Bourdieu's concepts . . ." The true task, of course, is to avoid both these options and to assert the universality of a theory as the result of hard theoretical work and struggle, a struggle that is not external to theory: the point is not (only) that Shanib had to do a lot of work to break the constraints of his local context and grasp Bourdieu—this appropriation of Bourdieu by an Abkhazian intellectual also affects the substance of the theory itself, transposing it into a different universe. Did—*mutatis mutandis*—Lenin not do something similar with Marx? The shift of Mao with regard to Lenin *and* Stalin concerns the relationship between the working class and the peasantry. Both Lenin and Stalin were deeply distrustful of the peasantry, they saw breaking the inertia of the peasantry as one of the main tasks of Soviet power: to uproot their substantial attachment to land, to "proletarianize" them and thus fully expose them to the dynamics of modernization—in clear contrast to Mao who, as we have noted, in his critical notes on Stalin's *Economic Problems of Socialism in the USSR* (from 1958) remarked that "Stalin's point of view [. . .] is almost altogether wrong. The basic error is mistrust of the peasants." The theoretical and political consequences of this shift are properly shattering: they imply no less than a thorough reworking of Marx's Hegelian notion of the position of the proletariat as that of "substanceless subjectivity," of those who are reduced to the abyss of their subjectivity.

As is well known by those who still remember their Marxism, the ambiguous central point of its theoretical structure concerns its premise that capitalism itself creates the conditions for its transcendence through proletarian revolution—how are we to read this? Is it to be read in a linear evolutionary way: revolution should take place when capitalism fully develops all its potential and exhausts all its possibilities, the mythical point at which it confronts its central antagonism ("contradiction") at its purest, in its naked form? And is it enough to add the "subjective" aspect and to emphasize that the working class should not just sit and wait for the "ripe moment," but "educate" itself through long struggle? As is also well known, Lenin's theory of the "weakest link in the chain" is a kind of compromise solution: although it accepts that the first revolution can take place, not in the most developed country, but in a country in which the antagonisms of capitalist development are most aggravated, even if it is less developed (Russia, which combined concentrated modern capitalist-industrial islands with agrarian backwardness and pre-democratic authoritarian government), it still perceived the October Revolution as a risky breakthrough which could only succeed if it was soon accompanied by a large-scale Western European revolution (all eyes were focused on Germany in this respect). The radical abandonment of this model occurred only with Mao, for whom the proletarian revolution should take place in the less developed part of the world, among the wide masses of the Third World's impoverished peasants, workers, and even the "patriotic bourgeoisie," who are exposed to the aftershocks of capitalist globalization, organizing their rage and despair. In a total reversal (perversion even) of Marx's model, the class struggle is thus reformulated as the struggle between First World "bourgeois nations" and Third World "proletarian nations." The paradox here is properly dialectical, perhaps in the ultimate application of Mao's teaching on contradictions: its very underdevelopment (and thus "unripeness" for the revolution) makes a country "ripe" for the revolution. Since, however, such "unripe" economic conditions do not allow the construction of properly post-capitalist socialism, the necessary correlate is the assertion of the "primacy of politics over economics": the victorious revolutionary subject does not act as an instrument of economic necessity, liberating its potential whose further development is thwarted by capitalist contradictions; it is, rather, a voluntarist agent which acts *against* "spontaneous" economic necessity, imposing its vision on reality through revolutionary terror.

One should bear in mind here the fundamental lesson of Hegelian "concrete universality": universal necessity is not a teleological force which, operative from the outset, pulls the strings and runs the process, guaranteeing its happy outcome; on the contrary, this universal necessity is always retroactive, it emerges out of the radical contingency of the process and signals the moment of the contingency's self-*Aufhebung*. One should thus say that, once the (contingent) passage from Leninism to Maoism took place, it cannot but appear as "necessary," that is, one can (re)construct the "inner necessity" of Maoism as the next "stage" of the development of Marxism. In order to grasp this reversal of contingency into necessity, one should leave behind the standard linear historical time structured as the realization of possibilities (at the temporal moment X, there are multiple possible directions history can take, and what actually takes place is the realization of one of the possibilities): what this linear time is unable to grasp is the paradox of a contingent actual emergency which retroactively creates its own possibility: only when the thing takes place can we "see" how it was possible. The rather tiresome debate about the origins of Maoism (or Stalinism) oscillates around three main options: (1) the "hard" anti-Communists and the "hard" partisans of Stalinism claim that there is a direct immanent logic which leads from Marx to Lenin and from Lenin to Stalin (and then from Stalin to Mao); (2) the "soft" critics claim that the Stalinist (or, prior to it, Leninist) turn is one of the historical possibilities present in Marx's theoretical structure—it could have turned out otherwise, but the Stalinist catastrophe is nonetheless inscribed as an option into the original theory itself; (3) finally, the defenders of the purity of the "original teaching of Marx" dismiss Stalinism (or indeed Leninism) as a simple distortion, betrayal, insisting on the radical break between the two: Lenin and/or Stalin simply "kidnapped" Marx's theory and used it for purposes totally at odds with Marx. One should reject all three versions as based on the same underlying linear-historicist notion of temporality, and opt for the fourth version, beyond the false question "to what extent was Marx responsible for the Stalinist catastrophe?": Marx *is* entirely responsible, but *retroactively*, that is, the same holds for Stalin as for Kafka in Borges's famous formulation: they both created their own predecessors.

This is the movement of "concrete universality," this radical "transubstantiation" through which the original theory has to reinvent itself in a new context: only by way of surviving this transplantation can it emerge as effectively universal. And, of course, the point is not that we are dealing here with the pseudo-Hegelian process of "alienation" and "dis-alienation," of how the original theory is "alienated" and then has to incorporate the foreign context, reappropriate it, subordinate it to itself: what such a pseudo-Hegelian notion misses is the way this violent transplantation into a new context radically affects the original theory itself, so that, when this theory "returns to itself in its otherness" (reinvents itself in the foreign context), its very substance changes—and yet this shift is not just the reaction to an external shock, it remains an inherent transformation of the *same* theory of the overcoming of capitalism. This is how capitalism is a "concrete universality": it is not the question of isolating what all the particular forms of capitalism have in common, their shared universal features, but of grasping this matrix as a positive force in itself, as something which all actual particular forms try to counteract, the destructive effects of which they strive to contain.

The limits of Mao's dialectics

The most reliable sign of capitalism's ideological triumph is the virtual disappearance of the very term over the last two or three decades: in the 1980s, "virtually no one, with the exception of a few allegedly archaic Marxists (an 'endangered species'), referred to capitalism any longer. The term was simply struck from the vocabulary of politicians, trade unionists, writers and journalists—not to mention social scientists, who had consigned it to historical oblivion."[42] So what about the upsurge of the anti-globalization movement over the last few years? Does it not clearly contradict this diagnostic? Not at all: a close examination quickly demonstrates that this movement also succumbs to "the temptation to transform a critique of capitalism itself (centred on economic mechanisms, forms of work organization, and profit extraction) into a critique of 'imperialism'."[43] In this way, when one talks about "globalization and its agents," the enemy is externalized (often in the form of vulgar anti-Americanism). From this perspective, the main task today is to fight "the American empire," and any ally is fine if it is anti-American, thus unbridled Chinese "Communist" capitalism, violent Islamicist anti-modernism, as well as the obscene Lukashenko regime in Belarus (see Chavez's visit to Belarus in July 2006), may appear as progressive anti-globalist comrades-in-arms . . . What we have here is thus another version of the ill-famed notion of "alternative modernity": instead of the critique of capitalism as such, instead of confronting its basic mechanism, we have the critique of the imperialist "excess," with the (tacit) idea of mobilizing capitalist mechanisms within another, more "progressive," framework.

This is how one should approach what is arguably Mao's central contribution to Marxist philosophy, his elaborations on the notion of contradiction: one should not dismiss them as a worthless philosophical regression (which, as one can easily demonstrate, relies on a vague notion of "contradiction" which simply means "struggle of opposing tendencies"). The main thesis of his great text "On Contradiction" regarding the two facets of contradiction, "the principal and the non-principal contradictions in a process, and the principal and the non-principal aspects of a contradiction," deserves a close reading. Mao's reproach to the "dogmatic Marxists" is that they "do not understand that it is precisely in the particularity of contradiction that the universality of contradiction resides":

> For instance, in capitalist society the two forces in contradiction, the proletariat and the bourgeoisie, form the principal contradiction. The other contradictions, such as those between the remnant feudal class and the bourgeoisie, between the peasant petty bourgeoisie and the bourgeoisie, between the proletariat and the peasant petty bourgeoisie, between the non-monopoly capitalists and the monopoly capitalists, between bourgeois democracy and bourgeois fascism, among the capitalist countries and between imperialism and the colonies, are all determined or influenced by this principal contradiction.
>
> When imperialism launches a war of aggression against such a country, all its various classes, except for some traitors, can temporarily unite in a national war against imperialism. At such a time, the contradiction between imperialism and the country concerned becomes the principal contradiction, while all the contradictions among the various classes within the country (including what was the principal contradiction, between the feudal system and the great masses of the people) are temporarily relegated to a secondary and subordinate position.[44]

This is Mao's key point: the principal (universal) contradiction does not overlap with the contradiction which should be treated as dominant in a particular situation—the universal dimension literally *resides* in this particular contradiction. In each concrete situation, a different "particular" contradiction is the predominant one, in the precise sense that, in order to win the battle for the resolution of the principal contradiction, one should treat a particular contradiction as the predominant one, to which all other struggles should be subordinated. In China under the Japanese occupation, patriotic unity against the Japanese was the predominant feature if Communists wanted to win in the class struggle—*in these conditions, any direct focus on class struggle harms the class struggle itself.* (Therein, perhaps, resides the main feature of "dogmatic opportunism": to insist on the centrality of the principal contradiction at the wrong moment.)

The further key point concerns the principal *aspect* of a contradiction; for example, with regard to the contradiction between the productive forces and the relations of production,

> the productive forces, practice and the economic base generally play the principal and decisive role; whoever denies this is not a materialist. But it must also be admitted that in certain conditions, such aspects as the relations of production, theory and the superstructure in turn manifest themselves in the principal and decisive role. When it is impossible for the productive forces to develop without a change in the relations of production, then the change in the relations of production plays the principal and decisive role.[45]

The political stakes of this debate are decisive: Mao's aim is to assert the key role, in the political struggle, of what the Marxist tradition usually refers to as the "subjective factor"—theory, the superstructure. This is what, according to Mao, Stalin neglected:

> Stalin's [*Economic Problems of Socialism in the USSR*] from first to last says nothing about the superstructure. It is not concerned with people; it considers things, not people. [. . .] [It speaks] only of the production relations, not of the superstructure nor politics, nor the role of the people. Communism cannot be reached unless there is a communist movement.[46]

Alain Badiou, a true Maoist here, applies this to the contemporary constellation, avoiding the focus on the anti-capitalist struggle, even ridiculing its main form today (the anti-globalization movement), and defining the emancipatory struggle in strictly political terms, as the struggle against (liberal) democracy, today's predominant ideologico-political form. "Today the enemy is not called Empire or Capital. It's called Democracy."[47] What, today, prevents the radical questioning of capitalism itself is precisely *the belief in the democratic form of the struggle against capitalism.* Lenin's stance against "economism" as well as against "pure" politics is crucial today, apropos the split attitude towards the economy in (what remains of) the Left: on the one hand, the "pure politicians" abandon the economy as the site of struggle and intervention; on the other hand, the "economists," fascinated by the functioning of the contemporary global economy, preclude any possibility of a political intervention proper. With regard to this split, today, more than ever, we should return to Lenin: yes, the economy is the key domain, the battle will be decided there, one has to break the spell of global capitalism—*but* the intervention should be properly *political*, not economic. Today, when everyone is "anti-capitalist," up to and including the Hollywood "socio-critical" conspiracy movies (from *The Enemy of the State* to *The Insider*) in which the enemy are the big corporations with their ruthless pursuit of profit, the signifier "anti-capitalism" has lost its subversive sting. What one should problematize is the self-evident opposite of this "anti-capitalism": the trust in democracy by honest Americans who break up the conspiracy. *This* is the hard kernel of today's global capitalist universe, its true Master-Signifier: democracy itself.[48]

Mao's further elaboration on the notion of contradiction in his "On the Correct Handling of Contradictions Among the People" (1957) also cannot be reduced to its best-known feature, the rather common-sense point of distinguishing between the antagonistic and the non-antagonistic contradictions:

> The contradictions between ourselves and the enemy are antagonistic contradictions. Within the ranks of the people, the contradictions among the working people are non-antagonistic, while those between the exploited and the exploiting classes have a non-antagonistic as well as an antagonistic aspect. [. . .] [U]nder the people's democratic dictatorship two different methods, one dictatorial and the other democratic, should be used to resolve the two types of contradictions which differ in nature—those between ourselves and the enemy and those among the people.[49]

One should always read this distinction together with its more "ominous" supplement, a warning that the two aspects may overlap: "In ordinary circumstances, contradictions among the people are not antagonistic. But if they are not handled properly, or if we relax our vigilance and lower our guard, antagonism may arise." Democratic dialogue, the peaceful coexistence of different orientations in the working class, is not something that is simply given, a natural state of things, it is something that is won and sustained by vigilance and struggle. Here, too, struggle has priority over unity: the very space of unity has to be won through struggle.

So what are we to do with these elaborations? One should be very precise in diagnosing, at the very abstract level of theory, where Mao was right and where he was wrong. Mao was right in rejecting the standard notion of "dialectical synthesis" as the "reconciliation" of the opposites, as a higher unity which encompasses their struggle; he was wrong in formulating this rejection, this insistence on the priority of struggle, of division, over every synthesis or unity, in terms of a general cosmology–ontology of the "eternal struggle of opposites"—this is why he got caught up in the simplistic, properly *non-dialectical*, notion of the "bad infinity" of struggle. Mao clearly regresses here to primitive pagan "wisdoms" on how every creature, every determinate form of life, sooner or later meets its end: "One thing destroys another, things emerge, develop, and are destroyed, everywhere is like this. If things are not destroyed by others, then they destroy themselves." One should give Mao his due at this level: he pushes to the end in this direction, applying this principle to communism itself—see the following passage, in which Mao accomplishes a gigantic ontological "leap forward" from the division of the atomic nucleus into protons, anti-protons, and so on, to the inevitable division of communism into stages:

> I don't believe that communism will not be divided into stages, and that there will be no qualitative changes. Lenin said that all things can be divided. He gave the atom as an example, and said that not only can the atom be divided, but the electron, too, can be divided. Formerly, however, it was held that it could not be divided; the branch of science devoted to splitting the atomic nucleus is still very young, only twenty or thirty years old. In recent decades, the scientists have resolved the atomic nucleus into its constituents, such as protons, anti-protons, neutrons, anti-neutrons, mesons and anti-mesons.[50]

He even goes a step further and moves beyond humanity itself, forecasting, in a proto-Nietzschean way, the "overcoming" of man—

> The life of dialectics is the continuous movement toward opposites. Mankind will also finally meet its doom. When the theologians talk about doomsday, they are pessimistic and terrify people. We say the

end of mankind is something which will produce something more advanced than mankind. Mankind is still in its infancy.[51]

Moreover, he envisages the rise of (some) animals themselves to the (what we consider today as exclusively human) level of consciousness:

In the future, animals will continue to develop. I don't believe that men alone are capable of having two hands. Can't horses, cows, sheep evolve? Can only monkeys evolve? And can it be, moreover, that of all the monkeys only one species can evolve, and all the others are incapable of evolving? In a million years, ten million years, will horses, cows and sheep still be the same as those today? I think they will continue to change. Horses, cows, sheep, and insects will all change.[52]

Two things should be added to this "cosmic perspective": first, one should remember that Mao is here talking to the inner circle of party ideologists. This is what accounts for the tone of sharing a secret not to be rendered public, as if Mao is divulging his "secret teaching"—and, in fact, Mao's speculations closely echo so-called "biocosmism," the strange combination of vulgar materialism and Gnostic spirituality which formed an occult shadow ideology, the obscene secret teaching, of Soviet Marxism. Repressed from public sight during the main period of the Soviet state, biocosmism was openly propagated only in the first and in the last two decades of Soviet rule; its main theses were: the goals of religion (collective paradise, the overcoming of all suffering, full individual immortality, the resurrection of the dead, the victory over time and death, the conquest of space far beyond the solar system) can be realized in terrestrial life through the development of modern science and technology. In the future, not only will sexual difference be abolished, with the rise of chaste post-humans reproducing themselves through direct biotechnical reproduction; it will also be possible to resurrect all the dead of the past (establishing their biological formulae through their remains and then re-engendering them—DNA had not yet been heard of . . .), thus even erasing all past injustices, "undoing" past suffering and destruction. In this bright biopolitical Communist future, not only humans, but also animals, all living beings, will participate in a directly collectivized Reason of the cosmos . . . Whatever one may say against Lenin's ruthless critique of Maxim Gorky's "God-building" (*bogogradi-telk'stvo*), the direct deification of man, one should bear in mind that

Gorky himself collaborated with biocosmists. It is interesting to note resemblances between this "biocosmism" and contemporary techno-gnosis.

Second, this "cosmic perspective" is for Mao not just an irrelevant philosophical caveat; it has precise ethico-political consequences. When Mao highhandedly dismisses the threat of the atomic bomb, he is not downplaying the scope of the danger—he is fully aware that such a war may led to the extinction of humanity as such, so, to justify his defiance, he has to adopt the "cosmic perspective" from which the end of life on Earth "would hardly mean anything to the universe as a whole." This "cosmic perspective" also grounds Mao's dismissive attitude towards the human costs of economic and political endeavors. If one is to believe the latest biography of Mao,[53] he caused the greatest famine in history by exporting food to Russia to buy atomic and other types of arms: 38 million people starved or were slave-driven to death in 1958–61. Mao supposedly knew exactly what was happening, saying: "half of China may well have to die." This is the instrumental attitude at its most radical: killing as part of a ruthless attempt to realize a goal, reducing people to disposable means—and what one should bear in mind is that the Nazi Holocaust was *not* the same: the murder of the Jews was not part of a rational strategy, but was autotelic, a meticulously planned "irrational" excess (recall the deportation of the last Jews from the Greek islands in 1944, just before the German retreat, or the massive use of trains for transporting Jews instead of war materiel in 1944). This is why Hei-degger was wrong when he reduced the Holocaust to the industrial production of corpses: it was *not* that, Stalinist Communism rather could be characterized better in this way.[54]

The conceptual consequence of this "bad infinity" that pertains to vulgar evolutionism is Mao's consistent rejection of the "negation of the negation" as a universal dialectical law. Thus the explicit polemic against Engels (incidentally, following Stalin who, in his "On Dialectical and Historical Materialism," also does not mention the "negation of the negation" among the "four main features of Marxist dialectics"):

Engels talked about the three categories, but as for me I don't believe in two of those categories. (The unity of opposites is the most basic law, the transformation of quality and quantity into one another is the unity of the opposites quality and quantity, and the negation of the negation does not exist at all.) [. . .] There is no such thing as the negation of the negation. Affirmation, negation, affirmation, negation . . . in the development of things, every link in the chain of events is both affirmation and negation. Slave-holding society negated primitive society, but with reference to feudal society it constituted, in turn, the affirmation. Feudal society constituted the negation in relation to slave-holding society but it was in turn the affirmation with reference to capitalist society. Capitalist society was the negation in relation to feudal society, but it is, in turn, the affirmation in relation to socialist society.[55]

Along similar lines, Mao scathingly dismissed the category of the "dialectical synthesis" of opposites, promoting his own version of "negative dialectics"—every synthesis was for him ultimately what Adorno in his critique of Lukács called "*erpreßte Versöhnung*" (enforced reconciliation), at best a momentary pause in the ongoing struggle, which occurs not when the opposites are united, but when one side simply wins over the other:

> What is synthesis? You have all witnessed how the two opposites, the Kuomintang and the Communist Party, were synthesized on the mainland. The synthesis took place like this: their armies came, and we devoured them, we ate them bite by bite. [. . .] One thing eating another, big fish eating little fish, this is synthesis. It has never been put like this in books. I have never put it this way in my books either. For his part, Yang Hsien-chen believes that two combine into one, and that synthesis is the indissoluble tie between two opposites. What indissoluble ties are there in this world? Things may be tied, but in the end they must be severed. There is nothing which cannot be severed.[56]

(Note, again, the tone of sharing a secret not to be rendered public, the cruel-realistic lesson that undermines the happy public optimism . . .) This was at the core of the famous debate, in the late 1950s, about the One and the Two (are the Two united into One, or is the One divided into Two?): "In any given thing, the unity of opposites is conditional, temporary and transitory, and hence relative, whereas the struggle of opposites is absolute." This brings us to what one is tempted to call Mao's ethico-political injunction—to paraphrase the last words of Beckett's *L'Innomable*: "in the silence you don't know, you must go on severing, I can't go on, I'll go on severing."[57] The paradox of Mao's radical politics of the eternally ongoing division which never reaches the final point of peace is that it rejoins its opposite, the rightist social-democratic revision whose founder Bernstein proposed the well-known formula: "The goal is nothing, the movement is everything."

So where does Mao fall short here? In the way he *opposes* this injunction to sever, to divide, to dialectical synthesis.

When Mao mockingly refers to "synthesizing" as the destruction of the enemy or his subordination, his mistake resides in this very mocking attitude — he does not see that this *is* the true Hegelian synthesis . . . After all, what is the Hegelian "negation of the negation"? First, the old order is negated within its own ideologico-political form; then, this form itself has to be negated. Those who vacillate, those who are afraid to take the second step of overcoming this form itself, are those who (to repeat Robespierre) want a "revolution without a revolution" — and Lenin displays all the strength of his "hermeneutics of suspicion" in discerning the different forms of this retreat. The true victory (the true "negation of the negation") occurs when the enemy talks your language. In this sense, a true victory is a victory in defeat: it occurs when one's specific message is accepted as a universal framework, even by the enemy. For example, in the case of rational science versus belief, the true victory of science takes place when the Church starts to defend itself in the language of science. Or, in the contemporary politics of the United Kingdom, as many a perspicuous commentator has observed, the Thatcher revolution was in itself chaotic, impulsive, marked by unpredictable contingencies, and it was only the "Third Way" Blairite government that was able to *institutionalize* it, to stabilize it into new institutional forms, or, to put it in Hegelese, to raise (what first appeared as) a contingency, a historical accident, into necessity. In this sense, Blair repeated Thatcherism, elevating it into a concept, in the same way that, for Hegel, Augustus repeated Caesar, transforming–sublating a (contingent) personal name into a concept, a title. Thatcher was not a Thatcherite, she was just herself — it was only Blair (more than John Major) who truly forged Thatcherism as a notion. The dialectical irony of history is that only a (nominal) ideologico-political enemy can do this to you, can elevate you into a concept — the empirical instigator has to be knocked off (Julius Caesar had to be murdered, Thatcher had to be ignominiously deposed).

This is the surprising lesson of the last decades, the lesson of West European Third Way social-democracy, but also the lesson of the Chinese Communists presiding over what is arguably the most explosive development of capitalism in the entirety of human history: *we can do it better*. Recall the classical Marxist account of the overcoming of capitalism: capitalism unleashed the breathtaking dynamics of self-enhancing productivity—in capitalism, "all that is solid melts into air," capitalism is the greatest revolutionizer in the history of humanity; on the other hand, this capitalist dynamic is propelled by its own inner obstacle or antagonism—the ultimate limit of capitalism (of capitalist self-propelling productivity) is Capital itself, that is, capitalism's incessant development and revolutionizing of its own material conditions, the mad dance of its unconditional spiral of productivity, is ultimately nothing but a desperate *fuite en avant* to escape its own debilitating inherent contradictions . . . Marx's fundamental mistake was here to conclude, from these insights, that a new, higher social order (communism) was possible, an order that would not only maintain, but even raise to a higher degree and fully release the potential of the upward spiral of productivity without it being thwarted by socially destructive economic crises. In short, what Marx overlooked is that, to put it in standard Derridean terms, this inherent obstacle/antagonism as the "condition of impossibility" of the full deployment of the productive forces is simultaneously its "condition of possibility": if we abolish the obstacle, the inherent contradiction of capitalism, we do not get the fully unleashed drive finally freed from its shackles, but rather we lose precisely this very productivity that seemed to be simultaneously generated and stifled by capitalism, for it simply dissipates . . . And it is as if this logic of the "obstacle as a positive condition" which underlay the failure of socialist attempts to overcome capitalism, is now returning with a vengeance in capitalism itself: capitalism can fully thrive not in the unencumbered reign of the market, but only when an obstacle (from minimal welfare-state intervention, up to and including the direct political rule of the Communist Party, as in the case of China) constrains its unimpeded rampage.

So, ironically, *this* is the "synthesis" of capitalism and Communism in Mao's sense: in a unique kind of poetic justice on a historic scale, it was capitalism which "synthetized" Maoist Communism. The key new feature in China over the last few years has been the emergence of a large-scale workers' movement, protesting against the work conditions which are the price China pays for rapidly becoming the world's foremost manufacturing power, a movement which has faced brutal repression—new proof, if it is still needed, that China is today the ideal capitalist state: freedom for capital, with the state doing the "dirty job" of controlling the workers. China as the emerging superpower of the twenty-first century thus seems to embody a new kind of capitalism: disregard for ecological consequences, disdain for workers' rights, everything subordinated to the ruthless drive to develop and become the new world force. The big question is: what will the Chinese do with regard to the biogenetic revolution? Is it not a safe wager that they will hurl themselves into unconstrained genetic manipulation of plants, animals, and humans, bypassing all our "Western" moral prejudices and limitations?

This is the ultimate price for Mao's theoretical mistake of rejecting the "negation of the negation," of his failure to grasp how the "negation of the negation" is not a compromise between a position and its excessively radical negation, but, on the contrary, the only true negation.[58] And it is because Mao is unable to theoretically formulate this self-relating negation of form itself that he gets caught in the "bad infinity" of endless negating, scissions into two, subdivision . . . In Hegelese, Mao's dialectic remains at the level of Understanding, of fixed notional oppositions; it is unable to formulate the properly dialectical self-relating of notional determinations. It is this "serious mistake" (to use a Stalinist term) which led Mao, when he was courageous enough to draw all the consequences from his stances, to reach a properly nonsensical conclusion that, in order to invigorate class struggle, one should directly open up the field to the enemy:

> Let them go in for capitalism. Society is very complex. If one only goes in for socialism and not for capitalism, isn't that too simple? Wouldn't we then lack the unity of opposites, and be merely one-sided? Let them do it. Let them attack us madly, demonstrate in the streets, take up arms to rebel—I approve all of these things. Society is very complex, there is not a single commune, a single *hsien*, a single department of the Central Committee, which one cannot divide into two.[59]

This notion of dialectics provides the basic matrix of Mao's politics, its repeated oscillation between "liberal" openness and then the "hard line" purge: first, let the proverbial "hundred flowers blossom," so that the enemies will actualize and fully express their reactionary hidden tendencies; then, once everyone's true positions are clearly articulated, engage in a ruthless struggle. Again, what Mao fails to do here is to proceed to the properly Hegelian "identity of opposites," and to recognize in the force the revolution is fighting and trying to annihilate *its own essence*, as is the case in G.K. Chesterton's *The Man Who Was Thursday*, in which the secret police chief organizing the search for the anarchist leader and this mysterious leader in the end appear to be one and the same person (God Himself, incidentally). And did Mao himself ultimately not play a similar role, that of a secular God who is at the same time the greatest rebel against himself? What this Chestertonian identity of the good Lord with the anarchist Rebel enacts is the logic of the social *carnival* brought to the extreme of self-reflexion: anarchist outbursts are not a transgression of Law and Order; in our societies, anarchism already *is* in power wearing the mask of Law and Order—our Justice is the travesty of Justice, the spectacle of Law and Order is an obscene carnival—the point made clear by arguably the greatest political poem in English, Shelley's "The Mask of Anarchy", which describes the obscene parade of the figures of power:

> And many more Destructions played
> In this ghastly masquerade,
> All disguised, even to the eyes,
> Like Bishops, lawyers, peers, or spies.

> Last came Anarchy: he rode
> On a white horse, splashed with blood;
> He was pale even to the lips,
> Like Death in the Apocalypse.

> And he wore a kingly crown;
> And in his grasp a sceptre shone;
> On his brow this mark I saw—
> "I AM GOD, AND KING, AND LAW!"

This identity is difficult to assume, even in cinema. Although *V for Vendetta* was praised (by none other than Toni Negri, among others) and, even more, criticized for its "radical"—pro-terrorist, even—stance, it does not push the logic to the end: it shirks from drawing the consequences from the parallels between Sutler and V, the totalitarian dictator and the anarchist-terrorist rebel. The "Norsefire" party is, we learn, the instigator of the terror it is fighting—but what about the further identity of Sutler and V? In both cases, we never see their real faces (except the scared Sutler at the very end, when he is about to die): Sutler we see only on TV screens, and V is a specialist in manipulating the screen. Furthermore, V's dead body is placed on the train packed with explosives, in a kind of Viking funeral strangely evoking the name of the ruling party: Norsefire. So when Evey is imprisoned and tortured by V in order to learn how to overcome fear and be free, is this not parallel to what Sutler does to the entire English population, terrorizing them so that they become free and rebel? But the film fails to draw this Chestertonian lesson of the ultimate *identity* between V and Sutler.[60]

Cultural revolution and power

Is not this Hegelian–Chestertonian shift from the criminal transgression of Law and Order to Law and Order itself as the highest criminal transgression directly enacted by Mao? This is why, while setting in motion and secretly pulling the strings of the self-destructive carnival, Mao nonetheless remained exempted from its process: at no moment was there ever a serious threat that Mao himself would be ritualistically deposed, treated as "yesterday a king, today a beggar"—he was not the traditional Master, but the "Lord of Misrule":

> In the European Middle Ages it was customary for great households to choose a "Lord of Misrule." The person chosen was expected to preside over the revels that briefly reversed or parodied the conventional social and economic hierarchies. [. . .] When the brief reign of misrule was over, the customary order of things would be restored: the Lords of Misrule would go back to their menial occupations, while their social superiors resumed their wonted status. [. . .] [S]ometimes the idea of Lord of Misrule would spill over from the realm of revel to the realm of politics. [. . .] [T]he apprentices took over from their guild masters for a reckless day or two, [. . .] gender roles were reversed for a day as the women took over the tasks and airs normally associated only with men.
>
> Chinese philosophers also loved the paradoxes of status reversed, the ways that wit or shame could deflate pretension and lead to sudden shifts of insight. [. . .] It was Mao's terrible accomplishment to seize on such insights from earlier Chinese philosophers, combine them with elements drawn from Western socialist thought, and to use both in tandem to prolong the limited concept of misrule into a long-drawn-out adventure in upheaval. To Mao, the former lords and masters

should never be allowed to return; he felt they were not his betters, and that society was liberated by their removal. He also thought the customary order of things should never be restored.[61]

Is, however, such a "terrible accomplishment" not the elementary gesture of every true revolutionary? Why make a revolution at all, if we do not think that "the customary order of things should never be restored?" What Mao did was to deprive the transgression of its ritualized, ludic character by taking it seriously: revolution is not just a temporary safety valve, a carnivalesque explosion destined to be followed by a process of sobering up. His problem was precisely the absence of the "negation of the negation," the failure of the attempts to transpose revolutionary negativity into a truly new positive order: all temporary stabilizations of the revolution amounted to just so many restorations of the old order, so that the only way to keep the revolution alive was the "spurious infinity" of endlessly repeated negation which reached its apex in the Great Cultural Revolution. In his *Logiques des mondes*, Badiou elaborated two subjective attitudes which counter an event: the "reactive subject" and the "obscure subject."[62] Insofar as one is ready to accept the risk of obscenely designating the reintroduction of capitalism into China a kind of event, one can claim that the Cultural Revolution and the revisionism identified by the name "Deng Xiaoping" stand, respectively, for the obscure and the reactive subject: Deng orchestrated the renaissance of capitalism in Communist China, while the Cultural Revolution aimed at its total annihilation and was as such precisely what Badiou calls *un désastre obscur*. Badiou himself concedes that the final result of the Cultural Revolution was negative:

> it all began when, between 1966 and 1968, saturating *in the real* the previous hypotheses, the Red Guardist high-school pupils and students, and then the workers of Shanghai, prescribed for the decades to come the *affirmative realization* of this beginning, of which they themselves, since their fury remained caught into what they were rising against, explored only the face of pure negation.[63]

One should take a step further here: what if the Cultural Revolution was "negative" not only in the sense of clearing the space and opening up the way for a new beginning, but *negative in itself*, negative as an index of its *impotence* in generating the New? This brings us back to the central weakness of Mao's thought and politics. Many a commentator has made ironic remarks about the apparent stylistic clumsiness of the titles of Soviet Communist books and articles, such as their tautological character, with the repeated use of the same word (like "revolutionary dynamics in the early stages of the Russian revolution," or "economic contradictions in the development of the Soviet economy"). However, what if this tautology points towards an awareness of the logic of betrayal best rendered by the classic reproach of Robespierre to the Dantonist opportunists: "What you want is a revolution without a revolution?" The tautological repetition thus signals the urge to repeat the negation, to relate it to itself—the true revolution is "revolution with a revolution," a revolution which, in its course, revolutionizes its own starting presuppositions. Hegel had a presentiment of this necessity when he wrote, "It is a modern folly to alter a corrupt ethical system, its constitution and legislation, without changing the religion, to have a revolution without a reformation."[64] He thereby announced the necessity of a cultural revolution as the condition for the successful social revolution. This, then, should be our precise version of Robespierre's retort: "What you want is a revolution without a reformation!" The problem with revolutionary attempts hitherto is thus not that they were "too extreme," but that they were *not radical enough*, that they did not question their own presuppositions. In a wonderful essay on *Chevengur*, Platonov's great peasant utopia written in 1927 and 1928 (just prior to forced collectivization), Fredric Jameson describes the two moments of the revolutionary process. It begins with the gesture of radical negativity:

> this first moment of world-reduction, of the destruction of the idols and the sweeping away of an old world in violence and pain, is itself the precondition for the reconstruction of something else. A first moment of absolute immanence is necessary, the blank slate of absolute peasant immanence or ignorance, before new and undreamed-of-sensations and feelings can come into being.[65]

Then follows the second stage, the invention of a new life—not only the construction of the new social reality in which our utopian dreams would be realized, but the (re)construction of these dreams themselves:

> a process that it would be too simple and misleading to call reconstruction or Utopian construction, since in effect it involves the very

effort to find a way to begin imagining Utopia to begin with. Perhaps in a more Western kind of psychoanalytic language [. . .] we might think of the new onset of the Utopian process as a kind of desiring to desire, a learning to desire, the invention of the desire called Utopia in the first place, along with new rules for the fantasizing or daydreaming of such a thing—a set of narrative protocols with no precedent in our previous literary institutions.[66]

The reference to psychoanalysis is here crucial and very precise: in a radical revolution, people not only "realize their old (emancipatory, etc.) dreams"; rather, they have to reinvent their very modes of dreaming. Is this not the exact formula of the link between the death drive and sublimation? Therein resides the necessity of the Cultural Revolution clearly grasped by Mao: as Herbert Marcuse put it in another marvelous circular formula from the same epoch, *freedom* (from ideological constraints, from the predominant mode of dreaming) *is the condition of liberation*, that is, if we only change reality in order to realize our dreams, and do not change these dreams themselves, sooner or later we regress back to the old reality. There is a Hegelian "positing of presuppositions" at work here: the hard work of liberation retroactively forms its own presupposition.

It is only this reference to what happens *after* the revolution, to the "morning after," that allows us to distinguish between pathetic libertarian outbursts and true revolutionary upheavals: the former lose their energy when one has to start the prosaic work of social reconstruction—at this point, lethargy sets in. In contrast, recall the immense creativity of the Jacobins just prior to their fall, the numerous proposals about a new civic religion, about how to defend the dignity of old people, and so on. Therein also resides the interest of reading the reports about daily life in the Soviet Union in the early 1920s, with the enthusiastic urge to invent new rules for quotidian existence: what are the new rules of courting? How should one celebrate a birthday? . . . [67]

At this point, the Cultural Revolution miserably failed. It is difficult to miss the irony of the fact that Badiou, who adamantly opposes the notion of the act as negative, locates the historical significance of the Maoist Cultural Revolution precisely in the negative gesture of signaling "the end of the party-state as the central production of revolutionary political activity"—it is here that he should have been consistent and denied the eventual status of the Cultural Revolution: far from being an Event, it was rather a supreme display of what Badiou likes to refer to as the "morbid death drive." Destroying old monuments was not a true negation of the past, it was, once again, rather an impotent *passage à l'acte* bearing witness to the failure to get rid of the past.

So, in a way, there is a kind of poetic justice in the fact that the final result of Mao's Cultural Revolution is today's unheard-of explosion of capitalist dynamics in China. That is to say, with the full deployment of capitalism, especially in today's "late capitalism," it is the predominant "normal" way of life which, in a way, becomes "carnivalized," with constant self-revolutionizing, reversals, crises, and reinventions. Brian Massumi clearly formulated this deadlock, which is based on the fact that contemporary capitalism has already overcome the logic of totalizing normality and adopted that of erratic excess:

> the more varied, and even erratic, the better. Normalcy starts to lose its hold. The regularities start to loosen. This loosening of normalcy is part of capitalism's dynamic. It's not a simple liberation. It's capitalism's own form of power. It's no longer disciplinary institutional power that defines everything, it's capitalism's power to produce variety—because markets get saturated. Produce variety and you produce a niche market. The oddest of affective tendencies are okay—as long as they pay. Capitalism starts intensifying or diversifying affect, but only in order to extract surplus-value. It hijacks affect in order to intensify profit potential. It literally valorises affect. The capitalist logic of surplus-value production starts to take over the relational field that is also the domain of political ecology, the ethical field of resistance to identity and predictable paths. It's very troubling and confusing, because it seems to me that there's been a certain kind of convergence between the dynamic of capitalist power and the dynamic of resistance.[68]

There *is* thus, beyond all cheap jibes and superficial analogies, a profound structural homology between Maoist permanent self-revolutionizing, the continuous struggle against the ossification of state structures, and the inherent dynamics of capitalism. One is tempted to paraphrase Brecht here, his "What is the robbing of a bank compared to the founding of a new bank?", yet again: what are the violent and destructive outbursts of a Red Guardist caught up in the Cultural Revolution compared to the true Cultural Revolution, the permanent dissolution of all life-forms necessitated by capitalist reproduction? Today, the tragedy of the Great Leap Forward itself is repeating itself as the farce of the capitalist Great Leap Forward into modernization, with the old slogan "an iron foundry in every village" re-emerging as "a skyscraper in every street."

It is the reign of contemporary global capitalism which is the true Lord of Misrule. No wonder, then, that, in order to curb the excess of social disintegration caused by the capitalist explosion, Chinese officials celebrate religions and traditional ideologies which sustain social stability, from Buddhism to Confucianism, that is, the very ideologies that were the target of the Cultural Revolution. In April 2006, Ye Xiaowen, China's top religious official, told the Xinhua News Agency that "religion is one of the important forces from which China draws strength," and he singled out Buddhism for its "unique role in promoting a harmonious society," the official formula for combining economic expansion with social development and care; the same week, China hosted the World Buddhist Forum.[69] The role of religion as a stabilizing force against capitalist turbulence is thus officially sanctioned—what bothers the Chinese authorities in the case of sects like Falun Gong is merely their independence from state control. (This is why one should also reject the argument that the Cultural Revolution strengthened socialist attitudes among the people and thus helped to curb the worst disintegrative excesses of today's capitalist development: quite the contrary, by undermining traditional stabilizing ideologies such as Confucianism, it rendered the people all the more vulnerable to the dizzying effects of capitalism.)

It is against this background that one should read the recent great campaign in China to resuscitate Marxism as effective state ideology (literally hundreds of millions of US dollars are being invested in this venture). Those who see in this operation a threat to capitalist liberalization, a sign that hardliners want to reassert their hegemony, are totally missing the point. Paradoxical as it might sound, this return of Marxism is the sign of the ultimate triumph of capitalism, the sign of its thoroughgoing *institutionalization*. (Recent legal measures which guarantee private property, hailed by the West as a crucial step towards legal stability, are part of the same thrust.) That is to say, what kind of Marxism is being offered as appropriate for today's China? Emphasis is on the distinction between Marxism and "leftism": Marxism is not the same as "leftism," a term which refers to any talk of workers' liberation, from free trade unions to the overcoming of capitalism. Based on the Marxist thesis of the development of the forces of production as the key factor of social progress, the main task of progressive forces is defined as that of creating the conditions for the continuing rapid "modernization," while avoiding all forms of instability, those caused by "leftism" as well as those caused by "rightism" (campaigns for multi-party democracy and so on), which will bring chaos and thus hinder the very modernization process. The conclusion is clear: in today's China, only the leading role of the Communist Party can sustain a rapid transformation of the conditions of social stability—the official (Confucian) term is that China should become a "harmonious society."

Consequently, to put it in the old Maoist terms, although it may appear that the main enemy is the "bourgeois" threat, the "principal contradiction" is, in the eyes of the ruling elite, the one between the existing "harmonious" order (unfettered capitalist development sustained by Communist Party rule) and the threat of workers' and peasants' revolts—which is why the recent strengthening of the oppressive apparatuses (the formation of special units of riot police to crush popular unrest, and so forth) is the actual social expression of what, in ideology, appears as a revival of Marxism. The problem with this revival is that, to put it in Kant's terms, it totally subordinates Marxism to the "private use of reason." For Kant, the public space of the "world civil society" designates the paradox of universal singularity, of a singular subject who, in a kind of short-circuit, bypassing the mediation of the particular, directly participates in the universal. This is what Kant, in the famous passage of his "What Is Enlightenment?", means by "public" as opposed to "private": "private" is not one's individual, as opposed to communal, ties, but the very communal-institutional order of one's particular identification; while "public" is the transnational universality of the exercise of Reason:

> The public use of one's reason must always be free, and it alone can bring about enlightenment among men. The private use of one's reason, on the other hand, may often be very narrowly restricted without particularly hindering the progress of enlightenment. By public use of one's reason I understand the use which a person makes of it as a scholar before the reading public. Private use I call that which one may make of it in a particular civil post or office which is entrusted to him.[70]

The paradox of Kant's formula "Think freely, but obey!" is thus that one participates in the universal dimension of the "public" sphere precisely as a singular individual extracted from or even opposed to one's substantial communal identification—one is truly universal only when radically singular, in the interstices of communal identities. Coming back to contemporary China: the artificially resuscitated form of Marxism is an exemplary case of the *private* use of reason: Marxism is mobilized not on account of its inherent universal truth, but in order to legitimize the present Chinese state interest of maintaining Communist Party power and thus guaranteeing stability in a period of fast-moving economic development—such a use of Marxism is "objectively cynical," with no cognitive value at all. The tragedy is that the Chinese state will sooner or later encounter the limits of the formula "capitalism with Confucian values," and, at that point, only an unconstrained "public use of reason" will be able to do the job of inventing new solutions. No wonder that, in today's China, the two terms, "public intellectual" and "civil society," are very negatively viewed in official eyes: although they are not explicitly prohibited, every intellectual knows that it is better to avoid them if one wants to remain on good terms with those in power. Anything (almost) is permitted—in closed academic debates, that is, as long as it does not reach the general public.

The paradoxical status of contemporary Chinese Marxism is conditioned by the fact that China in the twenty-first century is indeed no longer a totalitarian state, but rather what some would call an authoritarian state: there are passionate public debates, different opinions on key issues are openly defended, but within very precise limits (one cannot directly put into question the Communist Party's political monopoly); while one can draw attention to ecological problems, one is obliged to do it with great restraint, avoiding hot topics like the gigantic Yellow River dam; although one can write about the terrible conditions of unskilled manual workers, one should treat it as local anomaly and never propose the formation of any type of workers' defense organization such as independent labor unions; and one is often compelled to use a coded language, such as formulating a critique of socialism as advocacy of one socialist orientation against another one.

How, then, do leading Communist theorists react when confronted with the all too obvious contradiction: a Communist Party which still legitimizes itself in Marxist terms, but renounces Marxism's basic premise, that of workers' self-organization as a revolutionary force in order to overthrow capitalism? It is difficult to avoid the impression that all the resources of the legendary form of Chinese politeness are mobilized here:

it is considered impolite to directly raise (or insist on) these questions. This resort to politeness is necessary, since it is the only way to combine what cannot be combined: to enforce Marxism as official ideology while openly prohibiting its central axioms would cause the collapse of the entire ideological edifice, thereby rendering it meaningless. The result is thus that, while certain things are clearly prohibited, this prohibition cannot be publicly stated, but is itself prohibited: it is not merely prohibited to raise the question of workers' self-organization against capitalist exploitation as the central tenet of Marxism, it is also prohibited to publicly claim that it is prohibited to raise this question. (What one usually hears from theorists is a private admission that, of course, this is contradictory, but that, nonetheless, such a contradictory ideological edifice *works*, and works spectacularly: it is the only way to ensure fast economic growth and stability in China. Need we add that this is the "private use of reason" at its purest?)

This paradox is nicely rendered in the title of a recent report on China: "Even What's Secret Is a Secret in China."[71] Many troublesome intellectuals who report on political oppression, ecological catastrophes, rural poverty, and so on (for example, a Chinese woman who sent her husband, who lives abroad, clippings from a local Chinese newspaper), suffer years of imprisonment for betraying state secrets. However, "many of the laws and regulations that make up the state-secret regime are themselves classified, making it difficult for individuals to know how and when they're in violation." This secrecy of the prohibition itself serves two different purposes which should not be confused. Its commonly admitted role is that of universalizing guilt and fear: if you do not know what is prohibited, you cannot even know when you are violating a prohibition, which makes you potentially guilty all the time.

Of course, things are more precise here: except at the climax of the Stalinist purges when, effectively, everyone could be found guilty, people *do* know when they are doing something that will annoy those in power. The function of prohibiting prohibitions is thus not to give rise to "irrational" fears, but to let the potential dissidents (who think they can get away with their critical activity, since they are not breaking any laws, but only doing what laws guarantee them—freedom of opinion, and so on) know that, if they irk those in power too much, they can be punished at the latters' whim: "Don't provoke us, we can do whatever we want to you, no laws are protecting you here!" In ex-Yugoslavia, the infamous Article 133 of the penal code could always be invoked to prosecute writers and journalists. It criminalized any text that falsely presented the achievements of the socialist revolution or that *might arouse tension and discontent among the public* due to the way it dealt with political, social, or other topics. This last category is obviously not only infinitely plastic, but also conveniently self-referential: does not the very fact that you are accused by those in power obviously mean that you have *"aroused tension and discontent among the public"*? During those years, I remember asking a Slovene politician how he justified this law. He just smiled and, with a wink, told me: "Well, we have to have some tool to discipline when we want those who annoy us . . ."

But there is another function of prohibiting prohibitions which is no less crucial: that of *maintaining appearances*, and we all know how absolutely crucial appearances were under Stalinism: the Stalinist regime reacted with total panic whenever there was a threat that appearances would be disturbed (say, that some accident which made clear the failure of the regime might be reported in the public media: there were, in the Soviet media, no black chronicles, no reports on crimes and prostitution, not to mention workers' or other types of public protests). Which is why this prohibition of prohibitions is far from limited to Communist regimes: it is operative also in today's "permissive" capitalism. A "postmodern" boss insists that he is not a master but just a coordinator of our joint creative efforts, the first among equals; there should be no formalities among us, we should address him by his nickname, he shares a dirty joke with us . . . but during all this, he *remains our master*. In such a social link, relations of domination function through their denial: in order to be operative, they have to be ignored. We are not only obliged to obey our masters, we are also obliged to act as if we were free and equal, as if there was no domination—which, of course, makes the situation even more humiliating. Paradoxically, in such a situation, the first act of liberation is to demand from the master that he act like one: one should reject false collegiality from the master and insist that he treat us with cold distance, as a master. (The same goes for patriarchal domination over women: in modern societies, this domination is no longer admitted as such—which is why one of the subversive tactics of feminine resistance is mockingly to act as if subordinated . . .)

Things go even deeper here: the ultimate ground of this paradox is the shift in social relations that occurs with the rise of capitalism itself. One should apply here Marx's old formula of commodity fetishism in which relations between people appear as relations between things: this is why, in capitalism, we are *as people*, as persons, all equal, possessing the same dignity and freedom—the relations of domination, which were in previous societies directly hierarchical relations among persons, are now transposed onto relations between "things" (commodities). The logic of domination which necessarily denies itself as domination is inscribed into the very core of capitalist relations.

What one should bear in mind is that, while every social structure relies on certain exclusions and prohibitions, this exclusionary logic is always redoubled: not only is the subordinated Other (homosexuals, non-white races . . .) excluded/repressed, the excluding and repressive power itself relies on an excluded/repressed "obscene" content of its own (say, the exercise of power that legitimizes itself as legal, tolerant, Christian . . ., relies on a set of publicly disavowed obscene rituals of violent humiliation of the subordinated). More generally, we are dealing here with what one is tempted to call the ideological practice of disidentification. That is to say, one should turn around the standard notion of ideology as providing a firm identification for its subjects, constraining them to their "social roles": what if, at a different—but no less irrevocable and structurally necessary—level, ideology is effective precisely by way of constructing a space of false disidentification, of false distance towards the actual coordinates of the subject's social existence? Is this logic of disidentification not discernible from the most elementary case of "I am not only an American (husband, worker, Democrat, gay man . . .), but, beneath all these roles and masks, a human being, a complex and unique personality" (where the very distance towards the symbolic feature that determines my social place guarantees the effectiveness of this determination), up to the more complex case of cyberspace playing with one's multiple identities? The mystification operative in the perverse "just gaming" of cyberspace is thus double: not only are the games we are playing in it more serious than we tend to assume (is it not that, in the guise of a fiction, of "it's just a game," a subject can articulate and stage sadistic, "perverse," and so on, features of his symbolic identity that he would never be able to admit in his "real" intersubjective contacts?), but the opposite also holds, that is, the much-celebrated playing with multiple, shifting personae (freely constructed identities) tends to obfuscate (and thus falsely liberate us from) the constraints of social space in which our existence is caught.

This long detour brings us back to the paradox of contemporary Chinese Marxism: it is easy, from the standpoint of libertarian

Western Marxism, to mock this Marxism which dispenses with Marxism's central emancipatory premise (a truly decaffeinated Marxism, Marxism deprived of its subversive core). However, any direct ironic critique of this new Chinese state-ideology Marxism misses the point, which is that we are not dealing with a simple betrayal of Marxism, but, literally, with its symptom, a formula to resolve its inconsistency. There effectively was, in "original" Marxism itself, a dimension which potentially led to the enslavement of the workers to "progress" (the rapid development of the forces of production); while, under Stalinism, this "progress" was organized within the framework of the centralized state economy, today's China draws the logical conclusion that the most efficient motor of development are capitalist relations of production. The premise of classical Marxism (up to and including Toni Negri) was that "history is on our side": workers' resistance to capitalism "objectively" serves an even faster development of the forces of production; it is itself a sign that capitalism is no longer a motor, but more and more an obstacle to this development. What to do, then, when capitalism *de facto* proves itself as the most effective motor of social relations? The answer is the Chinese solution: to honestly admit that, in this phase of world history, we should fully embrace capitalism. Where Marxism enters is in the claim that only the leading role of the Communist Party can sustain such modernization and simultaneously maintain a "harmonious society," that is, prevent the social disintegration that characterizes Western liberal capitalism.

This capitalist reappropriation of revolutionary dynamics is not without its comic side effects. It was recently made public that, in order to conceptualize the Israeli Defense Forces' urban warfare against the Palestinians, the IDF military academies systematically refer to Deleuze and Guattari, especially to *Thousand Plateaus*, using it as "operational theory"—the catchwords used are "Formless Rival Entities," "Fractal Maneuver," "Velocity vs. Rhythms," "The Wahabi War Machine," "Postmodern Anarchists," "Nomadic Terrorists." One of the key distinctions they rely on is the one between "smooth" and "striated" space, which reflect the organizational concepts of the "war machine" and the "state apparatus." The IDF now often uses the term "to smoothe out space" when they want to refer to operation in a space as if it had no borders. Palestinian areas are thought of as "striated" in the sense that they are enclosed by fences, walls, ditches, roadblocks, and so on:

The attack conducted by units of the IDF on the city of Nablus in April 2002 was described by its commander, Brigadier-General Aviv Kokhavi, as "inverse geometry", which he explained as "the reorganization of the urban syntax by means of a series of micro-tactical actions". During the battle soldiers moved within the city across hundreds of metres of overground tunnels carved out through a dense and contiguous urban structure. Although several thousand soldiers and Palestinian guerrillas were manoeuvring simultaneously in the city, they were so "saturated" into the urban fabric that very few would have been visible from the air. Furthermore, they used none of the city's streets, roads, alleys or courtyards, or any of the external doors, internal stairwells and windows, but moved horizontally through walls and vertically through holes blasted in ceilings and floors. This form of movement, described by the military as "infestation", seeks to redefine inside as outside, and domestic interiors as thoroughfares. The IDF's strategy of "walking through walls" involves a conception of the city as not just the site but also the very medium of warfare, "a flexible, almost liquid medium that is forever contingent and in flux".[72]

So what follows from all this? Not, of course, the nonsensical accusation that Deleuze and Guattari are theorists of militaristic colonization—but the conclusion that the conceptual machinery articulated by Deleuze and Guattari, far from being simply "subversive," also fits the (military, economic, and ideologico-political) operational mode of contemporary capitalism. How, then, are we to revolutionize an order whose very principle is constant self-revolutionizing?

Although a failure, the Great Proletarian Cultural Revolution (GPCR) was unique in attacking the key point: not just the takeover of state power, but the new economic organization and reorganization of daily life. Its failure was precisely the failure to create a new form of everyday life: it remained a carnivalesque excess, with the state apparatus (under Zhou Enlai's control) guaranteeing the reproduction and maintenance of everyday life, of production. At the level of social reality, there is obviously some truth to the claim that the Cultural Revolution was triggered by Mao in order to re-establish his power (which had been seriously curtailed in the early 1960s, in the aftermath of the spectacular failure of the Great Leap Forward, when the majority of *nomenklatura* staged a silent inner-party coup against him); it is true that the Cultural Revolution brought incalculable suffering, that it cut deep wounds in the social fabric, that its story can be told as the story of fanatical crowds chanting slogans—however, this is simply not the entire story. In spite of (or, rather, *because of*) all its horrors, the Cultural Revolution undoubtedly did contain elements of an enacted utopia. At its very end, before the agitation was blocked by Mao himself (since he had by then achieved his goal of re-establishing his influence and getting rid of the top *nomenklatura* competitors), there was the "Shanghai Commune": one million workers who simply took the official slogans seriously, demanding the abolition of the state and even the party itself, and the direct communal organization of society. It is significant that it was at this very point that Mao ordered the army to intervene and to restore order. The paradox is that of a leader who triggers an uncontrolled upheaval, while trying to exert full personal power—the overlapping of extreme dictatorship and extreme emancipation of the masses. The argument that the GPCR was triggered by Mao in order to get rid of rivals in the inner-party struggle and reassert his authority, and that it was tamed by the intervention of the army the moment it threatened to spiral out of control, is irrelevant here, even if true: it simply confirms that the events acquired a dynamic of their own. This genuinely revolutionary aspect of the Cultural Revolution is sometimes admitted even by conservative critics compelled to take note of the "paradox" of the "totalitarian" leader teaching people to "think and act for themselves," to rebel and destroy the very apparatus of "totalitarian domination"—here is what Gordon Chang recently wrote in the conservative journal *Commentary*:

> Paradoxically, it was Mao himself, the great enslaver, who in his own way taught the Chinese people to think and act for themselves. In the Cultural Revolution, he urged tens of millions of radical youths [. . .] to go to every corner of the country to tear down ancient temples, destroy cultural relics, and denounce their elders, including not only mothers and fathers but also government officials and Communist-party members. [. . .] The Cultural Revolution may have been Mao's idea of ruining his enemies, but it became a frenzy that destroyed the fabric of society. As government broke down, its functions taken over by revolutionary committees and "people's communes," the strict restraints and repressive mechanisms of the state dissolved. People no longer had to wait for someone to instruct them what to do—Mao had told them they had "the right to rebel." For the radical young, this was a time of essentially unrestrained passion. In one magnificent

stroke, the Great Helmsman had delegitimized almost all forms of authority.[73]

What this means is that we can read the Cultural Revolution at two different levels. If we read it as a part of historical reality (being), we can easily submit it to a "dialectical" analysis which perceives the final outcome of a historical process as its "truth": the ultimate failure of the Cultural Revolution bears witness to the inherent inconsistency of the very project ("notion") of cultural revolution, it is the explication–deployment–actualization of these inconsistencies (in the same way that, for Marx, the vulgar, non-heroic, capitalist daily reality of profit-seeking is the "truth" of noble Jacobin revolutionary heroism). If, however, we analyze it as an Event, as an enactment of the eternal Idea of egalitarian justice, then the ultimate factual result of the Cultural Revolution, its catastrophic failure and reversal into the recent capitalist transformation, does not exhaust the real of the Cultural Revolution: the eternal Idea of the Cultural Revolution survives its defeat in socio-historical reality, it continues to lead an underground spectral life of the ghosts of failed utopias which haunt the future generations, patiently awaiting their next resurrection. This brings us back to Robespierre who expressed in a touching way the simple faith in the eternal Idea of freedom which persists through all defeats, without which, as was clear to Robespierre, a revolution "is just a noisy crime that destroys another crime," the faith most poignantly expressed in Robespierre's very last speech on 8 Thermidor 1794, the day before his arrest and execution:

> But there do exist, I can assure you, souls that are feeling and pure; it exists, that tender, imperious and irresistible passion, the torment and delight of magnanimous hearts; that deep horror of tyranny, that compassionate zeal for the oppressed, that sacred love for the home-land, that even more sublime and holy love for humanity, without which a great revolution is just a noisy crime that destroys another crime; it does exist, that generous ambition to establish here on earth the world's first Republic.[74]

Does the same not hold even more so for the last big installment in the life of this Idea, the Maoist Cultural Revolution—without this Idea which sustained revolutionary enthusiasm, the Cultural Revolution was to an even greater degree "just a noisy crime that destroys another crime"?

One should recall here Hegel's sublime words on the French Revolution from his *Lectures on the Philosophy of World History*:

> It has been said that the French revolution resulted from philosophy, and it is not without reason that philosophy has been called *Weltweisheit* [world wisdom]; for it is not only truth in and for itself, as the pure essence of things, but also truth in its living form as exhibited in the affairs of the world. We should not, therefore, contradict the assertion that the revolution received its first impulse from philosophy. [. . .] Never since the sun had stood in the firmament and the planets revolved around him had it been perceived that man's existence centers in his head, i.e. in thought, inspired by which he builds up the world of reality. [. . .] not until now had man advanced to the recognition of the principle that thought ought to govern spiritual reality. This was accordingly a glorious mental dawn. All thinking being shared in the jubilation of this epoch. Emotions of a lofty character stirred men's minds at that time; a spiritual enthusiasm thrilled through the world, as if the reconciliation between the divine and the secular was now first accomplished.[75]

This, of course, did not prevent Hegel from coldly analyzing the inner necessity of this explosion of abstract freedom in turning into its opposite, self-destructive revolutionary terror; however, one should never forget that Hegel's critique is immanent, accepting the basic principles of the French Revolution (and its key supplement, the Haitian Revolution). And one should proceed in exactly the same way apropos the October Revolution (and, later, the Chinese Revolution): it was, as Badiou pointed out, the first case in the entire history of humanity of the successful revolt of the exploited poor—they were the zero-level members of the new society, they set the standards. The revolution stabilized itself into a new social order, a new world was created and miraculously survived for decades, amid unthinkable economic and military pressure and isolation. This was effectively "a glorious mental dawn. All thinking being shared in the jubilation of this epoch." Against all hierarchical orders, egalitarian universality directly came to power.

There is a basic philosophical dilemma which underlies this alternative: it may seem that the only consistent Hegelian standpoint is the one which measures the Notion by the success or failure of its actualization, so that, in the perspective of the total mediation of the Essence by its Appearance, any transcendence of the Idea over its actualization is discredited. The consequence of this is that, if we insist on the eternal Idea which survives its historical defeat, this necessarily entails—in Hegelese—a regression from the level of the Notion as the fully actualized unity of Essence and Appearance, to the level of the Essence supposed to transcend its Appearance. Is it really so, however? One can also claim that the excess of the utopian Idea that survives its historical defeat does not contradict the total mediation of Idea and its Appearance: the basic Hegelian insight according to which the failure of reality to fully actualize an Idea is simultaneously the failure (limitation) of this Idea itself continues to hold. What one should simply add is that the gap that separates the Idea from its actualization signals a gap within this Idea itself. This is why the spectral Idea that continues to haunt historical reality *signals the falsity of the new historical reality itself, its inadequacy to its own Notion*—the failure of the Jacobin utopia, its actualization in utilitarian bourgeois reality, is simultaneously the limitation of this reality itself.

Consequently, one should invert the commonplace reading of Lacan's "Kant avec Sade" according to which Sadean perversion is the "truth" of Kant, more "radical" than Kant, that it draws out the consequences Kant himself did not have the courage to confront. But we would claim the contrary: Sadean perversion emerges as the result of the Kantian compromise, of Kant's avoidance of the consequences of his breakthrough. Sade is the *symptom* of Kant: while it is true that Kant retreated from drawing all the consequences of his ethical revolution, the space for the figure of Sade is opened up by this Kantian compromise, by his unwillingness to push through to the end, to retain full fidelity to his philosophical breakthrough. Far from being simply and directly "the truth of Kant," Sade is the symptom of Kant's betrayal of the truth of his own discovery—the obscene Sadean *jouisseur* is a stigma bearing witness to Kant's ethical compromise; the apparent "radicality" of this figure (the willingness of the Sadean hero to go to the end in his Will-to-Enjoy) is a mask of its exact opposite. In other words, the true horror is not a Sadean orgy, but the real core of the Kantean ethic itself—if we can be forgiven paraphrasing Brecht yet again, what is the miserable Evil of a Sadean group orgy in comparison with the "diabolical Evil" that pertains to a pure ethical act? And, *mutatis mutandis*, the same applies to the relationship between the Chinese Cultural Revolution and today's explosion of capitalist development as its "truth": this explosion is also a sign that Mao retreated from drawing all the consequences of the Cultural Revolution, that is, the space for the capitalist explosion was opened up by this compromise, by Mao's unwillingness to push through to the end, to retain full fidelity to the idea of the Cultural Revolution. And the lesson is, in both cases, that of Kant as well that of Mao, the same, namely that we take from Beckett's *Worstward Ho*: "Try again. Fail again. Fail better."[76]

5   Stalinism Revisited
Or, How Stalin Saved the Humanity of Man

The Stalinist cultural counter-revolution

A consistent conservative case can be made that, far from being the
greatest catastrophe that could have befallen Russia, Stalinism effectively
saved what we understand as the humanity of man. Crucial here is the
great shift of the early and mid–1930s from proletarian egalitarianism to
the full assertion of the Russian legacy. In the cultural sphere, figures
such as Pushkin and Tchaikovsky were elevated far above modernism;
traditional aesthetic norms of beauty were reasserted; homosexuality was
outlawed, sexual promiscuity condemned, and marriage proclaimed the
elementary cell of the new society. It was the end of the brief marriage of
convenience between Soviet power and the artistic and scientific modernists. In cinema, this passage is clearly discernible in the shift from
Eisenstein's silent films with their montage of "attractions" to his "organicist" sound films; in music, in the shift from Shostakovich's violent-
parodic provocative music with elements of circus and jazz from the
1920s to his return to more traditional forms in the late 1930s.

The standard reading of this shift sees it as the "cultural Thermidor,"
the betrayal of the authentic revolution. However, before accepting this
judgment at face value, one should take a closer look at the ideological
vision which sustained radical egalitarianism: we refer here again to so-
called "biocosmism."[1] A good example here is the following passage by
Trotsky:

> What is man? He is by no means a finished or harmonious being. No,
> he is still a highly awkward creature. Man, as an animal, has not
> evolved by plan but spontaneously, and has accumulated many contra-
> dictions. The question of how to educate and regulate, of how to
> improve and complete the physical and spiritual construction of man,

is a colossal problem which can only be understood on the basis of socialism. [. . .] To produce a new, "improved version" of man — that is the future task of communism. And for that we first have to find out everything about man, his anatomy, his physiology and that part of his physiology which is called his psychology. Man must look at himself and see himself as a raw material, or at best as a semi-manufactured product, and say: "At last, my dear *homo sapiens*, I will work on you."[2]

These were not just idiosyncratic theoretical principles, but expressions of a real mass movement in art, architecture, psychology, pedagogy, and organizational sciences, comprising hundreds of thousands of people. The officially supported cult of Taylorism, whose most radical exponent was Alexei Gastev, a Bolshevik engineer and poet who used the term "biomechanics" as early as 1922, explored the vision of society in which man and machine would merge. Gastev ran the Institute of Labor, which carried out experiments to train workers to act like machines. He saw the mechanization of man as the next step in evolution, envisaging

a utopia where "people" would be replaced by "proletarian units" identified by ciphers such as "A,B,C, or 325,075,0, and so on." [. . .] A "mechanized collectivism" would "take the place of the individual personality in the psychology of the proletariat." There would no longer be a need for emotions, and the human soul would no longer be measured "by a shout or a smile but by a pressure gauge or a speedometer."[3]

Is not this dream the first radical formulation of what, today, one usually calls biopolitics? Counterintuitive as this may sound, one can argue that this vision, had it really been imposed, would have been much more terrifying than Stalinism actually was. It was against this threat of full-scale modernist mechanization that Stalinist cultural politics reacted; it not only demanded a return to artistic forms that would be attractive to large crowds, but also — although it may appear cynical — the return to elementary traditional forms of morality. In the Stalinist show trials, the victims were held responsible for certain acts, forced to confess . . . in short, though it may appear obscene (and it was), they were treated as autonomous ethical subjects, not as objects of biopolitics. Against the utopia of "mechanized collectivism," high Stalinism of the 1930s stood for the return of ethics at its most violent, as an extreme measure to counteract the threat that traditional moral categories would be rendered meaningless, where unacceptable behavior would not be perceived as involving the subject's guilt, but as a malfunctioning measured by a special pressure gauge or a speedometer.

This is also why the imposition of "Socialist Realism" was sincerely welcomed by a large majority of people: it signaled that

> the regime [had] completely abandoned its commitment to the revolutionary idea of establishing a "proletarian" or "Soviet" form of culture that could be distinguished from the culture of the past. [. . .] Contemporary writers like Akhmatova could not find a publisher, but the complete works of Pushkin and Turgenev, Chekhov and Tolstoy (although not Dostoevsky) were issued in their millions as a new readership was introduced to them.[4]

This return to classical culture reached its peak in 1937, the centenary of Pushkin's death, when

> [t]he whole country was involved in festivities: small provincial theatres put on plays; schools organized special celebrations; Young Communists went on pilgrimages to places connected with the poet's life; factories organized study groups and clubs of "Pushkinists"; collective farms held Pushkin carnivals with figures dressed as characters from Pushkin's fairy tales.[5]

These facts are worth mentioning because they bring us to another paradox: how the very resistance to Stalinism, marginal and oppressed as it was, followed this cultural trend. That is to say, although hypocritical and censured, this massive reintroduction of the classical Russian cultural heritage was more than just a measure for enlightening the half-illiterate masses: the universe of great classics such as Pushkin and Tolstoy contained an entire vision of culture, with its own ethics of social responsibility, of solidarity with the oppressed against autocratic power:

> Dissidence in the USSR represented truthfulness, unexpurgated reality and ethical values—as against the fantasy reality of socialist realism and the pervasive falseness of Soviet public discourse with its concerted negation of traditional morality (an explicitly stated, indeed

fundamental, ingredient in the Soviet regime's forwarding of "revolutionary development").[6]

In this sense, Solzhenitsyn himself is the son of the Stalinist cultural politics of the 1930s. This is also why the "private" works of Shostakovich, full of melancholy, despair, and private anxieties (centered on his string quartets) are no less an organic part of the Stalinist culture than his great "public" works (centered in his officially celebrated symphonies, 5, 7, and 11).

And this brings us to the third paradox. Wilhelm Furtwängler remarked apropos Stravinsky's "Rite of Spring" that it shows the limitation of Russian spirituality: it exults in brilliant mechanic rhythmic explosions, but it cannot reach the level of organic living unity that characterizes German spirituality. The first irony is that the very same composers to which Furtwängler referred were perceived by the Russian traditionalists as Western modernizers endangering the Russian organic heritage. However, in a way, Furtwängler was right. Many Western travelers to Russia in the eighteenth and nineteenth centuries went there in search of an organic society, a living social Whole, as opposed to Western individualist societies which were held together by the external pressure of laws; they soon discovered that Russia was actually a vast chaotic empire, lacking precisely any inner organic form and therefore ruled by the iron hand of the brutal imperial autocracy. In other words, the notion of "old Russia" whose harmonious balance was disturbed by Western modernization was mythical: violent "modernism," the brutal imposition of a central order onto the chaotic texture of social life, is thus a key component of traditional Russian social identity—Stalin was correct to celebrate Ivan the Terrible as his precursor.

Is, then, the conclusion of this that, with regret, one should endorse Stalinism as the defense against a much worse threat? What about applying here too Lacan's motto *"le père ou le pire,"* and take the risk of *the choice of the worse*: what if the effective result of choosing to pursue to the end the biopolitical dream would have been something unpredictable that would have shaken the very coordinates of this dream?

A letter which did not reach its destination
(and thereby perhaps saved the world)

The Stalinist terror of the 1930s was a humanist terror: its adherence to a "humanist" core was not what constrained its horror, it was what sustained it, it was its inherent condition of possibility. What if the legacy of the humanist tradition resuscitated by high Stalinism not only created the ideological presuppositions for dissident resistance, but also "saved the world" in a quite literal way—namely, prevented global nuclear catastrophe during the Cuban missile crisis?

As far as one can reconstruct the events today, two things combined to facilitate the happy outcome. The first was polite tact, the rituals of polite feigned ignorance—if one is to believe recent revelations. Kennedy's stroke of genius, which was crucial for the resolution of the Cuban missile crisis, was to pretend that a key letter had *not* arrived at its destination, to act as if this letter did not exist—a stratagem which, of course, only worked because the sender (Khrushchev) participated in it. On Friday, October 26, 1962, a letter from Khrushchev to Kennedy confirms the offer previously made through intermediaries: the missiles would be removed if the US issued a pledge not to invade Cuba. On Saturday, October 27, before a US answer, another, harsher and more demanding, letter from Khrushchev arrived, adding the removal of US missiles from Turkey as a condition, and signaling a possible political coup in the Soviet Union. At 8.05 p.m. the same day, Kennedy sent a response to Khrushchev, informing him that he was accepting the proposal of October 26, that is, *acting as if the October 27 letter had never existed*. On Sunday, October 28, Kennedy received a letter from Khrushchev in which he agreed to the deal . . . The lesson of this is that, in such moments of crisis where the fate of everything hangs in the balance, saving appearances, politeness, the awareness that one is "playing a game," matters more than ever.

One can also claim that what triggered the crisis was a symmetrical fact, a letter which also did not arrive at its addressee, but, this time, because it was never sent. Soviet missiles were stationed in Cuba as the result of the secret mutual security pact between Cuba and the USSR; many observers (most notably Ted Sorensen) suggested that the US reaction would have been much less offensive if the mutual security pact had been made public in advance (as Castro had wanted, incidentally!). It was the secrecy on which Soviets had insisted that made the US believe that the missile emplacement could have no purpose other than to launch an attack upon the US: if the entire process of signing the pact and installing the missiles had been in the open and transparent, it would have been perceived as something much less threatening: not as the preparation of a real attack, but simply as demonstrative posturing which posed no real military threat.

This lesson was not learned by the US military establishment, which interpreted the peaceful resolution of the crisis in a quite different way.[7] Its opinion is best rendered by Raymond Garthoff, at the time an intelligence analyst in the State Department:

> If we have learned anything from this experience, it is that weakness, even only apparent weakness, invites Soviet transgression. At the same time, firmness in the last analysis will force the Soviets to back away from rash initiatives.[8]

The crisis is thus perceived as the eyeball-to-eyeball confrontation of two players, a macho game of "chicken," where the one with greater toughness, inflexibility, and resolve wins. This view, of course, does not fit reality: a whole series of details demonstrate Kennedy's flexibility and his concessions to the Soviet need to save face by way of salvaging something positive from the crisis. In order to buy some time and avoid a direct confrontation, he permitted on October 25 a Soviet tanker to proceed through the quarantine; on October 28, he ordered that no interview should be given and no statement made which would claim any kind of victory; furthermore, he made an offer of removing US missiles from Turkey, as well as a guarantee that the US would not invade Cuba, in exchange for which the Soviets would withdraw their missiles from Cuba.

The Soviet perception of the crisis was different: for them, it was not the threat of force that ended the crisis. The Soviet leadership believed the crisis had ended because both Soviet and US officials had realized they were at the brink and that the crisis was threatening to destroy humankind. They did not fear only for their immediate safety and were not worried merely about losing a battle in Cuba. Their fear was the fear of deciding the fate of millions of others, even of civilization itself. It was *this* fear, experienced by both sides at the peak of the crisis, which enabled them to reach a peaceful solution; and it was this fear which was at the very core of the famous exchange of letters between Khrushchev and Fidel Castro at the climax of the crisis.[9] In a letter to Khrushchev on October 26, Castro wrote that

> if the imperialists invade Cuba with the goal of occupying it, the danger that that aggressive policy poses for humanity is so great that following that event the Soviet Union must never allow the circum-

stances in which the imperialists could launch the first nuclear strike against it. I tell you this because I believe that the imperialists' aggressiveness is extremely dangerous and if they actually carry out the brutal act of invading Cuba in violation of international law and morality, that would be the moment to eliminate such danger forever through an act of clear legitimate defense, however harsh and terrible the solution would be, for there is no other.

Khrushchev answered Castro on October 30:

> In your cable of October 27 you proposed that we be the first to launch a nuclear strike against the territory of the enemy. You, of course, realize where that would have led. Rather than a simple strike, it would have been the start of a thermonuclear world war. Dear Comrade Fidel Castro, I consider this proposal of yours incorrect, although I understand your motivation. We have lived through the most serious moment when a nuclear world war could have broken out. Obviously, in that case, the United States would have sustained huge losses, but the Soviet Union and the whole socialist camp would have also suffered greatly. As far as Cuba is concerned, it would be difficult to say even in general terms what this would have meant for them. In the first place, Cuba would have been burned in the fire of war. There's no doubt that the Cuban people would have fought courageously or that they would have died heroically. But we are not struggling against imperialism in order to die, but to take advantage of all our possibilities, to lose less in the struggle and win more to overcome and achieve the victory of communism.

The essence of Khrushchev's argument can be best summed up by Neil Kinnock's argument for unilateral disarmament, when he was the Labour leader: "I am ready to die for my country, but I am not ready to let my country die for me." It is significant to note that, in spite of the "totalitarian" character of the Soviet regime, *this* fear was far more predominant in the Soviet leadership than in that of the US—so, perhaps, the time has come to rehabilitate Khrushchev, not Kennedy, as the real hero of the Cuban missile crisis. Castro answered Khrushchev on October 31:

> I realized when I wrote them that the words contained in my letter could be misinterpreted by you and that was what happened, perhaps

because you didn't read them carefully, perhaps because of the translation, perhaps because I meant to say so much in too few lines. However, I didn't hesitate to do it. Do you believe, Comrade Khrushchev, that we were selfishly thinking of ourselves, of our generous people willing to sacrifice themselves, and not at all in an unconscious manner but fully assured of the risk they ran? No, Comrade Khrushchev. Few times in history, and it could even be said that never before, because no people had ever faced such a tremendous danger, was a people so willing to fight and die with such a universal sense of duty. [. . .] We knew, and do not presume that we ignored it, that we would have been annihilated, as you insinuate in your letter, in the event of nuclear war. However, that didn't prompt us to ask you to withdraw the missiles, that didn't prompt us to ask you to yield. Do you believe that we wanted that war? But how could we prevent it if the invasion finally took place? [. . .] And if war had broken out, what could we do with the insane people who unleashed the war? You yourself have said that under current conditions such a war would inevitably have escalated quickly into a nuclear war. I understand that once aggression is unleashed, one shouldn't concede to the aggressor the privilege of deciding, moreover, when to use nuclear weapons. The destructive power of this weaponry is so great and the speed of its delivery so great that the aggressor would have a considerable initial advantage. And I did not suggest to you, Comrade Khrushchev, that the USSR should be the aggressor, because that would be more than incorrect, it would be immoral and contemptible on my part. But from the instant the imperialists attack Cuba and while there are Soviet armed forces stationed in Cuba to help in our defense in case of an attack from abroad, the imperialists would by this act become aggressors against Cuba and against the USSR, and we would respond with a strike that would annihilate them. [. . .] I did not suggest, Comrade Khrushchev, that in the midst of this crisis the Soviet Union should attack, which is what your letter seems to say; rather, that following an imperialist attack, the USSR should act without vacillation and should never make the mistake of allowing circumstances to develop in which the enemy makes the first nuclear strike against the USSR. And in this sense, Comrade Khrushchev, I maintain my point of view, because I understand it to be a true and just evaluation of a specific situation. You may be able to convince me that I am wrong, but you can't tell me that I am wrong without convincing me.

It is clear that it was Castro himself who (purposefully) misread Khrushchev here: Khrushchev understood very well what Castro wanted the USSR to do—not to attack the US "out of nowhere," but, in the case of the US invasion of Cuba (still an act of *conventional* war, and a limited one, at that—attacking a recent ally of the USSR, not the USSR itself), to retaliate with *total nuclear* counterattack. This is what the warning that the USSR "should never make the mistake of allowing circumstances to develop in which the enemy makes the first nuclear strike against the USSR" can only mean: that the USSR should be the first to deal a decisive nuclear strike—"once aggression is unleashed, one shouldn't concede to the aggressor the privilege of deciding, moreover, when to use nuclear weapons." To put it bluntly, Castro was demanding that Khrushchev choose the end of civilized life on earth over the loss of Cuba . . .[10]

So, again, what we witness here is a confrontation between Khrushchev's humanist considerations (ultimately, the legacy of traditional culture resuscitated by high Stalinism) and Castro's ruthless total wager, which echoes Mao Zedong's reflection on the possible annihilation of the human race. As we have noted earlier, Che Guevara approached the same line of thought when he praised the heroic readiness of the Cuban people to risk its own effacement.

Kremlinology

Stalinism's role in saving the "humanity of man" is discernible at the most elementary level of language. If the language of the new post-human being was to have been a language of signals, no longer properly representing the subject, no wonder that Stalinist language is the most violent imaginable opposite. What characterizes human language, in contrast to the most complex signals of bees, is what Lacan called "empty speech," speech whose denotative value (explicit content) is suspended on behalf of its function as an index of intersubjective relations between speaker and hearer, and this suspension is a key feature of Stalinist jargon, the object of the science of "Kremlinology":

> Before the Soviet-era archives opened wide, foreign scholars trying to make out what had happened, and what might come to pass, took abuse for relying upon hearsay: so-and-so had heard from so-and-so, who in turn had heard from someone in the camps, who was sure that . . . [insert fantastic particulars here]. Critics of such hearsay-scholar-

ship had a point. But what few people seem to realize, even now, is that the salient issue might not be the reliability in Stalin's Soviet Union of word of mouth and political divination, but its pervasiveness. Kremlinology arose not at Harvard, but in and around the Kremlin. [. . .] this was how the entire regime operated, and it was what everyone in the Soviet Union did to a degree, the more so the higher up. Amid the inter-ministerial warfare and Mobius-strip intrigues, Stalinist life and death remained opaque, no matter where you stood or whom you knew. It was at the same time formulaic and indeterminate.

In April 1939, [the nominal head of Comintern Georgi] Dimitrov frets over his sudden omission in *Pravda*'s coverage of one honor presidium and in *Izvestiya*'s of another. His agitation eases when he learns that his portraits were borne aloft at the May Day parade, which quieted the ominous chitchat about him. But then it happened again. "For the first time on International Women's Day I was *not elected* to the honor presidium," he records on March 8, 1941. "That, of course, is no accident." Ah, but what *did* it mean? Dimitrov—who could scarcely have been closer to the Kremlin—was an inveterate Kremlinologist, studying Mausoleum choreography, divining omens, drowning in rumors.[11]

Another comical detail along these lines: the public prosecutor in the show trial against the "United Trotskyite–Zinovievite Center" published a list of those that this "Center" was planning to assassinate (Stalin, Kirov, Zhdanov . . .); this list became "a bizarre honor since inclusion signified proximity to Stalin."[12] Although Molotov was on good personal terms with Stalin, he was shocked to discover that he was not on the list: what could this sign mean? Just a warning from Stalin, or an indication that soon it would be his turn to be arrested? Here indeed, the secrets of the Egyptians were secrets also for the Egyptians themselves. It was the Stalinist Soviet Union which was the true "empire of signs."

A story told by Soviet linguist Eric Han-Pira provides a perfect example of the total semantic saturation of this "empire of signs," a saturation which, precisely, relied on the emptying of direct denotative meaning. For many years, when the Soviet media announced the funeral ceremonies of a member of the senior *nomenklatura*, it used a cliché formulation: "buried on Red Square by the Kremlin wall." In the 1960s, however, because of the lack of space, most of the newly deceased dignitaries were cremated and urns with their ashes were placed in niches inside the wall itself—yet the same old formula was used in press statements. This incongruity compelled fifteen members of the Russian Language Institute of the Soviet Academy of Sciences to write a letter to the Central Committee of the Communist Party, suggesting that the phrase be modified to fit the current reality: "The urn with ashes was placed in the Kremlin wall." Several weeks later, a representative of the Central Committee phoned the Institute, informing them that the Central Committee had discussed their suggestion and decided to keep the old formulation; he gave no reasons for this decision.[13] According to the rules that regulate the Soviet "empire of signs," the CC was right: the change would not have been perceived as simply registering the fact that dignitaries were now cremated and their ashes placed in the wall itself; any deviation from the standard formula would have been interpreted as a sign, triggering frenzied interpretive activity. So, since there was no message to be delivered, why change things? One may oppose to this conclusion the possibility of a simple "rational" solution: why not change the formulation and add an explanation that it meant nothing, that it simply registered a new reality? Such a "rational" approach totally misses the logic of the Soviet "empire of signs": since, in it, *everything* has some meaning, even and *especially* a denial of meaning, such a denial would trigger an even more frantic interpretive activity—it would have been read not only as a meaningful sign within a given, well established, semiotic space, but as a much stronger meta-semantic indication that the very basic rules of this semiotic space were changing, thus causing total perplexity, panic even! Some Soviet leaders retained a sense of irony and displayed a dark sense of humor with regard to this total plasticity of facts; when, in early 1956, Anastas Mikoyan flew to Budapest to inform the Hungarian ultra-Stalinist leader Mátyás Rákosi of Moscow's decision to depose him, he told Rákosi: "The Soviet leadership has decided you are ill. You will need treatment in Moscow."[14]

It would be interesting to reread, from this perspective, the model post-World War II Soviet textbook on dialectical materialism, Mark Rozental's *The Marxist Dialectical Method*, whose first edition appeared in Moscow in 1951. In later reprints, long passages were omitted or rewritten; however, these changes had nothing whatsoever to do with the author's further reflections on immanent philosophical problems — they are all to be read strictly in Kremlinological terms, as signals of the shifts in the ideologico-political line. The book, of course, relies on

Stalin's "systematization" of the four "main features" of dialectical method (the unity of all phenomena; the dynamic nature of reality; the permanent development of reality; the "revolutionary" nature of this development which proceeds through sudden jumps, not only through continuous gradual change), from which, significantly, the "law" of the "negation of the negation" is absent. (See Stalin's "On Dialectical and Historical Materialism.") In the subsequent editions of Rozental's book, the description of these four "main features" subtly changes: at some point, the "negation of the negation" is silently readmitted, and so on and so forth. These changes are Kremlinological signals of the shifts in the ideologico-political constellation, the shifts of de-Stalinization which, paradoxically, began under Stalin himself at his instigation (see his two late essays on linguistics and the economy, which paved the way for recognizing the relative autonomy and independence from class struggle of — some — sciences). The fact that the "negation of the negation" is posited as a fundamental ontological feature of reality, has thus nothing to do with the cognition of the world and everything to do with shifts in the ideologico-political constellation.

Is then Kremlinology not a kind of obscene double of Sovietology, the latter studying the Soviet regime objectively, through sociological data, statistics, power shifts, and so forth, the former as an obscure semiotic system?[15]

From objective to subjective guilt

What kind of subjective position does such a universe imply? Let us take as our starting point Brecht's "learning play" *Die Massnahme* (*The Measures Taken*), in which a young revolutionary, part of a group of Communist agitators sent to China to stimulate revolutionary activity, is killed by fellow Communists because they consider him a security risk (and he dutifully assents to his execution). Although this play is often presented as a justification of the Stalinist show trials, there is a crucial distinction between the two:

> what separated Brecht's fictional agitators from Stalin's very real prosecutors like Vyshinsky and policemen like Beria was the latters' banal insistence that the defendants had really done this or that wicked, blood-soaked, conspiratorial deed — rather than pursuing the idea of a paradoxical "objective" guilt transcending the actual facts

[. . .] Brecht stacks the cards in such a way that we the audience are bound to embrace the executed hero. [Brecht's critical interpreter Herbert] Luthy admitted that no Communist country or organization has ever staged the play[16] — "The Party itself does not like so much candour . . ." — but failed to notice that Brecht's "candour" in exposing the ruthlessness of the Party line is incompatible with subscribing to it. The true believers invariably kept their knowledge to themselves.[17]

The problem with this reading is that it falsifies Brecht's position in two key ways: (1) Brecht does *not* justify the killing of the young comrade in terms of "objective guilt," but in terms of pragmatic expediency (the young comrade had removed his mask and revealed his face, thus compromising them all) — his killing was not a punishment. (2) For Brecht, the open exposition of the mechanism is *not* incompatible with subscribing to it — the great dramatic tension of the piece is that, while fully displaying the harshness of the "measure taken," the way the unfortunate young comrade's life is ruthlessly sacrificed, he still condones it.[18] The true question is: why can the logic of "objective guilt" not be explicitly asserted? Why does it have to remain a kind of obscene secret, admitted only in a semi-private place? Why would its full public assertion be self-destructive? We encounter here the mystery of appearance at its purest: "objective guilt" — the fact that "the more you are subjectively innocent (with regard to factual accusations) the more you are (objectively) guilty" — must not appear as such.

The question is thus: what kind of ethics enables us to talk about "objective guilt"? Obviously, an immoral ethics. *The* philosopher of immoral ethics was Friedrich Nietzsche, and we should remember that the title of his masterpiece is *The Genealogy of Morals* — *morals*, not ethics: the two are not the same. Morality is concerned with the symmetry of my relations with other human beings; its zero-level rule is "do not do to me what you do not want me to do to you";[19] ethics, on the contrary, deals with my consistency with myself, my fidelity to my own desires. On the back flyleaf of a 1939 edition of Lenin's *Materialism and Empiriocriticism*, Stalin made the following note in red pencil:

1) Weakness
2) Idleness
3) Stupidity

These are the only things than can be called vices. Everything else, in the absence of the aforementioned, is undoubtedly *virtue*.

NB! If a man is 1) strong (spiritually), 2) active, 3) clever (or capable), then he is good, regardless of any other "vices"!

1) plus 3) make 2).[20]

This is as concise as ever a formulation of *immoral ethics*; in contrast to it, a weakling who obeys moral rules and worries about his guilt, stands for *unethical morality*, the target of Nietzsche's critique of *ressentiment*.

There is, however, a limit to Stalinism: not that it is too immoral, but that it is secretly *too moral*, still relying on a figure of the big Other. As we have seen, in what is arguably the most intelligent legitimization of Stalinist terror, Merleau-Ponty's *Humanism and Terror* from 1946, the terror is justified as a kind of wager on the future, almost in the mode of the theology of Pascal who enjoins us to make a bet on God: if the final result of today's horror will be the bright Communist future, then this outcome will retroactively redeem the terrible things a revolutionary has to do today. Along similar lines, even some Stalinists themselves—when (half privately, usually) they were forced to admit that many of the victims of the purges were innocent, accused and killed because "the party needed their blood to fortify its unity"—would look to the future moment of final victory in which all the necessary victims would at last be given their due and their innocence and highest sacrifice for the cause would be recognized. This is what Lacan, in his *Ethics* seminar, refers to as the "perspective of the Last Judgment," a perspective even more clearly discernible in one of the key terms of the Stalinist discourse, that of the "objective guilt" and "objective meaning" of your acts: while you can be an honest individual who acted with the most sincere intentions, you are nonetheless "objectively guilty," if your acts serve reactionary forces—and it is, of course, the party which has the direct access to what your acts "objectively mean." Here, again, we not only have the perspective of the Last Judgment (which formulates the "objective meaning" of your acts), but also the present agent who already has the unique ability to judge today's events and acts from this perspective.[21]

We can see now why Lacan's motto *"il n'y a pas de grand Autre"* (there is no big Other) brings us to the very core of the ethical problematic: what it excludes is precisely this "perspective of the Last Judgment," the idea that somewhere—even if only as a thoroughly virtual point of reference, even if we concede that we cannot ever occupy its place and pass the actual judgment—there must be a standard which allows us to take a measure of our acts and pronounce their "true meaning," their true ethical status. Even Jacques Derrida's notion of "deconstruction as justice" seems to rely on a utopian hope which sustains the specter of "infinite justice," forever postponed, always to come, but nonetheless here as the ultimate horizon of our activity.

The harshness of Lacanian ethics is that it demands that we thoroughly relinquish this reference—and its further wager is that, not only does this abdication not leave us in the grip of an ethical insecurity or relativism, or even undermine the very foundations of ethical activity, but that renouncing the guarantee of some big Other is the very condition of a truly autonomous ethics. Recall that the dream about Irma's injection that Freud used as the exemplary case to illustrate his procedure of analyzing dreams is a dream about responsibility (Freud's own responsibility for the failure of his treatment of Irma)—this fact alone indicates that responsibility is a crucial Freudian notion. But how are we to conceive it? How are we to avoid the common misperception that the basic ethical message of psychoanalysis is, precisely, the one of relieving myself of my responsibility, of putting the blame on the Other: "since the unconscious is the discourse of the Other, I am not responsible for my unconscious formations, it is the big Other who speaks through me, I am merely its instrument"? Lacan himself pointed the way out of this deadlock by referring to Kant's philosophy as the crucial antecedent of psychoanalytic ethics.

According to the standard critique, the limitation of the Kantian universalist ethic of the "categorical imperative" (the unconditional injunction to do our duty) resides in its formal indeterminacy: the moral Law does not tell me *what* my duty is, it merely tells me *that* I should accomplish my duty, and so leaves the space open for empty voluntarism (whatever I decide to be my duty *is* my duty). However, far from being a limitation, this very feature brings us to the core of Kantian ethical autonomy: it is not possible to derive the concrete norms I have to follow in my specific situation from the moral Law itself—which means that it is the subject himself who has to assume the responsibility for translating the abstract injunction of the moral Law into a series of concrete obligations. The full acceptance of this paradox compels us to reject any reference to duty as an excuse: "I know this is heavy and can be painful, but what can I do, this is my duty . . ." Kant's ethics of unconditional duty is often taken as justifying such an attitude—no wonder Adolf Eichmann himself referred to Kantian ethics when he tried to justify his role in planning and executing the Holocaust: he was just doing his duty and obeying the Führer's orders. However, the aim of Kant's emphasis on the subject's full moral autonomy and responsibility is precisely to prevent any such maneuver of shifting the blame onto some figure of the big Other.

So, let us return to Stalin. The commonplace condemnation of Stalin comprises two propositions: (1) he was a cynic who knew very well how things stood (that the accused at the show trials were really innocent, and so on); and (2) he knew what he was doing, that is, he had full control over the events. Documents from the newly accessible archives rather point in the opposite direction: Stalin basically *did* believe (in the official ideology, in his role as an honest leader, in the guilt of the accused, and so on), and he did *not* really control the events (the actual results of his own measures and interventions often shocked him).[22] Lars T. Lih proposed a distressing conclusion: "The people of the Soviet Union would probably have been better off if Stalin had been more cynical than he was."[23] There is, however, a different way to read Stalin's "belief": it is not that he "personally" believed—*he wanted the big Other to believe*. Lih himself points in this direction when he condones Robert Tucker's amazement at

how much pain and suffering went into the mass production of confessions during 1937. These confessions served no earthly purpose; they were promptly filed away and forgotten. Tucker speculates that Stalin insisted on these confessions as proof to posterity that his vision of a world filled with enemies was basically correct.[24]

What if, however, we take the statement that the extorted confessions "served no earthly purpose" more literally: they were "filed away and forgotten" by actual people, because their addressee was not these actual people but the virtual "big Other," the same big Other that can only account for the well-known incident concerning the great Soviet encyclopedia which occurred in 1954, immediately after the fall of Beria. When Soviet subscribers received the volume of the encyclopedia which contained the entries under the letter B, there was, of course, a double-page article on Beria, praising him as the great hero of the Soviet Union; after his fall and denunciation as a traitor and spy, all subscribers received from the publishing house a letter asking them to cut out and return the page on Beria; in exchange they were promptly sent a double-page entry (with photos) on the Bering Strait, so that, when they inserted it into the volume, its wholeness was reestablished, there was no blank to bear witness to the sudden rewriting of history . . . The mystery here is: *for whom* was this (semblance of) wholeness maintained, if every subscriber *knew* about the manipulation (since he had to perform it *himself*)? The only answer is, of course, for the innocent gaze of the big Other. This is why the structure of Stalinism is inherently theological; this is why Stalinism so desperately strived to maintain proper appearances. Such a solution to the enigma also allows us to reject the dilemma, "Was Stalin a believer or a cynic?" as a false one: he was both at the same time. Personally, he, of course, was often aware of the lie in the official discourse; so, personally, he was a cynic, but he was simultaneously quite sincere in his efforts to safeguard the innocence and sincerity of the "big Other." The modern name for this Other who is "supposed to believe" in our stead is the "people"—when Golda Meir was asked whether she believed in God, she said: "I believe in the Jewish people, and the Jewish people believe in God." One should be very precise in interpreting this statement: it does not imply that the majority of the Jews believe in God (as a matter of fact, the State of Israel is arguably the most atheistic country in the world, the only one in which a clear majority of its citizens do not believe in God). What it implies is a certain fetishization of the "people": even if—to go to the extreme—no individual Jewish citizen of Israel believes, each of them presupposes that the "people" believes, and this presupposition is enough to make her act as if she believes . . .

A Stalinist acts not on behalf of real individuals, but on account of the "people," this virtual big Other which believes even if no empirical individual believes. In this way, he can combine his individual cynicism with his "objective" sincerity: he does not have to believe in a Cause, he only believes in the "people" supposed to believe . . . This brings us to the underlying subjective position of the Stalinist Communist: the position of a pervert. A true Stalinist politician loves mankind, but nonetheless performs horrible purges and executions—his heart is breaking while he is doing it, but he cannot help it, it is his Duty towards the Progress of Humanity. This is the perverse attitude of adopting the position of the pure instrument of the big Other's Will: it is not my responsibility, it is not me who is effectively doing it, I am merely an instrument of the higher Historical Necessity. As to the genesis of this perverse subjective position, it would be revealing to engage in a detailed account of how the Bolshevik movement related to medicine, to the doctors who took care of the leaders. Three documents are crucial here.

First, are Lenin's letters to Gorky from the fall of 1913[25] in which, deeply disturbed by Gorky's support for the humanist ideology of "God-building," Lenin implies that Gorky has succumbed to this deviation because of his bad nerves, and advises him to go to Switzerland and get the best medical treatment there. In one of the letters, after making it clear how he is shocked at Gorky's ideas—

> Dear Alexei Maximovitch, what are you doing, then? Really, it is terrible, simply terrible! Why are you doing this? It is terribly painful. Yours, V.I.

—Lenin adds a strange postscript:

> P.S. *Take care of yourself* more seriously, really, so that you will be able to travel in winter *without catching cold* (in winter, it is dangerous).

Obviously, Lenin is worried that, apart from catching cold, Gorky will catch a much more serious ideological disease, as is clear from the subsequent letter (posted together with the previous one):

> Perhaps I don't understand you *well*? Perhaps *you were joking* when you wrote "for the moment"? Concerning the "construction of God," perhaps you didn't write that seriously? Good heavens, take care of yourself a little bit better. Yours, *Lenin*.

What should surprise us here is the way the root of ideological deviation is located in a bodily condition (overexcited nerves) that needs medical treatment. Is it not a bit of a supreme irony that, in Trotsky's dream from 1935 in which the dead Lenin appears to him, he gives him exactly the same advice?

> He was questioning me anxiously about my illness. "You seem to have accumulated nervous fatigue, you must rest . . ." I answered that I had always recovered from fatigue quickly, thanks to my native *Schwung-kraft*, but that this time the trouble seemed to lie in some deeper processes . . . "then you should *seriously* (he emphasized the word) consult the doctors (several names) . . ."[26]

So, to bring this logic to its conclusion, one is tempted to imagine a scene between Lenin and Stalin in the last year of Lenin's life, after his stroke and collapse, when, with his last forces, he ferociously attacks Stalin, and Stalin answers him patronizingly: "Good heavens, comrade Lenin, you seem to have accumulated nervous fatigue, you must rest! You should consult the doctors more seriously!" . . . Here, Lenin would have received his own message in its inverted-true form—an appropriate punishment for his mistake.

Second, there is Stalin's speech at Lenin's funeral ("On the Death of Lenin") delivered on January 26, 1924, which begins with:

Comrades, we Communists are people of a special mould. We are made of a special stuff. We are those who form the army of the great proletarian strategist, the army of Comrade Lenin. There is nothing higher than the honor of belonging to this army. There is nothing higher than the title of member of the Party whose founder and leader was Comrade Lenin. It is not given to everyone to be a member of such a party. It is not given to everyone to withstand the stresses and storms that accompany membership in such a party.[27]

Lenin's obsession with the body of the revolutionary, which for him was merely an idiosyncrasy, is here, as it were, elevated into a concept: a Bolshevik "cadre" is perceived as the one who possesses a special body, not a body like others—which is why special care should be taken of it (and, eventually, the body deserves to be preserved in a mausoleum).

Third, is the fact that Stalin's last paranoid obsession concerned the so-called "doctor's plot": all the doctors who were treating him and the top Soviet leadership were arrested and tortured to make them confess that they were part of an international US–Jewish conspiracy to kill the Soviet leadership.[28] Again, the continuity with the previous two points is clear: the doctors' crime was not merely killing their ordinary human patients, but killing the sacred bodies of revolutionary cadres.

So what is a "cadre,"? One is tempted to play the Heideggerian game for a brief moment, discerning in "cadre" the ancient Greek *tetragonos*, as this word appears at the beginning of a poem by Simonides from the fifth century BC: "It is arduous to be an able, a truly able man: in hands and feet as well as in mind square [*tetragonos*], without fault . . ." (The intermediary link between this Greek notion and the Communist one is none other than Kazimir Malevich's "Black Square on White Surface":

the square figure against the nondescript background.) So, to put it in Heideggerese, the essence of the cadre is to provide a *cadre* (square, frame) for the essence itself.

Far from being a mere "metaphor," this notion of the cadre's special body is grounded in the logic of "objective meaning" shared by Lenin and Stalin: while ordinary individuals are caught in historical events which surpass them, blinded to their true meaning, so that their consciousness is "false," a revolutionary cadre has access to the true ("objective") meaning of events, that is, his consciousness is the direct self-consciousness of historical necessity itself. (It is this special position that allows him to criticize others in the well-known style of "your intentions may be good and your desire to help people sincere, but, nonetheless, objectively, what you claim means, in this precise moment of the struggle, support for the reactionary forces . . ." In Hegelese, what this position overlooks is how this "objective" meaning is already subjectively mediated. It is, for example, when the party decides to change its political line that the same politics can radically change its "objective" meaning: up until the Hitler–Stalin pact in 1939, fascism was the principal enemy, while if, after the pact, one continued to focus on the anti-fascist struggle, one "objectively" served imperialist reaction.) And the cadre's sublime body is the ethereal support of this direct self-consciousness of the historical absolute Subject.

There is nonetheless a crucial rupture here between Lenin and Stalin: while Lenin remained at this level, claiming access to the "objective meaning" of the events, Stalin took a fateful further step and *re-subjectivized* this objective meaning. In the Stalinist universe, there are, paradoxically, ultimately no dupes, everyone knows the "objective meaning" of their acts, so that, instead of illusory consciousness, we get direct hypocrisy and deceit: the "objective meaning" of your acts is what you *really wanted*, and your good intentions are merely a hypocritical mask. Furthermore, all of Lenin cannot be reduced to this subjective position of privileged access to "objective meaning": there is another, much more "open," subjective position at work in Lenin's writings, the position of total exposure to historical contingency. From this position, there is no "true" party line waiting to be discovered, no "objective" criteria to determine it: the party "makes all possible mistakes," and the "true" party line emerges out of the zigzag of oscillations, that is, "necessity" is constituted in praxis, it emerges through the mutual interaction of subjective decisions.

Historians who try to demonstrate the continuity between Lenin's politics and Stalinism like to focus on the figure of Felix Dzerzhinsky, the founder of the Cheka (later the GPU, NKVD, KGB . . .), the Bolshevik secret police: as a rule, he is portrayed as what Deleuze would have called the "dark precursor" of Stalinism, in the precise sense of the term as defined by Ian Buchanan: "Dark precursors are those moments in a text which must be read in reverse if we are not to mistake effects for causes."[29] In the context of the pre-Stalinist development of the Soviet Union in the first decade after the October Revolution, Dzerzhinsky has to be "read in reverse," as a voyager who traveled back in time from the Stalinist future a decade ahead. Such a reading often acquires properly fantasmatic dimensions, as in those historians who emphasize Dzerzhinsky's cold blank gaze, allegedly a bodily expression of his ruthless mind, deprived of all human warmth and compassion. No wonder, then, that the West received with chilled surprised the news that the Putin government in Russia decided to return the Dzerzhinsky statue to the square in front of the infamous Lubyanka palace, the seat of the dreaded KGB . . . There are, however, some surprises in store for those who cling to this received image. Lesley Chamberlain's *The Philosophy Steamer*—a book about the expulsion from the Soviet Union in 1921 of the group of most exposed non-Marxist intellectuals, a work which insists precisely on the straight path (if not direct continuity) between Leninism and Stalinism—has an Appendix of short biographical notes on all the persons involved. Here is the entry on Dzerzhinsky:

FELIKS DZERZHINSKY (1877–1926) Polish-born head of the Cheka, later the GPU, oversaw the expulsions. Dzerzhinsky spent a quarter of his life—eleven years—in tsarist prisons and Siberian exile, including three years of hard labor. "His identification with, and championship of, the underprivileged and the oppressed" (Leggett[30]) was unquestionable. Dzerzhinsky remains an enigmatic figure.[31]

There are many further details which throw an unexpected light on this emblematic figure; however, the point is not primarily to emphasize how much "softer," "more human," the early Bolsheviks were. One should in no way cover up the harshness of their rule—the point is elsewhere: precisely when they resorted to terror (and they often did it, openly, calling the beast by its name, "Red Terror"), this terror was different from the Stalinist kind. Of course, many a historian, while ready to concede this point, would nonetheless insist that there was a deeper necessity which led from the first to the second: is the shift of ruthless revolutionary purity into corrupted terror not a commonplace of the histories of revolutions? No doubt the early Bolsheviks would have been shocked at what the Soviet Union turned into in the 1930s (as many of them were, and were also ruthlessly exterminated in the great purges); however, their tragedy was that they were not able to perceive in the Stalinist terror the ultimate offspring of their own acts. What they needed was their own version of the old Oriental insight "tatvam asi" ("thou art that") . . . This accepted wisdom—which, let me state clearly, cannot be dismissed as cheap anti-Communism: it has its own coherent logic, and it does acknowledge a tragic grandeur in the Bolshevik old guard—is what one should nonetheless render problematic. Here, the Left should propose its own alternative to the now fashionable rightist what-if histories: the answer to the eternal leftist query "What would have happened if Lenin had survived ten years longer with his health intact, and succeeded in deposing Stalin?" is not as clear as it may appear (the liberal would answer: basically, *nothing*—that is to say, nothing really different: the same Stalinism, just deprived of its worst excesses), in spite of many good arguments on its behalf (did Rosa Luxemburg herself not already back in 1918 foretell the rise of bureaucratic Stalinism?).

So, although it is clear how Stalinism emerged from the initial conditions of the October Revolution and its immediate aftermath, one should not *a priori* discount the possibility that, had Lenin stayed healthy for a couple of years and removed Stalin, something entirely different would have emerged—not, of course, the utopia of "democratic socialism," but nonetheless something substantially different from Stalinist "socialism in one country," the result of a much more "pragmatic" and improvised series of political and economic decisions, fully aware of its own limitations. Lenin's desperate last struggle against reawakened Russian nationalism, his support for Georgian "nationalists," his vision of a much more decentralized federation, and so forth, were not just tactical compromises: they implied a vision of state and society totally incompatible with the Stalinist perspective.

Therein resides the importance of Trotsky. Although Trotskyism often functions as a kind of politico-theoretical obstacle, preventing the radical self-critical analysis needed by the contemporary Left, the figure of Trotsky nonetheless remains crucial inasmuch as it stands for an element which disturbs the alternative "either (social-)democratic socialism or Stalinist totalitarianism": what we find in Trotsky, in his writings and his revolutionary practice in the early years of the Soviet Union, is revolutionary terror, party rule, and so forth, but *in a different mode* from that of Stalinism. One should thus, in order to remain faithful to Trotsky's real achievements, dispel the popular myths of a warm democratic Trotsky who favored psychoanalysis, mixed with surrealist artists and had an affair with Frida Kahlo. And, again, the conclusion "even if Trotsky had won, the ultimate result would have been basically the same" (or, even more, the claim that Trotsky is at the origin of Stalinism, namely, that, from the late 1920s onwards, Stalin merely applied and developed measures first envisaged by Trotsky in the years of "war communism"[32]) is wrong: history is open, one cannot tell what would have happened if Trotsky had won. The problem lies elsewhere: in the fact that Trotsky's attitude made it *impossible for his orientation to win* in the struggle for state power.

The shift from the Leninism of the 1920s to the Stalinism proper of the 1930s is discernible even at the level of humor in the inner party debates.[33] A certain kind of humor was always part of Bolshevik debates—Lenin himself said at the Eleventh Party Congress in 1922 that "a joke is a very good thing: we cannot make speeches without cracking a joke here and there."[34] This humor was sometimes rough, sarcastic, laced with glacial irony, but still part of a dialogue of party comrades—to quote Hamlet on the way to his mother in Act III of the play: "I will speak daggers to her, but use none." Furthermore, humor and sarcasm in polemical exchanges were strictly symmetrical—say, during the debate between the Leninist majority and the Workers' Opposition in 1921, both sides not only resorted to sarcastic and ironic remarks, but also replied in the same way to their opponents' remarks, by turning them around, extrapolating them to the point of ridicule, and so on. In the 1930s, however, a much more cruel form of sarcasm predominated, which the Soviet press itself called "victors' laughter": making fun of and laughing at the ridiculous excuses of the impotent and humiliated victims who tried to convince others of their honesty. Examples abound—Vyshinsky, the public prosecutor, shouted at Kamenev and Zinoviev during the famous show trial: "Drop this clownish farce!" When Smirnov, a defendant at the same trial, denied that he was a terrorist, he was told: "The pathetic attempt to wriggle free is quite comical." Along the same lines, the Kafkaesque quality of the eerie laughter that erupted amongst the public during Bukharin's last speech in front of the Central Committee on February 23, 1937 hinges on the radical discord between the speaker's utter seriousness (he is talking about his possible suicide, and why he would not commit it, since it could hurt the party, but would rather go on with the hunger strike till his death) and the reaction of the Central Committee members:

> BUKHARIN: I won't shoot myself because then people will say that I killed myself so as to harm the party. But if I die, as it were, from an illness, then what will you lose by it? (Laughter.)
>
> VOICES: Blackmailer!
>
> VOROSHILOV: You scoundrel! Keep your trap shut! How vile! How dare you speak like that!
>
> BUKHARIN: But you must understand—it's very hard for me to go on living.
>
> STALIN: And it's easy for us?!
>
> VOROSHILOV: Did you hear that: "I won't shoot myself, but I will die"?!
>
> BUKHARIN: It's easy for you to talk about me. What will you lose, after all? Look, if I am a saboteur, a son of a bitch, then why spare me? I make no claims to anything. I am just describing what's on my mind, what I am going through. If this in any way entails any political damage, however minute, then, no question about it, I'll do whatever you say. (Laughter.) Why are you laughing? There is absolutely nothing funny about any of this . . .[35]

The same uncanny laughter also appeared in other places:

> BUKHARIN: Whatever they are testifying against me is not true. (Laughter, noise in the room.) Why are you laughing? There is nothing funny in all this.[36]

Do we not have here, enacted in real life, the uncanny logic of Josef K's first interrogation in *The Trial*?

> "Well, then," said the Examining Magistrate, turning over the leaves and addressing K. with an air of authority, "you are a house-painter?" "No," said K., "I'm the junior manager of a large Bank." This answer evoked such a hearty outburst of laughter from the Right party that K. had to laugh too. People doubled up with their hands on their knees and shook as if in spasms of coughing.[37]

In such a universe, of course, there is no place for even the most formal and empty right of subjectivity, on which Bukharin continues to insist:

BUKHARIN: [. . .] I confessed that from 1930 to 1932 I committed many political sins. I have come to understand this. But with the same forcefulness with which I confess my real guilt, with that same forcefulness I deny the guilt which is thrust upon me, and I shall deny it forever. And not because it has only personal significance, but because I believe that no one should under any circumstances take upon himself anything superfluous, especially when the party doesn't need it, when the country doesn't need it, when I don't need it. (Noise in the room, laughter.) [. . .]

The whole tragedy of my situation lies in this, that this Piatakov and others like him so poisoned the atmosphere, such an atmosphere arose that no one believes human feelings—not emotions, not the impulses of the heart, not tears. (Laughter.) Many manifestations of human feeling, which had earlier represented a form of proof—and there was nothing shameful in this—have today lost their validity and force.

KAGANOVICH: You practiced too much duplicity!

BUKHARIN: Comrades, let me say the following concerning what happened—

KHLOPLIANKIN: It's time to throw you in prison!

BUKHARIN: What?

KHLOPLIANKIN: You should have been thrown in prison a long time ago!

BUKHARIN: Well, go on, throw me in prison. So you think the fact that you are yelling: "Throw him in prison!" will make me talk differently? No, it won't.[38]

It is easy to see how this shift in humor depends on the passage from the Leninist notion of the "objective meaning" of one's acts to its Stalinist resubjectivization: since, in the Stalinist universe, there are ultimately no dupes, and everyone knows the "objective meaning" of their acts, disagreement with the official party line can only be the result of direct hypocrisy and deceit. What is more surprising is the readiness of Western Communist observers to perceive this hypocrisy as a true psychological fact about the accused. In a letter to Benjamin from 1938, Adorno reports a conversation he had with Hanns Eisler in New York:

I listened with not a little patience to his feeble defense of the Moscow trials, and with considerable disgust to the joke he cracked about the murder of Bukharin. He claims to have known the latter in Moscow, telling me that Bukharin's conscience was already so bad that he could not even look him, Eisler, honestly in the eyes.[39]

Eisler's psychological blindness is staggering here: he misreads Bukharin's terror, fearing contact with foreigners, knowing that he is under observation and close to arrest, as an inner feeling of guilt.

Shostakovich in Casablanca

Although, of course, the perverse position of the instrument of the big Other was reserved for the members of the *nomenklatura*, ordinary Soviet citizens were not reduced to the simple alternative of believers or non-believers; the split that characterized their predominant subjective position was of a different nature. Recall the debate about the true message of Shostakovich's work that raged in musicological circles until recently: where did the composer truly stand with regard to his (obviously tortured) relationship to Communism? The two opposed positions are that, in spite of all his (obvious) doubts and oscillations, Shostakovich was a faithful Soviet composer, or that in fact Shostakovich was a closet dissident whose music presents "disguised or coded challenges to the very political system he pretended to endorse." In the second case, we get caught in the interpretive madness in which every feature can be interpreted as a sign of its opposite: "complain that the 'triumphant' ending of the Leningrad Symphony was banal and you might get the response, 'Ah, but it's *meant* to be banal!' The message conveyed was what mattered."[40] It is thus only a thin line of reflexivity that separates the two readings: if banality is self-declaratory, if it is meant as such, then it cancels itself and reverts into irony . . . Where, then, does the truth reside? What I propose is a Hegelian "synthesis" of these opposed views, albeit a synthesis with an unexpected twist: what if what makes Shostakovich's music "Stalinist," part of the Soviet universe, is *his very distance towards it*? What if a distance towards the official ideological universe, far from undermining it, was *a key constituent of its functioning*? Shostakovich's spontaneously intimate attitude towards politics is probably best expressed in his remark to a friend: "Do you not think that history is really a whore?"[41] This generalized distrust of all politics (which also grounds his distance towards dissidents such as Solzhenitsyn) made his survival much easier.[42] This crucial insight compels us to give a specific twist to the standard argument for Shostakovich's "dissidence":

> even the most "official" writers [. . .] were, more often than not, privately skeptical about the Soviet regime and known to be within the dissident culture. It is, indeed, rare to find Russian writers under Soviet rule, however officially sanctioned or ostensibly conformist, who did not, at one time or other, voice a critical outlook on "Soviet reality". [. . .] [Shostakovich] was also [. . .] uniquely active in forwarding dissident values in his work (an enterprise substantially protected by the deniability inherent in non-verbal dissidence). But he was in no sense alone in privately maintaining a dissenting outlook on Soviet life while at the same time necessarily giving a contrary public impression of conformism.[43]

So why did Stalin not liquidate Shostakovich (and many other leading figures from Akhmatova to Pasternak whose views were "transparently" dissident)? "In the case of poets, Stalin's superstition seems to have played a part, but the main answer is that major figures could not be 'liquidated' without causing foreign uproar . . ."[44] — it looks really bad for a line of reasoning which has go so far as to evoke Stalin's superstition . . . Is it not much easier and more logical to admit that *the gap between "public" allegiance to the regime and "private" dissidence was part of the very identity of the Stalinist subject*? If there is a lesson to be learned from the functioning of Stalinist ideology, it is that (public) *appearances matter*, which is why one should reserve the category "dissidence" *exclusively* for the public discourse: "dissidents" were *only* those who disturbed the smooth functioning of the public discourse, announcing publicly — in one way or another — what, privately, everybody already knew.

Was, however, such a subjective position the only one possible (if one wanted to survive, of course . . .)? The fate of Sergei Prokofiev, the other great name of Soviet music, shows a radically different path. In his (disputed) memoirs, Dmitri Shostakovich dismissed Sergei Prokofiev, his great competitor, as refusing to take historical horrors seriously, always playing the "wise guy." However, to name just one supreme example, Prokofiev's First Violin Sonata (Opus 80) clearly demonstrates the obverse of Prokofiev's (in)famous "irony":

> Throughout its four movements [. . .] one senses a powerful undertow of struggle. Yet it is not the struggle of a work against something outside itself, but rather the struggle of something within the work, unmanifested, trying desperately to break out, and constantly finding its emergence "blocked" by the existing, outward form and language of the piece. This blocking of "something within" [. . .] has to do with the frustration of a desire for cathartic release into some supremely positive state of being, where meaning—musical and supra-musical—is transparent, un-ironizable: in short, a domain of spiritual "purity."[45]

It is here that Prokofiev pays the price for his ironic stance, and it is such passages that bear witness to his artistic integrity: far from signaling any kind of vain intellectual superiority, this ironic stance is just the falsely bright obverse of the *failure of Prokofiev's constant struggle to bring the "Thing from Inner Space" (the "something within") out.* The superficial "playfulness" of some of Prokofiev's works (such as his popular First Symphony) merely signals, in a negative way, the fact that Prokofiev is the ultimate anti-Mozart, a kind of Beethoven whose "titanic struggle" ended in disaster: if Mozart was *the* supreme musical genius, perhaps the last composer with whom the musical Thing transposed itself into musical notes in a spontaneous flow, and if in Beethoven, a piece only achieved its definitive form after a long heroic struggle with the musical material, Prokofiev's greatest pieces are monuments to the defeat of this struggle.[46]

Shostakovich never reached the level of such an immanent failure. His piece which can be compared to Prokofiev's First Violin Sonata in its exceptional subjectively engaged intensity is, of course, his String Quartet No. 8, and the difference between the two pieces is striking. Whatever subjective anguish is detectable beneath the quartet, its musical expression flows unhindered, pouring out and generating an easily recognizable emotional impact; Shostakovich's life and subjective experience may have been thwarted, marked by depressions and terrible and debasing compromises, but this blockade does not affect his musical expression. In Prokofiev's violin sonata, on the contrary, we are dealing with a much more radical immanent blockage of musical expression itself; the tragic failure, is here the failure of the form itself, and this failure accounts for the inner truth missing in Shostakovich.

In the last decade and a half of his life, Prokofiev was caught up in the Stalinist superego at its purest: whatever he did was wrong. When he stuck to his modernist roots, he was accused of "anti-people formalism" and bourgeois decadence. When, thereafter, he tried to do his best to bow to the pressure in his infamous *Cantata for the 20th Anniversary of the October Revolution*, using texts by Marx, Lenin, and Stalin, the cantata was again criticized for "Leftist deviation and vulgarity" (that is, for dragging Marx and Lenin into it). Desperate to contribute something—anything—to the twentieth anniversary, Prokofiev quickly threw together a concoction of folk-tunes and party singalongs entitled *Songs of Our Days*; the work was again dismissed as "pale and lacking in individuality"—which, of course, was true.

> Prokofiev must by now have been utterly bewildered. If he wrote like a simpleton, he was a depersonalized Left deviationist; if he wrote like Prokofiev, he was a mercenary Formalist. Individual, non-individual . . . there must have seemed no rhyme or reason to it—and, of course, none existed.[47]

But there definitely *was* a "rhyme and reason" to it: the rhyme and reason of the Stalinist superego in the eyes of which one is always guilty . . . However, the problem was a deeper one: the paradox of Prokofiev's late style was that the logic of his immanent musical development which led him away from expressionist pathos towards "new simplicity" strangely reverberated with the official demands for the easy-listening music accessible to ordinary Soviet people.

In the case of Prokofiev as well as in that of Shostakovich, the reason why critics so desperately look for the ultimate proof of secret dissidence is to avoid a highly embarrassing truth: their most popular works today in the West overlap to a surprising degree with the very works which got the greatest official (not only popular) support from the regime: Shostakovich's Fifth, Seventh, and Eleventh Symphonies, Prokofiev's *Peter and the Wolf* and the *Romeo and Juliet* ballet. Even among Shostakovich's chamber music, his Piano Quintet, which got the Stalin prize in 1940, is his most popular piece! How can this be? Here enters the hermeneutics of dissidence which shows the escape route. Shostakovich's Fifth Symphony—the most often performed twentieth-century symphony also in the West? It has to be the case that the triumphant finale is really meant ironically, mocking the emptiness of Stalinist triumphalism! The enduring popularity of the Seventh Symphony (the *Leningrad*)? It has to be that the inexorable brutal marching progress in the first movement does not "really" refer to the German conquest of Russia in 1941, but to the Communist conquest of Russia! Shostakovich's Eleventh Symphony ("1905") a hit? It has to be quickly confirmed that 1905 is just a pretext, that the revolutionary explosion "really" refers to Hungary in 1956! . . . But what about the Shostakovich symphonies which were effectively unacceptable for those in power, like the Thirteenth (*Babi-Yar*) and the last, the Fifteenth? The answer is clear: in a supreme twist of irony, the Thirteenth caused such a stir at its premiere precisely and only because of the political circumstances—it functioned as a gesture of political defiance—*not* because of its artistic strength. These works are today respected and praised, but not really enjoyed.

The publicity text for the new recording of Shostakovich's First Violin Concerto by Leila Josefowicz says that she "pays homage to the struggles Shostakovich faced under Stalin's regime"—the patent absurdity of this claim confirms Michael Tanner's thesis that "there is almost no other composer for whom the life-and-works mélange has achieved such orthodox status."[48] Tanner is fully justified in pointing out how the endless debates regarding how some symphony movements are to be read, with serious pathos or as ironic subversion, or regarding which victorious finales are meant to render the victories pyrrhic, "tell us, in fact, what the music itself fails to achieve." There is no greater monument to Shostakovich's artistic failure than the obsessive search for some private (extra-artistic) document that would definitely prove his intimate anti-Communist stance. This is why, in the ambiguities in which this politically engaged background no longer resonates, Shostakovich's music is simply "uninterestingly enigmatic," like the references to Rossini and Wagner in the last symphony—there is no deeper meaning to be discovered here, the "enigma" is musically flat. The irony here is that the very search for the extra-musical "smoking gun" demonstrates the truth of the Stalinist accusation about the "formalist" character of Shostakovich's music—not, of course, in the sense in which it was intended by Zhdanov *et consortes*, but in the sense that his music is neutral with regard to social commitments (which is why one has to look for extra-musical signs to pin it down).

So what if we read Shostakovich's popular symphonies along the lines of how we might read one of the great Hollywood classics? In the well-known brief scene three-quarters into *Casablanca*,[49] Ilsa Lund (Ingrid Bergman) comes to Rick Blaine's (Humphrey Bogart's) room to try to obtain the letters of transit that will allow her and her Resistance leader husband Victor Laszlo to escape from Casablanca to Portugal and then to America. After Rick refuses to hand them over, she pulls a gun and threatens him. He tells her, "Go ahead and shoot, you'll be doing me a favor." She breaks down and tearfully starts to tell him the story of why she left him in Paris. By the time she says, "If you knew how much I loved you, how much I still love you," they are embracing in a close-up. The movie dissolves into a three-and-a-half-second shot of the airport tower at night, its searchlight circling, and then dissolves back to a shot from outside the window of Rick's room, where he is standing, looking out and smoking a cigarette. He turns round and says, "And then?" She resumes her story . . .

The question that immediately pops up here, of course, is: what happened *in between*, during the three-and-a-half-second shot of the airport—did they *do it* or not? Maltby is right to emphasize that, as to this point, the film is not simply ambiguous; it rather generates two very clear, although mutually exclusive meanings—they did it, and they did not do it, that is, the film gives unambiguous signals that they did it, and simultaneously unambiguous signals that they cannot have done it. On the one hand, a series of codified features signal that they did do it, namely that the three-and-a-half-second shot stands for a longer period of time (the dissolve of the couple passionately embracing usually signals the act after the fade-out; the cigarette is also the standard sign of post-coital relaxation; up to the vulgar phallic connotation of the tower); on the other hand, a parallel series of features signals that they did *not* do it, namely that the three-and-a-half-second shot of the airport tower corresponds to the real diegetic time (the bed in the background is undisturbed; the same conversation seems to go on without a break; and so on). Even when, in the final conversation between Rick and Laszlo at the airport, they directly touch on the events of this night, their words can be read in both ways:

RICK: You said you knew about Ilsa and me?
VICTOR: Yes.
RICK: You didn't know she was at my place last night when you were . . . she came there for the letters of transit. Isn't that true, Ilsa?
ILSA: Yes.
RICK: She tried everything to get them and nothing worked. She did her best to convince me that she was still in love with me. That was

all over long ago; for your sake she pretended it wasn't and I let her pretend.

VICTOR: I understand.

Well, *I* certainly *do not* understand—is Rick saying to Victor that he made love to his wife or not? Maltby's solution is to insist that this scene provided an exemplary case of how *Casablanca* "deliberately constructs itself in such a way as to offer distinct and alternative sources of pleasure to two people sitting next to each other in the same cinema," that is, that it "could play to both 'innocent' and 'sophisticated' audiences alike."[50] While, at the level of its surface narrative line, the film can be constructed by the spectator as obeying the strictest moral codes, it simultaneously offers to the "sophisticated" enough clues to construct an alternative, sexually much more daring narrative line. This strategy is more complex than it may appear: precisely *because* you knew that you are as it were "covered" or "absolved from guilty impulses"[51] by the official story line, you are allowed to indulge in dirty fantasies—you know that these fantasies are not "serious," that they do not count in the eyes of the big Other . . . So our only correction to Maltby would be that we do not need *two* spectators sitting next to each other: *one and the same spectator,* split in two, is sufficient.

To put it in Lacanian terms: during the infamous three and a half seconds, Ilsa and Rick did not do it for the big Other, the order of public appearance, but they did do it for our dirty fantasmatic imagination—this is the structure of inherent transgression at its purest, that is, Hollywood needs *both* levels in order to function. To put it in terms of the discourse theory elaborated by Oswald Ducrot, we have here the opposition between presupposition and surmise: the presupposition of a statement is directly endorsed by the big Other, we are not responsible for it, while the responsibility for the surmise of a statement rests entirely on the reader's (or spectator's) shoulders—the author of the text can always claim "It's not my responsibility if the spectators draw dirty conclusions from the texture of the film!" And, to link this to psychoanalytic terms, this opposition is, of course, the opposition between symbolic Law (the ego ideal) and the obscene superego: at the level of the public symbolic Law, nothing happens, the text is clean, while, at another level, it bombards the spectator with the superego injunction "Enjoy!", that is, give way to your dirty imagination. To put it in yet another way, what we encounter here is a clear example of the fetishistic split, of the disavowal structure of *"je sais bien, mais quand même . . ."*: the very awareness that they did not do it gives free rein to your dirty imagination—you can indulge in it, because you are absolved from the guilt by the fact that, for the big Other, they definitely did *not* do it . . . And this double reading is not simply a compromise on the part of the Law, in the sense that the symbolic Law is interested only in keeping up appearances and leaves you free to exercise your fantasies, insofar as they do not encroach upon the public domain, namely insofar as they save the appearances: the Law itself needs its obscene supplement, it is sustained by it, so it generates it.

Maltby is thus right in emphasizing that the infamous Hollywood Production Code of the 1930s and 1940s was not simply a negative censorship code, but also a positive (productive, as Foucault would have put it) codification and regulation that generated the very excess whose direct depiction it hindered. Indicative is here the conversation between Josef von Sternberg and Breen reported by Maltby: when Sternberg said "At this point, the two principals have a brief romantic interlude," Breen interrupted him: "What you're trying to say is that the two of then hopped into the hay. They fucked." The indignant Sternberg answered: "Mr. Breen, you offend me." Breen: "Oh, for Christ's sake, will you stop the horseshit and face the issue. We can help you make a story about adultery, if you want, but not if you keep calling a good screwing match a 'romantic interlude.' Now, what do these two people do? Kiss and go home?" "No," said Sternberg, "they fuck." "Good," yelped Breen, pounding the desk, "now I can understand your story." The director completed his outline, and Breen told him how he could handle it in such a way as to get past the Code.[52] So the very prohibition, in order to function properly, has to rely on a clear awareness about what really happened at the level of the prohibited narrative line: the Production Code did not simply prohibit some content, it rather codified its ciphered articulation.

And, back to Shostakovich, what if exactly the same holds for his popular symphonies? What if they also operate at two levels simultaneously, one, public, intended for the ruling ideological gaze, and another which transgresses the public rules, but remains, as such, its inherent supplement? One can thus appreciate the ambiguity of these lines:

Since the Stalinist assault against his music in 1936, Shostakovich had developed a sort of double-speak in his musical language, using one idiom to please his masters in the Kremlin and another to satisfy his own moral conscience as an artist and a citizen. Outwardly he spoke in a triumphant voice. Yet beneath the ritual sounds of Soviet rejoicing there was a softer, more melancholic voice—the carefully concealed voice of satire and dissent only audible to those who had felt the suffering his music expressed. These two voices are clearly audible in Shostakovich's Fifth Symphony [. . .] which received a half-hour ovation of electrifying force when it was first performed [. . .]. Beneath the endless fanfares trumpeting the triumph of the Soviet state in the finale [. . .] the audience must have felt its sadness [. . .] and they responded to the music as a spiritual release.[53]

A strange hermeneutics indeed—a "carefully concealed voice" which is nonetheless clearly understood by thousands? Were the official censors really so stupid as not to get it? So what if we read the fragile coexistence of these two idioms along the lines of the ambiguity inscribed into the night encounter scene from *Casablanca*? What if the Stalinist rejection of both Prokofiev's propagandistic and intimate works was right on its own terms? What if what they wanted from him was precisely the coexistence of two levels, propagandistic and intimate, while he was offering them either the first or the second? After World War II, Prokofiev withdrew increasingly to the intimate domain of chamber music, where he could find expression for his private sadness—was this an act of silent defiance, writing music "for the drawer," as Shostakovich would have put it? How is it then that the most moving and desperate of these works, his Violin Sonata in D major whose haunting opening movement was meant to sound "like the wind in a graveyard," was awarded the Stalin Prize in 1947? Orlando Figes claims that the award was meant "ironically"—but what kind of strange irony is this?[54]

Let us return to Shostakovich. Can we really be so sure that the public bombast music is meant ironically, while the intimate confessional mood is meant sincerely? What if the irony is objective and we have to read this music in the same way Marx read the attitude of the Party of Order in the French parliament after the 1848 revolution? Recall Marx's coruscating analysis of how this conservative-republican party functioned as the coalition of the two branches of royalism (Orleanists and Legitimists) in the "anonymous kingdom of the Republic."[55] The parliamentary deputies of the Party of Order perceived their republicanism as mockery: in parliamentary debates, they generated royalist slips of the tongue and ridiculed the Republic to let it be known that their true aim was to restore the king. What they were not aware of is that they themselves were duped as to the true social impact of their rule. They unknowingly established the conditions of the bourgeois republican order that they despised so much (by, for instance, guaranteeing private property). So it is not that they were royalists who were just wearing republican masks: although they thought of themselves as such, it was their "inner" royalist conviction which was the deceptive front masking their true social role. In short, far from being the hidden truth of their public republicanism, their sincere royalism was the fantasmatic support of their actual republicanism—it was what provided the passion for their activity. Is it not, then, that the deputies of the Party of Order were also *feigning to feign* to be republicans, to be what they really were—in exactly the same way that Shostakovich was feigning to feign to be a faithful Communist?

Nonetheless, the subjective position of Prokofiev is here radically different from that of Shostakovich: one can propose the thesis that, in contrast to Shostakovich, Prokofiev was effectively *not* a "Soviet composer," even if he wrote more than Shostakovich's share of official cantatas celebrating Stalin and his regime. Prokofiev adopted a kind of proto-psychotic position of internal exclusion towards Stalinism: he was not internally affected or bothered by it, that is, he treated it as just an external nuisance. There was effectively something childish in Prokofiev, like the refusal of a spoilt child to accept one's place in the social order of things—he returned to the Soviet Union in 1936, at the height of the Stalinist purges, drove around in his imported American car, dressed eccentrically in fancy clothes delivered from Paris, ordered books and food from the West, ignoring the madness and poverty around him. This is why, in contrast to Shostakovich, he never really "got into" the Stalinist superego double-talk idiom of combining external accommodation with inner bitterness and sadness. Even the melancholy and despair of his late violin sonata is not a reaction to Stalinist oppression: the same style and mood are there already in his pre-revolutionary works. The different reaction of the two composers to Zhdanov's attacks in 1946–47 is exemplarily here: Prokofiev simply did not understand what the charges were about, he did not internalize the tension. When, in 1947, he was forced to attend a meeting of the Composer's Union and to listen to Zhdanov's speech attacking him and other Soviet composers, he arrived drunk, made loud rude comments interrupting the speech and then fell asleep on his chair in the midst of it—miraculously, nothing happened, so accepted was his eccentricity.

And Shostakovich? The popularity and public resonance of his music underwent a weird change: a couple of decades ago, the majority of critics dismissed him as a "socialist realist" out of touch with the proper development of modern music; however, today, the great musical modernists such as Schoenberg or Webern are perceived as a thing of the past, respectfully ignored, while Shostakovich has emerged as arguably the most popular "serious" composer of the twentieth century; dozens of volumes were written not only about his music, but also about his closet dissidence. What if, however, Shostakovich's popularity is the sign of a non-event, of the occultation of the true Event of modern music—broadly, a moment of the vast cultural counter-revolution whose political mark is the withdrawal from radical emancipatory politics, and the refocusing on human rights and the prevention of suffering?

The Stalinist carnival . . .

What did the trauma of 1935 (the public campaign against his "Lady Macbeth" triggered by the *Pravda* article "Muddle Instead of Music") do to his music? Perhaps the clearest indicator of the break is the change in the function of the scherzo in Shostakovich's work in the 1940s and early 1950s. Prior to 1935, his scherzos can still be perceived as the explosive expression of new aggressive and grotesque vitality and *joie de vivre*—there is something of the liberating force of the carnival in them, of the madness of the creative power that merrily sweeps away all obstacles and ignores all established rules and hierarchies. After 1935, however, his scherzos had clearly "lost their innocence": their explosive energy acquires a brutal-threatening quality, there is something mechanical in their energy, like the forced movements of a marionette. They either render the raw energy of social violence, of massacres of helpless victims, or, if they are meant as the explosion of the "joy of life," this is clearly intended in a sarcastic way, or as an impotent maniacal outburst of the aggressivity of the helpless victim. The "carnival" is here no longer a liberating experience, but the flash of thwarted and repressed aggression—it is the "carnival" of racist pogroms and drunken gang rapes. (The outstanding cases are the second and third movements of the Eighth Symphony, the famous second movement of the Tenth Symphony ("Portrait of Stalin"), and, among the string quartets, the third movement of Quartet No. 3 (which, today, almost sounds like Herrmann's score for *Psycho*), and the "furioso" movement of Quartet No. 10.)[56]

Does this mean that, in a disturbing way, the traumatic experience of Stalinist condemnation helped Shostakovich to achieve his bitter maturity? Would he otherwise have remained a composer of the new Soviet *joie de vivre*, mixing jazz with aggressive rhythmic modernism? What if the mixture of melancholic oppressive drama and the destructive scherzo explosions is not the only way to reply to the experience of Stalinist terror, but, rather, a reply that fits in with Stalinist humanism, its reaffirmation of the old Russian tradition? What if there is a different way which is also already prefigured in another old Russian tradition, the overlapping of horror and humor as the sign of distinction of the specifically Russian grotesque whose first great representative was Gogol? What is "The Nose," his most famous short story, about a low-level bureaucrat whose nose becomes detached and acquires a life of its own, other than a grotesque comedy or a horror story? Indicative is here the reception of Shostakovich's early "absurdist" short opera (1930) based on this story: although it is usually played as a satire or even a frenetic farce, Shostakovich himself called it "a horror story": "I tried not to make jokes in *The Nose*. [. . .] It's too cruel." So when The Opera Group which recently staged it called it, in their production leaflet, "the funniest opera ever, an operatic version of *Monty Python*," this designation should remind us of the underlying nightmarish dimension of Monty Python's comedy. Such a mixture of horror and humor is a trademark of the concentration-camp universe—this is how Primo Levi, in *If This Is a Man*, describes the dreadful "selekcja," the survival examination in the camp:

> The *Blockältester* [the elder of the hut] has closed the connecting-door and has opened the other two which lead from the dormitory and the *Tagesraum* [day room] outside. Here, in front of the two doors, stands the arbiter of our fate, an SSD subaltern. On his right is the *Blockältester*, on his left, the quartermaster of the hut. Each one of us, as he comes naked out of the *Tagesraum* into the cold October air, has to run the few steps between the two doors, give the card to the SS man and enter the dormitory door. The SS man, in the fraction of a second between two successive crossings, with a glance at one's back and front, judges everyone's fate, and in turn gives the card to the man on his right or his left, and this is the life or death of each of us. In three or four minutes a hut of two hundred men is "done", as is the whole camp of twelve thousand men in the course of the afternoon.[57]

Right means survival, left means the gas chambers. Is there not something properly *comic* in this, the ridiculous spectacle of trying to appear strong and healthy, to attract for a brief moment the indifferent gaze of the Nazi administrator who presides over life and death? Here, comedy and horror coincide: imagine the prisoners practicing their appearance, trying to hold their heads high and push their chests forward, walking briskly, pinching their lips to appear less pale, exchanging advice on how to impress the SS man; imagine how a simple momentary confusion of cards or a lack of attention of the SS man can decide their fate . . . No wonder, then, that obscene humor is also a key indicator of the carnivalesque dimension of Stalinist terror. Recall the adventure of Shostakovich's interrogation by the KGB in 1937:

I was given a [security] pass and went to the [NKVD] office. The investigator got up when I came in and greeted me. He was very friendly and asked me to sit down. He started asking questions about my health, my family, the work I was doing—all kinds of questions. He spoke in a very friendly, welcoming and polite way. Then suddenly he asked me: "So, tell me. Do you know Tukhachevsky?" I said yes, and he said "How?". So then I said: "At one of my concerts. After the concert, Tukhachevsky came backstage to congratulate me. He said he liked my music, that he was an admirer. He said he'd like to meet me when he came to Leningrad to talk about music. He said it would be a pleasure to discuss music with me. He said if I came to Moscow he'd be happy to see me." "And how often did you meet?" "Only when Tukhachevsky came here. He usually invited me for dinner."—"Who else was at the table?" "Just his family. His family and relatives."—"And what did you discuss?" "Mostly music."—"Not politics?" "No, we never talked politics. I knew how things were."—"Dmitri Dmitryevich, this is very serious. You must *remember*. Today is Saturday. I'll sign your pass and you can go home. But on Monday noon, you must be here. Don't forget now. This is very serious, very important." I understood this was the end. Those two days until Monday were a nightmare. I told my wife I probably wouldn't return. She even prepared a bag for me—the kind prepared for people who were taken away. She put in warm underwear. She knew I wouldn't be back. I went back there at noon [on Monday] and reported to reception. There was a soldier there. I gave him my [internal] passport. I told him I'd been summoned. He looked for my name: first, second, third list. He said: "Who summoned you?" I said: "Inspector Zakovsky." He said: "He won't be able to see you today. Go home. We'll notify you." He returned my passport and I went home. It was only later that evening that I learned that the inspector had been arrested.[58]

If ever there was a carnival in which today you are a king and tomorrow a beggar, this was it![59] A common-sense reproach nonetheless imposes itself here: is there not a rather obvious fundamental difference between the carnival proper and the Stalinist purges? In the first case, the entire social hierarchy is momentarily suspended, those who were up are cast down and vice versa, while, in the case of Stalinism, the unexpected and "irrational" changes of fortune affect only those who are subjected to power—far from being threatened, far from its power being even symbolically suspended, the Communist *nomenklatura* uses the "irrational" shifts of arbitrary terror to fortify its rule . . . There are, however, moments of paroxysm in which revolutionary terror effectively reaches carnivalesque dimensions, moments in which, like the proverbial snake, the ruling party starts to eat itself, gradually swallowing its own tail. The surprising fact that "the most dangerous place to be was close to the centers of power" clearly distinguishes Stalinism from fascist regimes — here are the results of the mere two years of *yezhovshchina*:

> Five of Stalin's Politburo colleagues were killed, and 98 out of 139 Central Committee members. Of the Central Committee of the Ukraine Republic only three out of 200 survived; 72 of the 93 members of the Komsomol organization Central Committee perished. Out of 1,996 party leaders at the Seventeenth Congress in 1934, 1,108 were imprisoned or murdered. In the provinces 319 out of 385 regional party secretaries and 2,210 out of 2,750 district secretaries died.[60]

In his analysis of the paranoia of the German judge Schreber, Freud reminds us that what we usually consider as madness (the paranoid scenario of the conspiracy against the subject) is effectively already an attempt at recovery: after the complete psychotic breakdown, the paranoid construct is an attempt by the subject to re-establish a kind of order in his universe, a frame of reference enabling him to acquire a form of "cognitive mapping." Along the same lines, one is tempted to claim that, when, in late 1937, the Stalinist paranoid discourse reached its apogee and set in motion its own dissolution as a social link, the 1938 arrest and liquidation of Yezhov himself, Stalin's main executioner in 1937, was effectively the attempt at recovery, at stabilizing the uncontrolled fury of self-destruction that broke out in 1937: the purge of Yezhov was a kind of meta-purge, the purge to end all purges (he was accused precisely of killing thousands of innocent Bolsheviks on behalf of foreign powers — the irony being that the accusation was literally true: he did organize the killing of the thousands of innocent Bolsheviks . . .). However, the crucial point is that, although we are here reaching the limits of the social, the level at which the social-symbolic link itself approaches its self-destructive dissolution, this excess itself was nonetheless generated by a precise dynamic of social struggle, by a series of shifting alignments and realignments at the very top of the regime (Stalin and his narrow circle), the upper *nomenklatura* and the rank-and-file party members:

> Thus in 1933 and 1935 Stalin and the Politburo united with all levels of the *nomenklatura* elite to screen, or purge, a helpless rank and file. The regional leaders then used those purges to consolidate their machines and expel "inconvenient" people. This, in turn, brought about another alignment in 1936, in which Stalin and the Moscow *nomenklatura* sided with the rank and file, who complained of repression by the regional elites. In 1937 Stalin openly mobilized the "party masses" against the *nomenklatura* as a whole; this provided an important strand in the Great Terror's destruction of the elite. But in 1938 the Politburo changed alignments and reinforced the authority of the regional *nomenklatura* as part of an attempt to restore order in the party during the terror.[61]

The situation thus exploded when Stalin made the risky move of directly appealing to the lower rank-and-file members themselves, soliciting them to articulate their complaint against the arbitrary rule of the local party bosses (a move similar to Mao's Cultural Revolution) — their fury at the regime, unable to express itself directly, exploded all the more viciously against the personalized substitute targets. Since the upper *nomenklatura* at the same time retained its executive power in the purges themselves, this set in motion a properly carnivalesque self-destructive vicious cycle in which virtually everyone was threatened (for example, of eighty-two district party secretaries, seventy-nine were shot). Another aspect of the spiraling vicious cycle was the very fluctuations of the directives from the top as to the thoroughness of the purges: the top demanded harsh measures, while at the same time warning against excesses, so the executors were put in an untenable position—ultimately, whatever they did was wrong. If they did not arrest a sufficient number of traitors and discover enough conspiracies, they were considered lenient and supportive of counter-revolution; so, under this pressure, in order to meet the quota, as it were, they had to fabricate evidence and invent plots— thereby exposing themselves to the criticism that they were themselves saboteurs, destroying thousands of honest Communists on behalf of foreign powers . . . Stalin's strategy of addressing directly the party masses, co-opting their anti-bureaucratic attitudes, was thus very risky:

> This not only threatened to open elite politics to public scrutiny but also risked discrediting the entire Bolshevik regime, of which Stalin himself was a part. [. . .] Finally, in 1937, Stalin broke all the rules of the game—indeed, destroyed the game completely—and unleashed a terror of all against all.[62]

One can discern very precisely the superego dimension of these events: this very violence inflicted by the Communist Party on its own members bears witness to the radical self-contradiction of the regime, namely to the fact that, at the origins of the regime, there was an "authentic" revolutionary project—incessant purges were necessary not only to erase the traces of the regime's own origins, but also as a kind of "return of the repressed," a reminder of the radical negativity at the heart of the regime. The Stalinist purges of high party echelons relied on this fundamental betrayal: the accused were effectively guilty insofar as they, as the members of the new *nomenklatura,* betrayed the Revolution. The Stalinist terror is thus not simply the betrayal of the Revolution, that is the attempt to erase the traces of the authentic revolutionary past; it rather bears witness to a kind of "imp of perversity" which compels the post-revolutionary new order to (re)inscribe its betrayal of the Revolution within itself, to "reflect" it or "remark" it in the guise of arbitrary arrests and killings which threatened all members of the *nomenklatura*—as in psychoanalysis, the Stalinist confession of guilt conceals the true guilt. (As is well known, Stalin wisely recruited into the NKVD people of lower social origins who were thus able to act out their hatred of the *nomenklatura* by arresting and torturing senior apparatchiks.) This inherent tension between the stability of the rule of the new *nomenklatura* and the perverted "return of the repressed" in the guise of the repeated purges of the ranks of the *nomenklatura* is at the very heart of the Stalinist phenomenon: purges are the very form in which the betrayed revolutionary heritage survives and haunts the regime . . . As already noted in the case of Mao, one should specify here the role of the Leader: he was exempted from these shifts of fortune because he was not the traditional Master, but the "Lord of Misrule": the very agent of carnivalesque subversion.

Because of this carnivalesque self-destructive dynamic, the Stalinist *nomenklatura* cannot yet be characterized as the "New Class"—as Andrzej Walicki noted, paradoxically, the stabilization of *nomenklatura* into a new class is incompatible with true Stalinist "totalitarianism": it was only in the Brezhnev years that this occurred:

> the consolidation of the Soviet *nomenklatura*, which for the first time in Soviet history "succeeded in emancipating itself from the subservience to higher authorities," and constituted itself as a stable privileged stratum enjoying not only physical security (which it had obtained under Khrushchev) but also job security, regardless of performance — in effect a status similar to that of the new ruling class. [. . .] The high-water mark of totalitarianism was the period of the permanent purges, which aimed at the absolute elimination not only of all possible deviations, but also of stable interest groups whose very existence might endanger ideological purity and undermine the monolithic structure of power.[63]

There are two further paradoxical conclusions to be drawn here: due to the specific ideological nature of the Stalinist regime (its nominal commitment to the goal of an egalitarian and just communist society), the terror and purges of the *nomenklatura* itself were not only inscribed into its very nature (the very existence of *nomenklatura* betrayed its proclaimed goals), they were also the revenge of the regime's own ideology against its *nomenklatura* which *was* indeed guilty of "betraying socialism." Furthermore, this is why the full stabilization of the *nomenklatura* into a new class was only possible when its members ceased to take seriously the regime's ideological goals—therein resides the role of the term "really-existing socialism," which emerged during the Brezhnev years: it signals that the regime had renounced its communist vision and limited itself to a pragmatic power politics. This also confirms the (often-noted) fact that the Khrushchev years were the last years in which the Soviet ruling elite was still possessed by a genuine historical (if not revolutionary) enthusiasm about its own mission—after Khrushchev, nothing like his defiant message to the Americans "We will bury you! Your grandchildren will be Communists!" was imaginable.

. . . in the films of Sergei Eisenstein

Besides Welles's *Magnificent Ambersons*, Eisenstein's *Bezhin Meadow* and Part III of *Ivan the Terrible* belong to the series of lost absolute master-pieces of the history of cinema.

The supreme irony of *Bezhin Meadow* is the film's title: it is taken from Ivan Turgenev's short story, one of the *Sketches from a Hunter's Album*, about peasant boys discussing supernatural signs of death. What does this to have to do with the film's story, based on the (in)famous case of Pavlik Morozov, about a boy from a peasant village in the years of dekulakization, who is killed by his counter-revolutionary father because he supported collective farms? One is almost tempted to repeat the question of the perplexed viewer in front of a painting showing Nadhezda Krupskaya in her office, engaged in wild sex with a young Komsomol member, entitled "Lenin in Warsaw"—"Where is Lenin?" (The guide's calm reply: "Lenin is in Warsaw.") So where is Bezhin meadow? There are echoes between the two stories, but not at the explicit narrative level; they concern the underlying fantasmatic "virtual" level. In the film, too, there is a group of peasant boys struggling with the earthly representative of the supernatural, the Church, but they "discuss supernatural signs of death" by destroying it in a carnivalesque orgy.[64]

It was the greatness of Eisenstein that, in his films, he rendered the shift in the libidinal economy from the Leninist revolutionary fervor to the Stalinist "Thermidor." Recall the archetypal Eisensteinian cinematic scene which portrays the exuberant orgy of revolutionary destructive violence (what Eisenstein himself called "a veritable bacchanalia of destruction"): when, in *October*, the victorious revolutionaries penetrate the wine cellars of the Winter Palace, they indulge in an ecstatic orgy of smashing thousands of expensive wine bottles; in *Bezhin Meadow*, the village Pioneers force their way into the local church and desecrate it, robbing it of its relics, squabbling over an icon, sacrilegiously trying on vestments, heretically laughing at the statuary . . . In this suspension of goal-oriented instrumental activity, we effectively have a kind of

Bataillean "unrestrained expenditure"—the pious desire to deprive the revolution of this excess is simply the desire to have a revolution without a revolution. Contrast this with what Eisenstein does in Part II of *Ivan the Terrible*, where the only scene shot in color (the penultimate reel) is the carnivalesque orgy in the great hall of the count, a Bakhtinian fantasmatic space in which "normal" power relations are inverted: here the tsar is the slave of the idiot, whom he proclaims a new tsar, and Ivan provides the imbecile Vladimir with all the imperial insignia, then humbly prostrates himself in front of him and kisses his hand. The scene begins with the obscene chorus and dance of the *"oprichniks"* (Ivan's private army), staged in an entirely "unrealistic" way: an odd mixture of Hollywood and Japanese theater, a musical number whose words tell a weird story (they celebrate the axe which cuts off the heads of Ivan's enemies). The song first describes a group of boyars having a rich meal: *"Down the middle . . . the golden goblets pass . . . from hand to hand."* The Chorus then asks with pleasurable nervous expectation: *"Come along. Come along. What happens next? Come on, tell us more!"* And the solo *oprichnik*, bending forward and whistling, shouts the answer: *"Strike with the axes!"* We are here at the obscene site where musical enjoyment meets political liquidation. And, taking into account the fact that the film was shot in 1944, does this not confirm the carnivalesque character of the Stalinist purges? We encounter a similar nocturnal orgy in the third part of *Ivan*, which was not shot— see the scenario,[65] where the sacrilegious obscenity is explicit: Ivan and his *oprichniks* perform their nightly drinking feast as a black mass, with black monastic robes over their normal clothing. Therein resides the true greatness of Eisenstein: that he detected (and depicted) the fundamental shift in the status of political violence, from the "Leninist" liberating outburst of destructive energy to the "Stalinist" obscene underside of the Law.

Interestingly, the main opponent of Ivan in both parts of the film is not a man, but a woman: the old powerful Euphrosyna Staritskaya, Ivan's aunt, who wants to replace Ivan with her imbecilic son Vladimir and thus effectively reign herself. In contrast to Ivan, who wants total power, but perceives it as a "heavy load," exercising it as a means to an end (the creation of a great and powerful Russian state), Euphrosyna is the subject of a morbid passion. For her, power is an end in itself. The aforementioned lines from Hegel's *Phenomenology of the Spirit* on the notion of womankind[66] fit perfectly the figure of Ortrud in Wagner's *Lohengrin*: for Wagner, there is nothing more horrible and disgusting than a woman who intervenes in political life, driven by the desire for power. In contrast to male ambition, a woman wants power in order to promote her own narrow family interests or, even worse, her personal caprice, incapable as she is of perceiving the universal dimension of state politics. And, does the same not hold for *Ivan the Terrible*? Is Euphrosyna not the necessary counterpoint of the poisoned Ivan's bride, a gentle woman totally dedicated and submitted to her husband?[67]

Ivan's paradigmatic gesture is the following one: he puts on a show of horror and repentance at the bloodshed he had to set in train, and then, in a sudden reflexive gesture, he fully endorses his cruelty, demanding even more. In a typical moment in Part II, inspecting the bodies of the boyars killed by his *oprichniks*, he humbly crosses himself. Suddenly, he stops and points at the ground, a gleam of mad fury in his eyes, saying hoarsely: "Too few!" This jolting shift is best exemplified by the elementary trait in his acting: repeatedly, we see Ivan staring ahead, with a pathetic expression on his face, as if passionately engrossed in a noble mission; then, all of a sudden, he looks around suspiciously with an expression bordering on paranoid madness. A variation of this shift is the famous shot when, during his illness in Part I, the priests prematurely and all too eagerly start to perform the rites for the dying. They cover his head with a gigantic sacred book; holding a burning handle on his breast, Ivan participates in the ritual, murmuring prayers; all of a sudden, however, he struggles to raise his head from under the Bible, glances around the room as if trying desperately to get a view of the situation, and then, exhausted, drops back on the pillow beneath the book.

This brings us to a scene which was planned as what Eisenstein called the *donnée* (the pivotal dramatic and emotional point) of the entire trilogy: in the middle of Part III, after the siege and destruction of Novgorod, a city which rebelled against his rule, Ivan, torn by inner doubts and qualms, asks for a priest and wants to confess. The shot is a long continuous close-up of Ivan's head covering half of the screen; the other half is filled by the confessor's cross hanging by him while Ivan enumerates to the priest the horrible deeds he was forced to carry out for the motherland. All of a sudden, Eustace, the confessor, gets all too interested in the names of those killed (a fact nicely signaled by the trembling of his cross), and eagerly asks about whether other names are also among the dead: "Phillip? And . . . Timothy? And Michael?" After reassuring him ("We will catch him!"), Ivan is suddenly taken aback. He seizes Eustace's cross and drags it down until he is face to face with his confessor. Then, his hands reach up the chain to the confessor's throat, and he starts to accuse him menacingly: "Can it be that you too belong to this accursed line?" Finally, he explodes: "Arrest him! Interrogate him! Make him talk!"[68]

In a further climactic moment of Part III, Ivan involves God himself in this dialectic. While, in the church, a monk slowly reads the names of all those killed in Novgorod, Ivan lies prostrate in the dust beneath the large painting of the Last Judgment, on which sparks shoot out of the eyes of the celestial judge and his grim face is full of rage. Ivan reflects on his bloodthirsty actions, trying to excuse them: "It's not wickedness. Not anger. Not cruelty. It is to punish treason. Treason against the common cause." Then, in anguish, he directly addresses God:

"You say nothing, Celestial Tsar?"

He waits. There is no reply. Angrily, as though hurling a challenge, the earthly Tsar repeats menacingly to the Celestial Tsar:

"You say nothing, Celestial Tsar?"

The earthly Tsar, with a sudden, violent gesture, hurls his bejeweled scepter at the Celestial Tsar. The scepter smashes against the flat wall.[69]

In what, exactly, resides the libidinal economy of this strange twist? It is not that Ivan is simply torn by an inner conflict between his personal ethical qualms and the duty of the ruler who has to perform cruel acts for the sake of his country; it is also not that Ivan is simply bluffing, just hypocritically feigning moral torment. While his will to repent is *absolutely sincere*, he does not subjectively identify with it. He is lodged within the subjective split introduced by the symbolic order: he wants the ritual of confession performed as a proper externalized ritual, and he plays the game of confession in a totally sincere way, while, at the same time, retaining the position of a suspicious external observer of the entire spectacle, constantly vigilant, watching for a sudden stab in the back. All he wants is that the agent whom he is addressing, and from whom he expects forgiveness, will do his job properly, and not meddle in politics. In short, Ivan's paranoia is that he cannot trust the agent to whom he is ready to confess his sins—he suspects that this agent (ultimately, God himself) also harbors a hidden political agenda of his own running counter to Ivan's. This is why Stalin was here too quick when, in the famous nighttime conversation with Eisenstein, he reduced Ivan's religiosity to a moral obstacle which prevented Ivan from ruthlessly finishing off the job of destroying his enemies:

> Ivan the Terrible was extremely cruel. It is possible to show why he had to be cruel. One of the mistakes of Ivan the Terrible was that he did not completely finish off the five big feudal families. If he had destroyed these five families then there would not have been the Time of Troubles. If Ivan the Terrible executed someone then he repented and prayed for a long time. God disturbed him on these matters. [. . .] It was necessary to be decisive.[70]

What Stalin, in spite of his genius, failed to grasp is how the spectacle of repentance was not an obstacle to the ruthless killing of his enemies, but rather helped constitute the self-propelling spiral of the endless oscillation between murder and repentance. This spiral would have reached its unbearable climax in Part III of *Ivan the Terrible*. In the script for the film, there is a scene in the great hall of the court in which Ivan accomplishes a proto-Stalinist purge among his own *oprichniks*. Addressing the gathered *oprichniks*, he ominously claims that "there are some amongst us who have traded the cause of the *oprichniks* for gold," without naming anyone; he goes on: "There is amongst you one who is both venerable and who enjoys the highest confidence [. . .] And this wretch has betrayed my confidence." All eyes, following Ivan's gaze, are fixed on Ivan's faithful Alexei Basmanov, including the eyes of Alexei's grief-stricken son Fyodor. Then, Ivan asks: "Who is worthy enough to cut off so wise a head?" His eyes rest on Fyodor whose head is lowered. Fyodor feels Ivan's gaze on him; he raises his head to look Ivan right in the eyes. With a scarcely perceptible movement, Ivan nods his head; Fyodor leaves the table, goes up to his father and leads him off.

In a dark place outside, Alexei confesses his guilt to his son, but tells him that he has piled up mountains of gold for his son and family, so that "our line continues"; he then implores his son to promise him that, after killing him, he will keep all the gold for their descendants; Fyodor swears the oath, father and son kiss, and the son then swiftly decapitates his father. The scene then returns to the great hall, where Ivan, in a state of mounting tension and full of torment, looks at the door. At last the door opens and Fyodor reappears; his head is bowed, his hair sticking to his forehead. He raises his head; Ivan looks him straight in the eye.

But already the gaze of Fyodor is impure; it cannot withstand that of Ivan. Ivan's lips twitch as he speaks hollowly: "You showed no pity to your father, Fyodor. Why should you pity or defend me?" Fyodor grasps that the Tsar has divined the secret talk between him and his father.

Ivan utters the order: "Arrest him!" Like a madman, Fyodor tries to throw himself on Ivan, but is stabbed by Staden's (a German *oprichnik*'s) dagger. "A single tear rolls down the grey beard of Tsar Ivan. It remains suspended on the point of his beard like a raindrop on a funeral wreath. IVAN: 'Have pity on me, O Lord, have pity . . .'" With the last atom of his strength, the dying Fyodor warns Ivan: "Do not trust the German, O Tsar! . . ." Ivan raises his heavy eyelids; his gaze stops on Staden: "How promptly the foreign guest comes to the defense of the Tsar against his own *oprichniks*!" The faithful Malyuta quickly grabs Staden's shoulder with his heavy hand . . .[71] Even here, the chain of betrayal and suspicion goes on: from Alexei to Fyodor, from Fyodor to Staden . . . In both cases, Ivan's suspicion falls on the very person who has just performed a murder to defend the tsar.

Whom can Ivan trust, if even the couple of faithful servants, Alexei Basmanov and his son Fyodor, end up betraying him (stealing and amassing treasures for the wealth and glory of their family)? Malyuta Skuratov, his most trusted and doggishly devoted executioner, first met him when he led the mob which broke into the church where Ivan's coronation was in progress, with murder on his mind. At the end of Part III, the dying Malyuta as it were nominates his successor (the person whom Ivan can absolutely trust): Peter Volynets, the young man who, at the end of Part II, had stabbed Vladimir to death, believing that he was killing Ivan—it is as through Ivan can truly trust only former traitors.

The minimal difference

One can imagine a Stalinist tragedy proper which would occur when the accused in a show trial (an ex-member of *nomenklatura*) is compelled to admit that the unjust punishment that befell him is the outcome of his own previous political activity, and is, in this sense, a sign of an ironic justice, that is, that, in this sense, he effectively *is* "objectively guilty." But can one imagine Stalin himself undergoing a similar experience, recognizing in the madness of counter-revolutionary plots popping up all around him the result of his own madness? For structural reasons, no. What one can imagine is a successful *coup d'état* staged by the upper *nomenklatura* against Stalin (say in the last years of his life, when they were all again threatened by Stalin's anti-Semitic paranoia); but it would have been impossible to organize a show trial against Stalin himself, compelling him to confess that he had headed a conspiracy against true socialism. The most they could have done was to kill him discreetly, while elevating him simultaneously into an untouchable dead Master. In a way, this *did* happen in the late 1930s. One should always bear in mind that the notion of the infallibility of the pope was forged in the late nineteenth century not to increase his power but to curb it: a pope cannot nullify the decisions of his predecessors, since they are, by definition, infallible. And a similar paradox holds for Stalin: his deification, elevation into the untouchable supreme Leader, coincides with the limitation of his "real" power. At the climax of the great purges, when the spiral of carnivalesque self-destruction threatened to swallow the upper *nomenklatura* itself, the Politburo stood up to Stalin, forcing him to share his authority with them.

The standard characterization of Stalinist regimes as "bureaucratic socialism" is totally misleading and (self-)mystifying: it is the way the Stalinist regime itself perceived its problem, the cause of its failures and troubles—if there were not enough products in the stores, if the authorities failed to respond to people's demands, and so on and so forth, what was easier than to blame the "bureaucratic" attitude of indifference, petty arrogance, etc.? No wonder that, from the late 1920s onwards, Stalin was writing attacks on bureaucracy, on bureaucratic attitudes. "Bureaucratism" was nothing but an effect of the functioning of Stalinist regimes, and the paradox is that it is the ultimate misnomer: what Stalinist regimes really lacked was precisely an efficient "bureaucracy" (a depoliticized and competent administrative apparatus).

One of the arguments of those who insist that Communism, not fascism, was the true ethico-political catastrophe of the twentieth century, rests on the fact that in all of Nazi Germany there were only 25,000 Gestapo secret policemen to control the population, while the tiny GDR alone employed 100,000 secret policemen to control its much smaller population—clear proof of the much more oppressive nature of the Communist regime. However, what if one reads this fact in a different way? Fewer Gestapo agents were needed because the German population was much more morally corrupted in supporting the Nazis (and thus collaborated with the regime) than the GDR population—why? Why did the GDR population resist much more? The answer is a paradoxical one: it is not that the people simply retained their ethical independence, so that the regime was alienated from the "substantial ethical life" of the majority; quite the contrary, resistance was an indication of the success of the ruling ideology. In their very resistance to the Communist regime, the people relied on the official ideology itself which often blatantly contradicted reality: actual freedom, social solidarity, true democracy . . . One should never forget the extent to which the dissident resistance was indebted to the official ideology.

For this precise reason, one can claim that today's North Korea is no longer a Communist country, not even in the Stalinist sense: it cut the links with the legacy of the Enlightenment, whose notion of universality compels a regime to expose *all* its citizens to official propaganda. Shin Dong Hyok, who escaped a "total-control zone" in North Korea and reached South Korea via China, reports that the prisoners sent to such zones can never come out: they are put to work in mines or logging camps until they die. The authorities do not even bother to give them ideological education: the children who are born to parents in these zones (and destined to spend their entire lives in them) are only taught the elementary skills necessary for mining and farming. There were up to 1,000 children but no textbooks in the school at Valley No. 2, the part of the camp where Shin lived. In all of North Korea, villages are decorated with Communist slogans and portraits of Kim Jong Il. Valley No. 2 had only one slogan carved into a wooden plaque: "Everyone obey the regulations!"[72] What we have here is thus the disciplinary mechanism at its purest, deprived of any ideological justification. All North Koreans are expected to look up to their beloved leader (when blind patients were asked by Western journalists why they wanted to see, they all claimed that it was in order to catch the sight of Kim Yong Il, to whom they owed everything) — all except those prisoners who are thus literally reduced to subhuman status, excluded from the social community.

It is worth returning here to Ernst Nolte's book on Heidegger because it seriously approaches the task of grasping Nazism as a feasible political project, of trying to recreate "the story the Nazis were telling themselves about themselves," which is a *sine qua non* of its effective criticism; the same has to be done for Stalinism.[73] Nolte also formulated the basic terms and topics of the "revisionist" debate whose first tenet is to "objectively compare" fascism and Communism: fascism and even Nazism was ultimately a reaction to the Communist threat and a repetition of its worst practices (concentration camps, mass liquidations of political enemies):

> Could it be the case that the National Socialists and Hitler carried out an "Asiatic" deed [the Holocaust] only because they considered themselves and their kind to be potential or actual victims of a [Bolshevik] "Asiatic" deed. Didn't the "Gulag Archipelago" precede Auschwitz?[74]

Reprehensible as it was, Nazism was thus temporally what appeared after Communism; it was also, with regard to its content, an excessive *reaction* to the Communist threat. Furthermore, all the horrors committed by Nazism merely copied the horrors already committed by Soviet Communism: the reign of the secret police, concentration camps, genocidal terror . . . Nolte's conclusion is thus that Communism and Nazism share the same totalitarian form, and that the difference concerns only the empirical agents which fill the same structural places ("Jews" instead of "class enemy," and so on and so forth). The standard liberal-leftist reaction to Nolte consisted in a moralistic outcry: Nolte relativizes Nazism, reducing it to a secondary echo of Communist Evil—but how can one even compare Communism, this thwarted attempt at liberation, with the radical Evil of Nazism? In contrast to this dismissal, one should fully concede Nolte's central point: yes, Nazism was in fact a reaction to the Communist threat; it did indeed just replace class struggle with the struggle between Aryans and Jews—the problem, however, resides in this "just," which is by no means as innocent as it appears. We are dealing here with displacement (*Verschiebung*) in the Freudian sense of the term: Nazism displaces class struggle onto racial struggle and thereby obfuscates its true site. What changes in the passage from Communism to Nazism is the form, and it is in this change of the form that the Nazi ideological mystification resides: the political struggle is naturalized into the racial conflict, the (class) antagonism inherent in the social structure is reduced to the invasion of a foreign (Jewish) body which disturbs the harmony of the Aryan community. The difference between fascism and Communism is thus "formal-ontological": it is not (as Nolte claims) that we have in both cases the same formal antagonistic structure, where only the place of the Enemy is filled in with a different positive element (class, race). In the case of race, we are dealing with a positive naturalized element (the presupposed organic unity of society is perturbed by the intrusion of the foreign body), while class antagonism is absolutely inherent in and constitutive of the social field—fascism thus obfuscates antagonism, translating it into a conflict of positive opposed terms.[75]

It is here that one has to make the choice: the "pure" liberal stance of equidistance towards leftist and rightist "totalitarianism" (they are both bad, based on the intolerance of political and other differences, the rejection of democratic and humanist values, and so on) is *a priori* false, one *has* to take sides and proclaim one fundamentally "worse" than the other—for this reason, the ongoing "relativization" of fascism, the notion that one should rationally compare the two totalitarianisms, etc., *always* involves the—explicit or implicit—thesis that fascism was "better" than Communism, an understandable reaction to the Communist threat.[76]

In a letter (to which I have already referred in Chapter 3) to Herbert Marcuse on January 20, 1948, Heidegger wrote:

> To the serious legitimate charges that you express "about a regime that murdered millions of Jews . . ." I can merely add that if instead of "Jews" you had written "East Germans," then the same holds true for one of the allies, with the difference that everything that has occurred since 1945 has become public knowledge, while the bloody terror of the Nazis in point of fact had been kept a secret from the German people.[77]

Marcuse was fully justified in replying that the thin difference between brutally expatriating people and burning them in a concentration camp is the line that, at that moment, separated civilization from barbarism. One should not shrink from going a step further: the thin difference between the Stalinist gulag and the Nazi annihilation camp was also, at that historical moment, the difference between civilization and barbarism.

Let us take Stalinism at its most brutal: the dekulakization of the early 1930s. Stalin's slogan was that "kulaks as a class should be liquidated"— what does this mean? It can mean many things—from taking away their property (land), to forcibly removing them to other areas (say, from Ukraine to Siberia), or simply into a gulag—but it did *not* mean simply to kill them all. The goal was to liquidate them *as a class*, not as individuals. Even when the rural population was deliberately starved (millions of dead in Ukraine, again), the goal was not to kill them all, but to break their backbone, to brutally crush their resistance, to show them who was the master. The difference—minimal, but crucial—persists here with regard to the Nazi de-Judaization, where the ultimate goal effectively was to annihilate them as individuals, to make them disappear as a race.

In this sense, then, Ernst Nolte is right: Nazism *was* a repetition, a copy of Bolshevism—in Nietzsche's terms, it was a profoundly *re-active* phenomenon.

6 Why Populism Is (Sometimes) Good Enough in Practice, but Not Good Enough in Theory

Gerald Fitzgerald, the Irish ex-Prime Minister, once formulated a proper Hegelian reversal of the commonplace wisdom "This may be good for theory, but it is not good enough for practice": "This may be good in practice, but it is not good enough in theory." This reversal best encapsulates the ambiguous position of populist politics: while it can sometimes be endorsed as part of a short-term pragmatic compromise, one should critically reject the notion in its fundamental dimension.

The positive dimension of populism is its potential suspension of democratic rules. Democracy—in the way this term is used today—concerns, above all, formal legalism: its minimal definition is unconditional adherence to a certain set of formal rules which guarantee that antagonisms are fully absorbed into the agonistic game. "Democracy" means that, whatever electoral manipulation took place, every political agent will unconditionally respect the results. In this sense, the US presidential elections of 2000 were effectively "democratic": in spite of obvious electoral manipulation, and of the patent meaninglessness of the fact that a couple of hundred Florida voices decided who would be the president, the Democratic candidate accepted his defeat. In the weeks of uncertainty after the elections, Bill Clinton made an appropriate acerbic comment: "The American people have spoken; we just don't know what they said." This comment should be taken more seriously than it was meant: even now, we do not know it—and, maybe, because there was no substantial "message" behind the result at all . . . Jacques-Alain Miller has shown how democracy implies the "barred" big Other;[1] however, the Florida example demonstrates that, nonetheless, there is a "big Other" which continues to exist in democracy: the procedural "big Other" of electoral rules which should be obeyed whatever the result—and it is *this* "big Other," this unconditional reliance on rules that populism (threatens to) suspend. Which is why there is in populism always something violent, threatening, for the liberal view: an open or latent pressure, a warning that, if elections are manipulated, the "will of the people" will have to find another way to impose itself; even if electoral legitimization of power is respected, it is made clear that elections play a secondary role, that they serve only to confirm a political process whose substantial weight lies elsewhere. This is why the regime of Hugo Chavez in Venezuela is genuinely populist: although it was legitimized by elections, it is clear that its exercise of power relies on a different dynamic (direct organization of the poor in favelas and other modes of local self-organization). This is what gives the "thrill" to populist regimes: the democratic rules are never fully endorsed, there is always an uncertainty that pertains to them, a possibility always looms that they will be redefined, "unfairly changed in the middle of the game." This aspect of populism should be fully endorsed—the problem is not its "undemocratic" character, but its reliance on a substantial notion of the "people": in populism, the "big Other," although (potentially) suspended in the guise of procedural *formalism*, returns in the guise of the People as the *substantial* agent legitimizing power.

There are thus two elementary and irreducible sides to democracy: the violent egalitarian rise of the logic of those who are "supernumerary," the "part of no part," those who, while formally included within the social edifice, have no determinate place within it; and the regulated (more or less) universal procedure of choosing those who will exert power. How do these two sides relate to each other? What if democracy in the second sense (the regulated procedure of registering the "people's voice") is ultimately *a defense against itself*, against democracy in the sense of the violent intrusion of the egalitarian logic that disturbs the hierarchical functioning of the social edifice, an attempt to re-functionalize this excess, to make it a part of the normal running of the social edifice?

However, the trap to be avoided here is to oppose these two poles as the "good" versus the "bad", that is, to dismiss institutionalized democratic procedure as an "ossification" of a primordial democratic experience. What truly matters is precisely the degree to which the democratic explosion succeeds in becoming institutionalized, translated into social order. Not only are democratic explosions easily recuperated by those in power, since "the day after" people awaken to the sober reality of power relations reinvigorated by fresh democratic blood (which is why those in power love "explosions of creativity" like the French May 1968); often, the "ossified" democratic procedure to which the majority continues to stick as to the "dead letter" is the only defense remaining against the onslaught of "totalitarian" passions of the crowd.

The problem is thus: how to regulate/institutionalize the very violent egalitarian democratic impulse, how to prevent it being drowned in democracy in the second sense of the term (regulated procedure)? If there is no way to do it, then "authentic" democracy remains a momentary utopian outburst which, on the proverbial morning after, has to be normalized. The harsh consequence to be accepted here is that this excess of egalitarian democracy over the democratic procedure can only "institutionalize" itself in the guise of its opposite, as revolutionary-democratic *terror*.

Good enough in practice . . .

The 2005 French and Dutch "nos" to the project of the European Constitution were clear-cut cases of what in "French theory" is referred to as a *floating signifier*: a "no" of confused, inconsistent, overdetermined meanings, a kind of container in which the defense of workers' rights coexists with racism, in which the blind reaction to a perceived threat and fear of change coexist with vague utopian hopes. We are told that the French "no" was really a "no" to many other things: to Anglo-Saxon neoliberalism, to Chirac and his government, to the influx of immigrant workers from Poland who lower the wages of the French workers, and so on and so forth. The real struggle is going on now: namely the struggle for the *meaning* of this "no"—who will appropriate it? Who—if anyone—will translate it into a coherent alternative political vision?

If there is a predominant reading of the "no," it is a new variation on the old Clinton motto "It's the economy, stupid!": the "no" was supposedly a reaction to Europe's economic lethargy, falling behind with regard to other newly emerging blocs of economic power, its economic, social, and ideologico-political inertia—*but*, paradoxically, an inappropriate reaction, a reaction *on behalf of* this very inertia of privileged Europeans, of those who want to cling on to old welfare-state privileges. It was the reaction of "old Europe," triggered by the fear of any real change, the refusal of the uncertainties of the Brave New World of globalist modernization.[2] No wonder that the reaction of "official" Europe was one of near-panic at the dangerous, "irrational," racist and isolationist passions that sustained the "no," at a parochial rejection of openness and liberal multiculturalism. One is used to hearing complaints about the growing apathy of the voters, about the decline of popular participation in politics, so worried liberals talk all the time about the need to mobilize people in the guise of civil-society initiatives, to engage them more in a political process. However, when the people awaken from their apolitical slumber, it is as a rule in the guise of a rightist populist revolt—no wonder many enlightened technocratic liberals now wonder whether the previous form of "apathy" was not a blessing in disguise.

One should be attentive here to how even those elements which appear as pure rightist racism are in fact a displaced version of working-class protests: of course there is a form of racism in demanding an end to the immigration of foreign workers who pose a threat to employment; however, one should bear in mind the simple fact that the influx of immigrant workers from the post-Communist countries is not the consequence of multiculturalist tolerance—it *is* indeed part of the strategy of capital to hold in check workers' demands—this is why, in the US, Bush did more for the legalization of the status of Mexican illegal immigrants than did the Democrats caught up by labor-union pressures. So, ironically, rightist racist populism is today the best argument that the "class struggle," far from being "obsolete," goes on—the lesson the Left should learn from it is that one should not commit the error symmetrical to that of the populist racist mystification/displacement of hatred onto foreigners, and to "throw the baby out with the bath water," that is, to merely oppose populist anti-immigrant racism with multiculturalist openness, obliterating its displaced class content—benevolent as it wants to be, the simple insistence on tolerance is the most perfidious form of antiproletarian class struggle . . .

Typical here is the reaction of German mainstream politicians to the formation of the new Linkspartei in the 2005 elections, a coalition of the East German PDS and leftist dissidents of the SPD—Joschka Fischer himself reached one of the lowest points in his career when he called Oskar Lafontaine "a German Haider" (because Lafontaine protested at the importation of cheap East European labor to lower the wages of German workers). The exaggerated and panicky way the political (and even cultural) establishment reacted when Lafontaine referred to "foreign workers," or when the secretary of the SPD called the financial speculators "locusts," is symptomatic—as if we were witnessing a full neo-Nazi revival. This total political blindness, this loss of the very capacity to distinguish Left from Right, betrays a panic at politicization as such. The automatic dismissal of entertaining any thoughts outside the established post-political coordinates as "populist demagoguery" is the hitherto purest proof that we effectively live under a new *Denkverbot*.[3]

It is not only that today's political field is polarized between post-political administration and populist politicization; phenomena such as Berlusconi demonstrate how the two opposites can even coexist in the same party: is the Berlusconi movement Forza Italia! not a case of post-political populism, that is, of a mediatic-administrative government legitimizing itself in populist terms? And does the same not hold to some degree even for the New Labour government in the UK, or for the Bush administration in the US? In other words, is populism not progressively replacing multiculturalist tolerance as the "spontaneous" ideological supplement to post-political administration, as its "pseudo-concretization," its translation into a form that can appeal to individuals' immediate experience? The key fact here is that pure post-politics (a regime whose self-legitimization would be thoroughly "technocratic," presenting itself as a competent administration) is inherently impossible: any political regime needs a supplementary "populist" level of self-legitimization.

This is why today's populism is different from the traditional version — what distinguishes it is the opponent against which it mobilizes the people: the rise of "post-politics," the growing reduction of politics proper to the rational administration of conflicting interests. In the highly developed countries of the US and Western Europe, at least, "populism" is emerging as the inherent shadowy double of institutionalized post-politics; one is almost tempted to say: as its *supplement* in the Derridean sense, as the arena in which political demands that do not fit the institutionalized space can be articulated. In this sense, there is a constitutive "mystification" that pertains to populism: its basic gesture is to refuse to confront the complexity of the situation, to reduce it to a clear struggle with a pseudo-concrete "enemy" figure (from the "Brussels bureaucracy" to illegal immigrants). "Populism" is thus, by definition, a negative phenomenon, a phenomenon grounded in a refusal, even an implicit admission of impotence. We all know the old joke about a man looking for the key he has dropped under the street light; when asked where he lost it, he admits that it was in an ill-lit spot; so why is he looking for it here, under the light? Because the visibility is so much better here . . . There is always something of this trick in populism. So, not only is populism not the arena within which today's emancipatory projects should inscribe themselves, but one should even go a step further and propose that the main task of contemporary emancipatory politics, its life-and-death problem, is to find a form of political mobilization that, while (like populism) critical of institutionalized politics, will *avoid* the populist temptation.

Where, then, does all this leave us with regard to Europe's imbroglio? The French voters were not given a clear symmetrical choice, since the very terms of the choice privileged the "yes": the elite proposed a choice to the people which was in fact no choice at all—people were called to ratify the inevitable, the result of enlightened expertise. The media and the political elite presented the choice as the one between knowledge and ignorance, between expertise and ideology, between post-political administration and the archaic political passions of the Left and the Right.[4] The "no" was thus dismissed as a shortsighted reaction unaware of its own consequences: a murky reaction of fear of the emerging new postindustrial global order, a conservative instinct to protect creaking welfare-state structures—a gesture of refusal lacking any positive alternative program. No wonder that the only political parties whose official stance was "no" were the parties at the opposite extremes of the political spectrum, Le Pen's Front National on the Right and the Communists and Trotskyists on the Left.

However, even if there is an element of truth in all this, the very fact that the "no" was not sustained by a coherent alternative political vision is the strongest possible condemnation of the political and mediatic elite, a monument to their inability to articulate, to translate into a political vision, the people's longings and dissatisfactions. Instead, in their reaction to the "no," they treated the people as retarded pupils who had not learnt the lesson of the experts: their self-criticism was the one of the teacher who admits that he failed to educate his students properly. What the advocates of this "communication" thesis (the French and Dutch "no" means that the enlightened elite has failed to communicate adequately with the masses) fail to see is that, on the contrary, the "no" in question was a perfect example of communication in which, as Lacan put it, the speaker gets from the addressee its own message in its inverted, that is, true, form: the enlightened European bureaucrats received from the electorate the shallowness of their own message to them in its true form. The project of European Union that was rejected by France and the Netherlands stood for a kind of cheap trick, as if Europe could redeem itself and beat its competitors by simply combining the best of both worlds: by beating the US, China, and Japan in scientific-technological modernization through keeping alive its cultural traditions. One should insist here that, if Europe is to redeem itself, it should, on the contrary, be ready to take the risk of *losing* (in the sense of radically questioning) *both*: dispelling the fetish of scientific-technological progress *and* stop relying on the superiority of its cultural heritage.

So, although the choice was not that between two political options, it was also not the choice between the enlightened vision of a modern Europe, ready to fit into the new global order, and old confused political passions. When commentators described the "no" as a message of bewilderment and fear, they were wrong. The main fear at issue here is the fear the "no" itself provoked in the new European political elite, the fear that the people would no longer swallow their "post-political" vision. For the rest of us, the "no" is a message and expression of hope: hope that *politics* is still alive and possible, that the debate about what the new Europe shall and should be is still wide open. This is why we, on the Left, should reject the sneering insinuation by liberals that, in our "no," we find ourselves with strange neo-fascist bedfellows. What the new populist Right and the Left share is just one thing: the awareness that *politics proper is still alive*.

There *was* a positive choice in the "no": the choice of the choice itself; the rejection of the blackmail by the new elite which offers us only the choice to confirm their expert knowledge or to display one's "irrational" immaturity. The "no" is the positive decision to start a real political debate about what kind of Europe we really want. Late in his life, Freud asked the famous question *Was will das Weib?*—What does the woman want?—admitting his perplexity when faced with the enigma of feminine sexuality. Does the imbroglio with the European Constitution not bear witness to the same puzzlement: what kind of Europe do we want?

The unofficial anthem of the European Union, heard at numerous political, cultural, and sporting public events, is the "Ode to Joy" from the last movement of Beethoven's Ninth Symphony, a true "empty signifier" that can stand for anything. In France, it was elevated by Romain Rolland into a humanist ode to the brotherhood of all peoples ("the 'Marseillaise' of humanity"); in 1938, it was performed as the highpoint of *Reichsmusiktage* and later for Hitler's birthday; in the China of the Cultural Revolution, in the febrile context of a mass rejection of European classics, it was redeemed as a piece of progressive class struggle, while in contemporary Japan, it has achieved a cult status, being woven into the very social fabric with its supposed message of "joy through suffering"; until the 1970s, that is, during the period when both West and East German Olympic teams had to perform together as one German team, the anthem played for German gold medallists was the Ode, and, simultaneously, the Rhodesian white supremacist regime of Ian Smith, which proclaimed independence in the late 1960s in order to maintain apartheid, also appropriated the same song as its national anthem. Even Abimael Guzman, the (now imprisoned) leader of Sendero Luminoso, when asked what music he loved, mentioned the fourth movement of Beethoven's Ninth. So it is easy to picture an imaginary performance at which all the sworn enemies, from Hitler to Stalin, from Bush to Saddam, forget their differences and participate in the same magic moment of ecstatic brotherhood . . .[5]

However, before we dismiss the fourth movement as a piece "destroyed through social usage," let us note some peculiarities of its structure. In the middle of the movement, after we hear the main melody (the "Joy" theme) in three orchestral and three vocal variations, at this first climax, something unexpected happens which has bothered critics over the last 180 years, ever since the first performance: at bar 331, the tone changes totally, and, instead of the solemn hymnic progression, the same "Joy" theme is repeated in *marcia Turca* ("Turkish march") style, borrowed from the military music for wind and percussion instruments that eighteenth-century European armies had adopted from the Turkish janissaries—the mode is here that of a carnivalesque popular parade, a mocking spectacle.[6] And after this point, everything goes wrong, the simple solemn dignity of the first part of the movement is never recovered: after this "Turkish" part and in a clear counter-movement to it, in a kind of retreat into inner religiosity, the choral-like music (dismissed by some critics as a "Gregorian fossil") tries to depict the ethereal image of millions of people who kneel down embracing one another, contemplating the distant sky in awe and searching for the loving paternal God who must dwell above the canopy of stars ("*überm Sternezelt muß ein lieber Vater wohnen*"); however, the music, as it were, gets stuck when the word *muß*, first rendered by the basses, is repeated by the tenors and altos, and finally by the sopranos, as if this repeated conjuration is a desperate attempt to convince us (and itself) of what it knows is not true, turning the line "a loving father must dwell" into a desperate act of beseechment, and thus attesting to the fact that there is nothing beyond the canopy of stars, no loving father to protect us and to guarantee our brotherhood. After this, a return to a more celebratory mood is attempted in the guise of the double fugue which cannot but sound false in its excessively artificial brilliance, a fake synthesis if there ever was one, a desperate attempt to cover up the void of the *absent* God revealed in the previous section. But the final cadenza is the strangest of them all, sounding less like Beethoven than a puffed-up version of the finale of Mozart's *Abduction from Seraglio*, combining the "Turkish" elements with the fast rococo spectacle. (And let us not forget the principal lesson of this Mozart opera: the figure of the oriental despot is presented there as a true enlightened Master.) The finale is thus a bizarre mixture of Orientalism and regression into late eighteenth-century classicism, a double retreat from the historical present, a silent admission of the purely fantasmatic character of the joy of all-encompassing brotherhood. If there ever was a music that literally "deconstructs itself," this is it: the contrast between the highly ordered linear progression of the first part of the movement and the precipitous, heterogeneous, and inconsistent, character of the second cannot be stronger—no wonder that already in 1826, two years after the first performance, some reviewers described the finale as "a festival of hatred towards all that can be called human joy. With gigantic strength the perilous hoard emerges, tearing hearts asunder and darkening the divine spark of gods with noisy, monstrous mocking."[7]

Beethoven's Ninth is thus full of what Nicholas Cook called "unconsummated symbols": elements which are in excess of the global meaning of the work (or of the movement in which they occur), which do not fit this meaning, although it is not clear what additional meaning they bring.[8] Cook lists the "funeral march" at bar 513 of the first movement, the abrupt ending of the second movement, the military tones in the third movement, the so-called "horror fanfares," the Turkish march, and many other moments in the fourth movement—all these elements "vibrate with an implied significance that overflows the musical scenario."[9] It is not simply that their meaning should be uncovered through attentive interpretation—the very relationship between texture and meaning is inverted here: if the predominant "musical scenario" seems to set to music a clear preestablished meaning (the celebration of joy, universal brotherhood . . .), here the meaning is not given in advance, but seems to float in some kind of virtual indeterminacy—it is as if we know *that* there is (or, rather, has to be) some meaning, without ever being able to establish *what* this meaning is.

What, then, is the solution? The only radical solution is to shift the entire perspective and to render problematic the very first part of the fourth movement: things do not really go wrong only at bar 331, with the entrance of the *marcia Turca*, they go wrong from the very start—one should accept that there is something of an insipid sham in the Ode, so that the chaos that enters after bar 331 is a kind of "return of the repressed," a *symptom* of what was wrong from the very beginning. What if we have domesticated the Ode to Joy too much, what if we have got all too used to it as a symbol of joyful brotherhood? What if we should confront it anew, reject in it what is false? Many of today's listeners cannot but be struck by the empty pompous character and pretentiousness of the Ode, by its somewhat ridiculous solemnity—recall what we see if we watch its performance on television: fat, self-satisfied, well-dressed singers with bulging veins, making a great effort, accompanied by ridiculous waving of hands, to get their sublime message through as loudly as possible . . . What if these listeners are simply *right*? What if the true obscenity is what takes place *before* the *marcia Turca*, not after it? What if we displace the entire perspective and perceive the *marcia* as a return to everyday normality that cuts short the display of preposterous portentousness and thus brings us back to earth, as if it were saying "You want to celebrate the brotherhood of men? Here it is then, real humanity . . ."?

And does the same not hold for Europe today? After inviting millions, from the highest to the lowest (the worm) to embrace, the second strophe ominously ends: "But he who cannot rejoice, let him steal weeping away" (*Und wer's nie gekonnt, der stehle weinend sich aus dem Bund*). The irony of Beethoven's Ode to Joy as the unofficial European anthem is, of course, that the main cause of today's crisis of the Union is precisely Turkey: according to most of the polls, one of the reasons motivating those who voted "no" in the last referendums in France and Netherlands was their opposition to Turkish membership. The "no" can be grounded in rightist-populist terms (no to the Turkish threat to our culture, no to Turkish cheap immigrant labor), or in liberal-multiculturalist terms (Turkey should not be allowed in because, in its treatment of the Kurds, it does not display sufficient respect for human rights). And the opposite view, the "yes," is as false as Beethoven's final cadenza . . . The case of contemporary Turkey is crucial for a proper understanding of capitalist globalization: the political proponent of globalization is the ruling "moderate" Islamist party of the Prime Minister Erdogan.[10] It is the ferociously nationalist and secular Kemalists who, focused on the fully sovereign nation-state, resist full integration into the global space (and also have misgivings about Turkey joining the European Union), while the Islamists find it easy to combine their religious-cultural identity with economic globalization. Insisting on one's particular cultural identity is no obstacle to globalization: the true obstacle is the transcultural nation-state universalism.

So, should Turkey be allowed into the Union or should it be let to "steal itself weeping out of the union" (*Bund*)? Can Europe survive the "Turkish march"? And, as in the finale of Beethoven's Ninth, what if the true problem is not Turkey, but the basic melody itself, the song of European unity as it is played to us by the Brussels post-political technocratic elite? What we need is a totally new melody, a new definition of Europe itself. The problem of Turkey, the perplexity of the European Union as to what to do about Turkey, is not about Turkey as such, but a confusion about what Europe itself is.

What, then, is Europe's predicament today? Europe is caught between the great pincers of America on the one side and China on the other. America and China, seen metaphysically, are both the same: the identical hopeless frenzy of unchained technology and of the rootless organization of the average man. When the farthest corner of the globe has been conquered technically and can be exploited economically; when any incident you like, in any place you like, at any time you like, becomes accessible as fast as you like; when, through TV "live coverage," you can simultaneously "experience" a battle in the Iraqi desert and an opera performance in Beijing; when, in a global digital network, time is nothing but speed, instantaneity, and simultaneity; when a winner in a reality TV show counts as the great man of the people; then, yes, still looming like a specter over all this uproar are the questions, What is it for? Where are we going? What is to be done?[11]

There is thus a need, amongst us Europeans, for what Heidegger called *Auseinandersetzung* (interpretive confrontation) with others as well as with Europe's own past in its totality, from its ancient and Judeo-Christian roots to the recently deceased welfare-state idea. Europe is today split between the so-called Anglo-Saxon model—accept "modernization" (adaptation to the rules of the new global order)—and the Franco-German model—save as much as possible of the "old European" welfare state. Although opposed, these two options are two sides of the same coin, and our true path is not to return to any idealized form of the past, for these models are clearly exhausted—nor to convince Europeans that, if we are to survive as a world power, we should accommodate ourselves as fast as possible to recent trends of globalization. Nor should we be tempted by what is arguably the worst option, the search for a "creative synthesis" between European traditions and globalization, with the aim of constructing something one is tempted to call "globalization with a European face."

Every crisis is in itself a stimulus for a new beginning; every collapse of short-term strategic and pragmatic measures (for the financial reorganization of the Union etc.) a blessing in disguise, an opportunity to rethink its very foundations. What we need is a retrieval-through-repetition (*Wieder-Holung*): through a critical confrontation with the entire European tradition, one should repeat the question "What is Europe?", or, rather, "What does it mean for us to be Europeans?", and thus formulate a new beginning. The task is difficult, it compels us to take the great risk of stepping into the unknown—yet its only alternative is slow decay, the gradual transformation of Europe into what Greece was for the mature Roman Empire, a destination for nostalgic cultural tourism with no effective relevance.[12]

The conflict on Europe is usually portrayed as one between Euro-centric Christian hardliners and liberal multiculturalists who want to open the doors of the European Union much more widely, to Turkey and beyond. What if this conflict is the wrong one? What if cases like Poland should compel us to *narrow* entry, to redefine Europe in such a way that it would exclude Polish Christian fundamentalism? Maybe it is time to apply to Poland the same criteria as to Turkey: the high-class mazurka should make us no less suspicious than the low-class Turkish march.

The lesson is thus clear: fundamentalist populism is filling in the void of the absence of a leftist dream. Donald Rumsfeld's infamous statement about the Old and the New Europe is acquiring a new unexpected actuality: the contours are emerging of the "new" Europe of the majority of post-Communist countries (Poland, the Baltic countries, Romania, Hungary . . .), with their Christian populist fundamentalism, belated anti-Communism, xenophobia and homophobia, and so on.

A further point apropos of which we should risk the hypothesis that Heidegger was right, although not in the sense he meant it, is, what if democracy is not the answer to this predicament? In his *Notes Towards a Definition of Culture*, the great conservative T.S. Eliot remarked that there are moments when the only choice is the one between sectarianism and non-belief, when the only way to keep a religion alive is to engage in a sectarian split from its main body. This is our only chance today: only by means of a "sectarian split" from the standard European legacy, by cutting ourselves off from the decaying corpse of old Europe, can we keep the renewed European legacy alive. Such a split should render problematic the very premises that we tend to accept as our destiny, as non-negotiable facts of our predicament—the phenomenon usually designated as the global New World Order and the need, through "modernization," to accommodate ourselves to it. To put it bluntly, if the emerging New World Order is the irrefragable framework for all of us, then Europe is lost, so the only solution for Europe is to take the risk and break this spell of destiny. *Nothing* should be accepted as inviolable in this new refoundation, neither the need for economic "modernization" nor the most sacred liberal and democratic fetishes.

So although the French and Dutch "no" is not sustained by a coherent and detailed alternative vision, it at least *clears the space for it*, opening up a void which demands to be filled in with new projects—in contrast to the pro-Constitution stance which effectively *precludes thinking*, presenting us with an administrative-political fait accompli. The message of the French "no" to all of us who care about Europe is: no, anonymous experts whose merchandise is sold to us in brightly-colored liberal-multiculturalist packages will not prevent us from *thinking*. It is time for us, citizens of Europe, to become aware that we have to make a properly *political* decision about what we want. No enlightened administrator will do the job for us.

. . . but not good enough in theory

The French–Dutch "no" thus presents us with the latest chapter in the story of populism. For the enlightened liberal-technocratic elite, populism is inherently "proto-fascist," the demise of political reason, a revolt in the guise of an outburst of blind utopian passions. The easiest reply to this distrust would be to claim that populism is inherently neutral: a kind of transcendental-formal political *dispositif* that can be incorporated into different political engagements. This option has been elaborated in detail by Ernesto Laclau.[13]

For Laclau, in a nice case of self-referentiality, the very logic of hegemonic articulation applies also to the conceptual opposition between populism and politics: "populism" is the Lacanian *objet a* of politics, the particular figure which stands for the universal dimension of the political, which is why it is "the royal road" to understanding the political. Hegel provided a term for this overlapping of the universal with part of its own particular content: "oppositional determination" (*gegensätzliche Bestimmung*) as the point at which the universal genus encounters itself among its particular species. Populism is not a specific political movement, but the political at its purest: the "inflection" of the social space that can affect any political content. Its elements are purely formal, "transcendental," not ontic: populism occurs when a series of particular "democratic" demands (for better social security, health services, lower taxes, against war, and so on) is enchained in a series of equivalences, and this enchainment produces "the people" as the universal political subject. What characterizes populism is not the ontic content of these demands, but the mere formal fact that, through their enchainment, "the people" emerge as a political subject, and all different particular struggles and antagonisms appear as parts of a global antagonistic struggle between "us" (the people) and "them." Again, the content of "us" and "them" is not prescribed in advance but, precisely, the stake of the struggle for hegemony: even ideological elements such as brutal racism and anti-Semitism can be enchained in a populist series of equivalences, in the way "them" is constructed.

It is clear now why Laclau prefers populism to class struggle: populism provides a neutral "transcendental" matrix of an open struggle whose content and stakes are themselves defined by the contingent struggle for hegemony, while "class struggle" presupposes a particular social group (the working class) as a privileged political agent; this privilege is not itself the outcome of hegemonic struggle, but grounded in the "objective social position" of this group—the ideologico-political struggle is thus ultimately reduced to an epiphenomenon of "objective" social processes, powers and their conflicts. For Laclau, on the contrary, the fact that some particular struggle is elevated into the "universal equivalent" of all struggles is not a predetermined fact, but itself the result of the contingent political struggle for hegemony—in some constellations, this struggle can be the workers' struggle, in other constellations, the patriotic anti-colonialist struggle, in yet others the anti-racist struggle for cultural tolerance . . . *there is nothing in the inherent positive qualities of some particular struggle that predestines it for such a hegemonic role* as the "general equivalent" of all struggles. The struggle for hegemony thus not only presupposes an irreducible gap between the universal form and the multiplicity of particular contents, but also the contingent process by means of which one among these contents is "transubstantiated" into the immediate embodiment of the universal dimension—say (Laclau's own example), in the Poland of 1980, the particular demands of Solidarność were elevated into the embodiment of the people's global rejection of the Communist regime, so that all different versions of the anti-Communist opposition (from the conservative-nationalist opposition through the liberal-democratic version and cultural dissidence to leftist workers' protests) recognized themselves in the empty signifier "Solidarność."

This is how Laclau tries to distinguish his position both from gradualism (which reduces the very dimension of the political: all that remains is the gradual realization of particular "democratic" demands within the differential social space) as well as from the opposite idea of a total revolution that would bring about a fully self-reconciled society. What both extremes miss is the struggle for hegemony in which a particular demand is "elevated to the dignity of the Thing," that is, comes to stand for the universality of "the people." The field of politics is thus caught in an irreducible tension between "empty" and "floating" signifiers: some particular signifiers start to function as "empty," directly embodying the universal dimension, incorporating into the chain of equivalences which they totalize a large number of "floating" signifiers.[14] Laclau mobilizes this gap between the "ontological" need for a populist protest vote (conditioned by the fact that the hegemonic power discourse cannot incorporate a series of popular demands) and the contingent ontic content to which this vote gets attached, to explain the supposed shift of many French voters who, till the 1970s, supported the Communist Party rather than the rightist populism of the Front National[15]—the elegance of this solution is that it releases us from the tiresome topic of the alleged "deeper (totalitarian, of course) solidarity" between the far Right and the "extreme" Left.

Although Laclau's theory of populism stands out as one of today's great (and, unfortunately for social theory, rare) examples of true conceptual stringency, one should note a couple of problematic features. The first concerns his very definition of populism: the series of formal conditions he enumerates are not sufficient to justify calling a phenomenon "populist"—what needs to be added is the way the populist discourse displaces the antagonism and constructs the enemy: in populism, the enemy is externalized/reified into a positive ontological entity (even if this entity is spectral), whose annihilation would restore balance and justice; symmetrically, our own—the populist political agent's—identity is also perceived as preexisting the enemy's onslaught. Let us take Laclau's own precise analysis of why one should count Chartism as populism:

> Its dominant leitmotiv is to situate the evils of society not in something that is inherent in the economic system, but quite the opposite: in the abuse of power by parasitic and speculative groups which have control of political power—"old corruption," in Cobbett's words. [. . .] It was for this reason that the feature most strongly picked out in the ruling class was its idleness and parasitism.[16]

In other words, for a populist, the cause of the trouble is ultimately never the system as such, but the intruder who corrupted it (financial manipulators, not capitalists as such, etc.); not a fatal flaw inscribed into the structure as such, but an element that does not play its part within the structure properly. For a Marxist, on the contrary (as for a Freudian), the pathological (the deviant misbehavior of some elements) is the symptom of the normal, an indicator of what is wrong in the very structure that is threatened with "pathological" outbursts: for Marx, economic crises are the key to understanding the "normal" functioning of capitalism; for Freud, pathological phenomena such as hysterical outbursts provide the key to the constitution (and hidden antagonisms that sustain the functioning) of a "normal" subject. This is also why fascism definitely is a populism: its figure of the Jew is the equivalential point of the series of (heterogeneous, inconsistent even) threats experienced by individuals: the Jew is simultaneously too intellectual, dirty, sexually voracious, hardworking, financially exploitative . . . Here we encounter another key feature of populism not mentioned by Laclau: not only is—as he is right to emphasize—the populist Master-Signifier for the enemy empty, vague, imprecise, and so on:

> to say that the oligarchy is responsible for the frustration of social demands is not to state something which can possibly be read out of the social demands themselves; it is provided from *outside* those social demands, by a discourse on which they can be inscribed. [. . .] It is here that the moment of emptiness necessarily arises, following the establishment of equivalential bonds. *Ergo*, "vagueness" and "imprecision," but these do not result from any kind of marginal or primitive situation; they are inscribed in the very nature of the political.[17]

In populism proper, this "abstract" character is, furthermore, always supplemented by the *pseudo-concreteness* of the figure that is selected as *the* enemy, the singular agent behind all the threats to the people. One can today buy laptops with a keyboard that artificially imitates the resistance to the fingers of the old typewriter, as well as the typewriter sound of the key hitting the paper—what better example of the recent need for pseudo-concreteness? Today, when not only social relations but also technology are becoming more and more opaque (who can visualize what goes on inside a PC?), there is a great thirst to recreate an artificial concreteness in order to enable individuals to relate to their complex environs as if it were a meaningful life-world. In computer programming, this was the step accomplished by Apple: the pseudo-concreteness of icons on the desktop. Guy Debord's old formula about the "society of spectacle" is thus receiving a new twist: images are created in order to fill in the gap that separates the new artificial universe from our old life-world surroundings, that is, to "domesticate" this new universe. And is the pseudo-concrete populist figure of the "Jew" that condenses the vast multitude of anonymous forces that determine us not analogous to a computer keyboard that imitates the old typewriter keyboard? The Jew as the enemy definitely emerges from outside the realm of social demands that experience themselves as frustrated.

This supplement to Laclau's definition of populism in no way implies any kind of regression to the ontic level: we remain at the formal-ontological level and, while accepting Laclau's thesis that populism is a certain formal political logic, not bound to any content, simply supplement it with the characteristic (no less "transcendental" than its other features) of "reifying" antagonism into a positive entity. As such, populism, by definition, contains a minimum, an elementary form, of ideological mystification; which is why, although it is effectively a formal frame/matrix of political logic that can be given different political twists (reactionary-nationalist, progressive-nationalist . . .), nonetheless, insofar as it displaces, in its very notion, the immanent social antagonism into the antagonism between the unified "people" and its external enemy, it harbors "in the last instance" a long-term proto-fascist tendency.[18]

In short, I agree with Laclau's attempt to define populism in a formal-conceptual way, also taking note of how, in his last book, he has clearly shifted his position from "radical democracy" to populism (he now reduces democracy to the moment of democratic demand *within* the system); however, as is clear to him, populism can also be very reactionary—so how are we to draw a line here?[19] So, again, is there a way to draw the line at a formal-conceptual level? My wager is that the answer is "yes."

Every construction of and action on behalf of the people as a political subject is not *eo ipso* populism. In the same way that Laclau likes to emphasize that Society does not exist, nor does the People, and the problem with populism is that, within its horizon, the people *does* exist— the People's existence is guaranteed by its constitutive exception, by the *externalization* of the Enemy into a positive intruder/obstacle. The formula of a truly democratic reference to the people should thus be a paraphrase of Kant's definition of beauty as *Zweckmässigkeit ohne Zweck*: the popular without the People, namely, the popular cleft, thwarted, by a constitutive antagonism which prevents it from acquiring the full substantial identity of a People. That is why populism, far from standing for the political as such, always involves a minimal *de-politicization*, "naturalization," of the political.

This accounts for the fundamental paradox of authoritarian fascism, which is that it almost symmetrically inverts what Chantal Mouffe calls the "democratic paradox": if the wager of (institutionalized) democracy is to integrate the antagonistic struggle itself into the institutional/differential space, transforming it into regulated agonism, fascism proceeds in the opposite direction. While fascism, in its mode of activity, brings the antagonistic logic to its extreme (talking about the "struggle to death" between itself and its enemies, and always maintaining—if not realizing—a minimal extra-institutional threat of violence, of "direct pressure of the people" bypassing the complex legal-institutional channels), it posits as its political goal precisely the opposite, an extremely ordered hierarchical social body (no wonder that fascism always relies on organicist-corporatist metaphors). This contrast can be nicely rendered in terms of the Lacanian opposition between the "subject of enunciation" and the "subject of the enunciated (content)": while democracy admits antagonistic struggle as its goal (in Lacanese: as its enunciated, its content), its procedure is regulated-systemic; fascism, on the contrary, tries to impose the goal of hierarchically structured harmony through the means of an unbridled antagonism.

In a homologous way, the ambiguity of the middle class, this contradiction embodied (as Marx put it apropos Proudhon), is best exemplified by the way it relates to politics: on the one hand, the middle class is against politicization—it just wants to sustain its way of life, to be left to work and live its life in peace, which is why it tends to support the authoritarian coups which promise to put an end to the crazy political mobilization of society, so that everybody can return to his or her work. On the other hand, members of the middle class—in the guise of the threatened patriotic hardworking moral majority—are the main instigators of grassroots mass mobilization in the guise of rightist populism—for example, in France today, the only force that truly disturbs the post-political technocratic-humanitarian administration is Le Pen's Front National.

Populism is ultimately always sustained by ordinary people's frustrated exasperation, by a cry of "I don't know what's going on, I just know I've had enough of it! It can't go on! It must stop!"—an impatient outburst, a refusal to understand, exasperation at complexity, and the ensuing conviction that there must be somebody responsible for all the mess, which is why an agent who is behind the scenes and explains it all is required. Therein, in this refusal-to-know, resides the properly *fetishistic* dimension of populism. That is to say, although, at a purely formal level, the fetish involves a gesture of transference (onto the fetish object), it functions as an exact inversion of the standard formula of transference (with the subject supposed to know): what the fetish gives body to is precisely my disavowal of knowledge, my refusal to subjectively assume what I know. Therein resides the contrast between the fetish and the symptom: a symptom embodies a repressed knowledge, the truth about the subject that the subject is not ready to accept. This is why Freud engaged in speculating on how the fetish is the last object seen before stumbling upon the fact that women do not have penises: it is the last support of the subject's ignorance.[20]

Linked to this are some further weaknesses of Laclau's analysis. The smallest unit of his analysis of populism is the category of the "social demand" (in the double meaning of the term: a request and a claim). The strategic reason for choosing this term is clear: the subject of the demand is constituted through raising this demand; the "people" thus constitutes itself through an equivalential chain of demands, it is the performative result of raising these demands, not a preexisting group. Laclau calls such an elementary demand, prior to its eventual enchainment into a series of equivalences, "democratic"; in his slightly idiosyncratic usage, such a term refers to a demand that functions within the socio-political system — in other words, it is encountered as a particular demand rather than being frustrated and thus, forced to inscribe itself into an antagonistic series of equivalences. Although he emphasizes how, in a "normal" institutiona-lized political space, there are, of course, multiple conflicts, but these conflicts are dealt with one by one, without setting in motion any transversal alliances/antagonisms, Laclau is well aware that chains of equivalences can also form themselves within an institutionalized demo-cratic space: recall how, in the UK under John Major's Conservative leadership in the late 1980s, the figure of the "unemployed single mother" was elevated into the universal symbol of what was wrong with the old welfare-state system—all "social evils" were somehow reduced to this figure (Why is there a state budget crisis? Because too much money is spent on supporting these mothers and their children. Juvenile delin-quency? Because single mothers do not exert enough authority to provide proper educational discipline; and so on and so forth).

What Laclau neglected to emphasize is not only the uniqueness of democracy with regard to his basic conceptual opposition between the logic of differences (society as a global regulated system) and the logic of equivalences (the social space as split into two antagonistic camps which equalize their inner differences), but also the full inner entwine-ment of these two logics. The first thing we should note here is how, only in a democratic political system, the antagonistic logic of equiv-alences is inscribed into the very political system, as its basic structural feature. It seems that Mouffe's work is here more pertinent, in its heroic attempt to bring together democracy and the spirit of agonistic struggle, rejecting both extremes: on the one side, the celebration of heroic struggle-confrontation that suspends democracy and its rules (Nietzsche, Heidegger, Schmitt); on the other side, the evacuation of true struggle from the democratic space, so that all that remains is anemic rule-regulated competition (Habermas).[21] Here, Mouffe is right to point out that violence returns with a vengeance in the exclusion of those who do not fit the rules of unconstrained communication. How-ever, the main threat to democracy in today's democratic countries resides in neither of these two extremes, but in the death of the political through the "commodification" of politics. What is at stake here is not primarily the way politicians are packaged and sold as merchandise at elections; a much deeper problem is that elections themselves are conceived along the lines of buying a commodity (power, in this case): they involve a competition between different merchandise-parties, and our votes are like money which buys the government we want. What gets lost in such a view of politics as just another service we buy is politics as a shared public debate of issues and decisions that concern us all.

Thus democracy, it seems, not only can include antagonism, it is the only political form that solicits and presupposes it, that *institutionalizes* it. What other political systems perceive as a threat (the lack of a "natural" pretender to power), democracy elevates into a "normal" positive condition of its functioning: the place of power is empty, there is no natural claimant for it; *polemos*/struggle is irreducible, and every positive government must be fought out, gained through *polemos*. This why Laclau's critical remark about Lefort misses the point:

> [F]or Lefort, the *place* of power in democracies is empty. For me, the question poses itself differently: it is a question of *producing* emptiness out of the operation of hegemonic logic. For me, emptiness is a type of identity, not a structural location.[22]

The two emptinesses are simply not comparable: the emptiness of the "people" is the emptiness of the hegemonic signifier which totalizes the chain of equivalences, that is, whose particular content is "transubstantiated" into an embodiment of the social whole, while the emptiness of the place of power is a distance which renders every empirical bearer of power "deficient," contingent and temporary.

The conclusion to be drawn is that populism (in the manner we have supplemented Laclau's definition of it) is not the only mode of existence of the excess of antagonism over the institutional-democratic framework of regulated agonistic struggle: not only the (now defunct) communist revolutionary organizations, but also the widescale phenomena of non-institutionalized social and political protest, from the student movements of the late 1960s and early 1970s to later anti-war protests and the more recent anti-globalization movement, cannot be properly called "populist." Exemplary is here the case of the anti-segregation movement in the US in the late 1950s and early 1960s, epitomized by the name of Martin Luther King: although it endeavored to articulate a demand that was not properly met within the existing democratic institutions, it cannot be called populist in any meaningful sense of the term—the way it led the struggle and constituted its opponent was simply not "populist." A more general remark should be made here about the single-issue popular movements, for example, the "tax revolts" in the US: although they function in a populist manner, mobilizing the people around a demand which is not met by the democratic institutions, they do *not* seem to rely on a complex chain of equivalences, but remain focused on one singular demand.

The "determining role of economy": Marx with Freud

The topic of populism versus class struggle also raises a series of fundamental conceptual problems. Let us begin with a precise theoretical point about the status of universality: we are dealing here with two opposed logics of universality to be strictly distinguished. On the one hand, there is the state bureaucracy as the universal class of a society (or, in a larger scope, the US as the world policeman, the universal enforcer and guarantor of human rights and democracy), the direct agent of the global Order; on the other hand, there is "supernumerary" universality, the universality embodied in the element which sticks out of the existing Order, which, while internal to it, has no proper place within it (what Jacques Rancière calls the "part of no-part"). Not only are the two not the same,[23] but the struggle is ultimately *a struggle between these two universalities*, not simply between the particular elements of the universality: not just about which particular content will "hegemonize" the empty form of universality, but a struggle between two exclusive *forms* of universality themselves.

This is why Laclau misses the point when he opposes the "working class" and the "people" along the axis of conceptual content versus the effect of radical nomination:[24] the "working class" designates a preexisting social group, characterized by its substantial content, while the "people" emerges as a unified agent through the very act of nomination—there is nothing in the heterogeneity of demands that predisposes them to be unified into a "people." However, Marx distinguishes between the "working class" and the "proletariat": the "working class" is indeed a particular social group, while the "proletariat" designates a subjective position.

This is why Laclau's critical debate about Marx's opposition between proletariat and lumpenproletariat also misses the point: the distinction is not one between an objective social group and a non-group, a remainder-excess with no proper place within the social edifice, but a distinction between two modes of this remainder-excess which generate two different subjective positions. The implication of Marx's analysis is that, paradoxically, although the lumpenproletariat seems more radically "displaced" with regard to the social body than the proletariat, it in fact fits much more smoothly into the social edifice: to refer to the Kantian distinction between negative and infinite judgment, the lumpenproletariat is not truly a non-group (the immanent negation of a group, a group which is a non-group), but not a group, and its exclusion from all strata not only consolidates the identity of other groups, but makes it a free-floating element which can be used by any stratum or class—it can be the radicalizing "carnivalesque" element of the workers' struggle, pushing them from compromising moderate strategies to an open confrontation, or the element which is used by the ruling class to denature from within opposition to its rule (the long tradition of the criminal mob serving those in power). The working class, on the contrary, is a group which is in itself, *as a group* within the social structure, a non-group, that is, whose position is in itself "contradictory": it is a productive force, society (and those in power) need it in order to reproduce themselves and their rule, but, nonetheless, they cannot find a "proper place" for it.

Based on this misunderstanding, Laclau puts forward a general argument rendered succinctly by Oliver Marchart:

> on a formal level, *every* politics is based on the articulatory logics of "a combination and condensation of inconsistent attitudes", not only the politics of fascism. As a result, the fundamental social antagonism will always be displaced to some degree since, as we have noted earlier, the ontological level—in this case, antagonism—can never be approached directly and without political mediation. It follows that distortion is constitutive for every politics: politics as such, not only fascist politics, proceeds through "distortion".[25]

This reproach remains caught in the "binary" tension between essence and appearance: the fundamental antagonism never appears as such, directly, in a transparent manner (in Marxist terms: the "pure" revolutionary situation in which all social tensions would be simplified/reduced to the class struggle never takes place, it is always mediated by other— ethnic, religious, etc.—antagonisms). So: the "essence" never appears directly, but always in a displaced/distorted way. While this statement is in principle true, there are at least two things to add to it. First, if this is the case, why even continue to talk about a "fundamental social antagonism"? All we have here is a series of antagonisms which (can) build a chain of equivalences, metaphorically "contaminating" each other, and which antagonism emerges as "central" is the contingent result of a struggle for hegemony. So does this mean that one should reject the very notion of a "fundamental antagonism" (as Laclau does)?

I would propose a Hegelian answer—let me make this point clear by (yet again) referring to one of my standard examples: Lévi-Strauss's exemplary analysis, from his *Structural Anthropology*, of the spatial disposition of buildings amongst the Winnebago, one of the Great Lake tribes. The tribe is divided into two subgroups ("moieties"), "those who are from above" and "those who are from below"; when we ask an individual to draw on a piece of paper, or on sand, the ground-plan of her village (the spatial disposition of cottages), we obtain two quite different answers, depending on her relationship to one or the other subgroup. Both perceive the village as a circle; but for one subgroup, there is within this circle another circle of central houses, so that we have two concentric circles, while for the other subgroup, the circle is split into two by a clear dividing line. In other words, a member of the first subgroup (let us call it "conservative-corporatist") perceives the ground-plan of the village as a ring of houses more or less symmetrically disposed around the central temple, whereas a member of the second ("revolutionary-antagonistic") subgroup perceives her village as two distinct heaps of houses separated by an invisible frontier.[26]

The point Lévi-Strauss wants to make is that this example should in no way entice us into cultural relativism, according to which the perception of social space depends on the observer's group belonging: the very split into the two "relative" perceptions implies a hidden reference to a constant—not the objective, "actual" disposition of buildings but a traumatic kernel, a fundamental antagonism the inhabitants of the village were unable to symbolize, to account for, to "internalize," to come to terms with, an imbalance in social relations that prevented the community from stabilizing itself into a harmonious whole. The two perceptions of the ground-plan are simply two mutually exclusive endeavors to cope with this traumatic antagonism, to heal its wound via the imposition of a balanced symbolic structure. It is here that one can see in what precise sense the Real intervenes through anamorphosis. We have first the "actual," "objective," arrangement of the houses, and then its two different symbolizations which both distort in an anamorphic way the actual arrangement. However, the "real" is here not the actual arrangement, but the traumatic core of the social antagonism which distorts the tribe members' view of the actual antagonism. The Real is thus the disavowed X on account of which our vision of reality is anamorphically distorted. It is simultaneously the Thing to which direct access is not possible *and* the obstacle which prevents this direct access; the Thing which eludes our grasp *and* the distorting screen which makes us miss the Thing. More precisely, the Real is ultimately the very shift of perspective from the first to the second standpoint: the Lacanian Real is not only distorted, but *the very principle of the distortion* of reality.

This three-level *dispositif* is strictly homologous to Freud's three-level *dispositif* of the interpretation of dreams: for Freud, too, unconscious desire in a dream is not simply its core which never appears directly, distorted by the translation into the manifest dream-text, but the very principle of this distortion. This is how, for Deleuze, in a strict conceptual homology, the economy exerts its role of determining the social structure "in the last instance": the economy in this role is never directly present as an actual causal agent, its presence is purely virtual, it is the social "pseudo-cause," but, precisely as such, absolute, non-relational, the absent cause, something that is never "in its own place": "that is why 'the economic' is never given properly speaking, but rather designates a differential virtuality to be interpreted, always covered over by its forms of actualization."[27] It is the absent X which circulates between the multiple series of the social field (economic, political, ideological, legal . . .), *distributing them in their specific articulation*. One should thus insist on the radical difference between the economic as this virtual X, the absolute point of reference of the social field, and the economic in its actuality, as one of the elements ("subsystems") of the actual social totality: when they encounter each other, that is, to put it in Hegelese, when the virtual economic encounters in the guise of its actual counterpart itself in its "oppositional determination," this identity coincides with absolute (self-) contradiction.

As Lacan put it in his *Seminar XI*, *il n'y a de cause que de ce qui cloche*, there is no cause but a cause of something that stumbles/slips/falters[28] —a thesis whose obviously paradoxical character is explained when one takes into account the opposition between cause and causality: for Lacan, they are in no way the same, since a "cause," in the strict sense of the term, is precisely something which intervenes at the points where the network of causality (the chain of causes-and-effects) falters, when there is a cut, a gap, in the causal chain. In this sense, a cause is for Lacan, by definition, a distant cause (an "absent cause," as one used to put it in the jargon of the happy "structuralist" of the 1960s and 1970s): it acts in the interstices of the direct causal network. What Lacan has in mind here is specifically the working of the unconscious. Imagine an ordinary slip of the tongue: at a chemistry conference, someone gives a paper about, say, the exchange of fluids; all of a sudden, he stumbles and makes a slip, blurting out something about the passage of sperm in the sexual act . . . an "attractor" from what Freud called "an Other Scene" intervenes like a type of gravity, exerting its invisible influence from a distance, curving the space of the speech-flow, introducing a gap into it. What makes this Lacanian thesis so interesting for the philosophical perspective is that it allows us to approach in a new way the old topic of "causality and freedom": freedom is opposed to causality, but not to the cause. The standard political trope "the cause of freedom" should be taken more literally than is usually intended, including *both* main meanings of the term "cause," a cause which produces effects and a political cause that mobilizes us. Perhaps, the two meanings are not as disparate as they may appear: the Cause that mobilizes us (the "cause of freedom") acts as the absent Cause which disturbs the network of causality. It is a cause which makes me free, extracting me from the network of causes-and-effects. And, perhaps, this is also how one should understand the infamous Marxist formula of the "determination in the last instance": the overdetermining instance of "economy" is also a distant cause, never a direct one, that is, it intervenes in the gaps of direct social causality.

With the class struggle, it is today a little bit like Freud's patient's answer to the question as to the identity of the woman in his dream: "Whatever this fight is about, it is not class struggle . . . (but: sexism, cultural intolerance, religious fundamentalism . . .)." One of the standard topics of post-Marxism is that, today, the working class is *no longer* the "predestined" revolutionary subject, that contemporary emancipatory struggles are plural, with no particular agent who can claim to occupy a privileged place. The way to answer this reproach is to concede even more: there *never was* such a privilege of the working class, the key structural role of the working class does not imply this kind of priority.

How, then, does the "determining role of economy" function, if it is not the ultimate referent of the social field? Imagine a political struggle fought in the terms of popular musical culture, as was the case in some post-"socialist" Eastern European countries in which the tension, in the field of popular music, between pseudo-folk and rock functioned as a displacement of the tension between the nationalist-conservative Right and the liberal Left. To put it in old-fashioned terms: a popular-cultural struggle "expressed" (provided the terms in which) a political struggle (was fought out). (As in the US today, where country music is predominantly conservative and rock predominantly left-liberal.) Following Freud, it is not enough to say that the struggle in popular music was here only a secondary expression, a symptom, an encoded translation, of the political struggle, which was what the whole thing "was really about." Both struggles have a substance of their own: the cultural struggle is not just a secondary phenomenon, a battlefield of shadows to be "deciphered" for its political connotation (which, as a rule, is obvious enough).

The "determining role of the economy" does not mean that, in this case, what all the fuss "really was about" was the economic struggle, so that we should imagine the economy as a hidden meta-Essence which then "expresses" itself with a two-level-distance in a cultural struggle (it determines politics, which in turn determines culture . . .). On the contrary, the economy inscribes itself in the course of the very translation/transposition of the political struggle into the popular-cultural struggle, into how this transposition is never direct, but always displaced, asymmetrical. The "class" connotation as it is encoded in cultural "ways of life" can often turn around the explicit political connotation — recall how, in the famous presidential TV debate in 1959 responsible for Nixon's defeat, it was the liberal Kennedy who was perceived as an upper-class patrician, while the rightist Nixon appeared as his opponent of more humble origins. This, of course, does not mean that the second opposition simply belies the first one, that it stands for the "truth" obfuscated by the first, namely, that Kennedy who, in his public statements, presented himself as Nixon's progressive-liberal opponent, in fact signaled through his life-style features enacted in the debate that he was "really" simply an upper-class patrician; but it does mean that the displacement bears witness to the limitation of Kennedy's progressivism, that is, it does point towards the contradictory nature of Kennedy's ideologico-political position.[29] And it is here that the determining instance of the "economy" enters: the economic is the absent cause that accounts for the displacement in representation, for the asymmetry (reversal, in this case) between the two series, the couple progressive/conservative politics and the couple upper/middle class.

The Laclauian solution would have been to conceive such "contaminations" as the enchainment of antagonisms into a contingent series of equivalences: the fact that the political opposition Left/Right "contaminates" the popular musical opposition of rock and country is a contingent result of the struggle for hegemony, namely, that there is no inner necessity for rock to be progressive or for country to be conservative. There is, however, an asymmetry here that is obfuscated by this straightforward solution: the political struggle is not one among other struggles (in a series alongside artistic, economic, religious, etc., struggles); it is the purely formal principle of antagonistic struggle as such. That is to say, there is no proper content of politics; all political struggles and decisions concern other specific spheres of social life (taxation, the regulation of sexual mores and procreation, the health service, and so on and so forth)—"politics" is merely a formal mode of dealing with these topics, insofar as they emerge as topics of public struggle and decision. This is why "everything is (or, rather, can become) political"—insofar as it becomes a stake in political struggle. The "economy," on the other hand, is not just one of the spheres of political struggle, but the "cause" of the mutual contamination–expression of struggles. To put it succinctly, Left–Right is the Master-Signifier "contaminated" by the series of other oppositions, while the economy is the *objet a*, the elusive object that sustains this contamination (and when that contamination is directly economic, the economy encounters itself in its oppositional determination).

Politics is thus a name for the distance of the "economy" from itself. Its space is opened up by the gap that separates the economic as the absent Cause from the economy in its "oppositional determination," as one of the elements of the social totality: there is politics *because* the economy is "non-all," because the economic is an "impotent" impassive pseudo-cause. The economic is thus here doubly inscribed in the precise sense which defines the Lacanian Real: it is simultaneously the hard core "expressed" in other struggles through displacements and other forms of distortion, and the very structuring principle of these distortions.[30]

In its long and twisted history, Marxist social hermeneutics has relied on two logics which, although often confounded under the ambiguous shared term of the "economic class struggle," are completely different. On the one hand, there is the (in)famous "economic interpretation of history": all struggles, artistic, ideological, political, are ultimately conditioned by the economic ("class") struggle, which is their secret meaning to be deciphered. On the other hand, "everything is political," that is, the Marxist view of history is thoroughly politicized: there are no social, ideological, cultural, and other phenomena that are not "contaminated" by the basic political struggle, and this goes even for the economy—the illusion of "trade unionism" is precisely that the workers' struggle can be depoliticized, reduced to a purely economic negotiation for better work conditions and so on. However, these two "contaminations"—the economic determines everything "in last instance"; "everything is political"—do not obey the same logic. The "economy" without the ex-timate political core ("class struggle") would be a positive social matrix of development, as it is in the (pseudo-)Marxist evolutionary-historicist notion of development to which Marx himself came dangerously close in his "Preface" to the *Critique of Political Economy*:

> In the social production of their existence, men inevitably enter into definite relations, which are independent of their will, namely relations of production appropriate to a given stage in the development of their material forces of production. The totality of these relations of production constitutes the economic structure of society, the real foundation, on which arises a legal and political superstructure and to which correspond definite forms of social consciousness. The mode of production of material life conditions the general process of social, political and intellectual life. It is not the consciousness of men that determines their existence, but their social existence that determines their consciousness. At a certain stage of development, the material productive forces of society come into conflict with the existing relations of production or—this merely expresses the same thing in legal terms—with the property relations within the framework of which they have operated hitherto. From forms of development of the productive forces these relations turn into their fetters. Then begins an era of social revolution. The changes in the economic foundation lead sooner or later to the transformation of the whole immense superstructure.
>
> In studying such transformations it is always necessary to distinguish between the material transformation of the economic conditions of production, which can be determined with the precision of natural science, and the legal, political, religious, artistic or philosophic—in short, ideological forms in which men become conscious of this conflict and fight it out. Just as one does not judge an individual by what he thinks about himself, so one cannot judge such a period of transformation by its consciousness, but, on the contrary, this consciousness must be explained from the contradictions of material life, from the conflict existing between the social forces of production and the relations of

production. No social order is ever destroyed before all the productive forces for which it is sufficient have been developed, and new superior relations of production never replace older ones before the material conditions for their existence have matured within the framework of the old society.[31]

The evolutionist logic of these lines is clear: the "motor" of social progress is the apolitical development of the forces and means of production; they determine the relations of production, and so on.

On the other hand, "pure" politics, "decontaminated" from the economy, is no less ideological: vulgar economism and ideologico-political idealism are two sides of the same coin. The structure is here that of an inward loop: the "class struggle" is politics in the very heart of the economic. Or, to put it paradoxically, one can reduce all political, juridical, cultural content to the "economic base," "deciphering" it as its "expression"—all *except* class struggle, which is the political in the economic itself.

Mutatis mutandis, the same holds for psychoanalysis: all dreams have sexual content *except* explicitly sexual dreams—why? Because the sexualization of a context is formal, the principle of its distortion: through repetition, the oblique approach, and so on, every topic—inclusive of sexuality itself—is sexualized. The ultimate properly Freudian lesson is that the explosion of human symbolic capacities does not merely expand the metaphoric scope of sexuality (activities that are in themselves thoroughly asexual can become "sexualized," everything can be "eroticized" and start to "mean that"), but, much more importantly, this explosion *sexualizes sexuality itself*: the specific quality of human sexuality has nothing to do with the immediate, rather stupid, reality of copulation, including the preparatory mating rituals; it is only when animal coupling gets caught in the self-referential vicious circle of the drive, in the protracted repetition of its failure to reach the impossible Thing, that we have what we call sexuality, that is, that sexual activity itself becomes sexualized. In other words, the fact that sexuality can spill over and function as a metaphoric content of every (other) human activity is not a sign of its power but, on the contrary, a sign of its impotence, failure, its inherent blockage. The class struggle is thus a unique mediating term which, while mooring politics in the economy (all politics is "ultimately" an expression of class struggle), simultaneously stands for the irreducible political moment in the very heart of the economic.

Drawing the line

The consequences of these conceptual elaborations for the dilemma of the "direct expression of the universal or its constitutive distortion" are clear. Laclau's basic political argument against me is that, due to my rigid class-reductionist pseudo-revolutionary vision, I am condemned to "waiting for the Martians": since the conditions I set for revolutionary agents "are specified within such a rigid geometry of social effects that no empirical actor can fit the bill." However, in order to sustain the appearance that I am talking about real agents, I have to have recourse to the "process of 'Martianization'": "to attribute to actually existing subjects the most absurd features, while keeping their names so that the illusion of a contact with reality is maintained." One cannot but take note of how close this process mockingly described by Laclau as "Martianization" resembles his own theory of hegemony: an empirical event is "elevated to the dignity of the Thing," it starts to function as the embodiment of the impossible fullness of Society. Referring to Joan Copjec, Laclau compares hegemony to the "breast-value" attached to partial objects: so, *mutatis mutandis*, is his thesis not that, since Martians are impossible but necessary, in the process of hegemony, an empirical social element is invested with "Martian value"—the difference between me and him being that I (am supposed to) believe in real Martians, while he knows that the place of Martians is forever empty, so that all we can do is invest empirical agents with "Martian value"?[32]

It is Laclau who is here (like Kant) all too naive in his critical stance, namely, in his assertion of the irreducible gap between empty universality and its distorted representation. From my Hegelian standpoint, this gap can be overcome. How? Not through the arrival of an adequate direct presentation of the universal, but so that *distortion as such is asserted as the site of universality*: universality *appears* as the distortion of the particular — in an exact homology with Freud's logic of dreams, where the "universal" unconscious desire (which, to put it in Marxist terms, determines the dream "in the last instance") is not the core of the dream expressed in the dream's text in a displaced/distorted form, but the process of the distortion itself. In this precise sense, it is wrong to say that the "central" social antagonism ("class struggle") is always expressed/articulated in a distorted/displaced way: it is the very *principle* of this distortion. Consequently, true "class politics" has nothing whatsoever to do with focusing exclusively on class struggle and reducing all particular struggles to secondary expressions and effects of the one and only "true" struggle. Let us return to Mao's "On Contradiction": his main claim there is that, in each concrete situation, a different "particular" contradiction is the predominant one, in the precise sense that, in order to win the battle for the resolution of the principal contradiction, one should treat a particular contradiction as the predominant one, to which all other struggles should be subordinated.

But the question remains: why does the economic occupy this structuring role? Again, a homology with psychoanalysis could help us to clarify matters, since one can (and often does) raise exactly the same objection against Freud: why is it unconscious desire which "overdetermines" the entanglement of all other dream-wishes of sexual nature? Why should we not assert open interaction in which the predominant role of a specific wish is itself the result of a "struggle for hegemony" between different wishes? Is the central role of sexuality not a clear reminder of Freud's "sexual essentialism," in an exact parallel to Marx's "economic essentialism"? The answer is simple for a true Freudian: sexuality spills over all other contents, every content can be "sexualized," because of sexuality's inherent failure ("there is no sexual relationship"); that is to say, the central event in the becoming-human of humanoids was "symbolic castration," the imposition of the bar of impossibility which extracted sexuality from the domain of instinctual satisfactions regulated by seasonal rhythms, transforming it into a "meta-physical" infinite search for the impossible Thing. The Freudian hypothesis is thus that sexuality is not just one *among* the possible innuendos (connotations) of every speech; it is, much more strongly, *inherent to the form of connotation as such*: the very fact that something "means much more than it seems" sexualizes it, that is, symbolic castration sustains the very indeterminacy of the space in which connotations can float around.[33] And the Marxist hypothesis is that, *mutatis mutandis*, the same goes for the "economy," for the collective process of production: the social organization of production (the "mode of production") is not just one among many levels of social organization, it is the site of "contradiction," of structural instability, of the central social antagonism ("there is no class relationship"), which, as such, spills over into all other levels.

Now we can also answer the reproach that commodity fetishism relies on the opposition between the direct expression of an idea (or a subject) and its distorted metaphoric representation. Let me explain this point by referring to the thesis that, today, we live in a post-ideological world.

There are two ways to understand this thesis: either we take it in a naive post-political sense (finally liberated from the burden of great ideological narratives and causes, we can dedicate ourselves to pragmatically solving real problems), or in a more critical way, as a sign of the contemporary predominant form of cynicism (power no longer needs a consistent ideological structure to legitimize its rule; it can afford to directly state the obvious truth—the search for profits, the brutal imposition of economic interests). According to the second reading, there is no longer a need for the refined procedure of *Ideologiekritik*, for a "symptomal reading" that detects the faults in an ideological edifice: such a procedure knocks at an open door, since the thoroughly cynical power discourse concedes all this in advance, like the analysand of today who calmly accepts the analyst's suggestions about his innermost obscene desires, no longer shocked by anything.

Is this really the case? If it is, then *Ideologiekritik* and psychoanalysis are ultimately of no use, since the wager of their interpretive procedure is that the subject *cannot* openly admit and really assume the truth about what she is doing. However, psychoanalysis opens up a way to unmask this apparent proof of its uselessness, by detecting, beneath the deceptive openness of post-ideological cynicism, the contours of fetishism, and thus opposing the *fetishistic* mode of ideology, which predominates in our allegedly "post-ideological" era, to its traditional *symptomal* mode, in which the ideological lie which structures our perception of reality is threatened by symptoms *qua* "returns of the repressed," cracks in the fabric of the ideological lie. The fetish is effectively a kind of *envers* of the symptom. That is to say, the symptom is the exception which disturbs the surface of false appearance, the point at which the repressed Other Scene erupts, while the fetish is the embodiment of the lie which enables us to sustain the unbearable truth. Let us take the case of the death of a beloved person: in the case of a symptom, I "repress" this death, I try not to think about it, but the repressed trauma returns in the symptom; in the case of a fetish, on the contrary, I "rationally" fully accept this death, and yet I cling to the fetish, to some feature that embodies for me the disavowal of this death. In this sense, a fetish can play a very constructive role by allowing us to cope with the harsh reality. Fetishists are not dreamers lost in their private worlds, they are thoroughly "realist," able to accept the way things effectively are—since they have their fetish to which they can cling in order to cancel the full impact of reality.

There is a wonderful early short story by Patricia Highsmith,

"Button," about a middle-class New Yorker who lives with his intellec-
tually impaired nine-year-old son who babbles meaningless sounds all the
time and smiles, with saliva drooling from his mouth. Late one evening,
unable to endure the situation any longer, the main character decides to
take a walk in the lonely Manhattan streets where he stumbles upon a
destitute homeless beggar who pleadingly extends his hand towards him.
In an act of inexplicable fury, the hero beats the beggar to death and tears
a button from his jacket. Afterwards, he returns home a changed man,
enduring his family nightmare serenely, capable of even a kind smile for
his handicapped son; he keeps this button all the time in the pocket of his
trousers—a perfect fetish, the embodied disavowal of his miserable
reality, the constant reminder that, at least once, he had been able to
strike back against his miserable destiny.

In *Stasiland*, Anna Funder describes an even crazier case of the fetish
which occurred in the real life of Hagen Koch, the GDR Stasi officer who
attracted the attention of the world's media on August 13, 1961, when the
GDR authorities started to build the Berlin Wall.[34] His (dubious) honor
was as the man who literally drew the line of the Wall: a worker in the
map department of the Stasi, he was ordered to mark with white paint the
exact line that separates East from West Berlin, so that the Wall could
then be constructed at the appropriate place. For a whole day, he was
seen and photographed, walking slowly with one foot in the East and the
other in the West and drawing the line. It is as if this in-between position
somehow symbolized his basic attitude towards political reality: he was
leading a life full of compromises and hesitations, oscillating between
fidelity to the GDR regime and acts of small rebellion (among other
things, he married a girl from a non-Communist family in spite of the
opposition of his Stasi superiors). Finally, he got sick and tired of his Stasi
job, asked for a transfer, and was allowed to move to a post in the regular
army.

At this precise point in his life, he committed something of an act.
When emptying his office in the Stasi building, he noticed for the first
time a cheap, kitsch gold-painted plastic plate hanging on the wall by his
desk, a ridiculous official recognition of the honorable third place his unit
had won in the Stasi ranking for work in culture. He smuggled this plate
out beneath his coat as his act of "small private revenge" for all the
compromises and humiliations of his life—stealing this plate was the only
thing for which he could summon enough courage. He drew the line here,
this time literally, and he held it—because, to his surprise and as befits the

German bureaucracy, there were reactions to and consequences of his act, more numerous and stronger than he had expected.

First, three weeks later, two Stasi superior officers visited him at home, accused him of stealing the plate and demanded that he return it. He denied it and, upon request, signed a sworn statement that he had not taken it. Then, years later, after *die Wende*, he improvised in his apartment a small private museum about the Wall, where things were presented from the Eastern perspective. Since he was also known as the person who had drawn the line of the Wall in 1961, this caused some interest and, in 1993, he was interviewed in his flat on TV, with the stolen plate hanging on the wall behind him. A technician asked him to remove the plate because it reflected the light and caused too much glitter; Koch furiously refused to do it: "I'll do anything for you, but the plate will stay where it is." The plate stayed there. However, a couple of days later, after the report on his museum was shown on TV, a Treuhand agent (Treuhand was the federal agency dealing with the fate of GDR state property) appeared at his door, again demanding the plate: according to the new law, GDR state property had now become the property of the united Federal Republic of Germany, and, since he had stolen the plate, he now had to return it. Koch furiously threw the agent out; the agent left with threats of a court procedure. Weeks later, the agent again visited him, informing him that the charges of the theft of state property against him had been dropped (the stolen object was of minimal value, and his crime had taken place years earlier, so that the deadline for a judicial action had passed long ago). However, the agent informed him, there was now a new charge raised against him, the charge of false testimony (to the Stasi, since, decades ago, he had signed the statement that he had not stolen the plate), and this false sworn statement still was a punishable crime. Koch threw the agent out again, but his troubles continued: because of rumors that he was a thief, his career suffered and his wife even lost her job . . . As Koch put it to Anna Funder: "All the courage I had is in that plate. The whole shitty little skerrick of it. That's all I had, that plate stays there." *This* is a fetish at its purest: a tiny stupid object to which I cling and which allows me to endure all the dirty compromises of my life. Do we not all have, in one or another form, such fetishes? They can be our inner spiritual experiences (which tell us that our social reality is mere appearance which does not really matter), our children (for whose good we do all the humiliating things in our jobs), and so on and so forth.

Let us turn to the standard reproach that commodity fetishism relies on the opposition between direct expression of an idea (or a subject) and its distorted metaphoric representation: this reproach only holds if one sticks to the simplistic notion of the fetish as an illusion obfuscating the true state of things. In psychiatric circles, there is a story told about a man whose wife was diagnosed with acute breast cancer and who died three months later; the husband survived her death unscathed, being able to talk coolly about his traumatic last moments with her—how? Was he a cold, distant, and unfeeling monster? Soon, his friends noticed that, while talking about his deceased wife, he always held a hamster in his hands, her pet object and now his fetish, the embodied disavowal of her death. No wonder that, when, a couple of months later, the hamster died, the man broke down and had to be hospitalized for a long period, treated for acute depression. So, when we are bombarded by claims that in our post-ideological cynical era nobody believes in the proclaimed ideals, when we encounter a person who claims he has been cured of any beliefs, accepting social reality the way it really is, one should always counter such claims with the question: OK, but *where is your hamster—the fetish which enables you to (pretend to) accept reality "the way it is"*? And does exactly the same not hold for the Marxian concept of commodity fetishism? Here is the very beginning of the famous subdivision 4 of the first chapter of *Capital*, on "The Fetishism of the Commodity and its Secret":

> A commodity appears at first sight an extremely obvious, trivial thing. But its analysis brings out that it is a very strange thing, abounding in metaphysical subtleties and theological niceties.[35]

These lines should surprise us, since they invert the standard procedure for demystifying a theological myth, that of reducing it to its terrestrial base: Marx does not claim, in the usual manner of Enlightenment critique, that critical analysis should demonstrate how what appears a mysterious theological entity emerged out of "ordinary" real-life process; he claims, on the contrary, that the task of critical analysis is to unearth the "metaphysical subtleties and theological niceties" in what appears at first sight just an ordinary object. In other words, when a critical Marxist encounters a bourgeois subject immersed in commodity fetishism, the Marxist's reproach to him is not "The commodity may seem to you to be a magical object endowed with special powers, but it really is just a reified expression of relations between people." The Marxist's reproach is, rather, "You may think that the commodity appears to you as a simple embodiment of social relations (that, for example, money is just a kind of voucher entitling you to a part of the social product), but this is not how things really seem to you—in your social reality, by means of your participation in social exchange, you bear witness to the uncanny fact that a commodity really appears to you as a magical object endowed with special powers."

It is in this precise sense that the contemporary era is perhaps less atheistic than any prior one: we are all ready to indulge in utter skepticism, cynical distance, exploitation of others "without any illusions," violations of all ethical constraints, extreme sexual practices, and so on and so forth—protected by the silent awareness that the big Other is ignorant about it. Niels Bohr provided the perfect example of how this fetishistic disavowal of belief works in ideology. Seeing a horseshoe hanging above the entrance to Bohr's country house, a surprised visitor said that he did not believe in the superstition that the horseshoe keeps the bad spirits out of the house and brings luck, to which Bohr snapped back: "Nor do I believe in it; I have it there because I was told that it also works if one does not believe in it!" Fetishism does not operate at the level of "mystification" and "distorted knowledge": what is literally "displaced" in the fetish, transferred onto it, is not knowledge but *illusion itself*, the belief threatened by knowledge. Far from obfuscating "realistic" knowledge of how things are, the fetish is, on the contrary, the means that enables the subject to accept this knowledge without paying the full price for it: "I know very well [how things really stand], and I am able to endure this bitter truth because of a fetish (a hamster, a button . . .) in which the illusion to which I stick is embodied."

Although, at a purely formal level, the fetish also involves a gesture of transference (onto the fetish object), it functions as an exact inversion of the standard formula of transference (with the subject supposed to know): what the fetish gives body to is precisely my disavowal of knowledge, my refusal to subjectively assume what I know. Therein— to emphasize a point I made earlier—resides the contrast between the fetish and the symptom: a symptom embodies a repressed knowledge, the truth about the subject that the subject is not ready to assume. In a certain kind of Christianity, Christ himself is elevated into a fetish, insofar as he is supposed to be the innocent subject who ignores the wicked ways of the world.

This dialectic of fetishism reaches its apogee in today's "virtual capitalism." Capitalism as such entails the radical secularization of social life—it mercilessly tears apart all aura of authentic nobility, sacredness, honor, etc.:

> It has drowned the most heavenly ecstasies of religious fervor, of chivalrous enthusiasm, of philistine sentimentalism, in the icy water of egotistical calculation. It has resolved personal worth into exchange value, and in place of the numberless indefeasible chartered freedoms, has set up that single, unconscionable freedom—Free Trade. In one word, for exploitation, veiled by religious and political illusions, it has substituted naked, shameless, direct, brutal exploitation.[36]

However, the fundamental lesson of the "critique of political economy" elaborated by the mature Marx in the years after the *Manifesto* is that this reduction of all heavenly chimerae to the brutal economic reality generates a spectrality of its own. When Marx describes the mad self-enhancing circulation of capital, whose solipsistic path of self-fecundation reaches its apogee in today's meta-reflexive speculation on futures, it is far too simplistic to claim that the specter of this self-engendering monster that pursues its path disregarding any human or environmental concern is an ideological abstraction, and that one should never forget that, behind this abstraction, there are real people and natural objects on whose productive capacities and resources capital's circulation is based and on which it feeds itself like a gigantic parasite. The problem is that this "abstraction" is not only in our (the financial speculator's) misperception of social reality, but that it is "real" in the precise sense of determining the structure of the very material social processes: the fate of whole strata of population and sometimes of whole countries can be decided by the "solipsistic" speculative dance of capital, which pursues its goal of profitability in blessed indifference as to how its movement will affect social reality. Today is this not more true than ever? Do phenomena usually designated as "virtual capitalism" (futures trading and similar abstract financial speculations) not point towards the reign of the "real abstraction" at its purest, much more radically than in Marx's time? In short, the highest form of ideology does not reside in getting caught up in the ideological spectrality, forgetting about its foundation in real people and their relations, but precisely in overlooking this Real of spectrality and in pretending to address directly "real people with their real worries." Visitors to the London Stock Exchange get a free leaflet which explains to them that the stock market is not about some mysterious fluctuations, but about real people and their products—*this* is ideology at its purest.

The standard Marxist topic of "reification" and "commodity fetishism" still relies on the notion of the fetish as a solid object whose stable presence obfuscates its social mediation. Paradoxically, fetishism reaches its acme precisely when the fetish itself is "dematerialized," turned into a fluid "immaterial" virtual entity; money fetishism will culminate with the passage to its electronic form, when the last traces of its materiality will disappear—electronic money is the third form, after "real" money which directly embodies its value (gold, silver) and paper money which, although a "mere sign" with no intrinsic value, still clings to its material existence. And it is only at this stage, when money becomes a purely virtual point of reference, that it finally assumes the form of an indestructible spectral presence: I owe you $1,000, and no matter how many material notes I burn, I still owe you $1,000, the debt is inscribed somewhere in the virtual digital space . . . It is only with this thoroughgoing "dematerialization," when Marx's claim from the *Manifesto* that, under capitalism, "all that is solid melts into air," acquires a much more literal meaning than the one Marx had in mind, it is only at this point that what Derrida called the spectral aspect of capitalism is fully actualized.

One should thus reject the enthusiastic claims regarding our entry into a new era of virtual capitalism: what this "new era" makes visible is a virtual dimension which was here all the time. Recall Kant's rejection of the ontological proof of God's existence which takes as its starting point his thesis that being is not a predicate: if one knows all predicates of an entity, its being (existence) does not follow, that is, one cannot conclude being from a notion. (The departure from Leibniz is clear here, according to whom two objects are indiscernible if all of their predicates are the same.) The implication for the ontological proof of God is clear: in the same way that I can have a perfect notion of 100 thalers and still do not have them in my pocket, I can have a perfect notion of God and God still does not exist. The irony is that Kant talks about thalers, money, whose existence *as money* is not "objective," but depends on "notional" determinations. True, as Kant says, having a concept of 100 thalers is not the same as having them in your pocket; but let us imagine a process of rapid inflation which totally devalues the thalers: yes, they are still there in my pocket, but they are no longer money, just meaningless, valueless coins. In other words, money is precisely an object whose status depends on how we "think" about it: if people no longer treat this piece of metal as money, if they no longer "believe" in it as money, it no longer *is* money.

The lesson of these paradoxes is the odd overlapping of cynicism and belief. While capitalism is resolutely "materialistic" (what ultimately matters is wealth, real power, pleasures, all other things are just "noble lies," chimerae covering up this hard truth), this cynical wisdom itself has to rely on a vast network of belief: the whole capitalist system functions only insofar as one plays the game and "believes" in money, takes it seriously, and practices a fundamental *trust* in others who are also supposed to participate in the game. Capital markets, now valued at an estimated $83 trillion, exist within a system based purely on self-interest, in which herd behavior, often based on rumors, can inflate or destroy the value of companies—or whole economies—in a matter of hours.

It is in this very imbrication of brutal cynicism with wide-eyed belief that the objective irony of capitalism resides. One can thus imagine, as a counterpoint to this virtual capitalism in which "real things" take place at a purely virtual level of financial transfers, totally disconnected from our ordinary reality, a purely virtual collapse, the collapse of virtual markets as an "end of the world" in which nothing in our material reality would "really change"—it is just that all of a sudden, people would refuse to give their trust, they would refuse to participate in the game. That is to say, the virtual status of money means that it functions like a nation: while the nation is the people's substance, the cause for which they are (sometimes) ready to sacrifice everything, it has no substantial reality of its own—it exists only insofar as people "believe" that it exists, it is a Cause posited retroactively by its own effects. One should then imagine a scenario similar to the one envisaged by Saramago in his *Seeing* (in which a people all of a sudden refuses to participate in voting), only transposed to the economic domain: people refusing to participate in the financial virtual game. Perhaps, such a refusal would be today the ultimate political act.

In "Murder in the Mews," an early Agatha Christie story, Hercule Poirot investigates the death of Mrs Allen, found shot in her apartment on Guy Fawkes night. Although her death looks like suicide, numerous details indicate that a murder is more likely and that a clumsy attempt has been made to make it look like Mrs Allen took her own life. She shared a flat with Miss Plenderleith who was away at the time. Soon a cufflink is found at the murder scene and its owner, Major Eustace, is implicated in the crime. Poirot's solution is one of the best in Christie's work: it inverts the standard plot of a murder made to look like a suicide. The victim, who, years ago, had been caught up in a scandal in India, where she had also met Eustace, was engaged to marry a Conservative MP. Knowing that the public exposure of her scandal would ruin her chances of marriage, Eustace had been blackmailing her. In despair, Mrs Allen shot herself. Coming home immediately after the suicide, Miss Plenderleith—who knew about Eustace's blackmail and hated him—quickly rearranged details at the scene of the death to make it look as though the murderer had tried clumsily to present the death as suicide, so that Eustace would be fully punished for driving Mrs Allen to kill herself. The story thus turns the question on its head: How should the inconsistencies noted on the scene of crime be read? Is it a murder masked as suicide or a suicide masked as murder? The story works because, instead of the murder being covered up (the usual narrative), its appearance is staged, that is, a crime is not concealed but fabricated as a lure.

Is this not what the instigators of populist violence do? In order to (re)direct the wrath of the deceived crowd, they misconstrue suicide as crime, in other words, they falsify the clues so that a catastrophe which is a "suicide" (the result of immanent antagonisms) appears as the work of a criminal agent. This is why, to put it in Nietzschean terms which are here fully appropriate, the ultimate difference between true radical-emancipatory politics and populist politics is that authentic radical politics is active, imposing, enforcing its vision, while populism is fundamentally *reactive*, a reaction to a disturbing intruder. In other words, populism remains a version of the politics of fear: it mobilizes the crowd by way of invoking the fear of the corrupt intruder.

The act

Is, however, this critique of Laclau really Lacanian? Yannis Stavrakakis's *The Lacanian Left*,[37] an attempt to supplement Laclau's and Mouffe's project of "radical democracy" with Lacanian theory, disputes it. According to Stavrakakis, I started off well, but then, in my work, I "move continuously into more bizarre and unfathomable directions."[38] The key reproach concerns my alleged idealization of Antigone, of the radical autonomy of her suicidal "pure" desire: such a stance excludes her from the socio-political field. I claim that the subject of an act "risks" an encounter with death and "momentarily" suspends the symbolic/legal framework, but Antigone clearly does not meet these criteria—she not only risks death, she desires it:

> Risk entails a minimum of strategic or pragmatic calculation, which is something alien to Antigone's pure desire. Suspension presupposes a before and an after, but for Antigone there is no after. In that sense, this was never a case of an act effecting a displacement of the status quo. Her act is a one-off and she couldn't care less about what will happen in the *polis* after her suicide.[39]

Really? Far from just throwing herself into the arms of death, Sophocles' Antigone insists up to her death on performing a precise symbolic gesture: the proper burial of her brother. Like *Hamlet*, *Antigone* is a drama of a failed symbolic ritual—Lacan insisted on this continuity (he analyzed *Hamlet* in his seminar that precedes *The Ethics of Psychoanalysis*). Antigone does not stand for some extra-symbolic real, but for the pure signifier—her "purity" is that of a signifier. This is why, although her act is suicidal, the stakes are symbolic, and her persistence till death has a cathartic effect not only on us, the public, but also on the Theban people themselves embodied in the Chorus. Stavrakakis's point here is that I elevate Antigone's radical suicidal act which excludes her from the symbolic community into the model for a political act, thereby ignoring not only that Lacan never conceived Antigone in this way, but also the later shifts in his position:

> To focus exclusively on Lacan's commentary of Antigone would amount to ignoring the radical shift in Lacan's own position following the *Ethics* seminar. Clearly, Antigone is not Lacan's last—or most insightful—word on the question of ethics and agency. His position continued to develop in a direction that undermined his earlier focus on Antigone's pure desire. [. . .] anyone taking seriously the important shift in Lacan's position has to abandon Antigone as a model of the ethico-political act, something that Žižek fails to do.[40]

Stavrakakis sees a strange regression in my work: in my early books, I insisted on the "lack in the Other" as Lacan's key insight, while in my more recent work, I criticize this notion as belonging to deconstructionism, thus handing over to the latter Lacan's most precious insight. My notion of the act involves a miraculous emergence of unconditional positivity which suspends lack, that is, I rely on a "strict opposition between lack, denoting finitude and negativity, and divine miracle, denoting immortality and positivity."[41] Assuming lack means assuming negativity and finitude, while I conceive the act as absolute-positive-eternal, external to the Symbolic; or, as Pluth and Hoens claim, quoted approvingly by Stavrakakis, "by neglecting the importance of an act's involvement with the symbolic, Žižek seems to be saying that the real of an act happens without the symbolic."[42] ("Seems" is a crucial word here, and, as we shall see, in Stavrakakis's book too: it registers his own doubt about the accuracy of his own reading.) Such an absolutization of the act, which extracts it from its socio-symbolic texture, also makes it impossible to distinguish between true and false acts or events, between events and their simulacra (a standard argument against Badiou) . . . as if I have not spent pages explaining how one *can* distinguish an event from its simulacrum by way of analyzing how the event relates to the symptomal knot, the inscription of the *lack* in a situation.

So while Stavrakakis's general line of argumentation is that I steer away from Lacan under the influence of Badiou, the ultimate joke is, predictably, that even Badiou is more Lacanian than me: what I do not see (and that Badiou does) is that "the true positivity of a real event depends on its inextricable relation to the void of the eventual site, to a registering of negativity."[43] No wonder that I criticize Badiou when he warns of the totalitarian danger of "enforcing" a truth on a situation, of ignoring the "nameless," the excess of the multiplicity of reality which resists being subsumed under a truth-procedure. This is what Stalinism did: in imposing forced collectivization and a centralized planned economy, it enacted its voluntarism which ignored the inertia of reality—and, in a quite consistent way, since Stalinism did not admit this excess of the "nameless," it had to interpret the resistance of reality to its projects as intentional counter-revolution.[44] And, as expected, for Stavrakakis, this also holds for my notion of the act as unconditional: insofar as it knows no limitation (for which Badiou allows when he warned against the excess of enforcement), it necessarily leads to a totalitarian assertion.

The reason I find Badiou problematic here is that, for me, something is wrong with the very notion that one can excessively "enforce" a truth: one is almost tempted to apply here the logic of the joke quoted by Lacan "my fiancée is never late for an appointment, because the moment she is late, she is no longer my fiancée": a Truth is never enforced, because the moment the fidelity to Truth functions as an excessive enforcement, we are no longer dealing with a Truth, with fidelity to a Truth-Event. In the case of Stalinism, its problem was not simply that of "enforcing" the Truth, ruthlessly imposing it onto the situation: the problem was rather that *the "truth" which was enforced—the vision of a centralized planned economy, and so forth—was in itself not a Truth*, so that the resistance of reality against it was a sign of its own falsity.[45]

The story goes on in a predictable way: my notion of a momentary miraculous act implies "an act without after,"[46] that is, I ignore the effects of the act, its inscription into the situation . . . as if I have not written many pages developing how what matters is not the act itself but "the day after," the way an act rearticulates the situation. (Furthermore, I am accused of privileging positivity, of obliterating negativity—but such an "act without after," just a rupture, a cut, would have been precisely a pure non-positivized negativity.) So I ignore the "positivization/institutionalization of lack": "Žižek seems [*sic*] to deny the very possibility of institutionalizing lack and division, of articulating a *positive* political order encircling—but not neutralizing—negativity and impossibility"[47] . . . as if the whole point of my reading of Hegel's political thought is not that the Hegelian state is a negativity institutionalized! As if my privileging of the Lenin of 1919–22 over the Lenin of 1917 is not precisely the privileging of the Lenin of the institutionalization of a new order which positivizes revolutionary negativity! Furthermore, because I ignore negativity, I do not see how the negative gesture of creating empty space is a condition of a positive act:

> Paul Klee once said, speaking of Mondrian: "To create emptiness is the principal act. And this is true creation, because this emptiness is positive" [. . .]. In politics, this is the radical democratic strategy, and this is what Žižek seems [*sic*] unable to understand.[48]

As if I have not written pages and pages on opening up empty space, on reaching the point at which *rien n'aura eu lieu que le lieu*—say, apropos the relation between the death drive and sublimation (the negativity of the death drive as the condition of positive sublimation) . . . How, then, does Stavrakakis react to the *massive* evidence that I have amply developed all the points he reproaches me for ignoring (lack in the Other, negativity, symbolic determination of the act . . .)? Instead of questioning his own reading of my notion of the act, he proclaims *me* a pervert (in theory):

I have no intention to teach Žižek Lacanian commonplaces. I take it for granted that he knows them very well, better than I do. *But this is exactly why it causes me great concern when Žižek himself seems to forget or abandon them.* It is not by coincidence that I have used the psycho-analytic term "disavowal" to describe this attitude. As is well known, disavowal, as the fundamental operation of perversion, involves the simultaneous recognition and denial of something—in the clinic, of castration. In fact, Žižek's response seems [*sic*] to come under this description.[49]

The sleight of hand is here truly breathtaking: every counter-argument of mine is in advance devalued. I am accused of claiming *A*; I cite proof that I am *not* claiming *A*, and the answer is that I merely disavow my sticking to *A*, that my reasoning is: "I know very well that *A* does not hold, but, nonetheless, I continue to act as if *A* holds . . ." So when, at the end of the chapter dedicated to my work, Stavrakakis writes "Why does [Žižek] bypass the whole Lacanian theorization of another (feminine) *jouis-sance?*,"[50] there is no point defending myself by referring to dozens of pages in which I deal precisely with *jouissance féminine*—such defense would be in advance devalued as a perverse "recital of absurdity"[51] . . . The only pervert here is Stavrakakis himself, what if *his* underlying logic is: "I know very well that my reproaches to Žižek are meaningless, but I continue to stick to them"? What if, however, Stavrakakis is simply *right* in his claims about my notion of the act? On what evidence are these claims based? Here is a passage in which he allegedly demonstrates how my work displays "the mechanism of disavowal in its unmistakable purity":

Consider the following two quotations. First, Žižek argues that, "in a situation like today's, the only way really to remain open to a revolu-tionary opportunity is to renounce facile calls to direct action. [. . .] The only way to lay the foundations for a true, radical change is to withdraw from the compulsion to act, to 'do nothing'—thus opening up the space for a different kind of activity". [. . .] Three pages later he condemns the resistance to political acts and the obsession with "radical Evil": "It is as if the supreme Good today is that nothing should happen". [. . .] What is one supposed to conclude from this? Surely "to do nothing" does not make sense as a remedy against those who supposedly argue that "nothing should happen".[52]

What one really concludes from this passage is that it exemplifies *misreading* "in its unmistakable purity": the appearance of contradiction vanishes the moment we take into account the (rather obvious) fact that I am systematically opposing true activity (fidelity to the act proper) and false activity (which merely reproduces the existing constellation—*plus ça change, plus ça reste le même*, we are active all the time to make sure that nothing will change). The condition for true change (a true act) is to stop false activity, or, as Badiou puts it in a sentence I quote repeatedly: "It is better to do nothing than to contribute to the invention of formal ways of rendering visible that which Empire already recognizes as existent."[53]

Another case: after quoting passages in which I assert contingency (every act is "embedded" in a contingent historical situation) and passages in which I assert the "unconditional" character of the act, Stavrakakis asks:

> How can an awareness of contingency be a necessary condition for something which actually presupposes that we abandon it and is located beyond any conditionality: *the unconditional revolutionary act*?[54]

Unfortunately, for me (as a Hegelian), there is no contradiction here: what I refer to as the "unconditional act" is not the nonsense imputed to me (an act outside history, outside the symbolic), but simply *the act irreducible to its conditions*. Such an act is not only rooted in its contingent conditions, these very conditions make it into an act: the same gesture, performed at a wrong moment (too early or too late), is no longer an act. The properly dialectical paradox here is that what makes an act "unconditional" is *its very contingency*: if the act were necessary, this would mean that it is fully determined by its conditions, that it can be deduced from them (as the optimal version arrived at through strategic reasoning or rational-choice theory). There is no need even to mention Hegel here: Derrida and Laclau suffice (in his reading of Kierkegaard, Derrida spoke about the "madness" of the act of choice/decision). The link between the situation and the act is thus clear: far from being determined by the situation (or from intervening in it from a mysterious outside), acts are possible on account of the ontological non-closure, inconsistency, gaps, in a situation.

Further "proof" of my practice of fetishistic disavowal is the alleged "perverse paradox" of my rejection of utopias while nonetheless claiming that today "it is more important than ever to hold this utopian place of the global alternative open"[55] — as if I have not repeatedly elaborated different meanings of utopia: utopia as simple imaginary impossibility (the utopia of a perfected harmonious social order without antagonisms, the consumerist utopia of contemporary capitalism), and utopia in the more radical sense of enacting what, *within the framework of the existing social relations*, appears as "impossible" — this second utopia is "a-topic" only with regard to these relations.[56] And so on — all Stavrakakis's "proofs" rely on such misreadings. Commenting on my "claim that, in Lacan's later versions of the act, this moment of 'madness' beyond strategic intervention remains," he writes: "Is this idea of the supposedly unconditional real act, of an act unbound by any relation to the symbolic field, what defines Lacan's notion of the act?"[57] Note the breathtakingly false paraphrase: from the claim that all authentic acts contain a "moment of 'madness' beyond strategic intervention," a claim found also in Derrida or Laclau, he jumps to "an act unbound by any relation to the symbolic field" . . . with such paraphrases, anything can be proven!

Since Stavrakakis also accuses me of totally ignoring the history of Marxism, let me recall Karl Kautsky's defense of multi-party democracy: Kautsky conceived the victory of socialism as the parliamentary victory of the Social-Democratic Party, and even suggested that the appropriate political form of the passage from capitalism to socialism would be the parliamentary coalition of progressive bourgeois parties and socialist parties. (One is tempted to push this logic to the brink and suggest that, for Kautsky, the only acceptable revolution would be one that took place after a referendum in which at least 51 percent of voters approved it.) In his writings of 1917, Lenin saved his utmost acerbic irony for those who engage in the endless search for some kind of "guarantee" for the revolution. This guarantee assumes two main forms: either the reified notion of social Necessity (one should not risk the revolution too early; one has to wait for the right moment, when the situation is "mature" with regard to the laws of historical development: "it is too early for the socialist revolution, the working class is not yet mature") or normative ("democratic") legitimacy ("the majority of the population is not on our side, so the revolution would not really be democratic"). As Lenin repeatedly puts it in other words, it is as if, before the revolutionary agent risks the seizure of state power, it should get permission from some figure of the big Other (organize a referendum which will ascertain that the majority supports the revolution). With Lenin, as with Lacan, the point is that a revolution *ne s'autorise que d'elle-même*: one should accept the revolutionary *act* not covered by the big Other—the fear of taking power "prematurely," the search for the guarantee, is the fear of the abyss of the act.

Democracy is thus not only the "institutionalization of the lack in the Other" (incidentally, the whole point of Hegel's theory of constitutional monarchy is that it is also exactly the same). By institutionalizing the lack, it neutralizes—normalizes—it, so that the inexistence of the big Other (Lacan's *il n'y a pas de grand Autre*) is again suspended: the big Other is again here in the guise of the democratic legitimization/authorization of our acts—in a democracy, my acts are "covered" as legitimate acts which carry out the will of the majority. In contrast to this logic, the role of emancipatory forces is not to passively "reflect" the opinion of the majority, but to instigate the working classes to mobilize their forces and thus to *create* a new majority—or, as Trotsky put it in *Terrorism and Communism*:

> If the parliamentary regime, even in the period of "peaceful," stable development, was a rather crude method of discovering the opinion of the country, and in the epoch of revolutionary storm completely lost its capacity to follow the course of the struggle and the development of revolutionary consciousness, the Soviet regime, which is more closely, straightly, honestly bound up with the toiling majority of the people, does achieve meaning, *not in statically reflecting a majority, but in dynamically creating it*.

This last point relies on a crucial philosophical premise which renders deeply problematic the standard dialectical-materialist theory of knowledge as "reflection" (propagated by Lenin himself in his *Materialism and Empiriocriticism*). Kautsky's worry that the Russian working class took power "too early" implies the positivist vision of history as an "objective" process which determines in advance the possible coordinates of political interventions; within this horizon, it is unimaginable that a radical political intervention would change these very "objective" coordinates and thus, in a way, create the conditions for its own success. An act proper is not just a strategic intervention into a situation, bound by its conditions—it retroactively creates its own conditions. Recall Borges's precise formulation of the relationship between Kafka and the multitude of his precursors, from ancient Chinese authors to Robert Browning:

Kafka's idiosyncrasy, in greater or lesser degree, is present in each of these writings, but if Kafka had not written we would not perceive it; that is to say, it would not exist. [. . .] [E]ach writer *creates* his precursors. His work modifies our conception of the past, as it will modify the future.[58]

The properly dialectical solution of the dilemma of "Is it really there, in the source, or did we only read it into the source?" is thus: it is there, but we can only perceive and state this retroactively, from today's perspective. This retroactivity was articulated by Deleuze. When Deleuze talks about genesis (of the actual out of the virtual), he does not mean temporal-evolutionary genesis, the process of the spatio-temporal becoming of a thing, but a "genesis without dynamism, evolving necessarily in the element of a supra-historicity, a *static genesis*."[59] This static character of the virtual field finds its most radical expression in Deleuze's notion of a *pure past*: a virtual past which already contains things still present. A present can become past because in a way it is already; it can perceive itself as part of the past—"what we are doing now is (will have become) history":

It is with respect to the pure element of the past, understood as the past in general, as an a priori past, that a given former present is reproducible and the present present is able to reflect itself.[60]

Does this mean that this pure past involves a thoroughly deterministic notion of the universe in which everything to happen (to come), all actual spatio-temporal deployment, is already part of an immemorial/atemporal virtual network? No, and for a very precise reason: because the pure past must be "amenable to change through the occurrence of any new present."[61] It was none other than T.S. Eliot who first clearly formulated this link between our dependence on tradition and our power to change the past:

[tradition] cannot be inherited, and if you want it you must obtain it by great labor. It involves, in the first place, the historical sense, which we may call nearly indispensable to anyone who would continue to be a poet beyond his twenty-fifth year; and the historical sense involves a perception, not only of the pastness of the past, but of its presence; the historical sense compels a man to write not merely with his own generation in his bones, but with a feeling that the whole of the literature of Europe from Homer and within it the whole of the literature of his own country has a simultaneous existence and composes a simultaneous order. [. . .] [W]hat happens when a new work of art is created is something that happens simultaneously to all the works of art which preceded it. The existing monuments form an ideal order among themselves, which is modified by the introduction of the new (the really new) work of art among them. The existing order is complete before the new work arrives; for order to persist after the supervention of novelty, the *whole* existing order must be, if ever so slightly, altered; and so the relations, proportions, values of each work of art toward the whole are readjusted; and this is conformity between the old and the new. Whoever has approved this idea of order, of the form of European, of English literature, will not find it preposterous that the past should be altered by the present as much as the present is directed by the past.[62]

When Eliot writes that, when judging a living poet, "*you must set him among the dead*," he provides a precise example of Deleuze's pure past. When he writes that "the existing order is complete before the new work arrives; for order to persist after the supervention of novelty, the *whole* existing order must be, if ever so slightly, altered," he no less clearly formulates the paradoxical link between the completeness of the past and our capacity to change it retroactively: precisely because the pure past is complete, each new work rearranges its entire balance. Recall Borges's idea of how Kafka created his predecessors—such retroactive causality exerted by the effect itself upon its causes, is the minimal *sine qua non* of freedom.

This is where Peter Hallward falls short in his otherwise excellent *Out of This World*, where he stresses only the aspect of the pure past as the virtual field in which the fate of all actual events is sealed in advance, since "everything is already written" in it. At this point where we view reality *sub specie aeternitatis*, absolute freedom coincides with absolute necessity and its pure automatism: to be free means to let oneself freely flow in/with the substantial necessity. But while Hallward is right to emphasize that, for Deleuze, freedom "isn't a matter of human liberty but of liberation *from* humanity,"[63] of fully submerging oneself in the creative flux of the absolute Life, his political conclusion from this seems too facile:

since a free mode or monad is simply one that has eliminated its resistance to the sovereign will that works through it, so then it follows that the more absolute the sovereign's power, the more "free" are those subject to it.[64]

Hallward ignores the retroactive movement on which Deleuze also insists, the way this eternal pure past which fully determines us is itself subjected to retroactive change. We are thus simultaneously less free and more free than we think: we are thoroughly passive, determined by and dependent on the past, but we have the freedom to define the scope of this determination, that is, to (over)determine the past which will determine us. Deleuze is here unexpectedly close to Kant, for whom I am determined by causes, but I (can) retroactively determine which causes will determine me: we, subjects, are passively affected by pathological objects and motivations; but, in a reflexive way, we ourselves have the minimal power to accept (or reject) being affected in this way, in other words, we retroactively determine the causes allowed to determine us, or, at least, the *mode* of this linear determination. "Freedom" is thus inherently retroactive: at its most elementary, it is not a free act which, out of nowhere, starts a new causal link, but a retroactive act of endorsing which link/sequence of necessities will determine me. Here, one should add a Hegelian twist to Spinoza: freedom is not simply "recognized/known necessity," but recognized/assumed necessity, the necessity constituted/actualized through this recognition. So, when Deleuze refers to Proust's description of Vinteuil's music that haunts Swann—"as if the performers not so much played the little phrase as executed the rites necessary for it to appear"—he is evoking the necessary illusion: generating the sense-event is experienced as a ritualistic evocation of a preexisting event, as if the event was already there, waiting for our call in its virtual presence.

What directly resonates in this topic is, of course, the Protestant trope of predestination: far from being a reactionary theological trope, predestination is a key element of the materialist theory of sense—on condition that we read it along the lines of the Deleuzian opposition between the virtual and the actual. That is to say, predestination does not mean that our fate is sealed in an actual text existing for eternity in the divine mind; the texture which predestines us belongs to the purely virtual eternal past which, as such, can be retroactively rewritten by our act. This, perhaps, is the ultimate meaning of the singularity of Christ's incarnation: it is an act which radically changes our destiny. Prior to Christ, we were determined by fate, caught in the cycle of sin and its payment, while Christ's erasure of our past sins means precisely that his sacrifice changes our virtual past and thus sets us free. When Deleuze writes that "my wound existed before me; I was born to embody it," does this variation on the theme of the Cheshire cat and its smile from *Alice in Wonderland* (the cat was born to embody its smile) not provide a perfect formula of Christ's sacrifice: Christ was born to embody his wound, to be crucified? The problem is the literal teleological reading of this proposition: as if the actual deeds of a person merely actualize its atemporal–eternal fate inscribed in its virtual idea:

> Caesar's only real task is to become worthy of the events he has been created to embody. *Amor fati*. What Caesar actually does adds nothing to what he virtually is. When Caesar actually crosses the Rubicon this involves no deliberation or choice since it is simply part of the entire, immediate expression of Caesarness, it simply unrolls or "unfolds" something that was encompassed for all times in the notion of Caesar.[65]

However, what about the retroactivity of a gesture which (re)constitutes this past itself? This, perhaps, is the most succinct definition of what an authentic *act* is: in our ordinary activity, we effectively just follow the (virtual-fantasmatic) coordinates of our identity, while an act proper is the paradox of an actual move which (retroactively) changes the very virtual "transcendental" coordinates of its agent's being — or, in Freudian terms, which not only changes the actuality of our world, but also "rouses its infernal regions." We have thus a kind of reflexive "folding back of the condition onto the given it was the condition for":[66] while the pure past is the transcendental condition for our acts, our acts not only create an actual new reality, they also retroactively change this very condition. In predestination, fate is substantialized into a decision that precedes the process, so that the stake of individuals' activities is not to performatively constitute their fate, but to discover (or guess) one's preexisting fate. What is thereby obfuscated is the dialectical reversal of contingency into necessity, or, the way the outcome of a contingent process is the appearance of necessity: things retroactively "will have been" necessary. This reversal was described by Jean-Pierre Dupuy:

> The catastrophic event is inscribed into the future as a destiny, for sure, but also as a contingent accident: it could not have taken place, even if, in *futur antérieur*, it appears as necessary. [. . .] [I]f an outstanding event takes place, a catastrophe, for example, it could not not have taken place; nonetheless, insofar as it did not take place, it is not inevitable. It is thus the event's actualization—the fact that it takes place—which retroactively creates its necessity.[67]

Dupuy takes as an example the French presidential elections in May 1995; here is the January forecast of the main polling institute: "If, on next May 8, Mr Balladur is elected, one can say that the presidential election was decided before it even took place." If—accidentally—an event takes place, it creates the preceding chain which makes it appear inevitable: *this*, not the commonplaces regarding how the underlying necessity expresses itself in and through the accidental play of appearances, is *in nuce* the Hegelian dialectic of contingency and necessity. The same goes for the October Revolution (once the Bolsheviks won and stabilized their hold on power, their victory appeared as an outcome and expression of a deeper historical necessity), and even of Bush's much contested first US presidential victory (after the contingent and contested Florida majority, his victory retroactively appears as an expression of a deeper US political trend). In this sense, although we are determined by destiny, we are nonetheless *free to choose our destiny*. This, according to Dupuy, is also how we should approach the ecological crisis: not to "realistically" appraise the possibilities of the catastrophe, but to accept it as Destiny in the precise Hegelian sense: like the election of Balladur, "if the catastrophe happens, one can say that its occurrence was decided before it even took place." Destiny and free action (blocking the "if") thus go hand in hand: freedom is at its most radical the freedom to change one's Destiny.

The Real

There is another curious point that should be mentioned here: Stavrakakis's reproach that I obliterate negativity (in my work, negativity magically disappears in the positivity of the Act), is, as Stavrakakis himself notes, the exact opposite of Peter Hallward's critique of my work: Hallward's reproach concerns my alleged morbid fascination with negativity, the death drive, and so on, which misses the positivity of the

Event. Is this not strange: two critical readings of the same work which attribute to me exactly opposite positions? Is the conclusion that imposes itself not that both of my critics merely use my theory as a kind of token to fill in a preestablished place in their matrix of "wrong" positions?[68]

Why, then, does Stavrakakis have to stick so stubbornly to the ridiculous notion of the act imputed to me? Obviously, it is not the case that the difference is only verbal, a mere misunderstanding—it is not that Stavrakakis and I claim the same thing and that he has merely misread me. His perversion is conditioned by a weakness in his basic theoretical apparatus, a fault line which also prevents him from articulating a viable political project, so that all he offers is a new version of the old Freudo-Marxist platitudes. This basic weakness is discernible already in his brief methodological reflection in the "Introduction," where he draws attention to the circularity of positive sciences which claim that their theories fully reflect reality and are proven by facts, thereby neglecting how the "objective facts" to which they refer are not the direct pre-Symbolic Real, but a Real which is already mediated/constructed by the Symbolic:

> contrary to a popular unconditional Enlightenment optimism, knowledge in general is never adequate; something always escapes. It looks as if theory is a straitjacket unable to contain our vibrant and unpredictable field of real experience.[69]

The underlying premise is here the identification of the couple knowledge–experience with the couple Symbolic–Real: one should assert the "constitutive tension between knowledge and experience, symbolic and real."[70] The Lacanian couple Symbolic/Real is thus reduced to the common-sense empiricist motif "theories are grey, while the tree of life is green": our knowledge is always limited, it cannot ever fully encompass and account for the wealth of experience. Since, however, one cannot step out of knowledge and directly grasp the Real, one should go on, pursuing the endless task of symbolizing the Real with the full awareness that every determinate symbolization is unstable, temporary, that it will be sooner or later destabilized through some traumatic encounter with the Real:

> In the face of the irreducibility of the real of experience, we seem to have no other option but to symbolize, to keep on symbolizing, trying to enact a positive encircling of negativity. But this should not be a

> fantasmatic symbolization attempting to mortify the real of experience
> [. . .] It will have to articulate a set of symbolic gestures (positiviza-
> tions) that will include a recognition of the real limits of the symbolic,
> the real limits of theory, and attempts symbolically to "institutionalize"
> real lack, the (negative) trace of experience, or rather of our failure to
> neutralize experience.[71]

We thus end with what Hegel called "spurious infinity": the subject
strives to fill in his constitutive lack and provide an identity for itself
through Symbolic and Imaginary identifications; however, no identification can produce a full identity, lack always reemerges . . . Stavrakakis is
here not radical enough in pursuing his own premise: *every* Symbolic field
needs a signifier of lack to suture itself—as Spinoza already recognized,
in traditional religion, "God" is such a signifier (from the standpoint of
true knowledge, "God" has no positive content, the signifier merely
positivizes our ignorance). In short, although Stavrakakis endlessly
varies the motif of how I do not take into account the possibility of lack
itself being symbolized–positivized–institutionalized, he himself does not
see it where it already operates.

There is nothing inherently "subversive" or "progressive" in the
notion of the "signifier of lack". Is the figure of the Jew in anti-
Semitism not its supreme ideological example? This figure has no
consistent positive content—what holds it together is *the name* "Jew"
as the empty signifier. That is to say, the structure is here the same as
that of the good old Polish anti-Communist joke from the epoch of
"really-existing socialism": "Socialism is the synthesis of the greatest
achievements of all previous modes of production: from pre-class tribal
society it takes primitivism, from the Asiatic mode of production it takes
despotism, from Antiquity it takes slavery, from feudalism it takes the
social domination of lords over serfs, from capitalism it takes exploitation, and from socialism it takes the name." The anti-Semitic figure of
the Jew takes from great capitalists their wealth and social control,
from the hedonists sexual debauchery, from commercialized popular
culture and the yellow press their vulgarity, from the lower classes their
filth and bad smell, from intellectuals their corrupted sophistry, *and from
Jews their name*. It is this intervention of the pure/empty signifier which
engenders the mysterious *X*, the *je ne sais quoi* which makes Jews Jews:
for a true anti-Semite, a Jew is not simply corrupt, promiscuous, and so
on—he is corrupt, promiscuous, etc., *because he is a Jew*. In this sense,

"Jew" is—within the anti-Semitic discourse—clearly a signifier of lack, the lack in the Other.

Consequently, Stavrakakis's equation of the Real with the experience of the excess of reality over its symbolization has nothing to do with the Lacanian (or, for that matter, Laclauian) Real. The Laclauian "antagonism" is not the positivity of the Real outside the Symbolic, it is totally inherent to the Symbolic, its immanent crack or impossibility. The Real is not the transcendent substantial reality which from outside disturbs the Symbolic balance, but the immanent obstacle, stumbling block, of the Symbolic order itself. This empiricist misreading of the Lacanian Real accounts for Stavrakakis's strange use of "negativity": the Real as the excess of experience over its symbolization is "negative" only in the superficial sense that it undermines symbolization, since it functions as the Otherness which resists it; in itself, however, this Real is a positivity of the exuberant wealth of experience. For Lacan, things are exactly opposite. It is true that the early Lacan (in his first seminars) sometimes uses "the Real" to designate pre-Symbolic reality; however, this Real is the pure positivity of being without any lack—as Lacan repeats again and again in these years, *rien ne manque dans le réel*, lack is introduced only by the Symbolic. This is why, for Lacan, negativity is not the Real undermining the Symbolic from outside, but the Symbolic itself, the process of symbolization with its violent abstraction, reduction of the wealth of experience to the signifying *trait unaire*. Lacan quotes Hegel: a word is the murder of the thing it designates, its mortification.

For Lacan, the elementary form of negativity is thus not the excess of experience over its symbolization, but the very gap that separates symbolization from experienced reality. Recall the big photo of an elephant on the cover of the French edition of Lacan's first seminar: the elephant is here in its signifier, even if there is no "real elephant" roaming around—this brutal reduction of the "real" elephant to its signifier is negativity (or the death drive) at its purest. Although Lacan later shifts his position (the "death drive" is later defined as the Symbolic system itself which operates autonomously, ignoring reality; finally, the "death drive" is conceived as the Real which resists symbolization), the Real remains immanent to the Symbolic, its inherent traumatic core: there is no Real without the Symbolic, it is the emergence of the Symbolic which introduces into reality the gap of the Real.

It is thus touching to find someone who can still (think and) write as if Hegel had not existed[72]—and not only Hegel: what about Lacan's notion of the *matheme*, of the scientific real as the set of mathematized formulae opposed to imaginary experience? This is why Lacan strictly opposes scientific "knowledge in the real" to imaginary hermeneutic understanding. Furthermore, Stavrakakis's approach also misses the properly dialectical relationship between theory and practice in psychoanalysis. Freud's claim was that psychoanalysis would only be fully possible in a society which would no longer need it, so that psychoanalytic theory is not only the theory of what goes on in the analytic practice, the theory of the conditions of possibility of practice, but simultaneously the theory of its impossibility, of why practice is always open to failure, even doomed to fail. In this sense, it is not simply practice which is in excess over theory, it is theory which conceptualizes the limit of practice, its *Real*.

Because he neglects this *real* (not merely symbolic) status of scientific knowledge, Stavrakakis identifies knowledge and understanding: in the same line of thought regarding the limitation of knowledge, he mentions Lacan's warning that "one of the things we must guard most against is to understand too much." However, Lacan's point here is not, as Stavrakakis claims, that "the registering of the limits of understanding allows for a better, or rather a different, type of understanding."[73] When Lacan talks about "a kind of refusal of understanding," he opposes understanding and analytic knowledge: the aim of analysis is not to understand the patient, to provide the hidden meanings of his signifiers, but, on the contrary, to reduce meaning to the "signifying non-sense," as he puts it in his *Seminar XI*.

The key point here is that the Lacanian Real, in its opposition to the Symbolic, has nothing whatsoever to do with the standard empiricist (or phenomenological, or historicist, or *Lebensphilosophie*) topic of the wealth of reality that cannot be reduced to abstract conceptual determinations. The Lacanian Real is even more "reductionist" than any symbolic structure: we touch it when we subtract from a symbolic field all the wealth of its differences, reducing it to a minimum of antagonism. It is because of this "minimalist"—purely formal and insubstantial—status of the Real that, for Lacan, *repetition precedes repression*—or, as Deleuze put it succinctly: "We do not repeat because we repress, we repress because we repeat."[74] It is not that, first, we repress some traumatic content, and then, since we are unable to remember it and thus to clarify our relationship to it, this content continues to haunt us, repeating itself in disguised forms. If the Real is a minimal difference, then repetition (that establishes this difference) is primordial; the primacy of repression emerges with the "reification" of the Real into a Thing that resists symbolization—only then does it appear that the excluded/repressed Real insists and repeats itself. The Real is primordially nothing but the gap that separates a thing from itself, the gap of repetition. The consequence of this is also the inversion of the relationship between repetition and re-memorialization. Freud's famous motto "what we do not remember, we are compelled to repeat" should thus be turned upside down: *what we are unable to repeat, we are haunted by and are compelled to remember*. The way to get rid of a past trauma is not to remember it, but to fully *repeat* it in the Kierkegaardian sense.

What is Deleuzian "pure difference" at its purest, if we may put it in this tautological way? It is the purely virtual difference of an entity which repeats itself as totally identical with regard to its actual properties:

> there are significant differences in the virtual intensities expressed in our actual sensations. These differences do not correspond to actual recognizable differences. That the shade of pink has changed in an identifiable way is not all-important. It is that the change is a sign of a rearrangement of an infinity of other actual and virtual relations.[75]

Is not such a pure difference what takes place in the repetition of the same actual melodic line in Robert Schumann's "Humoresque"? This piece is to be read against the background of the gradual loss of the voice in Schumann's songs: it is not a simple piano piece, but a song without the vocal line, with the vocal line reduced to silence, so that all we in fact hear is the piano accompaniment. This is how one should read the famous "inner voice" (*innere Stimme*) added by Schumann (in the written score) as a third line between the two piano lines, higher and lower: as the vocal melodic line which remains a non-vocalized "inner voice" (which exists only as *Augenmusik*, music for the eyes only, in the guise of written notes). This absent melody is to be reconstructed on the basis of the fact that the first and third levels (the right- and the left-hand piano lines) do not relate to each other directly, that is, their relationship is not that of an immediate mirroring: in order to account for their interconnection, one is thus compelled to (re)construct a third, "virtual" intermediate level (melodic line) which, for structural reasons, cannot be played. Schumann brings this procedure of absent melody to an apparently absurd self-reference when, later in the same fragment of "Humoresque," he repeats the same two effectively played melodic lines, yet this time the score contains no third absent melodic line, no inner voice — what is absent here is the absent melody, namely absence itself. How are we to play these notes when, at the level of what is in fact to be played, they exactly repeat the previous notes? The effectively played notes are deprived only of what is not there, of their constitutive lack, or, to refer to the Bible, they lose even that which they never had. The true pianist should thus have the *savoir-faire* to play the existing, positive, notes in such a way that one would be able to discern the echo of the accompanying non-played "silent" virtual notes or their absence . . . This, then, is pure difference: the nothing-actual, the virtual background, which accounts for the difference of the two melodic lines.

This logic of virtual difference can also be discerned in another paradox. The cinematic version of Edgar Doctorow's *Billy Bathgate* is basically a failure, but an interesting one: a failure which nonetheless evokes in the viewer the specter of the much better novel. However, when one then goes on to read the novel on which the film is based, one is disappointed — this is *not* the novel the film evoked as the standard with regard to which it failed. The repetition (of a failed novel in the failed film) thus gives rise to a third, purely virtual, element, the better novel. This is an exemplary case of what Deleuze deploys in the crucial pages of his *Difference and Repetition*:

> while it may seem that the two presents are successive, at a variable distance apart in the series of reals, in fact they form, rather, *two real series which coexist in relation to a virtual object of another kind*, one which constantly circulates and is displaced in them. [. . .] Repetition is constituted not from one present to another, but between the two coexistent series that these presents form in function of the virtual object (object = x).[76]

With regard to *Billy Bathgate*: the film does not "repeat" the novel on which it is based; rather, they both "repeat" the unrepeatable virtual x, the "true" novel whose specter is engendered in the passage from the actual novel to the film. The underlying movement is here more complex than it may appear. It is not that we should simply conceive the starting point (the novel) as an "open work," full of possibilities which can be deployed later, actualized in later versions; or — even worse — that we should conceive the original work as a pre-text which can later be incorporated in other con-texts and given a meaning totally different from the original one. What is missing here is the retroactive, backwards, movement that was first described by Henri Bergson, a key reference for Deleuze. In his "Two Sources of Morality and Religion," Bergson describes the strange sensation he experienced on August 4, 1914, when war was declared between France and Germany:

> In spite of my turmoil, and although a war, even a victorious one, appeared to me as a catastrophe, I experienced what [William] James spoke about, a feeling of admiration for the facility of the passage from the abstract to the concrete: who would have thought that such a formidable event can emerge in reality with so little fuss?[77]

Crucial is here the modality of the break between before and after: before its outburst, the war appeared to Bergson *"simultaneously probable and impossible*: a complex and contradictory notion which persisted to the end";[78] after its outburst, it all of a sudden becomes real *and* possible, and the paradox resides in this retroactive appearance of probability:

> I never pretended that one can insert reality into the past and thus work backwards in time. However, one can without any doubt insert there the possible, or, rather, at every moment the possible inserts itself there. Insofar as unpredictable and new reality creates itself, its image reflects itself behind itself in the indefinite past: this new reality finds itself all the time having been possible; but it is only at the precise moment of its actual emergence that it *begins to always have been*, and this is why I say that its possibility, which does not precede its reality, will have preceded it once this reality emerges.[79]

And *this* is what takes place in the example of *Billy Bathgate*: the film inserts back into the novel the possibility of a different, much better, novel. And do we not encounter a similar logic in the relationship between Stalinism and Leninism? Here also, *three* moments are in play: Lenin's politics before the Stalinist takeover; Stalinist politics; the specter of "Leninism" retroactively generated by Stalinism (in its official Stalinist version, but *also* in the version critical of Stalinism, as when, in the process of "de-Stalinization" in the USSR, the motto evoked was that of the "return to original Leninist principles"). One should therefore stop the ridiculous game of opposing the Stalinist terror to the "authentic" Leninist legacy betrayed by Stalinism: "Leninism" is a thoroughly

Stalinist notion. The gesture of projecting the emancipatory-utopian potential of Stalinism backwards, into a preceding time, signals the incapacity of the line of thought in enduring the "absolute contradiction," the unbearable tension, inherent to the Stalinist project itself. It is therefore crucial to distinguish "Leninism" (as the authentic core of Stalinism) from the actual political practice and ideology of Lenin's period: the actual greatness of Lenin is *not* the same as the Stalinist authentic myth of Leninism.

And the irony is that this logic of repetition, elaborated by Deleuze, *the* anti-Hegelian *par excellence*, is at the very core of the Hegelian dialectic: it relies on the properly dialectical relationship between temporal reality and the eternal absolute. The eternal absolute is the immobile point of reference around which temporal figurations circulate, their presupposition; however, precisely as such, it is posited by these temporal figurations, since it does not preexist them: it emerges in the gap between the first and the second—in the case of *Billy Bathgate*, between the novel and its repetition in the film. Or, back to "Humoresque": the eternal absolute is the third un-played melodic line, the point of reference of the two lines played in reality. It is absolute, but fragile—if the two positive lines are played wrongly, it disappears . . . This is what one is tempted to call "materialist theology": the notion that temporal succession itself creates eternity.

The vacuity of the politics of jouissance

The short-circuit between Stavrakakis's ontology and politics is not difficult to guess: the acceptance of the constitutive hole in the Symbolic, the "lack in the Other," provides the space for theorizing democracy as the institutionalization of contingency. This brings us to the political wager of Stavrakakis's book:

> [to] combine an ethical attitude that reinvigorates modern democracy with a real passion for transformation, capable of stimulating the body politic without reoccupying the obsolete utopianism of the traditional Left.[80]

Such a combination has to enact a "delicate balancing act,"[81] avoiding both extremes of passionless egalitarian democracy *à la* Habermas and of passionate totalitarian engagement. The balance is between lack and excess: lack is articulated in discourse theory, while excess points towards enjoyment as a political factor. For example, in recent debates about European identity, "the neglect of the affective side of identification leads to a displacement of cathectic energy which is now invested in anti-European political and ideological discourses."[82]

Modern society is defined by the lack of an ultimate transcendental guarantee, or, in libidinal terms, of total *jouissance*. There are three main ways to cope with this negativity: utopian, democratic, and post-democratic. The first (totalitarianism, fundamentalism) tries to reoccupy the ground of absolute *jouissance* by attaining a utopian and harmonious society which eliminates negativity. The second, the democratic, enacts a political equivalent of "traversing the fantasy": it institutionalizes the lack itself by creating the space for political antagonisms. The third, consumerist post-democracy, tries to neutralize negativity by transforming politics into apolitical administration: individuals pursue their consumerist fantasies in the space regulated by expert social administration. Today, when democracy is gradually evolving into consumerist post-democracy, one should insist that the democratic potential is not exhausted—"democracy as an unfinished project" could have been Stavrakakis's motto here. The key to the resuscitation of this democratic potential is to remobilize enjoyment: "What is needed, in other words, is *an enjoyable democratic ethics of the political.*"[83]

It is deeply symptomatic that Stavrakakis is silent about a key shift in Laclau's writings over the last few years: in his *Populist Reason*, Laclau clearly changed his position from "radical democracy" to populism, reducing democracy to the moment of democratic demand *within* the system. This shift has clear political grounds and implications—suffice it to mention Laclau's support for Hugo Chavez. One can easily imagine a situation determined by a tension between the institutionalized democratic power bloc and the oppositional populist bloc, in which Laclau (and, let me add to avoid a misunderstanding, here I would side with him) would opt for the populist bloc—when Stavrakakis criticizes my claim that a "progressive military dictatorship" can play a positive role, he is obviously not aware of my implicit reference to Laclau.[84]

But the key question here is, of course, *what kind of* enjoyment are we talking about?

Libidinal investment and the mobilization of *jouissance* are the necessary prerequisite for any sustainable identification (from nationalism to consumerism). This also applies to the radical democratic ethics of the political. But the type of investment involved has still to be decided.[85]

Stavrakakis's solution is: neither the phallic enjoyment of power nor the utopia of the incestuous full enjoyment, but a non-phallic (non-all) partial enjoyment. Predictably, I fit into this scheme as a representative of the incestuous utopia, among the "disillusioned leftists who, unable to mourn 'proletarian revolution' and 'utopia', opt for a nostalgic return to the old—defeated and dangerous—politics of reoccupation"[86]—again, as if my Lenin book, *Revolution at the Gates*, is not precisely a book of mourning—not of melancholic attachment, but of parting with Lenin:

> Consequently, to REPEAT Lenin does NOT mean a RETURN to Lenin—*to repeat Lenin is to accept that "Lenin is dead,"* that his particular solution failed, even failed monstrously, but that there was a utopian spark in it worth saving. To repeat Lenin means that one has to distinguish between what Lenin effectively did and the field of possibilities that he opened up, the tension in Lenin between what he effectively did and another dimension, what was "in Lenin more than Lenin himself." To repeat Lenin is to repeat not what Lenin DID, but what he FAILED TO DO, his MISSED opportunities.[87]

In the last pages of his book, trying to demonstrate how "democratic subjectivity is capable of inspiring high passions,"[88] Stavrakakis refers to the other Lacanian *jouissance*, "a *jouissance* beyond accumulation, domination and fantasy, an enjoyment of the not-all or not-whole."[89] How do we achieve this *jouissance*? By way of accomplishing "the sacrifice of the fantasmatic *objet petit a*" which can only "make this other *jouissance* attainable":[90]

> The central task in psychoanalysis—and politics—is to detach the *objet petit a* from the signifier of the lack in the Other [. . .] to detach (anti-democratic and post-democratic) fantasy from the democratic institutionalization of lack, making possible the access to a partial enjoyment beyond fantasy. [. . .] Only thus shall we be able to really enjoy our partial enjoyment, without subordinating it to the cataclysmic desire of fantasy. Beyond its dialectics of disavowal, this is the concrete challenge the Lacanian Left addresses to us.[91]

The underlying idea is astonishingly simplistic: in total contradiction to Lacan, Stavrakakis reduces the *objet petit a* to its role in fantasy—the *objet a* is that excessive X which magically transforms the partial objects which occupy the place of the lack in the Other into the utopian promise of the impossible fullness of *jouissance*. What Stavrakakis proposes is thus the vision of a society in which desire functions without an *objet a*, without the destabilizing excess which transforms it into a "cataclysmic desire of fantasy"—as Stavrakakis puts it in a symptomatically tautological way, we should learn to "really enjoy our partial enjoyment."

For Lacan, on the contrary, the *objet a* is a(nother) name for the Freudian "partial object," which is why it cannot be reduced to its role in fantasy which sustains desire; it is for this reason that, as Lacan emphasizes, one should distinguish its role in desire and in the drive. Following Jacques-Alain Miller, a distinction has to be introduced here between two types of lack, the lack proper and the hole: lack is spatial, designating a void *within* a space, while the hole is more radical, it designates the point at which this spatial order itself breaks down (as in the "black hole" in physics).[92] Therein resides the difference between desire and drive: desire is grounded in its constitutive lack, while drive circulates around a hole, a gap in the order of being. In other words, the circular movement of the drive obeys the weird logic of the curved space in which the shortest distance between the two points is not a straight line, but a curve: the drive "knows" that the shortest way to attain its aim is to circulate around its goal-object. (One should bear in mind here Lacan's well-known distinction between the aim and the goal of the drive: while the goal is the object around which the drive circulates, its (true) aim is the endless continuation of this circulation as such.)

Miller also proposed a Benjaminian distinction between "constituted anxiety" and "constituent anxiety," which is crucial with regard to the shift from desire to drive: while the first designates the standard notion of the terrifying and fascinating abyss of anxiety which haunts us, its infernal circle which threatens to draw us in, the second stands for the "pure" confrontation with the *objet petit a* as constituted in its very loss.[93] Miller is right to emphasize here two features: the difference which separates constituted from constituent anxiety concerns the status of the object with regard to fantasy. In a case of constituted anxiety, the object dwells within the confines of a fantasy, whereas we get the constituent anxiety only when the subject "traverses the fantasy" and confronts the void, the gap, filled up by the fantasmatic object. However, clear and convincing as it is, this formula of Miller's misses the true paradox or, rather, the ambiguity of the *objet a*. When he defines the *objet a* as the object which overlaps with its loss, which emerges at the very moment of its loss (so that all its fantasmatic incarnations, from breasts to voice and gaze, are metonymic figurations of the void, of nothing), he remains within the horizon of *desire*—the true object-cause of desire is the void filled in by its fantasmatic incarnations. While, as Lacan emphasizes, the *objet a* is also the object of the drive, the relationship is here thoroughly different: although, in both cases, the link between object and loss is crucial, in the case of the *objet a* as the object-cause of *desire*, we have an object which is originally lost, which coincides with its own loss, which emerges as lost, while, in the case of the *objet a* as the object of the drive, the "object" *is directly the loss itself*—in the shift from desire to drive, we pass from the *lost object* to *loss itself as an object*. That is to say, the weird movement called "drive" is not driven by the "impossible" quest for the lost object; it is *a push to directly enact the "loss"—the gap, cut, distance—itself*. There is thus a *double* distinction to be drawn here: not only between the *objet a* in its fantasmatic and post-fantasmatic status, but also, within this post-fantasmatic domain itself, between the lost object-cause of desire and the object-loss of drive.[94]

The startling thing is that Stavrakakis's idea of sustaining desire without the *objet a* contradicts not only Lacan, but also Laclau's notion of hegemony: Laclau is on the right track when he emphasizes the necessary role of the *objet a* in rendering an ideological edifice operative. In hegemony, a particular empirical object is "elevated to the dignity of the Thing"; it starts to function as the stand-in for, the embodiment of, the impossible fullness of Society. As we have noted, he refers to Joan Copjec, comparing hegemony to the "breast-value" attached to partial objects which stand in for the incestuous maternal Thing (breast). Laclau should in fact be criticized here for confounding desire (sustained by fantasy) with drive (one of whose definitions is also "that which remains of desire after its subject traverses the fantasy"): for him, we are condemned to searching for impossible fullness. Drive—in which we directly enjoy lack itself—simply does not appear on his horizon. However, this in no way entails that, in drive, we "really enjoy our partial enjoyment," without the disturbing excess: for Lacan, lack and excess are strictly correlative, the two sides of the same coin. Precisely insofar as it circulates around a hole, the drive is the name of the excess that pertains to human being, it is the "too-much-ness" of striving which insists beyond life and death (this is why Lacan sometimes even directly identifies the drive with the *objet a* as surplus-enjoyment.)

Because he ignores this excess of drive, Stavrakakis also operates with a simplified notion of "traversing the fantasy"—as if fantasy is a kind of illusory screen blurring our relation to partial objects. This notion fits perfectly with the common-sense idea of what psychoanalysis should do: of course it should liberate us from the hold of idiosyncratic fantasies and enable us to confront reality the way it effectively is . . . but this, precisely, is what Lacan does *not* have in mind—what he aims at is almost the exact opposite. In our daily existence, we are immersed in "reality" (structured–supported by the fantasy), and this immersion is disturbed by symptoms which bear witness to the fact that another repressed level of our psyche resists this immersion. To "traverse the fantasy" therefore paradoxically means *fully identifying oneself with the fantasy*—namely with the fantasy which structures the excess resisting our immersion into daily reality, or, to quote a succinct formulation by Richard Boothby:

> "Traversing the fantasy" thus does not mean that the subject somehow abandons its involvement with fanciful caprices and accommodates itself to a pragmatic "reality," but precisely the opposite: the subject is submitted to that effect of the symbolic lack that reveals the limit of everyday reality. To traverse the fantasy in the Lacanian sense is to be more profoundly claimed by the fantasy than ever, in the sense of being brought into an ever more intimate relation with that real core of the fantasy that transcends imaging.[95]

Boothby is right to emphasize the Janus-like structure of a fantasy: a fantasy is simultaneously pacifying, disarming (providing an imaginary scenario which enables us to endure the abyss of the Other's desire) *and* shattering, disturbing, inassimilable into our reality. The ideologico-political dimension of this notion of "traversing the fantasy" was rendered clear by the unique role the rock group *Top Lista Nadrealista* (*The Top List of the Surrealists*) played during the Bosnian war in besieged Sarajevo: their ironic performances which, in the midst of the war and hunger, satirized the predicament of the Sarajevo population, acquired a cult status not only in counterculture, but also among the citizens of Sarajevo in general (the group's weekly TV show went on throughout the war and was extremely popular). Instead of bemoaning the tragic fate of the

Bosnians, they daringly mobilized all the clichés about the "stupid Bosnians" which were a commonplace in Yugoslavia, fully identifying with them—the point thus made was that the path of true solidarity leads through direct confrontation with the obscene racist fantasies which circulated in the symbolic space of Bosnia, through playful identification with them, not through the denial of these obscenities in the name of "what people are really like."

No wonder, then, that, when Stavrakakis tries to provide some concrete examples of this new politics of partial enjoyment, things become really "bizarre." He starts with Marshall Sahlins's thesis that the Paleolithic communities followed "a Zen road to affluence": although deeply marked by divisions, exchange, sexual difference, violence and war, they lack the "shrine of the Unattainable," of "infinite Needs," and thus the "desire for accumulation". In them,

> enjoyment seems to be had without the mediation of fantasies of accumulation, fullness and excess. [. . .] [T]hey do show that another world may, in principle, be possible insofar as a detachment of (partial) enjoyment from dreams of completeness and fantasmatic desire is enacted. [. . .] Doesn't something similar happen in the psychoanalytic clinic? And isn't this also the challenge for radical democratic ethics?[96]

Again, is the idea here not precisely that of a society without lack? The way the Paleolithic tribesmen avoided accumulation was to cancel lack itself—it is the idea of such a society without the excess of "infinite Needs" which is properly utopian, the ultimate fantasy, the fantasy of a society before the Fall.[97] What then follows is a series of examples of how "political theorists and analysts, economists, and active citizens—some of them directly inspired by Lacanian theory—are currently trying to put this radical democratic orientation to work in a multitude of empirical contexts."[98] For example: "A group of cooperative workers [Byrne and Healy] have examined and tried to restructure their enjoyment in a non-fantasmatic way"[99]—it would be certainly interesting to hear in detail how this "restructuring" was carried out! Then comes Robin Blackburn's proposal for the democratization of pension funds, Roberto Unger's proposal to pass from a family to a social inheritance system, Toni Negri's proposal for a minimum citizenship income, the projects of participatory budgets in Brazil . . .[100]—what all this has to do with *jouissance féminine* remains a mystery. The vague underlying idea is that, in all these cases, we are dealing with modest pragmatic proposals, with partial solutions which avoid the excess of radical utopian re-foundation—definitely not enough to qualify them as cases of *jouissance féminine* which is precisely Lacan's name for absolute excess.

Stavrakakis's attempt to relate Lacanian concepts like feminine *jouissance*, the signifier of the lack in the Other, and so on, to concrete socio-political examples is thus thoroughly unconvincing. When he quotes Joan Copjec's precise thesis on how *suppléance* "allows us to speak well of our desire not by translating *jouissance* into language, but by formalizing it in a signifier that does not mean it but is, rather, directly enjoyed,"[101] he reads it as a "way to think of enjoyment and the production of a signifier of lack in a democratic perspective"[102]—but does Copjec's description not also perfectly fit nationalism? Is the name of the nation not such a *suppléance*? When a passionate patriot exclaims "America!" does he thereby not produce a signifier which "does not translate *jouissance* into language, but formalizes it in a signifier that does not mean it but is, rather, directly enjoyed"?

Stavrakakis's political vision is vacuous. It is not that his call for more passion in politics is in itself meaningless (of course the contemporary Left needs more passion); the problem is rather that it resembles all too much the joke quoted by Lacan about a doctor asked by a friend for free medical advice—unwilling to give his services without payment, the doctor examines the friend and then calmly states: "You need medical advice!" Paradoxically, for all his (justified) critique of Freudo-Marxism, Stavrakakis's position can be designated as "Freudo-radical democracy": he remains within Freudo-Marxism, expecting psychoanalysis to supplement the theory of radical democracy in the same way Wilhelm Reich, amongst others, expected psychoanalysis to supplement Marxism. In both cases, the problem is exactly the same: we have the appropriate social theory, but what is missing is the "subjective factor"—how are we to mobilize people so that they will engage in passionate political struggle? Here psychoanalysis enters, explaining what libidinal mechanisms the enemy is using (Reich tried to do this for fascism, Stavrakakis for consumerism and nationalism), and how the Left can practice its own "politics of *jouissance*." The problem is that such an approach is an ersatz political analysis: the lack of passion in political praxis and theory should be explained in its own terms, that is, in the terms of political analysis itself. The true question is: What is there to be passionate about? Which political choices fit people's experience as "realistic" and feasible?

The moment we pose the question in this way, the contours of our ideological constellation appear in a different manner, underlining W. B. Yeats's famous lines "The best lack all conviction, while the worst are full of passionate intensity." These lines seem to offer a perfect description of the current split between anemic liberals and impassioned fundamentalists ("the best" are no longer able fully to engage, while "the worst" engage in racist, religious, sexist fanaticism). Are, however, the terrorist fundamentalists, be they Christian or Muslim, really fundamentalists in the authentic sense of the term? Do they really believe? What they lack is a feature that is easy to discern in all authentic fundamentalists, from Tibetan Buddhists to the Amish in the US: the absence of resentment and envy, deep indifference towards the non-believer's way of life. If today's so-called fundamentalists really believe that they have found their way to Truth, why should they feel threatened by non-believers, why should they envy them? When a Buddhist encounters a Western hedonist, he hardly condemns the latter. He just benevolently notes that the hedonist's search for happiness is self-defeating. In contrast to true fundamentalists, terrorist pseudo-fundamentalists are deeply bothered, intrigued, fascinated, by the sinful life of non-believers. One senses that, in fighting the sinful other, they are fighting their own temptation. This is why the so-called Christian or Muslim fundamentalists are a disgrace to true fundamentalism.

It is here that Yeats's diagnosis falls short of the present predicament: the passionate intensity of a mob bears witness to a lack of true conviction. Deep inside themselves, terrorist fundamentalists also lack true conviction—their violent outbursts are proof. How fragile the belief of a Muslim must be, if he feels threatened by a stupid caricature in a low-circulation Danish newspaper? Fundamentalist Islamicist terror is *not* grounded in the terrorists' conviction of their superiority and in their desire to safeguard their cultural-religious identity from the onslaught of global consumerist civilization. The problem with fundamentalists is not that we consider them inferior to us, but, rather, that *they themselves* secretly consider themselves inferior. This is why our condescending politically correct assurances that we feel no superiority towards them only makes them more furious and feeds their resentment. The problem is not cultural difference (their effort to preserve their identity), but the opposite fact that the fundamentalists are already like us, that, secretly, they have already internalized our standards and measure themselves by them. (This clearly goes for the Dalai Lama who justifies Tibetan

Buddhism in the Western terms of the pursuit of happiness and the avoidance of pain.) Paradoxically, what fundamentalists really lack is precisely a dose of that true "racist" conviction of one's own superiority.

It would be instructive to refer here to Rousseau, who described the inversion of the libidinal investment from the object to the obstacle which prevents our access to the object. This is why egalitarianism itself should never be accepted at face value: the notion (and practice) of egalitarian justice, insofar as it is sustained by envy, relies on the inversion of the standard renunciation accomplished to benefit others: "I am ready to renounce it, *so that others will (also)* not (*be able to*) *have it!*" Far from being opposed to the spirit of sacrifice, Evil is thus the very spirit of sacrifice itself, ready to ignore one's own wellbeing—if, through my sacrifice, I can deprive the Other of his *jouissance* . . .[103] And do we not encounter the same negative passion also in politically correct multicultural liberalism? Is its inquisitorial pursuit of the traces of racism and sexism in the details of personal behavior not in itself indicative of the passion of resentment? Fundamentalism's passion is a false one, while anemic liberal tolerance relies on a disavowed perverse passion. The distinction between fundamentalism and liberalism is sustained by a shared underlying feature: they are both permeated by the negative passion of resentment.

III

WHAT IS TO BE DONE?

7   The Crisis of Determinate Negation

Back in the 1950s and 1960s, when the Frankfurt School adopted an increasingly critical attitude towards the classical Marxist notion of the historical necessity of revolution, this critique also culminated in their abandonment of the Hegelian notion of "determinate negation," the obverse of which is the rise of the notion of the "wholly Other" (*das ganz Andere*) as the prospect of the utopian overcoming of the global techno-capitalist order. The idea is that, with the "dialectic of Enlightenment" which tends towards the zero-point of the totally "administered" society, one can no longer conceptualize breaking out of the deadly spiral of this dialectic by means of the classical Marxist notion according to which the New will emerge from the very contradictions of the present society, through its immanent self-overcoming: the impetus for such an overcoming can only come from an unmediated Outside.[1]

This abandonment of "determinate negation" is, of course, the obverse of accepting capitalism's triumph. As we have already noted, the most reliable sign of capitalism's ideological triumph was the virtual disappearance of the very term over the last two or three decades.[2]

The contemporary Left has reacted in a wide spectrum of modes (which partially overlap) to the full hegemony of global capitalism and its political supplement, liberal democracy:

1. full acceptance of this framework: continuing to fight for emancipation *within* its rules (Third Way social democracy);
2. acceptance of this framework as something that is here to stay, but which one should nonetheless resist, withdrawing from its scope and operating from its "interstices" (Simon Critchley is an exemplar of this position);
3. acceptance of the futility of all struggle, since the framework is today all-encompassing, coinciding with its opposite (the logic of concentration camps, the permanent state of emergency), so noth-

ing can really be done, one can only wait for an outburst of "divine violence"—a revolutionary version of Heidegger's "only God can still save us" (a perspective embodied today by Giorgio Agamben and in a way, before him, by the late Adorno);

4. acceptance of the temporary futility of struggle ("in today's triumph of global capitalism, true resistance is not possible, at least not in the metropolis of capitalism, so all we can do till the renewal of the revolutionary spirit in the global working class is to defend what there still is of the welfare state, bombarding those in power with demands we know they cannot fulfill, and otherwise withdraw into cultural studies, where one can silently pursue critical work");

5. emphasis on the fact that the problem is a more fundamental one, that global capitalism is ultimately an ontic effect of the underlying ontological principle of technology or "instrumental reason" (Heidegger, but, in a way, again also Adorno);

6. belief that one can undermine global capitalism and state power, however, not by way of directly attacking them, but by refocusing the field of struggle on everyday practices, where one can "build a new world"—in this way, the foundations of the power of capital and the state will be gradually undermined, and, at some point, the state will collapse like a cat hovering over the precipice in the cartoons (one thinks here of the Zapatista movement);

7. a "postmodern" shift of the accent from anti-capitalist struggle to the multiple forms of the politico-ideological struggle for hegemony, conceptualized as a contingent process of discursive rearticulation (Ernesto Laclau);

8. a wager that one can repeat at the postmodern level the classical Marxist gesture and enact the "determinate negation" of capitalism: with today's rise of "cognitive work," the contradiction between social production and capitalist relations has reached an unprecedented height, rendering "absolute democracy" possible for the first time (Hardt and Negri).

One is tempted to categorize these versions as so many modes of the negations of politics proper, which follow the different modes of avoiding a traumatic Real in psychoanalysis: acceptance-through-denial (*Verneinung*: a version of "whoever that woman in my dream is, it is not my mother"—"whatever the new antagonisms are, they are not class struggle"), psychotic foreclosure (*Verwerfung*: the foreclosed class struggle returns in the real, in the paranoid guise of an invisible and all-powerful Enemy, like the "Jewish plot"), neurotic repression (*Verdrängung*: the repressed class struggle returns in the guise of a multiplicity of "new antagonisms"), and fetishistic disavowal (*Verleugnung*: the elevation into the principal Cause of some fetishistic ersatz of the class struggle as "the last thing which we see" prior to confronting the class antagonism).

We are not dealing here with a series of avoidances of some "true" radical leftist position—the trauma these avoidances try to blur is rather the lack of such a position. The lesson of the last decades, if there is one, is the indestructibility of capitalism—when (already) Marx compared it to a vampire, we should bear in mind the living-dead aspect of vampires: they always rise up again and again after being stabbed to death. Even the radical Maoist attempt in the Cultural Revolution to wipe out the traces of capitalism ended up with its triumphant return.

The humorous superego . . .

A fear is haunting (whatever remains of) the contemporary Left: the fear of directly confronting state power. Those who still insist on fighting state power, let alone directly taking it over, are immediately accused of being stuck in the "old paradigm": the task today is to resist state power by withdrawing from its scope, subtracting oneself from it, creating new spaces outside its control. This dogma of the contemporary academic Left is best encapsulated by the title of Negri's interview-book: *Goodbye Mister Socialism*. The idea is that the time of the old Left in its two versions, reformist and revolutionary, which both aimed at taking over state power and protecting the working class's corporate rights, is over. Today, the predominant form of exploitation is the exploitation of knowledge, and so on and so forth—there is a new "postmodern" social development going on which the old Left refuses to take into account, and, in order to renovate itself, the Left has to . . . read Deleuze and Negri and start to practice nomadic resistance, follow the theory of hegemony, and so on. But what if this very mode of defining the problem is part of the problem? Since the institutionalized Left (the Third Way social democrats, the trade unions, and others) so persistently refuses to learn this lesson, the problem must (also) reside with its "postmodern" critics.

Within this "postmodern" field, Simon Critchley's *Infinitely Demanding* is an almost perfect embodiment of the position to which my work is absolutely opposed,[3] and that at two distinct, but interconnected, levels:

that of the account of subjectivity as arising out of ethical commitment to a Good, and that of the proposed politics of resistance. When he includes himself among the "critical, secular, well-dressed metro-sexual post-Kantians,"[4] the irony of this self-characterization occludes its seriousness—no wonder Critchley included in the list of those who "resist" the clutches of state power Princess Diana herself.[5]

Critchley's starting point is the "motivational deficit" of our liberal-democratic institutions. This deficit sustains two main political attitudes, those of "passive" and "active" nihilism: on the one hand, cynical indifference, escape into consumerist hedonism, and so on, and, on the other hand, violent fundamentalism which aims at destroying the corrupt liberal universe. Critchley's problem is how to break out of this deadlock, how to resuscitate emancipatory political passion. This problem is a real one—in our allegedly "post-ideological" era, after the self-proclaimed end of great emancipatory projects, the gap between meaning and truth seems insurmountable: who still dares to claim access to a "cognitive mapping" of our constellation that would simultaneously open up space for a meaningful radical social transformation? Consequently, today, the very idea of a "politics of truth" is dismissed as totalitarian—above and beyond efficient social administration, the main acceptable political goals are negative: to prevent pain and suffering, to establish the minimal conditions for the toleration of different ways of life . . . To each their own truth, and the task of politics is seen as the art of pragmatic compromise, of the coordination of interests, of guaranteeing the peaceful coexistence of ways of life—as if economic uniformity and cultural diversity were the two sides of the same process. However, this liberal-democratic prospect remains haunted by the specter of "fundamentalism." Recall the public reaction to the pope's death. Who would like to live in a state which prohibits abortion and divorce? And yet *the same* people who reject the pope's views admire him for his firm, principled, ethical stance and his message of hope, thereby displaying the need for a firm standard of Truth beyond pragmatic relativism.

How, then, to break out of this deadlock? Critchley proceeds in two steps. First, in a combination of Levinas, Badiou, and Lacan, he deploys the notion of the subject as constituted by its recognition in an unconditional ethical Call engendered by the experience of injustice and wrongs. Then he proposes a notion of politics as resistance to state power on behalf of this ethical Call.

The subject emerges as a reaction to the traumatic encounter of the helpless suffering Other (Neighbor), which is why it is constitutively decentered, not autonomous, but split by the ethical Call, "a subject defined by the experience of an internalized demand that it can never meet, a demand that exceeds it";[6] the paradox constitutive of the subject is thus the demand that the subject cannot meet, so that the subject is constitutively divided, its autonomy "always usurped by the heteronomous experience of the other's demand."[7] Only an omnipotent and infinite God would have been able to meet such a demand; so, "knowing that there is no God, we have to subject ourselves to the demand to be God-like, knowing that we are sure to fail because of our finite condition."[8] Critchley refers here to Levinas's claim that

> my relation to the other is not some benign benevolence, compassionate care or respect for the other's autonomy, but is the obsessive experience of a responsibility that persecutes me with its sheer weight. I am the other's hostage.[9]

How, then, can the subject attenuate the crushing weight of the superego? "How can I respond in infinite responsibility to the other without extinguishing myself as a subject?"[10] Critchley turns here to Lacan, to the way Lacan elaborated Freud's notion of sublimation: aesthetic sublimation enables the subject to achieve a minimum of happiness.[11] The Beautiful interposes itself between the subject and the Good, it "places the subject in relation to the source of the ethical demand, but which protects the subject from the direct glare of the Thing."[12]

Critchley adds humor to the list of sublimations as the benevolent aspect of the superego: in contrast to the evil, punishing superego, the severe judge which crushes us with the weight of infinite guilt on account of our failure to live up to its Call, in humor—in which we also observe our finitude and ridiculous failure from the standpoint of the superego— our finitude appears as funny, ridiculous in its failures. Instead of installing anguish and despair, this superego enables us to laugh at our limitations, failures, and false pretensions. What Critchley strangely leaves out of consideration is *the brutal "sadistic" aspect of humor itself*: humor can be extremely cruel and denigrating. Let us take an extreme example: the infamous "Arbeit macht frei!" over the gates of Auschwitz is no argument against the dignity of work. Work truly makes us free, as Hegel put it in the famous passage of his *Phenomenology of Spirit* on Master and Servant; what the Nazis did with the motto at the gates of Auschwitz is simply an act of cruel mockery analogous to raping someone while wearing a T-shirt saying "Sex brings pleasure!"

Critchley's claim that "[s]ome versions of psychoanalysis, particularly Lacan's, have a problem with the superego"[13] is thus odd: Lacan was fully aware not only of the link between humor and the superego, but also of the brutal-sadistic aspect of humor. The Marx Brothers' *Duck Soup*, their masterpiece, is regarded as a work that makes fun of ridiculous totalitarian state rituals, denouncing their empty posturing, and so on: laughter is the mightiest weapon, no wonder that totalitarian regimes found it so threatening . . . This commonplace should be turned upside down: the powerful effect of *Duck Soup* does not reside in its mockery of the totalitarian state's machinery and paraphernalia, but in openly displaying the madness, the "fun," the cruel irony, which are *already present* in the totalitarian state. The Marx brothers' "carnival" is the carnival of totalitarianism itself.

What is the superego? Recall the strange fact, regularly evoked by Primo Levi and other Holocaust survivors, regarding how their intimate reaction to their survival was marked by a deep split: consciously, they were fully aware that their survival was just a meaningless accident, that they were not in any way responsible for it, that the only guilty perpetrators were their Nazi torturers; at the same time, they were (more than mildly) haunted by the "irrational" feeling of guilt, as if they had survived at the expense of others who had died and were thus somehow responsible for their deaths—as is well-known, this unbearable feeling of guilt drove many of the survivors to suicide. This feeling of guilt displays the agency of the superego at its purest: the obscene agency which manipulates us into a spiraling movement of self-destruction. What this means is that the function of the superego is precisely to obfuscate the cause of the terror constitutive of our being human, the inhuman core of being human, the dimension of what the German Idealists called negativity and what Freud called the death drive. Far from being the traumatic hard core of the Real from which sublimations protect us, the superego is itself the mask screening the Real.

The humorous superego is the cruel and insatiable agency which bombards me with impossible demands and which mocks my failed attempts to meet them, the agency in the eyes of which I am all the more guilty, the more I try to suppress my "sinful" strivings and meet its demands. As I have noted, the cynical Stalinist motto about the accused at the show trials who professed their innocence ("the more they are innocent, the more they deserve to be shot") is the superego at its purest. Consequently, for Lacan, the superego "has nothing to do with moral conscience as far as its most obligatory demands are concerned:"[14] the superego is, on the contrary, the anti-ethical agency, the stigmatization of our ethical betrayal. As such, the superego is, at its most elementary, not a prohibitive, but a productive agency: "Nothing forces anyone to enjoy except the superego. The superego is the imperative of *jouissance*—Enjoy!"[15] Although *jouissance* can be translated as "enjoyment," translators of Lacan often leave it in French in order to render palpable its excessive, properly traumatic character: we are not dealing with simple pleasures, but with a violent intrusion that brings more pain than pleasure. No wonder, then, that Lacan posited an equation between *jouissance* and the superego: to enjoy is not a matter of following one's spontaneous tendencies; it is rather something we do as a kind of weird and twisted ethical duty.

When, following Badiou, Critchley defines the subject as something that emerges through fidelity to the Good ("A subject is the name for the way in which a self binds itself to some conception of the good and shapes its subjectivity in relation to that good"),[16] from a strict Lacanian perspective, he is confusing subject and subjectivization. Lacan is here to be opposed to the discourse-theory *doxa* about the subject as an effect of the process of subjectivization: for Lacan, the subject *precedes* subjectivization, subjectivization (the constitution of the subject's "inner life" of experience) is a defense against the subject. As such, the subject is a (pre)condition of the process of subjectivization, in the same sense in which, back in the 1960s, Herbert Marcuse claimed that freedom is the condition of liberation. Insofar as, in a way, the subject, in its content, "is" nothing positively but the result of the process of subjectivization, one can also say that the subject *precedes itself*—in order to become subject, it already has to be subject, so that, in its process of becoming, it becomes what it already is. (And, incidentally, this feature distinguishes the properly Hegelian dialectical process from pseudo-Hegelian "dialectical evolution.") The obvious counter-argument to this is that we are dealing here with the archetypal case of ideological illusion: there is no subject prior to the process of subjectivization, its preexistence is precisely the inversion that bears witness to the success of the ideological constitution of the subject; once constituted, the subject necessarily experiences itself as the cause of the very process that constitutes it, that is, it perceives this process as its "expression." This, precisely, is the reasoning one should reject—but why exactly?

Let us return for a brief moment to Althusser. In Althusserian terms, the subject is constituted through its assumption of an ideological Call, through recognizing itself in ideological interpellation—this recognition subjectivizes the pre-ideological individual. Of course, as is clear to Critchley, this interpellation, the assumption of the call of the Good, ultimately always fails, the subject cannot ever act at the level of this call, its endeavors always fall short. It is here that, from the Lacanian perspective, one should supplement the Althusserian account: the subject in a way *is* the failure of subjectivization, the failure of assuming the symbolic mandate, of fully identifying with the ethical Call. To paraphrase Althusser's celebrated formula: an individual is interpellated into subjecthood, this interpellation fails, and *the "subject" is this failure*. This is why the subject is irreducibly divided: divided between its task and the failure to remain faithful to it. It is in this sense that, for Lacan, the subject is *as such* hysterical: hysteria is, at its most elementary, the failure of interpellation, the gnawing worm questioning the identity imposed on the subject by interpellation—"Why am I that name?", why am I what the big Other claims I am?

When Critchley emphasizes how the subject always fails with regard to the Call of the ethical Thing, he seems to fully endorse this dimension, this failure as constitutive of subjectivity. There is, however, a crucial accent to be added here: it is totally wrong to directly identify this failure of interpellation—the fact that the subject never rises to the level of its responsibility towards the Call of the Good—with the subject. What accounts for this failure is not simply the limitation of the subject's finitude, its inadequacy to the "infinitely demanding" task; that is, we are not dealing with the simple gap between the subject's infinite ethical task and its finite reality which makes it forever inadequate to this task. The "subject before subjectivization" is a positive force in itself, the infinite force of negativity called by Freud the "death drive." Which is why, from the Lacanian perspective, it is problematic to claim that we humans "seem to have enormous difficulty in accepting our limitedness, our finiteness, and this failure is a cause of much tragedy":[17] on the contrary, we humans have enormous difficulty in accepting the "infinity" (undeadness, excess of life) in the very core of our being, the strange "immortality" whose Freudian name is the death drive.

The ethical Call does not intervene directly upon the human animal, disturbing its balance with its "infinitely demanding" injunction; the ethical Call, on the contrary, already presupposes that the balance of animal reproduction is thrown off the rails, becomes out of joint, through the transformation of the animal instinct into the death drive. Consequently, ethics is, for Lacan, not directly the zero-level of the encounter with the Real Thing; it is, rather, already a screen which protects us from the destructive impact of the Real. It is here that Critchley falsifies in a strange way Lacan's notions of the Good and the Beautiful from *The Ethics of Psychoanalysis* in that he posits the Beautiful as the screen that protects us from the direct exposure to the Real Thing, whereas for Lacan, the Good occupies precisely the same structural place, that is, it is not the Real Thing itself, but a screen protecting us from its blinding impact.

For Critchley, the traumatic intrusion of the radically heterogeneous Real Thing which decenters the subject is *identical with* the ethical Call of the Good, while, for Lacan, the radically heterogeneous Thing whose traumatic impact decenters the subject is, on the contrary, the primordial "evil Thing," something that cannot ever be sublated (*aufgehoben*) into a version of the Good, something which forever remains a disturbing cut. This is where Critchley's reference to Sade falls short: he claims that the Sadean project still fits the coordinates of the commitment to the Good— Sade simply puts what we perceive as to its content as "evil" at the place of the Good; in other words, for Sade, the unbridled use of others as a means of sexual enjoyment is his Good to which he is totally committed (or, to quote Satan from Milton's *Paradise Lost*: "Evil, be thou my Good!"). One should rather invert this notion that "evil" is a content whose very form (the unconditional ethical commitment) remains that of the Good: the difference between Good and Evil is not that of content, but that of form—but, again, not in the sense that Good is the form of unconditional commitment to a Cause, and Evil the betrayal of this commitment. It is, on the contrary, the very unconditional "fanatical" commitment to a Cause which is the "death drive" at its purest and, as such, the primordial form of Evil: it introduces into the flow of (social) life a violent cut that throws it out of joint. The Good comes afterwards, it is an attempt to "gentrify," to domesticate, the traumatic impact of the Evil Thing. In short, the Good is the screened/domesticated Evil. (Was Kant himself not on the tracks of this paradox in the deadlock of his notion(s) of radical and diabolical Evil?)

Rousseau had already noted that egoism or the concern for one's own wellbeing is *not* opposed to the common good, since altruistic norms can easily be deduced from egotistic concerns. Individualism versus communitarianism, utilitarianism versus the assertion of universal norms, are *false* oppositions, since the two opposed options amount to the same in their result—the critics who complain how, in today's hedonistic-egotistic society, true values are lacking totally miss the point. The true opposite of egotistic self-love is not altruism, a concern for the common Good, but envy, *ressentiment*, which makes me act *against* my own interests. The conservative or communitarian critics complain that the "ethics" one can generate from utilitarian individualist premises can only be a "pact between wolves" who conclude it is in the best interest of each of them to constrain their aggressivity, rather than genuine solidarity and altruism. But they miss the ironic point: what utilitarian ethics cannot properly account for is not the true Good, but Evil itself, which is ultimately against my long-term interests.

. . . *and its politics of resistance*

Which form of political practice best fits this notion of subjectivity? Since, on the one hand, the liberal-democratic state is here to stay, that is, since the attempts to abolish the state failed miserably, and, since, on the other hand, the motivational deficit with regard to the institutions of liberal democracy is irreducible, the new politics has to be located at a distance from the state, a politics of resistance to the state, of bombarding the state with impossible demands, of denouncing the limitations of state mechanisms. The main argument for the extra-statal status of the politics of resistance is its link to the meta-political ethical dimension of the "infinitely demanding" call for justice: every state politics has to betray this infinity, since its ultimate goal is the "real-political" one of securing the state's reproduction (its economic growth, public safety, and so on). This is Antigone versus Creon: Creon stands for the *raison d'état*, his concern is a totally respectable one, that of preventing another round of civil war which may destroy the city; as such, he has to oppose Antigone whose unconditional ethical demand ignores the mortal threat its fulfillment poses to the city.[18]

Critchley refers positively to the young Marx's critique of Hegel, where Marx opposes the "true democracy" of the social link of free people to the state as the imposed unity;[19] however, in contrast to Marx, whose aim is to abolish the state for this reason, for Critchley, true democracy is only possible "as the interstitial distance within the state"— such a true democracy calls the state into question and calls the established order to account, not in order to do away with the state, desirable though that might well be in some utopian sense, but in order to better it or attenuate its malicious effect.[20]

Such politics is negative in the sense that

it should not seek to set itself up as the new hegemonic principle of political organization, but remains the negation of totality and not the affirmation of a new totality. Anarchy is a radical disturbance of the state, a disruption of the state's attempt to set itself up or erect itself into a whole.[21]

Thus, democracy is not a fixed political form of society, but rather [. . .] the *deformation* of society from itself through the act of material political manifestation.[22]

If, then, politics (as the aesthetic-carnivalesque manifestation of the anarchic *demos*) and democracy are "two names for the same thing,"[23] what does this mean for democracy as the state form? When Critchley writes that the motivational deficit with regard to the institutions of liberal democracy (the growing indifference towards elections, and so on) "has also had positive effects,"[24] giving rise to a series of non-electoral political activities, of NGOs, of social movements such as the anti-globalization movement, the indigenous-rights movements in Mexico and Australia, and so forth, his position becomes ambiguous: is it actually *better* for emancipatory politics if people are not committed to the democratic institutions? So what then should, say, the Democrats do in the US? Should they withdraw ("subtract" themselves) from competing for the state power into the interstices of state, leaving state power to Republicans and engage in anarchistic resistance to it?

Of course, history is habitually written by the people with the guns and sticks and one cannot expect to defeat them with mocking satire and feather dusters. Yet, as the history of ultra-leftist active nihilism eloquently shows, one is lost the moment one picks up the guns and sticks. Anarchic political resistance should not seek to mimic and mirror the archic violent sovereignty it opposes.[25]

But Critchley would certainly support "picking up the guns and sticks" when one faces an adversary like Hitler, would he not? Surely in this case one should "mimic and mirror the archic violent sovereignty one opposes"? So what should the Left do—distinguish the cases when one joins forces with the state in resorting to violence from the cases when all one can and should do is use "mocking satire and feather dusters"?

When Critchley writes that "one should approach al-Qaeda with the words and actions of bin Laden resonating against those of Lenin, Blanqui, Mao,"[26] and makes the same point at the book's conclusion with the claim that "neo-Leninism [. . .] is practically expressed in the vanguardism of groups like al-Qaeda,"[27] he engages in the purest ideological formalism, blurring the crucial difference between two opposed political logics: radical egalitarian violence (what Badiou calls the "eternal Idea" of the politics of revolutionary justice at work from the ancient Chinese "legists" through Jacobins to Lenin and Mao), and anti-modernist "fundamentalist" violence—a new version of the old liberal-conservative identification of right and left "totalitarianism."

Furthermore, according to Critchley, not only is the state here to stay—the same holds for capitalism itself:

> Capitalist dislocation, in its ruthless destruction of the bonds of tradition, local belonging, family and kinship structures that one might have considered natural, reveals the contingency of social life, that is, its structured character, which is to say, its *political* articulation. [. . .] Once the ideological illusions of the natural have been stripped away and revealed as contingent formations by capitalist dislocation, where freedom, for example, becomes the precarious experience of insecurity when one sells oneself on the labor market, then the only cement that holds political identities together is a hegemonic link.[28]

The (unintended) implication of this reasoning is that the very "anti-essentialist" experience of social life as contingent, with every identity the result of discursive articulation, the outcome of an open struggle for hegemony, is grounded in the "essentialist" predominance of capitalism, which, itself, no longer appears as one of possible modes of production, but as simply the neutral "background" of the open process of contingent (re)articulations.

According to this view, capitalism means permanent multiple dislocations, and this dislocation opens up the space for the formation of new political subjectivities; however, it is no longer possible to contain these subjectivities under the heading of the "proletariat." Multiple dislocations clear the space for multiple subjectivities (threatened indigenous populations, sexual and ethnic minorities, slum-dwellers, and so on), and what we should aim at is the "chain of equivalences" between these series of demands–grievances. As an exemplary case of creating a new political subjectivity through an act of naming, Critchley celebrates the impoverished Mexican peasants' reinvention as "indigenous" people. Is it not, however, that his example demonstrates its own limitations? As his own analysis makes clear, the poor peasants had to reinvent/rename themselves as the "indigenous" people, because the successful neoliberal ideological offensive had made a direct reference to the economic position of being exploited untenable, ineffective: in our "post-political" epoch of the culturalization of the political, the only way to formulate one's complaint is at the level of cultural and/or ethnic demands: exploited workers become immigrants whose "otherness" is oppressed, and so forth. The price we pay for this operation is at least a minimal level of ideological mystification: what the poor peasants are defending appears as their "natural" (ethnic) substantial identity.

The contemporary liberal-democratic state and the "infinitely demanding" anarchistic politics are thus engaged in a relationship of mutual parasitism: the state externalizes its ethical self-consciousness in an extra-statal ethico-political agency, and this agency externalizes its claim to effectiveness in the state — anarchic agents do the ethical thinking for the state, and the state does the work of really running and regulating society.

The way Critchley's anarchic ethico-political agent relates to the superego is double: not only is it crushed by the superego, it also acts itself like a superego agent, comfortably bombarding the state with superego demands — and the state is all the more guilty, the more it tries to comply with its demands. (In compliance with this superego logic, the anarchic extra-statal agents focus their protests not on open dictatorships, but on the hypocrisy of liberal democracies, which are accused of not following consistently their own ideological norms.) What Critchley offers is thus liberal-capitalist-democracy with a human face — we remain firmly within the Fukuyama universe. Or, to paraphrase Thomas De Quincey's "Simple Art of Murder": look how many people started with a wrong reading of Lacan and ended up celebrating Princess Diana as a figure of insurgency . . .

The lesson here is that the truly subversive thing is not to insist on

349

"infinite" demands we know those in power cannot fulfill (since they also know it that we know it, such an "infinitely demanding" attitude is easily acceptable for those in power: "so wonderful that, with your critical demands, you remind us what kind of world we would all like to live in — unfortunately, however, we live in the real world, where we are just honestly doing what is possible"), but, on the contrary, to bombard those in power with strategically well-selected *precise, finite* demands which cannot allow for the same excuse.

"Goodbye Mister Resisting Nomad"

In contrast to Critchley, Toni Negri is the most representative version of the heroic attempt to stick to fundamental Marxist coordinates and to demonstrate how the very "postmodern" turn of capitalism, the rise of the "postindustrial" society with its shift towards informational work, creates the conditions for revolutionizing society even more radically than Marx imagined it, opening up the possibility of "absolute democracy."

Negri's starting point is a rather standard one: today, immaterial cognitive work plays the key role in creating new value; and since these cognitive aspects of work predominate, one can no longer measure value with time (labor-time), so the Marxist notion of exploitation is no longer operative:

> Now, it has to be noted immediately that today there is no production of value if not immaterial value, which is carried out by free brains capable of innovation; freedom is the only value that doesn't simply reproduce wealth but that puts it into circulation.[29]

Today's basic productive force is thus the "cognitariat," the multitude of cognitive workers; their work produces freedom, and their freedom is productive. "Freedom is the fixed capital that is inside the brain of the people."[30] This, then, is our situation:

> the subaltern classes are already classes with a fixed capital richer than that of the bosses, a spiritual patrimony more important than what the others boast, and an absolute weapon: the knowledge essential for the reproduction of the world.[31]

Instead, today, when the General Intellect becomes hegemonic in capitalist production, when, that is, immaterial and cognitive labor become immediately productive, intellectual labor-power now frees itself from this relation of subjection and the productive subject appropriates for itself those labor instruments that capital preconstituted before. We can say that variable capital represents itself as fixed capital. [. . .] I am productive outside of my relation with capital, and the flow of cognitive and social capital no longer has anything to do with capital as a physical structure in the hands of the bosses.[32]

The idea is thus that, with the hegemonic role of the general intellect, capital loses its function of socially organizing production, of bringing together fixed and variable capital, the means of production, and the labor force: its function is now purely parasitic, which is why it finally becomes possible to lop it off. It is no longer even a question of a violent cut into the social texture: since production and (social) life itself are progressively organized, the multitude has simply to pursue its work of self-organization, and capital will all of a sudden notice that it is suspended in the air and will crash down, like the cartoon cat walking in the air above a precipice and falling into the abyss beneath its feet when it looks down and notices that the ground is no longer there.

The key category here is that of the formal and real subsumption of production under capital. In clear contrast to the evolutionary logic of the changes in relations of production following the development of the means of production, Marx emphasizes how formal subsumption precedes the real form: capitalists first only formally subsumed the production process to their rule (providing raw materials and buying the product from individual artisans who continued to produce the way they did before this subsumption); it is only afterwards that the subsumption becomes material, that is, that the means and organization of production are directly formed by capital (the introduction of machinery, the factory division of labor, Fordism, and so on). This process reaches its culmination in large-scale mechanized factory production, in which the subordination of the worker to capital is directly reproduced in the very material organization of the production process: the worker is materially reduced to a cog in the machine, performing a particular task, with no overview of the entire production process and no idea of the scientific knowledge that sustains it—both knowledge and organization are on the side of capital; here is Marx's description from his *Grundrisse*:

> The accumulation of knowledge and of skill, of the general productive forces of the social brain, is thus absorbed into capital, as opposed to labor, and hence appears as an attribute of capital, and more specifically of fixed capital, in so far as it enters into the production process as a means of production proper. Machinery appears, then, as the most adequate form of fixed capital, and fixed capital, in so far as capital's relations with itself are concerned, appears as the most adequate form of capital as such.[33]

However, with the post-Fordist shift to the hegemonic role of cognitive labor, knowledge and organization are again reappropriated by the collective of workers, so that, in a kind of "negation of the negation," capital once again subsumes production in a purely formal way: its role is more and more purely parasitic, trying to control and regulate a process fully able to run itself . . . The problem with Negri and Hardt here is that they are *too* Marxist, taking over the underlying Marxist schema of historical progress: like Marx, they celebrate the "deterritorializing" revolutionary potential of capitalism; like Marx, they locate the contradiction within capitalism in the gap between this potential and the form of capital, of the private-property appropriation of the surplus. In short, they rehabilitate the old Marxist notion of the tension between productive forces and the relations of production: capitalism already generates the "germs of the future new forms of life," it incessantly produces the new "commons," so that, in a revolutionary explosion, this New is simply to be liberated from the old social form. Here, they remain Deleuzian: when Deleuze and Guattari write in *Anti-Oedipus* that, by striving to reach the furthest limit of deterritorialization, a schizophrenic "seeks out the very limit of capitalism: he is its inherent tendency brought to fulfillment,"[34] do they thereby not confirm that their own socio-political project is a desperate attempt to realize capitalism's own inherent fantasy, its virtual coordinates? Is communism thereby not reduced to what none other than Bill Gates called "frictionless capitalism," capitalism elevated and intensified to the infinite speed of circulation? No wonder that Negri has recently praised "postmodern" digital capitalism, claiming that it is already communist and that it needs just a little push, a formal gesture, to openly become such. The basic strategy of contemporary capital is to cover up its superfluousness by finding news ways to once again subsume the free productive multitude:

If fixed capital is now singularly capable of imagination, in order to put it to work there is the need of a new machine. This is the paradoxical "communism of capital," the attempt to close by means of financialization the global machine of production above and beyond the productive singularities that compose it. It is the attempt to subsume the multitude.[35]

There is a feature of this account which cannot but strike the eye. According to philosophical common sense, when one neglects philosophical reflection, the result is that one finds oneself relying on the worst and most naive philosophical framework. *Mutatis mutandis*, the same rule holds for ferocious anti-Hegelians: it is as if the revenge for their total rejection of Hegel is that they unknowingly use the most superficial Hegelian categories.[36] This accounts for a detail which effectively functions as a symptom of Negri's work: his unconstrained and unreflexive (one is almost tempted to say "wild," in the sense of "wild psychoanalysis") use of Hegelian categories, which so blatantly contradicts his professed anti-Hegelianism.[37] For example, the contemporary multitude

is in itself, but not for itself, and the transition isn't easy. It is an alternation of moments, of taking conscience of some and not of others, of a totality of transitions, interruptions of tendencies and of drifts.[38]

Is this not a strange reliance on the Hegelian couplet of the In-itself and the For-itself?

Should, then, we be surprised that, when, in their *Empire*, Negri and Hardt refer to Bartleby as the figure of resistance, of the No! to the existing universe of social machinery, they interpret Bartleby's "I would prefer not to" as merely the first move of, as it were, clearing the decks, of acquiring a distance towards the existing social universe? What is then needed is a move towards the long-term work of constructing a new community—if we remain stuck at the Bartleby stage, we end up in a suicidal marginal position with no consequences . . . in short, for them, Bartleby's "I would prefer not to" is a Hegelian "abstract negation" which should then be overcome by the patient positive work of the "determinate negation" of the existing social universe. The pointedness of this Hegelian formulation is intentional: Negri and Hardt, the two great anti-Hegelians, make apropos Bartleby the most standard (pseudo-) Hegelian critical point.[39]

The irony is that Negri refers here to the process which the ideologists of contemporary "postmodern" capitalism themselves celebrate as the passage from material to symbolic production, from the centralist-hierarchical logic to the logic of autopoietic self-organization, multi-centered cooperation, and so forth. Negri is here indeed faithful to Marx: what he tries to prove is that Marx was right, that the rise of the "general intellect" is in the long term incompatible with capitalism. The ideologists of postmodern capitalism make the exactly opposite claim: it is Marxist theory (and practice) which remains within the constraints of hierarchical, centralized state-control logic, and thus cannot cope with the social effects of the new informational revolution. There are good empirical reasons for this claim: again, the supreme irony of history is that the disintegration of Communism is the most convincing example of the validity of the traditional Marxist dialectic of forces and relations of production, a dialectic on which Marxism counted in its endeavor to overcome capitalism. What indeed ruined the Communist regimes was their inability to accommodate the new social logic sustained by the "informational revolution": they tried to steer this revolution as yet another large-scale, centralized state-planning project. The paradox is thus that what Negri celebrates as the unique chance for overcoming capitalism, the ideologists of "informational revolution" eulogize as the rise of the new "frictionless" capitalism.

Who, then, is right here? What is the role of capital in "informational society"? Negri's basic reference, the famous passages about the "general intellect" from Marx's *Grundrisse*, is worth quoting *in extenso*; in it, Marx deploys a logic of the self-overcoming of capitalism which he totally abstracts from the active revolutionary struggle—it is formulated in purely economic terms:

> Capital itself is the moving contradiction, [in] that it presses to reduce labor time to a minimum, while it posits labor time, on the other side, as sole measure and source of wealth. The "contradiction" which will ruin capitalism is thus the contradiction between the capitalist exploitation which relies on labor time as the sole source of value (and thus the sole source of surplus-value), and the scientific-technological progress which leads to quantitative and qualitative reduction of the role of direct labor; this labor is reduced both quantitatively, to a smaller proportion, and qualitatively, as an, of course, indispensable but subordinate moment, compared to general scientific labor, technolo-

gical application of natural sciences, on one side, and to the general productive force arising from social combination [*Gliederung*] in total production on the other side—a combination which appears as a natural fruit of social labor (although it is a historic product). Capital thus works towards its own dissolution as the form dominating production. [. . .]

To the degree that large industry develops, the creation of real wealth comes to depend less on labor time and on the amount of labor employed than on the power of the agencies set in motion during labor time, whose "powerful effectiveness" is itself in turn out of all proportion to the direct labor time spent on their production, but depends rather on the general state of science and on the progress of technology, or the application of this science to production.

Marx's vision is here that of a fully automated production process in which the human being (the worker) "comes to relate more as watchman and regulator to the production process itself":

No longer does the worker insert a modified natural thing [*Naturgegenstand*] as middle link between the object [*Objekt*] and himself; rather, he inserts the process of nature, transformed into an industrial process, as a means between himself and inorganic nature, mastering it. He steps to the side of the production process instead of being its chief actor. In this transformation, it is neither the direct human labor he himself performs, nor the time during which he works, but rather the appropriation of his own general productive power, his understanding of nature and his mastery over it by virtue of his presence as a social body—it is, in a word, the development of the social individual which appears as the great foundation-stone of production and of wealth. The theft of alien labor time, on which the present wealth is based, appears a miserable foundation in face of this new one, created by large-scale industry itself.

As soon as labor in the direct form has ceased to be the great wellspring of wealth, labor time ceases and must cease to be its measure.

Crucial is here the radical transformation of the status of "fixed capital":

The development of fixed capital indicates to what degree general social knowledge has become a direct force of production, and to what degree, hence, the conditions of the process of social life itself have come under the control of the general intellect and been transformed in accordance with it. To what degree the powers of social production have been produced, not only in the form of knowledge, but also as immediate organs of social practice, of the real life process.

What this means is that, with the development of general social knowledge, the "productive power of labor" is "itself the greatest productive power. From the standpoint of the direct production process it can be regarded as the production of fixed capital, this fixed capital being man himself."[40] And, again, since capital organizes its exploitation by appearing as "fixed capital" against living labor, the moment the key component of fixed capital is "man himself," its "general social knowledge," the very social foundation of capitalist exploitation is undermined, and the role of capital becomes purely parasitic:

> Today capital can no longer exploit the worker; it can only exploit cooperation amongst workers, amongst laborers. Today capital has no longer that internal function for which it became the soul of common labor, which produced that abstraction within which progress was made. Today capital is parasitical because it is no longer inside; it is outside of the creative capacity of the multitude.

Negri's idea is that this immaterial labor opens up the possibility of "absolute democracy," it cannot be enslaved, because *it is immediately, in itself, the form (and practice) of social freedom.* In it, form and content coincide: it is immediately free (inventive, creative, an expression of the subject's productivity, active, not re-active) and socialized (always participating in common, cooperative in its very content). This is why it renders capital parasitical: since it is directly socialized, it no longer needs capital to confer on it the form of universality. Exploitation is today essentially "the capitalist expropriation of the cooperative power that the singularities of cognitive labour deploy in the social process. It isn't capital anymore that organizes labor, but labor that organizes itself in itself."[41] This notion of the direct productivity of social life itself leads Negri to assert "biopolitics," in manner different from Agamben: "biopolitics" means that human life itself is the direct topic and product of collective labor. It is precisely this directly biopolitical character of production which enables "absolute democracy": "Biopolitical power [*potenza*] is therefore contrasted to biopower."[42]

As we have noted, is this gesture of Negri not the last in the long Marxist series of identifications of a moment in the social relations of production and/or of technology itself as the moment that capitalism will no longer be able to integrate and, consequently, which will in the long term lead to its demise? For Negri, what is new in the "postmodern" capitalism of today is the very direct overlapping of the two dimensions (material production and its social form): new social relations are the essence and goal of production. In other words, production is increasingly "directly" socialized, socialized in its very content, which is why it no longer needs the social form of capital imposed onto it. Negri passes all too quickly over the fact that what characterizes our time is *biocapitalism*, which, in the narrower sense, designates the immense field of new capitalist investments into the direct production of new forms of biological life (from genetically modified crops to the human genome).

Surely, the first task of the Marxist approach here should be to redefine in more stringent terms the notion of the exploitation of "intellectual labor"? In what precise theoretical sense is, say, Bill Gates "exploiting" thousands of programmers who work for him, if his exploitation is no longer the "theft of alien labor time"? Is his role really purely "parasitical" upon the self-organization of the programmers? Does his capital not, in a more substantial way, provide the very social space for their cooperation? And in what precise sense is the intellectual labor the "source of value," if the ultimate measure of value is no longer time? Is the category of value still applicable here?

Negri's thesis, reduced to its core, is thus that, with the development of cyber-technologies, the primary means of production of profit is no longer the exploitation of labor, but the "harvesting" of information; with this shift, it becomes possible to liberate labor *from within* the limits of capitalist production, since the exchange of "harvested" information on the market no longer relies on the exploitation of labor, that is, on the appropriation of surplus-value:

> The current problem of political economy is to consider human beings when they live and not only when they work, as human beings are always producers. Always, that is, in any moment of life. How is the exploitation of life thinkable? It is not.

With today's global interactive media, creative inventiveness is no longer individual, it is immediately collectivized, part of the "commons," so any attempt to privatize it through copyrighting is problematic—more and more literally, "property is theft" here. So what about a company like Microsoft which does precisely this—organizing and exploiting the collective synergy of creative cognitive singularities? The only remaining task is thus to conceive of how cognitive workers will "be able to blow the bosses away, because the industrial command of cognitive labor is completely *dépassé*."[43] What new social movements signal is that

> the epoch of wage-labor is finished, and that the struggle has moved from the level of a fight between labor and capital regarding the wage to a fight between the multitude and the state around the citizen's income.[44]

Therein resides the basic feature of "today's social revolutionary transition": "There is the need to make capital aware of the common good, and if it doesn't want to understand it, it is necessary to impose it."[45] (Note Negri's precise formulation: not abolish capital, but compel it to recognize the common good—one remains thus *within* capitalism.)

From this brief description, one can see the proximity as well as the difference between Marx and Negri. What is not in Marx, what Negri projects onto Marx's "general intellect," is his own central notion of "biopolitics" as the direct production of life itself in its social dimension. Where Negri sees a direct *fusion* (with "cognitive work," the ultimate objects of production are social relations themselves), Marx posits a radical *gap*, the exclusion of the worker from the production process: Marx envisages a fully automated production process in which the worker "steps to one side" and is reduced to its "watchman and regulator"; what this unequivocally means is that the underlying logic is here that of the "Cunning of Reason": instead of engaging himself directly in the production process, man steps aside and lets nature work upon itself. When the worker no longer "inserts a modified natural thing as middle link between the object and himself," that is, when he no longer uses tools to work on the objects he wants to transform; when, instead, he "inserts the process of nature, transformed into an industrial process, as a means between himself and inorganic nature, mastering it," he turns into a wise manipulator, regulating the production process from a safe distance. Marx's systematic use of the singular ("man," the "worker") is a key indicator of how the "general intellect" is not intersubjective, it is "monological." This is why, in this Marxian vision, the objects of the production process are precisely *not* social relations themselves: the "administration of things" (control of and domination over nature) is here separated from the relations between people, it constitutes a domain of the "administration of things" which no longer has to rely on the domination over people.

From a "postmodern" view, it would be tempting to read this discrepancy between Marx and Negri as an indication of how Marx remained stuck in the "old paradigm" of centralized "instrumental reason" which controls and regulates the production process from the outside; however, there is also a moment of truth in Marx's description which is obfuscated by Negri: the remaining radical *duality* of the production process.[46] Today, this duality has acquired a form which was not envisaged by Marx: the "kingdom of freedom," the domain of "cognitive work," and the "kingdom of necessity," the domain of material production, are physically separated, often even by state borders. On the one side are the "postmodern" companies that exemplify Negri's criteria (free communities of "expressive multitudes" which immediately produce life-forms, and so on); on the other side, there is the material production process where full automatization is far from achieved, so that we have — often literally on the other side of the world — sweatshops with a strict "Fordist" organization of labor, where thousands assemble computers and toys, pick bananas or coffee beans, mine for coal or diamonds, and so forth. There is no "teleology" here, no prospect of sweatshops becoming gradually integrated into the free space of "cognitive work." Outsourcing being more rule than exception, the two sides do not even directly relate to each other: they are brought together, "mediated," precisely by *capital*. For each side, the opposite side appears as Capital: for the crowds in the sweatshops, Capital is the power which, on behalf of "cognitive work," employs them to materialize its results; for the "cognitive workers," Capital is the power which employs them in order to use their results as the blueprints for material production. It is because of this duality neglected by Negri that Capital is not yet purely parasitic, but still plays a key role in the organization of production: it brings the two sides together.

Negri in Davos

Negri is right apropos forums such as Davos: they are the enlightened capitalists' "general intellect," the space for formulating their general interest, the space to "listen to other voices," to confront ecology, poverty, and so on, to expound on problems of spirituality and the rest, with a view to combining the struggle against pollution and poverty, or whatever it may be, with capitalism. This really is "communist capitalism": capitalism which tries to include the communist topic of the endangered commons. The very fact of the importance of Davos Forum (much more than the old Trilateral Commission, its predecessor), the *need* for a forum like Davos, is proof of the crisis of capitalism, of the threat of the commons. Davos is the Collective Brain of the Empire, its "think tank." Negri even proposed to Davos a strategic pact against the American project: although, in the long term, the multitude and Davos are enemies, in the short term, they share the interest of defeating the US *coup d'état* against the global Empire.[47] A strange logic indeed! Instead of exploiting the inconsistency of the enemy, one helps him establish the most effective form . . . To put it in other words, what if the very idea of a "pure" Empire which leaves behind the nation-state form, and in which the capitalist general intellect runs things directly, is an impossible abstraction? What if the role of nation-states is irreducible and crucial (and, with it, the temptation of some nation-state(s) to carry out *coups d'état* against the Empire), so that the exception — the excessive role of a nation-state in the Empire — is in fact the rule?

Negri here is not Leninist enough. To put it in Deleuzian terms already evoked, Lenin's moment is the "dark precursor," the vanishing mediator, the displaced object never in its own place, between the two series, the initial "orthodox" Marxian series of revolution in the most developed countries, and the new "orthodox" series of Stalinist "socialism in one country" and then the Maoist identification of the Third World nations with the new world proletariat. The shift from Lenin to Stalinism is here clear and easy to determine: Lenin perceived the situation as desperate, unexpected, but as such one which had to be creatively exploited for new political choices; with the notion of "socialism in one country," Stalin re-normalized the situation into a new narrative of linear development in "stages." That is to say, while Lenin was fully aware that an "anomaly" had happened (revolution in a country which does not have the pre-suppositions for developing a socialist society), he rejected the vulgar evolutionist conclusion that revolution had taken place "prematurely," so that one should take a step back in order to develop a modern democratic capitalist society, which would then slowly create the conditions for socialist revolution, claiming that — to refer back to the crucial passage we quoted earlier—this very "complete hopelessness of the situation" offers "the opportunity to create the fundamental requisites of civilization in a different way from that of the West European countries."[48] What Lenin is proposing here is effectively an implicit theory of "alternate history": under the "premature" domination of the force of the future, the same "necessary" historical process (of modern civilization) can be (re)run in a different way.

Perhaps this attitude is today more relevant than ever: the situation is "completely hopeless," with no clear "realistic" revolutionary perspective; but does this not give us a kind of strange freedom, a *freedom to experiment*? One has only to throw away the deterministic model of "objective necessities" and obligatory "stages" of development? One has thus to sustain a minimum of anti-determinism: nothing is *ever* written off, in an "objective situation" which precludes any act, which condemns us fully to biopolitical vegetation. There is *always* a space to be created for an act—precisely because, to paraphrase Rosa Luxemburg's critique of reformism, it is not enough to wait patiently for the "right moment" of the revolution. If one merely waits for it, it will never come, for one has to start with "premature" attempts which—therein resides the "pedagogy of the revolution"—in their very failure to achieve their professed goal create the (subjective) conditions for the "right" moment. Recall Mao's slogan "from defeat to defeat, to the final victory," which echoes in Beckett's already-quoted motto: "Try again. Fail again. Fail better."

In this precise sense, Lenin was a Beckettian *avant la lettre*: what he basically proposed that the Bolsheviks should do in the desperate situation at the end of the Civil War was not to directly "construct socialism," but to *fail better* than a "normal" bourgeois state. It holds also for the revolutionary process that, to paraphrase Derrida's well-known dictum once again, the condition of impossibility is the condition of possibility: the condition of impossibility—Russian backwardness and isolation which made socialism impossible—is part of the same exceptional situation which made the first socialist revolution possible. In other words, instead of bemoaning the historical anomaly of a revolution in an exceptional and "immature" situation (with the expectation that the revolution would start in the most developed capitalist countries), one should bear in mind that revolution never arrives "on time," when the objective social process generates the "mature" conditions for it—the point of Lenin's famous notion of the "weakest link in the chain" is, again, that one should use the "anomaly" as a lever to exacerbate the antagonisms so that they render possible a revolutionary explosion.[49]

Negri is also right to point out that, in this new global order, wars in the old sense of the term are less and less feasible: what we refer to as "wars" are police interventions of a "global" state into an area which is experienced as a threat to the global order. War and politics are combined in military "policing," in imposing order in a chaotic area. It is, paradoxically, Bush's politics which has continued the tradition of old wars, being an attempt by a nation-state to carry out a *coup d'état* against the Empire, to subordinate the Empire. With regard to the Empire, it is the US which is the "banana republic." Here, however, Negri becomes ambiguous: on the one hand, he is clear that the capitalist general intellect is, in the long term, the true enemy; on the other hand, apropos Lula, he supports the policies which aim at breaking US hegemony and at establishing a pluricentric global capitalism (the US, Europe with, maybe, Russia, China and the Far East, Latin America, and so on).

Contrary to misleading appearances, the "American century" is over and we are already entering the period of the formation of multiple centers of global capitalism. Is the fact that, on his visit to the US in April 2006, the Chinese President was first the guest of Bill Gates not a sign of these new times? So, perhaps, in this new era, each of the new centers will stand for capitalism with a specific twist: the US for neoliberal capitalism; Europe (with, maybe, Russia) for what remains of the welfare state; China for "Eastern Values" and authoritarian capitalism; Latin America for populist capitalism . . . After the failure of the US attempt to impose itself as the sole superpower (the universal policeman), there is now the need to establish the rules of interaction between these local centers in case of conflicting interests.[50]

Although Emmanuel Todd's vision of the contemporary global order is clearly one-sided,[51] it is difficult to deny its moment of truth: that the US is an empire in decline. Its growing negative balance of trade demonstrates that the US is the unproductive predator: it has to suck up an influx of 1 billion dollars a day from other nations to meet its consumption needs and is, as such, the universal Keynesian consumer that keeps the world economy running. (So much for the anti-Keynesian economic ideology that seems to predominate today!) This influx, which is effectively like the tithe paid to Rome in Antiquity, relies on a complex economic mechanism: the US is "trusted" as the safe and stable center, so that all others, from the oil-producing Arab countries to Western Europe and Japan, and now even China, invest their surplus profits in the US. Since this "trust" is primarily ideological and military, not economic, the problem for the US is how to justify its imperial role—it needs a permanent state of war, so it had to invent the "War on Terror," offering itself as the universal protector of all other "normal" (non-"rogue") states.

The entire globe thus tends to function as a universal Sparta with three classes, now emerging as the First, Second, and Third Worlds: (1) the US as the military-political-ideological power; (2) Europe and parts of Asia and Latin America as the industrial-manufacturing region (crucial here are Germany and Japan, the world's leading exporters, plus rising China); (3) the undeveloped rest, today's helots. In other words, global capitalism has brought about a new general trend towards oligarchy, masked as the celebration of the "diversity of cultures": equality and universalism are rapidly disappearing as actual political principles . . . However, even before it has fully established itself, this neo-Spartan world system is breaking down: in contrast to 1945, the world does not need the US, it is the US which needs the world. Since the world of today is composed of too many regional centers which cannot be controlled, the only thing the US can do to assert itself as the global military power is to engage in theatrical wars or "crises" with weak adversaries (Iraq, Cuba, Korea, Iran . . .), not with true alternative centers of power (China, Russia). The violent outbursts of the recent Bush administration are thus not exercises in power, but rather exercises in panic, irrational *passages à l'acte*.[52]

Perhaps, this focus on thwarting the US *coup d'état* against Empire accounts for Negri's strange elevation of Lula at the expense of Chavez:

> There doesn't exist in Latin America an alternative to the political project promised by Lula and the Brazilian PT. Now, above all recently, the Bolivarian Venezuela of [Hugo] Chavez was presented as an alternative to the project of Lula. But, it is obvious that this alternative is purely ideological, very abstract. [. . .] In Venezuela in particular the relationship between political power and the capacity of developing economic-productive alternatives still seems to be in deficit.[53]

So what are these achievements of Lula's? Negri mentions only two: that Lula governs in a direct dialogue with the movements, and that he is practicing new measures (paying off the IMF debt and so on) to ensure the government's autonomy from (international) capital; Negri himself admits that this goal of establishing a new international equilibrium has priority over the struggle against social inequalities.[54]

So what will happen when the US *coup d'état* is defeated and the general intellect will run the Empire? Here enters another weird feature, Negri's unexpected Eurocentrism:

> In a subsequent period, when global multilateralism is stabilized and aristocratic global representations are determined on a continental basis, Europe will become the only democratic mediator within this new global constitution. We need Europe because of this. [. . .] Europe is the only occasion for a pluralist and *democratic* push of real and dynamic transformation at the global level.[55]

The problem here is not Eurocentrism as such, but rather the lack of conceptual justification: why, exactly, is only Europe capable of triggering "a pluralist and democratic push of real and dynamic transformation at the gloval level"?

Deleuze without Negri

Negri's Eurocentrism is discernible already in the opposition between expression and representation, on which his entire thought is based: the logic of political representation (the state—or political parties—as representing people) versus the logic of expression (social movements expressing the free creativity of the multitude). Representation deals with individuals who are "represented" in the universal sphere, marked by the gap between their empirical particularity and their transcendental or legal universality; singularities are atoms which are directly interactive and productive, expressing their creative power. Philosophically, this means Descartes/Kant versus Spinoza. (There are clearly discernible echoes here of Sartre's notion of the "pratico-inert," developed in his *Critique of Dialectical Reason*.) The theoretical problem here is: can one imagine a society fully organized in terms of expression of the multitude, a society of "absolute democracy," a society without representation? A society of permanent mobilization, a society in which every objective structure is a direct expression of subjective productivity? What we encounter here is the old philosophical logic of Becoming versus Being (living productivity versus the sterility of an inert structure of representation), where every re-presentation is parasitical upon productive expressivity.

Perhaps one should shift the accent here: from "no representation without expressive productivity" to "no expressive productivity without representation." It is structurally impossible to "totalize" the multitude of movements: "absolute democracy," the full and direct reign of multitude, is a perspectival illusion, a composite image of the false overlapping of two heterogeneous dimensions. Tarkovsky's *Solaris* ends with the director's archetypal fantasy of combining within the same shot the Otherness into which the hero is thrown (the chaotic surface of Solaris) and the object of his nostalgic longing, the home dacha to which he longs to return, the house whose contours are encircled by the malleable slime of Solaris's surface—within radical Otherness, we discover the lost object of our innermost longing. The same fantasmatic staging concludes Tarkovsky's *Nostalgia*: in the midst of the Italian countryside encircled by the fragments of a cathedral in ruins, that is, of the place in which the hero is adrift, cut off from his roots, there stands an element totally out of place, the Russian dacha, the stuff of the hero's dreams; here, too, the shot begins with a close-up of only the recumbent hero in front of his dacha, so that, for a moment, it may seem that he has in fact returned home; the camera then slowly pulls back to divulge the properly fantasmatic setting of the dacha against the backdrop of the Italian countryside. This concluding fantasy is an artificial condensation of opposed, incompatible perspectives, somehow like the standard optician's test in which we see through one eye a cage, through the other eye a parrot, and, if our two eyes are well coordinated in their axes, when we open both eyes, we should see the parrot in the cage. And what if it is the same with Negri's "absolute democracy," for the multitude directly ruling itself? What if the gap between the multitude and power is here to stay?

This does not mean that we should abandon Deleuze—what we should abandon is merely Negri's one-sided appropriation of Deleuze, an appropriation which leaves out the radical duality of Deleuze's thought.[56] There are two incompatible ontologies at work in Deleuze: the Deleuze who celebrates the productive power of the virtual flow is forever haunted by the Deleuze who conceives the virtual flow of sense as a sterile immaterial effect, positing an irreducible gap between material productivity and the virtual flow of Sense.

The elementary coordinates of Deleuze's ontology are provided by the opposition between the Virtual and and the Actual: the space of the actual (real acts in the present, experienced reality, and subjects as persons *qua* formed individuals) accompanied by its virtual shadow (the field of proto-reality, of multiple singularities, impersonal elements later synthetized into our experience of reality). This is the Deleuze of "transcendental empiricism," the Deleuze who gives to Kant's transcendental his unique twist: the proper transcendental space is the virtual space of multiple singular potentialities, of "pure" impersonal singular gestures, affects, and perceptions that are not yet the gestures-affects-perceptions *of* a preexisting, stable, and self-identical subject. This is why, for example, Deleuze celebrates the art of cinema: it "liberates" the gaze, images, movements, and, ultimately, time itself from their attribution to a given subject—when we watch a movie, we see the flow of images from the perspective of the "mechanical" camera, a perspective which does not belong to any subject; through the art of montage, movement is also abstracted/liberated from its attribution to a given subject or object—it is an impersonal movement which is only secondarily, *a posteriori*, attributed to some positive entities.

Here, however, the first crack in this edifice appears: in a move which is far from self-evident, Deleuze links this conceptual space to the traditional opposition between production and representation. The virtual field is (re)interpreted as that of generative, productive forces, opposed to the space of representations. Here we face all the standard topics of the molecular multiple sites of productivity constrained by the molar totalizing organizations, and so on and so forth. Under the heading of the opposition between becoming and being, Deleuze thus seems to identify these two logics, although they are fundamentally incompatible (one is tempted to attribute the "bad" influence which pushed him towards the second logic to Félix Guattari[57]). The proper site of production is *not* the virtual space as such, but, rather, the very *passage* from it to constituted reality, the collapse of the multitude and its oscillations into one reality—production is fundamentaly a limitation of the open space of virtualities, the determination/negation of the virtual multitude (this is how Deleuze reads Spinoza's *omni determinatio est negatio* against Hegel).

The line of Deleuze proper is that of the great early monographs (the key ones being *Difference and Repetition* and *The Logic of Sense*) as well as some of the shorter introductory writings (like *Proust and Signs* and the *Introduction to Sacher-Masoch*). In his late work, it is the two cinema books which mark the return to the topics of *The Logic of Sense*. This series is to be distinguished from the books Deleuze and Guattari co-wrote, and one can only regret that the Anglo-Saxon reception of Deleuze (and, also, the politicial impact of Deleuze) is predominantly that of a "Guattarized" Deleuze. It is crucial to note that not a single one of Deleuze's own texts is in any way directly political; Deleuze "in himself" was a highly elitist author, indifferent to politics. The only serious philosophical question is thus: what inherent impasse caused Deleuze to turn towards Guattari? Is *Anti-Oedipus*, arguably Deleuze's worst book, not the result of escaping the full confrontation of a deadlock via a simplified "flat" solution, homologous to Schelling escaping the deadlock of his *Weltalter* project via his shift to the duality of "positive" and "negative" philosophy, or Habermas escaping the deadlock of the "dialectic of Enlightenment" via his shift to the duality of instrumental and communicative reason? Our task is to confront again this deadlock. Was, therefore, Deleuze not pushed towards Guattari because Guattari presented an alibi, an easy escape from the deadlock of his previous position? Does Deleuze's conceptual structure not rely on *two* logics, on *two* conceptual oppositions, which coexist in his work? This insight seems so obvious, stating it so close to what the French call a *lapalissade*, that one is surprised it has not yet been generally perceived:

First, on the one hand, the logic of sense, of immaterial becoming as the sense-event, as the *effect* of bodily-material processes-causes, the logic of the radical gap between the generative process and its immaterial sense-effect:

> multiplicities, being incorporeal effects of material causes, are impassible or causally sterile entities. The time of a pure becoming, always already passed and eternally yet to come, forms the temporal dimension of this impassibility or sterility of multiplicities.[58]

And is cinema not the ultimate case of the sterile flow of surface becoming? The cinematic image is inherently sterile and impassive, the pure effect of corporeal causes, although nonetheless acquiring its pseudo-autonomy.

Second, on the other hand, the logic of becoming as the *production* of Beings:

> the emergence of metric or extensive properties should be treated as a single process in which a continuous *virtual spacetime* progressively

differentiates itself into actual discontinuous spatio-temporal structures.[59]

In, say, his analyses of films and literature, Deleuze emphasizes the
desubstantialization of affects: in a work of art, an affect (boredom, for
instance) is no longer attributable to actual persons, but becomes a free-
floating event. How, then, does this impersonal intensity of an affect-
event relate to bodies or persons? Here, we encounter the same ambiguity: either this immaterial affect is generated by interacting bodies as a
sterile surface of pure Becoming, or it is part of the virtual intensities out
of which bodies emerge through actualization (the passage from Becoming to Being).

And, is this opposition not, yet again, that of materialism versus
idealism? In Deleuze, this means: *The Logic of Sense* versus *Anti-Oedipus*.
Either the Sense-Event, the flow of pure Becoming, is the immaterial
effect (neutral, neither active nor passive) of the intrication of bodily-
material causes, or the positive bodily entities are themselves the product
of the pure flow of Becoming. Either the infinite field of virtuality is an
immaterial effect of interacting bodies, or the bodies themselves emerge,
actualize themselves, from this field of virtuality. In *The Logic of Sense*,
Deleuze himself develops this opposition in the guise of two possible
modes of the genesis of reality: the formal genesis (the emergence of
reality out of the immanence of impersonal consciousness as the pure flow
of Becoming) is supplemented by the real genesis, the latter accounting
for the emergence of the immaterial event-surface itself out of bodily
interaction.

Is this opposition of the virtual as the site of productive Becoming and
the virtual as the site of the sterile Sense-Event not, at the same time, the
opposition of the "body without organs" (BwO) and "organs without a
body" (OwaB)? Is, on the one hand, the productive flux of pure
Becoming not the BwO, the body not yet structured or determined as
functional organs? And, on the other hand, are the OwaB not the
virtuality of the pure affect extracted from its embeddedness in a body,
like the smile in *Alice in Wonderland* that persists alone, even when the
Cheshire cat's body is no longer present?

"All right," said the Cat; and this time it vanished quite slowly,
beginning with the end of the tail, and ending with the grin, which
remained some time after the rest of it had gone. "Well! I've often seen

a cat without a grin," thought Alice; "but a grin without a cat! It's the most curious thing I ever saw in my life!"

This notion of extracted OwaB reemerges forcefully in *The Time-Image*, in the guise of the *gaze* itself as such an autonomous organ no longer attached to a body. These two logics (Event as the power which generates reality; Event as the sterile, pure effect of bodily interactions) also involve two privileged psychological stances: the generative Event of Becoming relies on the productive force of the "schizo," this explosion of the unified subject in the impersonal multitude of desiring intensities, intensities that are subsequently constrained by the Oedipal matrix; the Event as sterile, immaterial effect relies on the figure of the masochist who finds satisfaction in the tedious, repetitive game of staged rituals whose function is to postpone forever the sexual *passage à l'acte*. Can one effectively imagine a stronger contrast than that of the schizo throwing himself without any reservation into the flux of multiple passions, and of the masochist clinging to the theater of shadows in which his meticulously staged performances repeat again and again the same sterile gesture?

So, what if we conceive Deleuze's opposition of the intermixing of material bodies and the immaterial effect of sense along the lines of the Marxist opposition of base and superstructure? Is not the flow of becoming the superstructure *par excellence* —the sterile theater of shadows ontologically cut off from the site of material production, and precisely as such the only possible space of the Event? The tension between Deleuze's two ontologies clearly translates into two different political logics and practices. The ontology of productive Becoming clearly leads to the leftist topic of the self-organization of the multitude of molecular groups which resist and undermine the molar, totalizing systems of power—the old notion of the spontaneous, non-hierarchical, living multitude opposing the oppressive, reified system, the exemplary case of leftist radicalism linked to philosophical idealist subjectivism. The problem is that this is the only model of the politicization of Deleuze's thought available: the other ontology, that of the sterility of the Sense-Event, appears "apolitical." However, what if this other ontology also involves a political logic and practice of its own, of which Deleuze himself was unaware? Should we not, then, proceed like Lenin in 1915 when, in order to ground anew revolutionary practice, he returned to Hegel—not to his directly political writings, but, primarily, to his *Logic*? What if, in the same way, there is another Deleuzian politics to be discovered here?

The first hint in this direction may be provided by the already-mentioned parallel between the couple *corporeal causes/immaterial flow of becoming* and the old Marxist couple *base/superstructure*: such a politics would take into account both the irreducible duality of "objective" material/socio-economic processes taking place in reality as well as the explosion of revolutionary Events, of the political logic proper. What if the domain of politics is inherently "sterile," the domain of pseudo-causes, a shadow theater, but nonetheless crucial in transforming reality?

What this means is that one should accept the gap between sterile virtual movements and the actuality of power. This solution is more paradoxical than it may appear: one should bear in mind that virtuality stands for expressive productivity, while actual state power operates at the level of representation: productivity is "real," the state is representative. This is the way to break out of the philosophical paradigm of productivity versus the positive order of Being: the true gap is not that between reality and its representation; reality and representation are not opposed but on the same side, they form the same order of positive Being. Productivity is thus not the metaphysical principle or source of reality, to be opposed to the mere appearance of substantial Being: substantial Being is "all there really is," while the causality of productivity is a pseudo-causality, since productivity operates in a "sterile" shadowy virtual domain.

Is this duality not prefigured in the Heideggerian struggle between World and Earth, which we encounter, today, in the antinomy that defines our experience? On the one hand, there is the fluidification (volatilization) of our experience, its desubstantialization; this exponentially exploding "lightness of being" culminates in the cyber-dream of the transformation of our very identity as a human being from hardware to software, to a program able to be reloaded from one to another hardware. Reality is here virtualized, any failure can be undone by rewinding and having another try at it. However, this virtualized world in which we dwell is threatened by the shadow of what we usually designate as the prospect of ecological catastrophe—the imponderable heaviness and complexity, the inertia of Earth catching up, reminding us of the fragile equilibrium which forms the invisible background foundation of our survival on Earth and which we can destroy (and thus destroy ourselves)—through global warming, through new viruses, through a gigantic asteroid hitting the Earth . . . Never in the history of humanity was the tension so palpable between the unbearable lightness of our being (the media providing us with the strangest sensations with a click, cutting through the resistance of reality, promising a "frictionless" world) and the unpredictable background of the Earth.

At the political level proper, is not Negri himself on the tracks of this solution of asserting the irreducible gap when he proposes the formula of "governance" as the tension/dialogue between state power and the self-organized multitude's movements? Mao was well aware of this duality, which is why he intervened at the climax of the Cultural Revolution, when the Shanghai commune attempted to get rid of the party–state apparatus itself and replace it with communal self-organization — such an organization, he warned, is "too weak when it comes to suppressing counter-revolution";[60] when it comes to this threat, one needs pure and raw power:

> Of all important things, the possession of power is the most important. Such being the case, the revolutionary masses, with a deep hatred for the class enemy, make up their minds to unite, form a great alliance, and seize power! Seize power! Seize power!!! All the party power, political power, and financial power usurped by the counterrevolutionary revisionists and those diehards who persistently cling to the bourgeois reactionary line must be recaptured.[61]

This intervention by Mao is usually quoted as the proof of his ruthless manipulation of the Red Guards: he only needed them to crush his opponents within the party *nomenklatura*, so that the moment this job was done and the Guardists persisted, wanting to dissolve the party–state apparatus and effectively take it over, he instructed the army, the only stable state apparatus still functioning, to intervene, crushing the Red Guards' resistance and sending millions of the Guardists to the countryside to "reeducate" them . . . What if, however, such a reading is all too simple and misses the point? What if Mao was aware that the very flourishing of movements of the multitude always-already had to rely on some *dispositif* of Power which structures and sustains the very space within which they operate? Today, the movements for gay rights, human rights, and so on, all rely on state apparatuses, which are not only the addressee of their demands, but also provide the framework for their activity (stable civil life).

The more fundamental reproach to Mao is the standard one of the postmodern Left to traditional "Leninist" Marxists: that they all focus on state power, on taking over state power. However, the various successes in taking state power miserably failed in their goals, so the Left should adopt a different, apparently more modest, but in fact much more radical strategy: to withdraw from state power and focus on directly transforming the very texture of social life, everyday practices which sustain the entire social structure. This position was given its most elaborated form by John Holloway: *Change the World without Taking Power*.[62] The continually contested separation of "doing" (human activity, living labor) and "the done" (dead labor, capital) means that relations between people are reduced to relations between things. The social flow of doing, what Holloway terms human "power-to," is broken by "power-over." Our everyday existence is a series of struggles, hidden and open, violent and suppressed, conscious and unconscious. "We are not a Sleeping Beauty, a humanity frozen in our alienation until our prince–party comes to kiss us, we live rather in constant struggle to free ourselves from the curse."[63] Any radical social change must therefore be anti-fetishistic in its approach, but the very opposite of fetishism is precisely the "dark void" which cannot be seen or plotted, the path we make by treading, the questions we ask in asking itself.

There is a moment of truth in this approach—this truth is the truth first given its classic formulation by La Boétie in his treatise on voluntary servitude: our passive endurement of power constitutes it, we do not obey and fear power because it is in itself so powerful; on the contrary, power appears powerful because we treat it as such. This fact opens up the space for a magical passive revolution which, instead of directly confronting power, gradually undermines it through the subterranean digging of the mole, through abstaining from participation in the everyday rituals and practices that sustain it. In a way, was Mahatma Gandhi not doing exactly this, when he led the anti-British resistance in India? Instead of directly attacking the colonial state, he organized movements of civil disobedience, of boycotting British products, of creating a social space outside the scope of the colonial state.

Another field of such undermining of the rule of capital is consumers' self-organization. On this view, one should drop the traditional leftist privileging of production as the only substantial reality of social life: the position of the worker-producer and that of consumer should be sustained as irreducible in their divergence, without privileging one as the "deeper truth" of the other.[64] Value is created in the production process; however, it is, as it were, created there only potentially, since it is only *actualized* as value when the produced commodity is sold and the circle

M–C–M' is thus completed. Crucial is this temporal *gap* between the production of value and its actualization: even if value is produced in production, without the successful completion of the process of circulation, there is *stricto sensu* no value — the temporality is here that of the *futur antérieur*, in other words, value "is" not immediately, it only "will have been," it is retroactively actualized, performatively enacted. In production, value is generated "in itself," while only through the completed circulation process does it become "for itself." This is how Kojin Karatani resolves the Kantian antinomy of value which *is and is not* generated in the process of production: it is generated there only "in itself." And it is because of this gap between in- and for-itself that capitalism needs formal democracy and equality:

> What precisely distinguishes capital from the master–slave relation is that the worker confronts him as consumer and possessor of exchange values, and that in the form of the possessor of money, in the form of money he becomes a simple center of circulation — one of its infinitely many centers, in which his specificity as worker is extinguished.[65]

What this means is that, in order to complete the circle of its reproduction, capital has to pass through this critical point at which the roles are inverted: "[. . .] surplus value is realized in principle only by workers *in totality* buying back what they produce."[66] This point is crucial for Karatani: it provides the key leverage from which to oppose the rule of capital today: is it not natural that the proletarians should focus their attack on that unique point at which they approach capital from the position of a buyer, and, consequently, at which it is capital which is forced to court them? — "[. . .] if workers can become subjects at all, it is only as consumers."[67]

Today, this key role of consumption has reasserted itself in an unexpected way. Referring to Georges Bataille's notion of the "general economy" of sovereign expenditure, which he opposes to the "restrained economy" of capitalism's endless profiteering, the German post-humanist philosopher Peter Sloterdijk provides the outlines of capitalism's split from itself, its immanent self-overcoming: capitalism culminates when it "creates out of itself its own most radical — and the only fruitful — opposite, totally different from what the classical Left, caught in its miserabilism, was able to dream about."[68] His positive mention of Andrew Carnegie shows the way: the sovereign self-negating gesture of the endless accumulation of wealth is to spend this wealth on things beyond price, and outside market circulation: the public good, the arts and sciences, health, and so on. This concluding "sovereign" gesture enables the capitalist to break out of the vicious cycle of endless expanded reproduction, of gaining money in order to earn more money. When he donates his accumulated wealth to the public good, the capitalist self-negates himself as the mere personification of capital and its reproductive circulation: his life acquires meaning. It is no longer just expanded reproduction as an autotelic goal. Furthermore, the capitalist thus accomplishes the shift from *eros* to *thymos*, from the perverted "erotic" logic of accumulation to public recognition and reputation. What this amounts to is nothing less than elevating figures such as Soros or Gates to personifications of the inherent self-negation of the capitalist process itself: their work of charity—their immense donations to public welfare—is not just a personal idiosyncrasy. Whether sincere or hypocritical, it is the logical concluding point of capitalist circulation, necessary from the strictly economic standpoint, since it allows the capitalist system to postpone its crisis. It reestablishes balance—a kind of redistribution of wealth to the truly needy—without falling into a fatal trap: the destructive logic of resentment and enforced statist redistribution of wealth which can only end in generalized misery. It also avoids, one might add, the other mode of reestablishing a kind of balance and asserting *thymos* through sovereign expenditure, namely wars . . . This paradox signals a sad predicament of ours: contemporary capitalism cannot reproduce itself on its own. It needs extra-economic charity to sustain the cycle of social reproduction.

Governance and movements

Every revolution thus consists of two different aspects: factual revolution plus spiritual reform, namely, actual struggle for state power plus the virtual struggle for the transformation of customs, of the substance of everyday life—what Hegel called the "silent weaving of the Spirit," which undermines the invisible foundations of power, so that the formal change is the final act of taking note of what has already taken place, for one has only to remind the dead form that it is dead, and it disintegrates. In his *Phenomenology*, again, Hegel quotes the famous passage from Diderot's *Nephew of Rameau* about the "silent, ceaseless weaving of the Spirit in the simple inwardness of its substance":

[. . .] it infiltrates the noble parts through and through and soon has taken complete possession of all the vitals and members of the unconscious idol; then "one fine morning it gives its comrade a shove with the elbow, and bang! crash! the idol lies on the floor." On "one fine morning" whose noon is bloodless if the infection has penetrated to every organ of spiritual life.[69]

This, however, is not Hegel's final word: he goes on to point out that this "Spirit concealing its action from itself, is only one side of the realization of pure insight": at the same time, being a conscious act, this Spirit "must give its moments a definite manifest existence and must appear on the scene as a sheer uproar and a violent struggle with its anti-thesis."[70] In the transition to the New, there is a passionate struggle going on, which is over once the opposing force notices how its very opposition is already impregnated with the opponent's logic.[71] This, then, is how we are to read the two apparently opposed features (the priority of the form; the "silent weaving of the Spirit") together: the latter does not concern content, but the form itself—again, in the case of a televangelist preacher, this "silent weaving" undermines his message at the level of its own form (the way he delivers the message subverts its content).

The lesson of failures such as the Cultural Revolution is that the focus should be shifted from the utopian goal of the full reign of productive expressivity that no longer needs representation, state order, capital, and so forth, to the question, "What kind of representation should replace the existing liberal-democratic representative state?" Is Negri's proposal of a "citizen's income" not an indication in this sense? It is an institutional-representative measure (not for *homini sacer*, for full citizens—it implies state representation); it is not linked to an individual's productivity, but is the representative *condition and framework* for opening up the possible space of expressive productivity.

Negri characterizes the contemporary situation as one of "permanent governance":

Power is broken in two. In order to be realized, it no longer has the possibility of determining a norm, then executing it subsequently in a concrete administrative act. The norm can't be realized without consensus, which has to be seen as the participation of subjects.[72]

Incidentally, this notion of "dual power," of "governance" as the interaction between representative state power and councils of "expressive" movements, has a long tradition on the Left—among others, it was advocated by Karl Kautsky in 1918–19, when he rejected the exclusive alternative "either the national assembly or the council assembly," seeking their integration, with each of them fulfilling different and specific tasks:

> The councils, Kautsky argued, ought not to be chosen as the sole form of electoral representation even if they enjoyed the support of the majority of the population, for they were deficient both technically and politically. To opt exclusively for the council form would be to introduce a system based on work place and occupation, that would exact particularist and corporatist tendencies. [. . .] In parliamentary elections to a national assembly, on the other hand, social interests were homogenized and great political parties came to the fore.[73]

Trotsky, the target of Kautsky's critique, advocates the same duality when he makes a plea for the interplay between class self-organization and political leadership of the revolutionary vanguard party.[74]

The main form of direct democracy of the "expressive" multitude in the twentieth century were so-called councils ("soviets")—(almost) everybody in the West loved them, including liberals such as Hannah Arendt who perceived in them the echo of the ancient Greek life of the *polis*. Throughout the epoch of "really-existing socialism," the secret hope of "democratic socialists" was the direct democracy of the "soviets," the local councils as the form of self-organization of the people; and it is deeply symptomatic how, with the decline of "really-existing socialism," this emancipatory shadow which haunted it all the time has also disappeared—is this not the ultimate confirmation of the fact that the conciliar model of "democratic socialism" was just a spectral double of "bureaucratic" "really-existing socialism," its inherent transgression with no substantial positive content of its own, that is, unable to serve as the permanent basic organizing principle of a society? What both "really-existing socialism" and conciliar democracy shared was the belief in the possibility of a self-transparent organization of society which would preclude political "alienation" (state apparatuses, institutionalized rules of political life, legal order, the police, and so on)—and is the basic experience of the end of "really-existing socialism" not precisely the rejection of this *shared* feature, the resigned "postmodern" acceptance of the fact that society is a complex network of "subsystems," which is why a certain level of "alienation" is constitutive of social life, so that a totally self-transparent society is a utopia with totalitarian potential?[75] No wonder, then, that the same holds for today's practices of "direct democracy," from the favelas to "postindustrial" digital culture (do the descriptions of the new "tribal" communities of computer-hackers not often evoke the logic of conciliar democracy?): they all have to rely on a state apparatus, that is, for structural reasons, they cannot take over the entire field.

Negri's motto "no governing without movements" should therefore be countered with "no movements without governing," without a state power sustaining the space for movements. Negri dismisses the representative-democratic system: "The parliamentary system of representation has gone bad—you can't do anything there. We need to invent new things."[76] However, insofar as "expressive" movements have to rely on a presupposed Ground, one can defend democracy (not the direct form, but precisely the representative form) as providing the necessary Ground for the movements' exercise of expressive freedom: its abstract-universal formal character (one person one vote and so on) is the only appropriate one for providing such a neutral ground.

It is the tension between representative democracy and the "movement's" direct expression that allows us to formulate the difference between an ordinary democratic political party and the "stronger" (upper-case) Party (as in Communist Party): an ordinary political party fully assumes the representative function, its entire legitimization is provided by elections, while the Party considers the formal procedure of democratic elections secondary as regards the real political dynamics of movements "expressing" their force. This, of course, does not mean that the Party looks for its legitimization in movements which are external to it; the Party rather perceives/posits itself as the movements' *Selbst-Aufhebung* (self-sublation): it does not negotiate with movements, it is a movement transubstantiated into the form of political universality, ready to assume full state power, and which, as such, *ne s'autorise que de lui-même*.

Where democracy is not enough is with regard to what Badiou called the constitutive excess of representation over the represented. At the level of the Law, state power only represents the interests and so on of its subjects, it serves them, it is responsible to them and is itself subjected to their control; however, at the level of the superego underside, the public message of responsibility and the rest is supplemented by the obscene message of unconditional exercise of Power: laws do not really bind me, I can do to you *whatever I want*, I can treat you as guilty if I decide so, I can destroy you if I say so . . . This obscene excess is a *necessary* constituent of the notion of sovereignty (whose signifier is the Master-Signifier) — the asymmetry is here structural, that is, the law can only sustain its authority if subjects hear in it the echo of the obscene unconditional self-assertion.

Democracy presupposes a minimum of alienation: those who exert power can only be held responsible to the people if there is a minimal distance of re-presentation between them and the people. In "totalitarianism," this distance is canceled, the Leader is supposed to directly present the will of the people — and the result is, of course, that the (empirical) people are even more radically alienated in their Leader: he directly *is* what they "really are," their true identity, their true wishes and interests, as opposed to their confused "empirical" wishes and interests. In contrast to the authoritarian power alienated from its subjects, the people, here the "empirical" people, are alienated *from themselves*.

This, of course, in no way implies a simple plea for democracy and rejection of "totalitarianism": there *is*, on the contrary, a moment of truth in "totalitarianism." Hegel had already pointed out how political representation does not mean that people already know in advance what they want and then charge their representatives with advocating their interests — they only know them "in themselves"; it is their representative who formulates their interests and goals for them, making them "for-themselves." The "totalitarian" logic thus makes explicit, posits "as such," a split which always-already cuts from within the represented "people."

One should not be afraid here to draw the radical conclusion concerning the figure of the leader: democracy as a rule cannot reach beyond pragmatic utilitarian inertia, it cannot suspend the logic of the "servicing of goods" (*"service des biens"*); consequently, in the same way that there is no self-analysis, since the analytic change can only occur through the transferential relationship onto the external figure of the analyst, a leader is necessary to trigger the enthusiasm for a Cause, to bring about the radical change in the subjective position of his followers, to "transubstantiate" their identity.[77]

What this means is that the ultimate question of power is not "is it democratically legitimized or not" but: *what is the specific character (the "social content") of the "totalitarian excess" that pertains to sovereign power as such, independently of its democratic or non-democratic character?* It is at this level that the concept of the "dictatorship of the proletariat" functions: in it, the "totalitarian excess" of power is on the side of the "part of no-part," not on the side of the hierarchical social order—to put it bluntly, ultimately, the people are in power in the full sovereign sense of the term, in other words, it is not only that their representatives temporarily occupy the empty place of power, but, much more radically, they "twist" the very space of state representation in their direction.

One could argue that Chavez and Morales are coming close to what could be the contemporary form of the "dictatorship of the proletariat": although interacting with many agents and movements, drawing on their support, their governments obviously have privileged links with the dispossessed of the favelas—Chavez is ultimately *their* president, *they* are the hegemonic force behind his rule, and although Chavez still respects the democratic electoral process, it is clear that his fundamental commitment and source of legitimization is not there, but in the privileged relationship with the poor. This is the "dictatorship of the proletariat" in the form of democracy.[78]

A convincing story can be told about the hypocrisy of the Western Left which to a large extent ignores the striking "liberal renaissance" that is going on in Iran's civil society: since the Western intellectual references of this "renaissance" are figures such as Habermas, Arendt, and Rorty— even Giddens—not the usual gang of anti-imperialist "radicals," the Left makes no fuss when leading figures of this movement lose their jobs and are arrested, and so on. With their advocacy of the "boring" topics of the division of powers, of democratic legitimization, of the legal defense of human rights, and so forth, they are viewed with suspicion—they do not appear as sufficiently "anti-imperalist" and anti-American.[79] However, one should nonetheless raise the more fundamental question: is bringing Western liberal democracy the real solution for getting rid of the religious-fundamentalist regimes, or are these regimes rather a *symptom* of liberal democracy itself? What to do in cases like those of Algeria or the Palestinian territories, where a "free" democratic election brings "fundamentalists" to power?

When Rosa Luxemburg wrote that "dictatorship consists in the *way in which* democracy is *used* and not in its *abolition*," her point was not that democracy is an empty framework which can be used by different political agents (Hitler also came to power through—more or less—free democratic elections), but that there is a "class bias" inscribed into this very empty (procedural) frame. This is why, when radical leftists come to power through elections, their *signe de reconnaissance* is that they move to "change the rules," to transform not only the electoral and other state mechanisms, but also the entire logic of the political space (relying directly on the power of mobilized movements; imposing different forms of local self-organization and so on), in short, to guarantee the hegemony of their base, they are in order guided by a correct intuition regarding the "class bias" of the democratic form.

8 Alain Badiou
Or, the Violence of Subtraction

Materialism, democratic and dialectical

In his *Logiques des mondes*, Badiou provides a succinct definition of "democratic materialism" and its opposite, "materialist dialectics": the axiom which condenses the first is *"There is nothing but bodies and languages . . ."* to which materialist dialectics adds *". . . with the exception of truths."*[1] This opposition is not so much the opposition of two ideologies or philosophies as the opposition between non-reflected presuppositions/ beliefs into which we are "thrown" insofar as we are immersed into our life-world, and the reflexive attitude of thought proper which enables us to subtract ourselves from this immersion—to "unplug" ourselves, as Morpheus would have put it in *The Matrix*, a film much appreciated by Badiou, in which one also finds a precise account of the need, evoked by Badiou, to control oneself (when Morpheus explains to Neo the lot of ordinary people totally caught in ["plugged into"] the Matrix, he says: "Everyone who is not unplugged is a potential agent."). This is why Badiou's axiom of "democratic materialism" is his answer to the question of our spontaneous (non-reflexive) ideological beliefs: "What do I think when I am outside my own control? Or, rather, "what is our (my) spontaneous belief?" Furthermore, this opposition is immediately linked to what one (once) called the "class struggle in philosophy," the orientation most identified by the names of Lenin, Mao Zedong, and Althusser—let us recall Mao's succinct formulation: "It is only when there is class struggle that there can be philosophy." The ruling class (whose ideas are those of the ruling ideas) is represented by spontaneous ideology, while the dominated class has to fight its way through intense conceptual work, which is why, for Badiou, the key reference is here Plato—not the caricatural Plato, the anti-democratic philosopher of aristocratic reaction against Athenian democracy, but the Plato who was the first to clearly assert the field of rationality freed from inherited beliefs. After all the negative judgments of the "phono-logocentric" character of Plato's criticism of writing, it is perhaps time to assert its positive, egalitarian-democratic, aspect: in the pre-democratic despotic state, writing was the monopoly of the ruling elite, its character was sacred, "so it is written" was the ultimate seal of authority, the pre-supposed mysterious meaning of the written text was the object of belief *par excellence*. The aim of Plato's critique of writing was thus double: to deprive writing of its sacred character, and to assert the field of rationality freed from beliefs, in other words, to distinguish *logos* (the domain of dialectics, of rational reasoning which admits no external authority) from *mythos* (traditional beliefs):

> The significance of Plato's criticism thus appears: *to remove from writing its sacred character*. The way to truth is not writing but dialectics, i.e. the spoken word with its implication of two or rather three parties: the speaker, the listener and the language they share. With his criticism, Plato, for the first time in man's history, distilled the notion of rationality as such, free from all mixture with belief.[2]

The further paradox here is that the notion of the pure self-present Voice represented/copied by writing, this ultimate support of the "metaphysics of presence" that is the object of Derrida's deconstruction, is itself a product of writing: when philosophers were attacking the Platonic primacy of speech over writing

> they were criticizing a by-product of phonetic writing. It is scarcely possible to imagine a philosophy such as Platonism emerging in an oral culture. It is equally difficult to imagine it in Sumeria. How could a world of bodiless Forms be represented in pictograms? How could abstract entities be represented as the ultimate realities in a mode of writing that still recalled the realm of the senses?[3]

The point is not just that speech is always-already affected/constituted by writing, and so on, but that speech becomes the metaphysical Word, the ethereal/pure medium of self-affection, of spiritual self-presence, through "abstract" phonetic writing: prior to phonetic writing, speech is perceived as a practice which is part of a complex material life-world — it is phonetic writing that "purifies" it. (The qualification I am tempted to add here is that, perhaps, one should nonetheless suspend Badiou's understandable reticence apropos "dialectical materialism" and invert the subject–predicate relationship between the two opposites: "materialist democracy" versus "dialectical materialism.") There is a more constrained anthropological version of this axiom: for democratic materialism, "*there is nothing but individuals and communities*," to which materialist dialectics adds: "*Insofar as there is a truth, a subject subtracts itself from all community and destroys all individuation.*"[4]

The passage from the Two to the Three is crucial here, and one should bear in mind all of its Platonic, properly meta-physical, thrust in the direction of what, *prima facie*, cannot but appear as a proto-idealist gesture of asserting that material reality is not all that there is, that there is also another level of incorporeal truths. Along these lines, one is tempted to supplement Badiou in two ways. First, are not bodies and languages synonymous with being, its multiplicity, and worlds? The Three we are dealing with is thus the Three of being, worlds, and truths: for democratic materialism, there is only the multiplicity of being (endlessly differentiated reality) and different worlds—linguistic universes—within which individuals and communities experience this reality.[5] Is this not indeed our spontaneous ideology? There is an endlessly differentiated, complex reality, which we, the individuals and communities embedded in it, always experience from a particular, finite perspective of our historical world. What democratic materialism furiously rejects is the notion that there can be an infinite universal Truth which cuts across this multitude of worlds—in politics, this means "totalitarianism" which imposes its truth as universal. This is why one should reject, say, the Jacobins, who imposed their universal notions of equality and other truths on the plurality of French society, and thus necessarily ended in terror . . .

This brings us to the second supplement: there is an even more narrow political version of the democratic-materialist axiom: "All that takes place in today's society is the dynamics of postmodern globalization, and the (conservative-nostalgic, fundamentalist, old leftist, nationalist, religious . . .) reactions and resistances to it"—to which, of course, materialist dialectics adds its proviso: ". . . with the exception of the radical-emancipatory (communist) politics of truth."

It is here that the materialist-dialectic passage from the Two to the Three gains all its weight: the axiom of communist politics is not simply the dualist "class struggle," but, more precisely, the Third moment as the subtraction from the Two of hegemonic politics. That is to say, the hegemonic ideological field imposes on us a field of (ideological) visibility with its own "principal contradiction" (today, it is the opposition of market-freedom-democracy and fundamentalist-terrorist-totalitarian-ism—"Islamo-fascism" and so on), and the first thing we must do is to reject (to subtract ourselves from) this opposition, to perceive it as a false opposition destined to obfuscate the true line of division. Lacan's formula for this redoubling is 1+1+a: the "official" antagonism (the Two) is always supplemented by an "indivisible remainder" which indicates its foreclosed dimension. In other terms, the *true* antagonism is always reflexive, it is the antagonism between the "official" antagonism and that which is foreclosed by it (this is why, in Lacan's mathematics, 1+1 = 3). Today, for example, the true antagonism is not between liberal multiculturalism and fundamentalism, but between the very field of their opposition and the excluded Third (radical emancipatory politics).

One is even tempted to link this threesome to three different mechanisms of keeping a social body together:

1. the traditional matrix of authority in which a community is established through sacrifice or is grounded in some primordial crime, so that it is guilt which keeps the members together and subordinates them to a leader;
2. the "invisible hand" of the market, namely, a social field in which, by means of the Cunning of Reason, the very competition among individuals, each following his or her egotistic concerns, results in a mysterious equilibrium which works for the good of all;
3. the open political process of social cooperation in which decisions are neither made by the supreme authority, nor are they the outcome of a blind mechanism, but are reached through the conscious interaction of individuals.

And, furthermore, do these three modes not form a kind of Lévi-Straussian triangle? Both market liberalism and the properly democratic space of civil public action and planned social cooperation are modes of societal self-organization, as opposed to externally imposed authority. How do these three modes relate to the three sources of social authority: the authoritarian, the technocratic, the democratic? Technocratic authority relies on qualification (those who know should exert authority) versus both authoritarian and democratic forms of authority, which lack qualifications (a king rules because he was born a king, not because of his qualities; in democracy, everyone has the right to a share of power, independently of what he or she is or is not able to do). On the other hand, both authoritarian and expert forms of authority are selective (only those who are qualified to rule—by their position or expertise—should rule), versus democracy in which everyone should rule. And, lastly, both democracy and technocratic rule are in some sense egalitarian,[6] in contrast to traditional authority where the whole point is that it is important *who* is claiming what. The two triads obviously do not directly overlap, which is why one can argue that the triangle should be extended into a Greimasian semiotic square, since the third mode is itself split between democratic self-organization proper and state power imposed from above onto society—"self-management versus bureaucracy." The two axes of the semiotic square are thus central authority (traditional authority; state power) versus self-organization from below (the market, self-management), and external organization (symbolic authority, the market) versus democratic organization (modern state power, self-management.)

This allows us also to approach in a new way Badiou's concept of the "point" as the point of decision, as the moment at which the complexity of a situation is "filtered" through a binary disposition and thus reduced to a simple choice: all things considered, are we *against* or *for* (should we attack or retreat? support that proclamation or oppose it? And so on). With regard to the Third moment as the subtraction from the Two of hegemonic politics, one should always bear in mind that one of the basic operations of hegemonic ideology is to *enforce a false point*, to impose on us a false choice—as when, in the "War on Terror," anyone who draws attention to the complexity and ambiguity of the situation, is sooner or later interrupted by a brutal voice telling him: "OK, enough of this muddle—we are in the middle of a difficult struggle in which the fate of our free world is at stake, so please, make it clear where you really stand: do you support freedom and democracy or not?"[7] The obverse of this imposition of a false choice is, of course, the blurring of the true line of division—here, Nazism is still unsurpassed with its designation of the Jewish enemy as the agent of the "plutocratic-Bolshevik plot." In this designation, the mechanism is almost laid bare: the true opposition ("plutocrats" versus "Bolsheviks," that is, capitalists versus proletarians) is literally obliterated, blurred into One, and therein resides the function of the name "Jew"—to serve as the operator of this obliteration.

The first task of emancipatory politics is therefore to distinguish between "false" and "true" points, "false" and "true" choices, that is, to bring back the third element whose obliteration sustains the false choice—as, today, the false choice between "liberal democracy or Islamo-fascism" is sustained by the occlusion of radical-secular emancipatory politics. So one should be clear here in rejecting the dangerous motto "the enemy of my enemy is my friend," which leads some to discover a "progressive" anti-imperialist potential in fundamentalist Islamist movements. The ideological universe of movements such as Hezbollah is based on the blurring of distinctions between capitalist neo-imperialism and secular progressive emancipation: within the ideological space of Hezbollah, women's emancipation, gay rights, and so on, are *nothing but* the "decadent" moral aspect of Western imperialism . . .

This, then, is where we stand today: the antagonism imposed on us by the space of the dominant ideology is the secondary antagonism between (what Badiou calls) "reactive" and "obscure" subjects, leading their struggle against the background of the obliterated Event. What other responses to an Event are possible? Instead of withdrawing from political engagement, one should remember the motto that, behind every fascism, there is a failed revolution—this motto is worth remembering especially today, when we face what some call "Islamo-fascism." Again, the opposition of liberal democracy and religious fundamentalism is misleading: a third term is missing.

Responses to the Event

In one of the early novels about Hannibal Lecter, the claim that Hannibal's monstrosity is the result of unfortunate circumstances is rejected: "Nothing happened *to* him. *He* happened." This is the most concise formula of the Event in Badiou's sense, an emergence of the New which cannot be reduced to its causes or conditions. Or, to quote the wise old saying with which one of the Gothic DVD games starts: "Each Event is preceded by Prophecy. But without the Hero, there is no Event." One can easily translate this obscure wisdom into Marxist terms: "The general outlines of each revolutionary event can be foretold by social theorists; however, this event can only really take place if there is a revolutionary subject." Or, as Badiou might put it: "Only if there is a subject, can an Event occur within an evental site." Which is why, for Badiou, the different modes of subjectivity are simultaneously the modalities by which the subject relates to the Event—echoing Kant's thesis that the conditions of our experience of the object are simultaneously the conditions of the object itself. Badiou elaborates four such responses: the faithful subject; the reactive subject; the obscure subject; resurrection. Perhaps, this list should be complicated a little bit, so that there are actually six responses:

The responses to the Freud-Event were: (1) fidelity (Lacan); (2) reactive normalization, reintegration into the predominant field (ego psychology, "dynamic psychotherapy"); (3) outright denial (cognitivism); (4) obscurantist mystification in a pseudo-Event (Jung); (5) total enforcement (Reich, Freudo-Marxism); (6) resurrection of the message of the "eternal" Freud in various "returns to Freud."

The responses to a love-Event are: (1) fidelity; (2) normalization, reintegration (marriage); (3) outright rejection of the evental status (libertinage, the transformation of the Event into sexual adventure); (4) thoroughgoing rejection of sexual love (abstinence); (5) obscurantist suicidal mortal passion à la Tristan; (6) resurrected love (reencounter).

The responses to the Marxism-Event are: (1) fidelity (Communism, "Leninism"); (2) reactive reintegration (social democracy); (3) outright denial of the evental status (liberalism, Furet); (4) catastrophic total counterattack in the guise of a pseudo-Event (fascism); (5) total enforcement of the Event, which ends up in an "obscure disaster" (Stalinism, Khmer Rouge); (6) renewal of Marxism (Lenin, Mao . . .).

So how do (1) and (6) coexist (in figures such as Lenin or Lacan)? This brings us to a further hypothesis: an Event is necessarily missed the first time, so that true fidelity is only possible in the form of resurrection, as a defense against "revisionism": Freud did not recognize the true dimension of his discovery, it was only Lacan's "return to Freud" that allowed us to discern the core of the Freudian discovery; or, as Stanley Cavell put it apropos the Hollywood comedies of remarriage, the only true marriage is the second marriage (to the same person). This point was recently reiterated by Jacques-Alain Miller:

> One might believe that there is no heresy without orthodoxy, but one often observes that it is when discourses which will later be heretical emerge that the future orthodoxies come about, and that it is rather through an after-the-fact effect that orthodoxy takes hold.[8]

The point is not just that orthodoxy is the triumphant heresy, the one which succeeded in crushing all others, but a more complex one. When a new teaching, from Christianity to Marxism or psychoanalysis, emerges, there is first confusion, blindness about the true scope of its own act; heresies are the attempts to clarify this confusion by retranslating the new teaching into the old coordinates, and it is only against this background that the core of the new teaching can be formulated.

It is against this background of multiple responses to an Event that Adrian Johnston[9] recently discerned the ideologico-critical potential of the Badiouian topic of evental breaks: when the balance of an ideological situation is disturbed by the emergence of "symptomal knots," elements which, while formally part of the situation, do not fit into it, the ideological defense mechanism can adopt two main strategies—false "eventalization" of the dynamics which remains thoroughly integrated into the existing situation, or disavowal of the signs which delineate true evental possibilities, their reading as minor accidents or external disturbances:

> one, making mere modifications appear to promise evental newness (a tactic that comes to the fore in the ideology of late-capitalism, whose noisily marketed "perpetual revolution" is really just an instance of the cliché "the more things change, the more they stay the same"—or, as Badiou puts it, "capitalism itself is the obsession of novelty and the perpetual renovation of forms"); two, making the sites sheltering potentially explosive evental upheavals appear to be, at a minimum, unremarkable features of the banal, everyday landscape, and, at most, nothing more than temporary, correctable glitches in the functioning of the established system.

Perhaps, this line of thought needs just one qualification: Johnston writes that

> the ideology of the worldly state, through a sort of bluff or masquerade, disguises its non-integrated weakest points, its Achilles' heels, as fully integrated cogs and components of its allegedly harmonious functioning—rather than as loci containing the potential to throw monkey wrenches in its gears and thereby generate evental dysfunctions of this regime, a regime that is never so deeply entrenched as it would like to appear to be in the eyes of its subjects.

Is it not rather that one of the ideological strategies is to fully admit the threatening character of a dysfunction, and to treat it as an external intrusion, not as the necessary result of the system's inner dynamic? The model is here, of course, the fascist notion of social antagonisms as the result of a foreign intruder — Jews — disturbing the organic totality of the social edifice.

Recall the difference between the standard capitalist and the Marxist notion of economic crisis: for the standard capitalist view, crises are "temporary, correctable glitches" in the functioning of the system, while from the Marxist perspective, they are its moment of truth, the "exception" which only allows us to grasp the functioning of the system (in the same way that, for Freud, dreams and symptoms are not secondary malfunctionings of our psychic apparatus, but moments through which one can discern the repressed basic functioning of the psychic apparatus). No wonder that Johnston uses here the Deleuzian term "minimal difference" — "a minimal/minuscule difference (here construed as the difference between the change-category statuses simultaneously assigned to a single intra-situational multiple both by the ideology of the state and, in opposition, by another, non-statist framework)": when we pass from the notion of crisis as occasional contingent malfunctioning of the system to the notion of crisis as the symptomal point at which the "truth" of the system becomes visible, we are talking about one and the same actual event — the difference is purely virtual, it does not concern any of its actual properties, but only the way this event is supplemented by the virtual tapestry of its ideological and notional background (like Schumann's melody for piano first played with and then without the third line of notes written only for the eyes). Johnston is right here in critically noting

> Badiou's quick dismissal of apparently gradualist measures of seemingly minor political adjustments and reforms (i.e., not-quite-evental gestures) in the spheres of legislation and socio-economics while awaiting the quasi-divine intervention of the system-shattering evental rupture ushering in an uncompromisingly "perfect" revolution. But, the preceding analyses call into question whether he can be entirely confident and sure that what appears to be gradual or minor really is so, or, rather, simply seems this way solely under the shadow of statist ideology's assignation of change-category statuses.

One cannot ever be sure in advance if what appears (within the register and the space of visibility of the ruling ideology) as "minor" measures will not set in motion a process that will lead to the radical (evental) transformation of the whole field. There are situations in which a minimal measure of social reform can have much stronger large-scale consequences than self-professed "radical" changes, and this "inherent incalculability to the factors involved in setting the pace of the cadence of socio-political change" points towards the dimension of what Badiou tried to capture under the title of the "materialist notion of grace." Johnston raises the following question: what if the pre-evental actors

> don't really know exactly what they're doing or quite where they're going? What if, under the influence of statist ideology, they anticipate that a particular gesture will effectuate a system-preserving modification only to find out, after-the-fact of this gesture, that their intervention unexpectedly hastened (rather than delayed) the demise of this very system?

Is not the first association that comes to mind here that of Mikhail Gorbachev's perestroika which, while aiming at minor improvements that would make the system more efficient, triggered the process of its total disintegration? These, then, are the two extremes between which political interventions have to find their way: the Scylla of "minor" reforms which eventually lead to total collapse (recall also the fear — justified, we can say today — of Mao Zedong that even a minimal compromise with market economy would open up the path that ends in total surrender to capitalism), and the Charybdis of "radical" changes which in the long run merely fortify the system (Roosevelt's New Deal, and so forth).

Among other things, this also opens up the question of how "radical" different forms of resistance are: what may appear as a "radical critical stance" or as subversive activity can in fact function as the system's "inherent transgression," so that, often, a minor legal reform which merely aims at bringing the system in accordance with its professed ideological goals can be more subversive than open questioning of the system's basic presuppositions. These considerations enable us to define the art of a "politics of minimal differences": to be able to identify and then focus on a minimal (ideological, legislative, and so on) measure which, *prima facie*, not only does not question the system's premises, but even seems to merely apply its own principles to its actual functioning and thus render it more consistent with itself; however, a critico-ideological "parallax view" leads us to surmise that this minimal measure, while in no way disturbing the system's explicit mode of functioning, effectively "moves underground," introduces a crack in its foundations. Today, more than ever, we effectively need what Johnston calls a "pre-evental discipline of time":

> This other sort of temporal discipline would be neither the undisciplined impatience of hurriedly doing anything and everything to enact some ill-defined, poorly conceived notion of making things different nor the quietist patience of either resigning oneself to the current state of affairs drifting along interminably and/or awaiting the unpredictable arrival of a not-to-be-actively-precipitated "x" sparking genuine change (Badiou's philosophy sometimes seems to be in danger of licensing a version of this latter mode of quietism). Those subjected to today's frenetic socio-economic forms of late-capitalism are constantly at risk of succumbing to various forms of what one could refer to loosely as "attention deficit disorder," that is, a frantic, thoughtless jumping from present to ever-new present. At the political level, such capitalist impatience must be countered with the discipline of what could be designated as a specifically communist patience (designated thus in line with Badiou's assertion that all authentic forms of politics are "communist" in the broad sense of being both emancipatory as well as "generic" *qua* radically egalitarian and non-identitarian)—not the quietist patience condemned above, but, instead, the calm contemplation of the details of situations, states, and worlds with an eye to the discerning of ideologically veiled weak points in the structural architecture of the statist system. Given the theoretical validity of assuming that these camouflaged Achilles' heels (as hidden evental sites) can and do exist in one's worldly context, one should be patiently hopeful that one's apparently minor gestures, carried out under the guidance of a pre-evental surveillance of the situation in search of its concealed kernels of real transformation, might come to entail major repercussions for the state-of-the-situation and/or transcendental regime of the world.

There is, however, a limit to this strategy: if followed thoroughly, it ends up in a kind of "active quietism": while forever postponing the Big Act, all one does is to engage in small interventions with the secret hope that somehow, inexplicably, by means of a magic "leap from quantity to quality," they will lead to global radical change. This strategy has to be supplemented by the readiness and ability to discern the moment when the possibility of the Big Change is approaching, and, at that point, to quickly alter the strategy, take the risk and engage in total struggle. In other words, one should not forget that, in politics, "major repercussions" do not come by themselves: true, one has to lay the groundwork for them by means of patient work, but one should also know to seize the moment when it arrives.

The "specifically communist form of patience" is not just patient waiting for the moment when radical change will explode in a manner reminiscent of what systems theory calls an "emergent property"; it is also the patience of losing the battles in order to win the final fight (recall again Mao's slogan: "from defeat to defeat, to the final victory"). Or, to put it in more Badiouian terms: the fact that the evental irruption functions as a break in time, introducing a totally different order of temporality (the temporality of the "work of love," fidelity to the event), means that, from the perspective of non-evental time of historical evolution, there is *never* a "right moment" for the revolutionary event, the situation is never "mature enough" for a revolutionary act—the act is always, by definition, "premature." Recall what truly deserves the title of the *repetition* of the French Revolution: the Haitian Revolution led by Toussaint L'Ouverture—it was clearly "ahead of its time," "premature," and as such doomed to fail, yet, precisely as such, it was perhaps even more of an Event than the French Revolution itself. These past defeats accumulate the utopian energy which will explode in the final battle: "maturation" is not waiting for "objective" circumstances to reach maturity, but the accumulation of defeats.

Progressive liberals today often complain that they would like to join a "revolution" (a more radical emancipatory political movement), but no matter how desperately they search for it, they just "do not see it" (they do not see anywhere in the social space a political agent with the will and strength to seriously engage in such activity). While there is a moment of truth here, one should nonetheless also add that the very attitude of these liberals is in itself part of the problem: if one just waits to "see" a revolutionary movement, it will, of course, never arise, and one will never see it. What Hegel says about the curtain that separates appearances from true reality (behind the veil of appearance there is nothing, only what the subject who is searching has put there), holds also for a revolutionary process: "seeing" and "desire" are here inextricably linked, in other words, revolutionary potential is not there to be discovered as an objective social fact, one "sees it" only insofar as one "desires" it (engages oneself in the movement). No wonder the Mensheviks and those who opposed Lenin's call for a revolutionary takeover in the summer of 1917 "did not see" the conditions for it as "ripe" and opposed it as "premature"—they simply did not *want* the revolution. Another version of this skeptical argument about "seeing" is that liberals claim that capitalism is today so global and all-encompassing that they cannot "see" any serious alternative to it, that they cannot imagine a feasible "outside" to it. The reply to this is that, insofar as this is true, they do not see *tout court*: the task is not to see the outside, but to see in the first place (to grasp the nature of contemporary capitalism)—the Marxist wager is that, when we "see" this, we see enough, including how to go beyond it . . . So our reply to the worried progressive liberals, eager to join the revolution, and just not seeing it having a chance anywhere, should be like the answer to the proverbial ecologist worried about the prospect of catastrophe: do not worry, the catastrophe will arrive . . .

To complicate the image further, we often have an Event which succeeds through the self-erasure of its evental dimension, as was the case with the Jacobins in the French Revolution: once their (necessary) job was done, they were not only overthrown and liquidated, they were even retroactively deprived of their evental status, reduced to a historical accident, to a freakish abomination, to an (avoidable) excess of historical development.[10] This theme was often evoked by Marx and Engels—how, once "normal" pragmatic-utilitarian bourgeois daily life was consolidated, its own violent heroic origins were disavowed. This possibility—not only the (obvious) possibility of an evental sequence reaching its end, but a much more unsettling possibility of an Event disavowing itself, erasing its own traces, as the ultimate indication of its triumph, is not taken into account by Badiou:

> the possibility and ramifications of there being radical breaks and discontinuities that might, in part due to their own reverberations unfolding off into the future, become invisible to those living in realities founded on such eclipsed points of origin.

Such a self-erasure of the Event opens up the space for what, in the Benjaminian mode, one is tempted to call the leftist politics of melancholy. In a first approach, this term cannot but appear as an oxymoron: is not a revolutionary orientation towards the future the very opposite of melancholic attachment to the past? What if, however, the future one should be faithful to is *the future of the past itself*, in other words, the emancipatory potential that was not realized due to the failure of the past attempts and that for this reason continues to haunt us? In his ironic comments on the French Revolution, Marx opposes the revolutionary enthusiasm to the sobering effect of the "morning after": the actual result of the sublime revolutionary explosion, of the Event of freedom, equality, and brotherhood, is the miserable utilitarian/egotistic universe of market calculation. (And, incidentally, is not this gap even wider in the case of the October Revolution?) However, one should not simplify Marx: his point is not the rather commonsensical insight into how the vulgar reality of commerce is the "truth" of the theater of revolutionary enthusiasm, "what it all really came down to." In the revolutionary explosion as an Event, another utopian dimension shines through, the dimension of universal emancipation which, precisely, is the excess betrayed by the market reality which takes over "the day after"—as such, this excess is not simply abolished, dismissed as irrelevant, but, as it were, *transposed into a virtual state*, continuing to haunt the emancipatory imaginary like a dream waiting to be realized. The excess of revolutionary enthusiasm over its own "actual social base" or substance is thus literally that of the future of/in the past, a spectral Event waiting for its proper embodiment.

Most of the Romantic liberal enthusiasts who first welcomed the French Revolution were appalled by the Terror, the "monstrosity" unleashed by the revolution, and started to doubt its very rationale. The notable exception here is Shelley who remained faithful to the revolution to the end, without idealizing it, without brushing terror under the carpet; in his poem *The Revolt of Islam*, he formulated a rejection of the reactionary claim that the tragic and violent outcome was in some way the "truth" of the bright revolutionary hopes and ideals of universal freedom. For Shelley, history is a series of possible outcomes, possibility has priority over actuality, there is a surplus in it beyond its actualization, the spark that persists underground, so that the very immediate failure of emancipatory attempts signals to those who harbor future revolutionary aspirations that they should be repeated *more* radically, *more* comprehensively.

Perhaps the reason Badiou neglects this dimension is his all too crude opposition between repetition and the cut of the Event, his dismissal of repetition as an obstacle to the rise of the New, ultimately as the death drive itself, the morbid attachment to some obscure *jouissance* which entraps the subject in the self-destructive vicious circle. In this sense, "life" as the subjective category of fidelity to an Event "keeps at a distance the conservation drive (the misnamed 'life instinct'), as well as the mortifying drive (the death instinct). Life is what breaks with the drives."[11] What Badiou misses here is the fact that the "death drive" is, paradoxically, the Freudian name for its very opposite, for the way immortality appears within psychoanalysis: for an uncanny excess of life, for an "undead" urge which persists beyond the (biological) cycle of life and death, of generation and corruption. As such, the death drive stands for the very antipode of the obscure tendency to self-annihilation or self-destruction — as is rendered clearly in the work of Wagner whom Badiou admires so much. It is precisely the reference to Wagner which enables us to see how the Freudian death drive has nothing whatsoever to do with the craving for self-extermination, for a return to the inorganic absence of any life-tension. The death drive does *not* reside in Wagner's heroes' longing to die, to find peace in death: it is, on the contrary, the very obverse of dying — a name for the "undead" eternal life itself, for the horrible fate of being caught in the endless repetitive cycle of wandering around in guilt and pain. The final passing-away of the Wagnerian hero (the death of the Dutchman, Wotan, Tristan, Amfortas) is therefore the moment of their liberation from the clutches of the death drive. Tristan in Act III is not desperate because of his fear of dying: what makes him desperate is that, without Isolde, he cannot die and is condemned to eternal longing — he anxiously awaits her arrival so as to be able to die. The prospect he dreads is not that of dying without Isolde (the standard complaint of a lover), but rather that of endless life without her.

The ultimate lesson of psychoanalysis is that human life is never "just life": humans are not simply alive, they are possessed by the strange drive to enjoy life to excess, passionately attached to a surplus which sticks out and derails the ordinary run of things. This excess inscribes itself into the human body in the guise of a wound which makes the subject "undead," depriving him of the capacity to die (apart from Tristan's and Amfortas's wound, there is, of course, *the* wound, the one from Kafka's "A Country Doctor"): when this wound is healed, the hero can die in peace. This notion of the drive embodied in an organ also allows us to propose a correction to Badiou's notion of the body of a truth procedure: there are no bodies of truth, truth has its organs (without bodies), in other words, a truth inscribes itself into a body through its autonomized organ(s). The child's wound in the lower chest in Kafka's "Country Doctor" is such an organ, part of the body yet sticking out of it, leading an immortal (undead) life of its own, secreting blood all the time yet, for that very reason, preventing the child from finding peace in death.

It is at this point that one should turn to Deleuze against Badiou, to Deleuze's precise elaborations on repetition as the very form of the emergence of the New. Of course, Badiou is too refined a thinker not to perceive the evental dimension of repetition: when, in *Logiques des mondes*, he deploys the three "subjective destinations" of an event (faithful, reactive, obscure), he adds a fourth, that of "resurrection," the subjective reactivation of an event whose traces were obliterated, "repressed" into the historico-ideological unconscious: "every faithful subject can thus reincorporate into its evental present a truth fragment which in the old present was pushed beneath the bar of occultation. This reincorporation is what we call resurrection."[12] His beautifully developed example is that of Spartacus: erased from official history, his name was resurrected first by the black slaves' rebellion in Haiti (the progressive governor Laveaux called Toussaint L'Ouverture "black Spartacus"), and, a century later, by the two German "Spartakists," Rosa Luxemburg and Karl Liebknecht. What matters here, however, is that Badiou shirks from calling this resurrection *repetition* . . .

Do we need a new world?

Badiou's ambiguity with regard to this crucial point hinges on his triad Being–World–Event, which functions in the same way as Kierkegaard's triad of the Aesthetic–Ethical–Religious: the choice is always between two terms, an either/or, that is, the three terms do not operate at the same ontological level. It is the same with Lacan's Imaginary (I)/Symbolic (S)/Real (R) or with Freud's Ego/Superego/Id: when we focus on one term, the other two get condensed into one (under the hegemony of one of them). If we focus on the Imaginary, the Real and the Symbolic get contracted into the Imaginary's opposite under the domination of the Symbolic; if we focus on R, I and S are contracted under the domination of S. (Therein resides the shift in Lacan's work announced by his *Seminar VII* on the ethics of psychoanalysis: the shift from the axis I–S to the axis S–R.) Or, in Freud's case, if we focus on the Ego, its opposite is the Id (which encompasses the superego); and so on and so forth.[13]

Logiques des mondes enacts the shift is from the axis Being–Event to the axis World–Event. What this means is that Being, World, and Event do not form a triad: we have either the opposition of Being and World (appearance), or the opposition of World and Event. There is an unexpected conclusion to be drawn from this: insofar as (Badiou emphasizes this point again and again) a true Event is not merely a negative gesture, but opens up a positive dimension of the New, an Event *is* the imposition of a new world, of a new Master-Signifier (a new Naming, as Badiou puts it, or, what Lacan called "*vers un nouveau signifiant*"). The true evental change is the passage from the old to the new world.

One should even go a step further and introduce the dimension of dialectics here: an Event *can* be accounted for by the tension between the multiplicity of Being and the World, its site is the symptomal torsion of a World, it is generated by the excess of Being over World (of presence over re-presentation). The properly Hegelian enigma is here not "how is an Event, the rise of something truly New, possible?", but, rather, how do we pass from Being to World, to (finite) appearance, that is, how can Being, its flat infinite multiplicity, *appear* (to itself)? Is it not that this presupposes a kind of "negativity" that has to be somehow operative in the midst of Being itself, some force of (not infinity, but, on the contrary) finitization, what Hegel called the "absolute power" of tearing apart what in reality belongs together, of giving autonomy to appearance. Prior to any "synthesis," Spirit is what Kant called "transcendental imagination," the power to abstract, to simplify/mortify, to reduce a thing to its "unary feature" (*le train unaire*; *der einzige Zug*), to erase its empirical richness. Spirit is the power to say, when it is confronted with the confusing wealth of empirical features: "All this doesn't really matter! Just tell me if the feature *X* is there or not!" And, insofar as world as such is sustained by a "point," by such a violent imposition of a "unary feature," is a point-less, atonal world not a name for worldlessness? Badiou himself recently claimed that our time is *devoid of worldliness*, referring to Marx's well-known passage from the *Communist Manifesto* about the "deterritorializing" force of capitalism which dissolves all fixed social forms:

> The passage where Marx speaks of the desacralization of all sacred bonds in the icy waters of capitalism has an enthusiastic tone; it is Marx's enthusiasm for the dissolving power of Capital. The fact that Capital revealed itself to be the material power capable of disencumbering us of the "superego" figures of the One and the sacred bonds that accompany it effectively represents its positively progressive character, and it is something that continues to unfold to the present

397

day. Having said that, the generalized atomism, the recurrent individualism and, finally, the abasement of thought into mere practices of administration, of the government of things or of technical manipulation, could never satisfy me as a philosopher. I simply think that it is in the very element of desacralization that we must reconnect to the vocation of thinking.[14]

Badiou thus recognizes the exceptional *ontological* status of capitalism whose dynamic undermines every stable framework of representation: the task that should normally be performed by critico-political activity (namely, the task of undermining the representational frame of the state), is already performed by capitalism itself—and, this poses a problem for Badiou's notion of "evental" politics. In pre-capitalist formations, every state, every representational totalization, implies a foundational exclusion, a point of "symptomal torsion," a "part of no-part," an element which, although part of the system, does not have a proper place within it—and emancipatory politics has to intervene from this excessive ("supernumerary") element which, although part of the situation, cannot be *accounted for* in terms of the situation. However, what happens when the system no longer excludes the excess, but directly posits it as its driving force—as is the case in capitalism which can only reproduce itself through its constant self-revolutionizing, through the constant overcoming of its own limits? To put it in a simplified way: if a political event, a revolutionary emancipatory intervention into a determinate historical world, is always linked to the excessive point of its "symptomal torsion," if it by definition undermines the contours of this world, how, then, are we to define the emancipatory political intervention into a universe which is already in itself world-less, which, for its reproduction, no longer needs to be contained by the constraints of a "world"? As Alberto Toscano noted in his perspicuous analysis, Badiou gets caught here in an inconsistency: he draws the "logical" conclusion that, in a "worldless" universe (which is the contemporary universe of global capitalism), the aim of emancipatory politics should be the precise opposite of its "traditional" *modus operandi*—the task today is to form a new world, to propose new Master-Signifiers that would provide "cognitive mapping":

[. . .] whilst in Badiou's theoretical writings on the appearance of worlds he cogently argues that events engender the *dysfunction* of worlds and their transcendental regimes, in his "ontology of the present" Badiou advocates the necessity, in our "intervallic" or world-less times, of *constructing* a world, such that those now excluded can come to invent new names, names capable of sustaining new truth procedures. As he writes, "I hold that we are at a very special moment, a moment *at which there is not any world*" [. . .] As a result: "Philosophy has no other legitimate aim except to help find the new names that will bring into existence the unknown world that is only waiting for us because we are waiting for it." In a peculiar inversion of some of the key traits of his doctrine, it seems that Badiou is here advocating, to some extent, an "ordering" task, one that will inevitably, if perhaps mistakenly, resonate for some with the now ubiquitous slogan "Another World is Possible".[15]

This inconsistency brings us back to the topic of "determinate negation": the "ordering" task of building a new world is a kind of "return of the repressed," not only the repressed of Badiou's theory, but also the repressed of the political event itself which serves Badiou as the main contemporary point of reference, and which, as we have seen, failed precisely in this task of "ordering," the Maoist Cultural Revolution.

The lessons of the Cultural Revolution

What, then, for Badiou is the historical result (lesson) of the Cultural Revolution? It is difficult to miss the irony of the fact that Badiou, who adamantly opposes the notion of the act as negative, locates the historical significance of the Maoist Cultural Revolution precisely in signaling

> the end of the party-state as the central production of revolutionary political activity. More generally, the Cultural Revolution showed that it was no longer possible to assign either the revolutionary mass actions or the organizational phenomena to the strict logic of class representation. That is why it remains a political episode of the highest importance.

These lines are from Badiou's "The Cultural Revolution: The Last Revolution?",[16] a text whose very title points towards an unexpected parallel with Heidegger: the Cultural Revolution holds for Badiou the same structural place as the Nazi Revolution did for Heidegger, that of the most radical political engagement whose failure signals the end of (the traditional mode of) political engagement as such. The conclusion of Badiou's text emphatically reiterates this point:

> In the end, the Cultural Revolution, even in its very impasse, bears witness to the impossibility truly and globally to free politics from the framework of the party-state that imprisons it. It marks an irreplaceable experience of saturation, because a violent will to find a new political path, to re-launch the revolution, and to find new forms of the workers' struggle under the formal conditions of socialism, ended up in failure when confronted with the necessary maintenance, for reasons of public order and the refusal of civil war, of the general frame of the party-state.

The key importance of the last truly great revolutionary explosion of the twentieth century is thus *negative*, it resides in its very failure which signals the exhaustion of the party/statist logic of the revolutionary process. However, what if one should here take a step further and conceive both poles, presentation ("direct" extra-statist self-organization of the revolutionary masses) and re-presentation, as two interdependent poles, so that, in a truly Hegelian paradox, the end of the party-state form of revolutionary activity guided by the telos of "taking over the state power" is simultaneously also the end of all forms of "direct" (non-representational) self-organization (workers' councils and other forms of "direct democracy")?

When, in his more recent *Logiques des mondes*, Badiou makes the same point about the Cultural Revolution, his accent changes almost imperceptibly:

> The Cultural Revolution in effect tested, for all of the world's revolutionaries, the limits of Leninism. It taught us that the politics of emancipation can no longer be subject to the paradigm of revolution, or remain captive to the party-form. Symmetrically, it cannot be inscribed in the parliamentary and electoral apparatus. Everything begins—and this is the sombre genius of the Cultural Revolution—when, by saturating the previous hypotheses in the real, the high-school Red Guards and students, and then the workers of Shanghai, between 1966 and 1968, prescribed for the decades to come the *affirmative realisation* of this beginning. But their fury was still so caught up in that against which they were rising up

that they only explored this beginning from the standpoint of pure negation.[17]

There is a tension between these two interpretations. According to "The Cultural Revolution: The Last Revolution?", the failure of the Cultural Revolution "bears witness to the impossibility truly and globally to free politics from the framework of the party-state that imprisons it," and the cause of this failure is specified at a rather commonsensical level ("the necessary maintenance, for reasons of public order and the refusal of civil war, of the general frame of the party-state"—in short, the exigencies of the "servicing of the goods": whatever the revolutionary perturbations, life must go on, people have to work, to consume, and so on, and the only agency to do this was the party-state . . . in personal terms, no Mao Zedong without Zhou Enlai making sure that the state functioned somehow during the turbulence of the Cultural Revolution). Contrary to this claim about the impossibility of freeing politics *from* the framework of the party-state, the passage from *Logiques des mondes* perceives as the lesson of the Cultural Revolution lying in the impossibility of pursuing radical political activity *within* the framework of the party-state ("the politics of emancipation can no longer be subject to the paradigm of revolution, or remain captive to the party-form"). So neither can we practice revolutionary politics outside the party-state framework, nor can we do it within this framework. No wonder that, when, in *Logiques des mondes*, Badiou confronts the key question, "Is the 'eternal Idea' of egalitarian-revolutionary politics with its four components (equality, terror, voluntarism, trust in the people) rooted in the statist-party model, relying on a revolutionary state, which exhausted its potential in the Cultural Revolution, with the consequence that we have to abandon it, or is it truly 'eternal' and, as such, waiting to be reinvented in our post-revolutionary epoch?"[18] he offers an answer which is not convincing:

In effect, what constitutes the trans-worldly subjectivity of the figure of the state revolutionary is precisely the fact that it tries to make the separation between state and revolutionary politics prevail, but with the twist that *it tries to do so from within state power*. Consequently, the figure in question only exists if we presuppose this separation. That is also why it is only philosophically constructible today, after a new thinking of politics has made it thinkable and practicable to situate oneself, in order to think action, from within a politics for which state power is neither an objective nor a norm.[19]

Badiou's resolution of this deadlock (neither within nor outside the state form) is thus: *at a distance from* the state form — outside, but not an outside that is destructive of the state form; rather, a gesture of "subtracting" oneself from the state form without destroying it. The true question here is: how is this externality with regard to the state to be operationalized? Since the Cultural Revolution signals the failure of the attempt to destroy the state from within, to abolish the state, is then the alternative to simply accept the state as a fact, as the apparatus that takes care of "servicing the goods," and to operate at a distance towards it (bombarding it with prescriptive proclamations and demands)? But does not such a position come close to that of Simon Critchley, who, as we have seen, argues that emancipatory politics is

> enacted or even simply acted — practically, locally, situationally — at a distance from the state. [. . .] It calls the state into question, it calls the established order to account, not in order to do away with the state, desirable though that might well be in some utopian sense, but in order to better it or attenuate its malicious effect.

The main ambiguity of this position resides in a strange *non sequitur*: if the state is here to stay, if it is impossible to abolish the state (and capitalism), why act with a distance towards state? Why not act *with(in)* *the state*? Why not accept the basic premise of the Third Way?

In other words, is Critchley's (and Badiou's) position not that of relying on the fact that *someone else* will assume the task of running the state machinery, enabling us to engage in taking the critical distance towards it? Furthermore, if the space of emancipatory politics is defined by a distance towards the state, are we not abandoning the field (of the state) all too easily to the enemy? Is it not crucial *what* form state power takes? Does this position not lead to the reduction of this crucial question to a secondary status: ultimately, it does not really matter what kind of state we have?[20]

So when Badiou claims that the Red Guardists "prescribed for the decades to come the *affirmative realization* of this beginning, of which they themselves, since their fury remained caught up in what they were rising against, explored only the face of pure negation," will this "affirmative realization" be the one of inventing a new way of dispensing with the state, of "abolishing" it, or a mere distance towards the state, or—much more radically—a new *appropriation* of state apparatuses?

There is, however, another, even more important, aspect of the failure of the Cultural Revolution. Badiou reads this failure—and, more generally, the demise of Communism—as signaling the end of the epoch in which, in politics, it was possible to generate truth at the universal level, as a global (revolutionary) project: today, in the aftermath of this historical defeat, a political truth can only be generated as (the fidelity to) a local event, a local struggle, an intervention into a specific constellation. However, does he not thereby subscribe to his own version of postmodernism, of the notion that, today, only local acts of "resistance" are possible? What Badiou (like Laclau and Butler) seems to lack is a meta-theory of history that would provide a clear answer to the alternative that haunts "postmodern" theorizations of the political: is the passage from "large" to "small" (hi)stories, from essentialism to contingency, from global to local politics, and so forth, itself a historical shift, so that, prior to it, universal politics *was* possible, or is the insight into the local character of political interventions an insight into the very essence of politics, so that the previous belief in the possibility of universal political intervention was an ideological illusion?

Along these lines, Badiou recently relegated capitalism to the naturalized "background" of our historical constellation: capitalism as "worldless" is not part of a specific situation, it is the all-encompassing background against which particular situations emerge. This is why it is senseless to pursue "anti-capitalist politics": politics is always an intervention into a particular situation, against specific agents; one cannot directly "fight" the neutral background itself. One does not fight "capitalism," one fights the US government, its decisions and measures and so on.

But does not this global background nonetheless let itself be felt, from time to time, as a very palpable and brutal limitation? The recurrent story of the contemporary Left is that of a leader or party elected with universal enthusiasm, promising a "new world" (Mandela, Lula)—but, then, sooner or later, usually after a couple of years, they stumble upon the key dilemma: does one dare touch the capitalist mechanisms, or does one decide to "play the game"? If one disturbs the mechanisms, one is very swiftly "punished" by market perturbations, economic chaos, and the rest. So although it is true that anti-capitalism cannot be directly the goal of political action—in politics, one opposes concrete political agents and their actions, not an anonymous "system"—one should apply here the Lacanian distinction between goal and aim: if not the immediate goal of the emancipatory politics, anti-capitalism should be its ultimate aim, the horizon of all its activity. Is this not the lesson of Marx's notion of the "critique of *political* economy" (totally absent in Badiou)? Although the sphere of the economy appears "apolitical," it is the secret point of reference and structuring principle of political struggles.

A few days before the Czech municipal and Senate elections, on October 16, 2006, the Ministry of the Interior of the Czech Republic banned the organization the Communist Youth League (KSM). What was its "criminal idea" on account of which, according to the Ministry of the Interior, the KSM deserved to be banned? The fact that its program advocates the transformation of private property of the means of production into social property, thereby contradicting the Czech constitution . . . To claim that the demand for social ownership of the means of production is a crime is to say that modern left-wing thought has criminal roots.[21]

The act proper is precisely an intervention which does not merely operate *within* a given background, but disturbs its coordinates and thus renders it visible *as* a background. So, in contemporary politics, a *sine qua non* of an act is that it disturbs the background status of the economy by rendering palpable its political dimension (which is why Marx wrote on *political* economy). Recall Wendy Brown's trenchant observation that "if Marxism had any analytical value for political theory, was it not in the insistence that the problem of freedom was contained in the social relations implicitly declared 'unpolitical'—that is, naturalized—in liberal discourse?"[22] This is why "the political purchase of contemporary American identity politics would seem to be achieved in part through a certain renaturalization of capitalism."[23] The crucial question to be asked is thus:

> [. . .] to what extent a critique of capitalism is foreclosed by the current configuration of oppositional politics, and not simply by the "loss of the socialist alternative" or the ostensible "triumph of liberalism" in the global order. In contrast with the Marxist critique of a social whole and the Marxist vision of total transformation, to what extent do identity politics require a standard internal to existing society against which to pitch their claims, a standard that not only

preserves capitalism from critique, but sustains the invisibility and inarticulateness of class—not incidentally, but endemically? Could we have stumbled upon one reason why class is invariably named but rarely theorized or developed in the multiculturalist mantra, "race, class, gender, sexuality"?[24]

Although Badiou's universalism is, of course, radically opposed to identity politics, does it not share with it this "renaturalization" of capitalism in the guise of the reduction of capitalism to an omnipresent background of political struggles? Furthermore, the irony here is that this "renaturalization" of capitalism into a presupposed background is the key ideological constituent of what Fukuyama called the End of History. The obvious choice apropos Fukuyama seems to be: either one accepts his pseudo-Hegelian thesis on the End of History, on the finally found rational form of social life, or one emphasizes that struggles and historical contingency go on, that we are far from any End of History. My point is that neither of the two options is truly Hegelian. One should, of course, reject the naive notion of the End of History in the sense of achieved reconciliation, of the battle in principle already won; however, with today's global capitalist liberal-democratic order, with this regime of "global reflexivity," we *did* reach a qualitative break with all history hitherto, history *did* in a way reach its end, we *do* in fact live in a post-historical society. Globalized historicism and contingency are definitive indexes of this "end of history." So, one can say that we should indeed assert that, today, although history is not at an end, the very notion of "historicity" functions in a different way than before. What this means is that, paradoxically, the "renaturalization" of capitalism and the experience of our society as a reflexive risk society in which phenomena are experienced as contingent, as the result of a historically contingent construction, are two sides of the same coin.[25]

The predominant notion of ideology is that it fixates on or "naturalizes" what is in fact the contingent result of a historical process; the antidote is thus to see things as dynamic, part of a historical process. Today, however, when the notion of universal historicity and contingency is part of the hegemonic ideology, one should rather turn the critico-ideological perspective upside down and ask: what is it that *remains the same* in the much celebrated nomadic dynamism of contemporary society? The answer is, of course, capitalism, capitalist relations. And the relationship between the Same and what has changed is here properly dialectical: that which remains the same — capitalist relations — is the very constellation which instigates the incessant change, since the deepest feature of capitalism is its dynamic of permanent self-revolutionizing. If we were to enact a truly radical change — a change of capitalist relations themselves — that would precisely cut the roots from under the incessant social dynamic of capitalist life.

Which subtraction?

One should always be attentive when opponents start to talk the same language, to share a premise — this shared point is, as a rule, their symptomal point. Let us take three contemporary philosophers as different as Badiou, Critchley, and Negri: as we have seen, they share the premise that the era of party-state politics in which the ultimate aim is to take control of the state apparatus is over — from now on, politics should subtract itself from the domain of the state, creating spaces outside, "sites of resistance." The obverse of this shift is the acceptance of capitalism as the "background" of our lives: the lesson of the fall of Communist states is that it is meaningless to "fight capitalism" . . . It is from this shared space that one should "subtract" oneself: "resistance presents itself as an exodus, as a departure outside the world."[26]

In a recent interview, Alain Badiou exposed the core of his political diagnosis of our predicament.[27] He starts by drawing a line of distinction between communism and Marxism: he still considers himself a communist ("Communism in the 'generic sense' simply means that everyone is equal to everyone else within the multiplicity and diversity of social functions"). "Marxism, however, is something else." The core of Marxism is what Lenin called the "ABC of communism": "the masses are divided into classes, the classes are represented by parties and the parties directed by leaders" — this is what no longer holds today: the disorganized masses of global capitalism are no longer divided into classes in the classical Marxist fashion, so while the task still is to organize the masses politically, it can no longer be done in the old class-party manner.

> The model of the centralized party made possible a new form of power that was nothing less than the power of the party itself. We are now at what I call a "distance from the State." This is first of all because the question of power is no longer "immediate": nowhere does a "taking power" in the insurrectional sense seem possible today.

Three points are to be noted here. First, the ambiguous definition of communism: equality "within the multiplicity and diversity of social functions"—what this definition avoids is the inequality generated by this very "multiplicity and diversity of social functions." Second, the notion of class antagonism as simply "the masses divided into classes" reduces it to a subdivision within the social body, ignoring its status as a cut that runs across the entire social body. Third, what is the exact status of the impossibility of a revolutionary seizure of power? Is this a mere temporary setback, a sign that we live in a non-revolutionary situation, or does it indicate the limitation of the party-state model of revolution? Badiou opts for the second version.

In this new situation, we need a new form of politics, the "politics of subtraction," political processes that are "independent of—'subtracted' from—the power of the State. Unlike the insurrectional form of the party, this politics of subtraction is no longer immediately destructive, antagonistic or militarized." This politics is at a distance from the state, no longer "structured or polarized along the agenda and timelines fixed by the State." How are we to think this externality with regard to state? Badiou proposes here his key conceptual distinction, that between destruction and subtraction:

> [a subtraction] is no longer dependent on the dominant laws of the political reality of a situation. It is irreducible, however, to the destruction of these laws as well. A subtraction might leave the laws of the situation still being in place. What subtraction does is bring about a point of autonomy. It's a negation, but it cannot be identified with the properly destructive part of negation. [. . .] We need an "originary subtraction" capable of creating a new space of independence and autonomy from the dominant laws of the situation.

The underlying philosophical category that Badiou problematizes here is the Hegelian notion of "determinate negation," of a negation/destruction whose result is not zero:

> Contrary to Hegel, for whom the negation of the negation produces a new affirmation, I think we must assert that today negativity, properly speaking, does not create anything new. It destroys the old, of course, but does not give rise to a new creation.

Crucial is this link between revolutionary politics and Hegelian dialectics: "Just as the party, which was once the victorious form of insurrection, is today outdated, so too is the dialectical theory of negation." Unfortunately, this leads Badiou to a pseudo-problem of "adjustment or calibration between the properly negative part of negation and the part I called 'subtractive'":

> What I call a "weak negation," the reduction of politics to democratic opposition, can be understood as a subtraction that has become so detached from destructive negation that it can no longer be distinguished from what Habermas calls "consensus." On the other hand, we are also witnessing a desperate attempt to maintain destruction as a *pure* figure of creation and the new. This symptom often has a religious and nihilistic dimension.

In short, the task is to find a proper measure between democratic pure subtraction, deprived of its destructive potential, and a purely destructive ("terrorist") negation—the problem here is that this "internal disjunction of negation" into its destructive and subtractive aspects exactly reproduces the disjunction to which the Hegelian notion of "determinate negation" tried to provide a solution. (Badiou is well aware that one should not renounce violence; one should rather reconceptualize it as defensive violence, a defense of the autonomous space created by subtraction, like the Zapatistas defending their liberated territory.) The example of this "proper measure" provided by Badiou raises more questions than it answers: that of the Solidarity movement in Poland which practiced

> a new dialectic between the means of actions that were classically understood to be negative—the strike, demonstrations and so on—and something like the creation of a space of autonomy in the factories. The objective was not to take power, to replace an existing power, but to force the State to invent a new relation with the workers.

However, the reason why this experiment was so brief, as Badiou himself notes, is that it clearly functioned as the second phase in the three phases of dissidence: (1) criticizing the regime on its own terms ("We want true socialism!"—that is, the reproach to the ruling party is: "you betrayed your own socialist roots"); (2) to the counter-reproach of the ruling party that this adherence to socialism is hypocritical, follows the open admission: yes, we *are* outside the scope of the ruling socialist ideology, *but* we do not want power, just our autonomy, plus our demand is that those in power respect certain elementary ethical rules (human rights, etc.); (3) to the reproach of the ruling party that this lack of interest in taking power is hypocritical, that the dissidents really want power, follows the open admission: yes, why not, we *want* power . . .

Badiou's other example, that of Hezbollah in Lebanon with its ambiguous relation to state power (participating in it while retaining a distance towards it, resuscitating something like the old Leninist notion of "dual power"—which was for Lenin also a temporary tactic, laying ground for the later full takeover), gives rise to a further problem: the religious foundation of these movements. Badiou makes the point that "there is an internal limitation to these movements, bound as they are to religious particularity." Is, however, this limitation only a short-term one, as Badiou seems to imply, something that these movements will (have to) overcome in the proverbial "second, higher" stage of their development, when they will (have to) universalize themselves? Badiou is right to note that the problem here is not religion as such, but its particularity—and is this particularity not *now* a fatal limitation of these movements, whose ideology takes a directly counter-Enlightenment form?

The adequate reply to Badiou's version of Bartleby politics should be the Hegelian one: the whole problem of "proper measure" is a false one. Subtraction *is* the "negation of negation" (or "determinate negation"), in other words, instead of directly negating–destroying the ruling power, remaining within its field, it undermines this very field, opening up a new positive space. The point is that there are subtractions and subtractions— Badiou himself commits a symptomatic conceptual regression when he qualifies the social-democratic position as a pure subtraction: the democratic subtraction is no subtraction at all. It is, rather, the "nihilist" terrorists who subtract, creating their space of fundamentalist religious identity: in them, radical destruction *overlaps with* radical subtraction. Another "pure" subtraction is New Age meditative withdrawal, which creates a space of its own while leaving the sphere of social reality the way it is. (There is also *pure* destruction: the outbursts of "meaningless" violence like the burning of the cars in the French *banlieues* of 2005.) So when is subtraction really creative of a new space? The only appropriate answer: *when it undermines the coordinates of the very system from which it subtracts itself*, striking at the point of its "symptomal torsion." Imagine the proverbial house of cards or a pile of wooden pieces which rely on one another in such a complex way that, if one single card or piece of wood is pulled out—*subtracted*—the whole edifice collapses: *this* is the true art of subtraction.

Recall the plot of Saramago's *Seeing*, in which voters massively refuse to vote and cast invalid ballots, throwing the entire political establishment (the ruling bloc *and* the opposition) into panic: this act put them in a situation of radical responsibility towards their subject. Such an act is subtraction at its purest: a mere gesture of withdrawing from participation in a legitimizing ritual makes state power appear as if suspended in the air above the precipice. Their acts no longer covered by democratic legitimization, those in power are all of a sudden deprived of the option of replying to the protestors "Who are you to criticize us? We are an elected government, we can do what we want!" Lacking legitimacy, they have to earn it the hard way, by their deeds. I remember the last years of Communist rule in Slovenia: there was no government so eager to earn its legitimacy and do something for the people, trying to please everyone, precisely because the Communists held power which—as everyone, including themselves, knew—was not democratically legitimized. Since the Communists knew that their end was approaching, they knew they would be harshly judged . . .

There is an obvious reproach that arises here: is this not the case already today, with the growing indifference and abstention of voters? Those in power feel no threat in these phenomena, so where is the subversive edge here? The answer is that one should focus on the big Other: the majority of those who do not vote do it not as an active gesture of protest, but in the mode of relying on others—"I do not vote, but I count on others to vote in my place . . ." Non-voting becomes an act when it affects the big Other.

In this precise sense, subtraction *already is* the Hegelian "negation of the negation": the first negation is a direct destruction, it violently "negates"/destroys the positive content that it opposes within the same shared field of reality; a subtraction proper, on the contrary, changes the coordinates of the field itself within which the struggle is taking place. In some of Badiou's formulations, this crucial point gets lost. Peter Hallward has drawn attention to the multiplicity of meanings of Badiouian "subtraction"—as if this notion covers a Wittgensteinian "family" of meanings.[28] The main axis is between subtraction as "withdrawing from" (from the domain of state, creating a space of one's own) and subtraction as "reduction to minimal difference" (moving from multiplicity to basic antagonism, and thus drawing the real line of separation). The difficult task is to make a move in which these two dimensions overlap.

The subtraction to be made is one *from* the hegemonic field which, simultaneously, forcefully intervenes *into* this field, reducing it to its occluded minimal difference. Such a subtraction is extremely violent, even more violent than destruction/purification: it is a reduction to minimal difference, to a difference of part(s)/no-part, 1 and 0, groups and the proletariat. It is not only a subtraction of the subject *from* the hegemonic field, but a subtraction which violently *affects* this field itself, laying bare its true coordinates. Such a subtraction does not add a third position to the two positions whose tension characterizes the hegemonic field (so that we have now, on the top of liberalism and fundamentalism, also radical leftist emancipatory politics); this third term rather "dena-turalizes" the whole hegemonic field, bringing out the underlying com-plicity of the opposed poles that constitute it.

Take Shakespeare's *Romeo and Juliet*: the hegemonic opposition is there the one between Capulets and Montagues—it is the opposition in the positive order of Being, a stupid issue of belonging to a particular, this or that, family clan. To make this issue into a "minimal difference," to subordinate all other choices to this one as the only choice that really matters, is the wrong move. Romeo and Juliet's gesture with regard to this hegemonic opposition is precisely that of subtraction: their love singularizes them, they subtract themselves from its hold, constituting their own space of love which, the moment it is practiced as marriage, not merely as a transgressive secret affair, perturbs the hegemonic opposi-tion. The crucial thing to take note of here is that such a subtractive gesture on behalf of love "works" only with regard to the "substantive" differences of particular (ethnic, religious) domains, not with regard to class differences: class differences are "non-subtractive," one cannot subtract from them because they are not differences between particular regions of social being, but cuts across the entire social space. When confronted with a class difference, there are only two solutions to the love bond, namely, the couple *has* to take sides: either the lower-class partner is graciously accepted into the higher class, or the higher-class partner renounces his or her class in a political gesture of solidarity with the subaltern class.

Therein resides the dilemma of subtraction: is it a subtraction/with-drawal which leaves the field from which it withdraws intact (or even functions as its inherent supplement, like the "subtraction" from social reality to one's true Self proposed by New Age meditation); or does it violently shake up the field from which it withdraws? The first subtraction fits post-political biopolitics perfectly; what, then, would be the opposite of biopolitics?

Give the dictatorship of the proletariat a chance!

What if we take the risk of resuscitating the good old "dictatorship of the proletariat" as the only way to break with biopolitics? This cannot but sound ridiculous today; it cannot but appear that these are two incompatible terms from different fields, with no shared space: the latest analysis of political power versus archaic and discredited Communist mythology . . . And yet: this is the only true choice today. The term "proletarian dictatorship" continues to point towards the key problem.

A commonsensical reproach arises here: why dictatorship? Why not true democracy or simply the power of the proletariat? The term "proletarian dictatorship" continues to point towards the crucial issue. "Dictatorship" does not mean the opposite of democracy, but democracy's own underlying mode of functioning—from the very beginning, the thesis on the "dictatorship of the proletariat" involved the presupposition that it is the opposite of other form(s) of dictatorship, since the entire field of state power is that of dictatorship. When Lenin designated liberal democracy as a form of bourgeois dictatorship, he did not imply a simplistic notion that democracy is really manipulated, a mere façade, that some secret clique is really in power and controls things, and that, if threatened with losing its power in democratic elections, it will show its true face and assume direct power. What he meant is that the very *form* of the bourgeois-democratic state, the sovereignty of its power in its ideologico-political presuppositions, embodies a "bourgeois" logic.

One should thus use the term "dictatorship" in the precise sense in which democracy is also a form of dictatorship, that is, as a purely *formal* determination. It is often pointed out that self-questioning is constitutive of democracy, that democracy always allows, solicits even, constant self-interrogation of its features. However, this self-referentiality has to stop at some point: even the most "free" elections cannot put in question the legal procedures that legitimize and organize them, the state apparatuses that guarantee (by force, if necessary) the electoral process, and so on. The state in its institutional aspect is a massive presence which cannot be accounted for in terms of the representation of interests—the democratic illusion is that it can. Badiou has conceptualized this excess as the excess of state representation over what it represents. One can also put it in Benjaminian terms: while democracy can more or less eliminate constituted violence, it still has to rely continuously on constitutive violence.[29]

Let us recall the lesson of Hegelian "concrete universality"—imagine a philosophical debate between a hermeneuticist, a deconstructionist, and an analytic philosopher. What they sooner or later discover is that they do not simply occupy positions within a shared common space called "philosophy": what distinguishes them is the very notion of what philosophy is as such; that is, an analytic philosopher perceives the global field of philosophy and the respective differences between the participants differently than a hermeneuticist: what is different between them are the differences themselves, which are what render their true differences, in a first approach, invisible—the gradual classificatory logic of "this is what we share, and here our differences begin" breaks down. For the contemporary cognitivist analytic philosopher, with the cognitivist turn, philosophy has finally reached the maturity of serious reasoning, leaving behind metaphysical speculation. For a hermeneuticist, analytic philosophy is, on the contrary, the end of philosophy, the final loss of a truly philosophical stance, the transformation of philosophy into another positive science. So when the participants in the debate are struck by this more fundamental gap that separates them, they stumble upon the moment of "dictatorship." And, in a homologous fashion, the same goes for political democracy: its dictatorial dimension becomes palpable when the struggle turns into the struggle about the field of struggle itself.[30]

So what about the proletariat? Insofar as the proletariat designates the "part of no-part" which stands for universality, the "dictatorship of the proletariat" is the power of universality where those who are the "part of no-part" set the tone. Why are they egalitarian-universalist? Again, for purely formal reasons: because, as the part of no-part, they lack the particular features that would legitimate their place within the social body—they belong to the set of society without belonging to any of its subsets. As such, their belonging is directly universal. Here, the logic of the representation of multiple particular interests and their mediation through compromises reaches its limit. Every dictatorship breaks with this logic of representation, which is why the simplistic definition of fascism as the dictatorship of finance capital is wrong: Marx already recognized that Napoleon III, that proto-fascist, broke with the logic of representation.

The term "dictatorship" designates the hegemonic role in the political space, and the term "proletariat" those "out of joint" in the social space, the "part of no-part" lacking their proper place within it. This is why the all too quick dismissal of the proletariat as the "universal class" misses the point: the proletariat is not the "universal class" in the same sense in which, for Hegel, the state bureaucracy was the "universal class," directly standing for the universal interest of society (in contrast to other "estates" which stand for their particular interests). What qualifies the proletariat for this position is ultimately a *negative* feature: all other classes are (potentially) capable of reaching the status of the "ruling class," while the proletariat cannot achieve this without abolishing itself as a class:

> what makes the working class into an agency and provides it with a mission is neither its poverty, nor its militant and pseudo-military organization, nor its proximity to the (chiefly industrial) means of production. It is only its structural inability to organize itself into yet another ruling class that provides the working class with such a mission. The proletariat is the only (revolutionary) class in history that abolishes itself in the act of abolishing its opposite. "The people," on the other hand, made up of a myriad of classes and sub-classes, social and economic strata, cannot structurally carry out such a mission. Quite on the contrary, whenever a "historical task" is assigned to "the people" as such, the outcome has always been that either a fetal bourgeoisie immediately took precedence and, through an accelerated growth process, organized itself into a ruling class (as in the case of "national liberation movements"), or a politico-ideological nucleus designated itself as a "caretaker" government for an indeterminate period (for the people or, more specifically, the working class), which unerringly ended up in empire (as it was in the case of Jacobins and Bolsheviks).[31]

There is thus more than hypocrisy in the fact that, at the highest point of Stalinism, when the entire social edifice was shattered by purges, the new constitution proclaimed the end of the "class" character of Soviet power (voting rights were restored to members of classes previously excluded), and that the Socialist regimes were called "people's democracies." The opposition of the proletariat and the "people" is crucial here: in Hegelese, their opposition is the very opposition of "true" and "false" universality. *The people is inclusive, the proletariat is exclusive; the people fights intruders, parasites, those who obstruct its full self-assertion, the proletariat fights a struggle which divides the people in its very core. The people wants to assert itself, the proletariat wants to abolish itself.*

One should thus thoroughly demystify the scarecrow of the "dictatorship of the proletariat": at its most basic, it stands for the tremulous moment when the complex web of representations is suspended due to the direct intrusion of universality into the political field. With regard to the French Revolution, it was, significantly, Danton, not Robespierre, who provided the most concise formula of the imperceptible shift from the "dictatorship of the proletariat" to statist violence, or, in Benjamin's terms, from divine to mythic violence: "Let us be terrible so that the people will not have to be."[32] For Danton, Jacobin revolutionary state terror was a kind of preemptive action whose true aim was not to take revenge on its enemies but to prevent the direct "divine" violence of the *sans-culottes*, of the people themselves. In other words, let us do what the people demand us to do *so that they will not do it themselves* . . .

From ancient Greece, we have a name for this intrusion: democracy. That is to say, what is democracy, at its most elementary? A phenomenon which, for the first time, appeared in ancient Greece when the members of the *demos* (those with no firmly determined place in the hierarchical social structure) not only demanded that their voice be heard against those in power. They not only protested the wrong they suffered and wanted their voice be recognized and included in the public sphere, on an equal footing with the ruling oligarchy and aristocracy; even more, they, the excluded, presented themselves as the embodiment of the Whole of Society, of true Universality: "we—the 'nothing', not counted in the order—are the people, we are All against others who stand only for their particular privileged interest." Political conflict proper designates the tension between the structured social body in which each part has its place, and "the part of no-part" which unsettles this order on account of the empty principle of universality, of what Etienne Balibar calls *égaliberté*, the principled equality of all men *qua* speaking beings—up to and including the *liumang*, "hoodlums," in the China of today, those who are displaced and float freely hither and thither, without work or home, but also without cultural or sexual identities and unregistered by the state.

This identification of the part of society with no properly defined place within it (or which rejects the allocated subordinated place within it) with the Whole is the elementary gesture of politicization, discernible in all great democratic events from the French Revolution (in which *le troisième état* proclaimed itself identical with the Nation as such, against the aristocracy and clergy) to the demise of East European socialism (in which dissident "fora" proclaimed themselves representative of the entirety of society against the party *nomenklatura*). In this precise sense, politics and democracy are synonymous: the basic aim of anti-democratic politics always and by definition is and was depoliticization, the demand that "things should return to normal," with each individual sticking to his or her particular job. And this brings us to the inevitable paradoxical conclusion: *the "dictatorship of the proletariat" is another name for the violence of the democratic explosion itself.* The "dictatorship of the proletariat" is thus the zero-level at which the difference between legitimate and illegitimate state power is suspended, in other words, when state power as such is illegitimate. Saint-Just said in November 1792: "Every king is a rebel and an usurper." This phrase is a cornerstone of emancipatory politics: there is no "legitimate" king as opposed to the usurper, since *being a king is in itself an usurpation*, in the same sense that, for Proudhon, property as such is theft. What we have here is the Hegelian "negation of the negation," the passage from the simple and direct negation ("this king is not legitimate, he is an usurper"), to the inherent self-negation (an "authentic king" is an oxymoron, being a king *is* usurpation). This is why, for Robespierre, the trial of the king was not a trial at all:

> There is no trial to be held here. Louis is not a defendant. You are not judges. You are not, you cannot be anything but statesmen and representatives of the nation. You have no sentence to pronounce for or against a man, but a measure of public salvation to implement, an act of national providence to perform. [. . .] Louis was king, and the Republic is founded: the famous question you are considering is settled by those words alone. Louis was dethroned by his crimes; Louis denounced the French people as rebellious; to chastise it, he called on the arms of his fellow tyrants; victory and the people decided that he was the rebellious one: therefore Louis cannot be judged; either he is already condemned or the Republic is not acquitted. Proposing to put Louis on trial, in whatever way that could be done, would be to regress towards royal and constitutional despotism; it is a counter-revolutionary idea, for it means putting the revolution itself in contention. In fact, if Louis can still be put on trial, then he can be

acquitted; he may be innocent; what am I saying! he is presumed to be so until he has been tried. But if Louis is acquitted, if Louis can be presumed innocent, what becomes of the revolution?[33]

This strange coupling of democracy and dictatorship is grounded in the tension that pertains to the very notion of democracy. There are two elementary and irreducible sides to democracy: violent egalitarian imposition by those who are "supernumerary"; and the regulated (more or less) universal procedure of choosing those who will exert power. How do these two sides relate to each other? What if democracy in the second sense (the regulated procedure of registering the "people's voice") is ultimately *a defense against itself*, against democracy in the sense of the violent intrusion of the egalitarian logic that disturbs the hierarchical functioning of the social system, an attempt to re-functionalize this excess, to make it a part of the normal running of things?

The problem is thus: how to regulate/institutionalize the very violent egalitarian democratic impulse, how to prevent it from being drowned in democracy in the second sense of the term (regulated procedure)? If there is no way to do it, then "authentic" democracy remains a momentary utopian outburst which, the proverbial morning after, has to be normalized.

The Orwellian proposition "democracy is terror" is thus democracy's "infinite judgment," its highest speculative identity. This dimension gets lost in Claude Lefort's notion of democracy as involving the empty place of power, the constitutive gap between the place of power and the contingent agents who, for a limited period, can occupy that place. Paradoxically, the underlying premise of democracy is thus not only that there is no political agent which has a "natural" right to power, but, much more radically, that the "people" itself, the ultimate source of the sovereign power in democracy, does not exist as a substantial entity. In the Kantian conception, the democratic notion of the "people" is a negative concept, a concept whose function is merely to designate a certain limit: it prohibits any determinate agent from ruling with total sovereignty.[34] The claim that the people *does* exist is the basic axiom of "totalitarianism," and its mistake is strictly homologous to the Kantian misuse ("paralogism") of political reason: "the People exists" through a determinate political agent which acts as if it directly embodies (not only re-presents) the People, its true Will (the totalitarian Party and its Leader), that is, in the terms of transcendental critique, as a direct phenomenal embodiment of the noumenal People . . . Let us cite once again Jacques-Alain Miller's formulation of the link between this notion of democracy and Lacan's notion of the inconsistency of the big Other:

> Is "democracy" a master-signifier? Without any doubt. It is the master-signifier which says that there is no master-signifier, at least not a master-signifier which would stand alone, that every master-signifier has to insert itself wisely among others. Democracy is Lacan's big S of the barred A, which says: I am the signifier of the fact that the Other has a hole, or that it doesn't exist.[35]

Of course, Miller is aware that every Master-Signifier bears witness to the fact that there is no Master-Signifier, no Other of the Other, that there is a lack in the Other, and so on—the very gap between S_1 and S_2 occurs because of this lack (as with God in Spinoza, the Master-Signifier by definition fills in the gap in the series of "ordinary" signifiers). The difference is that, with democracy, this lack is directly inscribed into the social structure, it is institutionalized in a set of procedures and regulations—no wonder, then, that Miller approvingly quotes Marcel Gauchet regarding how, in democracy, truth only offers itself "in division and decomposition" (and one cannot but note with irony how Stalin and Mao made the same claim, although with a "totalitarian" twist: in politics, truth only emerges through the ruthless divisions of the class struggle . . .).

It is easy to note how, from within this Kantian horizon of democracy, the "terroristic" aspect of democracy can only appear as its "totalitarian" distortion, in other words, how, within this horizon, the line that separates the authentic democratic explosion of revolutionary terror from the "totalitarian" party-state regime (or, to put it in reactionary terms, the line that separates the "mob rule of the dispossessed" from the party-state's brutal oppression of the "mob") is obliterated.[36]

It is against this background that one can formulate a critique of Jacques Rancière's political aesthetics, of his idea of the aesthetic dimension of the properly political act: a democratic explosion reconfigures the established hierarchical "police" order of social space, it stages a spectacle of a different order, of a different *partage* of the public space. Peter Hallward is right to point out that, in today's "society of the spectacle" such an aesthetic reconfiguration has lost its subversive dimension: it can easily be appropriated into the existing order.[37] The true task lies not in momentary democratic explosions which undermine the established "police" order, but in the dimension designated by Badiou as that of "fidelity" to the Event: translating/inscribing the democratic explosion into the positive "police" order, imposing on social reality a *new* lasting order. *This* is the properly "terroristic" dimension of every authentic democratic explosion: the brutal imposition of a new order. And this is why, while everybody loves democratic rebellions, the spectacular/carnivalesque explosions of the popular will, anxiety arises when this will wants to persist, to institutionalize itself—and the more "authentic" the rebellion, the more "terroristic" is this institutionalization.

The standard liberal counter-argument to those who warn about the "invisible hand" of the market that controls our destinies is: if the price of being freed from the *invisible* hand of the market is to be controlled by the *visible* hand of new rulers, are we still ready to pay it? The answer should be: *yes*—if this visible hand is visible to and controlled by the "part of no-part."

9   Unbehagen in der Natur

Beyond Fukuyama

Where, then, do we stand today? How can we break out of the crisis of determinate negation and enact a subtraction in all its authentic violence? Gerald A. Cohen has enumerated the four features of the classical Marxist notion of the working class: (1) it constitutes the majority of society; (2) it produces the wealth of society; (3) it consists of the exploited members of society; (4) its members are the needy people in society. When these four features are combined, they generate two further features: (5) the working class has nothing to lose from revolution; (6) it can and will engage in a revolutionary transformation of society.[1] None of the first four features applies to the contemporary working class, which is why features (5) and (6) cannot be generated. Even if some of the features continue to apply to parts of today's society, they are no longer united in single agent: the needy people in society are no longer the workers, and so on and so forth. Correct as it is, this enumeration should be supplemented by a systematic theoretical deduction: for Marx, they all follow from the basic position of a worker who has nothing but her labor-power to sell. As such, workers are by definition exploited; with the progressive expansion of capitalism, they constitute the majority which also produces the wealth; and so on. How, then, are we to redefine a revolutionary perspective in today's conditions? Is the way out of this predicament, the *combinatoire* of multiple antagonisms, their potential overlappings?

The underlying problem is: how are we to think the singular universality of the emancipatory subject as not purely formal, that is, as objectively-materially determined, but without the working class as its substantial base? The solution is a negative one: it is capitalism itself which offers a negative substantial determination, for the global capitalist system is the substantial "base" which mediates and generates the excesses (slums, ecological threats, and so on) that open up sites of resistance.

It is easy to make fun of Fukuyama's notion of the End of History, but the dominant ethos today *is* "Fukuyamaian": liberal-democratic capitalism is accepted as the finally found formula of the best possible society, all that one can do is render it more just, tolerant, and so forth. The only *true* question today is: do we endorse this "naturalization" of capitalism, or does contemporary global capitalism contain antagonisms which are sufficiently strong to prevent its indefinite reproduction? Let us cite four such antagonisms:

1. *Ecology*: in spite of the infinite adaptability of capitalism which, in the case of an acute ecological catastrophe or crisis, can easily turn ecology into a new field of capitalist investment and competition, the very nature of the risk involved fundamentally precludes a market solution—why? Capitalism only works in precise social conditions: it implies trust in the objectivized/"reified" mechanism of the market's "invisible hand" which, as a kind of Cunning of Reason, guarantees that the competition of individual egotisms works for the common good. However, we are currently experiencing a radical change. Up until now, historical Substance—history as an objective process obeying certain laws—played out its role as the medium and foundation of all subjective interventions: whatever social and political subjects did, it was mediated and ultimately dominated, overdetermined, by the historical Substance. What looms on the horizon today is the unprecedented possibility that a subjective intervention will intervene directly into the historical Substance, catastrophically disturbing its course by triggering an ecological catastrophe, a fateful biogenetic mutation, a nuclear or similar military–social catastrophe, and so on. No longer can we rely on the safeguarding role of the limited scope of our acts: it no longer holds that, whatever we do, history will carry on. For the first time in human history, the act of a single sociopolitical agent can really alter and even interrupt the global historical process, so that, ironically, it is only today that we can say that the historical process should effectively be conceived "not only as Substance, but also as Subject." This is why, when confronted with singular catastrophic prospects (say, a political group which intends to attack its enemy with nuclear or biological weapons), we can no longer rely on the standard logic of the "Cunning of Reason" which, precisely, presupposes the primacy of the historical Substance over acting subjects: we can no longer adopt the stance of "let us call the bluff of the enemy who

threatens us for he will thereby self-destruct"—the price for letting historical Reason do its work is too high since, in the meantime, we may all perish together with the enemy.

Recall a frightening detail from the Cuban missile crisis: only later did we learn how close to nuclear war we were during a naval skirmish between an American destroyer and a Soviet B–59 submarine off Cuba on October 27, 1962. The destroyer dropped depth charges near the submarine to try to force it to the surface, not knowing it had a nuclear-tipped torpedo. Vadim Orlov, a member of the submarine crew, told the conference in Havana that the submarine had been authorized to fire it if three officers agreed. The officers began a fierce shouting match over whether to sink the ship. Two of them said yes and the other said no. "A guy named Arkhipov saved the world," was the bitter comment of a historian on this incident.[2]

2. The inadequacy of *private property* for so-called "intellectual property." The key antagonism of the new (digital) industries is thus: how to maintain the form of (private) property, within which the logic of profit can be maintained (see also the Napster problem, the free circulation of music)? And do the legal complications in biogenetics not point in the same direction? A key element of the new international trade agreements is the "protection of intellectual property": whenever, in a merger, a big First World company takes over a Third World company, the first thing they do is close down the research department. Phenomena emerge here which push the notion of property towards extraordinary dialectical paradoxes: in India, the local communities suddenly discover that medical practices and materials they have been using for centuries are now owned by American companies, so they should be bought from the latter; with the biogenetic companies patenting genes, we are all discovering that parts of ourselves, our genetic components, are already copyrighted, owned by others . . .

The crucial date in the history of cyberspace was February 3, 1976, the day when Bill Gates published his (in)famous "Open Letter to Hobbyists," the assertion of private property in the software domain: "As the majority of hobbyists must be aware, most of you steal your software. [. . .] Most directly, the thing you do is theft." Bill Gates has built his entire empire and reputation on his extreme views about knowledge being treated as if it were tangible property. This was a decisive signal which triggered the battle for the "enclosure" of the common domain of software.

3. The socio-ethical implications of *new techno-scientific developments* (especially in biogenetics) — Fukuyama himself was compelled to admit that biogenetic interventions into human nature are the most serious threat to his vision of the End of History.

What is false about today's discussion concerning the "ethical consequences of biogenetics" (along with similar matters) is that it is rapidly turning into what Germans call *Bindenstrich-Ethik*, the ethics of the hyphen — technology-ethics, environment-ethics, and so on. This ethics does have a role to play, a role homologous to that of the "provisional ethic" Descartes mentions at the beginning of his *Discourse on Method*: when we engage on a new path, full of dangers and shattering new insights, we need to stick to old established rules as a practical guide for our daily lives, although we are well aware that the new insights will compel us to provide a fresh foundation for our entire ethical edifice (in Descartes's case, this new foundation was provided by Kant, in his ethics of subjective autonomy). Today, we are in the same predicament: "provisional ethics" cannot replace the need for a profound reflection regarding the emerging New.

In short, what gets lost here, in this hyphen-ethics, is simply ethics as such. The problem is not that universal ethics gets dissolved into particular topics, but, quite the contrary, that particular scientific breakthroughs are directly confronted with old humanist "values" (say, that biogenetics affects our sense of dignity and autonomy). This, then, is the choice we confront today: either we choose the typically postmodern stance of reticence (let's not go to the end — let's keep a proper distance towards the scientific Thing so that this Thing will not draw us into its black hole, destroying all our moral and human notions), or we dare to "tarry with the negative (*das Verweilen beim Negativen*)," that is, we dare to fully assume the consequences of scientific modernity, with the wager that "our Mind is a genome" will also function as an infinite judgment.

4. And, last but not least, *new forms of apartheid*, new walls and slums. On September 11, 2001, the Twin Towers were hit; twelve years earlier, on November 9, 1989, the Berlin Wall fell. November 9 announced the "happy nineties," the Fukuyama dream that liberal democracy had won, that the search was over, that the advent of a global, liberal world community was lurking just around the corner, that the obstacles to this ultra-Hollywoodesque happy ending were merely empirical and contingent (local pockets of resistance where the leaders had not yet grasped that their time was over). In contrast, 9/11 is the key symbol of the end of

the Clintonite happy nineties, of the era in which new walls are emerging everywhere, between Israel and the West Bank, around the European Union, along the US–Mexico border.

So what if the new proletarian position is that of the inhabitants of slums in the new megalopolises? The explosive growth of slums over the last decades, especially in the Third World mega-cities from Mexico City and other Latin American capitals through Africa (Lagos, Chad) to India, China, the Philippines, and Indonesia, is perhaps the crucial geopolitical event of our times.[3] The case of Lagos, the biggest node in the shanty-town corridor of 70 million people that stretches from Abidjan to Ibadan, is exemplary here: according to the official sources themselves, about two-thirds of Lagos State's total land mass of 3,577 square kilometers could be classified as shanties or slums; no one even knows the size of its population—officially it is 6 million, but most experts estimate it at 10 million. Since, sometime very soon (or maybe, given the imprecision of the Third World censuses, it has already happened), the urban population of the earth will outnumber the rural population, and since slum inhabitants will compose the majority of the urban population, we are in no way dealing with a marginal phenomenon. We are thus witnessing the fast growth of a population living outside state control, in conditions half outside the law, in terrible need of the minimal forms of self-organization. Although this population is composed of marginalized laborers, sacked civil servants and ex-peasants, they are not simply a redundant surplus: they are incorporated into the global economy in numerous ways, many of them working as informal wage workers or self-employed entrepreneurs, with no adequate health or social-security coverage. (The main source of their emergence is the inclusion of Third World countries in the global economy, with cheap food imports from the First World countries ruining local agriculture.) They are the true "symptom" of slogans such as "Development," "Modernization," and the "World Market": not an unfortunate accident, but a necessary product of the innermost logic of global capitalism.[4]

No wonder that the hegemonic form of ideology in slums is Pentecostal Christianity, with its mixture of charismatic miracles-and-spectacles-oriented fundamentalism and of social programs such as community kitchens and care of children and the old. While, of course, one should resist the easy temptation of elevating and idealizing the slum-dwellers into a new revolutionary class, one should nonetheless, in Badiou's terms, perceive slums as one of the few authentic "evental sites" in contemporary society—the slum-dwellers are literally a collection of those who are the "part of no-part," the "supernumerary" element of society, excluded from the benefits of citizenship, the uprooted and dispossessed, those who really "have nothing to lose but their chains." It is indeed surprising how many features of slum-dwellers fit the good old Marxist determination of the proletarian revolutionary subject: they are "free" in the double meaning of the word even more than the classic proletariat ("freed" from all substantial ties; dwelling in a free space, beyond the police regulations of the state); they are a large collective, forcibly thrown together, "thrown" into a situation where they have to invent some mode of being-together, and simultaneously deprived of any support in traditional ways of life, in inherited religious or ethnic life-forms.

Of course, there is a crucial difference between the slum-dwellers and the classical Marxist working class: while the latter is defined in the precise terms of economic "exploitation" (the appropriation of surplus-value generated by the situation of having to sell one's own labor-power as a commodity on the market), the defining feature of the slum-dwellers is socio-political, it concerns their (non-)integration into the legal space of citizenship with (most of) its incumbent rights—to put it in somewhat simplified terms, much more than a refugee, a slum-dweller is a *homo sacer*, the systemically generated "living dead" of global capitalism. The slum-dweller is a kind of negative of the refugee: a refugee from his own community, the figure that state power is not trying to control through concentration—where (to repeat the unforgettable pun from Ernst Lubitch's *To Be or Not to Be*) those in power do the concentrating while the refugees do the camping—but pushed into a space beyond control; in contrast to the Foucauldian micro-practices of discipline, with regard to slum-dwellers, state power renounces its right to exert full control and discipline, finding it more appropriate to let them vegetate in the twilight zone.[5]

What one finds in the "really-existing slums" is, of course, a mixture of improvised modes of social life, from criminal gangs and religious "fundamentalist" groups held together by a charismatic leader up to and including seeds of new forms of "socialist" solidarity. The slum-dwellers are the counter-class to the other newly emerging class, the so-called "symbolic class" (managers, journalists, and PR people, academics, artists, and so on) which is also uprooted and perceives itself as directly universal (a New York academic has more in common with a Slovene academic than with blacks in Harlem half a mile from his campus). Is this the new axis of class struggle, or is the "symbolic class" inherently split, so that one can make the emancipatory wager on a coalition between the slum-dwellers and the "progressive" part of the symbolic class? We should be looking for signs of the new forms of social awareness that will emerge from the slum collectives: they will be the germs of the future.

Peter Hallward was right to point out that the poetics of "resistance," of deterritorialized nomadic mobility, of creating *lignes de fuite*, of never being where one is expected to dwell, is not enough; the time has come to start creating what one is tempted to call liberated territories, the well-defined and delineated social spaces in which the reign of the System is suspended: a religious or artistic community, a political organization, and other forms of "a place of one's own." This is what makes slums so interesting: their territorial character. While contemporary society is often characterized as the society of total control, slums are the territories within a state's frontiers from which the state has (partially, at least) withdrawn its control, territories which function as white spots, blanks, in the official map of a state territory. Although they are *de facto* included in a state by the links of the black economy, organized crime, religious groups, and so forth, the state's control is nonetheless suspended, they are domains outside the rule of law. In the map of Berlin that one could buy in the now defunct GDR, the area of West Berlin was left blank, a weird hole in the detailed structure of the big city; when Christa Wolf, the well-known East German half-dissident writer, took her small daughter to East Berlin's TV tower, from which one had a nice view over prohibited West Berlin, the small girl shouted happily: "Look, mother, it is not white over there, there are houses with people like here!"—as if discovering a hidden slum zone . . .

This is why the "destructured" masses, poor and deprived of everything, situated in a non-proletarianized urban environment, constitute one of the principal horizons of the politics to come. These masses, therefore, are an important factor in the phenomenon of globalization. A genuine form of globalization, today, would be found in the organization of these masses—on a worldwide scale, if possible—whose conditions of existence are essentially the same. Whoever lives in the *banlieues* of Bamako or Shanghai is not essentially different from someone who lives in the *banlieue* of Paris or the ghettos of Chicago. Indeed, if the principal task of the emancipatory politics of the nineteenth century was to break the monopoly of the bourgeois liberals by politicizing the working class, and if the task of the twentieth century was to politically awaken the immense rural populations of Asia and Africa, the principal task of the twenty-first century is to politicize—organize and discipline—the "de-structured masses" of slum-dwellers.

Hugo Chavez's greatest achievement in the first years of his rule was precisely the politicization (inclusion into political life, social mobiliza-tion) of slum-dwellers; in other countries, they mostly persist in apolitical inertia. It was this political mobilization of the slum-dwellers which saved him from a US-sponsored coup: to the surprise of everyone, Chavez included, the slum-dwellers descended en masse to the affluent city center, tipping the balance of power to his advantage.

The course on which Chavez embarked from 2006 is the exact opposite of the postmodern Left's mantra regarding de-territorialization, rejection of statist politics, and so on: far from "resisting state power," he *grabbed* power (first by an attempted coup, then democratically), ruthlessly using the state apparatuses and interventions to promote his goals; furthermore, he is militarizing the favelas, organizing the training of armed units. And, the ultimate taboo: now that he is feeling the economic effects of the "resistance" to his rule by capital (temporary shortages of some goods in the state-subsidized supermarkets), he has anounced the constitution of his own political party! Even some of his allies are skeptical about this move: does it signal a return to the politics of the party-state? However, one should fully endorse this risky choice: the task is to make this party function not like the usual (populist or liberal-parliamentary) party, but as a focus for the political mobilization of new forms of politics (like the grassroots communal committees). So what should we say to someone like Chavez? "No, do not grab state power, just subtract yourself, leave the laws of the (state) situation in place"? Chavez is often dismissed as a clownish comedian—but would such a subtraction not really reduce him to a new version of Subcomandante Marcos of the Zapatista movement in Mexico, to whom many leftists now rightly refer as "Subcomediante Marcos"? Today, it is the big capitalists, from Bill Gates to the ecological polluters, who "resist" the state . . .

The four features presupposed in the Marxist notion of the proletariat are, of course, grounded in the singularly capitalist mechanism, they are four effects of the same structural cause. Is it possible to do the same with the four antagonisms that threaten the indefinite self-reproduction of global capital, to "deduce" them from the same cause? The task may appear almost as difficult as the great task of contemporary physics, the

development of a "unified theory" which would deduce the four fundamental forces (gravity, electricity/magnetism, weak atomic force, strong
atomic force) from one and the same underlying feature or law.

Perhaps one could even map Cohen's four features onto the second
tetrad: the "majority" principle appears as ecology, a topic which concerns us all; "poverty" characterizes those who are excluded and live in
slums; "wealth production" is more and more something which depends
on scientific and technological developments like biogenetics; and, finally, "exploitation" reappears in the impasses of intellectual property,
where the owner exploits the results of collective labor. The four features
form a kind of semiotic square, the intersection of two oppositions along
the lines of society/nature and inside/outside the social wall of a new
apartheid: ecology designates the outside of nature, slums the social
outside, biogenetics the natural inside and intellectual property the social
inside.

Why is this overlapping of the four antagonisms not the Laclauian
empty signifier (the "people"), filled in through the process of the
struggle for hegemony? Why is it not yet another attempt in the series
of the "rainbow coalitions" of oppressed sexual minorities, ethnic and
religious groups, and so forth? Because we still need a *proletarian* position,
the position of the "part of no-part." In other words, if one wants an older
model, it is rather the trusty Communist formula of the alliance of
"workers, poor farmers, patriotic petty bourgeoisie, and honest intellectuals": note how the four terms are not at the same level — only workers
are listed as such, while the other three are qualified ("*poor* farmers,
patriotic petty bourgeoisie, *honest* intellectuals").[6] Exactly the same goes
for today's four antagonisms: it is the antagonism between the Excluded
and the Included which is the zero-level antagonism, coloring the entire
terrain of struggle. Consequently, only those ecologists are included who
do not use ecology to legitimize the oppression of the "polluting" poor,
trying to discipline the Third World countries; only those critics of
biogenetic practices who resist the conservative (religious-humanist)
ideology which all too often sustains this critique; only those critics of
intellectual private property who do not reduce the problem to a legalistic
issue.

There is thus a qualitative difference between the gap that separates
the Excluded from the Included and the other three antagonisms, which
designate three domains of what Hardt and Negri call the "commons,"
the shared substance of our social being whose privatization is a violent

act which should also be resisted with violence, if necessary: *the commons of culture*, the immediately socialized forms of "cognitive" capital, primarily language, our means of communication and education (if Bill Gates were allowed a monopoly, we would reach the absurd situation in which a private individual would literally own the software texture of our basic network of communication), but also the shared infrastructure of public transport, electricity, post, etc.; *the commons of external nature* threatened by pollution and exploitation (from oil to forests and the natural habitat itself); *the commons of internal nature* (the biogenetic inheritance of humanity). What all these struggles share is the awareness of the destructive potential, up to and including the self-annihilation of humanity itself, if the capitalist logic of enclosing these commons is allowed a free run. It is this reference to "commons"—this substance of productivity which is neither private nor public—which justifies the resuscitation of the notion of communism. The commons can thus be linked to what Hegel, in his *Phenomenology*, deployed as *die Sache*, the shared social thing–cause, "the work of all and everyone," the substance kept alive by incessant subjective productivity.[7]

From fear to trembling

A further qualification should be added here: the solution is not to limit the market and private property by direct interventions of the state and state ownership. The domain of the state itself is also in its own way "private": private in the precise Kantian sense of the "private use of Reason" in state administrative and ideological apparatuses:

> The public use of one's reason must always be free, and it alone can bring about enlightenment among men. The private use of one's reason, on the other hand, may often be very narrowly restricted without particularly hindering the progress of enlightenment. By public use of one's reason I understand the use which a person makes of it as a scholar before the reading public. Private use I call that which one may make of it in a particular civil post or office which is entrusted to him.[8]

What one should add here, moving beyond Kant, is that there is a privileged social group which, on account of its lack of a determinate place in the "private" order of the social hierarchy, in other words, as a

429

"part of no-part" of the social body, directly stands for universality: it is only the reference to those Excluded, to those who dwell in the blanks of the space of the state, that enables true universality. There is nothing more "private" than a state community which perceives the Excluded as a threat and worries how to keep the Excluded at a proper distance. In other words, as we have already seen, in the series of the four antagonisms, the one between the Included and the Excluded is the crucial one, the point of reference for the others; without it, all others lose their subversive edge: ecology turns into a "problem of sustainable development," intellectual property into a "complex legal challenge," biogenetics into an "ethical" issue. One can sincerely fight for ecology, defend a broader notion of intellectual property, oppose the copyrighting of genes, while not questioning the antagonism between the Included and the Excluded—what is more, one can even formulate some of these struggles in terms of the Included threatened by the polluting Excluded. In this way, we get no true universality, only "private" concerns in the Kantian sense of the term. Corporations such as Whole Foods and Starbucks continue to enjoy favor among liberals even though they both engage in anti-union activities; the trick is that they sell products that claim to be politically progressive acts in and of themselves. One buys coffee made with beans bought from the growers at fair prices, one drives a hybrid vehicle, one buys from companies that provide good benefits for their employees (according to the corporation's own standards), and so on. Political action and consumption become fully merged. In short, without the antagonism between the Included and the Excluded, we may well find ourselves in a world in which Bill Gates is the greatest humanitarian fighting against poverty and diseases, and Rupert Murdoch the greatest environmentalist mobilizing hundreds of millions through his media empire.[9]

And, one should be clear at this point, the political expression of this radical antagonism, the way the pressure of the Excluded is experienced within the established political space, always has a flavor of terror. The lesson is thus the one rendered long ago by Athena towards the end of Aeschylus's *Eumenides*:

> As for terror,
> don't banish it completely from the city.
> What mortal man is truly righteous
> without being afraid? Those who sense the fear

revere what's right. With citizens like these
your country and your city will be safe,
stronger than anything possessed by men.[10]

How are we to read these famous lines? Do they really point towards
the manipulation of the politics of fear we know today?[11] The first
obstacle to such a reading is the obvious fact that Athena does not
evoke the fear of an external enemy whose threat justifies the disciplined unity and possible "defensive measures" of the city-state: the
fear is here the fear of divine Justice itself, of its blinding authority;
from the perspective of modern subjectivity (which is our perspective
here), the object of this fear is the abyss of subjectivity itself, its
terrifying power of self-relating negativity; it is the terrifying encounter of this traumatic core that Heidegger had in mind when he claimed
that terror (*Schrecken*) was necessary if "modern man" was to be
awakened from his metaphysico-technological slumber into a new
beginning:

> we must principally concern ourselves with preparing for man the very
> basis and dimension upon which and within which something like a
> mystery of his *Dasein* could once again be encountered. We should not
> be at all surprised if the contemporary man in the street feels disturbed
> or perhaps sometimes dazed and clutches all the more stubbornly at his
> idols when confronted with this challenge and with the effort required
> to approach this mystery. It would be a mistake to expect anything
> else. We must first call for someone capable of instilling terror into our
> *Dasein* again.[12]

Heidegger thus opposes wonder as the basic disposition of the first
(Greek) beginning to terror as the basic disposition of the second new
beginning: "In wonder, the basic disposition of the first beginning, beings
first come to stand in their form. Terror, the basic disposition of the other
beginning, reveals behind all progress and all domination over beings a
dark emptiness of irrelevance."[13] (The thing to note here is that Heidegger
uses the word "terror" and not "anxiety.")

Hegel said something similar in his analysis of the master and servant
(bondage), when he emphasized that, since the bondsman is also a self-
consciousness,

the master is taken to be the essential reality for the state of bondage; hence, for it, the truth is the independent consciousness existing for itself, although this truth is not taken yet as inherent in bondage itself. Still, it does in fact contain within itself this truth of pure negativity and self-existence, because it has experienced this reality within it. For this consciousness was not in peril and fear for this element or that, nor for this or that moment of time, it was afraid for its entire being; it felt the fear of death, the sovereign master. It has been in that experience melted to its inmost soul, has trembled throughout its every fibre, and all that was fixed and steadfast has quaked within it. This complete perturbation of its entire substance, this absolute dissolution of all its stability into fluent continuity, is, however, the simple, ultimate nature of self-consciousness, absolute negativity, pure self-referent existence, which consequently is involved in this type of consciousness. This moment of pure self-existence is moreover a fact for it; for in the master it finds this as its object. Further, this bondsman's consciousness is not only this total dissolution in a general way; in serving and toiling the bondsman actually carries this out. By serving he cancels in every particular aspect his dependence on and attachment to natural existence, and by his work removes this existence away.[14]

The servant is thus in-himself already free, his freedom being embodied outside himself in his master. It is in this sense that Christ is our master and simultaneously the source of our freedom. Christ's sacrifice set us free — how? Neither as the payment for our sins nor as legalistic ransom, but as when we are afraid of something (and fear of death is the ultimate fear that makes us slaves), and a true friend says: "Don't be afraid, look, I will do it. What are you so afraid of? I will do it, not because I have to but out of my love for you. I am not afraid!" He does it and in this way sets us free, demonstrating *in actu* that *it can be done*, that we too can do it, that we are not slaves . . . Recall, from Ayn Rand's *The Fountainhead*, the description of the momentary impact Howard Roark makes on the members of the audience in the courtroom where he is standing trial:

Roark stood before them as each man stands in the innocence of his own mind. But Roark stood like that before a hostile crowd — and they knew suddenly that no hatred was possible to him. For the flash of an instant, they grasped the manner of his consciousness. Each asked himself: do I need anyone's approval? — does it matter? — am I tied? —

And for that instant, each man was free—free enough to feel bene-
volence for every other man in the room. It was only a moment; the
moment of silence when Roark was about to speak.[15]

This is the way Christ brings freedom: when confronting him, we become
aware of our own freedom. And does not, *mutatis mutandis*, the same hold
for Che Guevara? The photos showing him under arrest in Bolivia,
surrounded by government soldiers, have a weird Christological aura, as
if we see a tired but defiant Christ on his way to crucifixion—no wonder
that, when, moments prior to his death, the executioner's pistol already
aimed at him, the hand holding it trembling, Guevara looked at him and
said: "Aim well. You are about to kill a man"[16]—his version of *ecce
homo* . . . And, indeed, is the basic message of Guevara not precisely this:
the message of how, in and through all his failures, he persisted, he went
on? One can imagine him thinking in the desperate last days in Bolivia a
version of the last words of Samuel Beckett's *The Unnameable*: "in the
silence you don't know, you must go on, I can't go on, I'll go on."[17] In an
unsurpassable irony of history, after the triumph of the Cuban revolution,
everything he did was a failure—the dismal failure of his economic
policies as the Cuban minister of economy (after a year, food had to be
rationed. . .), the failure of his Congo adventure, the failure of his last
mission in Bolivia; however, all these "human, all too human" failures
somehow fade into the background, the backdrop against which the
contours of his properly over-human (or, why not, *inhuman*) figure
appear, confirming Badiou's motto that the only way to be truly human
is to exceed ordinary humanity, tending towards the dimension of the
inhuman.

Ecology against nature

Do we not, today, once again need such a shattering experience of
negativity? That is to say, what if the true choice today were *between* fear
and terror? The expression "fear and trembling" assumes the identity of
the two terms, as if they point towards the two aspects of the same
phenomenon—what if, however, one has to introduce a gap between the
two, so that trembling (being-terrorized) is, at its most radical, the only
true opposition to fear? In other words, one can break out of this fear not
through a desperate search for safety, but, on the contrary, by pushing on
to the end, by accepting the nullity of that which we are afraid to lose.

Isaac Asimov said somewhere that there are two possibilities: either we are alone in the universe, there is nobody out there watching us, or there is somebody out there—and both possibilities are equally unbearable. So, from the fear of losing our anchorage in the big Other, we should pass to the terror of there being *no* big Other. The old formula "there is nothing to fear but fear itself" acquires thus a new and unexpected meaning: the fact that there is nothing to fear is the most terrifying fact imaginable. Terror is this "self-related" or "self-negated" fear: it is what fear changes into once we accept that there is no way back, that what we are afraid to lose, what is threatened by what we are afraid of (nature, the life-world, the symbolic substance of our community . . .) has always-already been lost. This terror whose contours Hegel outlined in his description of the servant's subjective experience of encountering the threat of death should serve us as the background against which one should read Marx and Engels's famous description of the capitalist dynamic in the *Communist Manifesto*:

> Constant revolutionizing of production, uninterrupted disturbance of all social conditions, everlasting uncertainty and agitation distinguish the bourgeois epoch from all earlier ones. All fixed, fast-frozen relations, with their train of ancient and venerable prejudices and opinions are swept away, all new-formed ones become antiquated before they can ossify. All that is solid melts into air, all that is holy is profaned, and man is at last compelled to face with sober senses his real conditions of life, and his relations with his kind. [. . .] In place of the old local and national seclusion and self-sufficiency, we have inter-course in every direction, universal inter-dependence of nations. And as in material, so also in intellectual production. The intellectual creations of individual nations become common property. National one-sidedness and narrow-mindedness become more and more im-possible, and from the numerous national and local literatures, there arises a world literature.[18]

Is this not, more than ever, our reality today? Ericsson phones are no longer Swedish, Toyota cars are manufactured 60 percent in the USA, Hollywood culture pervades the remotest parts of the globe . . . Further-more, does the same not go also for all forms of ethnic and sexual identity? Should we not supplement Marx's description in this sense, adding that also sexual "one-sidedness and narrow-mindedness become more and more impossible," that concerning sexual practices, it also true that "all that is solid melts into air, all that is holy is profaned," so that capitalism tends to replace standard normative heterosexuality with a proliferation of unstable shifting identities and/or orientations? And today, with the latest biogenetic developments, we are entering a new phase in which it is simply *nature itself* which melts into air: the main consequence of the scientific breakthroughs in biogenetics is the end of nature. Once we know the rules of its construction, natural organisms are transformed into objects amenable to manipulation. Nature, human and inhuman, is thus "desubstantialized," deprived of its impenetrable density, of what Heidegger called "earth." This compels us to give a new twist to Freud's title *Unbehagen in der Kultur*—discontent, uneasiness, in culture.[19] With the latest developments, the discontent shifts from culture to nature itself: nature is no longer "natural," the reliable "dense" background of our lives; it now appears as a fragile mechanism which, at any point, can explode in a catastrophic manner.

Biogenetics, with its reduction of the human psyche itself to an object of technological manipulation, is therefore effectively a kind of empirical instantiation of what Heidegger perceived as the "danger" inherent in modern technology. Crucial here is the interdependence of man and nature: by reducing man to just another natural object whose properties can be manipulated, what we lose is not (only) humanity but *nature itself*. In this sense, Francis Fukuyama is right: humanity relies on some notion of "human nature" as what we have inherited, as something that has simply been given to us, the impenetrable dimension in/of ourselves into which we are born/thrown. The paradox is thus that that there is man only insofar as there is impenetrable inhuman nature (Heidegger's "earth"): with the prospect of biogenetic interventions opened up by the access to the genome, the species freely changes/redefines *itself*, its own coordinates; this prospect effectively emancipates humankind from the constraints of a finite species, from its enslavement to "selfish genes." This emancipation, however, comes at a price:

> With interventions into man's genetic inheritance, the domination over nature reverts into an act of taking-control-over-oneself, which changes our generic-ethical self-understanding and can disturb the necessary conditions for an autonomous way of life and universalistic understanding of morals.[20]

How, then, should we react to this threat? Habermas's logic is here: since the results of science pose a threat to our (predominant notion of) autonomy and freedom, one should curtail science. The price we pay for this solution is the fetishistic split between science and ethics—"I know very well what science claims, but, nonetheless, in order to retain (the appearance of) my autonomy, I choose to ignore it and act as if I don't know it." This prevents us from confronting the true question: *how do these new conditions compel us to transform and reinvent the very notions of freedom, autonomy, and ethical responsibility?*

Science and technology today no longer aim only at understanding and reproducing natural processes, but at generating new forms of life that will surprise us; the goal is no longer just to dominate nature (the way it is), but to generate something new, greater, stronger than ordinary nature, including ourselves—exemplary here is the obsession with artificial intelligence, which aims at producing a brain more powerful than the human brain. The dream that sustains the scientific-technological endeavor is to trigger a process with no return, a process that would exponentially reproduce itself and go on and on autonomously. The notion of "second nature" is therefore today more pertinent than ever, in both its main meanings. First, literally, as the artificially generated new nature: monsters of nature, deformed cows and trees, or—a more positive dream—genetically manipulated organisms, "enhanced" in the manner that suits us. Then, "second nature" in the more standard sense of the autonomization of the results of our own activity: the way our acts elude us in their consequences, the way they generate a monster with a life of its own. It is *this* horror at the unforeseen results of our own acts that causes shock and awe, not the power of nature over which we have no control; it is *this* horror that religion tries to domesticate. What is new today is the short-circuit between these two senses of "second nature": "second nature" in the sense of objective Fate, of autonomized social process, is generating "second nature" in the sense of artificially created nature, of natural monsters, namely, the process which threatens to run out of control is no longer just the social process of economic and political development, but new forms of natural processes themselves, from unpredictable nuclear catastrophes to global warming and the unimaginable consequences of biogenetic manipulation. Can one even imagine what would be the unprecedented result of nanotechnological experiments: new life-forms reproducing themselves out of control in a cancerlike way, for example?[21] Here is a standard description of this fear:

Within fifty to a hundred years, a new class of organisms is likely to emerge. These organisms will be artificial in the sense that they will originally be designed by humans. However, they will reproduce, and will "evolve" into something other than their original form; they will be "alive" under any reasonable definition of the word. [. . .] [T]he pace of evolutionary change will be extremely rapid. [. . .] The impact on humanity and the biosphere could be enormous, larger than the industrial revolution, nuclear weapons, or environmental pollution.[22]

This fear also has its clear libidinal dimension: it is the fear of the asexual reproduction of Life, the fear of an "undead" life that is indestructible, constantly expanding, reproducing itself through self-division.[23] And, as always in the history of the last two millennia, the greatest master of exploiting this fear is the Catholic Church. Its predominant strategy today is that of trying to contain the scientific real within the confines of meaning—it is as an answer to the scientific real (materialized in biogenetic threats) that religion is finding its new *raison d'être*:

Far from being effaced by science, religion, and even the syndicate of religions, in the process of formation, is progressing every day. Lacan said that ecumenism was for the poor of spirit. There is a marvelous agreement on these questions between the secular and all the religious authorities, in which they tell themselves they should agree somewhere in order to make echoes equally marvelous, even saying that finally the secular is a religion like the others. We see this because it is revealed in effect that the discourse of science has partly connected with the death drive. Religion is planted in the position of unconditional defense of the living, of life in mankind, as guardian of life, making life an absolute. And that extends to the protection of human nature. [. . .] This is [. . .] what gives a future to religion through meaning, namely by erecting barriers—to cloning, to the exploitation of human cells—and to inscribe science in a tempered progress. We see a marvelous effort, a new youthful vigor of religion in its effort to flood the real with meaning.[24]

The Church's message of hope thus relies on a preexisting fear: it evokes and formulates the fear to which it then offers a solution of hope and faith.[25] The Life that it promises in its defense of the "culture of life" is not a positive life, but a reactive life, a defense against death. We are dealing here with the latest version of the fear first formulated in Mary Shelley's *Frankenstein*. The dilemma faced by many interpreters of *Frankenstein* concerns the obvious parallel between Victor and God, on the one side, and the monster and Adam, on the other: in both cases, we are dealing with a single parent creating a male progeny in a non-sexual way; in both cases, this is followed by the creation of a bride, a female partner. This parallel is clearly indicated in the novel's epigraph, Adam's complaint to God:

> Did I request thee, Maker, from my clay
> To mould Me man? Did I solicit thee
> From darkness to promote me?
>
> (*Paradise Lost*, X, 743–5)

It is easy to note the problematic nature of this parallel: if Victor is associated with God, how can he also be the Promethean rebel against God (recall the novel's subtitle: ". . . or The Modern Prometheus")? The answer seems to be a simple one, spelled out by Shelley herself: Victor's sin is precisely that of presumption, of "acting like God," engaging in an act of creation (of human life, the crown of the divine creation) which is and should remain the exclusive prerogative of God; if man tries to imitate God and do something for which he lacks qualifications, the result can only be monstrous . . .

There is, however, also a different (Chestertonian) reading: there is no problem here, Victor is "like God" precisely when he commits the ultimate criminal transgression and confronts the horror of its consequences, since *God is also the greatest Rebel* — against himself, ultimately. The King of the universe is the supreme criminal Anarchist. Like Victor, in creating man, God committed the supreme crime of aiming too high — of creating a creature "in his own image," new spiritial life, precisely like today's scientists who dream of creating an artificially intelligent living being; no wonder that his own creature escaped his control and turned against him. So what if the death of Christ (of himself) is the price God has to pay for his crime?

It is precisely within the domain of ecology that one can draw the line that separates the politics of emancipatory terror from the politics of fear at its purest. By far the predominant version of ecology is the ecology of fear, fear of a catastrophe — human-made or natural — that may deeply perturb, destroy even, human civilization, fear that pushes us to plan measures to protect our safety. This fear and pessimism are as a rule fake, as pointed out by Hans-Georg Gadamer: "The pessimist is disingenuous because he is trying to trick himself with his own grumbling. Precisely while acting the pessimist, he secretly hopes that everything will not turn out as bad as he fears."[26] Does the same tension between the enunciated and the position of enunciation not characterize today's ecological pessimism: the more those who predict a catastrophe insist on it, the more they secretly hope the catastrophe will not occur?

The first thing that strikes the eye apropos this fear is the way it remains conditioned by ideological trends. Two decades ago, everyone, especially in Europe, was talking about *Waldsterben*, the dying of the forests; the topic was present on the covers of all popular weeklies—now it has almost disappeared. Although concerns about global warming explode from time to time and are gaining more and more scientific credibility, ecology as an organized socio-political movement has to a large degree disappeared. Furthermore, ecology often lends itself to ideological mystifications: as a pretext for New Age obscurantisms (praising pre-modern "paradigms," and so forth), or for neo-colonialism (First World complaints that the fast development of Third World countries like Brazil or China threatens us all—"by destroying the Amazon rainforests, the Brazilians are killing the lungs of our Earth"), or as an honorable cause for "liberal communists" (buy green, recycle . . . as if taking ecology into account justifies capitalist exploitation).

This ecology of fear has every chance of developing into the predominant form of ideology of global capitalism, a new opium for the masses replacing declining religion:[27] it takes over the old religion's fundamental function, that of having an unquestionable authority which can impose limits. The lesson this ecology is constantly hammering away at is our finitude: we are not Cartesian subjects extracted from reality, we are finite beings embedded in a biosphere which vastly transcends our horizon. In our exploitation of natural resources, we are borrowing from the future, so we should start treating our Earth with respect, as something that is ultimately Sacred, something that should not be totally unveiled, that should and will forever remain a Mystery, a power we should trust, not dominate. While we cannot gain full mastery over our biosphere, it is unfortunately in our power to derail it, to disturb its balance so that it will run amok, wiping us away in the process. This is why, although ecologists are all the time demanding that we radically change our way of life, underlying this demand is its opposite, a deep distrust of change, of development, of progress: every radical change can have the unintended consequence of triggering a catastrophe.

It is this distrust which makes ecology the ideal candidate for the hegemonic ideology, since it echoes the anti-totalitarian post-political distrust of large collective acts. One of the most effective fictional versions of this distrust is Stephen Fry's *Making History*,[28] about a scientist traumatized by Hitler and the Nazi crimes who, in the 1950s, discovers a way to cross the time barrier and intervene in the past in a limited way. He decides to change the chemical composition of the stream from which the village of Hitler's parents was getting water, so that it renders women infertile; the experiment succeeds and Hitler is not born. However, when we switch into the alternate reality, the scientist discovers with horror what he has caused: instead of Hitler, a more intelligent upper-class high-ranking officer led the Nazis to victory, the Nazis win the war and kill many more Jews than perished in the Holocaust, even obliterating the memory of their act. The scientist spends the rest of his life trying to intervene again in the past in order to undo the results of his first intervention and to return us to the good old world with Hitler . . .

Such distrust was given a new impetus by biogenetics, which is on the verge of a crucial breakthrough.[29] Up until now, geneticists were confined to

> tinkering and tweaking what nature has already produced—taking a gene from a bacterium, say, and inserting it into the chromosome of corn or pigs. What we're talking about is producing life that is wholly new—not in any way a genetic descendant of the primordial Mother Cell. The initial members of each newly created breed will have no ancestors at all.

The genome itself of the organism will be artificially put together: first, individual biological building blocks are to be fabricated; then, they are to be combined in an entirely new synthetic self-replicating organism. Scientists designate this new life-form as "Life 2.0," and what is so unsettling about it is that "natural" life itself becomes thereby "Life 1.0"—it retroactively loses its spontaneous-natural character, becoming one in the series of synthetic projects. This is what the "end of nature" means: synthetic life is not just supplementing natural life, it turns natural life itself into a (confused, imperfect) species of synthetic life.

The prospects are, of course, breathtaking: from microorganisms which detect cancer cells and eliminate them, to whole "factories" which transform solar energy into usable fuel. However, the main limitation of this endeavor is no less obvious: the DNA of existing natural organisms is "a mess of overlapping segments and junk that has no purpose scientists can fathom," so when geneticists tinker with this mess, they cannot ever be sure not only of the outcome, but also of how, exactly, this outcome was generated—the logical conclusion is thus to try to "build new biological systems; systems that are easier to understand because we made them that way." However, this project will work only if we fully accept the thesis that "at least 90 percent of the human genome is 'junk DNA' that has no clear function." (The main function envisaged by scientists is that the junk serves as a guarantee against the danger of copying mistakes, a kind of back-up copy.) Only in this case we can expect a project of getting rid of the repetitious "junk" and generating the organism only from its "pure" genetic formula to work. What if, however, the "junk" does play a crucial role, unknown to us because we are unable to grasp all the higher-level complexity of the interaction of genes which can only account for how, out of a limited (finite) set of elements, an "infinite" (self-relating) organic structure arises as an "emergent property"?

Those who are opposed most ferociously to this prospect are religious leaders and environmentalists—for both, there is something of a transgression, of entering a prohibited domain, in this idea of creating a new form of life from scratch, from the zero-point. And this brings us back to the notion of ecology as the new opium of the masses; the underlying message is again a deeply conservative one—any change can only be a change for the worse:

> Behind much of the resistance to the notion of synthetic life is the intuition that nature (or God) created the best of possible worlds. Charles Darwin believed that the myriad designs of nature's creations are perfectly honed to do whatever they are meant to do—be it animals that see, hear, sing, swim or fly, or plants that feed on the sun's rays, exuding bright floral colours to attract pollinators.[30]

This reference to Darwin is deeply misleading: the ultimate lesson of Darwinism is the exact opposite, namely that nature tinkers and improvises, with great losses and catastrophes accompanying every limited success — is the fact that 90 percent of the human genome is "junk DNA" with no clear function not the ultimate proof? Consequently, the first lesson to be drawn is the one repeatedly made by Stephen Jay Gould: the utter contingency of our existence. There is no Evolution: catastrophes, broken equilibria, are part of natural history; at numerous points in the past, life could have taken a turn in an entirely different direction. The main source of our energy (oil) is the result of a past cataclysm of unimaginable dimensions.

Along these lines, "terror" means accepting the fact of the utter groundlessness of our existence: there is no firm foundation, place of retreat, on which one can safely count. It means fully accepting that "nature does not exist," in other words, fully consummating the gap that separates the life-world notion of nature and the scientific notion of natural reality: "nature" *qua* the domain of balanced reproduction, of organic deployment into which humanity intervenes with its hubris, brutally throwing its circular motion off the rails, is man's fantasy; nature is already in itself "second nature," its balance is always secondary, an attempt to bring into existence a "habit" that would restore some order after catastrophic interruptions.[31] The lesson to be fully endorsed is thus that of an environmental scientist who comes to the conclusion that, while one cannot be sure what the ultimate result of humanity's interventions in the geosphere will be, one thing is sure: if humanity were to abruptly stop its immense industrial activity and let nature on Earth take its balanced course, the result would be a total breakdown, an unimaginable catastrophe. "Nature" on Earth is already so "adapted" to human interventions, human "pollution" is already so completely included in the shaky and fragile balance of "natural" reproduction on Earth, that its cessation would cause a catastrophic imbalance.[32] This is what it means to say that humanity has nowhere to retreat to: not only is there no "big Other" (self-contained symbolic order as the ultimate guarantee of Meaning); there is also no *Nature qua* balanced order of self-reproduction whose homeostasis is disturbed, nudged off course, by unbalanced human interventions. Not only is the big Other "barred," but Nature too is barred. One should thus become aware not only of the limitation of the ideology of progress, but also of the limitation of the Benjaminian notion of the revolution as applying the emergency brake on the runaway train of progress: it is too late for that too.

In his *Reflections at the Edge of Askja*, Pall Skulason reports how he was affected by Askja, a volcanic lake and valley in the middle of Iceland, surrounded by snow-covered mountains:

> Askja is the symbol of objective reality, independent of all thought, belief and expression, independent of human existence. It is a unique natural system, within which mountains, lakes and sky converge in a volcanic crater. Askja, in short, symbolizes the earth itself; it is the earth as it was, is, and will be, for as long as this planet continues to orbit in space, whatever we do and whether or not we are here on this earth. [. . .] Coming to Askja is like coming to the earth itself for the first time; finding one's earthly grounding.[33]

Gilles Deleuze often played with the motif of how, in becoming post-human, we should learn to practice "a perception as it was before men (or after) [. . .] released from their human coordinates";[34] Skulason seems to be describing just such an experience, the experience of subtracting oneself from the immediate immersion into the surrounding world of objects which are "ready-at-hand," moments of our engaged relationship with reality—or is he? Let us take a closer look at what kind of experience he is rendering:

> the world suddenly strikes us in such a way that reality presents itself as a seamless whole. The question that then arises concerns the world itself and the reality that it orders into a totality. Is the world really a unified totality? Isn't reality just an infinitely variegated manifold of particular phenomena?[35]

One should be Hegelian here: what if this very experience of reality as a seamless Whole is a violent imposition of ours, something we "project onto it" (to use this old inappropriate term) in order to avoid directly confronting the totally meaningless "infinitely variegated manifold of particular phenomena" (what Alain Badiou calls the primordial multi-plicity of Being)? Should we not apply here the fundamental lesson of Kant's transcendental idealism: the world as a Whole is not a Thing-in-itself, it is merely a regulative Idea of our mind, something our mind imposes on the raw multitude of sensations in order to be able to experience it as a well-ordered meaningful Whole? The paradox is that the very In-itself of Nature as a Whole independent of us is the result of our (subjective) "synthetic activity"—do Skulason's own words, if we read them closely (i.e., literally), not already point in this direction? "Askja is used in this text as the symbol of a unique and important experience of the world and its inhabitants. There are numerous other symbols which men use to talk about the things that matter most."[36] So, exactly as is the case with the Kantian Sublime, the unfathomable presence of raw Nature-in-itself is reduced to a material pretext (replaceable with others) for "a unique and important experience." Why is this experience necessary?

> To live, to be able to exist, the mind must connect itself with some kind of order. It must apprehend reality as an independent whole [. . .] and must bind itself in a stable fashion to certain features of what we call reality. It cannot bind itself to the ordinary world of everyday experience, except by taking it on faith that reality forms an objective whole, a whole which exists independently of the mind. The mind lives, and we live, in a relationship of faith with reality itself. This relationship is likewise one of confidence in a detached reality, a reality which is different and other than the mind. We live and exist in this relationship of confidence, which is always by its nature uncertain and insecure. [. . .] [T]he relationship of confidence [. . .] is originally, and truly, always a relationship with reality as a natural totality: as Nature.[37]

One should note here the refined analysis of the tension between the inhabitable and the uninhabitable: in order to inhabit a small part of reality that appears within our horizon of meaning, we have to presuppose that Reality-in-itself, "different and other than the mind," which sustains our world is part of reality as an ordered and seamless Whole. In short, we have to have faith and confidence in Reality: nature-in-itself is not merely a meaningless composite of multiples, it is Nature. What, however, if this relationship of faith in Nature, in the primordial harmony between mind and reality, is the most elementary form of idealism, of reliance on the big Other? What if the true materialist position starts (and, in a way, ends) with the acceptance of the In-itself as a meaningless chaotic manifold? One is tempted here to turn again to Iceland's unique natural landscape: the magnificent misty-green coastal plain in the south, scattered with large rocks covered with wet green-brown moss, cannot but appear as nature run amok, full of pathological cancerous protuberances—what if this is much closer to "nature-in-itself" than the sublime images of seamless Wholes? Indeed, what we need is an *ecology without nature*: the ultimate obstacle to protecting nature is the very notion of nature we rely on.[38]

The true source of our problems is not "the most significant event to affect Western culture during recent centuries," namely the "breakdown of the relationship between man and nature,"[39] the retreat of the relationship of trust. On the contrary: this very "relationship of faith with reality itself" is the main obstacle that prevents us from confronting the ecological crisis at its most radical. That is to say, with regard to the prospects of an ecological catastrophe, it is too easy to attribute our disbelief in it to the impregnation of our minds by scientific ideology, which leads us to dismiss the sane concerns of our common reason, namely, the gut sense which tells us that something is fundamentally wrong with the scientific-technological attitude. The problem is much deeper. It resides in the unreliability of our common sense itself which, habituated as it is to our ordinary life-world, finds it difficult to really accept that the flow of everyday reality can be perturbed. Our attitude here is that of the fetishistic split: "I know very well (that global warming is a threat to the entire humanity), but nonetheless . . . (I cannot really believe it). It is enough to see the natural world to which my mind is connected: green grass and trees, the sighing of the breeze, the rising of the sun . . . can one really imagine that all this will be disturbed? You talk about the ozone hole—but no matter how much I look into the sky, I don't see it—all I see is the sky, blue or grey!"

The problem is thus that we can rely neither on the scientific mind nor on our common sense—they both mutually reinforce each other's blindness. The scientific mind advocates a cold objective appraisal of dangers and risks involved where no such appraisal is really possible, while common sense finds it hard to accept that a catastrophe can really occur. The difficult ethical task is thus to "un-learn" the most basic coordinates of our immersion into our life-world: what usually served as the recourse to Wisdom (basic trust in the background coordinates of our world) is now *the* source of danger. We should really "grow up" and learn to cut this ultimate umbilical cord to our life-sphere. The problem with the science-and-technology attitude is not its detachment from our life-world, but the abstract character of this detachment which compels the science-and-technology attitude to combine itself with the worst elements of our life-world immersion. Scientists perceive themselves as rational, able to appraise potential risks objectively; for them, the only unpredictable-irrational elements are the panic reactions of the uneducated masses: with ordinary people, a small and controllable risk can spread and trigger global panic, since they project onto the situation their disavowed fears and fantasies. What scientists are unable to perceive is the "irrational," inadequate, nature of their own "cold and distanced" appraisal. Contemporary science serves two properly *ideological* needs, "for hope and censorship," which were traditionally taken care of by religion:

> science alone has the power to silence heretics. Today it is the only institution that can claim authority. Like the Church in the past, it has the power to destroy, or marginalize, independent thinkers. [. . .] From the standpoint of anyone who values freedom of thought, this may be unfortunate, but it is undoubtedly the chief source of science's appeal. For us, science is a refuge from uncertainties, promising—and in some measure delivering—the miracle of freedom from thought, while churches have become sanctuaries for doubt.[40]

Indeed, as Nietzsche put it more than a century ago: "Oh, how much is today hidden by science! Oh, how much it is expected to hide!"[41] However, we are not talking here about science as such, so the idea of science sustaining "freedom from thought" is not a variation on Heidegger's notion that "science doesn't think." We are talking about the way science functions as a social force, as an ideological institution: at this level, its function is to provide certainty, to be a point of reference on which one can rely, and to provide hope (new technological inventions will help us against diseases, and so on). In this dimension, science is—in Lacanian terms—university discourse at its purest, S_2 (knowledge) whose "truth" is S_1 (Master-Signifier, power). The paradox effectively is that, today, science provides the security which was once guaranteed by religion, and, in a curious inversion, religion is one of the possible places from which one can develop critical doubts about contemporary society (one of the "sites of resistance," as it were).

Louis Dumont[42] noted the paradox of cognitivist reduction-naturalization: man finally master of himself, recreating his own genome—but *who* is the agent here? The blind circuit of neurons? Here the tension between the enunciated content and the position of enunciation (what Foucault referred to as the "transcendental-empirical doublet") is pushed to an extreme point: the more the enunciated content is limited to an objective material process, the more the position of enunciation is reduced to a *pure cogito*, the void of an empty subject. This brings us to the problem of free will. Compatibilists such as Daniel Dennett[43] have an elegant solution to the incompatibilists' complaints about determinism: when incompatibilists complain that our freedom cannot be combined with the fact that all our acts are part of the great chain of natural determinism, they secretly make an unwarranted ontological assumption. First, they assume that we (the Self, the free agent) somehow stand *outside* reality, and then go on to complain how they feel oppressed by the notion that reality with its determinism controls them totally. This is what is wrong with the notion of us being "imprisoned" by the chains of natural determinism: we thereby obfuscate the fact that we are *part of* reality, that the (possible, local) conflict between our "free" striving and external reality resisting it is a conflict inherent to reality itself. That is to say, there is nothing "oppressive" or "constraining" about the fact that our innermost strivings are (pre)determined: when we feel thwarted in our freedom by the constraining pressure of external reality, there must be something in us, some desires, strivings, which are thus thwarted, and where should these strivings come from if not from this same reality? Our "free will" does not in some mysterious way "disturb the natural course of things," it is part and parcel of this course. For us to be "truly" and "radically" free, this would entail there being no positive content that we want to impose as our free act—if we want nothing "external" and particular/given to determine our behavior, then "this would involve being free of every part of ourselves."[44] When a determinist claims that our free choice is "determined," this does not mean that our free will is somehow constrained, that we are forced to act *against* our free will— what is "determined" is the very thing that we want to do "freely," that is, without being thwarted by external obstacles.

The uses and misuses of Heidegger

What the ecology of fear obfuscates is thus a far more radical dimension of terror. Today, with the prospect of the biogenetic manipulation of human physical and psychic features, the notion of "danger" inscribed into modern technology, elaborated by Heidegger, becomes a commonplace. Heidegger emphasizes how the true danger is not the physical self-destruction of humanity, the threat that something will go terribly wrong with biogenetic interventions, but, precisely, that *nothing* will go wrong, that genetic manipulation will function smoothly—at this point, the circle will, in a certain manner, be closed and the specific openness that characterizes being-human abolished. That is to say, is the Heideggerian danger (*Gefahr*) not precisely the danger that the ontic will "swallow" the ontological (with the reduction of man, the *∂a* [here] of Being, to just another object of science)? Do we not encounter here again the formula of the fear of the impossible: what we fear is that that which cannot happen (since the ontological dimension is irreducible to the ontic) will nonetheless happen . . .

The same point is made in a cruder fashion by cultural critics from Fukuyama and Habermas to Bill McKibben, worried about how the latest techno-scientific developments (which potentially give the human species the capacity to redesign and redefine itself) will affect our being-human—the call we hear is best encapsulated by the title of McKibben's book: "Enough." Humanity as a collective subject has to set down limits and freely renounce further "progress" in this direction. McKibben endeavors to specify such limits empirically: somatic genetic therapy is still this side of the tipping point, one can practice it without leaving behind the world as we know it, since it simply involves intervention in a body formed in the old "natural" way; germline manipulations lie on the other side, in the world beyond meaning.[45] When we manipulate psychic and bodily properties of individuals before they are even conceived, we pass the threshold into full-fledged planning, turning individuals into products, preventing them from experiencing themselves as responsible agents who have to educate/form themselves by the effort of focusing their will, thus obtaining the satisfaction of achievement—such individuals no longer relate to themselves as responsible agents . . .

The insufficiency of this reasoning is double. First, as Heidegger would have put it, the survival of the being-human of humans cannot depend on an ontic decision of humans. Even if we try to define the limit of the permissible in this way, *the true catastrophe has already taken place*: we already experience ourselves as in principle manipulable; we just freely renounce the possibility of fully deploying this potential. "In the technological age, what matters to us most is getting the 'greatest possible use' out of everything."[46] Does this not throw a new light on how ecological concerns, at least in their predominant mode, remain within the horizon of technology? Is the point of using the resources sparingly, of recycling, and so forth, not precisely to maximize the use of everything?

But the crucial point is that, with biogenetic planning, not only will our universe of meaning disappear—in other words, not only are the utopian descriptions of the digital paradise wrong, since they imply that meaning will persist—but the opposite, negative, critical descriptions of the "meaningless" universe of technological self-manipulation also fall victim to a perspectival fallacy, for they too measure the future by inadequate present-day standards. That is to say, the future of technological self-manipulation only appears as "deprived of meaning" if measured by (or, rather, from within the horizon of) the traditional notion of what a meaningful universe is. Who knows what this "post-human" universe will reveal itself to be "in itself"? What if there is no singular and simple answer; what if the contemporary trends (digitalization, biogenetic self-manipulation) open themselves up to a multitude of possible symbolizations? What if the utopia—the perverted dream of the passage from hardware to software of a subjectivity freely floating between different embodiments—and the dystopia—the nightmare of humans voluntarily transforming themselves into programmed beings—are just the positive and the negative sides of the same ideological fantasy? What if it is only and precisely this technological prospect that fully confronts us with the most radical dimension of our finitude?[47]

Heidegger himself remains ambiguous here. It is true that Heidegger's answer to technology

is not nostalgic longing for "former objects which perhaps were once on the way to becoming things and even to actually presencing as things" ("The Thing"), but rather allowing ourselves to be conditioned by our world, and then learning to "keep the fourfold in things" by building and nurturing things peculiarly suited to our fourfold. When our practices incorporate the fourfold, our lives and everything around us will have importance far exceeding that of resources, because they and only they will be geared to our way of inhabiting the world.[48]

However, all the examples Heidegger provides of "keeping the fourfold in things"—from the Greek temples and van Gogh's shoes up to numerous examples from his Schwarzwald mountains are nostalgic, that is, they belong to a world which has passed, which is no longer ours—for example, he opposes traditional farming practices to modern technologized agriculture, the Black Forest farmer's house to a modern apartment block. So what would be examples that are appropriate to our technological times? Perhaps one should take very seriously Fredric Jameson's idea of reading Raymond Chandler's California as a Heideggerian "world," with Phillip Marlowe caught in a tension between heaven and earth, between his mortality and the "divine" shining through in the pathetic longing of his characters, and so on. And did Ruth Rendell not accomplish the same for British suburbia with its forlorn back gardens, grey shopping malls, and so forth? This is also why Hubert Dreyfus's notion that the way to be prepared for the upcoming *Kehre*, for the arrival of new gods, is to participate in practices which function as sites of resistance to technological total mobilization, is all too facile:

> Heidegger explores a kind of gathering that would enable us to resist postmodern technological practices. [. . .] [H]e turns from the cultural gathering he explored in "The Origin of the Work of Art" (that sets up shared meaningful differences and thereby unifies an entire culture) to local gatherings that set up local worlds. Such local worlds occur around some everyday thing that temporarily brings into their own both the thing itself and those involved in the typical activity concerning the use of the thing. Heidegger calls this event a *thing thinging* and the tendency in the practices to bring things and people into their own, *appropriation*. [. . .] Heidegger's examples of things that focus such local gathering are a wine jug and an old stone bridge. Such things gather Black Forest peasant practices [. . .] the family meal acts as a focal thing when it draws on the culinary and social skills of family members and solicits fathers, mothers, husbands, wives, children, familiar warmth, good humor, and loyalty to come to the fore in their excellence, or in, as Heidegger would say, their ownmost.[49]

From a strict Heideggerian position, such practices can—and as a rule *do*—function as the very opposite of resistance, as something that is in advance included in the smooth functioning of the technological mobilization (like the courses in transcendental meditation which make you more efficient in your job), which is why the path to salvation only leads through to full engagement in technological mobilization.

The flipside of constant capitalist innovation is, of course, the permanent production of piles of leftover waste:

> The main production of the modern and postmodern capitalist industry is precisely waste. We are postmodern beings because we realize that all our aesthetically appealing consumption artifacts will eventually end up as leftovers, to the point that it will transform the

earth into a vast waste land. You lose the sense of tragedy, you perceive progress as derisive.[50]

In these ever-growing piles of inert, dysfunctional "stuff"—the growing piles of useless waste, the mountains of used cars, computers, and so on, like the famous aeroplane "final resting place" in the Mojave desert . . .— which cannot but strike us with their pointless presence, one can, as it were, perceive the capitalist drive at rest. Therein resides the interest of Andrei Tarkovsky's films, such as his masterpiece, *Stalker*, with its post-industrial wasteland of wild vegetation growing in abandoned factories, concrete tunnels and railroads, pools of stale water, and stray cats and dogs wandering hither and thither. Nature and industrial civilization overlap here again, but through a process of common decay—civilization in decay is in the process of again being reclaimed (not by an idealized harmonious Nature, but) by nature in a state of decomposition. The ultimate Tarkovskian landscape is a river or pool on the edge of a forest, filled with the debris of human endeavor, pieces of rusty metal and decaying concrete blocks. The post-industrial wasteland of the *Second* World is indeed the privileged "evental site," the symptomal point out of which one can undermine the totality of contemporary global capitalism. One should *love* this world, including its grey decaying buildings and sulphureous smells—all this stands for *history*, threatened with erasure by the post-historical First World and pre-historical Third World.

Benjamin developed a notion of "natural history" as renaturalized history: it takes place when historical artifacts loose their meaningful vitality and are perceived as dead objects reclaimed by nature or, in the best case, as monuments of a past dead culture. (For Benjamin, it was when we confront such such dead monuments of human history re-claimed by nature that we experience history at its purest.) The paradox here is that this re-naturalization overlaps with its opposite, with de-naturalization: since for us human culture is our "second nature," we experience it as our natural habitat. Deprived of their function within a living totality of meaning, cultural artifacts dwell in an inter-space between nature and culture, between life and death, leading a ghostly existence, belonging neither to nature nor to culture, appearing as something akin to the monstrosity of natural freaks, like a cow with two heads and three legs.

Another less pathetic, but, perhaps, no less efficient strategy is that of *shindogu*, the Japanese movement popular a decade or more ago, which manufactured objects which were useless in their very over-functionality (like glasses with small "windscreen wipers" for better visibility when you go for a walk in the rain; or a "butter-stick," like a lipstick, for when you want to butter a slice of bread but don't have a knife; or an upwardly inverted umbrella with a water-collector which not only protects you from the rain but simultaneously provides you with fresh water . . .)— through this procedure, a kind of technological counterpart to ideological overidentification, our engagement with technology itself is turned into a means of distancing and releasing ourselves from its grip.

The challenge of technology is thus not that we should (re)discover how all our activity has to rely on our irreducible (*unhintergehbare*) embeddedness in our life-world, but, on the contrary, that of cutting onself off from this embeddedness and accepting the radical abyss of one's existence. This is the terror which even Heidegger did not dare confront. To put it in the terms of a problematic comparison, are we, insofar as we remain humans embedded in a pre-reflexive symbolic life-world, not something like "symbolic plants"? Hegel says somewhere in his *Philosophy of Nature* that a plant's roots are its entrails which, in contrast to an animal, the plant has externalized, plunging them into the earth to prevent it from cutting itself free from its roots and roaming where it will—for it, such a rupture would equal death. Is then our symbolic life-world in which we are always-already pre-reflexively embedded not something like our symbolic entrails which we have externalized? And is not the true challenge of technology that we repeat the passage from plant to animal, symbolically severing our roots and accepting the abyss of freedom? In this very precise sense one can accept the formula that humanity will/should pass into post-humanity—being embedded in a symbolic world is a definition of being-human. And in this sense too, technology is a promise of liberation through terror. The subject which emerges in and through this experience of terror is ultimately the *cogito* itself, the abyss of self-relating negativity that forms the core of transcendental subjectivity, the acephalous subject of (the death) drive. It is the properly in-human subject.

What is to be done?

What triggers this terror is the awareness of how we are in the midst of a radical change. Although individual acts can, in a direct short-circuit of levels, affect the "higher"-level social constellation, the way they affect it is unpredictable. The constellation is properly frustrating: although we (individual or collective agents) know that it all depends on us, we cannot ever predict the consequences of our acts — *we are not impotent, but, quite the contrary, omnipotent, without being able to determine the scope of our powers*. The gap between causes and effects is irreducible, and there is no "big Other" to guarantee the harmony between the levels, to guarantee that the overall outcome of our interactions will be satisfactory.

The deadlock is here deeper than it may appear (as has been repeatedly developed by Dupuy[51]): the problem is that the big Other continues to function, in the guise of "second nature," of the minimally "reified" social system which is perceived as an In-itself. Each individual perceives the market as an objective system confronting her, although there is no "objective" market, just the interaction of the multitude of individuals — so that, although each individual knows this very well, the specter of the "objective" market is this same individual's fact-of-experience, determining her beliefs and acts. Not only the market, but our entire social life is determined by such reified mechanisms. Scientists and technologists who keep scientific-technological progress alive with their incessant activity, nonetheless experience this Progress as an objective constraint that determines and runs their lives: this constraint is perceived as "systemic," no one is personally responsible for it, everyone just feels the need to adapt themselves to it. And the same goes for capitalism as such: no one is responsible, all are caught in the objectivized urge to compete and profit, to keep the circulation of capital flowing.[52]

Prosopopoeia is usually perceived as a mystification to which naive consciousness is prone, that is, as something to be "demystified." At the beginning of Monteverdi's *Orfeo*, the goddess of music introduces herself with the words "Io sono la musica . . ."—is this not something which soon afterwards, when "psychological" subjects had invaded the stage, became unthinkable, or, rather, unrepresentable? It is therefore all the more surprising to see "objective" social scientists practicing the "primitive" art of prosopopoeia—Dupuy underlines how sociologists interpret electoral results; say, when the government retains its majority, but only barely so, the result is read as "the voters prolonged their trust into the government, but with a warning that it should do its work better," as if the electoral result was the outcome of the decision of a single meta-Subject ("the voters") who wanted to deliver a "message" to those in power. And although Hegel is often dismissed as the very model of idealist prosopopoeia (the Spirit talks through us, finite mortals, or, in the inversion of the "materialist critique" of Hegel, we, mortal humans, project/transpose the results of our activity into autonomous Spirit . . .), Hegel's notion of "objective Spirit" precisely *undermines* such prosopopoeian mystification: "objective Spirit" is *not* a meta-subject who runs history.

It is crucial not to confuse Hegel's "objective spirit" with the Diltheyan notion of a life-form, a concrete historical world, as the "objectivized spirit," the product of a people, its collective genius. The moment we do this, we miss the point of Hegel's "objective spirit," which is precisely that it is spirit in its objective form, experienced by individuals as an external imposition, a constraint even—there is no collective or spiritual super-Subject that would be the author of "objective spirit," whose "objectivization" this spirit would be. There is, for Hegel, no collective Subject, no Subject–Spirit beyond and above individual humans. Therein resides the paradox of "objective spirit": it is independent of individuals, encountered by them as given, preexisting them, as the presupposition of their activity, yet it is nonetheless spirit, that is, something that exists only insofar as individuals relate their activity to it, only as *their* (pre)-supposition.[53]

So what is the problem today? The problem is that, although our (sometimes even individual) acts can have catastrophic (ecological and so forth) consequences, we continue to perceive such consequences as anonymous/systemic, as something for which we are not responsible, for which there is no clear agent. More precisely—and here we are back to the logic of the madman who knows that he is not a grain of corn, but is worried that the chickens have not realized this fact—we know we are responsible, but the chicken (the big Other) has not caught on. Or, insofar as knowledge is the function of the I, and belief the function of the Other, we know the real state of affairs very well, but we do not believe it—the big Other prevents us from believing in it, from assuming this knowledge and responsibility: "Contrary to what the promoters of the principle of precaution think, the cause of our non-action is not scientific uncertainty. We know it, but we cannot make ourselves believe in what we know."[54] Take global warming, as already noted: with all the data regarding its nature, the problem is not the uncertainty about facts (as those who caution us against panic claim), but our inability to believe that it can really happen: look through the window, the green grass and blue sky are still there, life carries on, nature follows its rhythm . . . And therein resides the horror of the Chernobyl accident: when one visits the site, with the exception of the sarcophagus, things look exactly the same as before, life seems to have deserted the site, leaving everything the way it was, and nonetheless we are aware that something is terribly wrong. The change is not at the level of the visible reality itself; it is more fundamental, it affects the very texture of reality. No wonder that there are some lone farmers around the Chernobyl site who continue to lead their lives as before — they simply ignore all the incomprehensible talk about radiation.

This situation confronts us with the deadlock of the contemporary "choice society" in its most radical form. In the standard situation of the forced choice I am free to choose on condition that I make the right choice, so that the only thing left for me to do is the empty gesture of pretending to accomplish freely what is in any case imposed on me. Here, on the contrary, the choice really *is* free and is, for this very reason, experienced as even more frustrating: we find ourselves constantly in the position of having to decide about matters that will fundamentally affect our lives, but without a proper foundation in knowledge:

> we have been thrown into a time in which everything is provisional. New technologies alter our lives daily. The traditions of the past cannot be retrieved. At the same time we have little idea of what the future will bring. *We are forced to live as if we were free.*[55]

It is thus not enough to vary the standard motif of the Marxist critique: "although we allegedly live in a society of choices, the choices effectively left to us are trivial, and their proliferation masks the absence of true choices, choices that would affect the basic features of our lives . . ." While this is true, the problem is rather that we are forced to choose without having at our disposal the knowledge that would permit an informed choice.

Here, perhaps, Dupuy is too quick when he attributes our disbelief in catastrophe to the impregnation of our minds by scientific ideology, which leads us to dismiss the sane concerns of our common sense, namely, the gut sense which tells us that something is fundamentally amiss with the scientistic attitude. The problem, as we have underlined, is much deeper, it resides in the unreliability of our common sense itself which, habituated as it is to our ordinary life-world, balks at accepting that the flow of everyday reality can be upset. The problem is thus that we can rely neither on the scientific mind nor on our common sense — they both reciprocally strengthen the myopia of the other. The scientific mind advocates a cold objective appraisal of dangers and risks involved where no such appraisal is actually possible, while common sense cannot accept that a catastrophe can really occur.

Dupuy refers to the theory of complex systems which accounts for the two opposite features of such systems: their robust and stable character and their extreme vulnerability. These systems can accommodate themselves to great disturbances, integrate them and find a new balance and stability—up to a certain threshold (a "tipping point"), beyond which a small disturbance can cause a total disaster and lead to the establishment of a totally different order. For many centuries, humanity did not have to worry about the impact on the environment of its productive activity— nature was able to accommodate itself to deforestation, to the use of coal and oil, and so on. However, one cannot be sure whether today we are not approaching a tipping point—one really cannot be sure, since the point at which certainty would be possible is when it is already too late. We touch here the paradoxical nerve of morality christened "moral luck" by Bernard Williams.[56] Williams evokes the case of a painter ironically named "Gauguin" who left his wife and children and moved to Tahiti in order to fully develop his artistic genius—was he morally justified in doing this or not? Williams's answer is that we can only answer this question *in retrospect*, after we learn the final outcome of his risky decision: did he develop into an artistic genius or not? As Dupuy has pointed out,[57] we encounter the same dilemma apropos the urgency of doing something about the contemporary threat of various ecological catastrophes: either we take this threat seriously and decide today to do things which, if the catastrophe does not occur, will appear ridiculous, or we do nothing and lose everything in the case of a catastrophe, the worst choice being that of a middle position, taking a limited number of measures—in which case, we fail whatever should happen (that is to say, there is no middle ground when it comes to an ecological catastrophe: either it will occur or it won't). In such a situation, the talk about anticipation, precaution, and risk control tends to become meaningless, since we are dealing with what, in the terms of Rumsfeldian epistemology, one should call the "unknown unknowns": we not only do not know where the tipping point is, we do not even know exactly *what* we do not know. The most unsettling aspect of the ecological crisis concerns the so-called "knowledge in the real" which can run amok: when the winter is too warm, plants and animals misread the hot weather in February as the signal that spring has already begun and start to behave accordingly, thus not only rendering themselves vulnerable to late onslaughts of cold weather, but also perturbing the entire rhythm of natural reproduction. In May 2007, it was reported that a mysterious disease, which is wiping out America's bees, could have a devastating effect on the country's food supply: about one-third of the human diet comes from insect-pollinated plants, and the bee is responsible for 80 percent of that pollination; even cattle, which feed on alfalfa, depend on bees. While not all scientists foresee a food crisis, noting that large-scale bee deaths have happened before, this one seems particularly baffling and alarming. This is how one should imagine a possible catastrophe: a small-level interruption with devastating global consequences.

One can learn even more from Rumsfeldian epistemology—the expression, of course, refers to the well-known incident in March 2003, when Donald Rumsfeld engaged in a little amateur philosophizing about the relationship between the known and the unknown: "There are known knowns. These are things we know that we know. There are known unknowns. That is to say, there are things that we know we don't know. But there are also unknown unknowns. There are things we don't know we don't know." What he forgot to add was the crucial fourth term: "unknown knowns," things we do not know that we know—which is precisely the Freudian unconscious, the "knowledge which does not know itself," as Lacan used to say. If Rumsfeld thought that the main dangers in the confrontation with Iraq were the "unknown unknowns," the threats from Saddam the nature of which we did not even suspect, what we should reply is that the main dangers are, on the contrary, the "unknown knowns," the disavowed beliefs and suppositions we are not even aware of adhering to ourselves. In the case of ecology, these disavowed beliefs and suppositions are the ones which prevent us from really believing in the possibility of a disaster, and they combine with the "unknown unknowns." The situation is like that of the blind spot in our visual field: we do not see the gap, the picture appears continuous.

Our blindness to the results of "systemic evil" is perhaps most clearly perceptible apropos debates about Communist crimes: there, responsibility is easy to allocate, we are dealing with subjective evil, with agents who committed them, and we can even identify the ideological sources (totalitarian ideology, the *Communist Manifesto*, Rousseau . . .). When one draws attention to the millions who died as the result of capitalist globalization, from the tragedy of Mexico in the sixteenth century through the Belgian Congo holocaust a century ago, responsibility is denied: this just happened as the result of an "objective" process, nobody planned and executed it, there was no *Capitalist Manifesto* . . . (Ayn Rand came closest to writing it). And therein also resides the limitation of the "ethical committees" which pop up everwhere to counteract the dangers of unbridled scientific-technological development: with all their good intentions, ethical considerations, and so forth, they ignore the more basic "systemic" violence.

The fact that the Belgian king Leopold who presided over the Congolese genocide was a great humanitarian, proclaimed a saint by the pope, cannot be dismissed as a mere case of ideological hypocrisy and cynicism: one can argue that, subjectively, he probably really was a sincere humanitarian, even modestly counteracting the catastrophic consequences of the vast economic project of ruthless exploitation of the natural resources of Congo over which he presided (Congo was his personal fiefdom!) — the ultimate irony is that most of the profits from this endeavor were directed for the benefit of the Belgian people, for public works, museums, and so on.

In the early seventeenth century, after the establishment of the shogun regime, Japan made a unique collective decision to isolate itself from foreign culture and to pursue its own path of a contained life of balanced reproduction, focused on cultural refinement, avoiding any tendencies towards wild expansion. Was the ensuing period which lasted till the middle of the nineteenth century really just an isolationist dream from which Japan was cruelly awakened by Commodore Perry on the American warship? What if the dream is that we can go on indefinitely in our expansionism? What if we all need to repeat, *mutatis mutandis*, the Japanese decision, and collectively decide to intervene in our pseudo-natural development, to change its direction? The tragedy is that the very idea of such a collective decision is discredited today. Apropos the disintegration of state socialism two decades ago, one should not forget that, at approximately the same time, the ideology of the Western social-democratic welfare state was also dealt a crucial blow, it also ceased to function as the imaginary able to arouse a collective passionate commitment. The notion that "the time of the welfare state has past" is today a piece of commonly accepted wisdom. What these two defeated ideologies shared is the notion that humanity as a collective subject has the capacity to somehow limit impersonal and anonymous socio-historical development, to steer it in a desired direction. Today, such a notion is quickly dismissed as "ideological" and/or "totalitarian": the social process is once again perceived as dominated by an anonymous Fate beyond social control. The rise of global capitalism is presented to us as such a Fate, against which one cannot fight—one either adapts oneself to it, or one falls out of step with history and is crushed. The only thing one can do is to make global capitalism as human as possible, to fight for "global capitalism with a human face" (this is what, ultimately, the Third Way is—or, rather, *was*—about). The sound barrier will have to be broken here, the risk will have to be taken to endorse once more large collective decisions.

If we are effectively to reconceptualize the notion of revolution in the Benjaminian sense of stopping the "train of history" which runs towards a catastrophe, it is not enough just to submit the standard notion of historical progress to critical analysis; one should also focus on the limitation of the ordinary "historical" notion of time: at each moment of time, there are multiple possibilities waiting to be realized; once one of them actualizes itself, others are canceled. The supreme case of such an agent of historical time is the Leibnizean God who created the best possible of worlds: before creation, He had in his mind the entire panoply of possible worlds, and His decision consisted in choosing the best one among these options. Here, the possibility precedes choice: the choice is a choice among possibilities. What is unthinkable within this horizon of linear historical evolution is the notion of a choice/act which retroactively opens up its own possibility: the idea that the emergence of something radically New retroactively changes the past—of course, not the actual past (we are not in science fiction), but the past possibilities, or, to put it in more formal terms, the value of the modal propositions about the past. Dupuy's point is that, if we are to confront properly the threat of a (cosmic or environmental) disaster, we need to break out of this "historical" notion of temporality: we have to introduce a new notion of time. Dupuy calls this time the "time of a project," of a closed circuit between the past and the future: the future is causally produced by our acts in the past, while the way we act is determined by our anticipation of the future and our reaction to this anticipation. This, then, is how Dupuy proposes to confront the forthcoming catastrophe: we should first perceive it as our fate, as unavoidable, and then, projecting ourself into it, adopting its standpoint, we should retroactively insert into its past (the past of the future) counterfactual possibilities ("If we had done this and that, the catastrophe we are in now would not have occurred!") upon which we then act today.[58] Therein resides Dupuy's paradoxical formula: we have to accept that, at the level of possibilities, our future is doomed, that the catastrophe will take place, it is our destiny—and, then, against the background of this acceptance, we should mobilize ourselves to perform the act which will change destiny itself and thereby insert a new possibility into the past. For Badiou, the time of the fidelity to an event is the *futur antérieur*: overtaking oneself towards the future, one acts now as if the future one wants to bring about is already here. The same circular strategy of the *futur antérieur* is also the only truly effective one in the face of a calamity (say, of an ecological disaster): instead of saying "the future is still open, we still have the time to act and prevent the worst," one should accept the catastrophe as inevitable, and then act to retroactively undo what is already "written in the stars" as our destiny.

And is not a supreme case of the reversal of positive into negative destiny the shift from classical historical materialism into the attitude of Adorno's and Horkheimer's "dialectic of Enlightenment"? While traditional Marxism enjoined us to engage and act in order to bring about the necessity (of communism), Adorno and Horkheimer projected themselves into the final catastrophic outcome perceived as fixed (the advent of the "administered society" of total manipulation and the end of subjectivity) in order to stimulate us to act against this outcome in our present. And, ironically, does the same not hold for the very defeat of Communism in 1990? It is easy, from today's perspective, to mock the "pessimists," from the Right to the Left, from Solzhenitsyn to Castoriadis, who deplored the blindness and compromises of the democratic West, its lack of ethico-political strength and courage in dealing with the Communist threat, and who predicted that the Cold War had already been lost by the West, that the Communist bloc had already won, that the collapse of the West was imminent—but it is precisely their attitude which was the most effective in bringing about the collapse of Communism. In Dupuy's terms, their very "pessimistic" prediction at the level of possibilities, of linear historical evolution, mobilized them to counteract it. We should thus ruthlessly abandon the prejudice that the linear time of evolution is "on our side," that History is "working for us" in the guise of the famous mole digging under the earth, doing the work of the Cunning of Reason.[59] But how, then, are we to counter the threat of ecological catastrophe? It is here that we should return to the four moments of what Badiou calls the "eternal Idea" of revolutionary-egalitarian Justice. What is demanded is:

1. strict *egalitarian justice* (all people should pay the same price in eventual renunciations, namely, one should impose the same world-wide norms of per capita energy consumption, carbon dioxide emissions, and so on; the developed nations should not be allowed to poison the environment at the present rate, blaming the developing Third World countries, from Brazil to China, for ruining our shared environment with their rapid development);
2. *terror* (ruthless punishment of all who violate the imposed protective measures, inclusive of severe limitations on liberal "freedoms," technological control of prospective law-breakers);
3. *voluntarism* (the only way to confront the threat of ecological catastrophe is by means of large-scale collective decisions which run counter to the "spontaneous" immanent logic of capitalist development);
4. and, last but not least, all this combined with *trust in the people* (the wager that a large majority of the people supports these severe measures, sees them as its own, and is ready to participate in their enforcement). One should not be afraid to assert, as a combination of terror and trust in the people, the reactivation of one of the figures of all egalitarian-revolutionary terrors, the "informer" who denounces the culprits to the authorities. (In the case of the Enron scandal, *Time* magazine rightly celebrated the insiders who tipped off the financial authorities as true public heroes.)[60]

Does, then, the ecological challenge not offer a unique chance to reinvent the "eternal Idea" of egalitarian terror?

Notes

All translations are mine except where otherwise indicated.

Introduction

1 This reversal obeys the same logic as the correct leftist-enlightened reply to Joseph Goebbels's infamous dictum "When I hear the word culture, I reach for my gun": "When I hear guns, I reach for my culture."

2 See his interview "Demokratie befordert Bullshit," *Cicero*, March 2007, pp. 38–41.

3 From the sermon "Jesus Entered," translated in Reiner Schuermann, *Wandering Joy*, Great Barrington, MA: Lindisfarne Books 2001, p. 7.

4 So what does this Leap of Faith mean with regard to taking sides on particular political issues? Is one not reduced to supporting the usual left-liberal postures, with the proviso that "they are not yet the Real Thing," that the Big Step still lies ahead? Therein resides a key point: no, this is not the case. Even if there seems to be no space, within the existing constellation, for radical emancipatory acts, the Leap of Faith sets us free for a thoroughly ruthless and open attitude towards all possible strategic alliances: it allows us to break the vicious cycle of left-liberal blackmail ("if you do not vote for us, the Right will limit abortion, implement racist legislation . . ."), and to profit from old Marx's insight into how intelligent conservatives often see more (and are more aware of the antagonisms of the existing order) than liberal progressives.

5 See Todd Dufresne, *Killing Freud: 20th Century Culture & the Death of Psychoanalysis*, London: Continuum 2004.

6 *Le Livre noir du communisme*, Paris: Robert Laffont 2000.

7 *Le Livre noir de la psychanalyse: vivre, penser et aller mieux sans Freud*, Paris: Éditions Les Arènes 2005.

8 Quoted from Eric Aeschimann, "Mao en chair," *Libération*, January 10, 2007.

9 François Regnault, *Notre objet a*, Paris: Verdier 2003, p. 17.

1 Happiness and Torture in the Atonal World

1 There is nonetheless an ingenious detail in the film, a detail which provides a perfect example of the "subject supposed to know": when the Mossad agents want to learn the whereabouts of those who organized the Munich killings (in order to execute them), they turn to a mysterious French group, a kind of extended family leading an ordinary rustic life in a large country house, with chickens and children running around in the garden, but whose male members, in a manner never accounted for, seem to know everything about the whereabouts of the entire terrorist and spy underground.

2 Epigraph of "Living Room Dialogues on the Middle East," quoted from Wendy Brown, *Regulating Aversion*, Princeton, NJ: Princeton University Press 2006.

3 *Von Trier on von Trier*, London: Faber and Faber 2003, p. 252.

4 As is (almost) always the case, I owe this point to Eric Santner.

5 To clarify these distinctions further, let us compare two politico-ideological examples. First, I am a Communist functionary who follows the ideological ritual with inner distance, convinced that I am just playing a superficial game which does not concern my true Self ("life is elsewhere," as Milan Kundera put it); or, as in an Eric Ambler novel, I am married to a rich woman and, in order to annoy her conservative relatives and friends, I start reading Communist literature and provocatively pretending to believe in it—gradually, however, I get caught up in my own game and really become a Communist . . .

6 Immanuel Kant, "The Conflict of Faculties," in *Political Writings*, Cambridge: Cambridge University Press 1991, p. 182.

7 Even the solution offered by the obvious exception, the Buddhist ethics of solidarity with every living being, is more a kind of universalized indifference—learning how to withdraw from too much empathy (which is why it can easily turn into the very opposite of universal compassion, into the advocacy of a ruthless military attitude, as the fate of Zen Buddhism aptly demonstrates).

8 This Benjaminian lesson is missed by Habermas who does precisely what one should *not* do: he posits ideal "language in general"—pragmatic universals—directly as the norm of the actually-existing language.

9 See Theodor W. Adorno, *Minima Moralia*, Frankfurt: Suhrkamp 1997, pp. 38–41.

10 Michael Baigent and Richard Leigh, *Secret Germany*, London: Arrow Books 2006, p. 14. Is this polite reluctance not the obverse of the memorable scene from the Ingmar Bergman film *The Serpent's Egg* (in other respects a failure), in which a group of Nazi thugs approaches a Jewish nightclub owner and politely asks him: "Could you please remove your glasses, so that they will not break?" After he does so, they brutally grab his hair and thereby beat his head on the table till it is smashed into bloody pulp.

11 See Robert Pippin, "The Ethical Status of Civility," in *The Persistence of Subjectivity*, Cambridge: Cambridge University Press 2005, pp. 223–38.

12 The politically correct vision enacts a weird reversal of racist hatred of Otherness—it stages a kind of mockingly Hegelian negation/sublation of openly racist dismissal and hatred of the Other, of the perception of the Other as the Enemy which poses a threat to our way of life. In the PC vision, the Other's violence against us, deplorable and cruel as it may be, is always a *reaction* against the "original sin" of *our* (white man's imperialist, colonialist, etc.) rejection and oppression of Otherness. We, white men, are responsible and guilty, the Other just reacts as a victim; we are to be condemned, the Other is to be understood; ours is a domain of morals (moral condemnation), whilst that of others involves sociology (social explanation). It is, of course, easy to discern how, beneath the mask of extreme self-humiliation and self-blame, such a stance of true ethical masochism repeats racism in its very form: although negative, the proverbial "white man's burden" is still here—we, white men, are the subjects of History, whilst others ultimately react to our (mis)deeds. In other words, it is as if the true message of the PC moralistic self-blame is: if we can no longer be the model of democracy and civilization for the rest of the world, we can at least be the model of Evil.

13 See Claude Lefort, *Essais sur le politique*, Paris: Éditions du Seuil 1986.

14 See Slavoj Žižek, *Looking Awry*, Cambridge, MA: MIT Press 1991.

15 See Marcel Mauss, "Essai sur le don," in *Sociologie et anthropologie*, Paris: PUF 1973.

16 See Claude Lévi-Strauss, "Introduction a l'œuvre de Marcel Mauss," in Mauss, "Essai sur le don."

17 Jean-Pierre Dupuy, *Avions-nous oublié le mal? Penser la politique après le 11 septembre*, Paris: Bayard 2002.

18 See Pierre Bourdieu, *Esquisse d'une thé orie de la pratique*, Geneva: Droz 1972.
19 Karl Marx, *Capital, Volume One*, Harmondsworth: Penguin 1990, p. 167.
20 See Marshall Sahlins, *Stone Age Economics*, Berlin and New York: Walter De Gruyter 1972.
21 A.C. Bradley, *Shakespearean Tragedy*, London: Macmillan 1978, p. 150.
22 Along these lines, one is tempted to claim that, of Shakespeare's great tragedies, only *Macbeth* and *Othello* are really tragedies: *Hamlet* is already a half-comical melodrama, while *King Lear* passes the threshold and is fully a comedy (comparable to *Titus Andronicus*, another superb comedy).
23 Alain Badiou, *Logiques des mondes*, Paris: Éditions du Seuil 2006, p. 443.
24 Jacques Lacan, *On Feminine Sexuality* (*The Seminar, Book XX*), New York: Norton 1998, p. 3.
25 Badiou, *Logiques des mondes*, p. 533.
26 Ibid., pp. 442–5.
27 See Fethi Benslama, *La Psychanalyse à l'épreuve de l'Islam*, Paris: Aubier 2002, pp. 77–85.
28 One of the ridiculous excesses of this joint venture of religious fundamentalism and scientific approaches is taking place today in Israel where a religious group convinced of the literal truth of the Old Testament prophecy that the Messiah will come when a totally red calf is born is spending enormous amounts of energy to produce, through genetic manipulations, such a calf.
29 We can also see how wrong are those who reproach Lacan with fetishizing the Symbolic in a quasi-transcendental Order: as was clear to Lacan back in 1938, when he wrote his *Complexes familiaux*, the very birth of psychoanalysis is linked to the crisis and disintegration of what he then called the "paternal image"—or, as he put it decades later, the subject of psychoanalysis is none other than the Cartesian subject of modern science. And to those who misread this diagnosis as implying a call for—or at least a hankering after—the good old days when paternal authority was still uncontested and fully functional, let us recall that, for Lacan, the crisis of paternal authority which gave birth to psychoanalysis (i.e., which is the main historical condition of its rise) is *stricto sensu* symptomal: the unique point of exception which allows us to formulate the underlying universal law.
30 I owe this idea to Alenka Zupančič, Ljubljana.
31 I owe this idea to Glyn Daly, University of Northampton.
32 Janusz Bardach and Kathleen Gleeson, *Man Is Wolf to Man*, London: Scribner 2003.
33 This is also why it is not enough to make the point that, if the priests' sexual urges do not find a legitimate outlet, they have to explode in a pathological way: allowing the Catholic priests to marry would not solve anything; it would not result in priests doing their job without harrassing young boys, since pedophilia is generated by the Catholic institution of the priesthood as its "inherent transgresion," as its obscene secret supplement.
34 The case of contemporary Turkey is crucial for the proper understanding of capitalist globalization: the political proponent of globalization is the ruling "moderate" Islamist party of the Prime Minister Erdogan.
35 Bill O'Reilly, *Culture Warrior*, New York: Broadway Books 2006, pp. 175–6.
36 Quoted from Antoine de Baecque, *Andrei Tarkovski*, Cahiers du Cinema 1989, p. 110.
37 In other words, what if Tarkovsky is doing the same thing as Nemanja (Emir) Kusturica, at a different level? Kusturica plays for the West the perfect Balkan, caught in authentic cycle of passionate violence, while Tarkovsky plays the role of authentically naive Russian spirituality.
38 John Gray, *Straw Dogs*, London: Granta 2003, p. 18.
39 Ibid., pp. 165–6.
40 This reversal is homologous to the one that characterizes the Hegelian dialectics of necessity and contingency. In a first approach, it appears that their encompassing

unity is necessity, i.e., that necessity itself posits and mediates contingency as the external field in which it expresses–actualizes itself—contingency itself is necessary, the result of the self-externalization and self-mediation of the notional necessity. However, it is crucial to supplement this unity with the opposite one, with contingency as the encompassing unity of itself and necessity: the very elevation of a necessity into the structuring principle of the contingent field of multiplicity is a contingent act, one can almost say: the outcome of a contingent ("open") struggle for hegemony. This shift corresponds to the shift from S to $, from Substance to Subject. The starting point is a contingent multitude; through its self-mediation ("spontaneous self-organization"), contingency engenders–posits its immanent necessity, in the same way that Essence is the result of the self-mediation of Being. Once Essence emerges, it retroactively "posits its own presuppositions," i.e., it sublates its presuppositions into subordinated moments of its self-reproduction (Being is transubstantiated into Appearance); this positing, however, is retroactive.

41 See Michael Bond, "The Pursuit of Happiness," *New Scientist*, October 4, 2003.

42 "Foreword by the Dalai Lama," in Mark Epstein, *Thoughts Without a Thinker*, New York: Basic Books 1996, p. xiii.

43 The "pursuit of happiness" is such a key element of the "American (ideological) dream" that one tends to forget the contingent origin of this phrase: "We hold these truths to be self-evident, that all men are created equal, that they are endowed by their Creator with certain unalienable Rights, that among these are Life, Liberty and the pursuit of Happiness." Where did the somewhat awkward "pursuit of happiness" come from in this famous opening passage of the US Declaration of Independence? The origin of it is John Locke, who claimed that all men had the natural rights of life, liberty, and property—the latter was replaced by "the pursuit of happiness" during negotiations of the drafting of the Declaration, *as a way to negate the black slaves' right to property*.

44 Thomas Metzinger, *Being No One. The Self-Model Theory of Subjectivity*, Cambridge, MA: MIT Press 2004, p. 620.

45 Ibid.

46 Ibid., p. 621.

47 Sam Harris, *The End of Faith*, New York: Norton 2005, p. 199.

48 Ibid., pp. 192–3.

49 Ibid., p. 197.

50 A more vulgar example: if an adolescent were to declare publicly in his class "I masturbate regularly," the shocked reaction of the class would be: "We all do it and we know it, so why are you saying it publicly?"

2 The Family Myth of Ideology

1 To this series, one should add Leon Uris's *Exodus* as an exercise in "Zionist realism."

2 He has already resorted to a similar reversal in *Disclosure*, the sexual-harassment novel, in which a woman harasses a man.

3 Michael Crichton, *Prey*, New York: Avon Books 2003. (All page references in brackets within the text refer to this edition.)

4 In a vulgar-Marxist reading, one is tempted to see in this fear of the collective of nanoparticles organizing itself free from the control of its human creators a displacement of the fear of class-consciousness of workers (or of other oppressed groups).

5 Jacques Lacan, *The Four Fundamental Concepts of Psycho-Analysis*, Harmondsworth: Penguin 1979, p. 198.

6 No wonder that the first climax of the novel is when a group of battling scientists destroy the swarm, entering a hidden cave in the desert, the site of Evil where the

swarm regenerates itself. Similarly, in *Eaters of the Dead*, a group of Viking warriors penetrates the cave of a Neanderthal tribe of cannibals in order to kill their matriarchal chief.

7 In fact they are not so surprising when one remembers the Stalinist fascination with the Hollywood-style dream-factory organization of cinema production. Boris Shumyatsky, the boss of Soviet cinema production in the 1930s, visited Hollywood and, impressed by it, planned to build a Soviet Hollywood on the Crimean Sea; unfortunately, a discovery in the late 1930s that he was an imperialist agent prevented this noble plan from being executed—instead, Shumyatsky himself was executed.

8 In a supreme twist of irony, the exception is provided by the very actor who played the film's hero, Gerd Wiesler, a Stasi agent whose duty is to plant the microphones and listen to everything the couple does: he discovered that, under the GDR, his wife had informed on him.

9 Roger Boyes, "Final Forgiveness for Spy Who Betrayed his Wife to the Stasi," *The Times*, January 6, 2007. There is one mystery about Vera's arrest in the GDR which is today easily explained: "When we were fingerprinted, we had to sit on a piece of fabric. This was later placed in an airless jar because they wanted to capture our smell. Can you tell me why?" Now we know: in order to track the movement of dissidents who tried to evade them, the Stasi used dogs, giving them the fabric to smell, so they could follow the scent.

10 Hegel's reading of *Antigone* is often reproached for ignoring the potential incestuous dimension of Antigone's attachment to her brother as the hidden reason she elevates him into the exception (recall the scandalous lines, so embarrassing that commentators, starting with Goethe, often dismiss them as a later interpolation, about how she would do what she is doing—putting at risk her life itself to ensure his proper funeral—only for her brother, never for her parents or children). While such a suspicion of incestuous attachment may be out of place in an ordinary family, Hegel should have remembered that we are dealing here with the family of Oedipus himself, the very site of paradigmatic incest. However, what should make us suspicious of this criticism is that the same ignorance is shared by Lacan in his detailed reading of *Antigone*: although he insists on the crucial role of Antigone's "fraternal exception," he never ventures into speculations about its incestuous dimension. So what is going on here? Lévi-Strauss mentions somewhere a tribe whose members believe that all dreams have sexual meaning—except dreams with explicit sexual content. Exactly the same goes for Antigone: for a true Freudian, such a strong sisterly attachment to a brother would signal an incestuous desire—except, of course, in Antigone's case since the family already *is* marked by incest.

11 Tom Holland, *Persian Fire*, London: Little, Brown 2005.

12 Filippo Del Lucchese and Jason Smith, "We Need a Popular Discipline: Contemporary Politics and the Crisis of the Negative", interview with Alain Badiou, Los Angeles, July 2, 2007, (unpublished).

13 Sigmund Freud, *Introductory Lectures on Psychoanalysis*, Harmondsworth: Penguin 1973, pp. 261–2.

14 A similar procedure is at work in the metaphoric dimension of everyday language. Let us say I am an editor who wants to criticize a submitted manuscript; instead of brutally saying "the text needs to be rewritten so that at least its most stupid parts will disappear," I ironically hint that "the text will probably need some fumigating"—does this metaphoric substitution not introduce a much more ominous reference to germs and insects, to killing, and so on?

15 Edmund Burke, *Letters on the Proposals for Peace with the Regicide Directory of France, Letter I* (1796), in *The Works and Correspondence of the Right Honorable Edmund Burke*, new edition (London 1852), vol. V, p. 256.

16 In 1937–38, while awaiting execution in the Lubyanka prison in Moscow, Nikolai

Bukharin wrote prolifically, finishing four substantial manuscripts (books on Marxist philosophy and on socialism and culture, a novel and a book of poems—the manuscripts miraculously survived and the first three are now available in English). The key to this extraordinary work is the constellation in which it was written and its addressee: Bukharin knew that he would be executed soon and that the books would not be published, and he was giving the manuscripts to his prison guards to be delivered to Stalin (who preserved them). Although written as books meant for the anonymous general public, their true addressee was thus only one person, Stalin himself, whom Bukharin, in this last desperate gesture, tried to fascinate with his intellectual brilliance.

17 I owe the instigation for this reading of Kafka to Avital Ronell's talk, delivered in Sass Fee on August 10, 2006. Kafka's letter to his father is available online at www.kafka-franz.com/KAFKA-letter.htm.

18 Jacques Lacan, *The Ethics of Psychoanalysis*, London: Routledge 1992, p. 310.

19 So what about figures like "odradek," a partial object along the lines of Beckett's later "unnameable," who is also defined as "father's shame"? In a parenthesis in his letter to his father, Kafka identifies himself with Josef K. from *The Trial*: "I had lost my self-confidence where you were concerned, and in its place had developed a boundless sense of guilt. (In recollection of this boundlessness I once wrote of someone, accurately: 'He is afraid the shame will outlive him.')" However, in "Odradek," the shame is the father's, and it is odradek itself which outlives the father as the latter's shame objectivized.

3 Radical Intellectuals, or, Why Heidegger Took the Right Step (Albeit in the Wrong Direction) in 1933

1 Available online at <books.eserver.org/fiction/innocence/brokensword.html>.

2 G.W.F. Hegel, *Phenomenology of Spirit*, Oxford: Oxford University Press 1977, p. 404.

3 Peter Sloterdijk, *Zorn und Zeit*, Frankfurt: Suhrkamp 2006, p. 260.

4 G.K. Chesterton, *The Man Who Was Thursday*, Harmondsworth: Penguin 1986, pp. 44–5.

5 The same insight was already formulated by Heinrich Heine in his *History of Religion and Philosophy in Germany* from 1834, although as a positive, admirable fact: "Mark you this, you proud men of action, you are nothing but the unconscious henchmen of intellectuals, who, often in the humblest seclusion, have meticulously plotted your every deed" (quoted from Dan Hind, *The Threat to Reason*, London: Verso 2007, p. 1).

6 Terry Eagleton, *Holy Terror*, Oxford: Oxford University Press 2005, pp. 50–1.

7 Jacques-Alain Miller, *Le Neveau de Lacan*, Paris: Verdier 2003, pp. 146–7.

8 Wendy Brown, *Politics out of History*, Princeton, NJ: Princeton University Press 2001, pp. 22–3.

9 Ibid. p. 28.

10 Ibid., p. 122.

11 Ibid., p. 128.

12 Ibid., pp. 122–3.

13 Ibid., p. 128.

14 Ibid., p. 137.

15 Nietzsche is as a rule strangely decontextualized/dehistoricized, by the same authors who are otherwise so eager to contextualize/historicize Lacan and others to demonstrate their metaphysical and repressive bias: in Deleuze's paradigmatic reading of Nietzsche, this dimension totally disappears. (While, typically, often the same authors go into great detail about Wagner's—Nietzsche's great opponent—anti-Semitism, locating it in its historical context. . .)

16 This parallel, of course, has its limits, the most obvious being that Foucault's Iranian

engagement was perceived as a lone idiosyncratic gesture, out of step with the hegemonic liberal-democratic consensus, while Heidegger's Nazi engagement followed the dominant trend among German radical-conservative intellectuals.

17 Janet Afary and Kevin B. Anderson, *Foucault and the Iranian Revolution*, Chicago: The University of Chicago Press 2005, pp. 3–4.

18 Quoted in ibid., p. 263.

19 Gilles Deleuze, *Negotiations*, New York: Columbia University Press 1995, p. 171.

20 Quoted in Afary and Anderson, *Foucault and the Iranian Revolution*, p. 265.

21 Is, however, this magic moment of enthusiastic unity of a collective will not an exemplary case of what Lacan refers to as imaginary identification? It is here, apropos this case, that one can observe at its purest the shift in Lacan's teaching: while the Lacan of the 1950s would undoubtedly have dismissed this enthusiastic unity as the imaginary misrecognition of symbolic overdetermination, the late Lacan would discern in it the eruption of the Real.

22 Quoted in Afary and Anderson, *Foucault and the Iranian Revolution*, p. 256.

23 Ibid., p. 253.

24 Ibid., p. 264.

25 Ibid., p. 265.

26 Ibid., p. 260.

27 Fethi Benslama, *La Psychanalyse à l'épreuve de l'Islam*, Paris: Aubier 2002, p. 320.

28 Ibid.

29 Ernst Nolte, *Martin Heidegger—Politik und Geschichte im Leben und Denken*, Berlin: Propylaen 1992, p. 296. Incidentally, the same line of defense of Heidegger's Nazi engagement had already been proposed by Jean Beaufret in a letter published in 1963 (see Emmanuel Faye, *Heidegger. L'introduction du nazisme dans la philosophie*, Paris: Albin Michel 2005, p. 502).

30 Mark Wrathall, *How to Read Heidegger*, London, Granta 2005, p. 87.

31 Ibid., p. 86.

32 Steve Fuller, *Kuhn vs. Popper*, Cambridge: Icon Books 2006, p. 191.

33 Miguel de Beistegui, *The New Heidegger*, London: Continuum 2005, p. 7.

34 Ibid., pp. 175–6.

35 Hannah Arendt, *The Origins of Totalitarianism*, New York: Harcourt Brace Jovanovich 1973, p. 328.

36 Hannah Arendt, *On Revolution*, London: Penguin 1990, p. 205.

37 Robert Pippin, *The Persistence of Subjectivity*, Cambridge: Cambridge University Press 2005, p. 165.

38 Ibid., p. 22.

39 De Beistegui, *The New Heidegger*, p. 182.

40 Ibid.

41 Wrathall, *How To Read Heidegger*, p. 82.

42 Ibid., pp. 79–80.

43 Ibid., pp. 81–2.

44 Martin Heidegger, *Introduction to Metaphysics*, New Haven, CT: Yale University Press 2000, p. 27.

45 Faye, *Heidegger. L'Introduction du nazisme dans la philosophie*, p. 358

46 Ibid., p. 333.

47 Ibid., p. 247.

48 Ibid., p. 217.

49 Ibid., p. 382.

50 Ibid., p. 367.

51 Jean-François Kervégan, "La vie éthique perdue dans ses extrêmes . . .," in *Lectures de Hegel*, sous la direction de Olivier Tinland, Paris: Livre de Poche 2005, p. 283.

52 Ibid., p. 291.

53 The problem is here, of course, whether the market dynamic really provides what it

promises. Does it not generate permanent destabilization of the social body, especially by way of increasing class distinctions and giving rise to a "mob" deprived of the basic conditions of life? Hegel's solution was here very pragmatic—he opted for secondary palliative measures such as colonial expansion and, especially, the mediating role of estates [Stande]. Hegel's dilemma is still ours today, two hundred years later.

The clearest indication of this historical limit of Hegel is his double use of the same term *Sitten* (customs, social ethical order): it stands for the immediate organic unity that has to be left behind (the ancient Greek ideal), and for the higher organic unity which should be actualized in a modern state.

54 Faye, *Heidegger*, p. 376.

55 Ibid., p. 221.

56 Ibid., p. 247.

57 Ibid., p. 240.

58 Ibid., p. 238.

59 G.W.F. Hegel, *Elements of the Philosophy of Right*, Cambridge: Cambridge University Press 1991, para. 279.

60 Ibid.

61 Ibid., para. 280.

62 Ibid.

63 Did the Marxists who mocked Hegel here not pay the price for this negligence in the guise of the leader who, once again, not only directly embodied the rational totality, but embodied it fully, as a figure of full Knowledge, not only as the idiotic point of dotting the "I"s. In other words, a Stalinist Leader is *not* a monarch, which makes him much worse . . .

64 Hegel, *Elements of the Philosophy of Right*, para. 280, Addition.

65 Faye, *Heidegger*, p. 239.

66 Heidegger, *Introduction to Metaphysics*, p. 102.

67 Faye, *Heidegger*, p. 457.

68 Ibid., p. 467.

69 Martin Heidegger, *Gesamtausgabe*, vol. 43, *Nietzsche: Der Wille zur Macht als Kunst*, Frankfurt: Klostermann 1985, p. 193.

70 Available online at www.slate.com/id/2107100.

71 Martin Heidegger, *Gesamtausgabe*, vol. 45, *Grundprobleme der Philosophie*, Frankfurt: Klostermann 1984, p. 41.

72 Authentic fidelity is the fidelity to the void itself—to the very act of loss, of abandoning/erasing the object. Why should the dead be the object of attachment in the first place? The name for this fidelity is the death drive. In the terms of dealing with the dead, one should, perhaps—against the work of mourning as well as against the melancholic attachment to the dead who return as ghosts—assert the Christian motto "let the dead bury their dead." The obvious reproach to this motto is: what are we to do when, precisely, the dead refuse to stay dead, but continue to live in us, haunting us with their spectral presence? Here, one is tempted to claim that the most radical dimension of the Freudian death drive provides the key to how are we to read the Christian "let the dead bury their dead": what the death drive tries to obliterate is not biological life, but the afterlife—it endeavors to kill the lost object the second time, not in the sense of mourning (accepting the loss through symbolization), but in a more radical sense of obliterating the very symbolic texture, the letter in which the spirit of the dead survives.

73 G.K. Chesterton, *Orthodoxy*, San Francisco: Ignatius Press 1995, p. 16.

74 So what about Heidegger's insistence on his ethnic roots? Although he always emphasized his Germanness as well as the unique role of the German language, he in a way had to betray his roots: his entire thought is marked by the tension between the Greeks and the Germans. The German roots had to be referred to the Greek origins;

the two could not simply be united into a linear story of the development of Western metaphysics. German roots have their own content, irreducible to Greek origins (see, for example, in *Unterwegs zur Sprache*, his analysis of *Geist* (spirit) as "a flame that ignites itself," paving the way for the German Idealist notion of the self-positing subjectivity—Heidegger points out that we do *not* find this notion of Spirit in Greek); and Greek nonetheless remains a *foreign* language to be deciphered.

75 Personal information from Professor Wolfgang Schirmacher, New York/Saas Fee.
76 See Jacques Derrida, *Of Spirit: Heidegger and the Question*, Chicago: The University of Chicago Press 1991.
77 See Bret W. Davis, *Heidegger and the Will*, Evanston, IL: Northwestern University Press 2007.
78 See Slavoj Žižek, *The Ticklish Subject*, London: Verso 1999, ch. 1.
79 In order to avoid the impression that we neglect the way the notion of the Will sustains not only the technological thrust to control and domination, but also the militaristic spirit of struggle and sacrifice, let us recall how *Gelassenheit* in no way protects us from the most devastating technological and military engagement—the fate of Zen Buddhism in Japan speaks volumes here.
80 Davis, *Heidegger and the Will*, p. 303.
81 Martin Heidegger, *Gesamtausgabe*, vol. 5, *Holzwege*, Frankfurt: Klostermann 1977, p. 355.
82 Hannah Arendt, *The Life of the Mind*, San Diego: Harcourt Brace 1978, p. 194.
83 Davis, *Heidegger and the Will*, p. 282.
84 Ibid., pp. 297–8.
85 Ibid., p. 297.
86 Ibid., p. 299.
87 Ibid., p. 289.
88 Ibid., p. 294.
89 Ibid.
90 Wrathall, *How to Read Heidegger*, p. 87.
91 See Gregory Fried, *Heidegger's Polemos: From Being to Politics*, New Haven, CT: Yale University Press 2000.
92 Incidentally, the very beginning of the fragment, in Greek, with the verb at the end (in Greek fashion), strangely recalls what every lover of popular culture today knows as the Yoda way, after the Heraclitean gnome in the *Star Wars* films, who pronounces profound sentences with the verb at the end—so the beginning (*polemos panton men pater esti*) should be translated in Yoda-ese "War father of all is . . .".
93 Heidegger, *Introduction to Metaphysics*, p. 47.
94 Joseph Stalin, "Dialectical and Historical Materialism (September 1938)," available online at http://www.marxists.org/reference/archive/stalin/works/1938/09.htm.
95 Heidegger, *Introduction to Metaphysics*, pp. 115–28.
96 In a standard move, Heidegger, of course, hastens to add how the first victim of this violence is the Creator himself who has to be erased with the advent of the new Order that he grounded; this erasure can take different forms, from physical destruction—from Moses and Julius Caesar onwards, we know that the founding figure has to be killed—to the relapse into madness, as in the case of Hölderlin.

4 Revolutionary Terror from Robespierre to Mao

1 See Alain Badiou, *Logiques des mondes*, Paris: Éditions du Seuil 2006, "Introduction."
2 The catch, of course, resides in the ambiguity of the term "the people": is the people that is to be trusted that composed of "empirical" individuals or are we referring to *the* People, on behalf of whom one can turn the terror of the people against the people's enemies into the terror against individual people themselves?

3 Its elements were, of course, already discernible in the earlier "millenarian" revolutionaries (from the Czech Hussites to Thomas Münzer) and in Cromwell's Commonwealth.

4 For a balanced historical description of the Terror, see David Andress, *The Terror. Civil War in the French Revolution*, London: Little, Brown 2005.

5 See "De quoi Mai est-il coupable?", *Libération*, May 3, 2007.

6 Maximilien Robespierre, *Virtue and Terror*, London: Verso 2007, p. 115.

7 Ibid., p. 117.

8 Ruth Scurr, *Fatal Purity*, London: Chatto and Windus 2006.

9 Antonia Fraser, "Head of the Revolution," *The Times*, April 22, 2006, Books, p. 9.

10 Badiou, *Logiques des mondes*, p. 98.

11 Louis-Antoine-Leon Saint-Just, *Œuvres choisies*, Paris: Gallimard 1968, p. 330.

12 And he was right: as we know today, during the last days of his freedom, King Louis XVI was plotting with foreign forces to start a major war between France and the European powers, where the king would pose as a patriot, leading the French army, and then negotiate an honourable peace for France, thus regaining his full authority—in short, the "gentle" Louis XVI was ready to plunge Europe into war to save his throne . . .

13 Robespierre, *Virtue and Terror*, p. 94.

14 See Walter Benjamin, "Critique of Violence," in *Selected Writings, Volume 1, 1913–1926*, Cambridge, MA: Harvard University Press 1996.

15 Friedrich Engels, "Introduction" (1891) to Karl Marx, *The Civil War in France*, in *Marx/Engels/Lenin On Historical Materialism*, New York: International Publishers 1974, p. 242.

16 Robespierre, *Virtue and Terror*, p. 59.

17 Ibid., p. 130.

18 Ibid., p. 43.

19 Ibid., p. 47.

20 See Alain Badiou, *The Century*, Cambridge: Polity 2007.

21 See the detailed analysis in Claude Lefort, "The Revolutionary Terror," in *Democracy and Political Theory*, Minneapolis, MN: University of Minnesota Press 1988, pp. 50–88.

22 Quoted from ibid., p. 63.

23 Quoted from ibid., p. 65.

24 Quoted from ibid., p. 64.

25 Mao Tse-Tung, *On Practice and Contradiction*, London: Verso 2007, p. 109.

26 Ibid., p. 87.

27 Quoted from Brian Daizen Victoria, *Zen War Stories*, London: Routledge 2003, p. 132.

28 Ibid., pp. 106–7.

29 In Latin: "quaeratur via *qua* nec sepultis mixtus et vivis tamen exemptus erres" (Seneca, *Oedipus*, 949–51).

30 Robespierre, *Virtue and Terror*, p. 103.

31 Margaret Washington, on http://www.pbs.org/wgbh/amex/brown/filmmore/reference/interview/washington05.html.

32 Ibid.

33 See Henry David Thoreau, *Civil Disobedience and Other Essays*, New York: Dover 1993.

34 Wendy Brown, *States of Injury*, Princeton, NJ: Princeton University Press 1995, p. 14.

35 So what about Robespierre's rather ridiculous attempt to impose a new civic religion celebrating a Supreme Being? Robespierre himself formulated succinctly the main reason for his opposition to atheism: "Atheism is aristocratic" (Maximilien Robespierre, *Œuvres Complètes*, Paris: Ernest Leroux 1910–67, vol. 10, p. 195). Atheism

was for him the ideology of the cynical-hedonistic aristocrats who had lost all sense of historical mission.

36 Along these lines, some Western Marxists attributed Stalinism to the "Asiatic mode of production," seeing the former as a new form of "Oriental despotism"—the irony being that, for traditional Russians, the exact opposite held: "It was always a Western fancy to see Lenin and Stalin as 'Oriental' despots. The great Russian tyrants in the eighteenth and the twentieth century were Westernizers" (Lesley Chamberlain, *The Philosophy Steamer*, London: Atlantic Books 2006, p. 270).

37 Emmanuel Levinas, *Les Imprévus de l'histoire*, Paris: Fata Morgana 1994, p. 172.

38 Martin Heidegger, *Schelling's Treatise on Human Freedom*, Athens, OH: Ohio University Press 1985, p. 146.

39 G.W.F. Hegel, *Phenomenology of Spirit*, Oxford: Oxford University Press 1977, p. 288.

40 F.W.J. Schelling, *Die Weltalter. Fragmente. In den Urfassungen von 1811 und 1813*, ed. Manfred Schroeter, Munich: Biederstein 1979, p. 13.

41 Georgi M. Derluguian, *Bourdieu's Secret Admirer in the Caucasus*, Chicago: The University of Chicago Press 2005.

42 Luc Boltanski and Eve Chiapello, *The New Spirit of Capitalism*, London: Verso 2005, p. ix.

43 Ibid., p. xvii.

44 Mao Zedong, *On Practice and Contradiction*, p. 87.

45 Ibid., p. 92.

46 Ibid., pp. 117–18.

47 Alain Badiou, "Prefazione all'edizione italiana," in *Metapolitica*, Naples: Cronopio 2002, p. 14.

48 And are the latest statements of Toni Negri and Michael Hardt not a kind of unexpected confirmation of this insight of Badiou? Following a paradoxical necessity, their very (focus on) anti-capitalism led them to acknowledge the revolutionary force of capitalism, so that, as they put it recently, one no longer needs to fight capitalism, because capitalism is already in itself generating communist potential— the "becoming-communist of capitalism," to put it in Deleuzian terms . . .

49 Mao Zedong, *On Practice and Contradiction*, pp. 131, 137.

50 Ibid., p. 183.

51 Ibid., p. 182.

52 Ibid., p. 176.

53 Jung Chang and Jon Halliday, *Mao: The Unknown Story*, New York: Knopf 2005. Of course, this work is highly tendentious and has been subject to harsh criticism: see, in particular, Andrew Nathan, "Jade and Plastic," *London Review of Books*, November 17, 2005.

54 Heidegger is also wrong in his letter to Marcuse, comparing the Holocaust to the 1946–47 deportation of Germans from Eastern Europe—Herbert Marcuse was correct in his reply: the difference between the fate of Jews and the Eastern European Germans was, at that moment, the thin line that separated barbarism from civilization.

55 Mao Zedong, *On Practice and Contradiction*, p. 181.

56 Ibid., pp. 179–80.

57 Samuel Beckett, *Trilogy*, London: Calder 2003, p. 418.

58 No wonder, then, that, when he describes the "democratic method of resolving contradictions among the people," Mao is obliged to evoke his own version of, precisely, the "negation of the negation," in the guise of the formula "unity–criticism–unity": "starting from the desire for unity, resolving contradictions through criticism or struggle, and arriving at a new unity on a new basis. In our experience this is the correct method of resolving contradictions among the people."

59 Mao Zedong, *On Practice and Contradiction*, pp. 172–3.

60 There is a brief hint in this direction in the middle of the film; however, it remains unexploited.

61 Jonathan Spence, *Mao*, London: Weidenfeld and Nicolson 1999, pp. xii–xiv.

62 Badiou, *Logiques des mondes*, pp. 62–70.

63 Ibid., pp. 543–4.

64 G.W.F. Hegel, *Enzyklopädie der philosophischen Wissenschaften*, Hamburg: Franz Heiner 1959, p. 436.

65 Fredric Jameson, *The Seeds of Time*, New York: Columbia University Press 1994, p. 89.

66 Ibid., p. 90.

67 Was Che Guevara's withdrawal from all official functions, even from Cuban citizenship, in 1965, in order to dedicate himself to world revolution—this suicidal gesture of cutting the links with the institutional universe—really an *act*? Or, was it an escape from the impossible task of the positive construction of socialism, from remaining faithful to the *consequences* of the revolution, namely, an implicit admission of failure?

68 Brian Massumi, "Navigating Movements," in Mary Zournazi, ed., *Hope*, New York: Routledge 2002, p. 224.

69 See the report "Renewed Faith," *Time*, May 8, 2006, pp. 34–5.

70 Immanuel Kant, "What Is Enlightenment?," in Isaac Kramnick, ed., *The Portable Enlightenment Reader*, New York: Penguin 1995, p. 5.

71 See "Even What's Secret Is a Secret in China," *The Japan Times*, June 16, 2007, p. 17.

72 Eyal Weizman, "Israeli Military Using Post-Structuralism as 'Operational Theory'," available online at www.frieze.com. See also, *Hollow Land*, London: Verso, 2007, ch. 7.

73 Gordon G. Chang, "China in Revolt," *Commentary*, December 2006, available online at http://www.commentarymagazine.com/cm/main/printArticle.html?article=com.-commentarymagazine.content.Article::10798

74 Robespierre, *Virtue and Terror*, p. 129.

75 G.W.F. Hegel, *Lectures on the Philosophy of World History*, Cambridge: Cambridge University Press 1980, p. 263.

76 Samuel Beckett, *Nohow On*, London: Calder 1992, p. 101.

5 *Stalinism Revisited, or, How Stalin Saved the Humanity of Man*

1 See above, Chapter 4.

2 Quoted from Orlando Figes, *Natasha's Dance*, London: Allen Lane 2001, p. 447.

3 Ibid., p. 464.

4 Ibid., pp. 480–1.

5 Ibid., p. 482.

6 Ian MacDonald, *The New Shostakovich*, London: Pimlico 2006, p. 299.

7 James G. Blight and Philip Brenner, *Sad and Luminous Days: Cuba's Secret Struggles with the Superpowers after the Cuban Missile Crisis*, New York: Rowman and Littlefield 2002.

8 Quoted in ibid., p. 23.

9 The letters are available online at http://www.cubanet.org/ref/dis/10110201.htm.

10 Castro's premise, according to which "the destructive power of this [nuclear] weaponry is so great and the speed of its delivery so great that the aggressor would have a considerable initial advantage," is very problematic: it is a safe bet—and the presupposition of the logic of Mutually Assured Destruction—that the surprise nuclear attack of one of the nuclear superpowers would fail to destroy all the opponent's nuclear arms, and that the opponent would have preserved a sufficently large stockpile to strike back. There is, nonetheless, a way to read Castro's demand as a case of "rational" strategic reasoning—what if it was sustained by a ruthless and

cynical calculation with the following scenario in view: the US army will invade Cuba with conventional forces; then, the US and the USSR will destroy each other (and, perhaps, Europe with it) with nuclear arms, making the US occupation of Cuba meaningless, so that Cuba (with most of the Third World) would survive and triumph?

11 Stephen Kotkin, "A Conspiracy So Immense", *The New Republic Online*, February 13, 2006.

12 Simon Montefiore, *Stalin. The Court of the Red Tsar*, London: Weidenfeld and Nicolson 2003, p. 168.

13 See Alexei Yurchak's wonderful *Everything Was Forever, Until It Was No More*, Princeton, NJ: Princeton University Press 2006, p. 52.

14 Quoted from Victor Sebestyen, *Twelve Days*, New York: Pantheon 2006.

15 Till recently, traces of such a totally semantically saturated space survived in Chinese official discourse; in philosophy, it is sometimes comically combined with other features which bear witness to the "organized" and planned character of philosophical research. I was told by a friend who visited the philosophy institute in one of the (for us, Europeans) anonymous 2–4-million-strong Chinese cities, that he had been surprised to discover in the entrance hall a large display board reporting on the achievements of the last five-year plan of philosophical research—which ontological, epistemological, aesthetic, etc., topics had been clarified. In conversation with a member of this institute, he asked him about the existence independent of his mind of the table in front of him; the researcher glibly answered: "Sorry, I cannot yet give you the definitive answer: according to our five-year plan, this topic will be dealt with only in 2008!"

16 This, incidentally, is not quite true: *The Measures Taken* was performed many times in front of large working-class crowds, with a large orchestra and chorus playing and singing the music composed by Hanns Eisler, in the early thirties, as part of the German Communist Party's propaganda and cultural activity. What is true is that the play provoked many critical responses in the official party press: careful not to repel Brecht, a very popular and prestigious author who had recently thrown his support behind the Communists, they nonetheless articulated their uneasiness about the play's "wrong political line." And, furthermore, the play then effectively disappeared from the stage for more than half a century: apart from a short revival by the Berliner Ensemble in the early fifties, its first public performance (again by the Berliner Ensemble) was in the late 1990s. Brecht himself and his literary executors (his wife, Helene Weigel, and daughter Barbara) rejected all requests to stage it.

17 David Caute, *The Dancer Defects*, Oxford: Oxford University Press 2003, p. 295.

18 One can argue that Brecht only pretends to subscribe to the mechanism that requires a politically justified murder, and that the underlying dialectical strategy is to make the spectators think autonomously and bring them to reject the explicit thesis of the play and to fully empathize with the victim; however, such a reading, if pursued to the end, leads to the absurd conclusion that, for decades, Brecht was pretending to be a Stalinist in order to generate in his public a revulsion against Stalinism . . .

19 Which is why the best psychoanalytic reply to this moral maxim is to imagine what it would mean for a *masochist* to promise us that he will abide by it in his relationship to us.

20 First published in Russian in *Pravda*, December 21, 1994. Beneath this note, Stalin appended in blue pencil: "Alas, what do we see, what do we see?" The translation is quoted from Donald Rayfield, *Stalin and His Hangmen*, London: Penguin 2004, p. 22.

21 The same goes for such a radical hedonist atheist as the Marquis de Sade: perspicuous readers of his work (such as Pierre Klossowski) pinpointed long ago that the compulsion to enjoy which drives the Sadean libertine implies a hidden

reference to a hidden divinity, to what Lacan called the "Supreme-Being-of-Evil," an obscure God demanding to be fed with the suffering of innocents.

22 See Lars T. Lih's outstanding "Introduction" to *Stalin's Letters to Molotov*, New Haven, CT: Yale University Press 1995, pp. 60–4.

23 Ibid., p. 48.

24 Ibid.

25 Available online at http://www.marxists.org/archive/lenin/works/1913/.

26 Leon Trotsky, *Diary in Exile 1935*, Cambridge, MA: Harvard University Press 1976, pp. 145–6.

27 Available online at www.marxists.org/reference/archive/stalin/works/1924/01/30.htm.

28 See Jonathan Brent and Vladimir P. Naumov, *Stalin's Last Crime*, New York: HarperCollins 2003.

29 Ian Buchanan, *Deleuzism*, Durham, NC: Duke University Press 2000, p. 5.

30 The reference is to George Leggett, *The Cheka: Lenin's Political Police*, Oxford: Oxford University Press 1981.

31 Lesley Chamberlain, *The Philosophy Steamer*, London: Atlantic Books 2006, pp. 315–16.

32 As is well known, after Stalin's death, Trotsky's *Terrorism and Communism* was found in his library, full of notes signaling Stalin's approval.

33 See Igal Halfin, "The Bolsheviks' Gallows Laughter," *Journal of Political Ideologies*, October 2006, pp. 247–68.

34 Ibid., p. 247.

35 J. Arch Getty and Oleg V. Naumov, *The Road to Terror. Stalin and the Self-Destruction of the Bolsheviks, 1932–39*, New Haven and London: Yale University Press 1999, p. 370.

36 Ibid., p. 394.

37 Franz Kafka, *The Trial*, Harmondsworth: Penguin Books 1985, p. 48.

38 Getty and Naumov, *The Road to Terror*, p. 322.

39 Theodor W. Adorno and Walter Benjamin, *The Complete Correspondence 1928–1940*, Cambridge, MA: Harvard University Press 1999, p. 252.

40 Stephen Johnson, "The Eighth Wonder," *The Gramophone*, July 2006, p. 28.

41 Quoted from Ian McDonald, *The New Shostakovich*, London: Pimlico 2006, p. 1.

42 At the opposite end, the lack of such a distance accounts for the tragic fate of Evald Ilyenkov, arguably the most talented of the Soviet Marxist philosophers: he took his Marxism seriously, as a deep personal engagement, and the price he paid for it was that, in 1979, he committed suicide in despair. Incidentally, Ilyenkov was also a passionate Wagnerian for whom "*The Ring of the Niebelungs* is Karl Marx's *Das Kapital* set to music."

43 MacDonald, *The New Shostakovich*, p. 300. Note the weird category of "non-verbal dissidence"—say, dissidence implied in the mood of the music, which can be verbally denied, so that the same work which officially celebrates socialism, like Shostakovich's Fifth or Seventh Symphony, is "really" its dissident rejection!

44 Ibid., p. 304.

45 Ronald Woodley, accompanying text to the recording by Martha Argerich and Gidon Kremer (Deutsche Grammophon 431 803–2).

46 Shostakovich is here more traditional than Prokofiev; the exemplary "explosion of the Thing" in his work is undoubtedly the second movement of his Tenth Symphony, a short but violently energetic scherzo with slashing chords that is usually referred to as the "Stalin portrait" (although one cannot but ask oneself why—why not simply an explosion of excessive vitality?). It is interesting to note how this shortest movement of them all (a little bit over four minutes, compared with twenty-three minutes of the first, and twelve of the third and fourth) nonetheless functions as the energetic focus of the entire symphony, its wild motif echoed and reverberating in other movements, its excessive energy spilling

over into others—as if it is here, in the second movement, that we court the danger of getting "burned by the sun" . . .

47 Ian MacDonald, "Prokofiev, Prisoner of the State," available online at http://www.siue.edu/~aho/musov/proko/prokofiev2.html.

48 Michael Tanner, "A Dissenting View," *The Gramophone*, July 2006, p. 23.

49 See Richard Maltby, "'A Brief Romantic Interlude': Dick and Jane Go to 3 1/2 Seconds of the Classic Hollywood Cinema," in David Bordwell and Noel Carroll, eds, *Post-Theory*, Madison, WI: University of Wisconsin Press 1996, pp. 434–59.

50 Ibid., p. 443.

51 Ibid., p. 441.

52 See Ibid., p. 445.

53 Figes, *Natasha's Dance*, pp. 492–3.

54 Ibid., p. 57.

55 See Karl Marx, "Class Struggles in France," *Collected Works*, vol. 10, London: Lawrence and Wishart 1978, p. 95.

56 See Bernd Feuchtner, *Dimitri Schostakowitsch*, Kassel, Stuttgart, and Weimar: Barenreiter/Metzler 2002, pp. 125–6.

57 Primo Levi, *If This Is a Man* and *The Truce*, London: Abacus 1987, pp. 133–4.

58 Available online at http://www.siue.edu/~aho/musov/basner/basner.html.

59 See Boris Groys, "Totalitarizm karnavala," *Bakhtinskii zbornik* vol. III, Moscow: Labirinth 1997.

60 Richard Overy, *The Dictators*, London: Penguin 2004, pp. 100–1.

61 Getty and Naumov, *The Road to Terror*, p. 14.

62 Ibid.

63 Andrzej Walicki, *Marxism and the Leap to the Kingdom of Freedom*, Stanford, CA: Stanford University Press 1995, p. 522.

64 The other breathtaking irony is that, when the first version of the film was rejected for not depicting Soviet village life in a truly optimistic Socialist Realist revolutionary spirit, the studio called in Isaac Babel to rewrite the script.

65 See Sergei Eisenstein, *Ivan the Terrible*, London: Faber and Faber 1989, pp. 225–64.

66 G.W.F. Hegel, *Phenomenology of Spirit*, Oxford: Oxford University Press 1977, p. 288.

67 The fluidity and interchangeability of sexual identity in *Ivan* has often been noted: Fyodor Basmanov takes the place of the poisoned Anastasia as Ivan's new partner; Vladimir is effeminate and his mother, Euphrosyna, masculinized; the Polish court is ridiculously feminized; and so on. This effeminization culminates in the scene at the English court in Part III, in which Elisabeth is played by a man (the director Mikhail Romm).

68 Eisenstein, *Ivan the Terrible*, pp. 240–1.

69 Ibid., p. 237.

70 Available online at http://revolutionarydemocracy.org/rdv3n2/ivant.htm.

71 Eisenstein, *Ivan the Terrible*, pp. 249–53.

72 See Choe Sang-Hun, "Born and Raised in a North Korean Gulag," *International Herald Tribune*, July 9, 2007, available on line at http://www.iht.com/articles/2007/07/09/news/korea.php.

73 Do we not find the opposite of the refusal to think of Nazism as a political project in the crucial theoretical scandal of Adorno (and the Frankfurt School in general): the total absence of an analysis of Stalinism in his work (not to speak of that of Habermas and others)?

74 Ernst Nolte, *Martin Heidegger—Politik und Geschichte im Leben und Denken*, Berlin: Propylaen 1992, p. 277.

75 Incidentally, Karl Kautsky, the main theorist of the Second International, already in the early 1920s, in his opposition to the Bolshevik dictatorship, perceived fascists as "copycat" terrorists, the Bolsheviks' "fraternal adversaries," claiming that Bolshevism had served as a school of repressive techniques for fascism: "Fascism is nothing

other than the counterpart of Bolshevism; Mussolini is simply aping Lenin" quoted from Massimo Salvadori, *Karl Kautsky and the Socialist Revolution*, London: Verso 1979, p. 290.

76 Anti-Communist writers such as Nolte who insist on the parallel between Nazism and Communism like to point out that Nazism also perceived (and designated) itself as a species of socialism ("National Socialism"), replacing class with nation. However, it is here that one should put all the weight on the difference between socialism and communism: one can well imagine a "national socialism," but (notwithstanding historical freaks like Ceausescu's Romania and the Khmer Rouge in Kampuchea) there never was a "national communism."

77 Quoted in Berel Lang, *Heidegger's Silence*, Ithaca, NY: Cornell University Press 1996, p. 21.

6 Why Populism Is (Sometimes) Good Enough in Practice, but Not in Theory

1 Jacques-Alain Miller, *Le Neveu de Lacan*, Paris: Verdier 2003, p. 270.

2 Many pro-European commentators favorably opposed the new Eastern European members of the Union's readiness to bear financial sacrifices to the egotistic intransigent behavior of the UK, France, Germany, and some other old members—however, one should also bear in mind the hypocrisy of Slovenia and other new Eastern members: they behaved like the latest members of an exclusive club, wanting to be the last allowed to enter. While accusing France of racism, they themselves opposed the entry of Turkey . . .

3 The tragedy, of course, is that, so far at least, the Linkspartei *is* in fact purely a protest party with no viable global program of change.

4 The limitation of post-politics is best exemplified not only by the success of rightist populism, but by the UK elections of 2005: in spite of the growing unpopularity of Tony Blair (he was regularly voted the most unpopular person in the UK), there is no way for this discontent with Blair to find a politically effective expression; such frustration can only foment dangerous extra-parliamentary explosions.

5 See Nicholas Cook, *Beethoven: Symphony No. 9*, Cambridge: Cambridge University Press 2003.

6 Some critics even compare the "absurd grunts" of the bassoons and bass drum that accompany the beginning of the *marcia Turca* to farts—see Cook, *Beethoven*, p. 103. The history of recognizing echoes of common obscenities in a musical piece is long and interesting. See what, in 1881, Eduard Hanslick wrote about Tchaikovsky's Violin Concerto: "The finale transports us to the brutal and wretched jollity of a Russian festival. We see the savage, vulgar faces, hear obscene curses and smell the vodka . . . Tchaikovsky's Violin Concerto brings us face to face with a hideous notion: that there may be music whose stink we can hear" (quoted from *Classic fm*, October 2005, p. 68). The spontaneous analytical answer to this is, obviously, that Hanslick is here brought face to face with *his own* repressed hideous fantasies . . .

7 Lines attributed to Gottfried Frank; quoted from Cook, *Beethoven*, p. 93. Of course, these lines are not meant as a criticism of Beethoven—on the contrary, in an Adornian mode, one should discern in this failure of the fourth movement Beethoven's artistic integrity: the truthful index of the failure of the very Enlightenment project of universal brotherhood.

8 Cook, *Beethoven*, p. 103.

9 Maynard Solomon, quoted in Cook, *Beethoven*, p. 93.

10 See Cihan Tugal, "NATO's Islamists," *New Left Review*, II, 44 (March–April 2007).

11 Anybody who is minimally acquainted with Heidegger's thought will easily recognize in this paragraph an ironic paraphrase of the well-known passage from Martin

Heidegger, *Introduction to Metaphysics*, New Haven, CT: Yale University Press 2000, pp. 28–9.

12 In March 2005, the Pentagon released the summary of a top-secret document, which sketches America's agenda for global military domination. It calls for a more "proactive" approach to warfare, beyond the weaker notion of "preemptive" and defensive actions. It focuses on four core tasks: to build partnerships with failing states to defeat internal terrorist threats; to defend the homeland, including offensive strikes against terrorist groups planning attacks; to influence the choices of countries at a strategic crossroads, such as China and Russia; and to prevent the acquisition of weapons of mass destruction by hostile states and terrorist groups. Will Europe accept this, satisfied with the role of anemic Greece under the domination of the powerful Roman Empire?

13 See Ernesto Laclau, *On Populist Reason*, London: Verso 2005.

14 This distinction is homologous to that deployed by Michael Walzer between "thin" and "thick" morality (see Michael Walzer, *Thick and Thin*, Notre Dame, IN: University of Notre Dame Press 1994). He gives the example of the great demonstration in the streets of Prague in 1989 that toppled the Communist regime: most of the banners read simply "Truth," "Justice," or "Freedom," general slogans even the ruling Communists had to agree with—the catch was, of course, in the underlying web of "thick" (specific, determinate) demands (freedom of the press, multi-party elections . . .) that indicated what the people *meant* by the simple general slogans. In short, the struggle was not simply for freedom and justice, but for the meaning of these words.

15 Laclau, *On Populist Reason*, p. 88.

16 Ibid., p. 90.

17 Ibid., pp. 98–9.

18 Many people sympathetic to the Hugo Chavez regime in Venezuela like to oppose Chavez's flamboyant and sometimes clownish *caudillo* style to the vast popular movement of the self-organization of the poor and dispossessed that surprisingly brought him back to power after he was deposed in a US-backed coup; the error of this view is to think that one can have the second without the first: the popular movement *needs* the identificatory figure of a charismatic leader. The limitation of Chavez lies elsewhere, in the very factor which enables him to play his role: oil money. It is as if oil is always a mixed blessing, if not an outright curse. Because of this supply, he can go on making populist gestures without "paying the full price for them," without really inventing something new at the socio-economic level. Money makes it possible to practice inconsistent politics (populist anti-capitalist measures that leave the capitalist edifice basically untouched), not acting but postponing the act, the radical change. (In spite of his anti-US rhetoric, Chavez takes great care that Venezuelan contracts with the US are regularly met—he is indeed a "Fidel with oil.")

19 One can easily imagine a situation determined by a tension between an institutionalized democratic power bloc and an oppositional populist bloc, in which one would definitely opt for the institutionalized democratic bloc—say, a situation in which a liberal-democratic regime in power is threatened by a large-scale racist-populist movement.

20 In Edith Wharton's *The Age of Innocence*, the young Newland's wife herself is his fetish: he can pursue his affair with the Countess Olenska only insofar as the wife is supposed *not* to know about it—the moment Newland learns that the wife knew about his affair all along, he is no longer able to pursue his love interest with the Countess, although his wife is now dead and there is no obstacle to his marrying the Countess.

21 See, especially, Chantal Mouffe, *The Democratic Paradox*, London: Verso 2000.

22 Laclau, *On Populist Reason*, p. 166.

23 The best anecdotal example of what is wrong with the first mode of universality is the story, from World War I, about a working-class English soldier on leave from the front, enraged by encountering an upper-class youth calmly leading a life of exquisite "Britishness" (tea rituals, and so on), not perturbed by the war at all. When he explodes against the youth: "How can you just sit here and enjoy it, while we are sacrificing our blood to defend our way of life?", the youth calmly responds: "But I *am* the way of life you are defending there in the trenches!"

24 See Laclau, *On Populist Reason*, p. 183.

25 Oliver Marchart, "Acting and the Act: On Slavoj Žižek's Political Ontology," in Paul Bowman and Richard Stamp, eds, *Truth of Žižek*, London: Continuum 2007, p. 174.

26 Claude Lévi-Strauss, "Do Dual Organizations Exist?" in *Structural Anthropology* (New York: Basic Books 1963), pp. 131–63; the drawings are on pp. 133–4.

27 Gilles Deleuze, *Difference and Repetition*, New York: Columbia University Press 1995, 186.

28 See Chapter 1 of Jacques Lacan, *The Four Fundamental Concepts of Psycho-Analysis*, Harmondsworth: Penguin 1979.

29 And the same reversal goes on today, when the opposition of liberal-left feminists and conservative populists is also perceived as the opposition of upper-middle-class feminists and multiculturalists against lower-class rednecks.

30 Can we say, then, that politics is All, a series of totalizations, of imposing Master-Signifiers which totalize a field through exceptions? But what about the Non-All as politics? "Everything is political" is misleading, the true formula is "there is nothing which is not political"—for it was Stalin who totalized politics, and had to pay the price for it in asserting the exception (technology, language, and so on) as apolitical, class-neutral. In other words, is it not politics which is the impassive pseudo-cause— a theater of shadows in which, nonetheless, everything is decided?

31 Karl Marx, "Preface," *A Contribution to the Critique of Political Economy*, Moscow: Progress Publishers 1977, pp. 7–8.

32 Ernesto Laclau, "Why Constructing a People Is the Main Task of Radical Politics," *Critical Inquiry* 32 (Summer 2006), pp. 657, 680. Furthermore, Laclau only develops hegemony as the particular elevated into the embodiment/representation of the impossible Thing; what is missing is how the particular element which represents All can only do it through negating the unifying feature of the All. Two worn-out examples should suffice here: for Marx, the only way to be a "royalist in general" is to be a republican; for Hegel, man (who creates himself) in general is a king (who is what he is by nature). This tension *precedes* the tension friend/enemy as reflected in hegemonic struggle.

33 Which is why, for example, when someone plays the game of postponing the revelation of the content to which he is referring, repeatedly giving hints and then withdrawing, we can accuse him of playing a sexualized game even if the content whose revelation is endlessly postponed is quite commonplace and asexual.

34 See Anna Funder, *Stasiland*, London: Granta Books 2003, pp. 177–82.

35 Karl Marx, *Capital, Volume One*, Harmondsworth: Penguin 1990, p. 163.

36 Karl Marx and Frederick Engels, *The Communist Manifesto*, Harmondsworth: Penguin 1985, p. 82.

37 Yannis Stavrakakis, *The Lacanian Left*, Edinburgh: Edinburgh University Press 2007.

38 Ibid., p. 30.

39 Ibid., p. 115.

40 Ibid., pp. 116–19.

41 Ibid., p. 122.

42 Ibid., p. 126.

43 Ibid., p. 154.

44 In more logical terms, Stalinism confused external and internal negation: the fact that the majority of the population did not share the revolutionary will to build a new society, that it was simply indifferent, was read as active negative willing, in other words, not-willing was turned into willing the no, the active negation of the Soviet order.

45 Of course, not every resistance to a truth-procedure is a sign of its falsity: Mao was right when he said that it is good—a sign of the correctness of our position—to be attacked by the enemy. The problem with the resistance to the Stalinist imposition of "Truth" was that it was the resistance of the people, the very source of the regime's legitimacy.

46 Stavrakakis, *The Lacanian Left*, p. 143.

47 Ibid., p. 141.

48 Ibid., p. 142.

49 Ibid., p. 130.

50 Ibid., p. 144.

51 Ibid., p. 133.

52 Ibid.

53 Alain Badiou, "Fifteen Theses on Contemporary Art," available online at http://www.lacan.com/frameXXIII7.htm.

54 Stavrakakis, *The Lacanian Left*, pp. 133–4.

55 Ibid., p. 142.

56 Similarly, when I claim that Stavrakakis does not take into account the capitalist utopia, he furiously replies that he elaborated in detail the capitalist consumerist utopia—as if it is not clear from the context that I am referring to the utopian nature of the market mechanism, discernible in the advocates of capitalism.

57 Ibid., p. 135.

58 Jorge Luis Borges, *Other Inquisitions: 1937–52*, New York: Washington Square Press 1966, p. 113.

59 Gilles Deleuze, *Difference and Repetition*, New York: Columbia University Press 1994, p. 183.

60 Ibid., p. 81.

61 James Williams, *Gilles Deleuze's "Difference and Repetition": A Critical Introduction and Guide*, Edinburgh: Edinburgh University Press 2003, p. 26.

62 T.S. Eliot, "Tradition and the Individual Talent," originally published in *The Sacred Wood: Essays on Poetry and Criticism* (1922).

63 Peter Hallward, *Out of this World*, London: Verso 2005, p. 135.

64 Ibid., p. 139.

65 Ibid., p. 54.

66 Williams, *Gilles Deleuze's "Difference and Repetition"*, p. 109.

67 Jean-Pierre Dupuy, *Petite métaphysique des tsunami*, Paris: Éditions du Seuil 2005, p. 19.

68 For Stavrakakis, my excessive assertion of positivity is contrasted to Laclau's excessive assertion of discursive negativity—and, as expected, whereas my thought regresses, Laclau's progresses: in his latest work, he is already filling in this lack, so that only I remain the "bad guy"

69 Stavrakakis, *The Lacanian Left*, p. 8.

70 Ibid., p. 8.

71 Ibid., pp. 9–10.

72 To anyone minimally acquainted with Hegel, Stavrakakis's implicit equation of positivity with infinity (immortality) and of negativity with finitude (mortality) is truly breathtaking: if there is something to be learned from Hegel above all, it is that negativity (negation of every finite positive/determinate being) is the only infinite power there is.

73 Stavrakakis, *The Lacanian Left*, p. 12.

74 Deleuze, *Difference and Repetition*, p. 105.
75 Williams, *Gilles Deleuze's "Difference and Repetition"*, p. 27.
76 Deleuze, *Difference and Repetition*, pp. 104–5.
77 Henri Bergson, *Œuvres*, Paris: PUF 1991, p. 1110–11.
78 Ibid.
79 Ibid., p. 1340.
80 Stavrakakis, *The Lacanian Left*, p. 16.
81 Ibid., p. 18.
82 Ibid., p. 222.
83 Ibid, p. 269.
84 And, incidentally, since, as is clear to Laclau, populism can also be reactionary, how are we to draw a line here? The problem of distinguishing between true and fake Events, attributed to Badiou, clearly reproduces itself here.
85 Stavrakakis, *The Lacanian Left*, p. 282.
86 Ibid., p. 275.
87 Slavoj Žižek, *Revolution at the Gates*, London: Verso 2004, p. 329.
88 Stavrakakis, *The Lacanian Left*, p. 278.
89 Ibid, p. 279.
90 Ibid., p. 279.
91 Ibid., pp. 280–2.
92 See Jacques-Alain Miller, "Le nom-du-père, s'en passer, s'en servir," available online at www.lacan.com.
93 See ibid.
94 For a more detailed account of how the distinction between desire and drive relates to capitalism, see Chapter 1 of my *Parallax* View (Cambridge, MA: MIT Press 2006).
95 Richard Boothby, *Freud as Philosopher*, New York: Routledge 2001, pp. 275–6.
96 Stavrakakis, *The Lacanian Left*, p. 281.
97 Not only Lévi-Strauss, but even Foucault was the victim of a similar fantasy when, in his last works, he constructed the image of ancient Greek ethics as preceding the Christian matrix of the Fall, sin and confession.
98 Stavrakakis, *The Lacanian Left*, p. 281.
99 Ibid., p. 281.
100 Ibid., p. 282.
101 Ibid., p. 279.
102 Ibid., p. 279.
103 It would be interesting to reread from this perspective Sayid Qutb's *Milestones*, this manifesto of fundamentalist Islamism: Qutb's formative experience was his period as a student in the US in the early 1950s: his book reveals the radical resentment apropos the sexual freedom and public activity of women he encountered there.

7 *The Crisis of Determinate Negation*

1 For a critique of this notion from a traditional Marxist standpoint see Wolfgang Fritz Haug, "Das Ganze und das ganz Andere: Zur Kritik der reinen revolutionären Transzendenz," in *Antworten auf Herbert Marcuse*, edited by Jürgen Habermas, Frankfurt: Suhrkamp 1968, pp. 50–72, and also Haug, *Bestimmte Negation*, Frankfurt: Suhrkamp 1973.
2 See Chapter 4.
3 See Simon Critchley, *Infinitely Demanding*, London: Verso 2007.
4 Ibid, p. 139.
5 See Simon Critchley, "Di and Dodi Die," *Theory & Event*, vol. 1, issue 4, 1997.
6 Critchley, *Infinitely Demanding*, p. 10.
7 Ibid., p. 11.

8 Ibid., p. 55.

9 Ibid., pp. 60–1.

10 Ibid., p. 69.

11 Ibid, p. 71.

12 Ibid., p. 74.

13 Ibid., p. 82.

14 Jacques Lacan, *The Ethics of Psychoanalysis*, London: Routledge 1992, p. 310.

15 Jacques Lacan, *On Feminine Sexuality* (*The Seminar, Book XX*), New York: Norton 1998, p. 3.

16 Critchley, *Infinitely Demanding*, p. 10.

17 Ibid., p. 1.

18 This is why it would be interesting to imagine *Antigone* rewritten in the style of Brecht's *Jasager* and *Neinsager*, from Creon's standpoint, presenting her as an obstinate girl not ready to listen to his reasonable arguments (a bloody civil war has just finished; if Polyneikos, the traitor who attacked the city, is properly buried, killing might explode again with hundreds of dead); or to imagine an alternate reality to *Antigone*'s, beginning in a city in ruins, devastated by fratricidal warfare, with people cursing a spoiled and obstinate girl of the court responsible for the destruction; we gradually learn that this girl is Antigone—she persuaded Creon to allow her to bury her brother properly, as a result of which war erupted once more . . .

19 Critchley, *Infinitely Demanding*, pp. 115–18.

20 Ibid., p. 117.

21 Ibid., p. 122.

22 Ibid., p. 129.

23 Ibid., p. 129.

24 Ibid., p. 151.

25 Ibid., p. 124.

26 Ibid., pp. 5–6.

27 Ibid., p. 146.

28 Ibid., pp. 100–1

29 Antonio Negri, *Goodbye Mister Socialism*, trans. Peter Thomas, New York: Seven Stories Press, forthcoming, p. 137.

30 Ibid., p. 185.

31 Ibid., p. 180.

32 Ibid., pp. 169–70.

33 Karl Marx, *Grundrisse*, Harmondsworth: Penguin 1973, p. 694.

34 Gilles Deleuze and Félix Guattari, *Anti-Oedipus*, New York: Viking Press 1977, p. 35.

35 Negri, *Goodbye Mister Socialism*, p. 170.

36 There is a rare, but interesting, inversion of this rule: when ferocious anti-Hegelians attack "Hegel" (the textbook simplified figure of Hegel), they unknowingly assert as their own anti-Hegelian position a central feature of Hegel's thought—Deleuze is perhaps the key example here.

37 Negri's version of the struggle between idealism and materialism is the struggle between the radically-democratic materialism of Machiavelli–Spinoza–Marx and the idealist supporters of capitalism from Descartes to Hegel. Ibid., p. 22.

38 Ibid., p. 168.

39 The same holds for Deleuze himself, their philosophical mentor. Fredric Jameson has drawn attention to the fact that the central reference of *Anti-Oedipus*, the underlying scheme of its larger historical framework, is "The Pre-Capitalist Modes of Production," the long fragment from the *Grundrisse* manuscripts in which we encounter Marx at his most Hegelian (its entire scheme of global historical movement relies on the Hegelian process from substance to subject).

40 Marx, *Grundrisse*, pp. 694–712.

41 Negri, *Goodbye Mister Socialism*, p. 215.

42 Ibid., p. 178. The first thing to draw attention to here is the oscillation of "biopower" between the more general feature that, according to Foucault, characterizes modernity as such (where the goal of power is no longer prohibitive legal rule, but the productive regulation of life), to the very specific field opened up by biogenetic discoveries: the prospect of direct generation of (new) forms of life.

43 Ibid., p. 189.

44 Ibid., p. 164, translation modified.

45 Ibid., pp. 189–90.

46 This duality also has the general form of the persistence of the gap between the "kingdom of necessity" and the "kingdom of freedom": in contrast to Negri who perceives the productive process of the general intellect as the direct enactment of freedom, Marx insists that freedom and necessity will remain separated, that work cannot turn into play.

47 Ibid., pp. 216–17.

48 V.I. Lenin, "Our Revolution", in *Collected Works*, Moscow: Progress Publishers 1965, vol. 33, p. 479.

49 The same is true today of Chavez in Venezuela: of course, one can say that Venezuela is an anomaly, that he can afford his opposition to the Empire precisely because he gets billions of dollars from it (for the oil); however, through this anomaly, Venezuela can nonetheless mobilize not only social movements within its own borders, but also introduce a new emancipatory dynamic in other, less "anomalous," Latin American countries.

50 Are recent trends in world cinema not an indicator of this gradual shift towards pluricentricity? Is the hegemony of Hollywood not gradually breaking down with global successes from Western Europe, from Latin America, even from China which, with films like *The Hero*, surpassed Hollywood in its home territory of grand historical spectacles and special-effects fights?

51 See Emmanuel Todd, *After the Empire*, London: Constable 2004.

52 Do the actual results of the US policy in the Middle East (the ultimate result of the US occupation of Iraq being the predominance of pro-Iranian political forces there—the intervention basically delivered Iraq to Iranian influence) not support the notion that Bush is "objectively" an Iranian agent?

53 Negri, *Goodbye Mister Socialism*, p. 154.

54 Ibid. Another of Negri's weirdly inadequate readings is his note on the post-Yugoslav war, where he fully endorses the disintegration of Yugoslavia as the result of a dark plot by Germany, Austria, and the Vatican, which sustained financially and ideologically murderous nationalisms; plus, as expected, he insists on the equally distributed guilt: "Milošević wasn't worse than Tudjman and the Kosovars weren't better than the Serbs . . . Things got to the point of a cannibalistic struggle between factions." The inadequacy of this reading, as well as its pro-Serb bias, cannot but strike the eye: if the agents of the disintegration of Yugoslavia were the separatist Croats and Slovenes, then the Serbs are *less* guilty . . . Plus it is not clear how to account in these terms for the original moment of the crisis, the Kosovan problem and the rise to power of Milošević. In this context, even I deserve a brief mention: "I remember Kusturica, the great director, an old friend of mine. We had organized a discussion on the history of Yugoslavia. Also there was Professor Grmek, very much linked to the right-wing Croat regime. Well, sometimes Kusturica slapped him . . . And then there was Žižek, the Slovenian, who has now become more or less a Trotskyist, who didn't know what to say. Kusturica was accused of being Philo-Milošević, even if all his work has always been libertarian, right from his splendid beginnings." (pp. 50–51).

I must admit that this passage leaves me a little bit perplexed. What my designation as "more or less a Trotskyite" refers to lies beyond my comprehension. I well remember the occasion: a small circle were assembled in a private apartment.

When Kusturica arrived (very late, as befits a star), he stayed for a long time in front of the entrance to the apartment, while the organizer of the debate (a Serb from Vojvodina, neither Negri nor Kusturica), tried to calm him down and dissuade him from starting a physical fight (Kusturica had threatened to punch some of us on the nose). When Kusturica finally sat down at the table, he engaged in a long hysterically poetic ramble to which most of us indeed "didn't know what to say," since it contained no clear line of argumentation. As to Kusturica and Milošević, throughout the war years, Kusturica traveled around on a Serb–Yugoslav diplomatic passport; his *Underground* was financed by Serbia, and so on and so forth, not to mention the fact that a person called Emir Kusturica literally no longer exists: since he recently underwent an Orthodox baptism and changed his name from the Muslim "Emir" to the resolutely Serb "Nemanja" (the name of some of Serbia's ancient saints and kings, among other things). Incidentally, when, a couple of years ago, a Montenegrin director put together a documentary consisting of numerous video-clips proving Kusturica's pro-Milošević and Serb nationalist bias (with many hair-raising moments), the director took him to court, and signatures in defense were collected all over ex-Yugoslavia.

55 Negri, *Goodbye Mister Socialism*, p. 245.
56 See Slavoj Žižek, *Organs Without Bodies*, New York: Routledge 2003.
57 I follow here Alain Badiou, on whose reading of Deleuze I rely extensively; see Badiou, *Deleuze: The Clamour of Being*, Minneapolis, MN: University of Minnesota Press 2000.
58 Manuel DeLanda, *Intensive Science and Virtual Philosophy*, New York: Continuum 2002, pp. 107–8.
59 Ibid., p. 102.
60 Quoted from Roderick MacFarquhar and Michael Schoenhals, *Mao's Last Revolution*, Cambridge, MA: Harvard University Press 2006, p. 168.
61 Quoted from ibid., pp. 168–9.
62 See John Holloway, *Change the World Without Taking Power: The Meaning of Revolution Today*, London: Pluto 2002.
63 Ibid., p. 31.
64 And, incidentally, did not the planned economy of state socialism pay a terrible price for privileging production at the expense of consumption, failing to provide consumers with goods they needed and wanted? When post-Marxist leftists speak of a "consumtariat" as the new form of proletariat (see Alexander Bard and Jan Soderqvist, *Netrocracy: The New Power Elite and Life after Capitalism*, London: Reuters 2002) what they indicate is the ultimate identity of worker and consumer—it is for *this* reason that, in capitalism, a worker has to be formally free.
65 Marx, *Grundrisse*, pp. 420–1.
66 Kojin Karatani, *Transcritique. On Kant and Marx*, Cambridge, MA: MIT Press 2003, p. 20.
67 Ibid., p. 290.
68 Peter Sloterdijk, *Zorn und Zeit*, Frankfurt: Suhrkamp 2006, p. 55.
69 G.W.F. Hegel, *Phenomenology of Spirit*, Oxford: Oxford University Press 1977, p. 332.
70 Ibid.
71 When, say, the reactionary counter-Enlightenment argumentation itself secretly relies on the ideological premises of the Enlightenment premises—as is the case from Robert Filmer's polemics against John Locke up to today's televangelists whose very delivering of their message undermines the message—in their performance, they display the very features they criticize so ferociously in their liberal opponents, from narcissistic self-indulgence to commercialized mediatic spectacles.
72 Negri, *Goodbye Mister Socialism*, pp. 139–40.
73 Quoted from Massimo Salvadori, *Karl Kautsky and the Socialist Revolution*, London: Verso 1979, p. 237.

74 Especially interesting is one of Trotsky's arguments on the need for a vanguard party: the self-organization in councils cannot replace the role of the party also for a politico-psychological reason—people "cannot live for years in an uninterrupted state of high tension and intense activity." See Ernest Mandel, *Trotsky as Alternative*, London: Verso 1995, p. 81.

75 For a clear articulation of this stance, see Martin Jay, "No Power to the Soviets," in *Cultural Semantics*, Amherst, MA: University of Massachusetts Press 1998.

76 Negri, *Goodbye Mister Socialism*, p. 143.

77 The figure of the Leader in no way guarantees the consistency of the political program; quite the contrary. As fascism demonstrates, the Leader's charismatic presence can also function as a fetish whose function is to *obfuscate* the inconsistency, the self-contradictory character, of the politics he stands for: the actual politics of fascism oscillated between concessions to different pressure groups, and this inconsistency and lack of a clear program was masked by the Leader's charisma.

78 One should, of course, refrain from utopian expectations: within the present global constellation, the probability is that the Chavez experiment will end in failure; nonetheless, as Beckett would have put it, this will be a "better failure."

79 See Danny Postel, *Reading "Legitimation Crisis" in Tehran*, Chicago: Prickly Paradigm Press 2006.

8 Alain Badiou, or, the Violence of Subtraction

1 Alain Badiou, *Logiques des mondes*, Paris: Éditions du Seuil 2006, p. 9.

2 Moustapha Safouan, "Why Are the Arabs Not Free: The Politics of Writing" (unpublished essay).

3 John Gray, *Straw Dogs*, London: Granta 2003, p. 57.

4 Badiou, *Logiques des mondes*, pp. 9–17. In one of his old songs, Wolf Biermann asked the question: "Is there life *before* death?"—an appropriate materialist reversal of the standard idealist question: "Is there life *after* death?" What bothers a materialist is: Am I really alive here and now, or am I just vegetating, as a mere human animal bent on survival?

5 One should then, against Badiou, insist on the strict equality between world and language: every world is sustained by language, and every "spoken" language sustains a world—this is what Heidegger was suggesting with his thesis on language as a "house of being."

6 Knowledge is also, in itself, accessible to all, no one is *a priori* excluded—as Plato demonstrated, a slave can learn mathematics in the same way that a noble can—logical reasoning and demonstrations exclude authority, their subject of enunciation is by definition universal, it does not matter *who* is reasoning

7 One can also imagine a humanitarian version of such a pseudo-ethical form of blackmail: "OK, enough of this muddle about neo-colonialism, the responsibility of the West, and so on—do you want to do something to really help the millions suffering in Africa, or do you just want to use them to score points in your ideologico-political struggle?"

8 Jacques-Alain Miller, "A Reading of the Seminar *From an Other to the other*," *lacanian ink*, 29 (2007), p. 40.

9 See Adrian Johnston, "The Quick and the Dead: Alain Badiou and the Split Speeds of Transformation" (unpublished essay).

10 It was none other than Hegel who, in his very "critique" of Jacobin "abstract freedom," perceived the necessity of this moment, dispelling the liberal dream of bypassing 1794, that is, of passing directly from 1789 to the established bourgeois quotidian reality. The dream denounced by Robespierre as the dream of those who

want "revolution without a revolution" is the dream of having 1789 without 1793, of having one's cake and eating it . . .

11 Badiou, *Logiques des mondes*, p. 531.

12 Ibid., p. 75.

13 The irony is thus that the title of Badiou's first great book to which *Logiques des mondes* is part two, *Being and Event*, should be read in the same way as Freud's *The Ego and the Id*: as an implicit reference to the missing third term, *World*, or, in Freud's case, *Superego*.

14 Alain Badiou, "L'entretien de Bruxelles," *Les Temps Modernes*, 526 (1990), p. 6.

15 Alberto Toscano, "From the State to the World? Badiou and Anti-Capitalism," *Communication & Cognition*, vol. 36 (2003), pp. 1–2.

16 A conference paper from 2002 translated by Bruno Bosteels.

17 Badiou, *Logiques des mondes*, pp. 543–44.

18 When Badiou talks about "eternal truths," transhistorical truths whose universality cuts across specific historical worlds, horizons of sense, this universality is not a mythical universality of a Jungian archetype (even if his description of the Idea of the horse from prehistoric cave paintings to Picasso sometimes comes dangerously close to it), but the sense-less universality of the Real, or what Lacan calls the "matheme."

19 Badiou, *Logiques des mondes*, p. 547.

20 With the temptation to go a step even further and say that it is *better* to have a "bad" state, because, in this way, the lines of demarcation are clearly drawn—the same logic that pushed German Communists in 1933 to claim that Hitler was *better* than Weimar democracy—with Hitler, we know where we stand, the fight is clear-cut. . .

21 This move is part of the curious but symptomatic phenomenon of "belated anti-Communism" which developed after 2000 in most of the Eastern European post-Communist countries (Lithuania, Poland, the Czech Republic, Hungary, Slovenia . . .): the attempt to directly criminalize Communism, to put it on the same level as fascism and Nazism (prohibiting the public display of its symbols, including the Red Star). It is easy to demonstrate that this "equality" is a fake, namely, that, implicitly, Communism is elevated into the primary Crime, with fascism reduced to a kind of political copycat-murder, a reaction to and imitation of Communism.

22 Wendy Brown, *States of Injury*, Princeton, NJ: Princeton University Press 1995, p. 14.

23 Ibid., p. 60.

24 Ibid., p. 61.

25 I am grateful to Saroj Giri (New Delhi), who has developed in detail this link between the assertion of socio-political contingency and the elevation of capitalism into a natural(ized) necessity.

26 Toni Negri, *Goodbye Mister Socialism*, Paris: Éditions du Seuil 2006, p. 125.

27 Filippo Del Lucchese and Jason Smith, "'We Need a Popular Discipline': Contemporary Politics and the Crisis of the Negative," interview with Alain Badiou, Los Angeles, July 2, 2007.

28 See Peter Hallward, *Badiou: A Subject to Truth*, Minneapolis, MN: Minnesota University Press 2003.

29 This limitation of democracy has nothing to do with the standard worry of the liberal exporters of democracy: what if the result is the victory of those who oppose democracy, and thus its self-cancellation? "This is a terrible truth that we have to face: the only thing that currently stands between us and the rolling ocean of Muslim unreason is a wall of tyranny and human rights abuses that we have helped to erect" (Sam Harris, *The End of Faith*, New York: Norton 2005, p.132). Here, then, is Harris's motto: "when your enemy has no scruples, your own scruples become another weapon in his hand" (ibid., p. 202). And, from here, predictably, he proceeds to justify torture . . . While this line of reasoning may appear convincing, it is not

pursued to the end; it remains stuck in the terms of the tiresome liberal debate: "Are the Muslim masses mature enough (culturally fit) for democracy, or should we support enlightened despotism amongst their rulers?" Both terms of the underlying choice (either we impose our democracy on them or we exploit their backwardness) are false. The true question is: *what if the "wall of tyranny and human rights abuses that we have helped to erect" is precisely what sustains and generates the "rolling ocean of Muslim unreason"?*

30 Or: "dictatorship" in a free debate is the element of the "final statements" whose evocation is considered conclusive. Today, in postmodern deconstructionism, it is the evocation of the nomadic versus the fixed identity, of change versus stasis, of the multitude versus the One, etc.—*this* is the moment of dictatorship.

31 Bulent Somay, personal letter, January 28, 2007. I am all the more content to quote this passage since Somay's letter is deeply critical of me.

32 Quoted in Simon Schama, *Citizens*, New York: Viking Penguin 1989, pp. 706–7.

33 Maximilien Robespierre, *Virtue and Terror*, London: Verso 2007 p. 42.

34 The only moment when the "people exists" is during an election, which is precisely the moment of the disintegration of the entire social structure—in elections, the "people" is reduced to a mechanical collection of individuals.

35 Jacques-Alain Miller, *Le Neveu de Lacan*, Paris: Verdier 2003, p. 270.

36 One can, of course, argue that direct "mob rule" is inherently unstable and that it turns necessarily into its opposite, a tyranny over the mob itself; however, this shift in no way changes the fact that, precisely, we are dealing with a shift, a radical inversion.

37 See Peter Hallward, "Staging Equality," *New Left Review*, II, 37 (January–February 2006).

9 Unbehagen in der Natur

1 G.A. Cohen, *If You're an Egalitarian, How Come You're So Rich?*, Cambridge, MA: Harvard University Press 2001.

2 David Rennie, "How Soviet Sub officer Saved World from Nuclear Conflict," *Daily Telegraph*, October 14, 2002.

3 See the excellent report by Mike Davis, "Planet of Slums. Urban Revolution and the Informal Proletariat," *New Left Review*, II, 26 (March–April 2004).

4 Are then slum-dwellers not to be classified as those whom Marx, with barely concealed contempt, dismissed as the "lumpenproletariat," the degenerate "refuse" of all classes which, when politicized, as a rule serves as the support of proto-fascist and fascist regimes (in Marx's case, of Napoleon III)? A closer analysis should focus on the changed structural role of these "lumpen" elements in the conditions of global capitalism (especially with large-scale migration).

5 The precise Marxian definition of the proletarian position is: substanceless subjectivity which emerges when a certain structural short-circuit occurs—not only do producers exchange their products on the market, but there are producers who are forced to sell on the market not the product of their labor, but directly their labor-power as such. It is here, through this redoubled/reflected alienation, that the surplus-object emerges: surplus-value is literally correlative to the emptied subject, it is the objectal counterpart of $. This redoubled alienation means not only that "social relations appear as relations between things," as in every market economy, but that the very core of subjectivity itself is posited as equivalent to a thing. One should be attentive here to the paradox of universalization: the market economy can only become universal when labor-power itself is also sold on the market as a commodity, that is, there can be no universal market economy with the majority of producers selling their own products.

6 The semiotic that sustains these qualifications obeys a very precise logic and deserves an analysis of its own: one cannot just mix the terms and propose, say, an alliance of "workers, patriotic farmers, honest petty bourgeoisie, and poor intellectuals." Each time, the line of separation is clear: only *poor* farmers, not the rich who belong to or form pacts with the ruling class; only the *patriotic* petty bourgeoisie, not those bourgeois who serve capitalist imperialism; only *honest* intellectuals, not those who have sold themselves to the ruling class and legitimize its domination. Should we then say that what we need today is an alliance between the Excluded, poor ecologists, patriotic intellectual workers, and honest biogeneticists?

7 The question is, how to distinguish this commons from the pre-modern commons of collective property?

8 Immanuel Kant, "What Is Enlightenment?," in Isaac Kramnick, ed., *The Portable Enlightenment Reader*, New York: Penguin 1995, p. 5.

9 See "Murdoch: I'm proud to be green. News Corp boss orders his entire empire to convert and become a worldwide enthusiast for the environment," *Independent on Sunday*, May 13, 2007, p. 3.

10 Aeschylus, *Eumenides*, Ian Johnston's translation (2003), available online at www.mala.bc.ca/~Johnstoi/aeschylus/aeschylus_eumenides.htm.

11 It is strange that Simon Critchley, who quotes these lines in his *Infinitely Demanding* (London: Verso 2007), reads them as prefiguring the politics of fear, although they fit much better the main motif of his book, the pressure of the "infinitely demanding" superego.

12 Martin Heidegger, *Gesamtausgabe*, vol. 29/30, *Die Grundbegriffe der Metaphysik. Welt — Endlichkeit — Einsamkeit*, Frankfurt: Klostermann 2004, p. 255.

13 Heidegger, *Gesamtausgabe*, vol. 45, *Grundprobleme der Philosophie*, Frankfurt. Klostermann 1984, p. 197.

14 G.W.F. Hegel, *Phenomenology of Spirit*, Oxford: Oxford University Press 1977, p. 189.

15 Ayn Rand, *The Fountainhead*, New York: Signet 1992, p. 677.

16 There are many further variants of Che Guevara's alleged "last words"—here are some of them: "I know you've come to kill me. Shoot, you are only going to kill a man." / "Shoot, coward, you are only going to kill a man." / "Know this now, you are killing a man." / "I knew you were going to shoot me; I should never have been taken alive." / "Tell Fidel that this failure does not mean the end of the revolution, that it will triumph elsewhere. Tell Aleida to forget this, remarry and be happy, and keep the children studying. Ask the soldiers to aim well." / "Don't shoot, I am Che Guevara and I am worth more to you alive than dead."

17 Samuel Beckett, *Trilogy*, London: Calder 2003, p. 418.

18 Karl Marx and Frederick Engels, *The Communist Manifesto*, Harmondsworth: Penguin 1985, pp. 83–4.

19 This title is usually translated as "Civilization and Its Discontents," thus missing the opportunity to bring into play the opposition of culture and civilization: the discontent is in culture, its violent break with nature, while civilization can be conceived as precisely the secondary attempt to patch things up, to "civilize" the cut, to reintroduce the lost balance and an appearance of harmony.

20 Quoted from Thorsten Jantschek, "Ein ausgezehrter Hase," *Die Zeit*, July 5, 2001, Feuilleton, p. 26.

21 Similarly, while scientists in the CERN particle collider are preparing the conditions to recreate the Big Bang explosion, some skeptics are warning about the possibility that the experiment will succeed all too well, effectively setting in motion a new Big Bang which will wipe out the world we know.

22 Doyne Farmer and Aletta Belin, "Artificial Life: The Coming Evolution," in C.G. Langton, C. Taylor, J.D. Farmer, and S. Rasmussen, eds, *Artificial Life*, Reading, MA: Addison-Wesley 1992, p. 815.

23 In the last decade, this topic has often been exploited in sci-fi thrillers—see, among others, Michael Crichton's *Prey* (New York: Avon Books 2002).

24 Jacques-Alain Miller, "Religion, Psychoanalysis," *lacanian ink*, 23 (2004), pp. 18–19.

25 Throughout modernity, the Church presented itself as the guardian against the danger of knowing-too-much. When, today, it presents itself as a beacon of the respect for freedom and human dignity, it is advisable to carry out a simple mental experiment. Till the early 1960s, the Church maintained the (in)famous Index of works whose reading was prohibited to (ordinary) Catholics; one can only imagine how the artistic and intellectual history of modern Europe would look if we erased from it all works that, at one time or another, found themselves on this Index—a modern Europe without Descartes, Spinoza, Leibniz, Hume, Kant, Hegel, Marx, Nietzsche, Sartre, not to mention a large majority of modern literary classics.

26 Jean Grondin, *Hans-Georg Gadamer*, New Haven, CT: Yale University Press 2003, p. 329.

27 I take this expression from Alain Badiou.

28 See Stephen Fry, *Making History*, New York: Arrow Books 2005.

29 See the report "Life 2.0" in *Newsweek*, June 4, 2007, pp. 37–43.

30 Ibid., p. 41.

31 In "Environmentalism as a Religion," a speech given to the Commonwealth Club of California, Michael Crichton described the similarities between the structure of various religious views (particularly Judeo-Christian dogma) and the beliefs of many modern urban atheists who he asserts have romantic ideas about Nature and our past, who he thinks believe in the garden of Eden, original sin, and Judgment Day. It is the tendency of today's environmentalists to cling stubbornly to elements of their faith in spite of scientific evidence to the contrary (Crichton cites the misconceptions about DDT, the dangers of passive smoking, and global warming as examples). Dubious as Crichton is—his bestsellers are one of the perfect embodiments of late capitalism's predominant ideology—he has a point here.

32 Another example: in order to counteract the policy of the ruthless destruction of forests, ecologists often succeeded in imposing strict measures of fire suppression—with the unexpected result that the virgin forests were altered even more irrevocably (since occasional fires played a key role in their self-reproduction). Or, at a more anecdotal level, there is the story about a valley in the UK which was heavily polluted by coal smoke. Once the coal-burning stopped, the immediate results were catastrophic: the birds and other organisms were already so used to coal pollution that they could not survive in new conditions, so they left, disturbing the fragile ecological balance in the valley . . . And what about animals like pigs reared on industrial farms, who are not able to survive on their own even for a couple of days (they are half blind, cannot stand on their own legs . . .)?

33 Pall Skulason, *Reflections at the Edge of Askja*, Reykjavik: The University of Iceland Press 2005, p. 21.

34 Gilles Deleuze, *Cinema 1: The Movement-Image*, Minneapolis, MN: University of Minnesota Press 1986, p. 122.

35 Skulason, *Reflections at the Edge of Askja*, p. 11.

36 Ibid., p. 19.

37 Ibid., pp. 31–3.

38 See Timothy Morton's outstanding *Ecology Without Nature*, Cambridge, MA: Harvard University Press 2007.

39 Ibid., p. 35.

40 John Gray, *Straw Dogs*, London: Granta 2003 p. 19.

41 Friedrich Nietzsche, *On the Genealogy of Morals*, Oxford: Oxford University Press 1998, p. 97.

42 See Louis Dumont, *Homo Aequalis*, Paris: Gallimard 1977, and *Essais sur l'individualisme*, Paris: Éditions du Seuil 1983.

43 See Daniel Dennett, *Freedom Evolves*, Harmondsworth: Penguin 2003.

44 Nicholas Fearn, *Philosophy. The Latest Answers to the Oldest Questions*, London: Atlantic Books 2005, p. 24.

45 Bill McKibben, *Enough. Staying Human in an Engineered Age*, New York: Henry Holt 2004, p. 127.

46 Mark Wrathall, *How to Read Heidegger*, London: Granta 2006, p. 102.

47 Giorgio Agamben refuses to enter the US: he does not want his fingerprints taken — for him, fingerprinting makes "the most private and incommunicable aspect of subjectivity" part of the system of state control. But, one is entitled to ask, why is the accidental shape of the ridges on the tip of my fingers "the most private and incommunicable aspect of subjectivity"?

48 Wrathall, *How to Read Heidegger*, p. 117.

49 See Hubert L. Dreyfus, "Highway Bridges and Feasts," available online at http://www.focusing.org/apm_papers/dreyfus.html.

50 Jacques-Alain Miller, "The Desire of Lacan," in *lacanian ink*, 14, (1999), p. 19.

51 Jean-Pierre Dupuy, *Retour de Tchernobyl*, Paris: Éditions du Seuil 2006.

52 Of course, the experience of Communist countries demonstrates that the central role of the state is no guarantee of better treatment of the interests of the "commons": ecological catastrophies were much worse in Communist countries. The opposition between state and commons regains all its significance here.

53 See Myriam Bienenstock, "Qu'est-ce que 'l'esprit objectif' selon Hegel?," in Olivier Tinland, ed., *Lectures de Hegel*, Paris: Livre de Poche 2005.

54 Dupuy, *Retour de Tchernobyl*, p. 147.

55 Gray, *Straw Dogs*, p. 110.

56 See Bernard Williams, *Moral Luck*, Cambridge: Cambridge University Press 1981.

57 See Jean-Pierre Dupuy, *Pour un catastrophisme éclairé*, Paris: Éditions du Seuil 2002, pp. 124–6.

58 Ibid.

59 However, this image should nonetheless be supplemented by its apparent opposite. Let us return to the last decade of the Cold War: the radical anti-Communists were nonetheless wrong when they dismissed human rights and other agreements between the West and the East (like the Helsinki Declaration on human rights, etc.) as a deception by the Communists who in reality conceded nothing. Although they, of course, perceived it as a deception, the dissident movement in the Communist countries used the Helsinki Declaration, which was adopted as a legally binding document, as a tool for a vast pro-democratic mobilization. As is often the case, the ruling Communists fatefully underestimated the power of appearances: they got caught up in the game of what they perceived as a mere appearance.

60 However, the temptation we must resist unconditionally here is to perceive ecological catastrophes themselves as a kind of "divine violence" of nature, the justice/vengeance of nature — such a conclusion would be an unacceptable obscurantist projection of meaning onto nature.

Index